The Christian Life and Character

OF THE CIVIL INSTITUTIONS
OF THE UNITED STATES

The Christian Life and Character

OF THE CIVIL INSTITUTIONS OF THE UNITED STATES

BENJAMIN F. MORRIS

The publication of this book was made possible by gifts from
Nicene Covenant Church,
sponsors of Grace Community Schools
and Grace Community Day Cares,
and their founding pastor,
Rev. Ellsworth E. McIntyre.

AMERICAN VISION PRESS
POWDER SPRINGS, GEORGIA

American Vision
EXERCISING SERVANTHOOD DOMINION

A Biblical Worldview Ministry

THE MISSION OF AMERICAN VISION, INC. IS TO PUBLISH AND DISTRIBUTE
MATERIALS THAT LEAD INDIVIDUALS TOWARD:

———

A personal faith in the one true God: Father, Son, and Holy Spirit

———

A lifestyle of practical discipleship

———

A worldview that is consistent with the Bible

———

An ability to apply the Bible to all of life

Typesetting by James DeMar and Luis Lovelace.
Cover design by Luis Lovelace

American Vision, Inc.
3150 Florence Road, Suite 2
Powder Springs, Georgia 30127-5385
www.AmericanVision.org
1-800-628-9460

———————

Library of Congress Cataloging-in-Publication Data

Morris, B.F., author.
   Christian Life and Character of the Civil Institutions of the United States / 2nd. ed.
   Includes bibliographical references and index.
   ISBN-13: 978-0-915815-70-8 Hardbound
   ISBN-13: 978-0-915815-96-8 Paperback

Table of Contents

Table of Contents

Foreword
Archie P. Jones, Ph.D.

Rev. Benjamin F. Morris' *magnum opus*, the *Christian Life and Character of the Civil Institutions of the United States*, could not be more pertinent to present day American life. The little-known information that it contains is just as true today as it was in 1864 and is far more needed than it was in the mid-nineteenth century. Moreover, American Christians have long neglected the heritage that God has given us through our Christian forefathers, so the vast majority of American Christians are ignorant of the Christian character of our civil government institutions. Furthermore, there has been a long-standing effort of anti-Christian scholars and propagandists to de-Christianize American civil government, law, and life. Largely because of their ignorance, many Christians have been misled by the disinformation generated by anti-Christian writers who have obscured or denied the Christian nature of our heritage of civil government and law. That heritage was not perfect but it was superior to the heritage of any other people on earth, and both Christians and non-Christians benefited immeasurably from our God-given heritage of Christian influence upon civil government and law in America. Hence, the interesting information presented by Rev. Morris is must reading for Christians and non-Christians alike.

Morris' great work is a magnificent contribution to our understanding of the Christian—or dominantly Christian—history of these United States of America. The evidence which he presents makes it unmistakably clear that early American citizens and statesmen knew what Romans 13 and the Bible as a whole make so clear: that civil government is not neutral among religions and philosophies of men but instead is a ministry of the sovereign God who created and rules His universe and world, and works out His eternal plan and holy will in history. Our forefathers in the faith did not retreat from involvement in society and politics. They did not turn civil government, the making, enforcement, and adjudication of laws, over to Satan and those who serve him. They did not surrender the ministry of civil government to those who are in rebellion against God. Instead, they sought to base civil government and law upon the truth. They understood that God is the Lord of history who rules the lives of nations by His divine providence, and that He is in authority over our nation as well over all others. They knew that our nation's civil government and law must be based upon God's laws and principles of justice if we are to enjoy His blessings upon our land and people. They comprehended that all men are sinners, and that man's sinful nature has particularly destructive consequences when it is allowed to vent itself through the power of civil government. They understood that true religion Christianity), virtue, and liberty are inseparably united, and that liberty cannot long be preserved in the absence of virtue among the people and their representatives.[1] As the record compiled and presented by B.F. Morris makes clear, they designed and conducted our civil governments accordingly.

The evidence so painstakingly assembled and beautifully presented by Morris is absolutely essential to the preservation of justice and liberty in these United States. The facts presented in this work should be known by all Christians everywhere, by all American Christians, and by all freedom-loving Americans regardless of their religious persuasion, for God's word applies to all men and nations. As M. Stanton Evans has pointed out in his important work,

---

[1]The knowledge that liberty depends upon virtue and virtue depends upon Christianity was no new thing to early Americans. See, for example, Patricia U. Bonomi, *Under the Cope of Heaven: Religion, Society and Politics in Early America* (New York: Oxford University Press, 1986) and Marvin Olasky, *Fighting for Liberty and Virtue: Political and Cultural Wars in Eighteenth-Century America—The American Experience, Book I* (Wheaton, Illinois: Crossway Books, 1995). This knowledge was basic to the Constitution, for such knowledge was widespread. The many quotations compiled in William J. Federer, *America's God and Country Encyclopedia of Quotations* (Coppell, Texas: Fame Publications, Inc., 1994) provide an inkling of this; Ellis Sandoz, *A Government of Laws: Political Theory, Religion and the American Founding* (Baton Rouge: Louisiana State University Press, 1990), and Ellis Sandoz, ed., *Political Sermons of the American Founding Era, 1750-1805* (Indianapolis: Liberty Press, 1991) provide, respectively, a comprehensive analysis and much neglected primary source evidence of our early citizens' and statesmen's awareness of the dependence of continued liberty upon true religion (Christianity), the foundation of moral virtue.

The Theme Is Freedom, it was Christianity—not paganism, "religious neutrality," or secularism—which produced freedom and justice in the West and in America.[2] The facts which are so ably presented by Rev. Morris massively document these truths. Moreover, such information glorifies God, for it is His plan and Divine Providence which made Christianity predominant in early America and brought manifold blessings to the people of this land.

That these facts have been obscured by secularists and neglected by Bible-believing Christians is a disaster of the first magnitude. It is a disaster which has worked its mischief quietly, subtly, and gradually. Yet it has had manifold effects, for it has robbed the American people of the godly vision of reality, civil government, and law which our forefathers possessed. Where there is no godly vision, no understanding of the nature of God and of His dealings with men, the people perish. They perish because, neglecting God and His whole counsel, they think and act in obedience to false views of the nature of reality, of God, men, and things. Following false views, the people are as the blind being led by the blind. They violate God's laws and principles, so God judges them. They fall into the "ditches" of history: as the Bible makes clear in Deuteronomy 28 and elsewhere, God brings all kinds of disasters upon them and their land, calamities which are the consequences of their own sinful actions. This is what has occurred in our history,[3] and this is the fundamental reason why American society is so troubled, American education is in a state of crisis, Americans have lost so much liberty, and justice is so perverted in our land today.

Benjamin F. Morris began compiling this great work in about 1853. He undertook this labor of love because by that time there were already forces in America which were seeking to deny the Christian origins and foundation, and to destroy the dominantly Christian nature of our Constitution and laws.

By that time Unitarianism had become a powerful force in the North and had spawned the virulent religious movement known

---

[2] M. Stanton Evans, *The Theme Is Freedom* (Washington, D.C.: Regnery Publishing, 1994).

[3] C. Gregg Singer, *A Theological Interpretation of American History* (Phillipsburg, New Jersey: Craig Press, 1982).

as Transcendentalism. Unitarianism exalted the unaided reason of man above the authority of the Scriptures, denied the inspiration and infallibility of the Bible, renounced the reality of Original Sin, rejected the Trinity—the divinity of Jesus Christ and the Holy Spirit—and waged war upon Biblical orthodoxy. Transcendentalism stretched Unitarianism's belief that man is naturally good into the notion that man is, or can become, God. Both denied the applicability of God's law as revealed in Scripture to man and society. Unitarians and Transcendentalists sought to use a combination of state-controlled education and civil government coercion to "reform" man and society along man-centered lines. Unitarians and socialists launched the drive to establish "public schools" in New England in the late 1830s and were influential in extending "free public education" across the states of the North into the Midwest before the "Civil War." They slyly worked to gradually remove the formerly dominant Christian content from education and to use government-controlled education to establish their own religious, ethical and political principles. Through the control of education they sought to change the views, values, politics and laws of the people of the United States.[4] Transcendentalists used the lecture circuit, the pulpit, and the pen to spread their perfectionistic and politically radical doctrines. Unitarians and Transcendentalists backed the abolitionist crusade which was a main cause of the War Between the States—the "Civil War" which did so much to destroy constitutional government and the rule of Christian laws in our Christian republic.[5] They financed and lauded the abolitionist terrorist John Brown, whose murderous designs and actions were a major cause of the sectional hostilities which produced the war.[6]

---

[4]See Samuel L. Blumenfeld, *Is Public Education Necessary?* (Boise, Idaho: The Paradigm Company, [1981] 1985).

[5]It should be noted, however, that some great Unitarian jurists and legal scholars were conservatives who affirmed that American law is basically Christian because American law was based on the English Common Law, which was fundamentally Christian in its nature and principles. See Perry Miller, *The Life of the Mind in America* (New York: Harcourt, Brace, and World, 1965), 194, 195 and passim.

[6]See Otto Scott, *The Secret Six: John Brown and the Abolitionist Movement* (New York: Times Books, 1979).

Added to this was the influence of many people engaged in manufacturing, commerce, and agriculture who were primarily interested in material gain. Many who were engaged in commerce and manufacturing sought to use civil government as a means of enriching themselves at the expense of others: sought to engage in legalized theft. This was true of both businessmen and their employees, for many employees, like their employers, voted primarily upon the basis of their own economic self-interest—at the expense of the economic interests of those in other occupations and in other regions of the nation. Such avarice was and is incompatible with the law of God and with the principles and spirit of the Constitution. It was also basic to the desire to increase the tariff and to use the money derived from this tax on imports to benefit Northern manufacturers. The misuse and increase of the tariff was a basic, though neglected cause of the War Between the States.[7] Much Southern support of slavery (which is usually pictured as being the cause of the war) was a result of the economic self-interest of slave owners.

The pre-"Civil War" years also saw a rise of rationalism, the view that man is not fallen in every area of his being and that man's reason is self-sufficient and does not need to base its reasoning upon God's revealed word in Scripture. Rationalism had been present, yet by no means dominant, before the War for Independence, yet it grew with the rise of Unitarianism in the early nineteenth century. As had been the case in Europe, rationalism spawned schemes for the radical transformation of society, civil government, and law. Rationalism was basic to socialism and other plans and movements for the "reform" of man and society which were so prominent in the early decades of the nineteenth century.

The decades from the 1820s to the 1850s also saw some attempts by rationalists, atheists and other unbelievers to have American courts declare that our laws are not fundamentally Christian. These pre-"Civil War" attempts were all resoundingly defeated, as the great mass of American lawyers and judges—so well-schooled in Blackstone's *Commentaries on the Laws of England*, the principal textbook of early American lawyers and gentlemen, and in the

---

[7]See Robert L. Dabney, *Essays: Secular* (Harrisonburg, Virginia: Sprinkle Press, [1897] 1979), 4:87–107.

Common Law—brought their knowledge of the law and of our history to bear crushingly upon the rationalists' arguments. Rationalists and unbelievers were defeated both in debate and in pre-"Civil War" court decisions.[8]

While these antagonistic modes of thought were developing, many Bible-believing Christians, under the influence of pietism and other theologies, were abandoning the traditional Christian view of the scope of the Bible's authority and of the Christian's proper concern in favor of much narrower views of the Bible's relevance. Pietism rightly stressed the importance of the individual's relationship to God but wrongly reduced the scope of the Christian's concern to his or her personal life, family life, and the affairs of the church as an ecclesiastical organization. Antinomianism (opposition to the law of God) denied that Biblical law, revealed in the Old Testament, is applicable to society and civil government. Revivalism tended to focus so much on the manipulation of people's emotions to produce professions of faith in Christ that it neglected the older emphasis on the covenant between a Christian society and our Savior and Lord Jesus Christ.[9] Widespread belief in the myth of neutrality, the idea that God is neutral in most areas of thought and life and is only particular about "religious" things, led many to abandon Christian education for "public education" and to forsake the application of all of Scripture to all areas of life. In the "public schools" Christians first accepted a watered-down, lowest-common-denominator Christianity which neglected the whole counsel of God revealed in the Bible. Then they acquiesced in the gradual de-Christianization of the textbooks. The result of these things was a Christian retreat from Biblically-principled educational, social, and political involvement. This in turn created a vacuum which non-Christian bodies of thought were eager to fill.

Such developments were "signs of the times" for Rev. Morris and other discerning Christians, and Morris, like the sons of Issachar,

---

[8]Miller, *The Life of the Mind in America*, 99-214.

[9]Perry Miller, "From the Covenant to the Revival," 90–120, in his *Nature's Nation* (Cambridge: Harvard University Press, 1967). Yet, as Miller himself notes in *The Life of the Mind in America*, early nineteenth-century American revivals continued to have a strong impact on society and law.

knew the times and understood what God's people ought to do. He knew that where there is no godly vision the people perish. He understood that Americans were losing a knowledge of the great work of God in the founding of America, a knowledge of the intimate connections between Christianity and our civil government, law, and liberty. He sought to give Christians and Americans a true vision of the hand of the Lord in our history and of the crucial, foundational place of Christianity in our civil government and public life. This great old work is the product of Morris's application of his knowledge, through a decade of study and hard work, to his times, for the good of the people of the nation, for the cause of Christ, for the future, for Christian liberty and justice, and for the glory of God.

A chief shortcoming of this great old work is its lack of footnotes or endnotes. The author quoted or paraphrased from works which were well known and readily available in his time (and listed most of them directly before the Table of Contents), works from which his information could have been more or less easily verified by his readers. Those works are not readily available now, having long since gone out of print and passed out of general circulation. Thus, although *Christian Life and Character* is an invaluable source of information, it lacks the scholarly apparatus which enables the researcher to check the author's sources easily. Many of these out-of-print historical sources can be found on the internet.

Despite this and other shortcomings, the *Christian Life and Character of the Civil Institutions of the United States* is a great and useful work. It provides a treasure trove of information about the Christian foundations and essence of our history, civil government, and constitutional order. It provides long-obscured facts about the role of Christian faith in our governmental system which not only Christians but also all Americans need to know.

Reverend Benjamin Franklin Morris (1810–1867) was the son of the Honorable Thomas Morris, a pioneer opponent of slavery who was United States Senator from Ohio. Morris had three daughters and two sons. One of the sons, George W. Morris, became Assistant Librarian of the Congressional Library in Washington, D.C.

A minister of the Congregational Church, Morris pastored churches in Rising Sun, Indiana, Lebanon, Ohio, and other places.

After his health began to fail, he retired from the ministry. He and his family moved to Washington, D.C. There he worked as a clerk in one of the departments of the Federal Government and was very active in working for the establishment of a Congregational Church in the city.

It was during the time he was in Washington, D.C. that Morris undertook the labor of writing *Christian Life and Character of the Civil Institutions of the United States.* He spent a decade absorbed in this project, working on it during his spare time. He followed this by compiling a book of accounts of events connected with the assassination and burial of President Abraham Lincoln.

Morris's deep concern about the loss of our Christian heritage in civil government and the threat of the de-Christianization of our nation's civil government, law, and public life led him to write the *Christian Life and Character* and was evident in his introduction to the book. The combination of failing health, full-time work for the Federal Government, active promotion of the establishment of a church, and the labor of study and writing these two books greatly weakened him. The very existence of the War Between the States—he would have called it the Civil War—and the subsequent assassination of Lincoln distressed him.

The things which led Morris to compile and write the *Christian Life and Character of the Civil Institutions of the United States* have had a much more extensive development since 1864. Late nineteenth century and twentieth century American thought, following the main currents of modern thought, became more man-centered, intellectually and morally relativistic, more openly rebellious against God and His law-word. American educational thought and practice followed suit, and became "progressively" more secularist, relativistic, manipulative, and anti-Christian. American political and legal thought and practice became increasingly more secularist, socialistic, and antinomian. In short, Americans rebelled against God and His holy word.

While this was occurring, American Christians continued to retreat from Bible-based involvement in social action, education, intellectual pursuits, the shaping of culture, and political thought and action. Many in the old "main-line" Protestant denominations abandoned belief in the full inspiration and inerrancy of the Bible in favor of faith in science, belief in the unscientific, false claims of evolutionism, and credence in various bodies of modern man-centered thought. Many followed baptized versions of modern pagan social and political thinking and programs. On the other hand, many who believed the truth of the Bible retreated from social and political involvement because those who had abandoned belief in the truth of the Bible were involved in politics. Meanwhile, many Bible-believing Christians became so convinced that the return of Jesus Christ was so close at hand that they forgot—or abandoned—the Biblical duty to occupy until He comes (Luke 19:13). Forsaking Bible-based educational thought and action, they allowed their children to be miseducated in "public schools" and secularist colleges (including nominally Christian institutions). Forsaking Bible-based social, cultural, and political action, they increased the size of the vacuum which their parents had created.

Consequently, the foundation of a godly nation was not maintained: indeed, it was permitted to be well-nigh destroyed. So the Constitution and its Christian principles were increasingly ignored in practice. Hence, the size and scope of civil government was increased; power was centralized in the national government; and the rule of law was abandoned in favor of the arbitrary rule of men.

Thus, presidents, congresses, and federal courts have made multitudes of decisions which have undermined not only the Constitution's principles but also Christian morality, the family, the social fabric, law and order, the safety of the individual and his property, economic freedom, liberty, and even domestic tranquility.

Now that Christians have begun to recover the knowledge that God and His word require us to be involved in all areas of life—including politics—for His glory and the good of our fellow men, it is time for Christians to recover our Christian forefathers' Biblical vision of the world and of life. It is time for Christians to grasp the vision of civil government under God which motivated the great majority of our early American citizens and statesmen. Christians must improve upon that vision and upon the practices of our forefathers. They must be equipped for the battles that such a restoration will involve. But they cannot do so if they remain ignorant of the truth about our heritage in civil government. The *Christian Life and Character of the Civil Institutions of the United States* is a powerful weapon which must be used in the battle to recover upon our godly heritage, and an important tool which should be used to improve upon that heritage. It should be read and enjoyed, studied and used by all Americans, and particularly by all American Christians.

Preface

THIS volume is committed to the American people, in the firm assurance that the invaluable facts which it records will be grateful to every patriotic and pious heart. In it, as from the richest mines has been brought out the pure gold of our history. Its treasures have been gathered and placed in this casket for the instruction and benefit of the present and future. We have a noble historic life; for our ancestors were the worthies of the world. We have a noble nation, full of the evidences of the moulding presence of Christian truth, and of the power and goodness of Divine wisdom in rearing up a Christian republic for all time. That this was the spirit and aim of the early founders of our institutions, the facts in this volume fully testify.

The field through which the reader will walk, in this work, must give wider expansion to his political views, quicken the pulses of his loyalty, add to his conscious dignity as an American citizen, strengthen his confidence in our future, and impart a higher tone to his piety.

The single object of the compiler was to link, in a connected form, the golden chain of our Christian history, and to reveal the basis on which our institutions stand.

The documents and facts are authentic, and have been collected, with laborious diligence, from standard historical works and from the political and Christian annals of the nation. The volume is the voice of the best and wisest men of the republic. It must, therefore, have weight with the American people, and be a political and Christian thesaurus and text-book to the scholar, the teacher, the patriot, the politician, the statesman, the jurist, the legislator, the divine, and, in a word, to all classes of American citizens.

The work is not speculative or theoretical, but a series of facts to unfold and establish the Christian life and character of the civil institutions of the United States, in the light of which every American citizen can trace to its source the true glory of the nation, and learn to appreciate its institutions and to venerate and imitate the great and good men who founded them.

It has been a delightful task of patriotism and piety to the compiler to prepare the volume, and to lay it as a grateful offering upon the common altar of his country and of Christianity.

The work has been the labor of years, performed in various States of the Union, and in the capital of the nation, within sight of the tomb of Washington, during the most eventful year of the Rebellion; and its last pages were prepared for the press in Philadelphia, where so many of the sacred scenes of the Revolution transpired. The volume, therefore, has in its preparation a national feature, and the reader will be impressed with the importance and appositeness of the facts to the present time.

It is also the ardent hope of the compiler that the facts and principles recorded in this volume, and in which, in our early struggle, all denominations of Christians uttered with such harmony their convictions that the only sure and stable basis of our civil institutions was in the Christian religion, may contribute to strengthen the union of patriotism and piety in all parts of the country, to save the nation from the perils of a wicked rebellion, and be the brightest hope of the future.

Care has been taken to give each author credit for his thoughts and language, though in a few instances it may have been overlooked. It was neither the desire nor the design of the compiler to elaborate his own views—though they are found in the volume—but to give those of the great leading minds of the republic, both past and present.

His grateful acknowledgments are tendered to the Librarians of the Young Men's Mercantile Library Association, and of the Mechanics' Institute Libraries of Cincinnati; of the State Library of Ohio; of the Historical and Astor Libraries of New York; of the Mercantile Library and Library Association of Philadelphia; of the Libraries of Congress, and of the Interior Department; to the Chief Clerk in the Department of State, for access to the manuscript papers of Washington; to Peter Force, of Washington City, for frequent examinations of his large and invaluable collection of books and periodicals illustrative of the early history of our country; and to the Honorable Thomas Corwin, of Ohio, for numerous visits to his valuable library. His thanks are due also to the late Honorable Samuel W. Parker,

of Indiana, for the frequent use of his large political and historical
library, and to the late Judge John McLean, of Ohio, who imparted
to the compiler valuable suggestions in reference to the preparation
of the work.

The Introduction to the work is written by Rev. Byron Sunderland, D.D., Pastor for the last twelve years of the First Presbyterian
Church of Washington City, and Chaplain to the Senate of the United States in the Thirty-Seventh Congress. Its high Christian tone
and sentiment, its finished literary excellence, and the important
truths it so forcibly enunciates will render it well worthy the attention of the reader.

The volume is committed to the blessing of God and to the judgment and favor of the American people, in humble trust that it may
aid in preserving and perpetuating to future generations the Union
of the States, the integrity of the best government ever instituted by
the wisdom of men, and the nationality of the American Republic.

Principal Authorities Consulted

Archives of American Annals by Peter Force

Journals of Congress and Official Records, Colonial and State Constitutions and Papers

History of the United States by George Bancroft

Han's History of the Puritans

Grahame's Colonial History of America

Webster's Works

Burke's Works

Annals of the American Pulpit by W. B. Sprague

Pulpit of the Revolution by John Wingate Thornton

Chaplains and Clergy of the Revolution by J. T. Headley

Dr. Beecher's Works

Power of the Pulpit by Gardiner Spring

Character of the American Government (Anonymous)

Rev. Jasper Adams' Sermon, with Notes, on the Relation of Christianity to the Civil Government of the United States

Principles and Acts of the American Revolution by H. Niles

Grimké's *Writings and Orations*

Chaplains of the American Government by L. D. Johnson

Nash's *Morality of the State*

Life and Times of Washington by John Frederick Schroeder D.D.

Writings of Washington by Jared Sparks

Recollections of Washington by George Washington Parke Custis

Religious Opinions and Character of Washington by B. C. McGuire

Presbyterian Review, New England Review, Bibliotheca Sacra, Rebellion Record by Frank Moore, and a large number of periodicals of the time of the Revolution and at the formation of the Constitution of the United States.

The Chapter on the "Christian Element in the Civil War" was compiled from the official acts and papers of the ecclesiastical denominations of benevolent organizations and of the national and State Governments.

The Bible

Commentaries on the Constitution by Joseph Story

Bayard's *Commentaries on the Constitution*

Rawle on the Constitution

Gardner's *Institutes of International Law*

Griswold's Republican Court, or *American Society in the Days of Washington*

Mrs. Ellett's *American Women*

Histories of the Various Colonies and States

Bough's *Thanksgiving Proclamations*

Lossing's *Field-Book of the Revolution*

Sanderson's *Biography of the Signers of the Declaration of Independence*

Introduction

THE story of Christianity in America is one of the most astonishing chapters in the annals of the world. The events of Providence in reserving and preparing the country of these United States to be the theater of its development and triumph, constitute one of the most remarkable passages of modern history.

This is a Christian nation, first in name, and secondly because of the many and mighty elements of a pure Christianity which have given it character and shaped its destiny from the beginning. It is pre-eminently the land of the Bible, of the Christian Church, and of the Christian Sabbath. It is the land of great and extensive and oft-repeated revivals of a spiritual religion—the land of a free conscience and of free speech—the land of noble charities and of manifold and earnest efforts for the elevation and welfare of the human race. The chief security and glory of the United States of America has been, is now, and will be forever, the prevalence and domination of the Christian Faith.

The materialist may find in other aspects of our country many grounds of complacency. Compared with other nations, we have had a wonderful career. The marvels of the republic stand thick along the line of our advancement. Whether we consider the colonial period, or that of the Revolution, or those of subsequent times, our growth in numbers, in territory, in wealth and power, has been almost unparalleled. The spirit of our Government and its institutions is singularly adapted to secure the general peace and happiness of human society. Our example has long been an object of jealousy and fear to the oppressors of man. Our country has thrown open an asylum to the unfortunate from every quarter of the globe. All the kindreds of the earth have been welcome to repose beneath the shadow of our Tree, which in less than a single century has spread its branches across the continent. And if our civil polity has not realized all the possible blessings of a free government, the reason lies less in the genius of the economy than in the acknowledged imperfections of human nature itself. In addition to these things, Providence has signally favored the nation in its geographical position, the fertility of its soil, the plenty of its seasons, and the salubrity of its climate. The vigor of the people has found ample scope in utilizing the physical resources of the country, by all the industries and arts of agriculture, manufacture, and commerce; while in conducting the educational and intellectual interests of society, no modern nation in the same space of time has contributed more to the great elements of that higher civilization towards which the world is everywhere slowly but surely tending. These are sources of just satisfaction to every friend and lover of his country. But they are, meanwhile, considerations which fall far below those great moral and spiritual principles in the absence of which no state on earth can perpetuate its existence.

The true theory of national life and prosperity is clearly unfolded in the revealed word of God. The secret of all stability and enduring greatness in human governments, as with individual men, is to be found alone in the quickening power of the Christian Faith. This only, imbuing and pervading the mind and heart of human society, can organize and preserve to the body politic its highest and most untroubled fortunes. Fallibility and corruption inhere indeed in the materials of every commonwealth,—the result of which is a liability to continual change. Growth succeeded by decay, and decay forcing another growth, is the philosophy of national vicissitude, as it is also the great fact of the physical creation. "One generation passeth away, and another generation cometh," and therefore the permanence of empire must rest in the *ideas* of a people. If then there be in such ideas no great enduring principle of spiritual life, there can be no perpetuity of national existence. If there be no grand, sublime, and imperishable *thought,* filling the soul of a people with its fire and fashioning their progress after its pattern, there can be no sense in which they may escape the inevitable mutations of the world, or avoid the fate of so many that have gone before them.

The most powerful empires of the past have perished because they were wanting in a principle strong enough and spiritual enough to resist the self-destructive energies of human nature. The pagan world could not furnish such a principle. It was in neither their philosophy nor their religion. It is not in the power of man unaided to discover and apply such a principle. Nothing short of divine wisdom and power can actualize among the nations that principle of spiritual life which not only originates but preserves the substance of social and civil welfare. Christianity is the divine method of imparting this principle to men and nations, and the only method revealed from Heaven for regulating our present state, and, after this, conferring upon us the lasting awards of a glorious immortality. The doctrines of Christianity form a system of perfect and saving truth, its duties comprise the sum of all genuine beneficence, while its ascendancy over the human soul is effectually secured by the regeneration of no less than the infinite Spirit of God.

The dispensation of this Spirit has been distinctly and constantly affirmed in our country, and the people have been instructed to expect "times of refreshing from the presence of the Lord," not more in the early and latter rains of heaven than in the silent but reformatory processes of our moral and religious condition. The Author of human nature is that same God who must re-supply its wasting energy, and diffuse in human society the life and light of truth, by turning men from the way of transgression unto "the wisdom of the just." According to this belief there is a direct and immediate connection between the human soul and the Divine Spirit; and wherever the sacred influence falls, there human beings are sure to "walk in newness of life," supporting and stimulating all that is precious and invaluable in the temporal and eternal well-being of mankind. This doctrine, which lies equally removed from the superstition of ignorance and from the levity of unbelief, has been more thoroughly explained and more widely disseminated among the people of America than anywhere else on the face of the earth. And it is due to the influence of evangelical religion among all classes of society, more than to all other considerations together, that our prosperity has been so great and our progress so unexampled. "Ye are the light of the world. Ye are the salt of the earth." This is the description of men whose views and conduct are the result of the inspiration of Jesus Christ. All time attests its truth. "Righteousness exalteth a nation, while sin is a reproach to any people," and must, if persisted in, pave the way to their final destruction. This divine maxim has been exemplified in all the old seats of human population, and is borne onward in the spirit of prophetic admonition from age to age. The voice of history is lifted in repeated accents of solemn warning, and rolls in thunder-blasts its own great lesson upon the ear of nations.

But while, without doubt, there has been, and is now, the presence of an evangelical power in this republic, that has left its impress and its influence upon our institutions and our society, and has reared so many sacred monuments for the gratitude and the admiration of mankind, it cannot and ought not to be denied that the nation as it stands to-day is far below that moral and religious condition which constitutes the essential safety, prosperity, and honor of any people. It is sadly true that a very large proportion of the population are strangers to the genuine spirit of the Christian religion, and almost, if not altogether, unacquainted even with the history of its facts and the extent of its influence in the land of our inheritance. The standing complaint of human degeneracy remains against us. Causes have been operating—and of late years with fearful rapidity and strength—to produce a state of moral obliquity and practical atheism among us, appalling in magnitude and of alarming consequence. It has become of late quite customary to sneer at the Puritanism of our fathers, and to speak with contempt of the severity of their manners and the bigotry of their faith. This impious treatment, by the present corruptors of society, of a generation of men whose lofty principles and illustrious virtues they seem utterly unable to comprehend, is well adapted not only to arouse the deepest indignation, but also to excite the most lively concern. There are two quarters from which these evil influences chiefly proceed. A class of men without conscience, and reckless of all moral restraint, have gained ascendency in public favor, and assume from their prominent position to mould and direct the public sentiment of the nation. Their general influence upon the public morals has been like the wind of the desert,—poisonous, withering, and destructive. Another and very large class of men moving in the lower walks of life form a significant element of our American population, whose hard and vicious instincts, gratified without compunction and paraded everywhere in the most offensive manner, would seem to render them well-nigh incapable of reformation. Apparently insensible to all the nobler sentiments of public morality and virtue, and ever ready to perform their congenial part in the general demoralization, they demand that all the higher classes shall pander to their depraved appetites, as the price of their patronage and support. In this reciprocal play of the baser passions the common principles of morality are daily sacrificed, and the strong and the weak join hands in carrying down the nation to the very verge of ruin. No man can observe the conditions of society in our country, and the obvious impulses of human conduct, without feeling that the perils against which the fathers warned us, and which have been so faithfully and constantly pointed out by the ministers of religion, have, notwithstanding, increased at a fearful rate, without seeing that the most alarming departures from the standard of individual rectitude and social integrity have occurred among us within the century that is past.

And, while every period has exhibited the signs of public degeneracy, none in our history presents more fearful proofs of the impiety and obduracy of great masses of the people. We have abandoned, in a great measure, the faith and practice of our ancestors, in putting aside from their lawful supremacy the Christian ordinances and doctrines. The natural result is, that we have corrupted our ways in all the circles of society and in all the pursuits of life. We have become as a field rank with the growth of all the vices and heaped with the pollution of mighty crimes. The rigid training of former times through family government, discipline, and instruction has been greatly relaxed, if not in many cases wholly neglected. Indeed, there are multitudes of parents in the land who from physical and moral causes are totally unfit to have the care of the children to whom they have given birth: so that a generation of human beings is growing up in one of the most favored regions of the globe, whose preparation for the responsibilities of their age and mission has been sadly at fault, and whose precocity in levity, mischief, and insubordination already equals the vitiating examples that are set before them. The education of the nation is going forward with rapid strides, but it is in a lamentable degree under the auspices of immorality and irreligion, alike in the high and the low places of the community. The unblushing venality and brazen wickedness of a large portion of the conductors of the public press and of the public men of the country have strongly tended to demoralize the nation, to undermine the foundations and destroy the influence of

Christian discipline, and to turn the mind and heart of many to infidelity and licentiousness. The same baleful spirit has moved upon the fountains of human learning and science, and so secularized the philosophy of the times as to have set the high faculty of human reason at variance with the sacred majesty of religion, and to have plunged thousands upon thousands of our young men into a sea of splendid sophistry and subtlety and all the ruinous speculation of a proud but vain imagination. Meanwhile, from the hearts of multitudes the dignity of honest labor and the dictates of a sober and frugal economy have died out, on the one hand increasing pauperism and crime and lending to misfortune the aggravation of human improvidence, and on the other fostering habits of false show, and thus increasing the temptation to deception, fraud, peculation, and all the dishonesties of the most high-pampered extravagance and excess. Moreover, the wanton neglect or abuse of our providential blessings, and the unconscious apostasy from every sentiment of purity and virtue, have served greatly to defile and degrade the mind of a large portion of the community, and ill the centers of population with a low and vulgar herd, who throng the open temples of obscenity and infamy. Thus the materials are prepared for human guilt and wretchedness, whose catalogue of crimes and woes exhausts the power of language to express them. Beyond all this, political controversy and partisan strife for the reins and spoils of power, conducted without principle, and reeking with abuse, have taken so fierce a form as often to have driven the best men from the arena and left the worst upon the field. The selfish and profligate stand forward to control the nominations and elections to office, and afterwards gamble with its duties and obligations without shame and without remorse. Nor is this all. Our wrongs to the Indian and the African, continued from the beginning, have brutalized the temper, darkened the understanding, and perverted the judgment of the nation in regard to the plainest principles of common humanity and justice. The tide of emigration from the Old World has borne to our shores a large element of the foreign-born, who speedily become imbued with our native and inexorable prejudice in this respect. Thus, while we claim to be a free government, we have cherished institutions in our midst which are a mockery of the name of liberty and have become our standing shame and curse in the sight of the whole world. Involved in a criminality so grave, we have not failed to exhibit its usual concomitants,—arrogance and self-conceit. Our vast facilities of production, trade, and transportation have filled us with high notions of our superiority, and at the same time degraded us to dispositions of covetousness and cruelty. And from the long period of our tranquility we have come at length to a pitch of wickedness that has culminated in one of the most gigantic and desolating civil wars the world has over seen. Our unparalleled liberty has degenerated into dissolute indulgence; we have been so long without the burdens of government as to have almost forgotten the price of our birthright and to have cast away the only safeguards of its continuance; we have proved ourselves unworthy of our inheritance, in our contempt of that virtue which alone affords protection to society, in our blind disregard of the Christian foundations on which alone the great interests of a nation can permanently rest. Thus, at last, a majority of the people have grown wholly unmindful of the authority and prerogative of God, and of the duties we owe to him and to his creatures. The true life and soul of Christianity has been to a great degree emasculated, and the very titles of Jehovah and the tokens of his awful majesty in the earth have become to multitudes among us as idle and unmeaning as the Grecian myths, used, indeed, to furbish a paragraph with classic elegance or round a period with sonorous emphasis, but completely divested of those great, grand, solemn, and glorious thoughts which never can dwell with vulgarity, profanation, and irreverence.

Now, if, under such conditions, Christianity should resume her sway and bring the masses of the nation back to the pure and simple virtues and to the stern and heroic spirit which marked the age of our Revolutionary fathers, it will prove to be a moral miracle equal to her first triumphs in apostolic days. Yet to this object all good men should devote their energies and their prayers. In the firm conviction that virtue must finally be supreme, and that a wise and beneficent Providence has designed this continent to be the theater of the yet more glorious conquests of Christianity, it is the mission and the duty of all friends of evangelical truth to combine in the attempt to hold and appropriate this country, with its resources, monuments, and institutions, for an empire devoted to the spread of God's kingdom in the earth, and the universal reign of Jesus Christ.

And it is high time that we had begun to see our duty and to feel our obligation. God's great "judgments are already in the land:" shall not its inhabitants begin "to learn righteousness"? The associated moral and spiritual power of a Christian people ought now to be making itself felt in every part of the land and in all that concerns the existence and welfare of the country. It is the settled conviction of many of the most intelligent and purest minds that the time has come when the Christian people of America should take into their own hands the work of reclaiming the government and wielding its power more decisively for the glory of God and the highest good of human nature, and that for this purpose the true and the good should sternly separate themselves from all connection with the openly vicious and corrupt, and from all countenance and support of those whose life and example will not bear the scrutiny of common decency and morality. And if in a representative government like ours there must be political divisions, and a conflict of the suffrages of the people, let there be a Christian party,—a party that will not sustain by their sympathy or their votes men who are known to be in sentiment and life, by precept and example, unchristian and untrue to the great principles of the Christian faith; for the highest treason of which mankind are capable is treason against the authority and law of the Divine government itself; and the most deadly enemies to human government are they who, with a great pretense of Loyalty, are nevertheless daily insulting the majesty of Him who has power to destroy nations at his will.

The fountain of political turbulence and corruption undoubtedly lies in the primary assemblies of the people, as conducted upon the principle of *party caucus,* which for a long period has amounted to little else than a system of chicanery and venality too humiliating to describe. This kind of imposition upon the free action of American citizenship has been carried to such an extent as well-nigh to neutralize the title of suffrage itself, and make of the boasted ballot-box a mockery of American privilege. For the *caucus,* then, let the Church be substituted—not any one sect or denomination of Christians, but the whole Church catholic—not with a view to exciting mutual jealousies and creating hostile prejudices, but standing on the platform of Christian character supposed to be exemplified in the sincere adherents of every Christian Church. Let the weight of every vote tell what is the conviction, the intelligent, sober, and matured judgment, of the Christian mind of this nation as to the value to our country of personal integrity and upright manhood. If it were well established that such would be the policy of the truly Christian portion of the people in all the Christian churches of the country, the very fact would carry with it a moral influence which even the most brazen and unscrupulous politician could not altogether despise or resist. And in connection with this position it must be seen that our Christian duty requires us also to set our faces as a flint against the current of social and moral degradation which flows in the popular fashions, tastes, customs, and amusements of the day—in the factitious and dishonest principles of business life—in the whole circle of immoral and dangerous practices and pursuits which ensnare the multitude and draw them on to ruin. We must be more diligent and faithful with the early years of childhood. Christian parents must resume the discipline and religious training over their sons and daughters which prevailed in the earlier and purer days of the republic. And all the departments of government must be filled with men who will administer their power for the suppression of whatever is deleterious in its influence, and for the encouragement of whatever is of a beneficent and elevating tendency. The Church of Christ must purge itself of worthless members, who now, through the laxity of discipline, continue a scandal and a reproach, cambering its progress and dragging down its sacred name into the dust. All the educational and eleemosynary institutions and organizations of the times should be pervaded by the ruling spirit of the Christian faith, and quickened and animated by the living principle of evangelical purity and power. In the liberal professions and in all the stations of political prominence from which decidedly Christian men have been pushed aside partly through their own timidity and partly by the audacity of bold and scheming demagogues, there must be made an earnest and persevering effort to establish the tried and faithful representatives of a higher morality and a more stainless character. In all these respects the evils of our delinquency have been multiplying from year to year. Christian men have been unwilling or afraid to unite upon the distinctive principles of a common Christianity, and have shrunk from the sacrifice, scarcely ready to suffer whatever of temporary defeat, expense, or reproach it might cost, and tamely submitting to be overruled by the boldness, the assiduity and energy of the evil-minded who assume to control and dictate the public policy and manners of the nation. In this way we have been swiftly sinking into the grossest perversions of ethical truth and the obligations of duty. We have confounded almost every distinction in morals; "we have put good for evil, and evil for good; we have called bitter sweet, and darkness light." In the unrestrained freedom of our experience, with no bonds and no restrictions of government or law that we could feel sensibly resting upon us, and permitted alike under divine and human authority to live in our lusts and to develop in monstrous proportions the sentiment of individual importance, we have come to exhibit little real regard for magistrates of our own choosing, and scarcely less disrespect for the very existence and form of civil government itself. Our very thoughts have been dissolved in the infatuation of personal sovereignty, until oaths and compacts, written charters and constitutions confirmed by the highest sanctions possible to man, are ruthlessly violated, rebellion is inaugurated, and we are brought to the very door of anarchy itself. It could not be otherwise with a people who have in the name of liberty struck at the vital interests of one whole race of men, and through these have aimed an impious blow at the prerogatives of God himself.

And now the day of vindication and of vengeance has burst upon us. The storm which uncovers the social and moral heart of the nation reveals the melancholy fact of a widespread demoralization amid the deepest corruption and the grossest profligacy of great multitudes of the people. Rebellion in favor of perpetuating a system of human bondage is held by many to be the crowning glory of men. Sedition, treachery, perjury, violence, and blood are counted as deeds of fame to immortalize their authors and abettors. Meanwhile, there are not wanting those who, utterly unprincipled, in the guise of pretended friendship, are gloating over the scene, and, like the fabled harpies of Tartarus, are plucking their gorge from the miseries of the nation, already reeling in the agonies of a mortal conflict. This is the spectacle which America presents to the world at the present moment. And were it not relieved by some brighter hues of Christian hope, by the spirit of an earnest and patriotic ardor, by the stupendous and heroic sacrifices of hundreds of thousands of men and women who freely lay all they possess on the altar of their country, and, finally, by the consciousness of the rectitude of our cause, our firm reliance on providential direction, and the assurance of the glorious purposes of God to be accomplished through this dreary and dreadful passage of the nation's history, it would he indeed the darkest and the saddest chapter yet recorded in the book of time.

Of what avail, then, is it for the enemies of a spiritual religion to attempt to delude us with the vain pretense that the true progress of mankind implies the rejection of the Bible as the divinely inspired word of God, and the denial of its authority in the affairs of men, and that in the onward march of civilization the dogmas of the Christian Church have become obsolete—that the human mind has outgrown its restrictions, and can no longer be controlled by its discipline or instructed by its counsels? And of what avail is it, by mocking at the sober habits and simple virtues of a purer age, to prepare society for the frightful scenes of its own dissolution? Here still are the great and solemn realities of life, here are the giant evils with which men have to grapple, and which, in despite of all the levities and impieties of an epicurean philosophy, cannot be treated as idle dreams, the vagrant fancies of a distempered mind. And in the effort to ignore both the mischiefs and the remedy of our subverted moral condition by the scoffing infidelity and the specious skepticism of our times, the nation with all its treasure has already been brought to the verge of destruction.

Every intelligent man knows it; every honest man confesses it. And yet the signals of evil omen are not removed. The spirit that humbles a nation before the God of heaven and supplies the conditions of the Divine interposition for our salvation has been strangely wanting to the people; while men are everywhere found among us who leave no means unused to bring the religion of our fathers into contempt, and to cut the nation loose from all her moorings in the ancient faith of martyrs and apostles. The men that do this, whether in the refuse that reeks from the daily press, or in the more pretentious eloquence of the forum, or in the more elaborate and finished chapters of the periodical, or in the more prurient and high-wrought pages of fiction that curse and corrupt the literature of the day, are the deadly enemies of the human soul not only in its relations to the present life, but also in its aspirations for the life to come. They are likewise the malignant and felonious torch-bearers of infidelity, setting the temple of our American greatness on fire, giving our heritage to the flames, and lighting a mighty people into the abyss of self-destruction.

Whoever, therefore, contributes his labor to raise a barrier against so vast and deplorable a calamity to ourselves and the world, whoever lifts his voice like a trumpet in admonition and warning of the danger, and especially whoever can succeed in recalling the mind of the nation to the Christian annals of the republic, in bringing back to the freshly opened fountains of the early inspiration the weary and exhausted body of the people, that they may once more be refreshed and strengthened, once more commune with the great principles, sentiments, achievements, and characters of former times, and be imbued with a sense of the value and importance of their recognition and imitation, will have rendered a noble service, and may justly be regarded as a public benefactor. For the facts of our past history, inspired by the faith of the Christian religion, authenticated and supported as they are by unquestionable proofs, comprise a body of evidence which no well-regulated mind can resist as to the divinity of the Christian religion itself and the reality of a superintending Providence over all the affairs of men. At the same time, they serve to acquaint us with the very purest and loftiest sentiments of the most illustrious men of America in every generation, and with an unbroken chain of testimony in regard to the influence of Christianity upon our national destiny from the beginning until now. And all this appears in connection with the history of most tragic and trying time; and is put forth in terms of thrilling eloquence, of stirring pathos, and of startling energy, kindling the soul to the sublimest fervor of grand and heroic enthusiasm. We shall find in this story of well-attested occurrences and events all the elements that can move the human heart to its profoundest depths, wise and steady counsels of the great and good men that adorned the secular professions and pursuits—the ringing trumpet-voice of the Christian ministry ever calling the host to the march or the conflict— the beauty and tenderness of woman, roused, amid the sweetness and charms of her gentler nature, as by some supernatural impulse, to all the high and lofty aims of truth and liberty, and imparting everywhere to the breast of manhood a portion of her own unspeakable endurance and devotion—the sublime unity of the Christian faith, in which were joined Catholic and Protestant, Churchman and Dissenter, clergyman and layman, the members of all parties and the parties of all creeds, as if animated by one spirit and glowing with one thought—the great idea of civil and religious liberty for all the tribes of men. Surely in these great outlines of essential unity there is enough to gratify and inspirit our generation upon the review of the records of those who have preceded us. It only needs to collect these scattered materials into one volume of available size and proportions to furnish to the American people one of the richest and most useful manuals of political and Christian information ever published in any country.

Such an attempt is made in the present volume, so far as is known the only work of the kind ever prepared for popular use and general circulation. The author and compiler, the Rev. B. F. Morris, a Protestant clergyman, for many years a successful pastor and preacher of the gospel in the great Valley of the West, and during the last year a pastor in Washington City, having mingled largely with all classes of the people and become extensively acquainted with many of the leading minds and most prominent and distinguished men of the nation both living and dead, and being peculiarly qualified also by extensive travel and observation throughout our country, and apparently moved to it by a natural aptitude for such a work and an earnest desire to serve the cause of Christianity and civil liberty, some ten years since conceived the idea of collecting from the national archives, and the various other sources of information in the country, the important and deeply interesting materials relating to Christianity in our history which are presented in this volume. In accomplishing this work he has not sought to express at length any opinions or speculations of his own, except so far as to give order, arrangement, and connection to the rich and copious materials thus brought together. Nor has it been his design, as the title of the work might possibly suggest, to give a complete account of the Christian Church in this country, or even a compendium of American ecclesiastical or theological history (which would properly be a distinct work in itself, and is held in reserve for some powerful pen of future times), but rather to show how the spirit of Christianity has entered into the foundations and elements of our national existence, and how it has affected our civil and political history and given shape and structure to our institutions—to exhibit the relations it has borne to the state and the impulse it has given to the actors in the great drama of American colonization and independence, the support it affords to the civil institutions of the American people, and its general influence upon their fortunes and their destiny. The conspicuity and moral grandeur of these great lessons are most powerfully and abundantly illustrated. No man can ponder them as presented here without discovering that they furnish an effectual antidote to the skeptical tendencies and moral laxities of the age, and without breathing an earnest prayer that all the people may become familiar with these great memorials of the past, these solemn and sublime tributes of a mighty nation to the one inspiring principle of their prosperity and greatness, and may learn to cherish it with increasing vigilance and care as the only solid foundation of their present peace or their future hope.

In undertaking a work of this magnitude years ago, how little could the author have anticipated that the period assigned in Providence for the consummation of his labor should be one in which the errors, follies, and sins of the nation have culminated in the awful storm that now desolates the land, and at a time when it may be hoped that the American people, chastened and sobered through so bitter an experience, will be more disposed to avail themselves of the opportunity to review the sacred monuments of the past, to mark their departures from the ways of wisdom, and to return to the only path of safety and of honor! Had the author been gifted with a foreknowledge of the events of the past few years, he could scarcely have set himself to perform a task more fitting to the exigency of the time or better adapted to promote the reformation which the present judgments of God must produce as the only alternative of our sure and swift destruction. No analysis of the book is here required. It will speak for itself in thunder-tones. As the common manual of the people, it should be in the hands of every individual in all our borders, and, if diligently perused and faithfully improved, who can tell but, under the blessing of God, it may become the morning star of the mightiest day of national regeneration the world has yet beheld.

Byron SUNDERLAND
WASHINGTON, D.C., April 14, 1863

1

Sources of Proof to Establish the Christian Life and Character of the Civil Institutions of the United States

Civil Institutions of the United States

The history and genius of the civil institutions of the United States must ever be a subject of profound thought and interest to the American citizen. Their establishment and progress to completed forms of government, and their influence and fruits upon thirty millions of people and on the nations of the earth, constitute a new era in the science of civil government and the progress of human liberty, and commend them to the reverent study of the statesman, the patriot, the Christian, and the citizen.

The institutions of the North American republic had their birth and baptism from the free inspirations and genius of the Christian religion. This fact has given to the state its political power and moral glory, and shed new light on the benign nature and adaptation of the Christian system to secure the highest political prosperity to a nation.

"Christianity is the principal and all-pervading element, the deepest and most solid foundation, of all our civil institutions. It is the religion of the people—the national religion; but we have neither an established church nor an established religion. An established *church* implies a connection between church and state, and the possession of *civil* and *political* as well as of ecclesiastical and spiritual power by the former. Neither exist in this country; for the people have wisely judged that religion, as a general rule, is safer in their hands than in those of rulers. In the United States there is no toleration; for all enjoy equality in religious freedom, not as a *privilege* granted, but as a *right* secured by the fundamental law of our social compact. Liberty of conscience and freedom of worship are not chartered immunities, but rights and duties founded on the *constitutional* republication of reason and revelation."

The theory and faith of the founders of the civil and political institutions of the United States practically carried out these statements. They had no state church or state religion, but they constituted the Christian religion the underlying foundation and the girding and guiding element of their systems of civil, political, and social institutions. This proposition will be confirmed by the following summary of historic facts, which have an extended record in the various chapters of this volume.

Object of the Founders of the Republic

First. The Christian inspirations and purpose of the founders and fathers of the republic.

It was a popular legend of the ancients, which gave to their laws, literature, and religion a sacred solemnity and power, that the founders of empires received immediate inspiration from the gods, and that their systems of government came from the responses of the deities who presided in their temples of religion. This myth, in a Christian sense, was a grand and glorious fact with the wise and skillful workmen who, under God, created and completed the civil institutions of the United States.

No claim to special inspiration from heaven is set up for the fathers of our republic. It would, however, be a violence to historic truth not to affirm and admit that they were under the special and constant guidance of an overruling Providence. The Bible, as the divine charter of their political rights, as well as of their hopes of immortality, they reverently studied, and on it laid the corner-stone of all their compacts and institutions. The Mosaic system of political jurisprudence, which "contains more consummate wisdom and common sense than all the legislators and political writers of the ancient nations," the founders of the American republic thoroughly understood, and incorporated its free spirit and democratic principles into their organic institutions.

Secondly. The Christian men who formed our civil institutions were trained and prepared for their work in scenes of conflict in which the truest ideas of liberty and religion were developed.

Great ideas, and the forward movements of the ages, have received their inspiration and impetus from civil and religious agitations and revolutions. This fact has its historic analogy in the conflicts that preceded the planting of a Christian republic on the North American continent. "The whole of the sixteenth century was a period of active preparation for future times; and all that is great in modern science may be said to have received its foundation in the agitations that grew out of that period of the world. It forms one of the grandest and richest eras in human history." Whilst it was an age replete with the most splendid triumphs in science and literature, it was pre-eminent, also, for its elaboration and vindication of the fundamental principles of civil and religious liberty.

The persecutions of the Puritans in England for non-conformity, and the religious agitations and conflicts in Germany by Luther, in Geneva by Calvin, and in Scotland by Knox, were the preparatory ordeals for qualifying Christian men for the work of establishing the civil institutions on the American continent. "God sifted," in these conflicts, "a whole nation, that he might send choice grain over into this wilderness;" and the blood and persecution of martyrs became the seed of both the church and the state.

It was in these schools of fiery trial that the founders of the American republic were educated and prepared for their grand Christian mission, and in which their faith and characters became strong and earnest with Christian truth. They were trained in stormy times, in order to prepare them to elaborate and establish the fundamental principles of civil and religious liberty and of just systems of civil government.

Brewster, and Winthrop, and Roger Williams, and Penn, and George Calvert, and Oglethorpe, and Otis, and Adams, and Jefferson, and Washington, with their illustrious co-laborers, could trace their true political parentage to Pym, and Hampden, and Wickliffe, and Milton, and Cromwell, and to the ages in which they vindicated the principles of liberty, and sealed, many of them, their faith by martyrdom.

Thirdly. Thus inspired and prepared, the Christian men of Puritan times and of the Revolution presented and developed the true symbol of civil government.

Symbols of Civil Governments

A nation, in the embodied form and spirit of its institutions, is the symbol of some one leading idea. This rules its civil administration, directs its social crystallization, and forms its political, martial, and moral character.

The Hebrew commonwealth was the symbol of a theocratic government. Its rituals of religion and liberty maintained the form and diffused the spirit of freedom and of a true republican government. Its nationality, growing out of peculiar and local causes, after ages of historic grandeur, passed away. It was the first and the last type of a national theocratic republic.

The Roman empire, in its colossal unity and form, was the symbol of law, of the stately grandeur of a strong government, of the reign of military rule and conquest. Its fabled origin, and the mythical communion of its founder (NUMA) with the divinities, gave a rigid religious cast to its civil and military institutions and transactions. The science of Roman jurisprudence educated the citizens of the empire in the cardinal virtues of loyalty and patriotism. Religion is a Roman word, signifying obligation to the government. A Roman citizen could no more be disloyal to his country than to the gods. This conviction gave to the government a religious character, and made it invincible in war and strong in governmental authority and influence. Cicero, in one of his addresses, refers to the religious element of the Roman empire in these words—"However much we may be disposed to exalt our advantages, it is, nevertheless, certain that we have been surpassed in population by the Spaniards, in physical force by the Gauls, in shrewdness and cunning by Carthage, in the fine arts by Greece, and in mere native talents by some of our Italian fellow-countrymen; but in the single point of attention to religion we have excelled all other nations, and it is to the favorable influence of this circumstance upon the character of the people that I account for our success in acquiring the political and military ascendency we now enjoy throughout the world."

This pervading religious element produced, also, the loftiest martial enthusiasm in the Roman citizen. "The attachment of the Roman soldier," says Gibbon, "was inspired by the united influence of religion and honor." In union with these civil and martial virtues in Roman citizens, the symbol of their government resulted in producing and blending some of the milder virtues of social and domestic life. Female character was formed on the most finished models of pagan excellence; chastity was a golden virtue; and to educate sons for statesmen or soldiers was the highest ambition of the most illustrious ladies of Rome.

The symbol of the Greek republic was the ideal and the actual of Beauty. "The Greek," says a writer, "saw the world almost only on the side of beauty. His name for it was *Kosmos,* divine order and harmony." This idea, in the mind of the Greek, was developed in artistic creations, and in the ornamental more than the useful. The fine arts—literature, painting, statuary, music, poetry, and oratory—were the natural and genial results of the Grecian symbol. It gave to the Greek religion and government the same ideal features, making the first a realm peopled with gods, and the second a system of but little political force or permanency. The Greek democracies were subject to sudden changes, and were wrecked amid the wild and tumultuous waves of liberty. "It was said of the popular assemblies of Athens that if every Athenian were a Socrates, still every Athenian assembly would be a mob." The political and civil institutions of the Greeks accomplished less, perhaps, for liberty and the rights of man than any other ancient republic.

The symbol of the British empire, from its earliest history till the present, was national aggrandizement and selfishness, originating in the feudal system. The landed estates became invested in a few, who grew into an aristocracy of wealth, of social caste, and of political power. The people were reduced to vassals, and had but few political rights and privileges. This aristocracy of wealth and of social position converted the government into a system of political selfishness and of national aggrandizement, at the expense, often, of international justice, honor, and right. Commerce, and territorial expansion, and the perpetuity of its nobility with all their hereditary privileges, have ever been the leading purposes of the British government. The prestige and unlimited power of this symbol of the empire of Great Britain have realized the words of Webster, who, alluding to the gigantic nationality of the empire, said that she "had dotted the surface of the whole globe with her possessions and military posts, whose morning drum-beats, following the sun, and keeping company with the hours, circle the earth daily with one continued and unbroken strain of the martial airs of England."

The symbol of the French empire is glory. This has ever been the star of destiny that has ruled the nation and converted its institutions into a mission of martial glory. The great evil of this symbol of the French empire was, that it displaced the moral basis on which every nation must permanently rest. Atheism, practical and theoretical, has ruled the French empire, and its fatal power has more than once threatened the very life of the nation. "Open the annals of the French nation," said Lamartine, "and listen to the last words of the political actors of the drama of our liberty. One would think that God was eclipsed from the soul—that his name was unknown in the language. The republic of these men without a God has been quickly stranded. The liberty won by so much heroism and so much genius has not found in France a conscience to shelter it, a God to avenge it, a people to defend it against the atheism which is called glory. All ended in a soldier. An atheistic republic cannot be heroic."

The founders of the Christian republic of North America adopted the symbol of civil and religious liberty as the great idea and end of all their civil institutions. They had the most glorious conceptions of the genius of the Christian religion, not only as a system of spiritual doctrines, but as designed and adapted to create and carry on the best and freest forms of civil government. They held to the faith that civil government was an ordination of God, and that its administration ought to harmonize with the law and will of

God as revealed in the Bible. This great object was kept before the minds of the founders and fathers of the republic, and their *beau-idéal* of civil government was that which was found in the Christian religion. As the fruits of this symbol, or leading idea and purpose, contrast the Christian republic of North America with the fruits of ancient and modern nations.

"What is the spirit," says Grimké, "of the civil and political institutions of America? Is it not free, magnanimous, and wise, frank and courteous, generous and just; in a degree far surpassing that of ancient Greece? Who would suffer, much less institute, a comparison between our national government and the council of Amphictyon, or between our State systems and the compound of monarchy, aristocracy, and democracy to be found in the Grecian States? As fountains of noble thoughts and high aspirations after public power, duty, and happiness, far above the triumphs of antiquity, who does not look with a virtuous pride, with grateful exultation, on the Senate of the United States, on the Chamber of National Representatives, and on the Supreme Court of the United States? If the system of the Grecian excelled that of other ancient states in its fitness to develop intellectual and moral freedom and power, who will not acknowledge, in the civil and political institutions of our country, a far superior capacity for the same ends? What is there in the constitution or administration of the Greek governments that can fill the soul of a freeman with such a sense of his own dignity, power, and duty as our written constitutions, the jury system, and the laws of evidence, the scheme of representation, the responsibility of rulers, and the independence of the judiciary? And what, in the most glorious age of Greece, was com-parable to the genius and past fruits of our government and country—so August, magnanimous, and benevolent in the eyes of the world—and to the prospect before us, not of selfishness, ambition, and violence, at home or abroad, but of harmony, virtue, wisdom, culture, at home; abroad, of duty, of usefulness, and love to all the nations of the earth?"

Christian Constitutions and State Papers

Fourthly, the Christian religion has a clear and full recognition in the civil constitutions and state papers of the fathers of the republic.

Official records express the faith and theory of those who form and administer the civil institutions of a nation. The fathers and founders of the American republic, being Christian men and designing to form a Christian republic, would be expected to imbue their state papers and their civil constitutions with the spirit and sentiments of the Christian religion. This fact is historic in the civil institutions of the country, and gives to its official documents a Christian feature and influence which belong only to American constitutions and American political annals. During the Revolution, the States assumed their separate sovereignties and formed State constitutions. These civil charters, as this work will show, were full and explicit in their incorporation of the fundamental doctrines of the Christian religion, and their constitutions prohibited men from holding office who did not publicly assent to their faith in the being of a God, the divinity of the Bible, and in the distinctive evangelical truths of Christianity.

The state papers of the Continental Congress were also full of the spirit and sentiments of the Christian system. Under the great seal of state, official documents were sent out to the nation and the world which affirmed the "merits and mediation of Jesus Christ to obtain forgiveness and pardon for sins," and prayed "that pure and undefiled religion may be universally diffused;" "that vice and irreligion may be banished, and virtue and piety established by grace;" "that the nation may be made a holy nation, and that the religion of our divine Redeemer, with all its benign influences, may cover the earth as the waters do the sea;" "that God would grant to his Church the plentiful effusions of divine grace, and pour out his Holy Spirit upon all ministers of the gospel;" "that he would establish the independence of these United States upon the basis of religion and virtue," and "diffuse and establish habits of sobriety, order, morality, and piety;" that he would "take under his guardianship all schools and seminaries of learning, and make them nurseries of virtue and piety, and cause pure religion and virtue to flourish," and that he would "fill the world with his glory." All their bills of rights, and remonstrances against the usurpations of the British government, glowed with the fervid and impassioned sentiments of liberty and religion, and their high Christian tone and diction form a rich part of the Christian political literature of the republic.

Fifthly, the popular utterances of the Christian men who formed our civil institutions declare the Christian religion to be the symbol of the republic.

Puritan divines and lawgivers, and the statesmen and patriots of the Revolution, unite their testimony on this point. They affirmed, in every form, the indissoluble union of religion and liberty. They uttered no such political atheism as "liberty first and religion afterwards;" but, maintaining the divine origin of both, they constituted their indissoluble union in the system of civil government which they formed. In the pulpit, before popular assemblies, in the forums of public justice, before the tribunes of the people, in the halls of legislation, in the public press—in tracts, essays, books, printed sermons and orations—did the men of Puritan and Revolutionary times utter their great thoughts, and declare the union of liberty and religion. A divine enthusiasm glowed in all their popular utterances, that swept with electric energy through the public mind and conscience, and which prepared the people for liberty, independence, and a Christian nationality. This historic fact will be conclusively established in the present volume.

The Revolution Inspired by Religion

Sixthly, the revolution for liberty, independence, and constitutional government had its source in religion, and was the cause of its energy and final victory.

History, as it records the events of ages, and the progress of nations to higher conditions of freedom and prosperity through revolutions, declares that "religion has been the companion of liberty in all her conflicts and in all her battles." The American Revolution adds another grand illustration of this great historic truth. That splendid victory for liberty and constitutional governments was not won by numbers, nor military genius, nor by armies and navies, nor by any combination of human means, but only through liberty intensified and made heroic through religion. This was the breath of its life, and carried it sublimely on till victory crowned our arms and our banners waved over a free republic. It was the inspirations of religion that girded our heroes for war, that guided our statesmen in civil councils, that fired and filled the hearts of the people with hope and courage, and gave to all the scenes of that grand conflict a Christian beauty, power, and glory.

Its influence flowed from every source. The cradle-songs of childhood; the home scenes of prayer and piety; the common and academic schools of the country; the Christian colleges of the republic; the literature of the age; the songs of patriotism and religion; the eloquence of the forum and the pulpit; the councils of civil cabinets and the military camps; public men and private citizens of all classes, became the medium of diffusing the religious spirit and power of the Revolution. This fact induced Washington to say, "I am sure that there never was a people who had more reason to acknowledge a divine interposition in their affairs than those of the United States; and I should be pained to believe that they have forgotten that agency which was so often manifested during the Revolution, or that they failed to consider the omnipotence of that God who is alone able to protect them. He must be worse than an infidel that lacks faith, and more than wicked that has not gratitude enough to acknowledge his obligations."

Christian Annals of the Republic

Seventhly, the Christian annals of the republic declare that religion was the ruling influence and moral power of the republic.

The historic grandeur and moral significance of the civil and political annals of the American nation consist in their Christian spirit and declarations. The inspirations and ideas of civil and religious liberty which they embody; the fundamental and inalienable rights of human nature which they announce and defend; the eternal laws of civil and political science which they affirm; the basis of just and orderly organic governments, and the civil structures which have risen and rest upon it, and which the annals of the republic present and unfold; the Christian nationality which they historically declare, and which they have contributed to form; the spirit and language in which the annals of the nation are written, and which permeate the state papers of the republic from the Puritan to the Revolutionary era, and in some good degree from the era of the Revolution to the present time; the philosophy and language of American history and

American literature, whether poetic, scientific, educational, political, or religious—all these constitute the facts and moral glory of the annals of the nation, and unite in recording and presenting them in a Christian form and spirit. Divest American annals of this their grandest and most important feature, and their value and glory would vanish.

The reverent and careful student of the annals of the American republic will find them imbued with the "benign, masculine, thoughtful spirit of the Christian religion." This feature gives them an interest, influence, and importance, a political and moral pre-eminence, over the annals of every other nation, whether ancient or modern.

Eighthly, Christian monuments and altars of religion and liberty.

Nations which are rich in historic grandeur have numerous memorials whose inspirations and influences aid in the diffusion of a healthy public sentiment and in the formation of a true nationality. They educate the people to admire and imitate the heroic virtues of the men and scenes of moral or martial glory which the memorials are designed to commemorate and perpetuate. The custom is coeval with time, and has a divine sanction. The annals of the Hebrew commonwealth record the consecration of numerous altars, places, and temples to religion and liberty. These were the symbols of their faith, and from them flowed beneficent and copious influences to form the intense religious nationality of that remarkable people, and to mould all their institutions. It was a divine injunction, as well as a work of piety and patriotism, for the Hebrew people to "walk about Zion, and go round about; tell the towers thereof; mark well her bulwarks; consider her palaces;" that they might tell it to future generations that "this God was our God."

The annals of American piety and patriotism have many similar memorials. A republic, the outgrowth of the Christian religion, whose history glows with the manifest presence and providences of God, and whose freedom is baptized with the sufferings and blood of martyred patriots and saints, would hallow many memorials of historic associations and grandeur. The American republic is rich in the monuments of piety and patriotism, and their influences and associations have had, and continue to have, the highest historic value and instruction for every American citizen, and are fraught with some of the noblest and purest lessons of religion and liberty. Their genial and inspiring power has been diffusive and beneficent in infusing fresher love for our civil institutions, and deepening and strengthening that intense enthusiasm for our freedom and free institutions which is characteristic of every loyal American. American history, in the Christian and patriotic scenes, achievements, and men which it records, is peculiarly grand and rich in this element and influence of our national sentiment and power. The altars of religion, the monuments of nature and art, the scenes of martial and moral glory, the halls of constitutional freedom, and the temples of legislation and organized civil governments, around all of which cluster memorable associations and glowing inspirations, are eminently worthy of record, and should be reverently studied by every patriot and Christian.

Christian Faith of the Men Who Formed Our Civil Institutions

Ninthly, the Christian faith and character, personal and political, of most of the men who originated and constructed our civil institutions, affirm the presiding genius and power of the Christian religion.

Sacred history, and the institutions which it unfolds, have their life and glory from the good and great men whom the providence and Spirit of God raised up and qualified for their varied and important missions. "In nothing does the superiority of the Bible over all other books appear more manifest than in its graphic and inimitable delineations of human character. From first to last it opens to our view, besides poets and orators, a magnificent succession of living characters—kings and statesmen, heroes and patriarchs, prophets and apostles," who constituted the glory of the age and nation in which they acted, and whose character and influence are a rich part of the political and moral wealth of the world.

The American republic, like the Hebrew commonwealth, has its chief glory from the good and great men who have adorned its civic and Christian history, and were the active agents in building up the organic forms of the social and political life of the republic. The Puritans, and the men of colonial history, were stalwart, noble Christian men. The men antecedent to and actors in the eventful drama of the Revolution were, most of them, men whose minds were illuminated by divine influences, and whose characters and lives bore the superscription and the image of Christ. All were not public professors of the Christian religion, but almost all acknowledged its divinity and necessity to the existence, welfare, and stability of the state. Their Christian faith and characters not only constitute the enduring glory of our republic, but are also the sources of the Christian features of our civil institutions.

The true and lasting fame of the American nation—its political and moral glory—consists in the eminent and illustrious characters which have, in each successive age of the republic, adorned the state and directed its political destinies. Trained in a Christian school and formed under Christian influences, and deriving their ideas of civil and religious liberty from the Bible, their practical faith led them to adopt it as the rule of life and to consult it as the source of their civil and political views and principles, as well as of their religious belief and hopes. The monument of these men of Puritan and Revolutionary times is in the great Christian ideas and truths they elaborated and incorporated into the civil institutions of the nation, and in the Christian virtues, public and private, which they bore as the fruits of their Christian faith.

The leaders of our Revolution were men of whom the simple truth is the highest praise. They were singularly sagacious, sober, thoughtful, wise. Lord Chatham spoke only the truth when he said to Franklin of the men who composed the first Colonial Congress, "The Congress is the most honorable assembly of statesmen since those of the ancient Greeks and Romans in the most virtuous times. They were most of them profound scholars, and studied the history of mankind that they might know men. They were so familiar with the lives and thoughts of the wisest and best minds of the past, that a classic aroma hangs about their writings and their speeches; and they were profoundly convinced of what statesmen know and mere politicians never perceive—that ideas are the life of a people— that the conscience, not the pocket, is the real citadel of a nation."

"Events," says a living American divine, "march in the train and keep step to the music of that divine LOGOS which was, and is, and is to come. In order to act the right part in them, and in order to understand them when they do come to pass, our intelligence must be in vital sympathy with that of their invisible Author and Arbiter. The divine purpose which is forcing its way into existence, and preparing for itself a local habitation and a name, must be reproduced in our own consciousness and embodied in our own life. This is the only way for men to become coworkers with the Most High in executing his sovereign behests.

"This is the ancient method by which from age to age mighty nations, and all the elect spirits of the race, have comprehended their heaven-appointed missions, fulfilled their tasks, and rendered themselves illustrious in human annals. This is the secret of that sacred enthusiasm which transformed Eastern shepherds and nomads of the desert into venerable patriarchs, seers, warriors, and kings, which changed fishermen into apostles and evangelists, and which is able still to bless the world with heroes, saints, and martyrs.

"It is the prevalence of some divine idea in the soul, actuating the whole being and illuminating the path of life. Let a man grasp, in honest conviction, a real thought of God, and spend his days in striving to realize it, and he is on the highway to glory, honor, and immortality. Let a whole people grasp, in honest conviction, some sacred cause, some principle of immortal justice, and consecrate themselves to the work of vindicating that cause and enthroning that principle, and we have the grandest spectacle ever witnessed on earth."

The grandeur of such a spectacle was seen in the faith and purpose of the fathers and founders of the American republic. These men, as well as the people, did grasp a great and "real thought of God," and devoted themselves to its glorious realization; and the result was the vindication of eternal right and justice, and the creation and establishment of civil institutions in conformity to the principles and teachings of the Christian religion. It is in the light of this great historic fact that the faith and labors of the Puritans and the men of the Revolution are to be read and studied.

Duty of American Citizens to Study the Christian Origin and Genius of Their Civil Institutions

This summary of the Christian facts and principles which belong to the history, formation, and progress of the civil institutions of the American republic impresses the patriotic and pious duty of giving diligent attention and study to the annals of our nation and the origin and genius of our institutions.

The ancient republics regarded it as a high political necessity and duty to educate their citizens into the history and spirit of their peculiar institutions. "The young men of the Roman empire," says Gibbon, "were so devoted to the study of the genius and structure of Roman law and government, that the celebrated Institutes of Justinian were addressed to the youth of his dominion who had devoted themselves to the science of Roman jurisprudence, and they had assurances from the reigning emperor that their skill and ability would in time be rewarded by an adequate share in the government of the republic."

"The Greek citizen," says Grimké, "was subjected, from the cradle to the grave, to the *full, undivided,* never-varying influence of the *peculiar* institutions of his own country. The spirit of those institutions was forever living and moving around him—was constantly acting upon him at home and abroad, in the family, at the school, in the temple, on national occasions. That spirit was unceasingly speaking to his eye and ear; it was his very breath of life; his soul was its habitation, till the battle-field or the sea, banishment, the dungeon, or the hemlock, stripped him equally of his country and his life."

If these duties were so faithfully discharged by the people of the ancient republics, how much higher and more important that the American people should know the history and nature of the civil institutions of their Christian republic, and live under their constant and full power, and thus be qualified to discharge with fidelity and conscientiousness all the duties of an American citizen!

"Be assured," says Grimké (changing a word of the passage), "if the American citizen rightly comprehends the genius of Christianity, the spirit of our institutions, the character of the age in which he lives, he must be deeply imbued with the benign, masculine, thoughtful spirit of religion. Let me commend to the profound study of every American citizen the institutions of their country, and the noble illustrations of them to be found in the writings of our historians and statesmen, judges, orators, scholars, and divines. Let me commend to their reverence, gratitude, and imitation the character of Washington, the noblest personification of patriotic duty, dignity, and usefulness that men ever have seen. Let me commend to them to enter with a deep seriousness, yet with a glowing enthusiasm, into the spirit of their institutions and of the age in which they live."

Nothing would have a happier influence on the public men and politics of our day, nothing raise, expand, and purify them, nothing would so exalt their conceptions and aims, or give them higher significance or greater weight, than a thorough and candid study of the Christian faith, characters, and actions of the great and good men who founded our civil institutions and watched over their history and development.

This duty, if faithfully discharged, would unfold the divine source of our civilization and system of civil government, give a higher appreciation of the inheritance received from our fathers, and a firmer purpose to preserve and transmit them, unimpaired, in their original purity and glory, to future ages and generations.

This study would impress the fact stated by Sir William Jones, a great English jurist, who said, with great truth and beauty, that "we live in the midst of blessings till we are utterly insensible of their greatness and of the source from whence they flow. We speak of our civilization, our arts, our freedom, our laws, and forget entirely how large a share is due to Christianity. Blot Christianity out of the pages of man's history, and what would his laws have been? what his civilization? Christianity is mixed up with our very being and our daily life; there is not a familiar object around us which does not wear a different aspect because the life of Christian love is on it—not a law which does not owe its gentleness to Christianity—not a custom which cannot be traced, in all its holy, healthful parts, to the gospel."

2

The Hand of God in the Settlement of the American Continent

God in History

G OD in human history is the key that solves the problem of human destiny and sheds a true and satisfactory light on the pathway and progress of nations. "In history," says D'Aubigné, "God should be acknowledged and proclaimed. The history of the world should be set as the annals of the government of the Sovereign of the universe. God is ever present on that vast theatre where successive generations of men and nations struggle. The history of the world, instead of presenting a confused chaos, appears as a majestic temple, in which the invisible hand of God himself is at work, and which rises to his glory above the rock of humanity.

"Shall we not recognize the hand of God in those grand manifestations, those great men, those mighty nations which arise and start as it were from the dust of the earth, and communicate a new form and destiny to the human race? Shall we not acknowledge him in those great heroes who spring from society at appointed epochs—who display a strength and an activity beyond the ordinary limits of humanity, and around whom, as around a superior and mysterious power, nations and individuals gladly gather? And do not those great revolutions which hurl kings from their thrones and precipitate whole nations to the dust—do they not all declare aloud a God in history? Who, if not God? What a startling fact, that men brought up amid the elevated ideas of Christianity regard as mere superstition that divine intervention in human affairs which the very heathen have universally admitted !"

Views of Divine Providence by Various Authors

That great scholar and Christian philosopher of Germany, the Chevalier Bunsen, says, in his "Philosophy of Human History," "The noblest nations have ever believed in an immutable moral order of the world, constituted by divine wisdom and regulating the destinies of mankind. The truly philosophical historian must believe that there is an eternal order in the government of the world, to which all might and power are to become and do become subservient; that truth, justice, wisdom, and moderation are sure to triumph; and that when the contrary appears to be the case, the fault lies in our mistaking the middle for the end. There must be a solution for every complication, as certainly as a dissonance cannot form the conclusion of a musical composition. In other words," says Bunsen, "the philosopher who will understand and interpret history must believe that God, not *accident*, governs the world."

"The principles that govern human affairs," says Bancroft, "extending like a path of light from century to century, become the highest demonstration of the superintending providence of God. Universal history does but seek to relate the sum of all God's works of providence. The wheels of providence are not turned about by blind chance, but they are full of eyes round about, and they are all guided by the Spirit of God." "Providence is the light of history, and the soul of the world. God is in history, and all history has a unity because God is in it."

Settlement of the American Continent

No era in human history is more signally and sublimely marked with the manifest providence and presence of God than that of the discovery and Christian colonization of the North American continent.

Discovered by Columbus

In 1492, Columbus hailed the opening of the New World with a song of praise, and by a solemn act of prayer consecrated it to God. In 1498, six years later, Cabot, an English navigator, discovered Newfoundland, and sailed along the coasts of the American continent. Columbus and Cabot were both Roman Catholics, and made their discoveries under the auspices of Ferdinand of Spain and Henry VIII of England, who were Roman Catholic sovereigns. It was more than a hundred years subsequent that any serious attempts were made to colonize the countries discovered by the Spanish and English navigators.

First Era of Colonization

"The intervening century," says a writer, "was in many respects the most important period of the world; certainly the most important in modern times. More marked and decided changes, affecting science, religion, and liberty, occurred in that period than had occurred in centuries before; and all these changes were just such as to determine the Christian character of this country.

Preparatory Means of the 16th Century

"Meantime, God held this vast land in reserve, as the great field on which the experiment was to be made in favor of civil and religious liberty. He suffered not the foot of Spaniard, or Portuguese, or Frenchman, or Englishman, to come upon it, until the changes had been wrought in Europe which would make it certain that it would always be a land of religious freedom. The changes then wrought, the advances then made, related to science and the arts, to religion, to the principles of liberty. The whole of the sixteenth century was a period of active preparation for future times, and all that is great in modern science and art may be said to have received its foundation in the agitations that grew out of that period of the world. The twelve decades, from 1480 to 1600, form one of the grandest and richest eras in the history of humanity. It was in that period that the foundation of our liberty was laid—in that period that it became sure that this would be a land of civil and religious freedom. England during all that time was a great laboratory in which these principles were brought out; and from the views which prevailed at the time of Henry VII., and which had prevailed for ages, it required one whole century to advance the world to that position which was maintained by Pym and Hampden and Milton, and was seen in the principles of Winthrop, and Robinson, and Brewster, of George Calvert, of Roger Williams, and of William Penn. Scarcely any thing has occurred in history which is more remarkable or which has been more certainly indicative of the designs of Providence."

Religious Acts and Character of Columbus

"Columbus came," says Irving, "as a religious man, an admiral of Christ, to find the continent, not for its material treasures, but because it held souls which he wished to bring as a trophy to the feet of Christ."

His Formal Consecration of the Continent to Christ

"A deep religious feeling mingled with his meditations and gave them at times a tinge of superstition, but it was of a sublime and lofty kind. He looked upon himself as being in the hand of Heaven, chosen from among men for the accomplishment of its high purpose; he read, as he supposed, his contemplated discoveries foretold in the mystic revelations of the prophets. The ends of the earth were to be brought together, and all nations and tongues and languages united under the banner of the Redeemer. This was to be the triumphant consum-mation of his enterprise, bringing the unknown regions of the earth into communion with Christian Europe—carrying the light of the true faith into benighted and pagan lands, and gathering their countless nations under the holy dominion of the Church. One of his principal objects was undoubtedly the propagation of the Christian faith. Columbus now considered himself about to effect this great work—to spread the light of revelation to the very ends of the earth, and thus to be the instrument of accomplishing one of the sublime predictions of Holy Writ.

"Whenever he made any great discovery, he celebrated it by solemn thanks to God. The voice of prayer and melody of praise rose from his ship when they first beheld the New World, and his first act on landing was to prostrate himself upon the earth and return thanksgiving. All his great enterprises were undertaken in the name of the Holy Trinity, and he partook of the communion before his embarkation. His conduct was characterized by the grandeur of his views and the magnanimity of his spirit. Instead of scouring the newly-found countries, like a grasping adventurer, eager only for immediate gain, as was too general with contemporaneous discoverers, he sought to ascertain their soil and productions, their rivers and harbors: he was desirous of colonizing and cultivating them, conciliating and civilizing the natives, introducing the useful arts, subjecting every thing to the control of law, order, and religion, and thus of founding regular and prosperous empires." In his will Columbus enjoins on his son Diego, or whoever might inherit after him, "to spare no pains in having and maintaining in the island of Hispaniola four good professors of theology, to the end and aim of their studying and laboring to convert to our holy faith the inhabitants of the Indias; and, in proportion as by God's will the revenue of the estate shall increase, in the same degree shall the number of teachers and devout persons increase, who are to strive to make Christians of the natives."

Webster's View of Columbus

"The great epitaph," said Webster, "commemorative of the character and the worth, the discoveries and the glory, of Columbus, was that he had *given a new world to the crowns of Castile and Aragon.* This is a great mistake. It does not come up to all the great merits of Columbus. He gave the territory of the Southern hemisphere to the crowns of Castile and Aragon; but, as a place for the plantation of colonies, as a place for the habitation of men, a place to which laws and religion, and manners and science, were to be transferred, as a place where the creatures of God should multiply and fill the earth under friendly skies and with religious hearts, he gave it to the whole world, he gave it to universal man! From this seminal principle, and from a handful, a hundred saints, blessed of God and ever honored of men, landed on the shores of Plymouth and elsewhere along the coast, united with the settlement of Jamestown, has sprung this great people."

3

Puritan Settlement—Its Christian Motives and Scenes

Puritan Settlement

THE Puritan settlement on the American continent, around which cluster the grandest associations and results, dates from the 22d of December, 1620, one hundred and twenty-eight years after a Christian navigator had greeted the New World with a song of praise, and consecrated it to Christ in prayer.

The motives that began this memorable era in American history were intensely religious. It opened a new chapter in the progress of events and in the history of colonizing countries. Hitherto, conquest, ambition, worldly glory, had often marked the settlement of newly discovered territory. God now changes the scene, and, for the first time in the history of the world, the colonization of a new and great continent begins from the purest and profoundest religious convictions and principles.

Previous Ages Preparatory

Previous ages had been preparatory to this new and important Christian era. Europe had been shaken and sifted by the conflicts of the Reformation. In England, Christian ideas and the principles of a purer and freer Christianity had, through Wickliffe's translation of the Bible, been generally diffused, and that book was the forerunner of coming revolutions. There was, in the providence of God, a peculiar fitness in the times to train and prepare Christian men for the great work of laying the foundation of a Christian empire in a new continent. They lived in an age of superior light, in which literature, philosophy, and the arts and sciences had enlightened and elevated the English nation; they were educated in schools of learning where the word of God had enthroned its power and diffused its light, and which created in their souls a longing desire for the simple forms of worship; their Christian faith was tried and strengthened in the furnace of persecution, in which it grew bolder for truth and freedom. Under such influences were the Puritan men educated and prepared for their Christian mission on the American continent. Their labors, as future ages showed, received the crowning and abundant blessing of God.

Pilgrims Emigrate to Holland

Under the convictions of a strong Christian faith, the Puritans, in 1608, bade farewell to England, where they had been persecuted for their pure faith and simple forms of Christian worship, and emigrated to Holland, where they hoped to find a permanent asylum. The love of country, the ties of home and kindred, the prospect of suffering, trials, and unnumbered privations, did not deter them from this Christian enterprise;—*"For their desires were set on the ways of God, and to enjoy his ordinances. But they rested on his providence, and knew whom they had believed."*

Webster's View of the Embarkation

"The embarkation of the Pilgrims for Holland," says Webster, "is deeply interesting from its circumstances, and also as a mark of the character of the times, independently of its connection with names now incorporated with the history of empires. Theirs was not the flight of guilt, but virtue. It was an humble and peaceable religion flying from causeless oppression. It was conscience attempting to escape from the arbitrary rule of the Stuarts. It was Robinson and Brewster leading off their little band from their native soil, at first to find a shelter on the shores of a neighboring continent, but ultimately to come hither, and, having surmounted all difficulties and braved a thousand dangers, to find here a place of refuge and rest. Thanks be to God that this spot was honored as the asylum of religious liberty! May its standard, reared here, remain forever! May it rise as high as heaven, till its banner shall fan the air of both continents, and wave as a glorious ensign of peace and prosperity to the nations!"

Emigration to the New World

After remaining in Holland twelve years, the Puritans resolved to seek rest and enlargement, and fulfil their Christian mission, by emigrating to the North American continent.

They had, as they affirmed, "a great hope and inward zeal of laying some good foundation, or at least to make some way thereunto, for the propagating and advancing of the kingdom of Christ unto those remote parts of the world; yea, though they should be but as stepping-stones unto others for performing so great a work."

Farewell Scenes

The farewell scenes are described by Governor Bradford, of the colony, as follows—

"So, being ready to depart, they had a day of solemn humiliation with their pastor—taking his text from Ezra the 8th, 21, '*I proclaimed a fast there, at the river Ahava, that we might afflict ourselves before God, and seek of him a right way for our little ones and our substance;*' upon which he spent a part of the day profitably, and very suitably to their present occasion. The rest of the time was spent in pouring out their prayers to the Lord with great fervency, mixed with abundance of tears. And the time being come when they must depart, they were accompanied with most of their brethren out of the city unto a town sundry miles off, called Delft Haven, where the ship lay ready to receive them. So they left that good and pleasant city, which had been their resting-place near twelve years. But they knew they were PILGRIMS, and looked not much on those things, but lifted up their eyes to heaven, their dearest country, and so quieted their spirits. When they came to the ship, and all things ready, and such of their friends as could not come with them followed after them, and sundry also came from Amsterdam to see them shipped and to take their leave of them.

"Little sleep was there to most of them that night. Friendly entertainment, Christian discourse, and expressions of deep affection in parting," held their eyes waking. "Never," says Winslow, "I persuade myself, never people on earth lived more lovingly together, and parted more sweetly, than we, the church of Leyden," ... "seeking, not rashly, but deliberately, the mind of God in prayer, and finding his gracious presence with us, and his blessing upon us."

The next day—July 22, 1620—the wind being fair, they went on board, and their friends with them; "when truly doleful was the sight of that sad and mournful parting; to see what sighs, and sobs, and prayers, did sound amongst them; what tears did gush from every eye, and pithy speeches pierced each other's heart;—that sundry of the Dutch strangers that stood on the quay as spectators could not refrain from tears. Yet comfortable and sweet it was to see such lively and true expressions of dear and unfeigned love. But the tide, which stays for no man, calling them away that were thus loth to depart, their reverend pastor, failing down upon his knees, and they all with him, with watered cheeks commended them with most fervent prayers to the Lord and his blessing; and then, with mutual embraces and many tears, they took leave of one another, which proved their last leave to many of them."

Robinson, the Pastor

Before they sailed, on the deck of the ship, their Pastor—JOHN ROBINSON—gave them the following farewell charge—

"Brethren, we are now quickly to part from one another; and whether I ever live to see your faces on earth any more, the God of heaven only knows; but whether the Lord has appointed that or no, I charge you, before God and his blessed angels, that you follow me no further than you have seen me follow the Lord Jesus Christ. If God reveals any thing to you by any other instrument of his, be as ready to receive it as ever you were to receive any truth by my ministry, for I am verily persuaded the Lord has more truth yet to break forth from his Holy Word. I charge you to take heed what you receive as truth; examine it, consider it, and compare it with the scriptures of truth before you receive it."

The farewell scenes closed, they set sail for the shores of the New World. "That embarkation," says Choate, "speaks to the nation as with the voices and melodies of an immortal hymn, which dilates and becomes actualized into the auspicious going forth of a colony whose planting has changed the history of the world—a noble colony of devoted Christians—educated, firm men, valiant soldiers, and honorable women—a colony on the commencement of whose heroic enterprise the selectest influences of religion seemed to be descending visibly, and beyond whose perilous path was hung the rainbow and the western star of empire."

"The Mayflower sought our shores," says Webster, "under no high-wrought spirit of commercial adventure, no love of gold, no mixture of purpose warlike or hostile to any human being. Like the dove from the ark, she had put forth only to find rest. Solemn supplications on the shore of the sea in Holland had invoked for her, at her departure, the blessings of Providence. The stars which guided her were the unobscured constellations of civil and religious liberty. Her deck was the altar of the living God. Fervent prayers on bended knees mingled morning and evening with the voices of the ocean and the sighing of the winds in her shrouds. Every prosperous breeze, which, gently filling her sails, helped the Pilgrims onward in their course, awoke new anthems of praise; and when the elements were wrought into fury, neither the tempest, tossing their fragile bark like a feather, nor the darkness and howling of the midnight storm, ever disturbed, in man or woman, the firm and settled purpose of their souls to undergo all and to do all that the meekest patience, the boldest resolution, and the highest trust in God could enable human beings to endure or to perform.

"That Mayflower was a flower destined to be of perpetual bloom! Its verdure will stand the sultry blasts of summer and the chilling winds of autumn. It will defy winter; it will defy all climate, and all time, and will continue to spread its petals to the world, and to exhale an ever-living odor and fragrance to the last syllable of recorded time."

On the 16th of September, 1620, they set sail from Southampton, and, after a stormy and perilous voyage, they fell in with land on the American coast on the 9th of November, "the which being made and certainly known to be it, they were not a little joyful. On their voyage they would set apart whole days of fasting and prayer, to obtain from heaven a good success in their voyage, especially when the weather was much against them, whereunto they had remarkable answers; so much so that the sailors were astonished, and said they were the first sea-fasts ever held in the world."

Arrival at Plymouth Rock

On the 22d of December, 1620, the Puritans, one hundred and one in number, landed from the Mayflower, and planted their feet on the Rock of Plymouth, and began a new era in the history of the world. The day and the rock became canonized in American history, and emblems of the grandest Christian ideas and associations. The first act of the Puritans, after landing, was to kneel down and offer their thanksgiving to God, and by a solemn act of prayer, and in the name and for the sake of Christ, to take possession of the continent. They thus repeated the Christian consecration which Columbus, more than a century before, had given to the New World, and so twice in the most formal and solemn manner was it devoted to Christ and Christian civilization. The seed thus planted bore an abundant harvest of Christian fruits, which have blessed the nation and enriched the world. How significant and sublime the lessons that gather round and flow from Plymouth Rock! How does it speak for God and of God! How grandly does it proclaim the Christian faith and fruits of those great and good men who, in prayer and faith, planted a Christian empire in the New World, and started a Christian nation on a noble career of progress and greatness!

Mrs. Sigourney's Poetry on the Pilgrims

"And can ye deem it strange
That from their planting such a branch should bloom
As nations envy? Should a germ embalm'd
With prayer's pure tear-drops strike no deeper root

Than that which mad Ambition's hand doth strew
Upon the winds to reap the winds again?
Hid by its Veil of waters from the hand
Of greedy Europe, *their* bold vine spread forth
In giant strength.

"Its early clusters, crush'd
In England's wine-press, gave the tyrant host
A draught of deadly wine. O ye who boast
In your free veins the blood of sires like these,
Lose not their lineaments. Should Mammon cling
Too close around your heart—or wealth beget
That bloated luxury which eats the core
From manly virtue—or the tempting world
Make faint the Christian purpose in your soul—
Turn ye to Plymouth's beach; and, on that rock,
Kneel in *their* footprints, and renew the vow
They breathed to God."

—Mrs. Sigourney

Macaulay's View of the Christian Character of the Pilgrims

The Christian life and character of the Puritans have the following description from the pen of England's historian, MACAULAY—

"The Puritans were men whose minds derived a peculiar character from the daily contemplation of superior beings and eternal interests. Not content with acknowledging in general terms an overruling Providence, they habitually ascribed every event to that great Being for whose power nothing was too vast, for whose inspection nothing was too minute. To know him, to serve him, to enjoy him, was with them the great end of existence. They rejected with contempt the ceremonious homage which other sects substituted for the worship of the soul. Instead of catching occasional glimpses of the Deity through an obscuring veil, they aspired to gaze full on the intolerable brightness, and to commune with him face to face. Hence originated their contempt for terrestrial distinctions. The difference between the greatest and meanest of mankind seemed to vanish when compared with the boundless interval which separated the whole race from Him on whom their own eyes were constantly fixed.

"They recognized no title to superiority but God's favor; and, confident of that favor, they despised all the accomplishments and all the dignities of the world. If they were unacquainted with the works of philosophers and poets, they were deeply read in the oracles of God. If their names were not found in the registers of heralds, they felt assured that they were recorded in the book of life. Their palaces were houses not made with hands; their diadems, crowns of glory which should not fade away. On the rich and the eloquent, on nobles and priests, they looked down with (comparative) contempt; for they esteemed themselves rich in more precious treasures, and eloquent in a more sublime language; nobles by the right of an earlier creation, and priests by the imposition of a mightier hand. The very meanest of them was a being to whose fate a mysterious and terrible importance belonged—on whose slightest action the spirits of light and darkness looked with anxious interest—who had been destined, before heaven and earth were created, to enjoy a felicity when heaven and earth should pass away. For his sake the Almighty had proclaimed his will by the pen of the evangelist and the harp of the prophet. He had been rescued by no common deliverer from the grasp of no common foe. He had been ransomed by the sweat of no vulgar agony, by the blood of no earthly sacrifice. It was for him the sun had been darkened, that the rocks had been rent, that the dead had arisen, that all nature had shuddered at the sufferings of an expiring God.

"Thus the Puritan was made of two different men: the one all self-abasement, penitence, gratitude, passion; the other, stern, calm, inflexible, sagacious. He prostrated himself in the dust before his Maker, but set his foot on the neck of his king. In his devotional retirement, he prayed with groans and tears; but when he took his seat in the council, or girt on his sword for war, these workings of the soul had left no perceptible trace behind them. The intensity of their feelings on one subject made them tranquil on all others."

Their Own Declarations

This description, in substance, corresponds with what the New England Puritans say of themselves. "We give ourselves," say they, "to the Lord Jesus Christ, and the word of his grace, for the teaching, ruling, and sanctifying of us, in matters of worship and conversation; resolving to cleave unto him alone for life and glory, and to reject all contrary ways, canons, and constitutions of men in his worship."

Webster's Remark

"Our fathers," says Webster, "had that religious sentiment, that trust in Providence, that determination to do right, and to seek, through every degree of toil and suffering, the honor of God, and the preservation of their liberties, which we shall do well to cherish, to imitate, to equal, to the utmost of our ability."

4

Civil Government Instituted in the Mayflower on a Christian Basis

Christian Signifigance of the Puritan Settlement

THE noblest significance of the Puritan settlement of the North American continent consists in its Christian origin and aim. As the design of Columbus was to "subject every thing to law, order, and religion," so the Puritans began practically to execute this great work. Their first act was to institute a form of civil government in conformity with the revealed will of God, and under whose benign legislation they were to enjoy all the rights and privileges of civil and religious freedom. The form of government was instituted in the cabin of the Mayflower, before they landed on Plymouth Rock, and signed and ratified under the solemnity of prayer and the most sacred sanctions of the Christian religion. That charter of a godly government is as follows—

The Charter

"In the name of God, Amen. We whose names are underwritten, the loyal subjects of our dread sovereign lord, King James, by the grace of God, of Great Britain, France, and Ireland, defender of the faith, &c., having undertaken, for the glory of God, and advancement of the Christian faith, and honor of our king and country, a voyage to plant the first colony on the northern part of Virginia, do, by these presents, solemnly and mutually, in the presence of God and one another, covenant and combine ourselves together into a civil body politic, for our better ordering and preservation, and furtherance of the ends aforesaid; and by virtue hereof to enact, constitute, and frame such just and equal laws, ordinances, acts, constitutions, and offices, from time to time, as shall be thought most meet and convenient for the general good of the colony; unto which we promise all due submission and obedience. In witness whereof, we have hereunto subscribed our names, at Cape Cod, the 11th of November, in the year of the reign of our sovereign lord, King James, of England, France, and Ireland the eighteenth, and of Scotland the fifty-fourth, Anno Domini 1620."

"This Constitution," said Webster, "invokes a *religious* sanction and the authority of God on their *civil* obligations; for it was no doctrine of the Puritans that civil obedience is a mere matter of expediency."

Views of Bancroft and Others

"This," says Bancroft, "was the birth of constitutional liberty. In the cabin of the Mayflower humanity recovered its rights, and instituted governments on the basis of equal rights, for the general good. As the Pilgrims landed, their institutions were already perfected. Democratic liberty and independent Christian worship at once existed in America."

"The compact of the Puritans," said John Quincy Adams, "is a full demonstration that the nature of civil governments, abstracted from the political institutions of their native country, had been an object of their serious meditation."

"Thou little Mayflower," said Carlyle, "hadst in thee a veritable Promethean spark, the life-spark of the largest nation on our earth! Honor to the brave and true! They verily carry fire from heaven, and have a power that themselves dream not of. Let all men honor Puritanism, since God has honored it."

"This compact was the first in the world," says Hall, the historian of the Puritans, "entered into by freemen, preserving the liberties of each, and guaranteeing to all equal privileges and rights. It was the germ of the first true republic on earth. The great idea, so novel, so startling to the world, so directly opposed to the divine right of kings and prelates, under whose sway the world had so long groaned in bondage—the great idea of such a republic, as founded in the nature and inalienable rights of man, the Pilgrims derived from the gospel scheme of a Christian church. For this stupendous discovery, which is now so simple that we wonder it could ever have been overlooked, we are wholly indebted to the diligent search which the Puritans made into the great principles of the rights of conscience, and into the true scriptural model of a Christian church." The charter of freedom formed in the Mayflower is a solemn, dignified, republican state paper, worthy of the founders of a free Christian republic. "Good authorities have pronounced it to have been the germ of American Constitutions." "It contained," says Pitkin, "the elements of those forms of government peculiar to the New World."

Synod of the New England Churches

The synod of the New England churches met at Cambridge, Massachusetts, September 30, 1648, and defined the nature of civil government, the functions of the civil magistrate, and the duties of the citizens, as follows—

"I. God, the Supreme Lord and King of all the world, hath ordained civil magistrates to be under him, over the people, and for his own glory and the public good; and to this end hath armed them with the power of the sword for the defence and encouragement of them that do well, and for the punishment of evil-doers.

"II. It is lawful for Christians to accept and execute the office of magistrate when called thereunto. In the management whereof, as they ought especially to maintain piety, justice, and peace, according to the wholesome laws of each Commonwealth, so for that end they may lawfully now, under the New Testament, wage war upon just and necessary occasions.

"III. They who, upon pretence of Christian liberty, shall oppose any lawful power, or the lawful exercises of it, resist the ordinances of God; and for their publishing such opinions or maintaining of such practices as are contrary to the light of nature, or the known principles of Christianity, or to the power of godliness, or such erroneous opinions and practices as either in their own nature, or in the manner of publishing or maintaining them, are destructive to the external peace and order which Christ hath established in the church, they may be called to account and proceeded against by the censure of the church and by the power of the civil magistrate; yet in such differences about the doctrines of the gospel, or the ways of the worship of God, as may befall men exercising a good conscience, manifesting it in their conversation, and holding the foundation and duly observing the rules of peace and order, there is no warrant in the magistrate to abridge them of their liberty.

"IV. It is the duty of the people to pray for magistrates, to honor their persons, to pay them tribute and other dues, to obey their lawful commands, and to be subject to their authority for conscience's sake. Infidelity or indifference does not make void the magistrate's just and legal authority, nor free the people from their due obedience to him. From which ecclesiastical persons are not exempted; much less has the Pope any power or jurisdiction over them in their dominions, or over any of their people; and least of all to deprive them of their dominions and lives, if he shall judge them to be heretics, or upon other pretext whatsoever."

Civil government on the basis of the Bible and the free principles of a pure Christianity was not the only object that the Puritans had in view in coming to the New World. They had also the great and good end of extending and establishing the kingdom of Christ, and of bringing the whole continent under the reign of Christianity and filling it with its saving blessings. Hence a grand part of the mission of the Puritans was to christianize and civilize the native Indians, who were the sole possessors of the North American continent.

Considerations for the Settlements of New England, by Mather.

Cotton Mather, in his work on New England, makes the following statements as to the motives and reasons that moved the Puritans to come to the New World—

"The God of heaven served, as it were, a summons upon the spirits of his people in the English nation, stirring up the spirits of thousands which never saw the faces of each other, with a most unanimous inclination to leave the pleasant accommodations of their native country, and go over a terrible ocean into a more terrible desert, for the pure enjoyment of all his ordinances. It is now fit that the reasons of this undertaking should be more exactly made known unto posterity; especially unto the posterity of those who were the undertakers, lest they come at length to forget and neglect the true interests of New England. Wherefore I shall transcribe some of them from a manuscript wherein they were tendered unto consideration.

General Considerations for the Plantation of New England

"First. It will be a service unto the church of great consequence, to carry the gospel into those parts of the world and raise a bulwark against the kingdom of Antichrist, which the Jesuits labor to rear up in all parts of the world.

"Secondly. All other churches of Europe have been brought under desolations; and it may be feared that the like judgments are coming upon us; and who knows but God has provided this place to be a refuge for many whom he means to save out of the general destruction?

"Thirdly. The land grows weary of her inhabitants, inasmuch that man, which is the most precious of all creatures, is here (in Europe) more vile and base than the earth he treads upon. Children, neighbors, and friends, especially the poor, are counted the greatest burdens; which, if things were right, would be counted the chiefest of earthly blessings.

"Fourthly. We are grown to that intemperance in all excess of riot, as no mean establishment will suffice a man to keep sail with his equals, and he that fails in it must live in scorn and contempt. Hence it comes to pass that all arts and trades are carried in that deceitful manner and unrighteous course, as it is almost impossible for a good, upright man to maintain his constant charge and live comfortably in them.

"Fifthly. The schools of learning and religion are so corrupted as (beside the unsupportable charge of education) most children, even the best, wittiest, and of the fairest hopes, are perverted, corrupted, and utterly overthrown by the multitudes of evil examples and licentious behavior in these seminaries.

"Sixthly. The whole earth is the Lord's garden, and he hath given it to the sons of Adam, to be tilled and improved by them: why then should we stand starving here for places of habitation, and in the mean time suffer whole countries, as profitable for the use of man, to be waste without improvement?

"Seventhly. What can be a better and nobler work, and more worthy of a Christian, than to erect and support a reformed particular church in its infancy, and unite our forces with such a company of faithful people, as by timely assistance may grow stronger and prosper, but for want of it may be put to great hazards, if not wholly ruined?

"Eighthly. If any such as are known to be godly, and live in wealth and prosperity here, shall forsake all this to join with this reformed church, and with it run the hazard of a hard and mean condition, it will be an example of great use, both for removing of scandal and to give more life unto the faith of God's people in their prayers for the plantation, and also to encourage others to join the more willingly in it."

In 1629, an Emigrant Aid Society was formed in England to promote the more rapid settlement of the North American Colonies; and in the instructions to John Endicott, who was to conduct the emigration, it is declared that the purpose is "for propagating of the gospel in these things we do profess ABOVE ALL to be our ayme in settling this plantacion."

In 1643, a confederation between the colonies of Massachusetts, New Plymouth, Connecticut, and New Haven was formed, in which it is affirmed that "wee all came into these parts of America with the same end and ayme, namely, to advance the kingdom of our Lord Jesus Christ, and to enjoy the liberties thereof with puritie and peace, and for preserving and propagating the truth and liberties of the gospel."

In the charter granted to Massachusetts, in 1640, by Charles I., the Colonies are enjoined by "their good life and orderly conversation to winne and invite the natives of the country to the knowledge of the only true God and Saviour of mankind, and the Christian faith which, in our royal intention and the adventurer's free possession, is the principal end of this plantation."

In 1658, John Eliot, pastor of Roxbury, Massachusetts, and after-wards a devoted and distinguished missionary, completed the trans-lation of the entire Bible, including the Old and New Testaments, for the use of the Indians. This fact having been communicated to the corporation established in London for the propagation of the gospel among the Indians of New England, that body declared, that "wee conceive" (the printing of the work) "will not only be acceptable unto God, but very proffitable to the poor heathen, and will much tend to the promotion of the sperituall part of this worke amongst them. And therefore wee offer it not only as our owne, but as the judgment of others, that the New Testament bee first printed in the Indian language."

The New Testament was, accordingly, printed at Cambridge, Massachusetts, in 1660; and its preface contained the following "Epistle Dedicatory"—

> "To the High and Mighty Prince, CHARLES the Second, by the Grace of God KING of *England, Scotland, France,* and *Ireland,* Defender of the faith, &c. The Commissioners of the Vnited Colonies in New England wish increase of all happiness, &c.

"The people of these four colonies (confederate for mutual defence in the time of the late distractions of our dear native country), your Majestie's natural born subjects, by the Favor and Grant of Your Royal Father and Grandfather of Famous Memory, put themselves upon this great and hazardous undertaking, of planting themselves at their own Charge in these remote ends of the Earth, that, with-out offence or provocation to our dear Brethren and Countrymen, we might enjoy the liberty to Worship God, which our own Con-sciences informed us was not only Right, but Duty; As also that we might (if it so pleased God) be instrumental to spread the light of the Gospel, the knowledge of the Son of God our Saviour, to the poor barbarous Heathen, which by His late Majesty, in some of our patents, is declared to be His principal aim.

"Our Errand hither hath been Endeavours and Blessings; many of the wild *Indians* being taught, and understanding the Doctrine of the Christian Religion, and with much affection attending Such

Preachers as are sent to teach them. Many of their Children are instructed to Write and Reade, and some of them have proceeded further, to attain the knowledge of the Latine and Greek tongues, and are brought up with our English youth in University-learning. There are divers of them that can and do reade some parts of the Scripture, and some Catechisms, which was formerly Translated into their own Language, which hath occasioned the undertaking of a greater Work, *viz.:* The Printing of the whole Bible, which (being Translated by a painful Labourer [Eliot] amongst them, who was desirous to see the Work accomplished in his dayes) hath already proceeded to the finishing of the New Testament, which we here humbly present to Your Majesty, as the first fruits and accomplishment of the Pious Design of your Royal Ancestors.

"And we do most humbly beseech your Majesty, that a matter of so much Devotion and Piety, tending so much to the Honour of God, may Suffer no disappointment. As this Book was begun, and now finished, in the first year of your Establishment; which doth not only presage the happy success of your Highness' Government, but will be a perpetual Monument, that, by your Majestic's Favour, the Gospel of our Lord and Saviour *Jesus Christ* was first made known to the Indians."

Webster's Views of the Civil Government of the Puritans

"Our ancestors," said Webster, "established their system of government on morality and religious sentiment. Moral habits, they believed, cannot be safely trusted on any other foundation than religious principles, nor any government be secure which is not supported by moral habits. Living under the heavenly light of revelation, they hoped to find all the social dispositions, all the duties which men owe to each other and to society, enforced and performed. Whatever makes good men makes good citizens. Our fathers came here to enjoy their religion free and unmolested; and, at the end of two centuries, there is nothing of which we can express a more deep and earnest conviction than of the inestimable importance of that religion to man, in regard to this life, and that which is to come. Let us not forget the religious character of our origin. Our fathers were brought hither by their high veneration of the Christian religion. They journeyed by its light and labored in its hope. They sought to incorporate it with the elements of their society, and to diffuse its influences through all their institutions—civil, political, social, and educational. Let us cherish their sentiments, and extend their influence still more and more, until the full conviction that that is the happiest society which partakes in the highest degree of the mild and peaceful spirit of Christianity." A set of men more conscientious in their doings, or simpler in their manners, or nobler in their character, or purer in their life and doctrines, never founded a commonwealth.

Choate's View

"There was," says Choate, "one influence on the history of the Puritans, whose permanent and Varied effects on its doctrines and destiny is among the most striking in the whole history of opinion. I mean its contact with the republican reforms of the continent, and particularly those of Geneva. I ascribe to the five years of Geneva an influence that has changed the condition of the world. I seem to myself to trace to it, as an influence on the English race, a new theology, a new politics, another tone of character, the opening of another era of time and liberty. I seem to myself to trace to it a portion, at least, of the great civil war of England, the republican constitution framed in the cabin of the Mayflower, the divinity of Jonathan Edwards, the battle of Bunker Hill, and the independence of America."

Bancroft's View of Calvin's Influence

Referring to the same influence, Bancroft says that "the genius of Calvin infused enduring elements into the institutions of Geneva, and made it, for the modern world, the impregnable fortress of popular liberty, the fertile seed-plot of democracy. He that will not honor the memory and respect the influence of Calvin knows but little of the origin of American liberty."

"Of the Puritans it may be said," remarks Judge Story, "with as much truth as of any men that have ever lived, that they acted up to their principles, and followed them out with an unfaltering firmness. They displayed at all times a downright honesty of heart and purpose. In simplicity of life, in godly sincerity, in temperance, in humility, and in patience, as well as in zeal, they seemed to belong to the apostolical age. Their wisdom, while it looked on this world, reached far beyond it in its aim and objects. They valued earthly pursuits no farther than they were consistent with religion. Amidst the temptations of human grandeur, they stood unmoved, unshaken, unreduced. Their scruples of conscience, if they sometimes betrayed them into difficulties, never betrayed them into voluntary sin. They possessed a moral courage which looked present dangers in the face as though they were distant and doubtful, seeking no escape, and indulging no terror. When, in defence of their faith, of what they deemed pure and undefiled religion, we see them resign their property, their preferments, their friends, and their homes; when we see them submitting to banishment and ignominy, and even to death; when we see them in foreign lands, on inhospitable shores, in the midst of sickness and famine, in desolation and disaster, still true to themselves, still confident in God's providence, still submissive to his chastisements, still thankful for his blessings, still ready to exclaim, in the language of Scripture, 'We are troubled on every side, yet not distressed; we are perplexed, but not in despair; persecuted, but not forsaken; cast down, but not destroyed;' when we see such things, where is the man whose soul does not melt within him at the sight? Where shall examples be sought or found, more fully to point out what Christianity is and what it ought to accomplish?

"What better origin could we desire than from men of characters like these? men to whom conscience was every thing, and worldly prosperity nothing; men whose thoughts belonged to eternity rather than to time; men who, in the near prospect of their sacrifices, could say, as our forefathers did say, 'When we are in our graves, it will be all one whether we have lived in plenty or in penury, whether we have died in a bed of down, or locks of straw. Only this is the advantage of the mean condition, THAT THERE IS MORE FREEDOM TO DIE, and the less comfort any have in the things of this world, the more liberty they have to lay up treasures in heaven.' Men who, in answer to the objections urged by the anxiety of friendship, that they might perish by the way, or by hunger, or the sword, could answer, as our forefathers did, 'We may trust God's providence for these things; either he will keep these evils from us, or will dispose of them for our good, and enable us to bear them.' Men who, in still later days, in their appeal for protection to the throne, could say with pathetic truth and simplicity, as our forefathers did, 'That we might enjoy divine worship, without human mixtures, without offence to God, man, our own consciences, with leave, *but not without tears*, we departed from our country, kindred, and fathers' houses, into this Patmos, in relation whereunto we do not say, "our garments are become old by reason of the very long journey," but that *ourselves*, who came away in our strength, are, by reason of our long absence, many of us become gray-headed, and some of us stooping for age.'

"If these be not the sentiments of lofty virtue, if they breathe not the genuine spirit of Christianity, if they speak not high approaches towards moral perfection, if they possess not an enduring sublimity, then indeed have I illy read the human heart; then indeed have I strangely mistaken the inspirations of religion."

5

Christian Colonization of the New England Colonies

Christian Colonization of the Various Colonies

T HE discovery of America," said Webster, "its colonization by the nations of Europe, the history and progress of the colonies, from their establishment to the time when the principal of them threw off their allegiance to the respective states by which they had been planted, and founded governments of their own, constitutes one of the most interesting portions of the annals of man. The Reformation of Luther broke out, kindling up the minds of men afresh, leading to new habits of thought, and awakening in individuals energies before unknown even to themselves. The religious controversies of this period changed society as well as religion." All the colonies, educated under the genius of Christianity and indoctrinated into the knowledge of the principles of just civil governments, laid the basis of their civil systems on the Bible, and made its truths the corner-stone of all their institutions. The fundamental doctrine of the men who planted each colony was, that the legislation of the Bible must be supreme and universal. They rejected as heretical the idea that civil governments could be rightly instituted, or wisely administered, without Christianity. Hence their institutions and their civilization began under the auspices of Heaven, and at once assumed the form of Christian order, and rose into Christian symmetry and completeness; their local democracies, in township, county, and colony, became the nurseries of freedom, and schools of science and art in civil government, and in which each independent colony was in process of preparation for working out the grand results of freedom, and the establishment of a Christian nation on the American continent.

Their Views of Civil Liberty

"Our fathers brought with them from England not merely a vague spirit of personal liberty, but certain ideas of the method of liberty in civil life. Taking the germ from certain Saxon institutions in England, they gave to it in the colonies a development which it had never had in the mother-country. The *township* in New England and the *churches* were the germs and prototypes of the sovereignty of states. It is De Tocqueville who says that the institutions of America are but the unfolding and larger application of the forms and principles of the townships of New England.

Their Local Government

New England townships are yet the purest, if not the only, specimens of absolute democracy in the world. The New England method was to reserve to the individual every right possible, consistently with the good of his neighbor; to retain in the town every particle of authority possible, consistently with the welfare of the state, and to yield to the Great and General Court, as the legislature was named, and to the executive, only such powers as were necessary for the welfare of the whole commonwealth. Thus the colonial governments were broad at the base. Authority was restricted to a few things at the top, but grew in breadth as it came near to the people. This was not an accident. It was the studious effort of sturdy and wise men to keep for the individual just as much personal liberty as was consistent with an equal liberty in all his fellows."

"The settlement of New England," says Trumbull, "purely for the purposes of religion and the propagation of civil and religious liberty, is an event which has no parallel in the history of modern ages. The piety, self-denial, suffering, patience, perseverance, and magnanimity of the first settlers of the country are without a rival. The happy and extensive consequences of the settlements which they made, and of the sentiments which they were careful to propagate to their posterity, to the Church, and to the world, admit of no description. They are still increasing, spreading wider and wider, and appear more and more important."

Massachusetts Colony

As an independent colony, was the first and most memorable of the Puritan family. Its Christian history and bold enunciation and vindication of the pure doctrines of Christianity, and their incorporation into forms of civil government and social life, is one of the most remarkable and instructive chapters in the Christian history of the world.

Charles II. reascended the throne of England in 1660, when the New England colonies had largely increased in population, prosperity, and political power. Grown strong in Christian faith, and in a fervent love for liberty, the people of Massachusetts enjoyed too much freedom for the despotic feelings and principles of the king. Hence, on the restoration of Charles II., they feared that their freedom would be abridged and their rights taken from them. The people of the commonwealth sent to the king a formal and a frank address. It was full of Christian sentiment and faith, and declared their purpose to submit to the government of the king in all things not conflicting with their duties to the King of kings.

They prayed for the continuance of civil and religious liberties. "Your servants are true men, fearing God and the king. We could not live without the public worship of God; and that we, therefore, might enjoy divine worship, without human mixtures, we, not without tears, departed from our country, kindred, and fathers' houses. To enjoy our liberty, and to walk according to the faith and order of the gospel, was the cause of our transporting ourselves, our wives, our little ones, and our substance, choosing the pure Christian worship, with a good conscience, in this remote wilderness, rather than the pleasures of England with submission to the impositions of the hierarchy, to which we could not yield without an evil conscience."

These professions of good faith and loyalty failed to secure the favor of Charles II. He demanded a surrender of their charter, and with it their independence as a free Christian commonwealth. The remonstrances against these usurpations are suggestive memorials of their Christian faith and firmness, and a vindication of the axiom that "resistance to tyrants is obedience to God." In their address to Charles II., 1664, they declare that they were "resolved to act for the glory of God, and for the felicities of his people;" and that, "having now above thirty years enjoyed the privilege of government within themselves, as their undoubted right in the sight of God and man, to be governed by rulers of our own choosing, and laws of our own, is the fundamental privilege of our charter."

This contest was a time of trial and of danger to their civil liberties, and they said their hope was in God alone. A day of fasting and humiliation was appointed, and the people prostrated themselves in humiliation and prayer before God, and implored his interposition. The civil court, when convened for the administration of business, spent a portion of each day in prayer—six elders praying, and a minister preaching a sermon. "We must," said they, "as well consider God's displeasure as the king's, the interests of ourselves and of God's things, as his majesty's prerogative; for our liberties are of concernment, and to be regarded as to preservation."

"Religion," says Bancroft, "had been the motive of settlement; religion was now its counsellor. The fervors of the most ardent devotion were kindled; a more than usually solemn form of religious observance was adopted; a synod of all the churches in Massachusetts was convened to inquire into the causes of the dangers to New England liberty, and the mode of removing the evils." "Submission," said they, "would be an offence against the majesty of Heaven. Blind obedience to the pleasure of the king cannot be without great sin, and incurring the high displeasure of the King of kings. Submission would be contrary unto that which has been the unanimous advice of the ministers, given after a solemn day of prayer. The ministers of God in New England have more of the spirit of John the Baptist in them, than now, when a storm hath overtaken them, to be reeds shaken with the wind.

The priests were to be the first that set their foot in the water, and there to stand till the danger be past. Of all men, they should be an example to the Lord's people, of faith, courage, and constancy.

"The civil liberties of New England are part of the inheritance of their fathers; and shall we give that inheritance away? Is it objected that we shall be exposed to great suffering? Better suffer than sin. It is better to trust the God of our fathers than to put confidence in princes. If we suffer because we dare not comply with the wills of men, against the will of God, we suffer in a good cause, and shall be accounted martyrs in the next generation and at the great day."

These were the noble utterances of Christian men and legislators, and display the nature of the principles which governed them in times of trial. They stood firm to their Christian faith and civil rights, and demonstrated the inseparable union between Christianity and civil liberty. These principles, maintained with such Christian heroism, were reproduced in the scenes of the Revolution, and contributed to the creation of a new and independent empire.

This Christian commonwealth declared that those "who should go about to subvert and destroy the Christian faith and religion by broaching and maintaining damnable heresies, as denying the immortality of the soul or the resurrection of the body, or denying that Christ gave himself a ransom for our sins, or shall deny the morality of the 4th Commandment, or shall deny the ordinance of the civil magistrate, shall be banished."

"Were a council," said Wise, in 1669, "called of all the learned heads of the whole universe, could they dictate better laws and advise better measures for the acquirement of learning, the increase of virtue and good religion, than are in the royal province of Massachusetts? If we take a survey of the whole land, we shall find religion placed in the body politic as the soul in the body natural. That is, the whole soul is in the whole body while it is in every part."

Colony of Connecticut

Unfolds, in its Christian colonization and civil institutions, the benign and beautiful fruits of the Christian religion. The aim of the crown and of the colonists in planting Connecticut was to establish and extend the reign of the Christian religion. For this purpose, the General Assembly of the Colony were instructed to govern the people "so as their good life and orderly conversation may win and invite the natives of the country to the knowledge and obedience of the only true God and Saviour of mankind, and the Christian faith; which, in our royal intentions and the adventurer's free possession, is the *only* and principal end of this plantation."

The first organization of civil society and government was made, in 1639, at Quinipiack, now the beautiful city of New Haven. The emigrants, men of distinguished piety and ability, met in a large barn, on the 4th of June, 1639, and, in a very formal and solemn manner, proceeded to lay the foundations of their civil and religious polity.

Government Instituted by the Church

The subject was introduced by a sermon from Mr. Davenport, the pastor, from the words of Solomon, "Wisdom hath builded her house, she hath hewn out her seven pillars." After a solemn invocation to Almighty God, he proceeded to represent to the Plantation that they were met to consult respecting the setting up of civil government according to the will of God, and for the nomination of persons who, by universal consent, were in all respects the best qualified for the foundation-work of a church. He enlarged on the great importance of thorough action, and exhorted every man to give his vote in the fear of God. A constitution was formed, which was characterized as "the first example of a written constitution; as a distinct organic act, constituting a government and defining its powers." The preamble and resolutions connected with its formation are as follows—

"FORASMUCH as it hath pleased the Almighty God, by the wise disposition of his divine providence, so to order and dispose of things that we, the inhabitants of Windsor, Hartford, and Wethersfield, are now cohabiting and dwelling in and upon the river of Connecticut, and the lands thereunto adjoining, and well knowing where a people are gathered together the word of God requireth that, to maintain the peace and union of such a people, there should be an orderly and decent government established according to God, to order and dispose of the affairs of the people at all seasons as occasion should require; do, therefore, associate and conjoin ourselves to be as one public STATE or COMMONWEALTH, and do enter into combination and confederation to maintain and preserve the liberty and purity of the gospel of our LORD JESUS, which we now profess, as also the discipline of the churches, which, according to the truth of said gospel, is now practised amongst us; as also in our civil affairs to be guided and governed according to such laws, rules, orders, and decrees as shall be made.

"I. That the Scriptures hold forth a perfect rule for the direction and government of all men in all duties which they are to perform to God and men, as well in families and commonwealths as in matters of the church.

"II. That as in matters which concerned the gathering and ordering of a church, so likewise in all public offices which concern civil order—as the choice of magistrates and officers, making and repealing laws, dividing allotments of inheritance, and all things of like nature—they would all be governed by those rules which the Scripture held forth to them.

"III. That all those who had desired to be received free planters had settled in the plantation with a purpose, resolution, and desire that they might be admitted into church fellowship according to Christ.

"IV. That all the free planters held themselves bound to establish such civil order as might best conduce to the securing of the purity and peace of the ordinance to themselves, and their posterity according to God."

When these resolutions had been passed, and the people had bound themselves to settle civil government according to the divine word, Mr. Davenport proceeded to state what men they must choose for civil rulers according to the divine word, and that they might most effectually secure to themselves and their posterity a just, free, and peaceable government. After a full discussion, it was unanimously determined—

"V. That church members only should be free burgesses; and that they only should choose magistrates among themselves, to have power of transacting all the public civil affairs of the plantation, of making and repealing laws, dividing inheritances, deciding of differences that may arise, and doing all things and businesses of a like nature."

That civil officers might be chosen and government proceed according to these resolutions, it was necessary that a church should be formed. Without this there could be neither freemen nor magistrates. Accordingly, in the most formal and solemn manner, a church was formed, with its proper officers. After this, those who constituted the church elected Theophilus Eaton governor of the civil commonwealth, and others to the offices of magistrates, secretary, and marshal.

The governor was then charged by the Rev. Mr. Davenport, in the most solemn manner, as to his duties, from Deut. i. 16,17—"And I charged your judges at that time, saying, Hear the causes between your brethren, and judge righteously between every man and his brother, and the stranger that is with him. Ye shall not respect persons in judgment, but ye shall hear the small as well as the great; ye shall not be afraid of the face of man; for the judgment is God's: and the cause that is too hard for you, bring it unto me, and I will hear it."

The General Court, established under this constitution, ordered—

"That God's word should be the only rule for ordering the affairs of government in this commonwealth."

Winthrop

In 1662, Winthrop, whose father had been Governor of Massachusetts Colony, obtained from Charles II. a charter for the colony of Connecticut, which gave the largest civil liberty to the colonists, and contained the great American doctrine of popular sovereignty. Winthrop was a truly godly magistrate, combining learning, piety, and practical wisdom with superior administrative talents. He was for fourteen consecutive years governor of the colony.

Bancroft's Picture of the Colony

"Religion," says Bancroft, "united with the pursuits of agriculture to give to the land the aspect of salubrity; religious knowledge was carried to the highest degree of refinement, alike in its application to moral duties, and to the mysterious questions on the nature of God, of liberty, and of the soul. Civil freedom was safe under the shelter of a masculine morality, and beggary and crime could not thrive in the midst of the severest manners. The government was in honest and upright hands; the state was content with virtue and single-mindedness; and the public welfare never suffered at the hands of plain men." Under this Christian government "Connecticut was long the happiest state in the world." "The contentment of Connecticut was full to the brim. In a public proclamation, under the great seal of the colony, it told the world that its days, under the charter, were the 'halcyon days of peace.'"

"In an age," says Trumbull, "when the light of freedom was but just dawning, the illustrious men of the colony of Connecticut, by voluntary compact, formed one of the most free and happy constitutions of government which mankind have ever adopted. Connecticut has ever been distinguished by the free spirit of its government, the mildness of its laws, and the general diffusion of knowledge among all classes of its inhabitants. They have been no less distinguished for their industry, economy, purity of manners, prosperity, and spirit of enterprise. For more than a century and a half they have had no rival as to the steadiness of their government, their internal peace and harmony, their love and high enjoyment of domestic, civil, and religious order and happiness. They have ever stood among the most illuminated, fervent, and boldest defenders of the civil and religious rights of mankind."

Rhode Island Colony

Became a distinct colony in 1662, by the grant of a charter from Charles II. This charter gave the utmost Christian liberty in the exercise of the rights of conscience in religion.

The object of colonizing Rhode Island is thus expressed in the charter—"The colonists are to pursue with peace and loyal minds their sober, serious, and religious intentions of godly edifying themselves and one another in the holy Christian faith and worship, together with the gaining over the conversion of the poor ignorant Indians to the sincere profession and obedience of the same faith and worship."

Roger Williams, a Baptist minister, and among the first emigrants to the colony of Massachusetts, was the founder of the Rhode Island Colony. Having seen and felt the evils of an intolerant spirit in matters of religion, he obtained a charter that granted freedom in religious matters to all denominations. "No person," declared the charter, "within the said colony, at any time hereafter, shall be in any wise molested or punished, disquieted or called in question, for any difference in opinion in matters of religion; every person may at all times freely and fully enjoy his own judgment and conscience in matters of religious concernments." This organic law was confirmed by the first legislative Assembly declaring, in 1665, that "liberty to all persons as to the worship of God had been a principle maintained in the colony from the very beginning thereof; and it was much in their hearts to preserve the same liberty forever." In 1680 the same fundamental law was re-enacted—"We leave every man to walk as God persuades his heart: all our people enjoy freedom of conscience."

"Roger Williams," says Bancroft, "asserted the great doctrine of intellectual liberty. It became his glory to found a state upon that principle, and to stamp himself upon its rising institutions so deeply that the impress can never be erased without the total destruction of the work. He was the first person in modern Christendom to assert in its plenitude the doctrine of the liberty of conscience, the equality of opinions before the law; and in its defence it was the harbinger of Milton, the precursor and the superior of Jeremy Taylor. Williams would permit persecutions of no opinion, of no religion, leaving heresy unharmed by law, and orthodoxy unprotected by the terrors of penal statutes." He had the honor of enunciating that fundamental principle of the Bible and of American institutions, "that the civil power has no jurisdiction over the conscience," a doctrine which, Bancroft says, "secures him an immortality of fame, as its application has given religious peace to the American world."

Civil Government of Rhode Island

The colony thus founded on a Christian basis enjoyed a Christian democracy, and this original charter of civil and religious liberty continued as the organic government of Rhode Island till 1842, "the oldest constituted charter in the world. Nowhere in the world were life, liberty, and property safer than in Rhode Island."

"Rhode Island," says Arnold, in his history of that commonwealth, "was a State whose founders had been doubly tried in the purifying fire; a State which more than any other has exerted, by the weight of its example, an influence to shape the political ideas of the present day, whose moral power has been in the inverse ratio with its material importance; of which an eminent historian of the United States has said, that, had its territory 'corresponded to the importance and singularity of the principles of its early existence, the world would have been filled with wonder at the phenomena of its history.'"

New Hampshire Colony

In 1679, was separated from Massachusetts and organized as an independent province. The colonists, having been so long a part of the Christian commonwealth of Massachusetts, constituted their institutions on the same Christian basis. Its legislature was Christian, and the colony greatly prospered and increased in population. It nourished a class of Christian men who loved liberty, and who have ever exerted a prominent influence on the civil and religious interests of the American nation.

January 1, 1680, a royal decree declared New Hampshire an independent province; and the policy of the king was to smooth the way to an unjust and an unconstitutional government. The colonists, in their remonstrances, declared that the policy "struck liberty out of existence, by denying them the choice of their own rulers; and they viewed the loss of liberty as a precursor to an invasion of their prosperity." A civil assembly was convened, and a solemn public fast proclaimed and observed to propitiate the favor of Heaven, and the continuance of their "precious and pleasant things."

In an address to the king, the colonists of New Hampshire say, "that your petitioners' predecessors removed themselves, and some of us, into this remote region and howling wilderness, in pursuance of the glorious cause proposed, *viz.*: The glory of God, the enlarging of his majesty's dominions, and spreading the gospel among the heathen."

The influence and results of the Christian constitutions and governments of New England are stated by Rev. John Wise, in a work on the Government of the New England Churches, as follows—

"1. Legislative power (that civil omnipotence) is doing very great things for religion, by their proclamations, and all penal laws enacted for the crushing of immorality and vice, and all their wise and exact precepts for the support of justice and piety. They are opening many civil channels, whereby they are conveying judgment, justice, and righteousness down our streets from the great fountain. Nay, this great and dread assembly puts awe upon all mankind. And the more daring and desperate are kept within compass, from a sense of this most terrible seat of thunder hanging over their heads, and upon every affront ready to break in strokes of vengeance and woes upon them, especially if they grow beyond the reach of common law.

"2. The executive power, or ministers of the law, are like a standing camp to awe, and a flying army to beat off, the enemy: they have their spies and scouts out in every quarter to observe his motions and break his measures, namely, in the innumerable number of all sorts of civil officers; and thus by the sword of justice they hunt down sin and impiety in the land. They are a terror to evil-doers, and a praise to them that do well; for the civil authority, by their wise and just precepts, their personal and noble examples and zealous administrations, outdo Plato himself, with all his moral reasons; for they can turn a Sodom into a Sion, and keep Sion to be Sion, evident by the history and chronicles of several governments of God's ancient people. For chief rulers, by their good or bad measures, can make or mar, kill or cure, a nation in a moral sense."

6

Christian Systems of Education in the New England Colonies

Christian Education

EDUCATION, next to the Christian religion, is an indispensable element of republican institutions, the basis upon which all free governments must rest.

Its Importance to the Civil State

"The state must rest upon the basis of religion, and it must preserve this basis, or itself must fall. But the support which religion gives to the state will obviously cease the moment religion looses its hold upon the popular mind. The very fact that the state must have religion as a support for its own authority demands that some means for teaching religion be employed. Better for it to give up all other instruction than that religion should be disregarded in its schools. The state itself has a more vital interest in this continued influence of religion over its citizens than in their culture in any other respect."

Christian education, from the very beginning of the New England colonies, engaged the attention of the Puritans, and ample provisions were made for the instruction of all the children and youth in every branch of human and divine knowledge. This, indeed, was one object they had in coming to the New World. Cotton Mather, in presenting the considerations for the plantation of the colonies, says—

"The schools of learning and religion are so corrupted as (besides the unsupportable charge of education) most children, even the best and wittiest, and of the fairest hopes, are perverted, corrupted, and utterly overthrown by the multitude of evil examples and licentious behavior in these seminaries."

John Eliot, the apostle to the Indians, in a prayer before the Civil Court, in Massachusetts, in 1645, uttered the following sentiments—

"Lord! for schools everywhere among us! That our schools may flourish! That every member of this Assembly may go home and procure a good school to be encouraged in the town where he lives! That before we die we may be so happy as to see a good school encouraged in every plantation in the country!"

Schools Established

In 1644, the Christian colonists, "to the end that all learning may not be buried in the graves of our forefathers, ordered," that every township, "after the Lord hath increased them to fifty householders, shall appoint one to teach all children to read and write; and where any town shall increase to the number of one hundred families, they shall set up a grammar school; the master thereof being able to instruct youth so far as they may be fitted for the university."

The Early School Laws

"One of the earliest legislative acts of the Massachusetts colony was the following—'Forasmuch as the good education of children is of singular behoofe and benefit to any commonwealth; and whereas parents and masters are too indulgent and negligent of their duty in that kind—

"'It is therefore ordered by this courte and authority thereof that the selectmen of every towne, in the several precincts and quarters where they dwell, shall have a vigilent eye over theire brethren and neighbours; to see, first, that none of them shall suffer so much barbarisme in any of their familyes, as not to endeavor to teach, by themselves or others, theire children and apprentices, so much learning as may inable them perfectly to read the English tongue, and knowledge of the capitall lawes.'"

As early as 1635, free schools were commenced in Boston. The union of the Massachusetts and New Hampshire colonies continued till 1680, and during this time the example of Boston was rapidly followed by smaller towns in both colonies. "In the subject of schools both rulers and ministers felt a deep interest, and schoolmasters were a commodity in great demand, and eagerly sought." As early as 1644, one town devoted a portion of its lands to the support of schools; but, before the lands could be productive, they raised in various ways the sum of twenty pounds to hire a schoolmaster.

The following was passed by the General Court, in the year 1647, for the promotion of common education—

"It is therefore ordered by this courte and authority thereof, That every towneshipp within this jurisdiction, after that the Lord hath increased them to the number of fifty howsholders, shall then forthwith appointe one within theire towne, to teach all such children as shall resorte to him, to write and read; whose wages shall be paid either by the parents or masters of such children, or by the inhabitants in generall, by way of supplye, as the major parte of those who order the prudentials of the towne shall appointe.

"And it is further ordered, That where any towne shall increase to the number of one hundred families or howsholders, they shall sett up a grammar schoole, the masters thereof being able to instruct youths so far as they may bee fitted for the university."

In 1636, the colonists began at Cambridge, Massachusetts, the first college on the American continent. Its commencement was as follows—

"The magistrates led the way by a subscription among themselves of two hundred pounds, in books for the library. The comparatively wealthy followed with gifts of twenty and thirty pounds. The needy multitude succeeded, like the widow of old, casting their mites into the treasury. A number of sheep was bequeathed by one man; a quantity of cotton cloth, worth nine shillings, presented by another; a pewter flagon, worth ten shillings, by a third; a fruit-dish, a sugar-spoon, a silver-tipt jug, one great set, and one smaller trencher set, by others."

"The ends," says Cotton Mather, "for which our fathers chiefly erected a college were that scholars might there be educated for the service of Christ and his churches, in the work of the ministry, and that the youth might be seasoned in their tender years with such principles as brought their blessed progenitors into this wilderness. There is no one thing of greater concernment to these churches, in present and after times, than the prosperity of that society. We cannot subsist without a college."

Harvard College Founded

A college, accordingly, was established in 1636, and in 1638 Rev. John Harvard, a learned and wealthy minister, died, and by his will gave one-half of his property and his entire library to the college at Boston; and hence it is called Harvard College, and now, also, Cambridge University.

Christian Facts Connected with Its Establishment

According to the rules for the government of this college, the president or professor, on being inaugurated, must first, "repeat his oath to the civil government; then he must declare his belief in the scriptures of the Old and New Testaments, and promise to open and explain the Scriptures to his pupils with integrity and faithfulness, according to the best light God shall give him." He also must promise "to promote true piety and godliness by his example and instruction."

"The rector or president shall also cause the Scriptures daily, except on the Sabbath mornings and evenings, to be read by the students at the times of prayer in the school; and upon the Sabbath he shall either expound practical theology, or cause the non-graduating students to repeat sermons; so that, through the blessing of God, it may be conducive to their establishment in the principles of the Christian Protestant religion.

"The exercises of the students had the aspect of a theological rather than a literary institution. *They were practised twice a day in reading the Scriptures*, giving an account of their proficiency in practical and spiritual truths, accompanied by theoretical observations on the language and logic of the sacred writings. They were carefully to attend God's ordinances, and be examined on their profiting; commonplacing the sermons, and *repeating them publicly in the hall.* In every year and every week of the college course, every class was practised *in the Bible and catechetical divinity."*

Rev. Thomas Shepard, D.D., a learned divine, and laborious minister of God, conceived the design of procuring voluntary contributions of corn—money being out of the question—from all parts of New England, for the purpose of maintaining poor students. He laid the following memorial before the commissioners of the united colonies of Massachusetts, Plymouth, Connecticut, and New Haven, which met at Hartford, in 1644.

"To the Honored Commissioners—

"Those whom God hath called to attend the welfare of religious commonwealths have been prompt to extend their care for the good of public schools, by means of which the commonwealth may be furnished unto knowing and understanding men in all callings, and the church with an able minister in all places; without which it is easy to see how both these estates may decline and degenerate into gross ignorance, and, consequently, into great and universal profaneness. May it please you, therefore, among other things of common concernment and public benefit, to take into your consideration some way of comfortable maintenance for that school of the prophets that now is established. ... If, therefore, it were recommended by you to the freedom of every family that is able and willing to give, throughout the plantations, to give but the fourth part of a bushel of corn, or something equivalent thereto," &c.

This memorial was received, and its policy cordially carried out by the commissioners, who recommended to the deputies of the several General Courts, and to the elders within the four colonies, to call for a voluntary contribution of one peck of corn, or twelve pence in money, or its equivalent in other commodities, from every family—a recommendation which was adopted and very generally responded to.

The constitution of Massachusetts, of 1780, thus refers to Harvard College—"Whereas our wise and pious ancestors, so early as the year 1636, laid the foundation of Harvard College, in which university many persons of great eminence have, by the blessing of God, been initiated into those arts and sciences which qualified them for public employment, both in Church and State; and whereas the encouragement of arts and sciences, and all good literature, *tends to the honor of God, the advantage of the Christian religion,* and the great benefit of this and the other United States of America, it is declared, that the President and Fellows of Harvard College," &c.

Yale College

At New Haven, Connecticut, the second successful effort was made to found a permanent college of learning. Common schools, where the elements of education were widely diffused among the rising population, did not satisfy the enlarged views of literary men, and the plan of an institution of higher pretensions and more extended scope occupied the thoughts of the first settlers of Connecticut.

After various consultations, chiefly in reference to the interests of the Church, and confined in a great measure to the liberal and enlightened clergy of the times, a definite proposition was at length submitted with regard to the establishment of a college in New Haven. The following resolution is the earliest record on the subject—

"At a General Court, held at Guilford, June 28th, A.D. 1652, Voted, the matter about a college at New Haven was thought to be too great a charge for us of this jurisdiction to undergo alone, especially considering the unsettled state of New Haven town, being publicly declared, from the deliberate judgement of the most understanding men, to be a place of no comfortable subsistence for the present inhabitants there. But, if Connecticut do join, the planters are generally willing to bear their just proportion for erecting and maintaining of a college there."

In 1700, ten of the principal ministers in the colony were nominated and agreed upon, by a general consent, both of the ministers and people, to stand as trustees or undertakers to found, erect, and govern a college. They soon met at Branford, and laid the foundation of Yale College. Each member brought a number of books and presented them to the body, and, laying them on the table, said—*"I give these books for the founding of a college* in this colony." The object of a college at New Haven was stated by a large number of ministers and laymen, who petitioned the Colonial Assembly for a charter. They said that, "from a sincere regard to, and zeal for upholding the Protestant religion by a succession of learned and orthodox men, they had proposed that a collegiate school should be erected in this colony, wherein youth should be instructed in all parts of learning, to qualify them for public employment in Church and civil State."

The legislature of the colony promptly responded to the application, and a charter was granted, in which it was said—

"Whereas, several well-disposed and public-spirited persons, out of their sincere regard to, and zeal for upholding and propagating the Christian Protestant religion by a succession of learned and orthodox men, have expressed by petition their earnest desire that full liberty and privilege be granted unto certain undertakers for the founding, suitably endowing and ordering a Collegiate School within his Majesty's Colony of Connecticut, wherein youth may be instructed in the arts and sciences, who, through the blessing of Almighty God, may be fitted for public employment both in Church and State. To the intent, therefore, that all due encouragement be given to such pious resolutions, and that so necessary and religious an undertaking may be set forward and well managed, be it enacted," &c.

The charter being granted, at a meeting of the collegiate undertakers, held at Saybrook, November 11, A.D. 1701, they sent out the following circular—

"Whereas, it was the glorious public design of our now blessed fathers in their removal from Europe into these parts of America, both to plant, and (under the Divine blessing) to propagate in this wilderness, the blessed Reformed Protestant religion, in the purity of its order and worship, not only to their posterity, but also to the barbarous natives; in which great enterprise they wanted not the royal commands and favor of his Majesty Ring Charles the Second to authorize and invigorate them.

"We, their unworthy posterity, lamenting our past neglect of this grand errand, and sensible of the equal obligations better to prosecute the same end, are desirous in our generation to be serviceable thereunto. Whereunto the religious and liberal education of suitable youth is, under the blessing of God, a chief and most probable expedient:

"Therefore, that we might not be wanting in cherishing the present observable and pious disposition of many well-minded people to dedicate their children and substance unto God in such a good service, and being ourselves with sundry other reverend elders, not only desired by our godly people to undertake, as Trustees, for erecting, forming, ordering, and regulating a Collegiate School, for the advancement of such an education; but having also obtained of our present religious government both full liberty and assistance by their donation to such use; tokens, likewise, that particular persons will not be wanting in their beneficence; do, in duty to God and the weal of our country, undertake in the aforesaid design.

"For the orderly and effectual management of this affair, we agree to, and hereby appoint and confirm, the following rules—

"1st. That the Rector take special care, as of the moral behaviour of the students, at all times, so with industry to instruct and ground them well in theoretical divinity; and to that end shall take effectual measures that the said students be weekly caused *memoriter* to recite the Assembly's Catechism in Latin; and he shall make, or cause to be made, from time to time, such explanations as may (through the blessing of God) be most conducive to their establishment in the principles of the Christian Protestant religion.

"2d. The Rector shall also cause the Scriptures daily (except on the Sabbath), morning and evening, to be read by the students, at the times of prayer in the school, according to the laudable order and usage of *Harvard College*, making expositions upon the same; and upon the Sabbath shall either expound practical theology, or cause the non-graduating students to repeat sermons; and in all other ways, according to his best discretion, shall at all times studiously endeavor, in the education of the students, to promote the power and purity of religion and the best edification of these New England churches."

Rev. Henry B. Smith, of the Union Theological Seminary at New York, in behalf of the Society for the Promotion of Collegiate and Theological Education at the West, presents the following view of the history and fruits of the colleges at Cambridge and New Haven—

"For our encouragement it may be said that no people ever began its institutions under better auspices or with ampler promise. This we owe, under God, to the pious zeal of our Pilgrim Fathers, many of them eminent in learning as well as faith. John Cotton, of Boston, had been the head-lecturer and dean of Immanuel College in Cambridge, England. John Newton, of Ipswich, afterwards of Boston, was offered a fellowship in the same college. John Davenport, of New Haven, was termed a 'universal scholar.' Thomas Hooker, of Hartford, was a fellow of Cambridge, and was here called the 'light of the Western churches.' Thomas Thatcher, of Weymouth, composed a Hebrew lexicon. Charles Chauncey, president of Harvard, had been Professor of Greek in Cambridge, England. Cotton Mather was the author of three hundred and eighty-two publications, including the 'Magnalia.'

Influence of These Colleges on the State

"Established under such auspices, it is no wonder that all our earlier colleges, and, following in their train, most of the later, have been animated by the conviction that institutions of learning are needed by Christianity, and should have this faith as the basis of all their instructions. The earliest were not so much colleges as schools for the training of the ministry. The Pilgrims, when they numbered only five thousand families, founded the University of Cambridge, in 1636, with its perennial motto, '*Christo et Ecclesiae*;' and Cotton Mather says that this university was 'the best thing they ever thought of.' In 1696, there were one hundred and sixteen pastors in the one hundred and twenty-nine churches, and one hundred and nine of these were from Harvard. Harvard has educated one thousand six hundred and seventy-three ministers: three hundred and fifty-one are still living. Yale College dates from 1700, and in its earlier years the Assembly's Catechism in Greek was read by the freshmen; the sophomores studied Hebrew; the juniors, sophomores, and the seniors, both at Harvard and Yale, were thoroughly instructed in divinity in the admirable compend of Wollebius.

"Yale has given to our churches one thousand six hundred and sixty-one ministers, of whom seven hundred and forty-one are still living. In the State of Connecticut, down to 1842, out of nine hundred and forty-seven ministers, only thirty-three were not graduates. Princeton was started in 1741, one of the fruits of the great re-vival, and by the New Side of that day. Dartmouth was a missionary school from its inception in 1769; and its catalogue gives the names of more than seven hundred ministers, a quarter-part of all its grad-uates. And almost all of our later colleges are the fruit of Christian beneficence, and their foundations have been laid with the prayers of our churches; and He who heareth prayer has breathed upon them his divine blessing, and through their influence sanctified our youth for the service of Christ and his Church. They have aspired to realize that ideal of education which Milton had in vision when he said, 'The end of learning is to repair the ruins of our first parents by regaining to know God aright, and out of that knowledge to love him, to imitate him, to be like him, as we may the nearest by pos-sessing our souls of true virtue, which, being united to the heavenly grace of faith, makes up the highest perfection.'"

"Yale College," says Lossing, "aside from its intrinsic worth as a seminary of learning, is remarkable for the great number of the lead-ing men of the Revolution who were educated within its walls. That warm and consistent patriot, President Daggett, gave a political tone to the establishment favorable to the republican cause, and it was regarded as the nursery of Whig principles during the Revolution. When New Haven was invaded by Tryon, Yale College was marked for special vengeance; but the invaders retreated hastily, without burning the town. There were very few among the students, during our war for independence, who were imbued with tory principles, and they were generally, if known, rather harshly dealt with."

Judge Story's Views

"Among the most striking acts of the legislation of the Puritans," says Judge Story, "are those which respect the cause of learning and education. Within ten short years after their first settlement, they founded the University of Cambridge, and endowed it with the sum of four hundred pounds—a sum which, considering their means and their wants, was a most generous benefaction. Perhaps no language could more significantly express the dignity of their design than their own words. 'After God had carried us safe to New England,' said they, 'and we had builded our houses, provided necessaries for our households, reared convenient places for God's worship, and settled the civil government, one of the next things we longed for, and looked after, was *to advance learning and perpetuate it to posterity*, dreading to leave an illiterate ministry to the churches when our present ministers shall lie in the dust.' The truest glory of our forefathers is in that system of public instruction which they instituted by law, and to which New England owes more of its character, its distinction, and its prosperity than to all other causes. If this system be not altogether without example in the history of other nations (as I suspect it to be in its structure and extent), it is, considering the age and means of the projectors, an extraordinary instance of wise legislation, and worthy of the most profound statesmen of any times. At the distance of centuries, it stands alone and unrivalled. It was on this system of public instruction that our fathers laid the foundation for the perpetuity of our institutions, and for that growth of sound morals, industry, and public spirit, which has never yet been wanting in New England, and, we may fondly hope, will forever remain her appropriate praise.

"I know not what more munificent donation any government can bestow than by providing instruction at public expense, not as a scheme of charity, but of municipal policy. If a private person deserves the applause of all good men, who founds a single hospital or college, how much more are they entitled to the appellation of public benefactors who by the side of every church in every village plant a school of letters! Other monuments of the art and genius of man perish; but these, from their very nature, seem absolutely immortal."

Bancroft's Views

"In these measures," says Bancroft, "especially in the laws establishing common schools, lies the secret of the success and character of New England. Every child, as it was born into the world, was lifted from the earth by the genius of the country, and in the statutes of the land received, as its birthright, a pledge of the public care for its morals and its mind."

7

Christian Colonization of Pennsylvania—New York— New Jersey— Delware

Colonization of Pennsylvania

IN 1682, another important era in the Christian colonization of the North American continent was inaugurated. William Penn was singularly qualified to be the founder of a Christian commonwealth. He had been educated under the influence of the gospel. He had studied the origin of government, the nature of civil liberty, and the rights of man, in the light of the pure word of God, and formed the purpose of founding a Christian empire on the free and peaceful precepts of Christianity. He had a firm faith in the great American idea that man, educated by Christianity, was capable of self-government. Finding no place in Europe to try the experiment of a Christian government, he resolved to seek it in America.

The settlement of the province of Pennsylvania by William Penn formed a new era in the liberties of mankind. It afforded a resting-place where the conscientious and oppressed people of Europe might repose, and enjoy the rights of civil and religious freedom which mankind had derived as an inheritance from the Creator.

He obtained from Charles II. a grant of territory that now embraces the States of Pennsylvania, New Jersey, and Delaware. He was legally inducted to the governorship of this immense domain, in England, by the officers of the crown, and in 1682 arrived in the New World and assumed the civil government of the colony. He avowed his purpose to be to institute a civil government on the basis of the Bible and to administer it in the fear of the Lord. The acquisition and government of the colony, he said, was "so to serve the truth and the people of the Lord, that an example may be set to the nations."

Based on the Bible

The frame of government which Penn completed in 1682 for the government of Pennsylvania was derived from the Bible. He deduced from various passages "the origination and descent of all human power from God; the divine right of government, and that for two ends—first, to terrify evil doers; secondly, to cherish those who do well;" so that government, he said, "seems to me to be a part of religion itself,"—"a thing sacred in its institutions and ends." "Let men be good, and the government cannot be bad." "That, therefore, which makes a good constitution must keep it—namely, men of wisdom and virtue—qualities that, because they descend not with worldly inheritance, must be carefully propagated by a virtuous education of youth."

Christian Legislation

The first legislative act, passed at Chester, the seventh of the twelfth month, December, 1682, announced the ends of a true civil government. The preamble recites, that, "Whereas the glory of Almighty God and the good of mankind is the reason and end of government, and, therefore, government in itself is a venerable ordinance of God, and forasmuch as it is principally desired and intended by the proprietary and governor, and the freemen of Pennsylvania and territories thereunto belonging, to make and establish such laws as shall best preserve true Christian and civil liberty, in opposition to all unchristian, licentious, and unjust practices, whereby God may have his due, Caesar his due, and the people their due, from tyranny and oppression."

The frame of government contained the following article on religious rights—

"That all persons living in this province who confess and acknowledge the one almighty and eternal God to be the creator, upholder, and ruler of the world, and who hold themselves obliged in conscience to live peaceably and justly in civil society, shall in no wise be molested or prejudiced for their religious persuasion or practice in matters of faith and worship; nor shall they be compelled at any time to frequent or maintain any religious worship, place, or ministry whatsoever."

William Penn, when about planting his colony and establishing his government in Pennsylvania, in 1682, caused the following law to be made—

"To the end that looseness, irreligion, and atheism may not creep in under the pretence of conscience in this province, be it further enacted by the authority aforesaid, That, according to the good example of the primitive Christians, and for the ease of the creation, every *first* day of the week, called the Lord's day, people shall abstain from their common toil and labor, that, whether masters, parents, children, or servants, they may better dispose themselves to read the Scriptures of truth at home or to frequent such meetings of religious worship abroad, as may best suit their respective persuasions."

Bancroft's View of Penn

"In the judgment of this Quaker patriarch and legislator," says Bancroft, "government derived neither its obligations nor powers from man. God was to him the beginning and the end of government. He thought of government as a part of religion itself. Christians should keep the helm and guide the vessel of state."

His Colony a New Era in Liberty

His object also was to carry the Christian religion to the natives. This Christian design is expressed in the charter granted by Charles II. It says, "Whereas our trusty and beloved William Penn, out of a commendable desire to enlarge the British empire, as also to reduce the savages, by just and gentle measures, to the love of civil society and the Christian religion, hath humbly besought our leave to translate a colony." This purpose was expressed by Penn in the petition he sent to the king. He says he "should be able to colonize the province, which might enlarge the British empire, and promote the glory of God by the civilization and conversion of the Indian tribes." He urged all who proposed to join the colony "to have especial respect to the will of God."

He continued to act as Governor of Pennsylvania till June, 1684, when he returned to England. Before his embarkation, he uttered these farewell words to the colony, as his parting benediction—"I bless you in the name and power of the Lord; and may God bless you with his righteousness, peace, and plenty, all the land over. Oh that you would eye God in all, through all, and above all the works of his hand."

One of the great features of the Christian polity of Penn was his faith and fair dealings with the Indians. Every rood of land he obtained by honest purchase, and his integrity and frankness won for him and his colony the confidence and friendship of the Indian race. Treaties of mutual advantage were entered into between them, in which it was covenanted that as long as the grass grew and the waters ran, the links in the chain of their mutual friendship should be kept bright and strong. His transactions with the Indian tribes were marked with Christian integrity, and added new lustre to his fame.

Means of Education

Penn, as the wise founder of a civil commonwealth, provided measures for the general diffusion of the blessings of a Christian education.

"Let men," he says, "be good, and the government cannot be bad. That, therefore, which makes a good constitution must keep it—namely, men of wisdom and virtue, qualities that, as they descend not with worldly inheritance, must be carefully propagated by a virtuous education of the youth."

One of the last acts of William Penn on leaving the country for England was to grant a charter to the public school in Philadelphia, in order to secure good school-instruction equally *to all the children of the community*. On the seal of this institution he placed the motto, "GOOD INSTRUCTION IS BETTER THAN RICHES;" with the impressive adage, "Love ye one another."

The Christian Colonization of New York

Is cotemporaneous with its first settlement. Commerce and Christianity are always in genial sympathy and co-operation; and as commerce, from the beginning of the colony in 1609, was a leading motive of the first settlers, so the Christian religion pioneered its way side by side with commerce. As early as 1613, four years after the discovery of Manhattan by Hudson, Holland merchants had established several trading-posts, and in 1623 measures were taken to found an agricultural and Christian settlement. The first emigrants were those who had fled from the severity of religious persecution in the seventeenth century in the French Belgic provinces, and came with a faith tried in a fiery furnace.

The East India Company, formed in 1621, stipulated that "where emigrants went forth under their auspices, and that of the States-General of Holland, it should be their duty to send out a schoolmaster, being a pious member of the church, whose office it was to instruct the children, and preside in their religious meetings on the Sabbath and other days, leading in the devotions, and reading a sermon, until the regular ministry should be established over them. An individual was often designated as a *Zickentrooster*, (comforter of the sick,) who for his spiritual gifts was adapted to edify and comfort the people."

In 1633 the first minister came over, and associated with him was a schoolmaster, who organized a church school. The introduction, at this early period of the settlement of the colony, of the church and school combined, cannot, therefore, be claimed as the peculiar distinction of the Puritan emigrants, as the direct aim and the provision made in the early settlements by the Dutch was to extend and preserve in the midst of them the blessings of education and religion.

The Dutch Reformed Church

The Collegiate Reformed Dutch Church of New York was the first founded in North America, and dates from the first settlement on

Manhattan Island. The first religious meetings were held in a temporary building, till in 1626 an emigrant, in building a horse-mill, provided a spacious room above for the congregation. At an interview, in 1642, between a famous navigator, De Vries, and the Governor of the Colony, the former remarked "that it was a shame that the English when they visited Manhattan saw only a mean barn in which we worshipped. The first they built in New England, after their dwelling-houses, was a fine church: we should do the same." This led to the erection of a new and spacious church-edifice.

In a letter written on the 11th of August, 1628, by Rev. Jonas Michaëllus, the first minister of the Dutch Reformed Church in the United States, there is found the following statement—

"We have established the form of a church, and it has been thought best to choose two elders for my assistance, and for the proper consideration of all such ecclesiastical matters as might occur. We have had at the first administration of the Lord's Supper full fifty communicants, not without great joy and comfort for so many— Walloons and Dutch; of whom a portion made their first confession, and others exhibited their church certificates. We administer the Holy Sacrament of the Lord's Supper once in four months.

"We must have no other object than the glory of God in building up his kingdom and the salvation of many souls. As to the natives of this country, I find them entirely savage and wild, proficient in all wickedness, who serve nobody but the devil. Let us then leave the parents in their condition, and begin with the children who are still young, and place them under the instruction of some experienced and godly schoolmaster, where they may be taught especially in the fundamentals of our Christian religion. In the mean time it must not be forgotten to pray to the Lord, with ardent and continual prayers, for his blessing."

Puritan and Presbyterian Settlements

In 1636, the Puritans of New England began to add largely to the New York colony. In ten years after the Puritan emigration began, "there were so many at Manhattan as to require preachers who could speak in English as well as Dutch." "Whole towns," says Bancroft, "had been settled by New England men, who had come to America to serve God with a pure conscience, and to plant New England liberties in a congregational way."

The colony of New York, after being under the jurisdiction of the Dutch for fifty years, passed, in 1664, to that of England. This political revolution secured a rapid colonization from various quarters. "English, Irish, Scotch, French, and Dutch, chiefly Presbyterians and Independents," now began to emigrate to the colony of New York. The Episcopalians claimed "that the province was subject to the ecclesiastical government of the Church of England, and that theirs was the religion of the state." The Duke of York, afterwards James II., maintained an Episcopal chapel in New York at his own private expense. "Ministers," said Andros, the civil Governor of the colony, in 1683, "are scarce, and religion wanes." "There were about twenty churches, of which half were destitute of ministers. But the Presbyterians and Independents, who formed the most numerous and thriving portions of the inhabitants, were the only class of the people who showed much willingness to procure and support ministers."

The Huguenots

The seventeenth century, constituting an important era of Christian colonization of the New World, brought to the North American colonies the rich Christian contribution from the Huguenots of France. All the colonies gave them a heart-welcome as refugees from a frenzied and cruel religious persecution. They were ardent lovers of liberty, and declared that, with "their ministers, they had come to adore and serve God with freedom." These Christian exiles were warmly welcomed to the colony of New York, and became one of the richest portions of the population. In 1682 they had become so numerous that the colonial laws and official papers were published in French as well as in Dutch and English. The French church in the city of New York became the metropolis of Calvinism, where the Huguenot emigrants out of the city came to worship.

"The character of the first Huguenot settlers," says Dr. De Witt, "was eminently worthy, both here and in other parts of the State and the United States. An interesting fact is related concerning the first settlers of New Rochelle, in Westchester county. When they entered the forests, and with toilful labor engaged in clearing and cultivating the fields, they resolved, in the spirit of deep piety which they brought with them, to unite with their brethren in New York in the public worship of the Sabbath, though at a distance of twenty miles. Such was their reverence for the sanctification of the Sabbath that they would take up their march on foot in the afternoon of Saturday, and reach New York by midnight, singing the hymns of Clement Marot by the way. Engaging in the worship of the Sabbath, they remained till after midnight, and then took their march in return to New Rochelle, relieving the toil of the way by singing Marot's hymns." "Happy and proud," says Bancroft, "in the religious liberty they enjoyed, they ceased not to write to their brethren in France of the grace which God had shown them."

Christian Legislation of the Colony

In 1665, the colonial legislature of New York passed the following act in reference to Christianity and its ordinances—

"Whereas, The public worship of God is much discredited for want of *painful* [laborious] and able ministers to instruct the people in the true religion, it is ordered that a church shall be built in each parish, capable of holding two hundred persons; that ministers of every church shall preach every Sunday, and pray for the king, queen, the Duke of York, and the royal family; and to marry persons after legal publication of license."

It was also enacted that "Sunday is not to be profaned by travelling, by laborers, or vicious persons," and "church-wardens to report twice a year all misdemeanors, such as swearing, profaneness, Sabbath-breaking, drunkenness, fornication, adultery, and all such abominable Sins." "Persons were punished with death who should in any wise deny the true God or his attributes." These were the laws of the colony of New York until 1683.

The following paper will show better the attention that the early settlers of New York paid to education, and is an amusing relic of colonial antiquity. It belongs to the ancient local history of Flatbush, Long Island—

A School Relic

ART. 1. The school shall begin at 8 o'clock and go outt att 11; shall begin again att 1 o'clock and ende att 4. The bell shall bee rung beefore the school begins.

ART. 2. When school opens, one of the children shall reade the morning prayer as it stands in the catechism, and close with the prayer before dinner; and inn the afternoon the same. The evening school shall begin with the Lord's prayer and close by singing a psalm.

ART. 3. Hee shall instruct the children inn the common prayers and the questions and answers off the catechism on Wednesdays and Saturdays, too enable them too say them better on Sunday inn the church.

ART. 4. Hee shall bee bound too keep his school nine months in succession, from September too June, one year with another, and shall always bee present himself.

ART. 5. Hee shall bee choirister off the church; ring the bell three tymes before service, and reade a chapter off the Bible inn the church between the second and third ringinge off the bell; after the third ringinge he shall reade the ten commandments and the twelve articles off ffaith and then sett the psalm. In the afternoone after the third ringinge off the bell hee shall reade a short chapter or one off the psalms off David as the congregatione are assemblinge; afterwards he shall again sett the psalm.

ART. 6. When the minister shall preach at Broockland or Utrecht he shall be bounde to reade twice before the congregatione from the booke used for the purpose. Hee shall heare the children recite the questions and answers off the catechism on Sunday and instruct them.

ART. 7. Hee shall provide a basin off water for the baptism, ffor which hee shall receive twelve stuyvers in wampum ffor every baptism from parents or sponsors. Hee shall furnish bread and wine ffor communion att the charge off the church. Hee shall also serve as messenger ffor the consistories.

ART. 8. Hee shall give the funerale invitations and toll the bell; and ffor which hee shall receive for persons off fifteen years off age and upwards twelve guilders; and ffor persons under fifteen, eight guilders; and if hee shall cross the river to New York hee shall have four guilders more.

[The compensation of the schoolmaster was as follows:]

1st. Hee shall receive ffor a speller or reader three guilders a quarter; and for a writer ffour guilders for the daye school.

Inn the evening four guilders for a speller or reader, and five guilders for a writer per quarter.

2nd. The residue off his salary shall bee four hundred guilders in wheat (of wampum value) deliverable at Broockland Fferry with the dwellinge, pasturage and meadowe appurtaininge to the school.

Done and agreede on inn consistorie, in the presence off the Honourable Constable and Overseers, this 8th daye off October, 1682.

Constable and Overseers   *The Consistorie*

Cornelius Berrian,   Casparus Vanzuren,

Ryniere Aertsen,   *Minister.*

Jan Remben.   Adriaen Ryerse,

           Cornelius B. Vanderwyck

I agree to the above articles, and promise to observe them.

           Johnnes Von Echkellen

New Jersey Colony

Became an independent colony in 1664. "Its moral character was moulded by New England Puritans, English Quakers, and Dissenters from Scotland." An association of church-members from the New Haven colony resolved with one heart "to carry on their spiritual and town affairs according to Godly Government;" and in 1668 the colonial legislative Assembly, under Puritan influence, transferred the chief features of the New England codes to the statute-book of New Jersey. New Jersey increased in population and prosperity under the genial presence of Christian institutions, and became distinguished for intelligence, industry, and enterprise. "The people," says Bancroft, "rejoiced under the reign of God, confident that he would beautify the meek with salvation."

The Christian Standard in Legislation

The Christian teachings of the Quakers, in union with Presbyterian and Anabaptist influences, made New Jersey, in its colonial structure, a model Protestant republic. "These were interwoven into the earliest elements of the political society of New Jersey, and constitute one of the beautiful historical incidents of the age. The people have always enjoyed a high reputation for piety, industry, economy, and good morals." They received and practised such Christian lessons as the following, given by their friends in England, in 1681—

"Friends that are gone to make plantations in America, keep the plantations in your own hearts, that your own vines and lilies be not hurt. You that are governors and judges, you should be eyes to the blind, feet to the lame, and fathers to the poor, that you may gain the blessing of those who are ready to perish, and cause the widow's heart to sing for gladness. If you rejoice because your hand hath gotten much, if you say to the fine gold, Thou art my confidence, you will have denied the God that is above. The Lord is ruler among nations; he will crown his people with dominion."

The high standard of Christian morality in the colony of New Jersey was indicated by the motto on the provincial seal— *"Righteousness exalteth a nation."* A proclamation made by Governor Basse, in 1697, contains the following Christian record—"It being very necessary for the good and prosperity of this province that our principal care be, in obedience to the laws of God, to endeavor as much as in us lyeth the extirpation of all sorts of looseness and profanity, and to unite in the fear and love of God and one another, that, by the religious and virtuous carriage and behavior of every one in his respective station and calling, the blessing of Almighty God may accompany our honest and lawful endeavors, I do therefore, by and with the advice of the Council of this province, strictly prohibit cursing, swearing, immoderate drinking, Sabbath-breaking, and all sorts of lewdness and profane behavior in word and action; and do strictly charge and command all justices of the peace, sheriffs, constables, and all other officers within the province, that they take due care that all laws made and provided for the suppression of vice and encouraging of religion and virtue, particularly the observance of the Lord's day, be duly put into execution."

One Colony of Delaware

Had a Christian colonization. Gustavus Adolphus, of the royal family of Sweden, projected an enterprise to aid in the Christian settlement of the New World. Its object, though in part commercial, was declared to be for the benefit of the "whole Protestant world." In 1637, two vessels, fitted out by the Government of Sweden, carried out a band of emigrants with their Christian teachers, and in the spring of 1638 they sailed into Delaware Bay and began the Christian colonization of that region. In 1640 the colony received Christian emigrants from New England. It continued a political connection with the colony of Pennsylvania till 1704, when it became an independent commonwealth.

8

Christian Colonization of Virginia—
Maryland—South Carolina—
North Carolina–Georgia

The Colonization of Virginia

Began in 1607, fourteen years previous to the Puritan settlement in New England, and seventy-five before William Penn gave to Pennsylvania the basis of a Christian government. In April, 1606, James, King of England, granted to a colony forming to emigrate to America a charter for the possession of those territories lying on the sea-coast between the 34th and 45th degrees of north latitude, and all the islands within a hundred miles of those shores. That charter declared the design of the colonists to be "to make habitation and plantation and to deduce a colony of sundry of our people into that part of America commonly called Virginia; and that so noble a work may, by the providence of Almighty God, hereafter tend to the glory of his divine majesty in propagating of the Christian religion to such people as yet live in darkness and in miserable ignorance of the true knowledge and worship of God, and may, in time, bring the infidels and savages living in those parts to human civility and a quiet government."

Its Christian Objects

It is, moreover, in the Virginia charter of 1609 declared "that it shall be necessary for all such as inhabit within the precincts of Virginia to determine to live together in the fear and true worship of Almighty God, Christian peace, and civil quietness;" and that "the principal effect which we [the crown] can desire or expect of this action is the conversion and reduction of the people in those parts unto the true worship of God and the Christian religion."

Preaching of the Gospel Enjoined

In a code of laws for the government of the Virginia colony, which the king assisted to frame, were "enjoined the preaching of the gospel in America, and the performance of divine worship in conformity with the doctrines and rites of the Church of England." In 1619, twelve years after the first settlement of Virginia, "The King of England having formerly issued his letters to the bishops of the kingdom, for collecting money to erect a college in Virginia for the education of Indian children, nearly fifteen hundred dollars had been already paid to this benevolent and pious design, and Henrico had been selected as a suitable place for the seminary. The Virginia Company granted ten thousand acres of land to be laid off for the University at Henrico. The first design was to erect and build a college in Virginia for the training up and educating infidel [Indian] children in the true knowledge of God." The principal design of William and Mary College was to instruct and christianize the Indians.

Jefferson's Remarks

Jefferson, in his "Notes on Virginia," says, "The purposes of the institution would be better answered by maintaining a perpetual mission among the Indian tribes, the object of which, besides instructing them in the principles of Christianity, as the founder required, should be to collect their traditions, laws, customs, languages, and other circumstances which might lead to a discovery of their relation with one another or descent from other nations. When these objects are accomplished with one tribe, the missionary might pass to another."

Acts of Christian Legislation

"The colony of Virginia consisted of Church-of-England men, and many of their first acts related to provision for the Church. The ministers were considered, not as pious and charitable individuals, but as officers of state, bound to promote the true faith and aid sound morality by authority of the community by which they were paid, and to which they were held responsible for the performance of their duty. The very first act of the Assembly required every settlement in which the people worship God to build a house to be appropriated exclusively for that purpose; the second act imposed a penalty of a pound of tobacco for absence from divine service on Sunday; and another act prohibited any man from disposing of his tobacco until the minister's portion was paid."

Episcopacy Established

When the population had increased to fifty thousand, in 1668, there were "nearly fifty Episcopal parishes, with as many glebes, church-edifices, and pastors. Episcopacy was established by law; attendance was enforced by penalties: even the sacramental services of the Church were legally enjoined upon the people; every thing wore the appearance of a very strict religious economy." The Christian religion was the underlying basis and the pervading element of all the social and civil institutions of the Virginia colony.

In 1662, the Assembly of Virginia passed an act to make permanent provision for the establishment of a college. The preamble of the act establishing it recites "that the want of able and faithful ministers in this country deprives us of those great blessings and mercies that always attend upon the service of God;" and the act itself declares "that for the advancement of learning, education of youth, supply of the ministry, and promotion of piety, there be land taken up and purchased for a college and free school, and that with all convenient speed there be buildings erected upon it for the entertainment of students and scholars." In 1693 the College of William and Mary was founded.

Colonization of Maryland

Began her colonial settlement in 1632, under the auspices of Lord Baltimore, a British nobleman and a Roman Catholic. His object was to "people a territory with colonists of his own religions faith, and to erect an asylum in North America for the Catholic religion."

He obtained a charter from Charles I., in which it was declared that the "grantee was actuated by a laudable zeal for extending the Christian religion and the territory of the British empire; and if any doubt should ever arise concerning the true meaning of the charter, there should be no construction of it derogatory to the Christian religion."

The first band of colonists, consisting of two hundred men of rank, led by Leonard Calvert, brother of Lord Baltimore, sailed from England in November, 1632, and landed on the coast of Maryland early in 1633. As soon as they landed, the governor erected a cross, and took possession of the country "for our Lord Jesus Christ, and for our sovereign lord the King of England." "To every emigrant fifty acres of land were given in absolute fee; and the recognition of Christianity as the established faith of the land, with an exclusion of the political predominance or superiority of any particular sect or denomination of Christians was enacted." The colonists "soon converted a desolate wilderness into a flourishing commonwealth enlivened by industry and adorned by civilization."

Religious toleration was, from the beginning, proclaimed as one of the fundamental laws of the colony. The Assembly, mostly of the Roman Catholic faith, passed, in 1650, a memorable Christian act, entitled, an "Act concerning Religion." The preamble declared that "the enforcement of the conscience had been of dangerous consequence in those countries where it had been practised;" and therefore it was ordained "that no person professing to believe in Jesus Christ should be molested on account of their faith, or denied the free exercise of their particular modes of worship." This act of religious toleration was as honorable to the first Catholic colony as it was a fitting tribute to the genius and sanction of the Christian religion. "It was the earliest example," says Judge Story, "of a legislator inviting his subjects to the free indulgence of religious opinion."

"With all that was excellent and grand and far-reaching in the principles of the Pilgrims, and with all the mighty influences of the religion of the Pilgrims in its bearing on the liberties of this nation—ultimately infinitely more far-reaching than those which had gone out from Maryland—still, it cannot be denied that the principles adopted in that colony were in advance of those which were held by the settlers of either Plymouth or Jamestown; and though coming short of those held by Roger Williams and William Penn, yet they were such as the age, in its progress, was carrying to that result." This beneficent and fundamental law exerted a highly favorable influence on the prosperity of the Maryland colony, and largely increased its population. It was, in time, incorporated in the legislation of the less tolerant colonies, and finally became the supreme law in all the State Constitutions, as well as in the Constitution of the United States.

Colonization of South Carolina

Began her colonial existence and history under the auspices of the Christian religion. In 1662, a company of emigrants, generally grandees of England and courtiers of Charles II., obtained a charter and settled in South Carolina. In the charter, it was stated that the colonists, "excited with a laudable and pious zeal for the propagation of the gospel, have begged a certain country in the parts of America, not yet cultivated and planted, and only inhabited by some barbarous people, who have no knowledge of God."

Frame of Government Formed by Locke

In 1669, a second charter was obtained, and the outlines of its government, under the title of "the Fundamental Constitution of Carolina," was drawn up by John Locke, the great Christian philosopher, who declared that Christianity had "God for its Author, salvation for its end, and truth without any mixture of error for its matter." In that constitution it is declared that—

"Since the natives of the place, who will be concerned in our plantations, are utterly strangers to Christianity, whose idolatry, ignorance, or mistake gives us no right to expel or treat them ill, and those who remove from other parts to plant there will undoubtedly be of different opinions concerning matters of religion, the liberty whereof they will expect to have allowed them, and it will not be reasonable on this account to keep them out; that civil peace may be maintained amidst the diversity of opinions, and our agreement and compact with all men may be duly and faithfully observed; the violation whereof, upon what pretence soever, cannot be, without great offence to Almighty

God, and great scandal to the true religion which we profess; and also that Jews, heathens, and other dissenters from the purity of the Christian religion may not be scared and kept at a distance from it, but, by having opportunity of acquainting themselves with the truth and reasonableness of its doctrines and the peaceableness and inoffensiveness of its professors, may by good usage and persuasion, and all those convincing methods of gentleness and meekness suitable to the rules and designs of the gospel, be won over to embrace and unfeignedly to receive the truth: therefore any seven or more persons, agreeing in *any religion*, shall constitute a *Church or profession*, to which they shall give some name, to distinguish it from others."

In the terms of communion of every such *Church* or *profession*, it was required that the three following articles should appear—that there is a God; that public worship is due from all men to this Supreme Being; and that every citizen shall, at the command of the civil magistrate, deliver judicial testimony with some form of words indicating a recognition of *divine justice and human responsibility*. Only the acknowledged members of some Church or profession were capable of becoming freemen of Carolina, or of possessing any estate or habitation within the province; and all persons were forbidden to revile, disturb, or in any way persecute the members of any religious association allowed by law. What was *enjoined* to freemen was *permitted* to slaves, by an article which declared that "since charity obliges us to wish well to the souls of all men, and religion ought to alter nothing in any man's civil estate or right, *it shall be lawful* for slaves, as well as others, to enter themselves and be of what Church or profession any of them shall think best and thereof be as fully members as any freeman."

In another of the articles of "the Fundamental Constitution" it was declared that "whenever the country should be sufficiently peopled and planted, the provincial parliament should enact regulations for the building of churches, and the public maintenance of divines, to be employed in the cause of religion according to the canons of the Church of England;" "which, being the only *true* and orthodox and the national religion of all the king's dominions, is so also of Carolina; and therefore it alone shall be allowed to receive public maintenance by grant of parliament."

After twenty years of experiment, the form of government instituted by Locke was abolished. The French Protestants, and Dissenters from England, became the ruling power, and established a more just and liberal system of government.

The Huguenots formed an important part of the colony of South Carolina.

The same lovely picture of piety as in the New York colony was presented by these Christian refugees who had settled in South Carolina. "There it was," says Bancroft, "that these Calvinist exiles could celebrate their worship, without fear, in the midst of the forests, and mingle the voice of their psalms with the murmur of the winds which sighed among the mighty oaks. Their church was in Charleston. They repaired thither every Sunday from their plantations, which were scattered in all directions on the banks of the Cooper." The descendants of these Christian colonists became distinguished in American history, and exerted a prominent influence in achieving the independence of the nation. American patriotism, eloquence, oratory, and jurisprudence are adorned by many noble names, descendants of the Huguenots.

Colonization of North Carolina

From the beginning of her colonial history, laid the basis of her institutions on Christianity. The first permanent settlements were made by fugitives from Virginia, who sought refuge from the rigid, intolerant laws of that colony, which bore so heavily on all that could not conform to the ceremonies of the established Church. When the Puritans were driven from Virginia, some eminently pious people settled along the seaboard, where they might be free from the oppression of intolerant laws and bigoted magistrates. About the year 1707, a colony of Huguenots located on the Trent River, and one of Palatines at Newbern, each maintaining the peculiar religious services of the fatherland. The Quakers were, like other sects, compelled to flee from the severe laws passed against them in Virginia, and sought refuge in Carolina. As early as 1730, scattered families of Presbyterians from the north of Ireland were found in various parts of the colony. In 1736 a colony of Presbyterians came from the province of Ulster, Ireland, and made a permanent settlement. Subsequently several other colonies of Presbyterians came from Ireland, and settled in different sections of the colony. These Presbyterian bands rapidly increased, and formed numerous large congregations, which multiplied into other congregations; and thus the colony became thoroughly Christian, and the people imbued with a fervent love of liberty.

In 1746 and 1747 a large emigration of Scotch came into the colony of North Carolina. In the efforts of Prince Charles Edward to obtain the crown of England, the Scotch were in sympathy with him. George II. granted pardon to a large number on condition of their emigration and taking the oath of allegiance. This is the origin of the Scotch settlements in North Carolina. A large number who had taken up arms for the Pretender preferred exile to death or to subjugation in their native land, and during the years 1746 and 1747 emigrated with their families and those of many of their friends, to North Carolina. In the course of a few years, large companies of industrious Highlanders joined their countrymen.

This Christian people, both in Scotland and this country, contended "that obligation to God was above all human control, and for the government of their conscience in all matters of morality and religion the Bible is the storehouse of information—acknowledging no Lord of the conscience but the Son of God, the head of the Church, Jesus Christ, and the Bible as his divine communication for the welfare and guide of mankind."

The Scotch-Irish Presbyterians, who formed so large a proportion of the people of North Carolina, and moulded its religious and political character, were eminently pious and ardent lovers of liberty. "Their religious principles swayed their political opinions; and in maintaining their form of worship and their creed they learned republicanism before they emigrated to America."

Bible the Basis of Their Institutions

The religious creed of these Christian emigrants formed a part of their politics so far as to lead them to decide that no law of human government ought to be tolerated in opposition to the expressed will of God. Their ideas of religious liberty have given a coloring to their political notions on all subjects—have been, indeed, the foundation of their political creed. The Bible was their text-book on all subjects of importance, and their resistance to tyrants was inspired by the free principles which it taught and enforced.

Christian Instructions to Civil Delegates

The following instructions to the delegates of Mecklenburg county exhibit the sentiments of the people on the Christian religion as the basis of civil government. It bears date September 1, 1775. The first Provincial Congress of North Carolina was then in session.

"13th. You are instructed to assent and consent to the establishment of the Christian religion, as contained in the Scriptures of the Old and New Testament, to be the religion of the state, to the utter exclusion forever of all and every other (falsely so called) religion, whether pagan or papal; and that a full and free and peaceable enjoyment thereof be secured to all and every constituent member of the state, as their individual right as freemen, without the imposition of rites and ceremonies, whether claiming civil or ecclesiastical power for their source; and that a confession and profession of the religion so established shall be necessary in qualifying any person for public trust in the state.

"14th. You are also to oppose the establishment of any mode of worship to be supported to the oppression of the rights of conscience, and at the destruction of private judgment."

This political paper declares that the people of North Carolina believed the Bible, and from it drew their principles of morals, religion, and polities. To abjure the Christian religion would have been, with them, to abjure freedom and immortality. They asserted in every political form the paramount authority of the Christian religion as the sole acknowledged religion of the state and community.

These Christian men, and others like them, constituted the celebrated Mecklenburg Convention of North Carolina convened in 1775. The convention was composed largely of Presbyterians, the most distinguished of whom were ministers. The delegates met on the 15th of May, 1775, and during their sittings news arrived of the battle of Lexington. Every delegate felt the value and importance of the prize of liberty, and the awful and solemn crisis which had arrived. Every bosom swelled with indignation at the malice, inveteracy, and insatiable revenge developed in the late attack at Lexington.

After a full and free discussion of various subjects, it was unanimously—

"2. *Resolved*, That we, the citizens of Mecklenburg county, do hereby dissolve the political bands which have connected us with the mother-country, and hereby absolve ourselves from allegiance to the British crown, and abjure all political connection, contract, and association, with that nation which has wantonly trampled on our rights and liberties, and inhumanly shed the innocent blood of American patriots at Lexington.

"3. *Resolved*, That we do hereby declare ourselves a free and independent people—that we are, and of right ought to be, a sovereign and self-governing association, under the control of no power other than that of God and the general government of the Congress; to the maintenance of which independence we solemnly pledge to each other our mutual co-operation, our lives, our fortunes, and our most sacred honor."

This declaration of independence preceded the one made by Congress in 1776 more than a year, and is a noble monument of the patriotism and piety of the people of North Carolina.

The colony of North Carolina is particularly distinguished for the large number of able and patriotic ministers who were diligent laborers in the fields of intellectual and Christian culture and in sowing broadcast the seeds of liberty and of future independence. The annals of Biblical learning and of freedom are adorned with the names of Campbell, Hall, Hunter, McAden, Craighead, Alexander, McWhorter, McCane, Petillo, and others, who were master-workmen in their department of Christian labor, and ardent and fearless patriots. These men were the pioneers of freedom and independence, and in all the measures preparatory to the coming revolution they were the foremost leaders.

Colonization of Georgia

Has a suggestive Christian history. James Oglethorpe, a member of the British Parliament, imbued with the philanthropic spirit of the gospel, obtained in 1732 a charter from George II. to establish a colony in North America. He had in former years devoted himself to the benevolent work of relieving multitudes in England who were imprisoned for debt and suffering in loathsome jails. Actuated by Christian motives, he desired to see these poor sufferers placed in an independent condition, and projected a colony in America for that purpose. "For them, and for persecuted Protestants," says Bancroft, "he planned an asylum and a destiny in America, where former poverty would be no reproach, and where the simplicity of piety could indulge the spirit of devotion without fear of persecution from men who hated the rebuke of its example." This Christian enterprise enlisted "the benevolence of England; the charities of an opulent and enlightened nation were to be concentrated on the new plantation; the Society for Propagating the Gospel in Foreign Parts sought to promote its interests; and Parliament showed its good will by contributing ten thousand pounds."

In January, 1732, Oglethorpe, with one hundred and twenty emigrants, landed in America, and on the basis of the Christian religion laid the future commonwealth of Georgia. The Christian liberality and philanthropy of the founder of the colony spread its fame far and wide; for it was announced that the rights of citizenship and all the immunities of the colony "would be extended to all Protestant emigrants from any nation of Europe, desirous of refuge from persecution, or willing to undertake the *religious* instruction of the Indians." The Moravians, or United Brethren—a denomination of Christians founded by Count Zinzendorf, a German nobleman of the fifteenth century—were invited to emigrate to the colony of Georgia. They accepted the invitation, and arrived in the winter of 1736. Their object was to Christianize and convert the Indians, and to aid in planting the institutions of the New World on the basis of Christianity. The journal of John Wesley during the voyage exhibits the godly manner of the emigrants. "Our common way," says he, "of living was this. From four of the morning till five, each of us used private prayer. From five to seven we read the Bible together, carefully comparing it (that we might not lean to our own understanding) with the writings of the earliest ages. At eight were public prayers. At four were the evening prayers—when either the second lesson was explained, or the children were catechized and instructed before the congregation. From five to six we again used private prayer. At seven I joined with the Germans in their public service. At eight we met again, to exhort and instruct one another. Between nine and ten we went to bed, where neither the roaring of the sea nor the motion of the ship could take away the refreshing sleep which God gave us." What a Christian way of spending the time, for emigrants sailing over the mighty deep to aid in founding a Christian empire on the shores of a new world!

When these Christian emigrants touched the shore, their first act was "to kneel and return thanks to God for their having safely arrived in Georgia." "Our end in leaving our native country," said they, "is not to gain riches and honor, but singly this—to live wholly to the glory of God." Their object was "to make Georgia a religious colony, having no theory but devotion, no ambition but to quicken the sentiment of piety."

Christian Element in Georgia

The Christian founder of the commonwealth of Georgia carried his Christian principles into all the official transactions of the colony. The survey and division of the lots in the city of Savannah were conducted under the sanctions of religion. On the 7th of July, 1733, the emigrants met in a body upon the bluff of the river, before Oglethorpe's tent, and, having returned thanks to Almighty God and joined in prayer for his blessing to rest upon the colony and city they were about to found, they proceeded to lay out the lots and divide them in a Christian manner. They felt and said, "Except the Lord keep the city, the watchman waketh but in vain."

Under the administration of Oglethorpe, the colony greatly prospered and increased in numbers. "His undertaking will succeed," said Johnson, Governor of South Carolina; "for he nobly devotes all his powers to serve the poor and rescue them from wretchedness." "He bears a great love to the servants and children of God," said the pastor of a Moravian church. "He has taken care of us to the utmost of his ability. God has so blessed us with his presence and his regulations in the land, that others would not in many years have accomplished what he has brought about in one."

In 1734, after a residence of fifteen months in Georgia, Ogle-thorpe returned to England. He succeeded in obtaining additional patronage for the colony, and in October, 1735, set sail with three hundred emigrants, and after a long and stormy voyage they reached the colony of Georgia in February, 1736, where they were joined a few days after by a band of Christian emigrants from the highlands of Scotland.

These colonists were accompanied by John and Charles Wesley, the founders of the Methodist Episcopal Church. Their purpose was to aid Oglethorpe in his philanthropic labors and to convert the Indians to Christianity. Charles Wesley held the office of Secretary for Indian Affairs, and also that of a chaplain to Governor Oglethorpe.

Rev. Mr. Stevens, a historian of Georgia, says that "John Wesley established a school of thirty or forty children, and hired a teacher, in which he designed to blend religious instruction with worldly wisdom; and on Sunday afternoon Mr. Wesley met them in the church before evening service, and heard the children recite their catechism, questioned them as to what they had learned in the Bible, instructed them still further in the Bible, endeavoring to fix the truth in their understandings as well as in their memories. This was a regular part of their Sunday duties; and it shows that John Wesley, in the parish of Christ's Church, in Savannah, had established a Sunday-school nearly fifty years before Robert Raikes originated his noble scheme of Sunday-instruction in Gloucester, England, and eighty years before the first school in America on Mr. Raikes's plan was established in New York."

George Whitefield visited Georgia, and preached with wonderful eloquence and zeal, and labored with apostolic faith and perseverance in founding an Orphan Asylum, a "Bethesda," a "House of Mercy," for orphan children. His fame and influence soon spread over the colonies, and wherever he went tens of thousands of people hung with breathless interest on his preaching. He made a number of voyages to England and back to America, and died in Newburyport, Massachusetts, in 1770. In consequence of his Christian services to Georgia, and especially his efforts for the orphans, the legislature of the colony proposed to remove his remains to Savannah and to bury them at public cost. Dr. Franklin wrote to Dr. Jones, of Georgia, on the subject as follows—"I cannot forbear expressing the

pleasure it gives me to see an account of the respect paid to Whitefield's memory, by your Assembly. I knew him intimately upwards
of thirty years: his integrity, disinterestedness, and indefatigable
zeal in prosecuting every good work *I have never seen equalled*, I
shall never see excelled." And such was the effect of Whitefield's
preaching in Philadelphia that Franklin said, "It was wonderful to
see the change soon made in the manner of our inhabitants. From
being thoughtless or indifferent about religion, it seemed as if all the
world were growing religious, so that one could not walk through
the town in an evening without hearing psalms sung in different
families in every street."

"It is a matter of great interest," says the historian of Georgia, "that
religion was planted with the first settlers, and that the English, the
Salzburgers, the Moravians, the Methodists, the Presbyterians, and
the Israelites severally brought with them the ministers or the worship
of their respective creeds. The Christian element of colonization—that
without which the others are powerless to give true and lasting elevation—entered largely into the colonization of Georgia, and did much
for her prosperity and glory. No colony can point to a leader or founder in whose character meet more eminent qualities or more enduring
worth than in that of James Oglethorpe, the father of Georgia."

Lessons of the Colonization of the Continent

These Christian facts in the colonial history of our country suggest
the following lessons—

1. The faith of the Puritans, and of the founders of the various
colonies, in the divine origin and authority of civil government.

They held firmly to the declarations of the Bible, that "there is no
power but of God: the powers that be are ordained of God. Whosoever therefore resisteth the power, resisteth the ordinance of God."
And the doctrine of the divine origin of civil government led these
Christian men to regard the civil ruler as the "minister of God to the
people for good; and that he that ruleth should rule in the fear of
God." This true and noble faith in reference to civil government and
the character of the men who administered it placed the entire administration of government under the direction of God and in har-

mony with his will. The results of this faith and practice will always be in perfect harmony with the just ends of government and with the highest political and moral propriety of a nation. This grand idea was one that was always supreme in the minds and purposes of the Puritan and other colonial legislators in respect to civil government. They ever regarded government as from God; and this view invested it with all the dignity and authority of a divine institution.

"The first settlers," says Lord Brougham, "of all the colonies, were men of irreproachable character. Many of them fled from *persecution*; others on account of honorable poverty; and all of them with their expectations limited to the prospect of a bare subsistence in freedom and peace. All idea of wealth or pleasure was out of the question. The greater part of them viewed their emigration as a taking up the cross, and bounded their hopes of riches to the gifts of the Spirit, and their ambition to the desire of a kingdom beyond the grave. A set of men more conscientious in their doings, or simpler in their manners, never founded an empire. It is indeed the peculiar glory of North America that, with very few exceptions, its empire was founded in charity and peace."

2. The subordination of civil government to the power of the Christian religion.

"They looked upon their commonwealths as institutions for the preservation of the Churches, and the civil rulers as both members and fathers of them." Hence it was a favorite doctrine with the first settlers of the colonies of Massachusetts and Connecticut, that all freemen and civil rulers must be in communion with the Churches, and so promote the interest and spread of Christianity.

This doctrine had an eminent advocate in the celebrated John Cotton, the first minister of Boston.

"The government," says he, "might be considered as a theocracy, wherein the Lord was judge, lawgiver, and king; that the laws which he gave Israel might be adopted so far as they were of a moral and perpetual equity; that the people might be considered as God's people in covenant with him; that none but persons of approved piety and eminent gifs should be chosen rulers." At the desire of the court, he compiled a system of laws, which were considered by the legislative body as the general standard.

The same fact was stated by President Stiles, of Yale College, in 1783. "It is certain," said he, "that civil dominion was but the second motive, religion the primary one, with our ancestors in coming hither and settling this land. It was not so much their design to establish religion for the benefit of the state, as civil government for the benefit of religion, and as subservient and even necessary towards the peaceable and unmolested exercise of religion—of that religion for which they fled to these ends of the earth. They designed, in thus laying the foundations of a new state, to make it a model for the glorious kingdom of Christ."

Rev. John Norton, in 1661, declared, in an election sermon, that they came into this wilderness to live under the *order of the gospel*; "that our policy may be a *gospel policy*, and may be complete according to the Scriptures, answering fully to the word of God: this is the work of our generation, and the very work we engaged for in this wilderness; this is the scope and end of it, that which is *written upon the forehead* of New England, *viz.*, the complete walking in the faith of the gospel according to the *order of the gospel*."

3. The end and operations of civil government to propagate and subserve the Christian religion.

"The Pilgrims," says Rev. R. S. Storrs, "would have held that state most imperfect which contented itself and complacently rested in its own advancement and special prosperities, without seeking to benefit others around it. They esteemed that progress to be radically wanting in greatness and value which was a mere progress in power and wealth and in physical success; which gained no results of great character and culture, and blossomed out to no wealthy fruits of enlarged Christian knowledge. The moral, to them, was superior to the physical; the attainments of Christian wisdom and piety, above accumulations of worldly resources; the alliance of the soul with God, through faith, above the conquest and mastery of nature. And to these they held the state to be tributary, as they held all things else that existed on the earth—the very earth itself and its laws. Not a mere police establishment was the state, on their theory, accomplishing its office in protecting its subjects and punishing criminals. It was to them a place and a power of the noblest education; a teeming nursery of all good influences and heavenly growths, from which letters, charities, and salvation should proceed, and in which they should perpetually be nourished. Philanthropic endeavors, and missionary enterprises, were to be its results, the proofs of its prosperity, the real and imperishable rewards of its founders. It existed in order that characters might be formed, commanding, large, and full of light, whose record should make all history brighter, whose influence should link the earth with the skies. And they expected the Millennium itself, with its long eras of peace and of purity, of tranquil delight and illuminated wisdom, to spring as the last and crowning fruitage from the states they were founding, and from others like them."

4. The position and influence of the ministers of the gospel in the civil affairs of the state.

They were consulted on all matters pertaining to the civil affairs of the New England colonies, and had the controlling influence in forming and directing the civil government. The very first written code of laws for Massachusetts, under the charter of 1629, was drawn up by a minister. And the instruction of the civil court, appointed to frame the laws of the commonwealth, was to make them "as near the law of God as they can." "They had great power in the people's heart," says Winthrop. "Religion ruled the state through its ministers."

Ministers were selected as agents to obtain charters and petition the king and Parliament, as well as to direct the character of the civil government at home. "The clergy were generally consulted on civil matters, and the suggestions they gave from the pulpit on election-days and other special occasions were enacted into laws."

Remarkable Prophecy of an English Bishop

Before the Declaration of Independence, the Bishop of St. Asaph, in England, published a discourse, in which are found the following remarkable passages in reference to the North American colonies—

"It is difficult," says he, "for man to look into the destiny of future ages: the designs of Providence are vast and complicated, and our own powers are too narrow to admit of much satisfaction to our curiosity. But when we see so many great and powerful causes constantly at work, we cannot doubt of their producing proportional effects.

"The colonies in North America have not only taken root and acquired strength, *but seem hastening with an accelerated progress to such a powerful state as may introduce a new and important change in human affairs.*

"Descended from ancestors of the most improved and enlightened part of the Old World, they receive as it were by inheritance all the improvements and discoveries of their mother-country. And it happens fortunately for them to commence their flourishing state at a time when the human understanding has attained to the free use of its powers and has learned to act with vigor and certainty. And let it be well understood what rapid improvements, what important discoveries, have been made, in a few years, by a few countries, with our own at the head, which have at last discovered the right method of using their faculties.

"May we not reasonably expect that a number of provinces possessed of these advantages and quickened by mutual emulation, with only the progress of the human mind, should very considerably enlarge the boundaries of science? It is difficult even to imagine to what height of improvement their discoveries may extend.

"And perhaps they may make as considerable advances in the arts of civil government and the conduct of life. May they not possibly be more successful than their mother-country has been in preserving that reverence and authority which are due to the laws—to those who make them, and to those who execute them? May not a method be invented of procuring some tolerable share of the comforts of life to those inferior useful ranks of men to whose industry we are indebted for the whole? Time and discipline may discover some means to correct the extreme inequalities between the rich and the poor, so dangerous to the innocence and happiness of both. They may, fortunately, be led by habit and choice to despise that luxury which is considered with us the true enjoyment of wealth. They may have little relish for that ceaseless hurry of amusements which is pursued in this country without pleasure, exercise, or employment. And perhaps, after trying some of our follies and caprices, and rejecting the rest, they may be led by reason and experiment to that old simplicity which was first pointed out by nature, and has produced those models which we still admire in arts, eloquence, and manners.

A New Scene of Providence Opened in the Settlement of America

"The diversity of the new scenes and new situations, which so many growing states must necessarily pass through, may introduce changes in the fluctuating opinions and manners of men which we can form no conception of; and not only the gracious disposition of Providence, but the visible preparation of causes, seems to indicate strong tendencies towards a general improvement."

John Adams, in contemplating the Christian colonization of the American continent, uttered the following views of the design of Providence—"I always consider," said he, "the settlement of America with reverence and wonder, as the opening of a grand scheme and design of Providence for the illumination of the ignorant and the emancipation of the slavish part of mankind all over the earth."

9

Statesmen of the Revolution— Their Views of Christianity and Its Relations to Civil Society and Government

Christian Statesmen of the Revolution

WISE and good men are God's workmen in laying the foundations and in completing the structures of human society. Every great and important era in history has been distinguished by the providential appearance and the successful labors of superior men, whose minds have been illuminated and whose steps have been guided by divine wisdom, and who have given progress to the interests of liberty and religion. As representative men—men of God, ordained and prepared for their special mission—contemplate Moses, the man of Providence, whose wisdom and genius have moulded the civil and religious institutions of all Christian nations; Paul, whose Christian faith, inspired writings, and heroic life have kindled the fires of freedom and truth among the nations of the earth, and exerted a boundless influence upon the intellectual and spiritual elevation and regeneration of the world; Luther, who by his masterly intellect and genus, his invincible Christian faith, iron will, indomitable energy, richness of Learning, and earnest devotion to truth, has liberated the human intellect from the shackles of ecclesiastical and civil despotism, and put into ceaseless activity agencies and influences which are working out the emancipation of nations and the moral regeneration of the world; Calvin, the profound thinker and theologian, "who," says Bancroft, "infused enduring elements into the institutions of Geneva, and made it for the modern world the impregnable fortress of popular freedom, the fertile seed-plot of democracy. He spread the fires of freedom in Scotland and carried the seeds of civil liberty and revolution to New England;" Wickliffe, the Oxford professor, and the translator of the Bible into the English language, who planted the seeds of the English Reformation, and started influences that resulted in Puritan emigration and the founding of a Christian nation on the American continent; Wesley, who by his practical wisdom and piety, and his sanctified genius, revived "Christianity in earnest," and put into intense and benevolent activity Christian and educational forces which are working effectually among the nations for their deliverance from error, ignorance, and despotism; Washington— the defender of his country, the founder of a Christian republic—whose fame and influence are as boundless as the world, and whose great example, illustrious life, profound practical wisdom, and unaffected piety have made him the ornament of the race and the benefactor of the world. These men were men of God, and divinely endowed and prepared for their great Christian work in giving the blessings of civil and religious liberty to nations.

"The affairs of men," says Lord Brougham, "the interests and history of nations, the relative value of institutions as discovered by their actual working, the merit of different systems of policy as tried by their effects, are all very imperfectly examined without a thorough knowledge of the individuals who administered the systems and presided over the management of public concerns. The history of empires is indeed the history of men—not only of the nominal rulers of the people, but of the leading persons who exerted a sensible influence over the destinies of their fellow-creatures, whether the traces of that influence resided in themselves, or, as in the case of lesser minds, their power was confined to their own times."

Views of the Men of the Revolution of the Christian Religion

The men of the Revolution had been, under the providence of God, trained and qualified for their great work. The Christian conflicts in Europe antecedent to American colonization, their Christian ancestors who had established their civil and social institutions on the

Bible, the Christian schools in which they had been educated, and the purity and manly vigor of the Christian faith which had formed their character and directed their conduct—these agencies had been at work to qualify the men who wrought the American Revolution and instituted our present forms of civil government. An outline sketch of the faith and declarations of the men who founded our civil institutions, in relation to the Christian religion and its necessity to civil government, will be recorded in the present chapter.

James Otis

Of Massachusetts, was among the first and foremost champions of freedom. He was educated, under Christian influences, by Rev. Jonathan Russell, minister of his parish, and in this Christian school caught the indomitable spirit of resistance to despotism. "Otis," said John Adams, "is a flame of fire,"—referring to a speech he made in Boston, in 1761, against the oppression of the British Government. "With a promptitude of classical allusions, a depth of research, a rapid summary of historical events and dates, a profusion of legal authorities, a prophetic glance of his eyes into futurity, and a rapid torrent of impetuous eloquence, he hurried all before him. American independence was then and there born. The seeds of patriot, and heroes to defend the vigorous youth were there and then sown. In fifteen years—*i.e.* in 1776—he grew up to manhood and declared himself free."

"There can be," said Otis, "no prescriptions old enough to supersede the law of nature, and the grant of Almighty God, who has given all men a right to be free. Government springs from the necessities of our nature, and has an everlasting foundation in the unchangeable will of God. The first principle and great end of government being to provide for the best good of all the people, this can be done only by a supreme legislature and executive, ultimately in the people, or the whole community, where God has placed it.

"The right of every man to his life, his liberty, no created being can rightfully contest. They are rights derived from the Author of nature—inherent, inalienable, and indefeasible by any law, compacts, contracts, covenants, or stipulations which man can devise. God made all men naturally equal."

Joseph Warren

Was as eminent for his virtues as for his intense patriotism. He fell a martyr to liberty at Bunker Hill, the 17th of June, 1775. He combined in a remarkable degree the qualities requisite for excellence in civil pursuits, with a strong taste for the military. He was educated at Cambridge University, and had in high perfection the gift of eloquence. His fine accomplishments as an orator, a patriot, and a professional and literary man were crowned with the virtues of religion. "There is hardly one," says Sparks, "whose example exercised a more inspiring and elevating influence upon his countrymen and the world than that of the brave, blooming, generous, self-devoted martyr of Bunker Hill. Such a character is the noblest spectacle which the moral world affords. It is declared by a poet to be a spectacle worthy of the gods. The friends of liberty, from all countries and throughout all time, as they kneel upon the spot that was moistened by the blood of Warren, will find their better feelings strengthened by the influence of the place, and will gather from it a virtue in some degree allied to his own."

On the morning of the battle of Bunker Hill, at a meeting of the Committee of Safety, Elbridge Gerry earnestly requested him not to expose his person. "I am aware of the danger," replied Warren; "but I should die with shame if I were to remain at home in safety while my friends and fellow-citizens are shedding their blood and hazarding their lives in the cause." "Your ardent temper," replied Gerry, "will carry you forward into the midst of peril, and you will probably fall." "I know that I may fall," replied Warren; "but where is the man who does not think it glorious and beautiful to die for his country?"

"Dulce et decorum est pro patria mori."

"In the private walks of life," said an orator who pronounced a eulogy on Warren in Boston, April 8, 1776, at the reinterment of his remains, "he was a pattern for mankind. In *public* life, the sole object of his ambition was to acquire the conscience of virtuous enterprises: *amor patriæ* was the spring of his actions, and *mens conscia recti* as his guide. And on this security he was, on every occasion, ready to sacrifice his health, his interest, and his ease to the calls of his country. When the liberties of his country were attacked, he appeared an early champion in the contest; and though his knowledge and abilities would have insured riches and preferment (could he have stooped to prostitution), yet he nobly withstood the fascinating charm, tossed fortune back her plume, and pursued the inflexible purpose of his soul in guiltless competence. The greatness of his soul shone even in the moment of death. In fine, to complete the great character, like *Harrington* he wrote, like *Cicero* he spoke, and like *Wolfe* he died. The *name* and the *virtues* of *Warren* shall remain immortal."

In an oration delivered in Boston, March 5, 1772, Warren, after discussing the principles of liberty, closes as follows—

"If you with united zeal and fortitude oppose the torrent of oppression; if you feel the true fire of patriotism burning in your breasts; if you from your souls despise the most gaudy dress that slavery can wear; if you really prefer the lonely cottage (whilst blest with liberty) to gilded palaces surrounded with the ensigns of slavery— you may have the fullest assurances that tyranny, with her whole accursed train, will hide their hideous heads in confusion, shame, and despair. If you perform your part, you must have the strongest confidence that THE SAME ALMIGHTY BEING who protected your venerable and pious forefathers, who enabled them to turn a barren wilderness into a fruitful field, who so often *made bare his arm* for their salvation, will be still mindful of you, their offspring.

"May *this* ALMIGHTY BEING graciously preside in all our councils. May he direct us to such measures as he himself will approve and be pleased to bless. May we ever be a people favored of God. May our land be a land of liberty, the seat of virtue, the asylum of the oppressed, *a name and a praise in the whole earth*, until the last shock of time shall bury the empires of the world in one common undistinguished ruin."

Samuel Adams

A true Christian statesman and hero, wise, ardent, fearless, and influential, was "a member of the church, and in a rigid community was an example of morals and the scrupulous observance of every ordinance. Evening and morning his house was a house of prayer; and no one more revered the Christian Sabbath." He was among the foremost patriots of the Revolution, and one of the signers of the Declaration of Independence. After that act had been passed, he stood on the steps of the Continental State-House, on the 1st of August, 1776, in Philadelphia, and, before thousands of patriots, delivered an oration, in which are the following passages—

"The time at which this attempt on our liberties was made, when we were ripened into maturity, had acquired a knowledge of war, and were free from intestine enemies—the gradual advances of our oppressors, enabling us to prepare for our defence—the unusual fertility of our lands—the success which at first attends our feeble arms, producing unanimity among our friends and reducing our internal foes to acquiescence—these are strong and palpable assurances that Providence is yet gracious unto our Zion, that it will turn away our captivity.

"These are instances of, I would say, an almost astonishing providence in our favor; so that we may truly say that it is not our arm that has saved us. The hand of Heaven appears to have led us on to be, perhaps, humble instruments and means in the great providential dispensation which is completing. Brethren and fellow-countrymen, if it was ever granted to mortals to trace the designs of Providence and interpret its manifestations in favor of its cause, we may, with humility of soul, cry out, 'Not unto us, not unto us, but to thy name be the praise.'

"My countrymen, from the day on which an accommodation takes place between England and America on any other terms than as independent states, I shall date the ruin of this country. We are now, to the astonishment of the world, three millions of souls united in one common cause. This day we are called on to give a glorious example of what the wisest and best of men were rejoiced to view only in speculation. This day presents the world with the most August spectacle that its annals ever unfolded—millions of freemen voluntarily and deliberately forming themselves into a society for the common defence and common happiness. Immortal spirits of Hampden, Locke, and Sidney! will it not add to your benevolent joys to behold your posterity rising to the dignity of *men*, and evincing to the world the reality and expediency of your systems, and in the actual enjoyment of that equal liberty which you were happy, when on earth, in delineating and recommending to mankind!"

Patrick Henry

The passionate and eloquent orator of liberty and the Revolution, was a profound believer in the divinity of Christianity, and declared its necessity to nations and governments as well as to the salvation and happiness of the soul. In April, 1775, he uttered the following Christian sentiments—

"He had no doubt that that God who, in former ages, had hardened Pharaoh's heart, that he might show his power and glory in the redemption of his chosen people, for similar purposes had permitted the flagrant outrages which had occurred throughout the continent. It was for them now to determine whether they were worthy of divine interference—whether they would accept the high boon now held out to them by Heaven;—that, if they would, though it might lead them through a sea of blood, they were to remember that the same God whose power divided the Red Sea for the deliverance of Israel still reigned in all his glory, unchanged and unchangeable—was still the enemy of the oppressor and the friend of the oppressed—that he would cover them from their enemies by a pillar of cloud by day, and guide them through the night by a pillar of fire."

In an impassioned burst of patriotism, he exclaimed, "We must fight. I repeat it, sir, we must fight. An appeal to arms and the God of hosts is all that is left us. Nor shall we fight our battles alone. That God who presides over the destinies of nations will raise up friends for us."

In reference to resolutions against the scheme of taxing the colonies, passed by the Virginia legislature in 1765, he stated, "Whether they will prove a blessing or a curse will depend on the use which our people make of the blessings which a gracious God hath bestowed on us. If they are wise, they will be great and happy. If they are of a contrary character, they will be miserable. *Righteousness alone can exalt them as a nation.*" Reader, whoever thou art, remember this, and in thy sphere practise virtue thyself, and encourage it in others.

"He was," says Wirt, his biographer, "a sincere Christian. His favorite religious works were Doddridge's Rise and Progress of Religion in the Soul, Butler's Analogy of Religion Natural and Revealed, and Jenyns's Views of the Internal Evidences of the Christian Religion." "Here," said he to a friend (holding up the Bible), "is a book worth more than all other books that were ever printed."

His last will bears this testimony, to his children and his countrymen, to the truth and importance of religion—"I have now disposed of all my worldly property to my family: there is one thing more I wish I could give them, and that is the Christian religion. If they had this, and I had not given them one shilling, they would be rich; and if they had it not, and I had given them all the world, they would be poor."

John Hancock

The son of a clergyman of Braintree, Massachusetts, was distinguished for his patriotism, piety, and benevolence. His great wealth and eminent talents were consecrated to his country. He was President of the Congress of 1776, and his name, in a bold, broad hand, stands first on the Declaration of Independence. Early in the struggle for independence and freedom he inspired his patriot companions with such stirring Christian words as these—

"I have the most animating confidence that the present noble struggle for liberty will terminate gloriously for America. And let us play the men for our God, and for the cities of our God: while we are using the means in our power, let us humbly commit our righteous cause to the great Lord of the Universe, who loveth righteousness and hateth iniquity. And, having secured the approbation of our hearts by a faithful and unwearied discharge of our duty to our country, let us joyfully leave our concerns in the hands of Him who raiseth up and putteth down the empires and kingdoms of the earth as he pleaseth, and, with cheerful submission to his sovereign will, devoutly say, '*Although the fig tree shall not blossom, neither shall fruit be in the vines; the labor of the olive shall fail, and the field shall yield no meat; the flock shall be cut off from the fold, and there shall be no herd in the stall: yet we will rejoice in the Lord, we will joy in the God of our salvation.*'"

John Adams

The orator of the Revolution, signer of the Declaration of Independence, the first Vice-President and second President of the United

States, was a firm believer in Christianity. He was early trained in its heavenly lessons, being the son of a deacon of the Congregational Church, of which he himself became a member. "His faith and soul clung to the Christian religion as the hope of himself and his country." In every position, he exerted his great powers to extend its beneficent reign. He was a faithful attendant on the public worship of God at home and when attending to his public duties abroad. Jefferson said of Adams that "a man more perfectly honest never came from the hands of the Creator."

"The Christian religion," Adams said, "as I understand it, is the brightness of the glory and the express portrait of the character of the eternal, self-existent, independent, benevolent, all-powerful, and all-merciful Creator, Preserver and Father of the universe, the first good, the first perfect, and the first fair. It will last as long as the world. Neither savage nor civilized man, without a revelation, could have discovered or invented it." "Religion and virtue are the only foundations, not only of republicanism and of all free governments, but of social felicity under all governments and in all the combinations of human society. Science, liberty, and religion are the choicest blessings of humanity: without their joint influence no society can be great, flourishing, or happy."

Mr. Adams was the first minister to England after peace was established. On the 9th of June, 1785, he was presented to the court of Great Britain, and made to the Queen of England the following address—

"Permit me, madam, to recommend to your majesty's royal goodness a rising empire and an infant virgin world. Another Europe, madam, is rising in America. To a philosophical mind like your majesty's, there cannot be a more pleasing contemplation than the prospect of doubling the human species and augmenting at the same time their prosperity and happiness. It will in future ages be the glory of these kingdoms to have planted that country and to have sown there those seeds of science, of liberty, of virtue, and, permit me, madam, to add, of PIETY, which alone constitute the prosperity of nations and the happiness of the human race."

When the Declaration of Independence was passed, Adams wrote to his wife as follows—

"The fourth day of July, 1776, will be a memorable epoch in the history of America. I am apt to believe that it will be celebrated by succeeding generations as the great anniversary festival. It ought to be commemorated as the day of deliverence, by solemn acts of devotion to Almighty God. It ought to be solemnized with pomp, shows, games, sports, guns, bells, bonfires, and illuminations, from one end of the continent to the other, from this time forward forever.

"You will think me transported with an enthusiasm; but I am not. I am well aware of the toil and blood and treasure that it will cost us to maintain this declaration and support and defend these States; yet through all the gloom I can see the rays of light and glory. I can see that the end is worth more than all the means, and that posterity will triumph, although you and I may rue it—which I hope we shall not."

Robert Treat Paine

A signer of the Declaration of Independence, had studied prayerfully and thoroughly the whole range of theology before he entered upon the study of law. He was for a short time chaplain in the army, and preached occasionally in Boston. "He was a decided, firm believer in the Christian revelation, and was fully convinced of its divine origin. He received it as a system of moral truth and righteousness given by God for the instruction, consolation, and happiness of man. His intellectual, moral, and religious character was strongly marked with integrity."

Elbridge Gerry

Also a signer of the Declaration of Independence, and Vice-President of the United States, was a statesman who recognized the providence of God in human affairs, and had faith in the divinity of Christianity. In a letter to Samuel Adams, December 13, 1775, he says, "History can hardly produce such a series of events as has taken place in favor of American opposition. The hand of Heaven seems to have directed every occurrence. Had such an event as lately occurred at Essex happened to Cromwell, he would have published it as a miracle in his favor, and excited his soldiers to enthusiasm and bravery." "It is the duty of every citizen," he said, "though he had but one day to live, to devote that day to the service of his country." "May that Omnipotent Being," (in addressing the Senate in 1814,) "who with infinite wisdom and justice presides over the destinies of nations, confirm the heroic patriotism which has glowed in the breasts of the national rulers, and convince the enemy that, whilst a disposition to peace on honorable and equitable terms will ever prevail in their public councils, one spirit, animated by the love of country, will inspire every department of the national government."

Matthew Thornton

A native of Ireland, was distinguished in the cause of liberty. He was a signer of the Declaration of Independence, and the disciple and friend of Washington. "No man was more deeply impressed with a belief in the existence and bounties of an overruling Providence—which he strongly manifested by a practical application of the strongest and wisest injunctions of the Christian religion. A believer in the divine mission of our Savior, he followed the great principles of his doctrines."

Stephen Hopkins

Was a pure-minded patriot and Christian statesman. He signed the Declaration of Independence, and bore a distinguished part in securing our liberties and forming our free institutions. He was a Quaker, and took an active interest in their church-affairs, and opened his house for their religious worship. He was well acquainted with the evidences of Christianity, and was frequently heard to confound the cavils of infidels and to establish the divinity of the Christian religion.

William Ellery

An ardent patriot, active and influential in Congress, and a signer of the Declaration of Independence, was a Christian statesman. "He studied the Scriptures with reverence and diligence; feeling their value, seeking for the truth, and aiming at the obedience they require." He had firm faith in the justice and goodness of God. In the most gloomy periods of the Revolution, he always ended his cheering addresses by saying, "Let us be hopeful and trusting; for 'the Lord reigneth.'"

Roger Sherman

Was a wise legislator, an ardent and incorruptible patriot, and a ripe Christian statesman. He had the unbounded confidence of Congress, and was on the committee to draft the Declaration of Independence. In Congress he advocated the Christian duty and propriety of appointing days of fasting and prayer and thanksgiving to Almighty God, and was the author of several of those eminently Christian state papers. He had great influence in imbuing the public and legislative transactions of the country with a scriptural sense of the need of God's presence and blessing. Washington esteemed and revered him as an eminent Christian and as a wise statesman. Adams said, "He was one of the soundest and strongest pillars of the Revolution." In early youth he made a public profession of religion, and for more than a half-century he defended its doctrines and illustrated its virtues. He applied Christian principles to every department of society, and considered all governments sadly defective that were not based on the moral teachings and principles of the Bible.

At his funeral it was said by his pastor, Jonathan Edwards, Jun., D.D., that, "whether we consider him as a politician or a Christian, he was a great and good man. The words of David concerning Abner may with great truth be applied on this occasion—' Know ye not that there is a great man fallen this day in Israel?' He ever adorned the profession of Christianity which he made in youth, was distinguished through life for public usefulness, and died in prospect of a blessed immortality."

The predominant traits in Mr. Sherman's character were his practical wisdom and his strong common sense. Mr. Jefferson, on one occasion, when pointing out the various members of Congress to a friend, said—"That is Mr. Sherman, of Connecticut, *a man who never said a foolish thing in his life.*" He possessed a singular power of penetrating into the characters and motives of men, while the rectitude and integrity of his own nature enabled him to acquire an extraordinary influence. "Though a man naturally of strong passions, he obtained a complete control over them, by means of his deep religious spirit, and became habitually calm, sedate, and self-possessed."

Samuel Huntington

Acted a prominent part in achieving our independence, and was a signer of the Declaration of Independence. "He was a firm friend of order and religion, a member of the Christian Church, and punctual in his devotions of the family. He was, occasionally, the people's mouth to God when destitute of preaching. As a professor of Christianity and a supporter of its institutions, he was exemplary and devout."

William Williams

Was the son of Rev. Solomon Williams, who for fifty-four years was the pastor of the Congregational church of Lebanon, Connecticut. "He was a man of piety, and from his early youth a member of the church. In all relations and transactions of life he preserved an unblemished Christian character." His high Christian character won for him the distinction of an honest politician. He signed the Declaration of Independence, and aided in forming our free institutions.

Oliver Wolcott

Has an honorable record in the annals of freedom. He was a Christian statesman, and signed the charter of our independence. "His integrity was inflexible, his morals were strictly pure, and his faith that of an humble Christian, untainted by bigotry or intolerance."

Philip Livingston

Belonged to a family of eminent Christian celebrity. He was a statesman of the highest order, consecrated himself to the cause of his country, and exercised great influence in forming our free institutions. He was a firm believer in the Christian religion, and an humble follower of our Divine Redeemer.

Richard Stockton

Was a true patriot, a ripe statesman, an eloquent orator, a profound jurist, and an honor to the Christian Church. He signed the Declaration of Independence, and aided greatly in our struggle for freedom. His will attests his views of the truth and importance of the Christian religion, in these words—"As my children will have frequent occasion of perusing this instrument, and may be particularly impressed with the last words of their father, I think proper here not only to subscribe to my entire belief in the great leading doctrines of the Christian religion, such as the being of a God, and 'the universal defection and depravity of human nature, the divinity of the PERSON and the completeness of the redemption purchased by the blessed Saviour, the necessity of the operations of the Divine Spirit, of divine faith accompanied with an habitual virtuous life, and the universality of the Divine Providence, but also, in the bowels of a father's affection, to charge and exhort them to remember that the fear of the Lord is the beginning of wisdom."

John Witherspoon

Was a Christian patriot, and a learned minister of the gospel. He was from Scotland, the land of learning and of liberty, and a descendant of John Knox, the Reformer. His great learning attracted the attention of the friends of education, and he was called to the presidency of Princeton College. Soon after his arrival the scenes of the Revolution opened, and the college was suspended. "Under his auspices," says Dr. Rogers, a contemporary, "have been formed a large proportion of the clergy of the Presbyterian Church, and to his instructions America owes many of her most distinguished patriots and legislators. In the civil councils of his adopted country he shone with equal lustre, and his talents as a legislator and senator showed the extent and the variety of the powers of his mind. His distinguished abilities pointed him out to the citizens of New Jersey as one of the most proper delegates to the convention which formed their republican Constitution. In this assembly he appeared to all the professors of law as profound a civilian as he had before been known to be a philosopher and divine. Early in the year 1776 he was sent, as a representative of the people of New Jersey, to the Congress of the United States. He was seven years a member of that illustrious body, which, under Providence, in the face of innumerable difficulties and dangers, led us on to the establishment of our independence. He was one of the signers of the Declaration of Independence. While he was thus engaged in serving his country in the character of a civilian, he did not lay aside his ministry." He advocated the cause of the country, with admirable simplicity, by his pen; exalting it in the pulpit by associating the interests of civil and religious liberty, and zealously co-operating in its active vindication in Congress. He was an eminent Christian statesman, as well as a pious and learned divine. "If the pulpit of America," says Headley, "had given only this one man to the Revolution, it would deserve to be held in everlasting remembrance for the service it rendered the country."

A sermon which Dr. Witherspoon preached at Princeton, on the 17th of May, 1776, being the general fast appointed by the Congress through the United Colonies, entitled "The Dominion of Providence over the Passions of Men," was rich in profound thought, and eloquent and just in its views of civil and religious liberty. His object in the discourse was to show that public calamities and commotions, the ambition of mistaken princes, and the passions and wickedness of men, are under the dominion of God, and will be overruled for the advancement and establishment of religion and liberty. The passage on which he based this noble discourse was, "*Surely the wrath of man shall praise thee: the remainder of wrath shalt thou restrain.*"—(Psalm lxxvi. 10.) The following extracts are given—

"There is no part of Divine Providence in which a greater beauty and majesty appears, than when the Almighty Ruler turns the councils of wicked men into confusion, and makes them militate against themselves." This he illustrates by many marked events in sacred and profane history. And, applying the doctrine of the discourse to the condition of the colonies struggling for liberty, he says, "You may perceive what ground there is to give praise to God for his favors already bestowed on us respecting the public cause. It would be a criminal inattention not to observe the singular interposition of Providence hitherto in behalf of the American colonies. How many discoveries have been made of the designs of the enemy in Britain and among ourselves, in a manner as unexpected to us as to them, and in such season as to prevent their effect! What surprising success has attended our encounters in almost every instance! Has not the boasted discipline of regular and veteran soldiers been turned into confusion and dismay before the new and maiden courage of freemen in defence of their property and rights? In what great mercy has blood been spared on the side of this injured country! Some important victories have been gained in the South, with so little loss that enemies will probably think it dissembled. The signal advantage we have gained by the evacuation of Boston, and the shameful flight of the army and navy of Britain, was brought on without the loss of a man. To all this we may add, that the counsels of our enemies have been visibly confounded, so that I believe I may say with truth that there is hardly any step which they have taken but it has operated strongly against themselves, and been more in our favor than if they had followed a contrary course.

"While we give praise to God, the supreme disposer of all events, for his interposition in our behalf, let us guard against the dangerous error of trusting in or boasting of an arm of flesh. I could earnestly wish that, while our arms are crowned with success, we might content ourselves with a modest ascription of it to the power of the Highest. The Holy Scriptures in general, and the truths of the glorious gospel in particular, and the whole course of Providence, seem intended to abase the pride of man and lay the vain-glorious in the dust. The truth is, that, through the whole frame of nature and the whole system of human life, that which promises most performs the least. The flowers of finest colors seldom have the sweetest fragrance. The trees of greatest growth or fairest form are seldom of the greatest value or duration. Deep waters run with the least noise. Men who think most are seldom talkative. And I think it holds as much in war as in any thing, that every boaster is a coward. I look upon ostentation and confidence to be a sort of outrage upon Providence; and when it becomes general and infuses itself into the spirit of a people, it is the forerunner of destruction.

"From what has been said you may learn what encouragement you have to put your trust in God, and hope for his assistance in the present important conflict. He is the Lord of Hosts, great in might and strong in battle. Whoever has his countenance and approbation shall have the best at last. If your cause is just, you may look with confidence to the Lord and entreat him to plead it as his own. I would neither have you to trust in an arm of flesh, nor to sit with folded hands and expect that miracles shall be wrought in your defence. In opposition to it, I would exhort as Joab did the host of Israel, who in this instance spoke like a prudent general and a pious man—'Be of good courage, and let us behave ourselves valiantly for our people, and for the cities of our God; and the Lord do that which is good in his sight.'" (2 Sam. x. 12.)

"He is the best friend to American liberty who is the most sincere and active in promoting true and undefiled religion, and who sets himself with the greatest firmness to bear down profanity and immorality of every kind. Whoever is an avowed enemy to God, I scruple not to call him an enemy to his country. It is your duty in this important and critical season to exert yourselves, every one in his proper sphere, to stem the tide of prevailing vice, to promote the knowledge of God, the reverence of his name and worship, and obedience to his laws. Your duty to God, to your country, to your families, and to yourselves, is the same. True religion is nothing else but an inward temper and outward conduct suited to your state and circumstances in Providence at any time. And as peace with God and conformity to him add to the sweetness of created comforts while we possess them, so in times of difficulty and trial it is the man of piety and inward principle that we may expect to find the uncorrupted patriot, the useful citizen, and the invincible soldier. God grant that in America true religion and civil liberty may be inseparable, and that the unjust attempts to destroy the one may in the issue tend to the support and establishment of both."

In affixing his name to the Declaration of Independence, he rose in that illustrious body of men and uttered the following thrilling words—

"Mr. President—That noble instrument on your table, which insures immortality to its author, should be subscribed this very morning by every pen in the House. He who will not respond to its accents, and strain every nerve to carry into effect its provisions, is unworthy the name of freeman. Although these gray hairs must descend into the sepulchre, I would infinitely rather they should descend thither by the hand of the executioner, than desert at this crisis the sacred cause of my country."

The appeal was electric. Every member rose and affixed his name to that immortal Declaration.

In a discourse he preached at a public thanksgiving, after peace, from the text, "*Salvation belongeth unto the Lord*," in which he showed "what the United States of America owed to Divine Providence in the course of the present war," he closed with the following remarks—

"Those who are vested with civil authority ought also with much care to promote religion and good morals among all under their government. If we give credit to the Holy Scriptures, he that ruleth must be just, ruling in the fear of God. Those who wish well to a state ought to choose, to places of trust, men of inward principle, justified by exemplary conversation. Those who pay no regard to religion and sobriety, in the persons whom they send to the legislature of any state, will soon pay dear for their folly. Let a man's zeal, profession, or even principles, as to political measures, be what they will, if he is without personal integrity and private virtue as a man, he is not to be trusted. I think we have had some instances of men who have roared for liberty in taverns, and were most noisy in public meetings, who yet have turned traitors in a little while. If the people in general ought to have regard to the moral character of those whom they invest with authority, either in the legislative, executive, or judicial branches, such as are so promoted may perceive what is and will be expected of them. They are under the strongest obligations to promote *religion*, sobriety, industry, and even social virtue, among those who are committed to their care. If you ask me what are the means which civil rulers are bound to use for attaining these ends, further than the impartial support and faithful guardianship of the rights of conscience, I answer, that example itself is none of the least. Those who are in high stations and authority are exposed to continual observation; and therefore their example is better seen and hath greater influence than that of persons of inferior rank. Reverence for the name of God, a punctual attendance on the public and private duties of religion, as well as sobriety and purity of conversation, are especially incumbent on those who are honored with places of power and trust. But I cannot content myself with this. It is certainly the duty of magis-trates to be a terror to evil-doers, and a praise to them that do well."

"Let us cherish a love of piety, order, industry, purity. Let us check every disposition to luxury, effeminacy, and the pleasures of a dissipated life. Let us in public measures put honor upon modesty and self-denial, which is the index of real merit. And in our families let us do the best, by religious instruction, to sow the seeds which may bear fruit in the next generation. Whatever state among us shall continue to make piety and virtue the standard of public honor will enjoy the greatest inward peace, the greatest national happiness, and in every conflict will discover the greatest constitutional strength."

Benjamin Franklin

The civilian, the philosopher, the patriot, the wise and virtuous statesman, and signer of the Declaration of Independence, had a profound reverence for the Christian religion and faith in its divinity. He was, in his childhood and youth, trained in the school of Puritan piety, and the foundation of his character and eminent usefulness was formed by the teachings of a Christian minister. In early life, he read Dr. Cotton Mather's little book, entitled "Essays to Do Good," and in his old age he said, "All the good I have ever done to my country or my fellow-creatures must be ascribed to the impressions produced on my mind by perusing that little work in my youth."

In writing, in 1790, to Dr. Stiles, President of Yale College, Dr. Franklin said—

"You desire to know something of my religion. Here is my creed. I believe in one God, the Creator of the universe. That he governs it by his Providence. That he ought to be worshipped. That the most acceptable service we render him is in doing good to his other children. That the soul of man is immortal, and will be treated with justice in another life respecting its conduct in this. These I take to be the fundamental points in all sound religion. As to Jesus of Nazareth, my opinion of whom you particularly desire, I think the system of morals, and his religion, as he left them to us, is the best the world ever saw, or is likely to see. I apprehend it has received various corrupting changes; and I have, with most of the present dissenters in England, some doubt as to his divinity, though it is a question I do not dogmatize upon, having never studied it, and think it needless to busy myself with it now, when I soon will have an opportunity of knowing the truth, with less trouble. I see no harm, however, in its being believed, if that belief has the good consequence, as probably it has, of making his doctrines more respected and observed, especially as I do not perceive that the Supreme takes it amiss, by distinguishing the believers in his government of the world with any peculiar marks of his displeasure. I shall only add, respecting myself, that, having experienced the goodness of that Being in conducting me prosperously through a long life, I have no doubt of its continuance in the next, though without the smallest conceit of meriting such goodness. My sentiments on this subject you will see in the copy of an old letter enclosed, which I wrote in answer to one from an old religionist (Whitefield) whom I had relieved in a paralytic case by electricity, and who, being afraid I should grow proud upon it, sent me his serious though rather impertinent caution.

"With great and sincere esteem and affection, I am, &c.,

"Benjamin Franklin."

Letter from Dr. Franklin to Rev. George Whitefield.
Philadelphia, June 6, 1753.

Dear Sir—

I received your kind letter of the 2d inst., and am glad to hear that you increase in strength: I hope you will continue mending until you recover your former health and firmness. Let me know whether you still use the cold bath, and what effect it has. As to the kindness you mention, I wish it could have been of more serious service to you; but if it had, the only thanks that I should desire are, that you would always be ready to serve any other person that may need your assistance; and so let offices go round, for mankind are all of a family. For my own part, when I am employed in serving others, I do not look upon myself as conferring favors, but as paying debts. In my travels, and since my settlement, I have received much kindness from men to whom I shall never have an opportunity of making the least direct return, and numberless mercies from God, who is infinitely above being benefited by our services. These kindnesses from men I can, therefore, only return to their fellow-men; and I can only show my gratitude to God by a readiness to help his other children and my brethren; for I do not think that thanks and compliments, though repeated weekly, can discharge our real obligation to each other, and much less to our Creator.

You will see, in this my notion of good works, that I am far from expecting to merit heaven by them. By heaven we understand a state of happiness infinite in degree and eternal in duration. I can do nothing to deserve such a reward. He that, for giving a draught of water to a thirsty person, should expect to be paid with a good plantation, would be modest in his demands, compared with those who think they deserve heaven for the little good they do on earth. Even the mixed imperfect pleasures we enjoy in this world are rather from God's goodness than our merit: how much more so the happiness of heaven! For my part, I have not the vanity to think I deserve it, the folly to expect, or the ambition to desire it, but content myself in submitting to the disposal of that God who made me, who has hitherto preserved and blessed me, and in whose fatherly goodness I may well confide that he will never make me miserable, and that the affliction I may at any time suffer may tend to my benefit.

The faith you mention has, doubtless, its uses in the world. I do not desire to lessen it in any man, but I wish it were more productive of good works than I have generally seen it. I mean real good works—works of kindness, charity, mercy, and public spirit; not in holyday-keeping, sermon hearing or reading, performing church ceremonies, or making long prayers, filled with flatteries and compliments, despised even by wise men, and much less capable of pleasing the Deity.

The worship of God is a duty; the hearing and reading may be useful; but if men rest in hearing and praying—as too many do—it is as if the tree should value itself on being watered and putting forth leaves, though it never produced any fruit.

Your good Master thought less of these outward appearances than many of his modern disciples. He preferred the doers of the word to the hearers; the son that seemingly refused to obey his father and yet performed his commands, to him that professed his readiness but neglected the work; the heretical but charitable Samaritan, to the uncharitable and orthodox priest and sanctified Levite; and those who gave food to the hungry, drink to the thirsty, and raiment to the naked, entertainment to the stranger, and never heard of his name, he declares, shall, in the last day, be accepted, when those who cry, Lord, Lord, who value themselves on their faith, though great enough to perform miracles, but having neglected good works, shall be rejected.

Being your friend and servant.
Benjamin Franklin

Thomas Paine wrote a little volume entitled "The Age of Reason." He sent the manuscript to Dr. Franklin, and received the following reply—

Dear Sir—

I have read your manuscript with some attention. By the argument which it contains against a particular Providence, though you allow a general Providence, you strike at the foundations of all religion. For, without the belief of a Providence that takes cognizance of, guards and guides, and may favor particular persons, there is no motive to worship a Deity, to fear its displeasure, or to pray for its protection. I will not enter into any discussion of your principles, though you seem to desire it.

At present I shall only give you my opinion that, though your reasonings are subtle, and may prevail with some readers, you will not succeed so as to change the general sentiments of mankind on that subject; and the consequence of printing this piece will be, a great deal of odium drawn upon yourself, mischief to you, and no benefit to others. He that spits against the wind spits in his own face. But were you to succeed, do you imagine any good will be done by it? You yourself may find it easy to live a virtuous life without the assistance afforded by religion—you having a clear perception of the advantages of virtue and the disadvantages of vice, and possessing a strength of resolution sufficient to enable you to resist common temptations. But think how great a portion of mankind consists of ignorant men and women and of inexperienced, inconsiderate youth of both sexes, who have need of the motives of religion to restrain them from vice, support their virtue, and retain them in the practice of it till it becomes habitual, which is the great point for its security. And perhaps you are indebted to her originally, that is, to your religious education, for the habits of virtue upon which you now justly value yourself.

You might easily display your excellent talents of reasoning upon a less hazardous subject, and thereby obtain a rank with our most distinguished authors. For among us it is not necessary, as among the Hottentots, that a youth, to be raised into the company of men, should prove his manhood by beating his mother.

I would advise you, therefore, not to attempt unchaining the tiger, but to burn this piece before it is seen by any other person; whereby you will save yourself a great deal of mortification from the enemies it may raise against you, and perhaps a good deal of regret and repentance. If men are so wicked *with* religion, what would they be *without* it? I intend this letter itself as a proof of my friendship, and therefore add no professions to it, but subscribe simply,

Yours, B. Franklin

A Lecture on the Providence of God in the Government of The World.

by Benjamin Franklin

I propose at this time to discourse on the providence of God in the government of the world. It might be judged an affront should I go about to prove this first principle, the existence of a Deity, and that he is the creator of the universe, for that all mankind, in all ages, have agreed in. I shall, therefore, proceed to observe that he must be a being of infinite wisdom, as appears in his admirable order and disposition of things— whether we consider the heavenly bodies, the stars and planets, and their wonderful regular motions; or this earth, compounded of such an excellent mixture of all elements; or the admirable structure of animate bodies, of such infinite variety, and yet every one adapted to its nature and way of life it is to be placed in, whether on earth, in the air, or in the water, and so exactly that the highest and most exquisite human reason cannot find a fault and say that this would have been better so, or in such a manner; which whoever considers attentively and thoroughly will be astonished and swallowed up in admiration.

That the Deity is a being of great goodness, appears in his giving life to so many creatures, each of which acknowledges it a benefit by their unwillingness to leave it; in his providing plentiful sustenance for them all, and making those things most useful most common and easy to be had; such as water, necessary for almost every creature to drink; air, without which few could subsist; the inexpressible benefits of light and sunshine to almost all animals in general; and to men the most useful vegetables, such as corn, the most useful of metals, as iron, &c., the most useful of animals, as horses, oxen, and sheep, he has made the easiest to raise or procure in quantity or numbers; each of which particulars, if considered seriously and carefully, would fill us with the highest love and affection.

That he is a being of infinite power, appears in his being able to form and compound such vast masses of matter as this earth, the sun, and innumerable stars and planets, and give them such prodigious motion; and yet so to govern them in their greatest velocity as that they shall not fly out of their appointed bounds, nor dash one against another for their mutual destruction. But 'tis easy to conceive of his power when we are convinced of his infinite knowledge and wisdom; for if weak and foolish creatures as we are, by knowing the nature of a few things, can produce such wonderful effects, such as, for instance, by knowing the nature only of nitre and sea-salt mixed we can make a water which will dissolve the hardest iron, and by adding one ingredient more can make another water which will dissolve gold and make the most solid bodies fluid; and by knowing the nature of saltpetre, sulphur, and charcoal, those mean ingredients mixed, we can shake the air in the most terrible manner, destroy ships, houses, and men at a distance, and in an instant overthrow cities, and rend rocks into a thousand pieces, and level the highest mountains; what power must He possess who not only knows the nature of every thing in the universe, but can make things of new natures with the greatest ease at his pleasure?

Agreeing, then, that the world was at first made by a being of infinite wisdom, goodness, and power, which being we call God, the state of things existing at this time must be in one of these four following manners, viz.—

1. Either he unchangeably decreed and appointed every thing that comes to pass, and left nothing to the course of nature, nor allowed any creature free agency.

2. Without decreeing any thing, he left all to general nature and the events of free agency in his creatures, which he never alters or interrupts; or,

3. He decreed some things unchangeably, and left others to general nature and the events of free agency, which also he never alters or interrupts; or,

4. He sometimes interferes by his particular providence, and sets aside the effects which would otherwise have been produced by any of the above causes.

I shall endeavor to show the first three suppositions to be inconsistent with the common light of reason, and that the fourth is most agreeable to it, and therefore most probably true.

In the first place: If you say he has in the beginning unchangeably decreed all things, and left nothing to nature or free agency, three strange conclusions will necessarily follow. 1. That he is now no more a God. It is true, indeed, before he made such unchangeable decrees, he was a being of power almighty; but now, having determined every thing, he has divested himself of all further power; he has done, and has no more to do; he has tied up his hands, and has no greater power than an idol of wood or stone; nor can there be any more reason for praying to him or worshipping of him than of such an idol, for the worshippers can never be better for such a worship. Then, 2. He has decreed some things contrary to the very notion of a wise and good being; such as that some of his creatures or children shall do all manner of injury to others, and bring every kind of evil upon them without cause; and that some of them shall even blaspheme their Creator in the most horrible manner; and, which is still more highly absurd, that he has decreed that the greatest part of mankind shall in all ages put up their earnest prayers to him both in private and publicly in great assemblies, when all the while he had so determined their fate that he could not possibly grant them any benefits on that account, nor could such prayers be in any way available. Why then should he ordain them to make such prayers? It cannot be imagined that they are of any service to him. Surely it is not more difficult to believe that the world was made by a God of wood or stone than that the God who made the world should be such a God as this.

In the second place, if you say he has decreed nothing, but left all things to general nature and the events of free agency, which he never alters or interrupts, then these conclusions will follow: he must either utterly hide himself from the works of his own hands, and take no notice at all of their proceedings natural or moral, or he must be, as undoubtedly he is, a spectator of every thing, for there can be no reason or ground to suppose the first. I say there can be no reason to imagine he would make so glorious a universe merely to abandon it. In this case imagine the Deity looking on and beholding the ways of his creatures. Some heroes in virtue he sees incessantly endeavoring the good of others; they labor through vast difficulties, they suffer incredible hardships and miseries to accomplish this end, in hopes to please a good God, and attain his favors, which they earnestly pray for. What answer can he make, then, within Himself but this? *Take the reward chance may give you: I do not intermeddle in these affairs.* He sees others doing all manner of evil, and bringing by their actions misery and destruction among mankind: what can he say here, but this?—*If chance rewards, I shall not punish you. I am not to be concerned.* He sees the just, the innocent, and the beneficent in the hands of the wicked and violent oppressor, and when the good are on the brink of destruction they pray to him, *Thou, O God, art mighty and powerful to save: help us, we beseech thee!* He answers, *I cannot help you; it is none of my business, nor do I at all regard those things.* How is it possible to believe a wise and infinitely good being can be delighted in this circumstance, and be utterly unconcerned what becomes of the beings and things he has created? for thus, we must believe him idle and inactive, and that his glorious attributes of power, wisdom, and goodness are no more to be made use of.

In the third place. If you say he has decreed some things and left others to the events of nature and free agency, which he never alters nor interrupts, you *un-God* him, if I may be allowed the expression: he has nothing to do; he can cause us neither good nor harm; he is no more to be regarded than a lifeless image, than Dagon or Baal, or Bel and the Dragon, and, as in both the other suppositions foregoing, that being which from its power is most able to act, from its wisdom knows best how to act, and from its goodness would always certainly act best, **is in** this opinion supposed to become the most inactive of all beings, and remain everlastingly idle, an absurdity which, when considered, or but barely seen, cannot be swallowed without doing the greatest violence to common reason and all the faculties of the understanding.

We are then necessarily driven to the fourth supposition, that the Deity sometimes interferes by his particular providence, and sets aside the events which would otherwise have been produced by the course of nature or by free agency of men; and this is perfectly agreeable with what we can know of his attributes and perfections. But, as some may doubt whether it is possible there should be such a thing as free agency in creatures, I shall just offer one short argument on that account, and proceed to show how the duty of religion necessarily follows a belief of a Providence. You acknowledge that God is infinitely powerful, wise, and good, and also a free agent, and you will not deny that he has communicated to us a part of his wisdom, power, and goodness—that is, he has made us in some degree wise, potent, and good. And is it then impossible for him to communicate any part of his freedom, and make us also in some degree free? Is even his infinite power sufficient for this? I should be glad to hear what reason any man can give for thinking in that manner. It is sufficient for me to show that it is not impossible, and no man, I think, can show it is improbable. Much more might he offered to demonstrate clearly that men are free agents and accountable for their actions.

Lastly. If God does not sometimes interfere by his providence, it is either because he cannot or because he will not. Which of these positions will you choose? There is a righteous nation grievously oppressed by a cruel tyrant: they earnestly entreat God to deliver them. If you say he cannot, you deny his infinite power, which you at first acknowledged. If you say he will not, you must directly deny his infinite goodness. You are of necessity obliged to allow that it is highly reasonable to believe a Providence, because it is highly absurd to believe otherwise.

Now, if it is unreasonable to suppose it out of the power of the Deity to help and favor us particularly, or that we are out of his hearing and notice, or that good actions do not procure more of his favor than ill ones, then I conclude that believing a Providence, we have the foundation of all true religion; for we should love and revere that Deity for his goodness, and thank him for his benefits; we should adore him for his wisdom, fear him for his power, and pray to him for his favor and protection. And this religion will be a powerful regulator of our actions, give us peace and tranquillity in our own minds, and render us benevolent, useful, and beneficial to others.

The following maxim of Franklin's is characteristic of the man, and reveals, in brief words, the whole genius and theory of giving stability and progress to free governments and to the diffusion of liberty—

"A Bible and a newspaper in every house, a good school in every district—all studied and appreciated as they merit—are the principal supports of virtue, morality, and civil liberty."

Thomas Jefferson

Was the penman of the Declaration of Independence, and his great abilities, genius, and ripe statesmanship have exerted a moulding influence on the civil and political affairs of the nation. "He poured the soul of the continent," said Dr. Stiles, in 1782, "into the monumental act of Independence." His views of the Christian religion have occasioned much discussion among the Christian public, and he has generally been regarded as an unbeliever in the divine inspiration of the Holy Scriptures. The following facts and statements will shed light on his views on this subject.

"I shall need" (he remarked, in his first message as President,) "the favor of that Being in whose hands we are, who led our fathers, as Israel of old, from their native land, and planted them in a Country flowing with all the necessaries and Comforts of life; who has covered our infancy with his providence, and our riper years with his wisdom and power; and to whose goodness I ask you to join with me in supplications that he will so enlighten the minds of your servants, guide their counsels, and prosper their measures, that whatsoever they do shall result in your good and shall secure to you the friendship and approbation of all nations."

"Can the liberties of a nation," said he, "be thought secure, when we have removed their only firm basis, a conviction in the minds of the people that these liberties are the gifts of God?—that they are not to be violated except with his wrath? Indeed, I tremble for my country when I reflect that God is just, and that his justice cannot sleep forever."

"Never," says a writer in the "National Magazine," "were a man's religious sentiments more grossly misrepresented than Jefferson's. He was not an atheist. He believed in God the Creator of all things, in his overruling providence, infinite wisdom, goodness, justice, and mercy. He believed that God hears and answers prayer, and that human trust in him is never misplaced nor disregarded. He believed in a future state of rewards and punishments. He believed in the Bible precepts and moralities. No man in Washington ever gave so much to build so many churches as Jefferson. He respected and cherished the friendship of truly pious men. He never wrote, for the public eye, one word against Christianity. Religiously, Jefferson would now be classed with the liberal Unitarians."

Mr. Jefferson, in a letter of condolence to John Adams on the death of his wife, in 1818, expressed his views of a future life as follows—"It is some comfort to us both that the term is not very distant at which we are to deposit in the same cerement our sorrowing and suffering bodies, and to ascend in essence to an ecstatic meeting with the friends we have loved and lost, and whom we shall still love and never lose again. God bless you and support you under your heavy affliction."

"Mr. Jefferson," says Randall, "was a public professor of his belief in the Christian religion. In all his most important early state papers, such as his Summary View of the Rights of British America, his portion of the Declaration made by Congress on the causes of taking up arms, the Declaration of Independence, the draft of a Constitution for Virginia, &c., there are more or less pointed recognitions of God and Providence. In his two inaugural addresses as President of the United States, and in many of his annual messages, he makes the same recognitions, clothes them on several occasions in the most explicit language, substantially avows the God of his faith to be the God of revelation, declares his belief in the efficacy of prayer and the duty of ascriptions of praise to the Author of all mercies, and speaks of the Christian religion, as professed in his country, as a benign religion, evincing the favor of Heaven.

"Had his wishes been consulted, the symbol borne on the national seal would have contained our public profession of Christianity as a nation.

"He contributed freely to the erection of Christian churches, gave money to Bible societies and other religious objects, and was a liberal and regular contributor to the support of the clergy. He attended church with as much regularity as most members of the congregation, sometimes going alone on horseback when his family remained at home. He generally attended the Episcopal church, and, when he did so, always carried his prayer-book and joined in the responses and prayers of the congregation."

The establishment of the University of Virginia occupied the closing years of Jefferson's life. His wish was to make the institution rival the Universities of Oxford and Cambridge in England, and afford opportunities for young men to become thoroughly accomplished in every branch of learning. A part of his plan was a theological seminary in connection with the university. Rev. Mr. Tucker, of Virginia, in the Presbyterian synod, met in 1859, said that "the establishment of a theological seminary near the University of Virginia was carrying out the original idea of Mr. Jefferson. He had seen in Mr. Jefferson's own handwriting, the pains-taking style of the olden time, a sketch of his plan. The University of Virginia was the crowning glory of that great man's life, and he felt it his duty to vindicate his memory, as he had it in his power to do, from any intention to exclude religious influences from the institution. He had invited all denominations to establish theological schools around the university, so that all might have the literary advantages of the institution, without making it subservient to one denomination."

George Mason

Of Virginia, was one of the purest and ablest of the men who conducted the important events of the Revolution to a fortunate and triumphant issue. He was a man endowed by nature with a vigorous understanding, which had been well cultivated by a liberal education. In temperament he was like the younger Cato, constitutionally stern, firm, and honest. His profound legal learning, and his political views and public duties, as well as his private life and character, were all under the guidance of virtue and religion, which gave him an illustrious and influential position in the cause of liberty and independence.

He was among the earliest and most distinguished of all the champions of freedom and an independent constitutional government; and no man exerted a greater influence on the fortunes of the country. He was a member of the Convention of Virginia which, on the 15th of May, 1776, declared that State independent, and formed a State constitution; and to him belongs the honor of having drafted the first declaration of rights ever adopted in America. It was made a part of the Constitution of Virginia, where it yet remains. In this declaration of Mason's, man seems to stand erect in all the majesty of his nature—to assert the inalienable rights and equality with which he has been endowed by his Creator, and to declare the fundamental principles by which all rulers should be governed and on which all governments should rest. Three of the fundamental articles are here inserted.

"1. That all men are created equally free and independent, and have certain inherent natural rights, of which they cannot, by any compact, deprive or divest their posterity; *among which* are the enjoyment of life and liberty, with the means of acquiring and procuring property and pursuing and obtaining happiness and safety.

"2. That all power is by *God and nature* vested in, and consequently derived from, the people; that magistrates are their trustees and servants, and at all times amenable to them.

"3. That government is, or ought to be, instituted for the common benefit, protection, and security of the people, nation, or community.

"15. That no free government, or the blessings of liberty, can be insured to any people, but by a firm adherence to justice, moderation, temperance, frugality, and virtue, and by frequent recurrence to fundamental principles.

"16. That religion, or the duty which we owe to our Creator, and the manner of discharging it, can be directed only by reason and conviction, not by force and violence, and, therefore, *that all men should enjoy the fullest toleration in the exercise of religion, according to the dictates of conscience, unpunished and unrestrained by the magistrate; unless under color of religion any man disturb the peace or the safety of society; and that it is the mutual duty of all to practise Christian forbearance, love, and charity towards each.*"

"If I can only live to see," said Mason, "the American Union firmly fixed, and free government well established in our Western world, and can leave to my children but a crust of bread and liberty, I shall die satisfied, and say, with the Psalmist, 'Lord, now lettest thou thy servant depart in peace.'"

The following extract from Mr. Mason's last will and testament attests his passionate patriotism, and presents his view of public life—

"I recommend it to my sons, from my own experience in life, to prefer the happiness of independence and a private station to the troubles and vexatious of public business; but, if their own inclinations or the necessity of the times should engage them in public affairs, I charge them, on a father's blessing, never to let the motives of private interest or ambition induce them to betray, nor the terrors of poverty and disgrace, or the fear of danger and death, deter them from asserting, the liberty of their country, and endeavoring to transmit to their posterity those sacred rights to which themselves were born."

This great man, whose soul was ever inflamed with liberty, and whose masterly intellect illuminated the grand era of the Revolution with its clear and steady light, died in a ripe old age, chastened and sanctified by providential afflictions in his family, leaving a legacy of glory and virtue to his country.

Gouverneur Morris

Of New York, was an eminent statesman of the Revolution, and exerted a prominent influence in the formation of our republican institutions. He was for many years in Congress and an ambassador to France. During the terrific reign of atheism in that country, he drew up a constitution for France, one article of which was as follows—

"Religion is the solid basis of good morals: therefore education should teach the precepts of religion and the duties of man towards God. These duties are—internally, love and adoration; externally, devotion and obedience: therefore provision should be made for maintaining divine worship as well as education. But each has a right to entire liberty as to religious opinions, for religion is the relation between God and man: therefore it is not within the reach of human authority."

"The education of young citizens," another article declared, "ought to form them to good manners, to accustom them to labor, to inspire them with a love of order, and to impress them with respect for lawful authority."

To a nobleman of France, Mr. Morris wrote, in June, 1792, "I believe that religion is the only solid basis of morals, and that morals are the only possible support of free governments."

In 1816, Mr. Morris was elected the first president of the New York Historical Society. In his inaugural address he presented his views of Christianity as follows—

"The reflection and experience of many years have led me to consider the holy writings not only as most authentic and instructive in themselves, but as the clue to all other history. They tell us what man is, and they alone tell us what he is. All of private and of public life is there displayed. From the same pure fountain of wisdom we learn that vice destroys freedom, that arbitrary power is founded on public immorality, and that misconduct in those who rule a republic, the necessary consequence of general licentiousness, so disgusts and degrades that, dead to generous sentiment, they become willing slaves.

"There must be religion. When that ligament is torn, society is disjointed, and its members perish. The nation is exposed to foreign violence and domestic convulsion. Vicious rulers, chosen by a vicious people, turn back the current of corruption to its source. Placed in a situation where they can exercise authority for their own emolument, they betray their trust. They take bribes. They sell statutes and decrees. They sell honor and office. They sell conscience. They sell their country. By this vile practice they become odious and contemptible.

"The most important of all lessons from the Scriptures is the denunciation of the rulers of every state that rejects the precepts of religion. Those nations are doomed to death who bury in the corruption of criminal desire the awful sense of an existing God, cast off the consoling hope of immortality, and seek refuge from despair in the dreariness of annihilation. Terrible, irrevocable doom— loudly pronounced, repeatedly, strongly exemplified in the sacred writings, and fully confirmed by the long record of time! It is the clue which leads through the intricacies of universal history. It is the principle of all sound political science.

"Hail! Columbia! child of science, parent of useful arts, dear country, hail! Be it thine to ameliorate the condition of man. Too many thrones have been reared by arms, cemented by blood, and reduced again to dust by sanguinary conflict of arms. Let mankind enjoy at last the consolatory spectacle of thy throne, built of industry on the basis of peace, and sheltered under the wings of justice. May it be secured by a *pious obedience* to the *divine will*, which prescribes the moral orbit of the empire with the same precision that his wisdom and power have displayed in the wheeling millions of planets round millions of suns, through the vastness of infinite space."

Charles Cotesworth Pinckney

Was a distinguished Revolutionary officer of South Carolina, and among the most brilliant lawyers of his age. His eminent abilities and virtues induced Washington to proffer him several of the highest places of trust in the Government—Judge of the Supreme Court, Secretary of War, and Secretary of State—all of which he declined from private considerations. He was a member of the convention which framed the Constitution of the United States. He was profoundly read in legal learning, and in his practice liberal and benevolent, never taking a fee from the widow and orphan. His great talents and attainments were sanctified and directed by the Christian religion, and his character adorned by its virtues. He had practical faith in the divinity of the Bible and its essential need to a republican government, and for more than fifteen years before his death he acted as President of the Bible Society in Charleston, an office to which he was elected with unanimity by Christians of every sect.

Benjamin Rush

An eminent physician and philanthropist, and one of the immortal men who signed the Declaration of Independence, was as eminent as a Christian as he was distinguished for his influence in the councils of the country. John Adams declared him to be "one of the greatest and best of Christians." He delighted in acts of Christian charities, and "esteemed the poor his best patients; for God," said he, "is their paymaster. He was an earnest advocate of introducing and reading the Bible, daily, as a common-school book, in all public schools and in every seminary of learning. He wrote as follows on this important subject—

The Bible as a School-Book

"Before I state my arguments in favor of teaching children to read by means of the Bible, I shall assume the five following propositions—

"I. That Christianity is the only true and perfect religion, and that in proportion as mankind adopt its principles and obey its precepts, they will be wise and happy.

"II. That a better knowledge of this religion is to be acquired by reading the Bible than in any other way.

"III. That the Bible contains more knowledge necessary to man in his present state than any other book in the world.

"IV. That knowledge is most durable, and religious instruction most useful, when imparted in early life.

"V. That the Bible, when not read in schools, is seldom read in any subsequent period of life.

"My arguments in favor of the use of the Bible as a schoolbook are founded, first, in the constitution of the human mind. The memory is the first faculty which opens in the minds of children. Of how much consequence, then, must it be to impress it with the great truths of Christianity before it is preoccupied with less interesting subjects! There is also a peculiar aptitude in the minds of children for religious knowledge. I have constantly found them, in the first six or seven years of their lives, more inquisitive upon religious subjects than upon any others; and an ingenious instructor of youth has informed me that he has found young children more capable of receiving just ideas upon the most difficult tenets of religion than upon the most simple branches of human knowledge.

"There is a wonderful property in the memory, which enables it, in old age, to recover the knowledge it had acquired in early life, after it had been apparently forgotten for forty or fifty years. Of how much consequence, then, must it be to fill the mind with that species of knowledge, in childhood and youth, which, when recalled in the decline of life, will support the soul under the infirmities of age and smooth the avenues of approaching death! The Bible is the only book which is capable of affording this support to old age; and it is for this reason that we find it resorted to with so much diligence and pleasure by such old people as have read it in early life. I can recollect many instances of this kind, in persons who discovered no attachment to the Bible in the meridian of their lives, who have, notwithstanding, spent the evening of them in reading no other book.

"My second argument in favor of the use of the Bible in schools, is founded upon an implied command of God, and upon the practice of several of the wisest nations of the world. In the sixth chapter of Deuteronomy we find the following words, which are directly to my purpose—'And thou shalt love the Lord thy God with all thine heart, and with all thy soul, and with all thy might. And these words which I command thee this day shall be in thine heart: and thou *shalt teach them diligently unto thy children*, and shalt talk of them when thou sittest in thine house, and when thou walkest by the way, and when thou liest down, and when thou risest up.'

"I have heard it proposed that a portion of the Bible should be read every day by the master, as a means of instructing children in it. But this is a poor substitute for obliging children to read it as a school-book; for by this means we insensibly *engrave*, as it were, its contents upon their minds; and it has been remarked that children instructed in this way in the Scriptures seldom forget any part of them. They have the same advantage over those persons who have only heard the Scriptures read by a master, that a man who has worked with the tools of a mechanical employment for several years has over the man who has only stood a few hours in the workshop and seen the same business carried on by other people."

Dr. Rush was an active friend of every philanthropic and Christian reform. He was an earnest advocate of temperance, and wielded his pen powerfully in its defence.

In an address to the people of the United States, in 1787, Dr. Rush said—

"There is nothing more common than to confound the terms of the *American Revolution* with those of the *late American War*. The American War is over; but this is far from being the case with the American Revolution. On the contrary, nothing but the first act of the great drama is closed. It remains yet to establish and perfect our new forms of government, and to prepare the principles, morals, and manners of our citizens for these forms of government, after they are established and brought to perfection.

"To conform the principles, morals, and manners of our citizens to our republican forms of government, it is absolutely necessary that knowledge of every kind should be disseminated through every part of the United States.

"For this purpose let Congress found a federal university. In this university let every thing connected with government—such as history, the law of nature and nations, the civil law, the municipal laws of our country, and the principles of commerce—be taught by competent professors. Let masters be employed likewise to teach gunnery, fortification, and every thing connected with defensive and offensive war. Above all, let a professor of, what is called in the European universities, economy, be established in this federal seminary. His business should be to unfold the principles and practice of agriculture and manufactures of all kinds; and, to make his lectures more extensively useful, Congress should support a travelling correspondent for him, who should visit all the nations of Europe, and transmit to him, from time to time, all the discoveries and improvements that are made in agriculture and manufactures.

"Let every man exert himself in promoting virtue and knowledge in our country, and we shall soon become good republicans. Every man in a republic is public property. His time and talents, his youth and manhood, his old age, nay, more, his life, his all, belong to his country."

Fisher Ames

A distinguished lawyer, a pure patriot, a fascinating orator, and an eminent Christian statesman, was active and influential in giving form and direction to the civil government of the United States. As a representative in the legislature of Massachusetts, he advocated the adoption of the Federal Constitution, and during eight years, the whole of Washington's administration, was a member of Congress from that State. His character as a patriot rests on the highest grounds. He loved his country with equal purity and fervor. This affection was the spring of all his efforts to promote her welfare. The glory of being a benefactor to a great people he justly valued. In the character of Mr. Ames the circle of the virtues seemed to be complete, and each virtue in its proper place.

"The objects of religion presented themselves with a strong interest to his mind. The relation of the world to its Author, and of this life to a retributory scene in another, could not be contemplated by him without the greatest solemnity. The religious sense was, in his view, essential in the constitution of man. He placed a full reliance on the divine origin of Christianity. He felt it his duty and interest to inquire, and discovered on the side of faith a fulness of evidence little short of demonstration. At about thirty-five he made a public profession of his belief in the Christian religion, and was a regular attendant on its services. In regard to articles of belief, his conviction was confined to those leading principles about which Christians have little diversity of opinion. He loved to view religion on the practical side, as designed to operate by a few simple and grand truths on the affections, actions, and habits of men. He cherished the sentiment and experience of religion, careful to ascertain the genuineness and value of impressions and feelings by their moral tendency. His conversation and behavior evinced the sincerity of his religious impressions. No levity upon these subjects ever escaped his lips; but his manner of recurring to them in conversation indicated reverence and feeling. The sublime, the affecting character of Christ he never mentioned without emotion."

This distinguished orator, in all his writings and speeches, imbued them with the pure and lofty sentiments of religion. In an article, written in 1801 for a periodical in Boston, on the subject of books for children, he thus speaks of the Bible, as adapted to the tender years and opening minds of children—

"Why, then, should not the Bible regain the place it once held as a school-book? Its morals are pure, its examples captivating and noble. The reverence for the sacred book, that is thus early impressed, lasts long, and probably, if not impressed in infancy, never takes firm hold of the mind. One consideration more is important. In no book is there so good English, so pure, and so elegant; and by teaching all the *same* book, they will speak alike, and the Bible will justly remain the standard of language as well as of faith."

John Hart

A signer of the Declaration of Independence, and a fearless patriot, was a munificent benefactor of the Baptist Church, and always known as a sincere but unostentatious Christian.

James Smith

Was educated by Rev. Dr. Alison, and was an ardent and active patriot, and one of the signers of the Declaration of Independence. "He ever retained a veneration for religion and its ministers, as well as his regular attention to public worship."

Robert Morris

Was the great financier of the Revolution, a signer of the Declaration of Independence, and a member of the convention that framed the Constitution of the United, States. It may be truly said of him, as it was of the Roman Curtius, that he sacrificed himself for the safety of the commonwealth. He was a great and good man. "The Americans owed, and still owe, as much acknowledgment to the financial operations of Robert Morris as to the negotiations of Benjamin Franklin, or even to the arms of George Washington."

Alexander Hamilton

The intimate friend and companion of Washington, was a statesman of the highest order, and had pre-eminent influence in forming the national Constitution and the present government. He was educated by Rev. Hugh Knox, a Presbyterian minister, to whom Hamilton was greatly attached. The fervent piety of this gentleman gave a strong religious bias to his feelings. When Hamilton was appointed aid-de-camp and secretary to Washington, Knox wrote him as follows—

"We rejoice in your good character and advancement, which is indeed the only just reward of merit. May you still live to deserve more and more of America, and justify the choice and merit the approbation of the great and good Washington, a name dear to the friends of the liberties of mankind! Mark this: you must be the annalist and biographer, as well as the aid-de-camp, of General Washington, and the historiographer of the American war. I aver, few men will be so well qualified to write the history of the present glorious struggle. God only knows how it will terminate. But, however that will be, it will be an interesting story."

"Hamilton was stamped by the Divine hand with the impress of genius. He had indeed a mind of immense grasp and unlimited original resources." He uttered such views of moral government as follows—

"The Supreme Intelligence who rules the world has constituted an eternal law, which is obligatory upon all mankind, prior to any human institution whatever. He gave existence to man, together with the means of preserving and beautifying that existence, and invested him with an inviolable right to pursue liberty and personal safety. Natural liberty is the gift of the Creator to the whole human race. Civil liberty is only natural liberty modified and secured by the sanctions of civil society. It is not dependent on human caprice, but it is conformable to the constitution of man, as well as necessary to the well-being of society. The sacred rights of mankind are not to be rummaged for among old parchments or musty records. They are written, as with a sunbeam, in the whole volume of human nature, by the hand of Divinity itself, and can never be erased or obscured by human power. This is what is called the law of nature, which, being coeval with mankind and dictated by God himself, is, of course, superior in obligation to any other. No human laws are of any validity if contrary to this. It is binding over all the globe, in all countries, and at all times."

In reference to the death of Washington, Hamilton said, "If virtue can secure happiness in another world, he is happy. This seal is now upon his glory. It is no longer in jeopardy by the fickleness of fortune."

"It is difficult," says Fisher Ames, speaking of Hamilton, after his death, "in the midst of such varied excellences, to say in what particular the effect of his greatness was most manifest. No man more promptly discerned truth; no man more clearly displayed it: it was not merely made visible; it seemed to come bright with illumination from his lips. He thirsted only for that fame which virtue would not blush to confer, nor time to convey to the end of his course. Alas! the great man who was at all times the ornament of our country is withdrawn to a purer and more tranquil region. May Heaven, the guardian of our liberty, grant that our country may be fruitful of Hamiltons and faithful to their glory."

Charles Carroll

The last survivor of the signers of the Declaration of Independence, was a member of the Roman Catholic Church, and distinguished for his Christian patriotism and virtues. Lord Brougham says, "He was among the foremost to sign the celebrated Declaration of Independence. As he set his hand to the instrument, some one said, 'There go some millions of property;' but, as there were many of the same name, he was told he might get clear. 'They will never know which to take.' 'Not so,' he replied, and instantly added—'of Carrollton.' He was universally respected for his patriotism and virtues. He had talents and acquirements which enabled him effectually to help the cause he espoused. His knowledge was various, and his eloquence was of a high order. It was like his character, mild and pleasant—like his deportment, correct and faultless."

In the year 1826, after all save one of the band of patriots whose signatures are on the Declaration of Independence had descended to the tomb, and the venerable Carroll alone remained among the living, the government of the city of New York deputed a committee to wait on the illustrious survivor, and obtain from him, for deposit in a public hall of the city, a copy of the Declaration of 1776, graced and authenticated anew with his sign-manual. The aged patriot yielded to the request, and affixed with his own hand to a copy of the instrument the grateful, solemn, and pious supplementary declaration which follows—

"Grateful to Almighty God for the blessings which, through Jesus Christ our Lord, he has conferred on my beloved country in her emancipation, and in permitting me, under circumstances of mercy, to live to the age of eighty-nine years, and to survive the fiftieth year of American Independence, adopted by Congress on the 4th of July, 1776, which I originally subscribed on the 2d day of August of the same year, and of which I am now the last surviving signer, I do hereby recommend to the present and future generations the principles of that important document as the best inheritance their ancestors could bequeath to them, and pray that the civil and religious liberties they have secured to my country may be perpetuated to remotest posterity and extended to the whole family of man."

Chas. Carroll, of Carrollton
August 2, 1826

Charles Thomson

Was the Secretary of the Continental Congress, a Quaker by birth and education, and a man of distinguished virtue and integrity of character. He possessed in an eminent degree the confidence of Congress, and was the active and steadfast friend of the Christian religion. His selection as secretary has a historic interest and singularity.

The Continental Congress first sat in the building then called Carpenter's Hall, up the court of that name in Chestnut Street. On the morning of the day that they first convened, their future secretary, Charles Thomson, who resided at that time in the Northern Liberties, and who afterwards so materially assisted to launch our first-rate republic, had ridden into the city and alighted in Chestnut Street. He was immediately accosted by a messenger from Congress; they desired to speak with him. He followed the messenger, and, entering the building, he said he was struck with awe upon viewing the aspects of so many great and good men impressed with the weight and responsibility of their situation, on the perilous edge of which they then were advancing. He walked up the aisle, and, bowing to the president, desired to know their pleasure. "Congress request your services, sir, as their secretary." He took his seat at the desk, and never looked back until the vessel was securely anchored in the haven of independence.

George Wythe

Was a statesman and a jurist of the highest accomplishments, and a signer of the Declaration of Independence. "His virtues were of the purest kind, his integrity inflexible, and his justice exact. It was his daily endeavor to live a Christian life; and he effectually succeeded."

James Wilson

A signer of the Declaration of Independence, and an eminent jurist and judge, was educated under Christian auspices by Dr. Isaac Watts and Dr. Robert Blair. He was an ornament to the American nation, and in public and private life maintained the faith and diffused the spirit and the principles of Christianity.

Samuel Chase

Was a signer of the Declaration of Independence, a member of Congress, and a Judge of the Supreme Court of the United States. "Among his Virtues may be included a heartfelt piety and a firm belief in the great truths of Christianity. He partook of the sacrament but a short time before his death, and said he was at peace with all mankind."

Richard Henry Lee

Was an accomplished orator of the Revolution, a signer of the Declaration of Independence, and a Christian statesman. "In the vigor of his mind, amid the honors of the world and its enjoyments, he publicly declared his belief in Jesus Christ as the Saviour of men."

Francis Lightfoot Lee

The brother of Richard Henry, was an upright and virtuous politician. He lived and died a Christian.

John Jay

As a Christian legislator, statesman, and judge, exerted a large and active influence in the Revolution, and in founding and administering the civil government of the United States. In private and public life he was an eminent Christian. His recognition of God and belief in the Christian religion were striking elements of his character.

"Whoever," said he, "compares our present with our former constitution will find abundant reasons to rejoice in the exchange, and readily admit that all the calamities incident to this war will be amply compensated by the many blessings flowing from this revolution.

"We should always remember that the many remarkable and unexpected means and events by which our wants have been supplied and our enemies repelled or restrained are such strong and striking proofs of the interposition of Heaven, that our having been hitherto delivered from the threatened bondage of Britain ought to be forever ascribed to its true cause (the favor of God), and, instead of swelling our breasts with arrogant ideas of our prowess and importance, kindle in them a flame of gratitude and piety which may consume all remains of vice and irreligion."

During a most gloomy period of the Revolution, when New York was in the hands of the British, and Washington was retreating through New Jersey, with an almost naked army, and the country desponding, Jay animated his countrymen with such stirring words as the following—

"Under the auspices of divine Providence your forefathers removed to the wilds and wilderness of America. By their industry they made it a fruitful, and by their virtues a happy, country; and we should still have enjoyed the blessings of peace and plenty, if we had not forgotten the source from which these blessings flowed, and permitted our country to be contaminated by the many shameful vices which have prevailed among us. It is a well-known fact that no virtuous people were ever oppressed, and it is also true that a scourge was never wanting to those of an opposite character. Even the Jews, those favorites of Heaven, met with the frowns whenever they forgot the smiles of their benevolent Creator. They for their wickedness were permitted to be scourged; and we for our wickedness are scourged by tyrants as cruel and implacable as theirs. If we turn from our sins, God will turn from his anger. Then will our arms be crowned with success, and the pride and power of our enemies, like the pride and arrogance of Nebuchadnezzar, will vanish away.

"Let a general reformation of manners take place; let universal charity, public spirit, and private virtue be inculcated, encouraged, and practised. Unite in preparing for a vigorous defence of your country as if all depended on you. And when you have done all these things, then rely on the good providence of Almighty God for success, in full confidence that without his blessing all our efforts will inevitably fail.

"Rouse, then, brave citizens! Do your duty like men, and be persuaded that Divine Providence will not let this Western World be involved in the horrors of slavery. Consider that from the earliest ages of the world religious liberty and reason have been bending their course towards the setting sun. The holy gospels are yet to be preached to these western regions; and we have the highest reason to believe that the Almighty will not suffer slavery and the gospel to go hand in hand. It cannot, it will not be."

In September, 1777, Jay, as Chief-Justice of the Supreme Court of New York, delivered a charge to the Grand Jury of Ulster county, on the political condition of the country. It was given at a time when the Assembly and Senate were convening, and the whole system of government, established by the Constitution of New York, about being put in motion. The grand inquest was composed of the most respectable characters in the county. In that charge are found the following Christian passages—

"GENTLEMEN—It affords me very sensible pleasure to congratulate you on the dawn of that free, mild, and equal government which now begins to rise and break from amidst those clouds of anarchy, confusion, and licentiousness which the arbitrary and violent domination of the King of Great Britain had spread throughout this and the other American States. This is one of those signal instances in which Divine Providence has made the tyranny of princes instrumental in breaking the chains of their subjects, and rendering the most inhuman designs productive of the best consequences to those against whom they were intended—a revolution which, in the whole course of its rise and progress, is distinguished by so many marks of the divine favor and interposition that no doubt can remain of its being finally accomplished. It was begun, and has been supported, in a manner so singular and, I may say, miraculous, that when future ages shall read its history they will be tempted to consider great part of it as fabulous. Will it not appear extraordinary that thirteen colonies, divided by a variety of governments and manners, should immediately become one people, and, though without funds, without magazines, without disciplined troops, in the face of their enemies, unanimously determine to be free, and, undaunted by the power of Great Britain, refer their cause to the justice of the Almighty, and resolve to repel force by force—thereby presenting to the world an illustrious example of magnanimity and virtue scarcely to be paralleled? However incredible these things may in future appear, we know them to be true, and we should always remember that the many remarkable and unexpected means and events by which our wants have been supplied and our enemies repelled or restrained are such strong and striking proofs of the interposition of Heaven, that our having been hitherto delivered from the threatened bondage of Britain ought, like the emancipation of the Jews from Egyptian servitude, to be forever ascribed to its TRUE CAUSE, and, instead of swelling our breasts with arrogant ideas of our own prowess and importance, kindle in them a flame of gratitude and piety which may consume all remains of vice and irreligion.

"The Americans are the first people whom Heaven has favored with an opportunity of deliberating upon and choosing the forms of government under which they should live. While you possess wisdom to discern and virtue to appoint men of worth and abilities to fill the offices of the state, you will be happy at home and respected abroad. Your life, your liberties, your property, will be at the disposal only of your Creator and yourselves.

"Security under our Constitution is given to the rights of conscience and private judgment. They are by nature subject to no control but that of Deity, and in that free situation they are now left. Every man is permitted to consider, to adore, and to worship his Creator in the manner most agreeable to his conscience. No opinions are dictated, no rules of faith are prescribed, no preference given to one sect to the prejudice of others. The Constitution, however, has wisely declared that the 'liberty of conscience, thereby granted, shall not be so construed as to excuse acts of licentiousness or justify practices inconsistent with the peace or safety of the state.' In a word, the convention by whom that Constitution was formed were of opinion that the gospel of CHRIST, like the ark of God, would not fall, though unsupported by the arm of flesh; and happy would it be for mankind if that opinion prevailed more generally.

"But let it be remembered that whatever marks of wisdom, experience, and patriotism there may be in the Constitution, yet, like the beautiful symmetry, the just proportions, and elegant forms of our first parents before their Maker breathed into them the breath of life, it is yet to be *animated,* and, till then, may indeed excite admiration, but will be of no use. From the people it must receive its spirit, and by them be quickened. Let virtue, honor, the love of liberty and science, be and remain the soul of the Constitution, and it will become the source of great and extreme happiness to this and future generations. Vice, ignorance, and want of vigilance will be the only enemies that can destroy it. Against these provide, and of these be forever jealous. Every citizen ought diligently to read and study the Constitution of his country, and teach the rising generation to be free."

"Providence," said he, "has given to our people the choice of their rulers, and it is the duty, as well as the privilege and interest, of a Christian nation to select and prefer Christians for their rulers."

Mr. Jay, from 1822 till his death in 1827, was President of the Bible Society, and at each annual meeting delivered an address. He demonstrated the divinity of the Bible, showed its relations and results to civil government and human society, and urged its universal circulation as the means to illumine and regenerate the world. He was an active and devout member of the Episcopal Church, but eminently liberal and charitable in his Christian views. His life was a beautiful exhibition of Christian faith, and his public career a noble illustration of the value of Christianity in forming the character and acts of a Christian statesman. Webster said of this eminent Christian jurist, that "when the ermine fell on him it touched nothing less pure than itself."

He was eminently a man of prayer, and drew up a form, full of spirituality and of Christian truths, as an extract will show—

"Enable me, merciful Father, to understand thy holy gospels, and to distinguish the doctrines thereof from erroneous expositions of them; and bless me with that fear of offending thee, which is the beginning of wisdom. Let thy Holy Spirit purify and unite me to my Saviour forever; and enable me to cleave unto him as unto my very life, as indeed he is. Perfect and confirm my faith, my trust, my hope of salvation in him, and in him only.

"Give me grace to love and obey, and be thankful unto thee, with all my heart, with all my soul, with all my mind, and with all my strength, and to worship and to serve thee in humility of spirit, and in truth. Give me grace also to love my neighbor as myself, and wisely and diligently to do the duties incumbent on me according to thy holy will, and not from worldly consideration. Condescend, merciful Father, to grant, as far as proper, these imperfect petitions, these inadequate thanksgivings, and to pardon whatever of sin hath mingled in them, for the sake of Jesus Christ, our blessed Lord and Saviour, unto whom, with thee and the blessed Spirit, even one God, be rendered all honor and glory, now and forever."

In his dying hour, he was asked if he had any farewell counsels to leave his children. His reply was, "THEY HAVE THE BOOK."

Elias Boudinot

Acted a prominent part in the scenes of the Revolution, and was an able and active member of the Continental Congress. He was a brilliant lawyer, an upright judge, a wise legislator, and a true Christian statesman. His Christian feelings thus found utterance on the propriety of observing the memory of American indepen-dence—

"The history of the world, as well sacred as profane, bears witness to the use and importance of setting apart a day as a memorial of great events, whether of a religious or a political nature. No sooner had the great Creator of the heavens and the earth finished his almighty work, and pronounced all very good, but he set apart (not as anniversary, or one day in a year, but) one day in seven, for the commemoration of his inimitable power in producing all things out of nothing.

"The deliverance of the children of Israel from a state of bondage to an unreasonable tyrant was perpetuated by eating the paschal lamb, and enjoining it to their posterity as an annual festival forever, with a 'remember this day, in which ye came out of Egypt, out of the house of bondage.'

"The resurrection of the Saviour of mankind is commemorated by keeping the first day of the week, not only as a certain memorial of his first coming in a state of humiliation, but the positive evidence of his future coming in glory.

"Let us, my friends and fellow-citizens, unite all our endeavors this day to remember with reverential gratitude to our Supreme Benefactor all the wonderful things he has done for us, in a miraculous deliverance from a second Egypt—another house of bondage. 'And thou shalt show thy son, on this day, saying, This day is kept as a day of joy and gladness, because of the great things the Lord has done for us, when we were delivered from the threatening power of an invading foe. And it shall be a sign unto thee upon thine hand,

and for a memorial between thine eyes, that the law of the Lord may be in thy mouth; for with a strong hand hast thou been delivered from thine enemies. Thou shalt therefore keep this ordinance, in its season, from year to year forever."

"Who knows but the country for which we have fought and bled may hereafter become a theater of greater events than have yet been known to mankind? May these invigorating prospects lead us to the exercise of every virtue, religious, moral, and political. And may these great principles, in the end, become instrumental in bringing about that happy state of the world when from every human breast, joined by the grand chorus of the skies, shall arise, with the profoundest reverence, that divinely celestial anthem of universal praise, 'Glory to God in the highest; peace on earth; good will towards men.'"

In 1816, Mr. Boudinot was elected the first President of the American Bible Society: In accepting, he said, "I am not ashamed to confess that I accept the appointment of President of the American Bible Society as the greatest honor that could be conferred on me this side of the grave." He served, also, from 1812 till his death in 1821, as a member of the American Board of Commissioners for Foreign Missions. His great wealth was consecrated to objects of Christian benevolence. He gave a liberal sum to the New Jersey Bible Society, to purchase spectacles for the aged poor to enable them to read the Bible.

James Madison

Was an eminent statesman and civilian of the Revolution, and was called the "Father of the Constitution." He was educated at Princeton College, under Dr. John Witherspoon, the eminent Christian scholar and patriot, who delighted to bear testimony to "the excellency of his character." He remarked to Mr. Jefferson, when they were colleagues in the Continental Congress, that in the whole course of Mr. Madison's career at college "He never knew him to say or do an indiscreet thing."

He was a friend to universal toleration in religions matters, and objected to the word "toleration" in our constitutions, because it implied an established religion. He labored to remove the legal disabilities from the Baptists in Virginia, and demonstrated that all men are equally entitled to the free exercise of religion according to the dictates of conscience.

The following paragraphs from his messages exhibit his views on God as the Governor of nations—

"We have all been encouraged to feel the guardianship and guidance of that almighty Being whose power regulates the destinies of nations, whose blessings have been so conspicuously displayed to this rising republic, and to whom we are bound to address our devout gratitude for the past, as well an our fervent supplications and best hopes for the future."

"Recollecting *always* that, for *every* advantage which may contribute to distinguish our lot from that to which others are doomed by the unhappy spirit of the times, we are indebted to that Divine Providence whose goodness has been so remarkably extended to this rising nation, it becomes us to cherish a devout gratitude, and to implore from the same omnipotent source a blessing on the consultations and measures about to be undertaken for the welfare of our beloved country."

"Invoking the blessings of Heaven on our beloved country, and on all the means that may be employed in vindicating its rights and advancing its welfare."

Again, in 1812, after the war, he says, "The appeal was made, in a just cause, to the just and all-powerful Being who holds in his hands the chain of events and the destiny of nations." The war "is stamped with that justice which invites the smiles of Heaven on the means of conducting it to a successful termination." "We are under sacred obligation to transmit entire to future generations that precious patrimony of national rights and independence, which is held in trust by the present *from the goodness* of Providence." "We may humbly repose our trust in the smiles of Heaven on so righteous a cause."

In closing his last message, Madison says, "May I not be allowed to add to this gratifying spectacle, that the destined career of my country will exhibit a government pursuing the public good as its sole object, and regulating its means by those great principles consecrated in its charter, and by those *moral* principles to which they are so well allied?—a government, in a word, whose conduct within and without may bespeak the most noble of all ambitions—that of promoting peace on earth, and good will to men."

James Monroe

Was an active patriot and statesman of Revolutionary and of more modern times, taking a leading part in the political affairs of the nation, and was twice elected President. He has left but little in reference to his views on the subject of religion. The following sentences occur in his messages—

"I enter on the trust with my fervent prayers to the Almighty, that he will he graciously pleased to continue to us that protection which he has already so conspicuously displayed in our favor."

"The fruits of the earth have been unusually abundant, commerce has flourished, the revenue has exceeded the most favorable anticipations, and peace and amity are preserved with foreign nations on conditions just and honorable to our country. For these inestimable blessings we cannot be too grateful to that Providence which watches over the destinies of nations."

"When we view the great blessings with which our country has been favored, those which we now enjoy, and the means which we possess of handing them down unimpaired to our latest posterity, our attention is irresistibly drawn to the source from whence they flow. Let us, then, unite in offering our most grateful acknowledgment for these blessings to the Divine Author of all good."

"With a firm reliance on the protection of Almighty God, I shall forthwith commence the duties of the high trust to which you have called me."

"Deeply impressed with the blessings which we enjoy, and of which we have such manifold proofs, my mind is irresistibly drawn to that Almighty Being, the great source from whence they proceed, and to whom our most grateful acknowledgments are due."

Oliver Ellsworth

Was an eminent statesman of the Revolution, and by Washington appointed Chief-Justice of the Supreme Court of the United States.

He was designed for the ministry, and studied theology under Dr. Bellamy, an eminent divine of Connecticut. In this Christian school his principles were received and his character formed. "Amiable and exemplary in all the relations of the domestic and social life and Christian character, pre-eminently useful in all the offices he sustained; whose great talents, under the guidance of inflexible integrity, consummate wisdom, and enlightened zeal, placed him among the first of the illustrious statesmen who achieved our independence and established the constitution of the American republic. In all the public stations which he ever filled he evinced an inflexible integrity, the purest morality, and the most unshaken firmness and independence."

William Henry Drayton

Of South Carolina, an eminent jurist and statesman, who devoted his great learning and abilities to achieve our independence and to form our free institutions, in April, 1776, gave utterance, in an official paper, to the following sentiments—

"I think it my duty to declare, in the awful seat of justice and before Almighty God, that, in my opinion, the Americans can have no safety but by the Divine favor, their own virtue, and their being so prudent as not to leave it in the power of British rulers to injure them. The Almighty created America to be independent of Britain: let us beware of the impiety of being backward to act as instruments in the Almighty's hand, now extended to accomplish his purpose, and by the completion of which alone America can be secure against the craft and insidious designs of HER ENEMIES, WHO THINK HER PROSPERITY AND POWER ALREADY BY FAR TOO GREAT."

"In a word, our piety and political safety are so blended, that to refuse our labors in this divine work is to refuse to be a great, a free, a pious, and a happy people! And now, having left the important alternative, political happiness or wretchedness, under God, in a great degree in your hands, I pray the Supreme Arbiter of the affairs of men so to direct your judgment as that you may act agreeably to what seems to be his will, revealed in his miraculous works in behalf of America bleeding at the altar of liberty."

Major-General Greene

Of Revolutionary renown, was eminently distinguished in the military service of his country, and was the confidential companion of Washington. He was as eminent for his virtues as for his patriotism and devotion to his country. Alexander Hamilton, in an eulogium on him, pronounced July 4, 1789, before the Society of Cincinnati, says of him—

"The name of Greene will at once awaken in your minds the image of whatever is noble and estimable in human nature. As a man, the virtues of Greene are admitted; as a patriot, he held a place in the foremost rank; as a statesman, he is praised; as a soldier, he is admired.

"But where, alas! is now this consummate general, this brave soldier, this discerning statesman, this steady patriot, this virtuous citizen, this amiable man? Why could not so many talents, so many virtues, so many bright and useful qualities shield him from a premature grave? It is not for us to scan, but to submit to, the dispensations of Heaven."

"He was a great and good man," was the comprehensive eulogy passed upon him by Washington, when he heard the news of General Greene's death. "Thus," says Washington, "some of the pillars of the Revolution fall. Others are mouldering by insensible degrees. May our country never want props to support the glorious fabric."

Henry Knox

Major-general in the American army during the Revolutionary War, was the right hand of Washington, and one whose resources for the emergencies of the war were infinite. His parents were of Scottish descent, and educated him in that piety which has ever distinguished the people of that country. He possessed a taste for literary pursuits, which he retained through life; and this, in union with his fine military genius and personal qualities, constituted him an accomplished gentleman and an able officer in the army and in the War Department, to which he was appointed by Congress before the adoption of the Constitution, and, after the government was organized, by Washington to the same office.

"The amiable virtues of the citizen and the man were as conspicuous in the character of General Knox as the more brilliant and commanding talents of the hero and statesman. The afflicted and destitute were sure to share of his compassion and charity. 'His heart was made of tenderness.' Mildness ever beamed in his countenance; 'on his tongue were the words of kindness. The poor he never oppressed; the most obscure citizen could never complain of injustice at his hands.'

"To these amiable qualities and moral excellencies of General Knox we may justly add his prevailing disposition to piety. With much of the manners of the gay world, and opposed as he was to all superstition and bigotry, he might not appear, to those ignorant of his better feelings, to possess religion and devout affections. He was a firm believer in the natural and moral attributes of the Deity and his overruling and all-prevailing providence."

Gilbert Mothier Lafayette

Deserves an eminent place among American heroes, as the champion of freedom and the friend of humanity. His chivalrous and heroic devotion in the American cause constitutes a romantic chapter in the history of the Revolution. He was a member of the Catholic Church, a friend of Christianity, and his sentiments and life were of a high moral tone. His inspirations of liberty, his just and rational views of the rights of all men, and his devotion to humanity and a Christian civilization, entitle Lafayette to be enrolled among the Christian champions of freedom. In reference to American slavery he said that if he had supposed he was fighting to perpetuate the system, he never would have unsheathed his sword for American liberty in our Revolutionary struggle.

John Quincy Adams, in his eulogy on Lafayette, prepared at the request of Congress, in 1834, says, "The self-devotion of Lafayette in the cause of America was twofold. First, to the maintaining a bold and seemingly desperate struggle against oppression and for national existence. Secondly and chiefly, to the principles of their declaration, which then first unfurled before his eyes the consecrated standard of human rights.

"To the *moral* principle of political action, the sacrifices of no other man were comparable to his. Youth, health, fortune, the favor of the king, the enjoyment of ease and pleasure, even the choicest blessings of domestic felicity—he gave them all for toil and danger in a distant land, and an almost hopeless cause; but it was the cause of justice, and of the rights of human kind."

Mr. Clarkson, of England, describes Lafayette "as a man who desired the happiness of the human race in consistence with strict subservience to the cause of truth and the honor of God."

At the close of the Revolution, Congress appointed a committee to receive and, in the name of Congress, to take leave of Lafayette, and to express to him their grateful and admiring sense of his services. A memorable sentence of his reply is as follows—

"May this immense temple of freedom ever stand a lesson to oppressors, an example to the oppressed, a sanctuary for the rights of mankind! And may these happy United States attain that complete splendor and prosperity which will illustrate the blessings of their Government, and for ages to come rejoice the departed souls of its founders."

William Livingston

Was a Christian lawyer of New York, and afterwards distinguished as a Christian statesman and Governor of New Jersey. In the earliest conflicts of the Revolution he said—

"Courage, Americans! liberty, religion, and science are on the wing to these shores. The finger of God points out a mighty empire to your sons. The savages of the wilderness were never expelled to make room for idolaters and slaves. The land we possess is the gift of Heaven to our fathers, and Divine Providence seems to have decreed it to our latest posterity. So legible is this munificent and celestial deed in past events, that we need not be discouraged by the bickerings between us and the parent country. The angry cloud will soon be dispersed, and America advance to felicity and glory with redoubled activity and vigor. The day dawns in which the foundation of this mighty empire is to be laid by the establishment of a regular American Constitution.

"Let us, both by precept and example, encourage a spirit of economy, industry, and patriotism, and that public integrity which cannot fail to exalt a nation—setting our faces at the same time like a flint against that dissoluteness of manners and political corruption which will ever be the reproach of any people. May the foundation of our infant state be laid in virtue and the fear of God, and the superstructure will rise gloriously and endure for ages. Then we may humbly expect the blessing of the Most High, who divides to nations their inheritance and separates the sons of Adam. While we are applauded by the whole world for demolishing, the old fabric, rotten and ruinous as it was, let us unitedly strive to approve ourselves master-builders, by giving beauty, strength, and stability to the new. May we, in all our deliberations and proceedings, be influenced by the great Arbiter of the fate of nations, by whom empires rise and fall, and who will not always suffer the sceptre of the wicked to rest on the lot of the righteous, but in due time avenge an injured people on their unfeeling oppressor and his bloody instruments."

Governor Livingston, in 1778, published the following views on the liberty of conscience in matters of religion—

"If in our estimate of things we ought to be regulated by their importance, doubtless every encroachment upon religion, of all things the most important, ought to be considered as the greatest imposition, and the unmolested exercise of it a proportionate blessing.

"By religion I mean an inward habitual reverence for, and devotedness to, the Deity, with such external homage, either public or private, as the worshipper believes most acceptable to him. According to this definition, it is impossible for human Jaws to regulate religion without destroying it; for they cannot compel *inward* religious reverence, that being altogether mental and of a spiritual nature; nor can they enforce *outward* religious homage, because all such homage is either a man's own choice, and then it is not compelled, or it is repugnant to it, and then it cannot be religion.

"The laws of England, indeed, do not peremptorily inhibit a man from worshipping God according to the dictates of his own conscience, nor positively constrain him to violate it, by conforming to the religion of the state. But they punish him for doing the former, or, what amounts to the same thing, for omitting the latter, and, consequently, punish him for his religion. For what are the civil disqualifications and the privation of certain privileges he thereby incurs, but so many punishments? And what else is the punishment

for not embracing the religion of others but a punishment for practising one's own? With how little propriety a nation can boast of
its freedom under such restraints of religious liberty, requires no
great sagacity to determine. They affect, it is true, to abhor the imputation of intolerance, and applaud themselves for their pretended
toleration and lenity. As contra-distinguished, indeed, from actual
prohibition, a permission may doubtless be called a toleration; for if
a man is permitted to enjoy his religion under whatever penalties or
forfeitures, he is certainly tolerated to enjoy it. But as far as he pays
for such enjoyment by suffering those penalties and forfeitures, he
as certainly does not enjoy it freely. On the contrary, he is persecuted in the proportion that his privilege is so regulated and qualified. I call it persecution, because it is harassing mankind for their
principles; and I deny that such punishments derive any sanction
from law, because the *consciences of men are not the objects of human legislation.* And to trace this stupendous insult on the dignity
of reason to any other source than the abominable combinations
of KINGCRAFT and PRIESTCRAFT (in everlasting indissoluble league
to extirpate liberty and to erect on its ruin boundless and universal
despotism) would, I believe, puzzle the most assiduous inquirer. For
what business, in the name of common sense, has the magistrate
(distinctly and singly appointed for our political and temporal happiness) with our religion, which is to secure our happiness spiritual and eternal? And, indeed, among all the absurdities chargeable
upon human nature, it never yet entered into the thoughts of any
one to confer such authority upon any other.

"In reality, such delegation of power, had it ever been made,
would be a mere nullity, and the compact by which it was ceded
altogether nugatory, the *rights of conscience being immutably personal and absolutely inalienable*; or can the state or the community,
as such, have any concern in the matter. For in what manner doth it
affect society what are the principles we entertain in our minds, *or
in what outward form we think it best to pay* our adoration to God?

"But, to set the absurdity of the magistrate's authority to interfere
in matters of religion in the strongest light, I would fain know what
religion it is that he has the authority to establish? Has he a right to
establish only the true religion? or is any religion true because he

does establish it? If the former, his trouble is as vain as it is arrogant, because *the true religion, being not of this world, wants not the princes of this world to support it, but has, in fact, either languished or been adulterated wherever they meddled with it.*

"If the supreme magistrate, as such, has authority to establish any religion he thinks to be true, and the religion so established is therefore right and ought to be embraced, it follows, since all supreme magistrates have the same authority, that all established religions are equally right and ought to be embraced. The Emperor of China, therefore, as supreme magistrate in his empire, has the same right to establish the precepts of Confucius, and the Sultan in his the imposture of Mahomet, as hath the King of Great Britain the doctrine of Christ in his dominion. It results from these principles that the religions of Confucius and Mahomet are equally true with the doctrine of our Saviour and his apostles, and equally obligatory upon the respective subjects of China and Turkey as Christianity is on those within the British realm—a position which, I presume, the most zealous advocate for ecclesiastical domination would think it blasphemy to avow.

"*The English ecclesiastical government, therefore, is, and all the* RELIGIOUS ESTABLISHMENTS IN THE WORLD are manifest violations of the rights of *private judgment in matters of religion.* They are impudent outrages on common sense, in arrogating a power of controlling the devotional operations of the mind and external acts of divine homage not cognizable by any human tribunal, and for which we are accountable only to the great Searcher of hearts, whose prerogative it is to judge them.

"In contrast with this spiritual tyranny, how beautiful appears our catholic constitution in *disclaiming all jurisdiction over the souls of men,* and securing, by a never-to-be-repealed section, the voluntary, unchecked, moral suasion of every individual, and by his own self-directed intercourse with the Father of spirits, *either by devout retirement or public worship of his own election!* How amiable the plan of intrenching with the sanctions of an ordinance, immutable and irrevocable, the sacred rights of conscience, and *renouncing all discrimination between men on account of their sentiments* about the various modes of church government or the *different articles of their faith!*"

Jonathan Trumbull

Was, says Sparks, "one of the firmest of patriots and best of men." He was Governor of Connecticut nearly twenty years—elected with great unanimity, and continuing till the close of the Revolution. His services were of very great importance throughout the whole war, not only in regulating the civil affairs of Connecticut, but in keeping alive a military ardor among the people. General Washington leaned on him as one of his main pillars of support. The following extracts from Governor Trumbull's letter to Washington will show the spirit prevailing at that day, as well as the religious cast of his mind—

"Suffer me to congratulate you on your appointment to be general and commander-in-chief of the troops raised, or to be raised, for the defence of American liberty. Men who have tasted of freedom, and who have felt their personal rights, are not easily taught to bear with encroachments on either, or brought to submit to oppression. Virtue ought always to be made the object of government; justice is firm and permanent.

"The honorable Congress have, with one united voice, appointed you to the high station you possess. The Supreme Director of all events has caused a wonderful union of hearts and counsels to subsist amongst us. Now, therefore, be strong and very courageous. May the God of the armies of Israel shower down the blessings of his divine providence on you, give you wisdom and fortitude, cover your head in the day of battle and danger, and, by giving success, convince our enemies of their mistaken measures, and that all their attempts to deprive the colonies of their inestimable constitutional rights and liberties are injurious and vain."

Washington replied as follows—

Cambridge, 18 July, 1775

Allow me to return you my sincere thanks for the kind wishes and favorable sentiments expressed in yours of the 13th instant. As the cause of our common country calls us both to active and dangerous duty, I trust that Divine Providence, which wisely orders the affairs of men, will enable us both to discharge it with fidelity and success. The uncorrupted choice of a brave and free people has raised you to deserved eminence.

Dr. Ezra Stiles, President of Yale College, in a sermon, entitled "The United States Elevated to Glory And Honor," preached, May 7, 1783, before Governor Trumbull and the General Assembly of Connecticut, paid the highest tribute of praise to this pure patriot and exalted Christian statesman. He said—

"Endowed with a singular strength of the mental powers, with a vivid and clear perception, with a penetrating and comprehensive judgment, embellished with the acquisition of academical, theological, and political erudition, your excellency became qualified for a very singular variety of usefulness in life. We adore the God of our fathers, the God and Father of the spirits of all flesh, that he hath raised you up for such a time as this, and that he hath put into your heart a wisdom which I cannot describe without adulation, a patriotism and intrepid resolution, a noble and independent spirit, an unconquerable love of liberty, religion, and our country, and that grace by which you have been carried through the arduous duties of a high office, never before acquired by an American governor. Our enemies revere the names of Trumbull and Washington."

George Washington and Others

"First in war, first in peace, and first in the hearts of his countrymen," was also first as a Christian hero and statesman. His Christian faith and sentiments pervaded his life, formed his character, guided all his private and public acts, and were repeated and recorded in every variety of form in all his state papers. He regarded Christianity not only as a divine system, worthy of the confidence of all men, and essential to man's happiness here and hereafter, but he profoundly felt, and everywhere taught, that all good government must be founded and administered in conformity to its benign and heavenly precepts. It is a suggestive fact that Washington, who led the armies of the Revolution to final victory, who presided in the council that formed the old Articles of Confederation, who was president of the convention that formed the Constitution, and who was the first President elected to administer the government, was a devout Christian. He has had more to do in shaping the destinies of the American Government and nation than all others combined, and in every official act he diffused the spirit and proclaimed, directly or indirectly, the principles of religion. This historical fact is unprecedented in the annals of the world, and displays the guiding hand of God in raising up and qualifying such a Christian leader for the American nation. Washington opened and closed his administration with the following sentiments—

"It is impossible," said he, "to govern the universe without the aid of a Supreme Being. Let us, therefore, unite in imploring the Supreme Ruler of nations to spread his holy protection over these United States; to stop the machinations of the wicked; to confirm our Constitution; to enable us, at all times, to suppress internal sedition and put invasion to flight; to perpetuate to our country that prosperity which his goodness has already conferred, and to verify the anticipations of this government's being a safeguard to human rights."

"The situation in which I now stand, for the last time, in the midst of the representatives of the people of the United States, naturally recalls the period when the administration of the present form of government commenced; and I cannot omit the occasion to congratulate you and my country on the success of the experiment, nor to repeat my fervent supplications to the Supreme Ruler of the Universe and Sovereign Arbiter of nations, that his providential care may still be extended to the United States; that the virtue and happiness of the people may be preserved; and that the government which they have instituted for the protection of their liberties may be perpetual."

Their State Papers

An appeal to the God of the Bible and of providence, from such Christian statesmen, would be expected, on all suitable and solemn occasions, in their state papers. These solemn appeals are as follow—

"We hold these truths to be self-evident: that all men are created equal; that they are endowed by their Creator with certain inalienable rights; that among these are life, liberty, and the pursuit of happiness. That to defend these rights government was instituted. ... We, therefore, the Representatives in General Congress assembled, appealing to the Supreme Ruler of the World for the rectitude of our intentions, do, in the name and by the authority of the good people of these colonies, solemnly publish and declare that these

United Colonies are, and of right ought to be, free and independent States; and for the support of this declaration, with a firm reliance on Divine Providence, we mutually pledge to each other our lives, our fortunes, and our sacred honor."

"Our cause is just. Our union is perfect. Our internal resources are great, and, if necessary, foreign assistance is undoubtedly at hand. We gratefully acknowledge, as signal instances of the Divine favor towards us, that his providence would not permit us to be called into this severe controversy until we had grown up to our present strength, had previously been exercised in warlike operations, and possessed of the means of defending ourselves. With hearts fortified with these animating reflections, we most solemnly, BEFORE GOD and the world, *declare* that, exerting the utmost energies of those powers which our beneficent Creator hath graciously bestowed on us, the arms we have been compelled to assume we will, in defiance of every hazard, with unabating firmness and perseverance, employ for the preservation of our liberties; being with one mind resolved to die freemen rather than live slaves.

"With an humble confidence in the mercies of the supreme and impartial Judge and Ruler of the Universe, we most devoutly implore his divine goodness to protect us happily through this great conflict, to dispose our adversaries to reconciliation on reasonable terms, and thereby to relieve the empire from the calamities of civil war."

A manifesto by Congress, in 1778, closes as follows—

"We appeal to that God who searcheth the hearts of men for the rectitude of our intentions, and in his holy presence declare, as we are not moved by any light or hasty suggestions of anger or revenge, so through every possible change of fortune we will adhere to this our determination."

"Appealing to the Being who searches thoroughly the heart," says a petition to the king in 1774, "we solemnly profess that our councils have been influenced by no other motives than a dread of impending destruction. We doubt not the purity of our intention and the integrity of our conduct will justify us at that grand tribunal before which all mankind must submit to judgment."

"Appealing to Heaven for the justice of our cause, we determine to die or be free."

"If it were possible for men, who exercise their reason, to believe that the Divine Author of our existence intended a part of the human race to hold an absolute property in and an unbounded power over others, marked out by his infinite goodness and wisdom as the objects of a legal domination never rightfully resistible, however severe and oppressive, the inhabitants of these colonies might at least require from the Parliament of Great Britain some evidence that this dreadful authority over them had been granted to that body."

"The Bills of Rights of the colonies sparkle with sentiments of humanity, of right, of liberty. The papers and resolves of the old colonial legislatures had in them that which fed the deep love of liberty in the human soul. The remonstrances addressed to the throne, the letters of eminent men, the declarations of Congress, were all aglow with a divine enthusiasm."

All the state papers emanating from these Christian men were not only replete with political wisdom, but were, in spirit and sentiment, Christian. Lord Chatham, in the British Parliament, says of them—

Lord Chatham's Eulogy

"When your lordships look at the papers transmitted from America—when you consider their decency, firmness, and wisdom—you cannot but respect their cause and wish to make it your own. For myself, I must declare and avow that in all my reading and observation—and it has been my favorite study—I have read Thucydides, and have studied and admired the master states of the world—that for solidity of reasoning, force of sagacity, and wisdom of conclusion, under such a complication of difficult circumstances, no nation or body of men can stand in preference to the General Congress in Philadelphia. I trust it is obvious to your lordships that all attempts to impose servitude upon such men, to establish despotism over such a mighty continental nation, must be vain, must be fatal."

Webster's View

Mr. Webster said he never could read this splendid eulogy on the men and state papers of the Revolutionary era without weeping.

Webster also said, "At that day there could not be found convened on the surface of the globe an equal number of men possessing such enlightened views of government or animated by a higher and a more patriotic motive. They were men full of the spirit of the occasion, imbued deeply with the general sentiment of the country, of large comprehension, long foresight, and of few words. They made no speeches for ostentation; they sat with closed doors, and their great maxim was, *'faire sans dire.'*

"They knew the history of the past, and were alive to all the difficulties and all the duties of the present, and they acted from the first as if the future was all open before them. In such a constellation it would be invidious to point out bright particular stars. Let me only say, what none will consider injustice to others, that George Washington was one of that number.

"The proceedings of this assembly were introduced by religious observances and devout supplications to the throne of grace for the inspirations of wisdom and the spirit of good counsel.

"Regarding the public characters who presided over our affairs during the stormy period of the war, and those on whom was devolved the yet more difficult and even more important duty of creating a system of government for the republic they have conducted to independence, we cannot refrain from a conviction that they were specially called to their high mission by a wise and an all-beneficent Providence. The extraordinary intelligence and virtue displayed in the Continental Congress were recognized by sagacious and dispassionate observers throughout the world. Mirabeau, the great French statesman, spoke of it as a company of demi-gods."

These great and good men, inspired with the sentiments of religion and liberty, felt the incompatibility of human slavery with the Christian life and character of the civil institutions which they founded, and on all suitable occasions declared it to be their first and fervent desire and purpose to have it removed and destroyed.

The first General Congress assembled in 1774, two years before the Declaration of Independence. Their first and main work was the formation of the *"Association"* which formed a *bond of union between the colonies.* The articles of the association contain the following declarations on the subject of slavery—

"We do, for ourselves and the inhabitants of the several colonies whom we represent, firmly agree and associate, under the sacred ties of virtue, honor, and love of our country, as follows—

"2. That we will neither import nor purchase any slave after the first day of December next, after which time we will wholly discontinue the SLAVE-TRADE, and will neither be concerned in it ourselves, nor will we hire our vessels nor sell our commodities or manufactures to those who are concerned in it.

"11. That a committee be chosen in every county, city, and town, by those who are qualified to vote for representatives in the legislature, whose business it shall be attentively to observe the conduct of all persons touching the Association; and when it shall be made to appear, to the satisfaction of a majority of any such committee, that any person within the limits of their appointment has violated this Association, that such majority do forthwith cause the truth of the case to be published in the Gazette, to the end that all such FOES to the rights of British America may be publicly known, and universally contemned as the ENEMIES OF AMERICAN LIBERTIES, and thenceforth we respectively will break off all dealings with him or her.

"14. And we do further agree and resolve that we will have no trade, commerce, dealings, or intercourse whatever with any colony or province in North America which shall not accede to, or which shall hereafter molest, this Association, but will hold them as UN-WORTHY OF THE RIGHTS OF FREEMEN, and as inimical to the liberties of this country.

"The foregoing Association, being determined upon by the Congress, was ordered to be subscribed by the several members thereof; and, therefore, we have hereunto set our respective names accordingly.

"In Congress, Philadelphia, October 20, 1774

"PEYTON RANDOLPH, *President*"

"NEW HAMPSHIRE—John Sullivan, Nathaniel Folsom.

"MASSACHUSETTS BAY—Thomas Cushing, Samuel Adams, John Adams, Robert Treat Paine.

"RHODE ISLAND—Stephen Hopkins, Samuel Ward.

"CONNECTICUT—Eliphalet Dyer, Roger Sherman, Silas Deane.

"NEW YORK—Isaac Low, John Alsop, John Jay, James Duane, Philip Livingston, William Floyd, Henry Wisner, Simon Boerum.

"NEW JERSEY—James Kinsey, William Livingston, Stephen Crane, Richard Smith, John D. Hart.

"PENNSYLVANIA—Joseph Galloway, John Dickinson, Charles Humphreys, Thomas Mifflin, Edward Biddle, John Morton, George Ross.

"THE LOWER COUNTIES, NEWCASTLE, &c.—Caesar Rodney, Thomas McKean, George Read. "MARYLAND—Matthew Tilghman, Thomas Johnson, Jr., William Paca, Samuel Chase.

"VIRGINIA—Richard Henry Lee, George Washington, Patrick Henry, Jr., Richard Bland, Benjamin Harrison, Edmund Pendleton.

"NORTH CAROLINA—William Hooper, Joseph Hawes, Richard Caswell.

"SOUTH CAROLINA—Henry Middleton, Thomas Lynch, Christopher Gadsden, John Rutledge, Edward Rutledge."

Views of the Statesmen of the Revolution on American Slavery

Societies having in view the abolition of slavery were formed in a number of States, in the early period of the republic, including Virginia and Maryland; and in 1794 a general convention of delegates from all the abolition societies in the United States was held in Philadelphia, to consult measures for the removal of slavery; and this general convention met annually for twelve years. To the first convention Dr. Rush was a delegate, and chairman of a committee to draft an address to the people of the United States, which contained the following condemnation of slavery—

"Many reasons concur in persuading us to abolish domestic slavery in our country.

"It is inconsistent with the safety of the liberties of the United States.

"Freedom and slavery cannot long exist together. An unlimited power over the time, labor, and posterity of our fellow-creatures necessarily unfits men for discharging the public and private duties of citizens of a republic.

"It is inconsistent with sound policy, in exposing the states which permit it to all those evils which insurrections and the most resentful war have introduced into one of the richest islands in the West Indies.

"It is unfriendly to the present exertions of the inhabitants of Europe in favor of liberty. What people will advocate freedom with a zeal proportioned to its blessings, while they view the purest republic in the world tolerating in its bosom a body of slaves?

"In vain has the tyranny of kings been rejected while we permit in our country a domestic despotism which involves in its nature most of the vices and miseries that we have endeavored to avoid.

"It is degrading to our rank as men in the scale of being. Let us use our reason and social affections for the purposes for which they were given, or cease to boast a pre-eminence over animals that are unpolluted with our crimes.

"But higher motives to justice and humanity towards our fellow-creatures remain yet to be mentioned.

"Domestic slavery is repugnant to the principles of Christianity. It prostrates every benevolent and just principle of action in the human heart. It is rebellion against the authority of a common Father. It is a practical denial of the extent and efficacy of the death of a common Saviour. It is a usurpation of the prerogatives of the great Sovereign of the universe, who has solemnly claimed an exclusive property in the souls of men.

"But, if this view of the enormity of domestic slavery should not affect us, there is one consideration more, which ought to alarm and impress us, especially at the present juncture.

"It is a violation of a divine precept of universal justice, which has in no case escaped with impunity."

Congress gave countenance and encouragement to these abolition societies, formed in various States of the Union, and as late as 1809 the Speaker of the House of Representatives, by a resolution, was directed to return a letter of thanks to an abolition convention for a gift of Clarkson's "History of Slavery," which was ordered to be placed in the Congressional library.

The patriot and statesman, the philanthropist and Christian, the politician and divine, the guardians of public liberty and morality, were all united to exterminate this moral and political evil from the republic. They deemed it a duty to imbue their schools, colleges, churches, legislatures, and domestic circles with the belief that slavery was a national crime, offensive to God, and destructive to the safety, happiness, and prosperity of the people.

Washington said, "There is not a man living who wishes more sincerely than I do to see a plan adopted for the abolition of slavery; but there is only one proper and effectual mode by which it can be accomplished, and that is by legislative authority; and this, so far as my suffrages will go, shall not be wanting."—*Letter to Robert Morris, April 12, 1786.*

"I never mean, unless some particular circumstance should compel me to it, to possess another slave by purchase—it being among the first wishes of my heart to see some plan adopted by which slavery in this country may be abolished by law."— *Letter to John H. Mercer, 1786.*

"There are in Pennsylvania laws for the gradual abolition of slavery, which neither Virginia nor Maryland have at present, but which nothing is more certain than that they must have, and at a period *not remote."—Letter to John Sinclair.*

Washington wrote to Lafayette as follows—

"The benevolence of your heart, my dear marquis, is so conspicuous on all occasions that I never wonder at fresh proofs of it; but your late purchase of an estate in the colony of Cayenne with a view of emancipating the slaves, is a generous and noble proof of your humanity. Would to God a like spirit might diffuse itself generally into the minds of the people of this country!"

Jefferson, the great apostle of democracy, declared, "The way, I hope, is preparing, under the auspices of Heaven, for a total emancipation. The hour of emancipation is advancing in the march of time. This enterprise is for the young, for those who can follow it up and bear it through to its consummation. It shall have all my prayers; and these are the only weapons of an old man. What execrations should the statesman be loaded with who, permitting one half the citizens thus to trample on the rights of the other, transforms the one into despots and the other into enemies, destroying the morals of one part and the *amor patriæ* of the other! And can the liberties of a nation be thought secured, when we have removed their only firm basis, a conviction in the minds of the people that their liberties are the gift of God? Indeed, I tremble for my country when I reflect that God is just, and that justice cannot sleep forever. The Almighty has no attribute that can take sides with us in such a contest."

Jefferson, writing from Paris, February, 1788, said—

"We must wait with patience the workings of an overruling Providence, and hope that that is preparing the deliverance of these [slaves] our suffering brethren. When the measure of their tears shall be full, when their tears shall involve heaven itself in darkness, doubtless a God of justice will awaken to their distress, and, by diffusing light and liberty among their oppressors, or at length by his exterminating thunder, manifest his attention to things of this world, and that they are not left to the guidance of blind fatality.

"I am very sensible of the honor you propose to me, of becoming a member of the Society for the Abolition of the Slave-Trade. You know that nobody wishes more ardently to see an abolition, not only of the trade, but of the condition of the slave; and certainly nobody will be more willing to encounter every sacrifice for that object."

Jefferson wrote to Edward Coles, of Illinois, August 25, 1814, as follows—

"The love of justice and love of country plead equally the cause of these people; and it is a moral reproach to us that they should have pleaded so long in vain, and should have produced not a single effort—nay, I fear, not much serious willingness—to relieve them and ourselves from our present condition of moral and political reprobation. It is an encouraging observation that no good measure was ever proposed which, if duly pursued, failed to prevail in the end. We have proof of this in the history of the endeavors in the British Parliament to suppress that very trade which brought this evil upon us. And you will be supported by the religious precept, 'Be not weary in well-doing.'"

Lafayette said, "While I am indulging in my views of American prospects and American liberty, it is mortifying to be told that in that very country a large portion of the people are slaves! It is a dark spot on the face of the nation. Such a state of things cannot always exist.

"I see in the papers that there is a plan for the gradual abolition of slavery in the District of Columbia. I would be doubly happy of it for the measure in itself, and because a sense of American pride makes me recoil at the observations of diplomatists, and other foreigners, who gladly improve the unfortunate existing circumstances into a general objection to our republican and, saving that deplorable evil, our matchless system."

"I never," said Lafayette, on another occasion, "would have drawn my sword in the cause of America, if I could have conceived that thereby I was founding a land of slavery."

John Jay said, in 1780, "An excellent law might be made out of the Pennsylvania one for the gradual abolition of slavery. Till America comes into this measure, her prayers to Heaven will be impious. This is a strong expression, but it is just. I believe God governs the world, and I believe it to be a maxim in his as in our court, that those who ask for equity should grant it."

"The word slaves," he said, "was avoided, probably on account of the existing toleration of slavery, and its discordancy with the principles of the Revolution, and from a consciousness of its being repugnant to some of the positions in the Declaration of Independence."

Monroe, in a speech in the Virginia Convention, said, "We have found that this evil has preyed upon the very vitals of the Union, and has been prejudicial to all the States in which it has existed."

Henry Laurens, of South Carolina, for two years President of the Continental Congress, wrote to his son, the 14th of August, 1776, as follows—

"You know, my dear son, I abhor slavery. I was born in a country where slavery had been established by British kings and Parliaments, as well as by the laws of that country, ages before my existence. I found the Christian religion and slavery growing together under the same authority and cultivation. I nevertheless disliked it. In former days there was no combating the prejudices of men supported by interest. The day, I hope, is approaching when, from principles of gratitude, as well as justice, every man will strive to be foremost in showing his readiness to comply with the Golden Rule."

Patrick Henry, the impassioned orator of the Revolution, affirmed, "Slavery is detested; we feel its fatal effects; we deplore it with all the pity of humanity. It would rejoice my very soul to know that every one of my fellow-beings was emancipated. I believe the time will come when an opportunity will be offered to abolish this lamentable evil."

"Believe me, I honor the Quakers for their noble efforts to abolish slavery. It is a debt we owe to the purity of our religion to show that it is at variance with that law that warrants slavery."

In the Convention of Virginia, met to ratify the Constitution of the United States, Patrick Henry argued "the power of Congress, under the United States Constitution, to abolish slavery in the States."

Randolph, in the Convention of Virginia, met to ratify the Federal Constitution, said, "I hope that there are none here who, considering the subject in the calm light of philanthropy, will advance an objection dishonorable to Virginia, that, at the moment they are securing the rights of their citizens, there is a spark of hope that those unfortunate men now held in BONDAGE may, by the operation of the General Government, be made FREE."

John Marshall, the friend and biographer of Washington, a distinguished member of Congress under the administrations of Washington and Adams, and for forty years Chief-Justice of the Supreme Court of the United States, saw with prophetic sagacity the evils of slavery and its future results. In an interview Harriet Martineau had with this venerable Christian judge in 1835, he made the following statement, published in a British magazine of that year. Marshall and Madison were then the only surviving representatives of the old ideas of Virginia on the subject of slavery. Miss Martineau says—

"When I knew the chief-justice, he was eighty-three—as bright-eyed and warm-hearted as ever, while as dignified a judge as ever filled the highest seat in the highest court of any country. He said he had seen Virginia the leading State for half his life; he had seen her become the second, and sink to be (I think) the fifth. Worse than this, there was no arresting her decline, if her citizens did not put an end to slavery; and he saw no signs of any intention to do so, east of the mountains at least. He had seen whole groups of estates, populous in his time, lapse into waste. He had seen agriculture exchanged for human stock-breeding; and he keenly felt the degradation. The forest was returning over the fine old estates, and the wild creatures which had not been seen for generations were reappearing; numbers and wealth were declining, and education and manners were degenerating. It would not have surprised him to be told that on that soil would the main battles be fought when the critical day should come which he foresaw."

Madison, the father of the Constitution, "thought it wrong to admit in the Constitution the idea that there could be property in man." "I object to the word slave appearing in a Constitution which I trust is to be the charter of freedom to unborn millions; nor would I willingly perpetuate the memory of the fact that slavery ever existed in our country. It is a great evil, and, under the providence of God, I look forward to some scheme of emancipation which shall free us from it. Do not, therefore, let us appear as if we regarded it perpetual, by using in our free Constitution an odious word opposed to every sentiment of liberty."

After the Constitution went into operation, Madison in Congress said, on the question of abolishing the slave-trade—

"The dictates of humanity, the principles of the people, the national safety and happiness, and prudent policy, require it of us. It is to be hoped that by expressing a national disapprobation of the trade we may *destroy it*, and save our country from reproaches, and our posterity from the imbecility ever attendant on a country filled with slaves."

Harriet Martineau in 1835 spent some days with Madison at his residence in Virginia. She thus relates the opinions of Madison on the subject of slavery—

"To Mr. Madison despair was not easy. He had a cheerful and sanguine temper, and if there was one thing rather than another which he had learned to consider secure, it was the Constitution which he had so large a share in making. Yet he told me that he was nearly in despair, and that he had been quite so till the Colonization Society arose. Rather than admit to himself that the South must be laid waste by a servile war, or the whole country by a civil war, he strove to believe that millions of negroes could be carried to Africa and so got rid of. I need not speak of the weakness of such a hope. What concerns us now is that he saw and described to me, when I was his guest, the dangers and horrors of the state of society in which he was living. He talked more of slavery than of all other subjects together, returning to it morning, noon, and night. He said that the clergy perverted the Bible, because it was altogether against slavery; that the colored population was increasing faster than the white; and that the state of morals was such as barely permitted society to exist. Of the issue of the conflict, whenever it should occur, there could, he said, be no doubt. A society burdened with a slave system could make no permanent resistance to an unencumbered enemy; and he was astonished at the fanaticism which blinded some Southern men to so clear a certainty.

"Such was Mr. Madison's opinion in 1835."

James Wilson, a leading member of the convention that formed the Constitution of the United States, and in the ratification convention of his State, speaking of the clause relating to the power of Congress over the slave-trade, said—

"I regard this clause as laying the foundation for banishing slavery out of this country. The new States which are to be formed will be under the control of Congress in this particular, and slavery will never be introduced among them. It presents us with the pleasing prospect that the rights of mankind will be acknowledged and established throughout the Union. If there was no other feature in the Constitution but this one, it would diffuse a beauty over its whole countenance. Yet the lapse of a few years, and Congress will have power to exterminate slavery from within our borders."

Dr. Benjamin Franklin was the unwearied friend of emancipation. He was President of the Pennsylvania Society for promoting the ABOLITION of slavery, and addressed the following memorial to Congress on the subject, on behalf of the society—

> Your memorialists, particularly engaged in attending to the distresses arising from SLAVERY, believe it to be their indispensable duty to present this subject to your notice. They have observed with real satisfaction that many important and salutary powers are vested in you, for promoting the welfare and securing the blessings of liberty to the people of the United States; and as they conceive that these blessings ought cheerfully to be administered, WITHOUT DISTINCTION or COLOR, to all descriptions of people, so they indulge themselves in the pleasing expectation that nothing which can be done for the relief of the unhappy objects of their care will be omitted or delayed.

From a persuasion that equal liberty was originally the portion of, and is still the birthright of, all men, and influenced by the strong ties of humanity and the principles of their institutions, your memorialists conceive themselves bound to use all justifiable endeavors to LOOSEN THE BONDS OF SLAVERY and promote a general enjoyment of the blessings of freedom. Under these impressions, they earnestly entreat your attention to the subject of *slavery*; that you will be pleased to countenance the RESTORATION TO LIBERTY of those unhappy men who alone, in this land of freedom, are degraded into perpetual bondage, and who, amid the general joy of surrounding freemen, are groaning in servile subjection; THAT YOU WILL DEVISE MEANS OF REMOVING THIS INCONSISTENCY OF CHARACTER FROM THE AMERICAN PEOPLE; that you will promote mercy and justice towards this distressed race; and that you will step to the very verge of the power vested in you for discouraging every species of traffic in the persons of our fellow-men.

Benjamin Franklin, *President.*
Philadelphia, Feb. 3, 1790.

Dr. Franklin was the personal friend of Granville Sharpe, who was a member of the British Parliament, and devoted his life to abolishing the slave-trade and to the promotion of universal freedom. The following letter of this distinguished philanthropist to Dr. Franklin is a rare and interesting paper touching the subject of slavery as affected by the Constitution—

TO HIS EXCELLENCY DR. FRANKLIN, PRESIDENT OF THE PENNSYLVANIA SOCIETY FOR PROMOTING THE ABOLITION OF SLAVERY.
Leadenhall Street, London, 10th Jan'y, 1788.

Dear Sir—
I ought long ago to have acknowledged the deep sense which I entertain of my obligations to the Pennsylvania Society for Promoting the Abolition of Slavery, for the honor they have

been pleased to confer upon me by inserting my name in the number of their corresponding members, as signified in your Excellency's letter of the 9th of July last.

I read with particular satisfaction their excellent remonstrance against slavery, addressed to the convention. If our most solemn and unanswerable appeals to the consciences of men in behalf of humanity and common justice are disregarded, the crimes of slavery and slave-dealing become crying sins, which presumptuously invite the divine retribution; so that it must be highly dangerous to the political existence of any state, that is duly warned against injustice, to afford the least sanction to such enormities by their legislative authority.

Having been always zealous of your government, I am the more sincerely grieved to see the new Federal Constitution stained by the insertion of two most exceptionable clauses of the kind above mentioned; the one in direct opposition to a most humane article ordained by the first American Congress to be perpetually observed, and the other in equal opposition to the express command of the Almighty not to deliver up the servant that had escaped to his master; and both clauses of the 9th Section of the 1st Article and the latter part of the 2d Section of the 3d Article are so clearly null and void by their iniquity, that it would be even a crime to regard them as law.

Though I have, indeed, too plainly proven myself a very unworthy and dilatory correspondent, through the unavoidable impediments of a variety of affairs and trusts which have been devolved upon me, yet I must request your Excellency to inform the Pennsylvania Society that I have never knowingly omitted any favorable opportunity of promoting the great objects of their institution, and trust in God I never shall.

With true esteem and respect, dear sir,

Yours, &c.,

Granville Sharpe.

This testimony of the fathers and founders of our civil institutions, as briefly put on record in this volume, confirms the declarations of Mr. Leigh in the convention of Virginia, in 1832, who said—

"I thought, till very lately, that it was known to everybody that during the Revolution, and for many years after, the abolition of slavery was a favorite topic with many of our ablest statesmen, who entertained with respect all the schemes which wisdom or ingenuity could suggest for its accomplishment."

Salmon P. Chase, in the Senate of the United States, in February, 1854, declared the same fact in reference to the faith and policy of the statesmen of the Revolution. He designated that as the "era of enfranchisement," and said—

"It commenced with the earliest Struggles for independence. The spirit which inspired it animated the hearts and prompted the efforts of Washington, of Jefferson, of Patrick Henry, of Wythe, of Adams, of Jay, of Hamilton, of Morris—in short of all the great men of our early history. All these hoped, all these labored, all these believed in the final deliverance of the country from the curse of slavery. That spirit burned in the Declaration of Independence, and inspired the provisions of the Constitution and of the Ordinance of 1787. Under its influence, when in full vigor, State after State provided for the emancipation of slaves within their limits, prior to the adoption of the Constitution."

In these notices of the men of the Revolution and their views on the Christian religion, it is appropriate in this volume to record the faith and declarations of four other eminent men, born during the Revolutionary struggle, and who have exerted a commanding influence on the legislation and politics of this country.

John Quincy Adams

The sixth President of the United States, was an eminent statesman and politician. Fifty years of his active life were spent in the service of his country, with dignity, honor, and usefulness. "The fear of God," says Edward Everett, "was the last great dominant principle of his life and character. There was the hiding of his power. Offices, and affairs, and honors, and studies, left room in his soul for *faith.* No man laid hold with a firmer grasp of the realities of life, and no man dwelt more steadily on the mysterious realities beyond life. He entertained a profound reverence for sacred things. He attended the public offices of social worship with a constancy seldom witnessed in this busy and philosophic age. The daily and systematic perusal of the BIBLE was an occupation with which no other duty was allowed to interfere. The daily entry of his journal, for the latter part of his life, begins with a passage extracted from Scripture, followed with his own meditations and commentary; and, thus commencing the day, there is little doubt that of his habitual reflections as large a portion was thrown forward to the world of spirits as was retained by the passing scenes. In all the private and public positions he occupied, he displayed the principles of the Christian religion."

His inaugural address as President of the United States says—

"'Except the Lord keep the city, the watchman waketh but in vain.' With fervent supplications for his favor, to his overruling providence I commit, with humble but fearless confidence, my own fate and the future destinies of my country.'"

His first message declares that "In taking a survey of the concerns of our beloved country with reference to subjects interesting to the common welfare, the first sentiment which impresses itself upon the mind is of gratitude to the Omnipotent Dispenser of all good, for the continuance of the signal blessings of his providence, and especially for that health which to an unusual extent has prevailed within our borders, and for that abundance which, in the vicissitudes of the seasons, has been scattered with profusion over our land. Nor ought we less to ascribe to him the glory that we are permitted to enjoy the bounties of his hand in peace and tranquillity—peace with all the other nations of the earth, in tranquillity among ourselves." In the year 1809, Mr. Adams was appointed Minister Plenipotentiary of the United States to the court of St. Petersburg. During his residence there he addressed to his eldest son, who was then ten years old, a series of letters on the study of the Bible. Extracts from these letters are here given embodying the views of this statesman on the Bible and its influence. The letters were written during the years 1811 and 1813. The extracts are given without reference to their dates.

"So great is my veneration for the Bible, and so strong my belief that, when duly read and meditated upon, it is of all books in the world that which contributes to make men good, wise, and happy, that the earlier my children begin to read it, and the more steadily they pursue the practice of reading it throughout their lives, the more lively and confident will be my hopes that they will prove useful citizens to their country, respectable members of society, and a real blessing to their parents.

"I have, myself, for many years made it a practice to read through the Bible once every year. My custom is to read four or five chapters every morning, immediately after rising from bed. It employs about an hour of my time, and seems to me the most suitable manner of beginning the day.

"You know the difference between right and wrong. You know some of your duties, and the obligation you are under of becoming acquainted with them all. It is in the Bible you must learn them, and from the Bible how to practise them. Those duties are—to *God*, to your *fellow-creatures*, to *yourself*. 'Thou shalt love the Lord thy God with all thy heart, and with all thy soul, and with all thy mind, and with all thy strength, and thy neighbor as thyself.' On these two commandments (Jesus Christ expressly says) 'hang all the law and the prophets.' That is to say that the whole purpose of divine revelation is to inculcate them efficaciously upon the minds of men.

"Let us, then, search the Scriptures. The Bible contains the revelation of the will of God; it contains the history of the creation of the world and of mankind. It contains a system of religion and morality which we may examine upon its own merits, independent of the sanction it receives from being the word of God. In what light soever we regard it, whether with reference to revelation, to history, to morality, or to literature, it is an inexhaustible mine of knowledge and virtue.

"The first words of the Bible are, 'In the beginning *God created* the heaven and the earth.' This blessed and sublime idea of God, the Creator of the universe—this source of all human virtue and all human happiness, for which all the sages and philosophers of Greece and Rome groped in darkness and never found—is *revealed* in the first verse of the book of Genesis. I call this the source of all human virtue and happiness.

"Here, then, is the foundation of all morality—the source of all our obligations as accountable creatures. This idea of the transcendent power of the Supreme Being is essentially connected with that by which the whole duty of man is summed up in obedience to his will.

"'And God said, Let there be light, and there was light.' This verse only exhibits one of the effects of that transcendent power which the first verse discloses in announcing God as the Creator of the world. The true sublimity is in the idea given us of God. To such a God, piety is but a reasonable service.

"The moral character of the Old Testament, then, is that *piety to* God is the foundation of all virtue, and that virtue is inseparable from it, but that piety without the practice of virtue is itself a crime and an aggravation of all iniquity. All the virtues which were recognized by the heathens are inculcated not only with more authority, but with more energy of argument and more eloquent persuasion, in the Bible, than in all the writings of the ancient moralists.

"The sum of Christian morality, then, consists in *piety to God*, and *benevolence to man*—piety manifested not by formal solemnities and sacrifices of burnt-offerings, but by *repentance*, by *obedience*, by *submission*, by *humility*, by the worship of the heart; and *benevolence* not founded upon selfish motives, but superior even to the sense of wrong or the resentment of injuries.

"The whole system of Christian morality appears to have been set forth by its Divine Author in the Sermon on the Mount. What I would impress upon your mind as infinitely important to the happiness and virtue of your life is the general spirit of Christianity, and the duties which result from it.

"The true Christian is the '*justum et tenacem propositi virum*' of Horace. The combination of these qualities, so essential to the heroic character, with those of *meekness, lowliness of heart*, and *brotherly love*, is what constitutes that moral *perfection* of which Christ gave an example in his own life, and to which he commended his disciples to aspire. Endeavor to discipline your own heart and to govern your conduct through life by these principles thus combined. Be meek, be gentle, be kind, be affectionate to all mankind, not excepting your enemies—but never tame or abject. Never give way to the wishes of impudence, or show yourself yielding or complying to prejudices, wrong-headedness, or intractability, which would lead or draw you astray from the dictates of your conscience and your sense of right. 'Till you die, let not your integrity depart from you.' Build your house upon the Rock; and then let the rain descend, and the floods come, and the winds blow, and beat upon that house: it shall not fall, for it will be founded upon a Rock. So promises your blessed Lord and Master."

"By admitting the Bible as a divine revelation, we have hopes of future felicity inspired, together with a conviction of our present wretchedness. The blood of the Redeemer has washed out the pollution of our original sin; and the certainty of eternal happiness in a future life is again secured to us in the primitive condition of obedience to the will of God.

"Jesus Christ came into the world to preach repentance and remission of sins, to proclaim glory to God in the highest, and on earth peace, good will to man, and, finally, to bring life and immortality to light in the gospel; and all this is clear if we consider the Bible as a divine revelation.

"Let us conclude by resuming the duties to God, to our fellow-creatures, and to ourselves, which are derived as immediate consequences from the admission of the Bible as divine revelation. 1. Piety. From the first chapter of the Old Testament to the last of the New, obedience to the will of God is inculcated as including the whole duty of man. 2. Benevolence. The love of our neighbor was forcibly taught in the Old Testament; but to teach it more effectually was the special object of Christ's mission upon earth. 'Love,' says St. Paul, 'is the fulfilling of the law.' But Christ says, 'A NEW commandment I give unto you, that ye love one another; as I have loved you, that ye also love one another. By this shall all men know that ye are my disciples, if ye have love one to another.' 3. Humility. The profound sense of our infirmities which must follow from the doctrine of original sin, and of its punishment inflicted upon all human kind, necessarily inspires meekness and. lowliness of spirit. These two are commanded expressly by Jesus Christ; and, as principles of morality, they are not only different from the maxims of every other known system of ethics, but in direct opposition to them.

"Of the ten commandments, emphatically so called for the extraordinary and miraculous distinction with which they were promulgated, the first four are religious laws. The fifth and tenth are properly and peculiarly *moral*, and the other four are of the criminal department of municipal law. The unity of the Godhead, the prohibition of making graven images for worship, that of taking 'in vain' the name of the Deity, and the injunction to observe the Sabbath as a day sanctified and set apart for his worship, were all intended to inculcate that reverence for the one only and true God, that profound and penetrating sentiment of *piety*, which is the great and only immediate foundation of all human virtue.

"Next to the duties towards the Creator, that of honoring the earthly parents is enjoined. It is to them that every individual owes the greatest obligations, and to them he is consequently bound by the first and strongest of earthly ties. The following commands are negative, and require all to abstain from wrong-doing—1. In their persons; 2. In *their property*; 3. In their conjugal rights; and 4. In their good name. The tenth and closing commandment goes to the very source of all human action, the heart, and positively forbids all those *desires* which first prompt and lead to every transgression upon the property and rights of our fellow-creatures. Vain indeed would be the search among all the writings of profane antiquity—not merely of that remote antiquity, but even in the most refined and most philosophic ages of Greece and Rome—to find so broad, so complete, so solid a basis for morality as this decalogue lays down."

As the life of Mr. Adams was closing, he was called to preside at the anniversary of the Bible Society of the city of Washington. On taking the chair, he said—

"Fellow-citizens and members of the Bible Society—In taking the chair as the oldest Vice-President of the Society, I deem myself fortunate in having the opportunity, at this stage of a long life drawing rapidly to its close, to bear at this place, the capital of our National Union, my solemn testimonial of reverence and gratitude to that Book of books, the Holy Bible."

Mr. Adams died in the Capitol of the nation, on the 23d of February, 1848, exclaiming, "This is the last of earth: I am content."

General Andrew Jackson's View of Christianity

The admired military hero and popular President, was a thorough believer in the Christian religion and its evangelical doctrines. He embraced the system of the gospel with a cordial and a warm-hearted faith. He had a pious Presbyterian mother, who in her earliest years planted the seeds of divine truth which in later life germinated into a practical faith and bore the fruits of genuine piety.

In his public life at Washington, as President, he bore unvarying testimony to the divinity of the Bible, as a book essential to civil government and to the salvation of the soul. During his eight years' residence at Washington as President, he was regular in his attendance on the public worship of God, and had a pew in the First Presbyterian Church. The Bible was a book which had a prominent place in the Presidential mansion during his administration, and its perusal was his constant habit and delight.

It was a long-cherished desire of his heart to make a public profession of his faith in Christ and join himself to a Christian church, but he was deterred, like most of our political and public men, by the fear his motives would be misunderstood and impugned. The following letter will explain his feelings on this point. It was written to a friend in Boston.

HERMITAGE, AUGUST 24, 1838.

DEAR SIR—I thank you kindly for the perusal of your pious uncle's letter, which you were good enough to enclose for my perusal. Should you live to see this pious divine, your uncle, present him my kind regards, with my prayers for a long-continued life of usefulness and a happy immortality. Say to him I would long since have made this solemn *public* dedication to Almighty God, but knowing the wretchedness of this world, and how prone many are to evil, and that the scoffer of religion would have cried out, 'Hypocrisy! *he has joined the Church for political effect*,'—I thought it best to postpone this public act until my retirement to the shades of private life, when no false imputations could be made that might be injurious to religion. Please say to him I well remember the pleasure I had of taking him by the hand and receiving his kind benediction, for which I was grateful. It would give me pleasure *now* in retirement to receive and shake him by the hand. Present our kind regards to your amiable family, and receive for yourself our best wishes.

I remain, very respectfully, yours, etc.,

Andrew Jackson.

P.S.—I am so much debilitated that I can scarcely wield my pen.

A. J.

To Dr. Lawrence.

His faith in an overruling Providence was expressed to Congress and the country in these words, which were in substance repeated in all his messages—

His second inaugural address says—

"It is my fervent prayer to that Almighty Being before whom I now stand, and who has *kept us in his hands* from the infancy of our republic to the present day, that he will so overrule all my intentions and actions, and inspire the hearts of my fellow-citizens, that we may be preserved from dangers of all kinds, and continue forever a UNITED AND HAPPY PEOPLE."

His message of 1835 says, "Never in any former period of our history have we had greater reason than we now have to be thankful to Divine Providence for the blessings of health and general prosperity."

His message of 1836 —"Our gratitude is due to the Supreme Ruler of the universe; and I invite you to unite with me in offering to him fervent supplication that his providential care may ever be extended to those who follow us.... I shall not cease to invoke that beneficent Being to whose providence we are already so signally indebted, for the continuance of his blessings on our beloved country."

"For relief and deliverance, let us firmly rely on that kind Providence which, I am sure, watches with peculiar care over the destinies of our republic, and on the intelligence and wisdom of our countrymen. Through *His* abundant goodness and *their* patriotic devotion, our liberty and Union will be preserved."

"May the Great Ruler of nations grant that the signal blessings with which he has favored us may not, by the madness of party or personal ambition, be lost; and may his wise providence bring those who have produced this crisis to see their folly before they feel the misery of civil strife, and inspire a returning veneration for the Union, which, if we may dare to penetrate his designs, he has chosen as the only means of attaining the high destinies to which we may reasonably aspire."

Commodore Elliott brought from Asia a sarcophagus, which was presented, through the National Institute, to General Jackson. His answer is as follows—

HERMITAGE, March 27, 1845.

Dear Sir—

Your letter of the 18th instant, together with a copy of the proceedings of the National Institute, have been received. . . . With the warmest sensations that can inspire a grateful heart, I must decline accepting the honor intended to be conferred. I cannot consent that my mortal body shall be laid in a repository prepared for an emperor or a king. My republican feelings and principles forbid it; the simplicity of our system of government forbids it. Every monument erected to perpetuate the memory of our heroes and statesmen ought to bear evidence of the economy and simplicity of our republican institutions and the plainness of our republican citizens, who are the sovereigns of our glorious Union and whose virtue is to perpetuate it. True virtue cannot exist where pomp and parade are the governing passions: it can only dwell with the people—the great laboring and producing classes, that form the bone and sinew of our confederacy.

For these reasons, I cannot accept the honor you and the president and directors of the National Institute intended to bestow. I cannot permit my remains to be the first in these United States to be deposited in a sarcophagus made for an emperor or a king. . . . I have prepared an humble depository for my mortal body beside that wherein lies my beloved wife, where, without any pomp or parade, I have requested, when my God calls me to sleep with my fathers, to be laid—for both of us there to remain until the last trumpet sounds to call the dead to judgment, when we, I hope, shall rise together, clothed with that heavenly body promised to all who believe in our glorious Redeemer, who died for us that we might live, and by whose atonement I hope for a blessed immortality.

Andrew Jackson.

The sublime system of divinity so clearly taught in the Holy Scriptures was the joy and rejoicing of his heart. He had a firm faith in the providential government of God over nations, men, and events. When rehearsing facts that had occurred in his military or political life, he would pause and say, "It was the hand of God: Divine Providence ordered it so." "Such an officer was cut down: he was a noble man. I felt his loss much; but it was the hand and counsel of God." In an address at a dinner given in Georgetown, in honor of the hero of the battle of New Orleans, he closed by saying, "But to HEAVEN and to the bravery of our soldiers were we indebted for the victory; to HEAVEN and them let it be ascribed."

The following sketch of the religious feelings and dying scenes of Andrew Jackson was written by the Rev. John S. C. Abbott—

"One Sunday morning in the year 1827, as General Jackson and his wife were walking towards the little Hermitage church, she entreated him to take a decided stand as a Christian and to unite with the Church. He replied—

"'My dear, if I were to do that now, it would be said all over the country that I had done it for the sake of political effect. My enemies would all say so. I cannot do it *now*; but I promise you that when once more I am clear of politics I will join the Church.'

"On the 23d of December, 1828, Mrs. Jackson died. It was a terrible blow to her husband, who loved her with singular fervor and constancy. He never quite recovered from the shock. His spirit became very much subdued, and he gave up entirely the use of profane language, to which he had been awfully addicted in his younger days.

"Mr. Nicholas P. Trist, of Virginia, was the private secretary of President Jackson. On one occasion it seemed necessary for him to enter the President's apartment after he had retired for the night. He found the President in his night-dress, sitting at a table with his wife's miniature propped up against some books before him, and between him and the miniature lay his wife's well-worn prayer-book, from which, according to his invariable custom, he was reading a prayer before he slept.

"About this time there was a season of special religious interest in Washington. The pastor of the church which the President attended, and from whom the writer has the anecdote, called at the White House and entered into conversation with the President upon the subject of personal religion. He replied, 'No man respects religion more than I do, or feels more deeply its importance. I promised my wife that I would attend to the salvation of my soul as soon as the election was over; but now the cares which engross me are so over-whelming, and my cabinet in such a divided state, that I have not a moment's time to think of any thing but the urgencies of the passing hour. But I am resolved, so soon as I leave the Presidential chair and retire to the seclusion of the Hermitage, to take up in earnest the subject of religion.'

"It was the old excuse: Go thy way for this time, till I have a conve-nient season. The hour of retirement came, and still the general did not keep his promise. To one who addressed him upon the subject, he wrote, in August, 1838, 'I would long since have made this sol-emn dedication to Almighty God, but, knowing the wretchedness of this world, and how prone many are to evil, and that the scoffer of religion would have cried out, "Hypocrisy! he has joined the Church for political effect," I thought it best to postpone this public act until my retirement to the shades of private life, 'when no false imputa-tions could be made that might be injurious to religion.'

"About a year from this time, in 1839, there was a protracted meeting at the Hermitage. General Jackson attended all the services with deep solemnity. He was deeply impressed by the last sermon, and urged the preacher, Rev. Dr. Edgar, of Nashville, to go home with him. An engagement prevented this.

General Jackson, a sin-convicted man, with his eyes open to his true condition, passed the evening and most of the night in read-ing the Bible and in meditation and prayer. The anguish and tears of that night eternity alone can reveal. With the light of the morn-ing peace dawned upon his soul. It was communion Sabbath at the little Hermitage church. That very day the general made a public profession of his faith in Christ. The church was crowded to its ut-most capacity, the very windows being darkened with eager faces. As in great infirmity he leaned upon his staff, giving his assent to the creed and covenant of the Church, tears trickled freely down his furrowed cheeks, and all were overcome with emotion.

"From this time until his death he spent most of his time read-ing the Bible. Scott's Family Bible he read through twice, and daily conducted family prayers, summoning all the household servants. On the 8th of June, 1845, the summons came for the weary pilgrim, then seventy-eight years of age, to appear before his final Judge. As he lay upon his dying bed, after a severe spasm, he swooned away, and all for a few moments thought him dead. But he revived, and, raising his eyes, said—

"'My dear children, do not grieve for me. It is true, I am going to leave you. I am well aware of my situation. I have suffered much bodily pain; but my sufferings are but as nothing compared with that which our blessed Saviour endured upon that accursed cross, that we might all be saved who put our trust in him.'

"He then took an affectionate leave of each one of his family, taking them one by one by the hand and addressing to each a few words of counsel. 'He then,' writes Dr. Efselman, who was present, 'delivered one of the most impressive lectures upon the subject of religion that I have ever heard. He spoke for nearly half an hour, and apparently with the power of inspiration; for he spoke with calmness, with strength, and even with animation. In conclusion, he said, "My dear children and friends and servants, I hope and trust to meet you in heaven, both white and black." The last sentence he repeated—"both white and black."'

"All present were in tears. 'Oh, do not cry,' said the general: 'be good children, and we will all meet in heaven.' These were his last words. He ceased to breathe, and died without a struggle or a pang. 'Major Lewis,' writes the biographer, 'removed the pillows, drew down the body upon the bed, and closed the eyes. Upon looking again upon the face, he observed that the expression of pain which it had worn so long had passed away. Death had restored it to naturalness and serenity. The aged warrior slept.'"

During his last illness, to a friend he pointed to the family Bible on the stand, and said— "That book, sir, is the rock on which our republic rests. It is the bulwark of our free institutions."

Henry Clay's Views

As an American statesman and a leading politician, wielded a masterly and moulding influence in shaping the legislative and political policy of his country. "His public life," says Dr. Robert C. Breckenridge, in an oration on the occasion of laying the corner-stone of a monument to Mr. Clay, "from the commencement of the practice of the law till his death, lasted about fifty-five years—a public life hardly matched in its duration and splendor by any other in our annals. He lived over seventy-five years: three-quarters of a century more fruitful in events or more decisive in their influence upon society had hardly ever occurred in the history of mankind. It was about eight months after the Continental Congress had issued from the city of Philadelphia the immortal Declaration of Independence, in the name of the people of the United States, that the pious wife of a faithful and laborious Baptist minister, far off in Virginia, gave birth to Henry Clay. The language which he learned to speak was replenished with the divine truth which pervades a Christian household. The first words which he understood were words which sunk into his heart forever—COUNTRY, LIBERTY, INDEPENDENCE. The first names he heard beyond his father's household were names that will live forever—the name of his neighbor HENRY, the prince of orators and patriots, the name of his fellow-Virginian, WASHINGTON, the first of mortals.

"God had bestowed on him a personal presence and bearing as impressive as any mortal ever possessed. The basis of his moral character was akin to that which lies at the foundation of supreme moral excellence—integrity and love of truth. His was a high, fair, brave, upright nature. His intellectual character, by which he will be chiefly known to posterity, was, as all men acknowledge, of the highest order, clear, powerful, and comprehensive: no subject seemed to be difficult under its steady insight, and it embraced with equal readiness every department of human knowledge to which it became his duty to attend. No genius was ever capable of a wider diversity of use than his. And the vast and searching common sense which was the most striking characteristic of his mind revealed the purity, the truth, and the force with which the ultimate elements of our rational nature dwelt and acted in his noble understanding.

"Mr. Clay was the child of Christian parents, all the more likely to be jealous of the heritage of God's love to their boy, as they had little else to bestow upon him. His own repeated declarations, made in the most public and solemn manner at every period of his life, that he cherished the highest veneration for the Christian religion, and the most profound conviction of the divine mission of the Saviour of sinners, fully justify the importance which I have attached to this element of his destiny, even if he had not attested in his latter years the sincerity of his life-long convictions, by openly professing his faith in the Son of God and uniting himself with his professed followers. He lived some years, and closed his days, in the communion of the Protestant Episcopal Church, to which his venerable wife had long been attached. It was my fortune to have personal knowledge, under circumstances which do not admit of any doubt in my own mind, that, according to the measure of the light he had, he was during a few years immediately preceding his death a penitent and believing follower of the divine Redeemer. It may be well allowed that the frank and habitual avowal even of speculative faith in the Christian religion, by a man of his character and position, was not without its value, and was not free from reproach, during that terrible season of unbelief which marked the close of the last century and stretched forward upon the first quarter of the present. And that the crowning efforts of his life were sustained by a sense of Christian duty, and its last sufferings assuaged by the consolations of Christian hope, are facts too important, as they relate to him, and too significant in their own nature, to be omitted in any estimate of him. It is not, however, on account of such considerations as these that I reiterate with so much emphasis the undeniable fact that Mr. Clay never was an infidel, that he was always an avowed believer in true religion. But it is because such is my sense of the shallowness, the emptiness, and the baseness of that state of the human soul in which it can deny the God who created it and the Saviour who redeemed it, and can empty itself of its own highest impulses and disallow its own sublimest necessities, that I have no conception how such a soul could be what this man was, or do what he did. It is because I do understand with perfect distinctness that belief in God, and belief in a mission given to us by him, and to be executed with success only by means of his blessing upon our efforts, must be a conviction, at once profound and enduring, in every soul that is great in itself, or that can accomplish any thing great. Wonderful as Mr. Clay's career was, it would be a hundredfold more wonderful to suppose that such a career was possible to a scoffer and a skeptic."

Mr. Clay died in the city of Washington, on the 29th of June, 1852. Rev. Dr. Butler, chaplain of the Senate, delivered, in the Senate-Chamber, a funeral sermon in the presence of the President and Congress of the United States, in which he gave the following just views of the character and principles of an American statesman, and the views of Mr. Clay on the subject of the Christian religion—

"A great mind, a great heart, a great orator, a great career, have been consigned to history. I feel, as a man, the grandeur of this career. But as an immortal, with this broken wreck of mortality before me, with this scene as the 'end-all' of human glory, I feel that no career is truly great but that of him who, whether he be illustrious or obscure, lives to the future in the present, and, linking himself to the spiritual world, draws from God the life, the rule, the motive, and the reward of all his labor. So would that great spirit which has departed say to us, could he address us now. So did he realize, in the calm and meditative close of life. I feel that I but utter the lessons which, living, were his last and best convictions, and which, dead, would be, could he speak to us, his solemn admonitions, when I say that statesmanship is then only glorious when it is *Christian,* and that man is then only safe and true to his duty and his soul, when the life which he lives in the flesh is the life of faith in the Son of God. Great, indeed, is the privilege, and most honorable and useful is the career, of a Christian American statesman. He perceives that civil liberty came from the freedom wherewith Christ made its early martyrs and defenders free. He recognizes it as one of the twelve manner of fruits on the tree of life, which, while its lower branches furnish the best nutriment of earth, hangs on its topmost boughs, which wave in heaven, fruits that exhilarate the immortals. Recognizing the state as God's institution, he will perceive that his own ministry is divine. Living consciously under the eye and in the love and fear of God, 'redeemed by the blood of Jesus,' sanctified by his Spirit, 'loving his law,' he will give himself, in private and in public, to the service of his Saviour. He will not admit that he may act on less lofty principles in public than in private life, and that he must be careful of his moral influence in the small sphere of home and neighborhood, but need take no heed of it when it stretches over continents and crosses seas. He will know that his moral responsibility cannot be divided and distributed among others. When he is told that adherence to the strictest moral and religious principles is

incompatible with a successful and eminent career, he will denounce
the assertion as a libel on the venerated fathers of the republic—a
libel on the honored living and the illustrious dead—a libel against
a great and Christian nation—a libel against God himself, who has
declared and made 'godliness profitable for the life that now is.' He
will strive to make laws the transcripts of the character, and institutions illustrations of the providence, of God. He will scan with
admiration and awe the purposes of God in the future history of the
world, in throwing open this continent, from sea to sea, as the abode
of freedom, intelligence, plenty, prosperity, and peace, and feel that
in giving his energies with a patriot's love to the welfare of his country he is consecrating himself, with a Christian zeal, to the extension
and establishment of the Redeemer's kingdom. Compared with a
career like this, which is equally open to those whose public sphere
is large or small, how paltry are the trades in patriotism, the tricks
of statesmanship, the rewards of successful baseness! This hour, this
scene, the venerated dead, the country, the world, the present, the
future, God, duty, heaven, hell, speak trumpet-tongued to all in the
service of their country, to *beware* how they lay polluted or unhallowed hands

'upon the ark
Of her magnificent and awful cause.'

"Such is the character of that statesmanship which alone would have
met the full approval of the venerated dead. For the religion which
always had a place in the convictions of his mind had also, within a recent period, entered into his experience and seated itself in his heart.
Twenty years since, he wrote, 'I am a member of no religious sect, and
I am not a professor of religion. I regret that I am not. I wish that I
was, and trust that I shall be. I have, and always have had, a profound
regard for Christianity, the religion of my fathers, and for its rites, its
usages and observances.' That feeling proved that the seed sown by
pious parents was not dead, though stifled. A few years since, its dor-
mant life was reawakened. He was baptized in the communion of the
Protestant Episcopal Church, and during his sojourn in this city he
was in full communion with Trinity Parish. He avowed his full faith
in the great leading doctrines of the gospel, the fall and sinfulness of

man, the divinity of Christ, the reality and necessity of the atonement, the need of being born again by the Spirit, and salvation through faith in a crucified Redeemer. He said, with much feeling, that he endeavored to, and trusted that he did, repose his salvation upon Christ; that it was too late for him to look at Christianity in the light of speculation—that he had never doubted of its truth, and that he now wished to throw himself upon it as a practical and blessed remedy. Very soon after this I administered to him the sacrament of the Lord's Supper. It was a scene long to be remembered. There, in that still chamber, at a weekday noon, the tides of life flowing all around us, three disciples of the Saviour—the minister of God, the dying statesman, and his servant, a partaker of the like precious faith—commemorated their Saviour's dying love. He grew in grace and in the knowledge of our Lord and Saviour Jesus Christ. Among the books which, in connection with the word of God, he read most, were Jay's 'Morning and Evening Exercises,' the 'Life of Dr. Chalmers,' and 'The Christian Philosopher Triumphant in Death.'"

Mr. CASS, an eminent Christian statesman, whose life, private and public, has illustrated the virtues of the Christian religion, and who in his official positions and public addresses has unfolded its benign relations and influence on society and civil states, was a co-Senator with Mr. Clay, and, in his remarks in the Senate, on his character and death, said—

"I was often with him during his last illness, when the world and the things of this world were fast fading away before him. After his duty to his Creator and his anxiety for his family, his first care was for his country, and his first wish for the preservation and perpetuation of the Constitution and Union—dear to him in the hour of death as they had ever been in the vigor of life—of the Constitution and Union, whose defence in the last and greatest crisis of their peril had called forth all his energies, and stimulated those memorable and powerful exertions which he who witnessed can never forget, and which no doubt hastened the final catastrophe a nation now deplores with a sincerity and unanimity not less honorable to themselves than to the memory of the object of their affections. And when we shall enter that narrow valley, through which he has passed before us, and which leads to the judgment-seat of God, may we be able to say, through faith in his Son our Saviour, and in the beautiful language of the hymn of the dying Christian—dying, but ever living and triumphant—

> 'The world recedes, it disappears!
> Heaven opens on my eyes! my ears
> With sounds seraphic ring:
> Lend, lend your wings! I mount—I fly!
> O Grave! where is thy victory?
> O Death: where is thy sting?'

"Let me die the death of the righteous, and let my last end be like his."

Daniel Webster's Views

Genius and influence on the political and legislative history of the American republic has been, and is, pre-eminently pure and powerful. As an American Senator, he was unequalled in his profound views of the genius of our civil institutions, and won for himself the title of the Great Expounder of the Constitution. For forty years he occupied the highest eminence in Congress and in the politics of the country, and acquired a fame that will be enduring and historic. As a lawyer, a statesman, a politician, an expounder of the Constitution, and a scholar, Mr. Webster had no equal among modern statesmen. His works constitute the richest treasures of the civil and political literature of the republic, and are distinguished as profound expositions of the genius of our institutions, and for their classic beauty, eloquence, and purity. In the Senate of the United States, before the Supreme Court of the United States, and on political, literary, and commemorative occasions, he vindicated the divinity of the Christian religion, and unfolded its relations to civil society and government and to the present and eternal well-being of man. The following declarations in reference to the Christian religion will present his views on this important subject.

In 1844, Mr. Webster made an elaborate argument before the Supreme Court of the United States against the validity of the will of Stephen Girard, of Philadelphia. Mr. Girard had, by his immense wealth, founded an institution of learning for the education of orphan children. A provision in the will contained the following restriction—

"Secondly, I enjoin and require *that no ecclesiastic, missionary, or minister of an sect whatever shall ever hold or exercise any station or duty whatever in the said College; nor shall any such person ever be admitted for any purpose, or as a visitor, within the premises appropriated to the purposes of the said College.*

"My desire is, that all the instructors and teachers in the College shall take pains to instil into the minds of the scholars the *purest morality,* so that on their entrance into active life they may, from *inclination* and habit, evince *benevolence towards their fellow-creatures, and a love of truth, sobriety, and industry,* adopting at the same time such religious tenets as their *matured reason* may enable them to prefer."

The heirs-at-law of Stephen Girard tried the question of the validity of the will. Mr. Webster was their lawyer, and made a masterly argument against it and in favor of the Christian religion. The speech produced a deep impression on the public mind, and led to a meeting of the citizens of Washington, belonging to different denominations, who passed the following resolution—

"1st. That, in the opinion of this meeting, the powerful and eloquent argument of Mr. Webster, on the before-mentioned clause of Mr. Girard's will, demonstrates the vital importance of Christianity to the success of our free institutions, and its necessity as the basis of all useful moral education; and that a general diffusion of that argument among the people of the United States is a matter of deep public interest."

The speech was published and widely circulated. The extracts in this volume touch upon various fundamental features of the Christian religion.

On the Christian ministry Mr. Webster said—

"Now, I suppose there is nothing in the New Testament more clearly established by the Author of Christianity than the appointment of a Christian ministry. The world was to be evangelized, was to be brought out of darkness into light, by the influences of the Christian religion spread and propagated by the instrumentality of man. A Christian ministry was, therefore, appointed by the Author of the Christian religion himself, and it stands on the same authority as any other part of religion. And after his resurrection, in the appointment of the great mission to the whole human race, the Author of Christianity commanded his disciples that they should 'go into all the world and preach the gospel to every creature.' This was one of his last commands; and one of his last promises was the assurance, 'Lo, I am with you always, even unto the end of the world.' I say, therefore, there is nothing set forth more authentically in the New Testament than the appointment of a Christian ministry; and he who does not believe this does not and cannot believe the rest.

"Why should we shut our eyes to the whole history of Christianity? Is it not the preaching of the minister of the gospel that has evangelized the more civilized part of the world? Why do we at this day enjoy the rights and benefits of Christianity ourselves? Do we not owe it to the instrumentality of the Christian ministry? And where was Christianity ever received—where were its truths ever poured into the human heart—where did its waters, springing up into everlasting life, ever burst forth—except in the track of the Christian ministry? Do we not all know that wherever Christianity has been carried and wherever it has been taught by human agency, that agency was the agency of Christian ministers?"

On the Christian Sabbath Mr. Webster said—

"What becomes of the Christian Sabbath in a school thus established? The observance of the Sabbath is a part of Christianity in all its forms. All Christians admit the observance of the Sabbath. There can be no Sabbath in this college, there can be no religious observance of the Lord's day; for there are no means of attaining that end. Where can these little children go to learn the truth, to reverence the Sabbath? They are just so far from the ordinary observance of the Sabbath as if there was no Sabbath day at all. And where there is no observance of the Christian Sabbath, there will, of course, be no public worship of God.

"As a part of my argument, I will read an extract from an address of a large convention of clergymen and laymen, held recently in Columbus, Ohio, to lead the public mind to a more particular observance of the Sabbath, and which bears with peculiar force upon this case—

"'It is alike obvious that the Sabbath exerts its salutary power by making the population acquainted with the being, perfections, and laws of God, with our relations to him as his creatures, and our obligations to him as rational and accountable subjects, and with our characters as sinners, for whom his mercy has provided a Saviour, under whose government we live to be restrained from sin and reconciled to God, and fitted by his word and Spirit for the inheritance above.

"'It is by the reiterated instruction and impression which the Sabbath imparts to the population of a nation, by the moral principle which it forms, by the conscience which it maintains, by the habits of method, cleanliness, and industry it creates, by the rest and renovated vigor it bestows on exhausted human nature, by the lengthened life and higher health it affords, by the holiness it inspires, and cheering hopes of heaven and the protection and favor of God which its observance insures, that the Sabbath is rendered the moral conservator of nations.

"'The omnipresent influence which the Sabbath exerts, however, is by no secret charm or compendious action, upon masses of unthinking minds; but it arrests the stream of worldly thoughts, interests, and affections, stopping the din of business, unlading the mind of its cares and responsibilities and the body of its burdens, while God speaks to men, and they attend, and hear, and fear, and learn to do his will.

"'You might as well put out the sun and think to enlighten the world with tapers, destroy the attraction of gravity and think to wield the universe by human powers, as to extinguish the moral illumination of the Sabbath, and break this glorious mainspring of the moral government of God.'"

On the relation of the Christian religion to morality, Mr. Webster said, "This scheme of education is derogatory to Christianity, because it proceeds upon the assumption that the Christian religion is not the only true foundation, or any necessary foundation, of morals. The ground taken is that religion is not necessary to morality, that benevolence may be insured by habit, and that all the virtues may flourish, and be safely left to the chance of flourishing, without touching the waters of the living spring of religious responsibility. With him who thinks thus, what can be the value of the Christian revelation? So the Christian world has not thought; for by that Christian world, throughout its broadest extent, it has been, and is, held as a fundamental truth that religion is the only solid basis of morals, and that moral instruction not resting on this basis is only building upon sand."

On the importance of early religious instruction, Mr. Webster said—

"This first great commandment teaches man that there is one, and only one, great First Cause—one, and only one, proper object of human worship. This is the great, the ever fresh, the overflowing fountain of all revealed truth. Without it, human life is a desert, of no known termination on any side, but shut in on all sides by a dark and impenetrable horizon. Without the light of this truth, man knows nothing of his origin and nothing of his end. And when the Decalogue was delivered to the Jews, with this great announcement and command at its head, what said the inspired lawgiver? That it should be kept from children?—that it should be revered as a communication fit only for mature age? Far, far otherwise. 'And these words, which I command thee this day, shall be in thy heart. And thou shalt teach them diligently unto thy children, and shalt talk of them when thou sittest in thy house, and when thou walkest by the way, when thou liest down, and when thou risest up.'

"There is an authority still more inspiring and awful. When little children were brought into the presence of God, his disciples proposed to send them away; but he said, 'Suffer little children to come unto me.' Unto *me*: he did not send them first to learn the lessons in morals to the schools of the Pharisees or to the unbelieving Sadducees, nor to read the precepts and lessons *phylacterized* on the garments of the Jewish priesthood; he said nothing of different creeds or clashing doctrines; but he opened at once to the youthful mind the everlasting fountain of living waters, the only source of eternal truths—'Suffer little children to come *unto me*.' And that injunction is of perpetual obligation. It addresses itself to-day with the same earnestness and the same authority which attended its first utterance to the Christian world. It is of force everywhere and at all times. It extends to the ends of the earth, it will reach to the end of time, always and everywhere sounding in the ears of men, with an emphasis which no repetition can weaken, and with an authority which nothing can supersede, 'Suffer little children to come unto me.' And not only my heart and my judgment, my belief and my conscience, instruct me that this great precept should be obeyed, but the idea is so sacred, the solemn thoughts connected with it so crowd upon me, it is so utterly at variance with this system of philosophical morality which we have heard advocated, that I stand and speak here in fear of being influenced by my feelings to exceed the proper line of my professional duty."

On the nature and purpose of true charity and its union with the Christian religion, Mr. Webster said—"There is nothing in the history of the Christian religion, there is nothing in the history of English law, either before or after the conquest; there can be found no such thing as a school of instruction in a Christian land, from which the Christian religion has been, of intent and purpose, rigorously and opprobriously excluded, and yet such a school regarded as a charitable trust or foundation. A school of instruction for children, from which the Christian religion and Christian teachers are excluded—there is no such thing in the history of religion, there is no such thing in the history of human laws, as a charity school of instruction for children, from which the Christian religion and Christian teachers are excluded, as unsafe and unworthy intruders. There can be no charity in that man of education that opposes Christianity.

"I maintain that in any institution for the instruction of youth, where the authority of God is disowned, and the duties of Christianity derided and despised, and its ministers shut out from all participation in its proceedings, there can no more charity, true charity exist, than evil can spring out of the Bible, error out of truth, or hatred and animosity come forth from the bosom of perfect love. No, sir! No, sir! If charity denies its birth and parentage—if it turns infidel to the great doctrines of the Christian religion, if it turns unbeliever—it is no longer charity. This is no longer charity, either in a Christian sense, or in the sense of jurisprudence; for it separates itself from the fountain of its own creation."

The faith of the Christian religion, which Mr. Webster had through his whole public career maintained with such masterly eloquence, was his stay in the last scenes of life. He died at Marshfield, Massachusetts, October 24, 1852. On that day he said, "All that is mortal of Daniel Webster will soon be no more." He then prayed, in his full, clear, and strong voice, ending with the petition, "Heavenly Father, forgive my sins, and receive me to thyself, through Christ Jesus."

His physician repeated to him, "Though I walk through the valley of the shadow of death, I will fear no evil: for thou art with me; thy rod and thy staff they comfort me."

Mr. Webster instantly rejoined "The fact! the fact! That is what I want! Thy rod! thy rod! Thy staff! thy staff!" His last words were, "I still live."

A few days before his death he drew up and signed the following declaration of his religious faith, which was by his direction inscribed on his tomb—

"Lord, I believe: help thou mine unbelief. Philosophical argument, especially that drawn from the vastness of the universe in comparison with the insignificance of this globe, has sometimes shaken my reason for the faith which is in me; but my heart has always assured and reassured me that the gospel of Jesus Christ must be a divine reality. The Sermon on the Mount cannot be a merely human production. This belief enters into the very depth of my conscience. The whole history of man proves it.

"Daniel Webster."

Contrast of Christian and Infidel Statesmen

Lamartine, a French statesman and writer, presents the following view of infidel and Christian influences, contrasted, on men and nations—

"I know—I sigh when I think of it—that hitherto the French people have been the least religious of all the nations of Europe. Is it because the idea of God—which arises from all the evidences of nature and from the depths of reflection—being the profoundest and weightiest idea of which human intelligence is capable, and the French mind being the most rapid, but the most superficial, the lightest, the most unreflective of all European races, this mind has not the force and severity necessary to carry far and long the greatest conception of the human understanding?

"Is it because our Governments have always taken upon themselves to think for us, to believe for us, and to pray for us? Is it because we are, and have been, a military people, a soldier nation, led by kings, heroes, ambitious men, from battle-field to battle-field, making conquests and never keeping them, ravaging, dazzling, charming, and corrupting Europe, and bringing home the manners, vices, bravery, lightness, and impiety of the camp to the fireside of the people?

"I know not; but certain it is that the nation has an immense progress to make in serious thought if she wishes to remain free. If we look at the characters, compared as regards religious sentiments, of the great nations of Europe, America, even Asia, the advantage is not for us. The great men of other countries live and die on the scene of history, looking up to heaven; our great men appear to live and die, forgetting completely the only idea for which it is worth living and dying: they live and die looking at the spectator, or, at most, at posterity.

"Open the history of America, the history of England, and the history of France; read the great lives, the great deaths, the great martyrdoms, the great words at the hour when the ruling thought of life reveals itself in the last words of the dying; and compare.

"Washington and Franklin fought, spoke, suffered, always in the name of God, for whom they acted; and the Liberator of America died, confiding to God the liberty of the people and his own soul.

"Sidney, the young martyr of a patriotism guilty of nothing but impatience, and who died to expiate his country's dream of liberty, said to his jailer, 'I rejoice that I die innocent towards the king, but a victim resigned to the King on high, to whom all life is due.'

"The Republicans of Cromwell only sought the way of God even in the blood of battles. Their politics were their faith; their reign, a prayer; their death, a psalm. One hears, sees, feels, that God was in all the movements of these great people.

"But cross the sea, traverse the Channel, come to our times, open our annals, and listen to the great words of the great political actors of the drama of our liberty. One would think that God was eclipsed from the soul, that his name was unknown in the language. History will have the air of an atheist when she recounts to posterity these annihilations rather than deaths of celebrated men in the greatest year of France! The victims only have a God; the tribune and lictors have none.

"Look at Mirabeau on the bed of death. 'Crown me with flowers,' said he; 'intoxicate me with perfumes; let me die to the sound of delicious music.' Not a word of God, or of his soul. Sensual philosopher, he desired only supreme sensualism, a last voluptuousness in his agony.

"Contemplate Madame Roland, the strong-hearted woman of the Revolution, on the cart that conveyed her to death. She looked contemptuously on the besotted people who killed their prophets and sibyls. Not a glance towards heaven! Only one word for the earth she was quitting—'O Liberty!'

"Approach the dungeon-door of the Girondins. Their last night is a banquet; the only hymn, the Marseillaise!

"Follow Camille Desmoulins to his execution. A cool and indecent pleasantry at the trial, and a long imprecation on the road to the guillotine, were the two last thoughts of this dying man on his way to the last tribunal.

"Hear Danton on the platform of the scaffold, at the distance of a line from God and eternity. 'I have a good time of it: let me go to sleep.' Then to the executioner, 'You will show my head to the people: it is worth the trouble.' His faith, annihilation; his last sigh, vanity! Behold the Frenchman of this latter age!

"What must one think of the religious sentiment of a free people whose great figures seem thus to march in procession to annihilation, and to whom that terrible minister, death itself, recalls neither the threatenings nor promises of God?

"The republic of these men without a God has quickly been stranded. The liberty won by so much heroism and so much genius has not found in France a conscience to shelter it, a God to avenge it, a people to defend it against that atheism which has been called glory. All ended in a soldier and some apostate republicans travestied into courtiers. An atheistic republicanism cannot be heroic. When you terrify it, it bends; when you would buy it, it sells itself. It would be very foolish to immolate itself. Who would take any heed? The people ungrateful, and God non-existent! So finish atheistic revolutions!"

10

Christian Legislation of the Continental Congress

Christian Legislation of tbe Continental Congress

PLUTARCH declares that the great care of the legislators of the republics of Greece and Rome was to inspire men with a sense of the favor and displeasure of the gods, and that religion is the cement of civil union, and the essential support of civil government. "A city might as well be built," says he, "on the air, without any earth to stand upon, as a commonwealth or a kingdom be constituted or preserved without religion." "No state," says an American writer, "ever yet existed without the basis of some religion. The earliest state constitution of which we have any clear record is the Egyptian, and this was distinctly a theocracy. The Hebrew state was at first theocratic; and when God gave the people a king, the religious element in their constitution was not withdrawn. The old kingdoms of Assyria, Phenicia, Media and Persia, all made use of some special religion as auxiliary to their civil state."

The testimony of Polybius, an ancient writer and philosopher, to the beneficial effects which resulted from the system of pagan superstition, in fortifying the sentiments of moral obligation and supporting the sanctity of oaths, is so weighty and decisive that it would be injustice not to insert it—more especially as it is impossible to attribute it to the influence of credulity on the author himself, who was evidently a skeptic. It is scarcely necessary to remark that all the benefits which might in any way flow from superstition are secured to an incomparably greater degree by the belief of true religion.

"But among all the useful institutions," says Polybius, "that demonstrate the superior excellence of the Roman government, the most considerable, perhaps, is the opinion which people are taught to hold concerning the gods; and that which other men regard as an object of disgrace appears, in my judgment, to be the very thing by which this republic is cherished and sustained. I mean superstition, the Roman religion, which is impressed with all its terrors, and influences the private actions of the citizens and the public administration of the state, to a degree that can scarcely be excelled."

Religion the Basis of Civil States

"In almost all of the distinguished states," said A. H. Everett, in the Legislature of Massachusetts, "the principal care of the community has been to provide for the support of religion. In Egypt, Palestine, and the Oriental nations, religion has always been the main object of the government. In Greece it was the only bond of union that held together the several members of that illustrious commonwealth of states."

"Seeing therefore it doth appear," says the great and venerable Hooker, "that the safety of states dependeth upon religion; that religion unfeignedly loved perfecteth men's abilities unto all kinds of virtuous services in the commonwealth; that men's desire is, in general, to hold no religion but the true, and that whatever good effects do grow out of their religion, who embrace, instead of the true, a false, the roots thereof are certain sparks of the light of truth intermingled with the darkness of error, because no religion can wholly and only consist of untruths: we have reason to think that all true virtues are to honor *true religion* as their parent, and all well-ordered commonwealths to love her as their chiefest stay."

Christianity is for all the wants of the civil state, as it is for all the wants of the soul and immortality. Hence it "has entered on a career of universal conquest: first the conquest of men, then of customs, institutions, corporations, and governments. She aims to carry out her spirit in the extremities even of the living framework of society. Accordingly, Christianity holds it to be as much the duty of the state to be born again from a life of selfishness and ambition and worldly glory, to a life of universal love, and justice, and liberty, and devotion to God and his service. A nation and a government thus regenerated would realize John Milton's idea of a civil government, that it should be "ONE HUGE CHRISTIAN PERSONAGE, ONE MIGHTY OUTGROWTH AND STATURE OF AN HONEST MAN."

Religious Convictions of the Men Who Formed Our Civil Institutions

The American colonies had a profound conviction of the essential need of religion as the only true basis of civil government. They had been schooled in the faith and practice of the Protestant religion, and when the time came for them to institute governments for themselves they were prepared to found them, and carry them on according to the religion of the Bible.

Burke's Views

"The people of the colonies," said Burke in the British Parliament, "are descendants of Englishmen. England is a nation which still, I hope, respects, and formerly adored, freedom. The colonists went from you when this part of your character was most predominant; and they took this bias and direction the moment they parted from your hands. They are, therefore, not only devoted to liberty, but to liberty according to English ideas and on English principles. Their governments are popular in a high degree. If any thing were wanting to this necessary operation of the form of government, RELIGION would have given it a complete effect. Religion—always a principle of energy in this new people—is no way worn out or impaired; and their mode of professing is also one main cause of this free spirit. The people are Protestants, and of that kind which is most adverse to all implicit submission of mind and opinion. This is a persuasion, sir, not only favorable to liberty, but built upon it. The dissenting interests have sprung up in direct opposition to all the ordinary powers of the world, and could justify that opposition only on a strong claim to natural liberty. All Protestantism, even the most cold and passive, is a sort of dissent. But the religion most prevalent in our Northern colonies is a refinement on the spirit of the principle of resistance: it is the dissidence of dissent, and the *protestantism of the Protestant religion.* This religion, under a variety of denominations, agreeing in nothing but in the communion of the spirit of liberty, is predominant in most of the Northern Provinces. The colonists left England when this spirit was high, and in the emigrants was highest of all; and even the stream of foreigners which has been constantly flowing into these colonies has, for the greater part, been composed of dissenters of their own countries, and have brought with them a temper and a character far from alien to that of the people with whom they mixed. A fierce spirit of liberty has grown up; it has grown up with the growth of your people, and increased with the increase of their population and wealth—a spirit that, unhappily, meeting with an excess of power in England, which, however lawful, is not reconcilable to any idea of liberty, much less with theirs, has kindled this flame which is ready to consume us."

This thorough education of the colonists in the Protestant school of Christianity, from their earliest history down to the Revolution, prepared the statesmen who instituted our forms of government to found them on the principles of Christianity. This policy but reflected the will of the people, as well as the views and convictions of the men who framed our free institutions.

"That some religion," said Bishop McIlvaine, "and that the Christian religion, is recognized as the religion of this nation and government, and as such is interwoven in its laws, and has a legal preference, though not 'establishment' in technical language, over whatever else has the name of religion, and especially over all forms of infidelity, all must admit. We are thankful that our system of government, our common law, and administration of justice, were instituted by men having the wisdom to see how entirely the liberties and interests of this nation are dependent on the teachings and keeping of the truths and institutions of Christianity."

Webster's Views

"There is nothing," says Webster, "we look for with more certainty than this principle, that Christianity is a part of the law of the land. Every thing declares this. The generations which have gone before speak to it, and pronounce it from the tomb. We feel it. All, all proclaim that Christianity, general, tolerant Christianity, independent of sects and parties, that Christianity to which the sword and the fagot are unknown, general, tolerant Christianity, is the law of the land."

The statesmen of the Continental Congress, in their deliberations, officially recognized the Christian religion, and incorporated its principles into their legislative acts. That body of great men is thus spoken of by Webster. He says—

First Congress

"No doubt the assembly of the first Continental Congress may be regarded as the era at which the Union of these States commenced. This event took place in Philadelphia, the city distinguished by the great civil events of our early history, on the 5th of September, 1774, on which day the first Continental Congress assembled. Delegates were present from New Hampshire, Massachusetts, Rhode Island, Connecticut, New York, New Jersey, Pennsylvania, Delaware, Maryland, Virginia, North Carolina, South Carolina, and Georgia.

"Let this day be ever remembered! It saw assembled from the several colonies those great men whose names have come down to us and will descend to all posterity. Their proceedings are remarkable for simplicity, dignity, and unequalled ability. At that day, probably, there could have been convened on no part of the globe an equal number of men possessing greater talents and ability, or animated by a higher and more patriotic motive. They were men full of the spirit of the occasion, imbued deeply with the general sentiment of the country, of large comprehension, of long foresight, and of few words. They made no speeches for ostentation: they sat with closed doors, and their great maxim was, *'faire sans dire.'* They knew the history of the past, they were alive to all the difficulties and all the duties of the present, and they acted from the first as if the future were all open before them. In such a constellation it would be invidious to point out the bright particular stars. Let me only say—what none can consider injustice to others—that George Washington was one of the number.

"This first Congress, for the ability which it manifested, the principles which it proclaimed, and the characters which composed it, makes an illustrious chapter in American history. Its members should be regarded not only individually, but in a group; they should be viewed as living pictures, exhibiting young America as it then was, and when the seeds of its public destiny were beginning to start into life, well described by our early motto as being full of energy and prospered by Heaven—

'Non sine Diis animosus infans.'

"For myself, I love to travel back in imagination, to place myself in the midst of this assembly, this union of greatness and patriotism, and to contemplate, as if I had witnessed, its profound deliberations, and its masterly exhibitions both of the rights and wrongs of the country."

The proceedings of the Assembly were introduced by religious observances and devout supplications to the throne of grace, for the inspiration of wisdom and the spirit of good counsels.

The first act of the first session of the Continental Congress was to pass the following resolution—

> *Tuesday, September 6, 1774.—Resolved,* That the Rev. Mr. Duché be desired to open Congress to-morrow morning with prayer, at Carpenter's Hall, at nine o'clock.
>
> *Wednesday, September 7, 1774, A.M.*—Agreeable to the resolve of yesterday, the meeting was opened with prayer by the Rev. Mr. Duché.

John Adams, in a letter to his wife, thus describes that scene—

"When the Congress first met, Mr. Cushing first made a motion that it should be opened with prayer. It was opposed by one or two, because we were so divided in religious sentiments—some were Episcopalians, some Quakers, some Anabaptists, some Presbyterians, and some Congregationalists—that we could not agree in the same act of worship. Mr. Samuel Adams rose and said, 'he was no bigot, and could hear a prayer from a gentleman of piety and virtue, who was at the same time a friend to his country. He was a stranger in Philadelphia, but had heard that Mr. Duché deserved that character, and therefore he moved that Mr. Duché, an Episcopalian clergyman, might be desired to read prayers to the Congress to-morrow morning.' The motion was seconded, and passed in the affirmative. Mr. Randolph, our President, waited on Mr. Duché, and received for answer that if his health would permit he certainly would. Accordingly, next morning he appeared, with his clerk and in his pontificals, and read the collect for the seventh day of September, which was the thirty-first Psalm. You must remember that this was the first morning after we heard the horrible rumor of the cannonade of Boston. I never saw a greater effect produced upon an audience. It seemed as if Heaven had ordained that Psalm to be read on that morning. It has had an excellent effect upon everybody here. I must beg you to read that Psalm." It is as follows—

1. In thee, O Lord, do I put my trust; let me never be ashamed: deliver me in thy righteousness.

2. Bow down thine ear to me; deliver me speedily: be thou my strong rock, for a house of defence to save me.

3. For thou art my rock and my fortress; therefore for thy name's sake lead me, and guide me.

4. Pull me out of the net that they have laid privily for me: for thou art my strength.

5. Into thine hand I commit my spirit: thou hast redeemed me, O Lord God of truth.

6. I have hated them that regard lying vanities: but I trust in the Lord.

7. I will be glad and rejoice in thy mercy: for thou best considered my trouble; thou hast known my soul in adversities;

8. And hast not shut me up into the hand of the enemy: thou hast set my feet in a large room.

9. Have mercy upon me, O Lord, for I am in trouble: mine eye is consumed with grief, yea, my soul and my belly.

10. For my life is spent with grief, and my years with sighing: my strength faileth because of mine iniquity, and my bones are consumed.

11. I was a reproach among all mine enemies, but especially among my neighbors, and a fear to mine acquaintance: they that did see me without fled from me.

12. I am forgotten as a dead man out of mind: I am like a broken vessel.

13. For I have heard the slander of many: fear was on every side: while they took counsel together against me, they devised to take away my life.

14. But I trusted in thee, O Lord: I said, Thou art my God.

15. My times are in thy hand: deliver me from the hand of mine enemies, and from them that persecute me.

16. Make thy face to shine upon thy servant: save me for thy mercies' sake.

17. Let me not be ashamed, O Lord; for I have called upon thee:

let the wicked be ashamed, and let them be silent in the grave.

18. Let the lying lips be put to silence; which speak grievous things proudly and contemptuously against the righteous.

19. Oh how great is thy goodness, which thou hast laid up for them that fear thee; which thou best wrought for them that trust in thee before the sons of men!

20. Thou shalt hide them in the secret of thy presence from the pride of man: thou shalt keep them secretly in a pavilion from the strife of tongues.

21. Blessed be the Lord: for he bath showed me his marvellous kindness in a strong city.

22. For I said in my haste, I am cut off from before thine eyes: nevertheless thou heardest the voice of my supplications when I cried unto thee.

23. Oh love the Lord, all ye his saints: for the Lord preserveth the faithful, and plentifully rewardeth the proud doer.

24. Be of good courage, and he shall strengthen your heart, all ye that hope in the Lord.

"After this," says Adams, "Mr. Duché, unexpectedly to everybody, struck out into an extemporaneous prayer, which filled the bosom of every man present. I must confess I never heard a better prayer, or one so well pronounced. Episcopalian as he is, Dr. Cooper himself never prayed with such fervor, such ardor, such earnestness and pathos, and in language so elegant and sublime, for America, for the Province of Massachusetts, and especially for the town of Boston."

In Adams's Diary, Sept. 7, 1774, the same scene is recorded—

"Went to Congress again; heard Mr. Duché read prayers; the collect for the 7th of the month was most admirably adapted—though this was accidental, or, rather, providential. A prayer which he gave us of his own composition was as pertinent, as affectionate, as sublime, as devout, as I ever heard offered up to Heaven. He filled every bosom present."

We give below the prayer as it is printed in Thatcher's "Military Biography," under date of December, 1777.

> O Lord our heavenly Father, high and mighty King of kings and Lord of lords, who dost from thy throne behold all the dwellers on earth, and reignest with power supreme and uncontrolled over all the kingdoms, empires, and governments; look down in mercy, we beseech thee, on these American States who have fled to thee from the rod of the oppressor, and thrown themselves on thy gracious protection, desiring to be henceforth dependent only on thee; to thee they have appealed for the righteousness of their cause; to thee do they now look up for that countenance and support which thou alone canst give; take them, therefore, heavenly Father, under thy nurturing care; give them wisdom in council, and valor in the field; defeat the malicious designs of our cruel adversaries; convince *them* of the unrighteousness of their cause, and if they still persist in their sanguinary purposes, oh, let the voice of thine own unerring justice, sounding in their hearts, constrain them to drop the weapons of war from their unnerved hands in the day of battle. Be thou present, O God of wisdom, and direct the councils of this honorable assembly: enable them to settle things on the best and surest

foundation, that the scene of blood may be speedily closed, that order, harmony, and peace may be effectually restored, and truth and justice, religion and piety, prevail and flourish amongst thy people. Preserve the health of their bodies and the vigor of their minds; shower down on them and the *millions* they here represent, such temporal blessings as thou seest expedient for them in this world, and crown them with everlasting glory in the world to come. All this we ask in the name and through the merits of Jesus Christ, thy Son, our Saviour. Amen!

Described by Webster and Goodrich

"It must have been an interesting scene," says Goodrich—"a minister, bound to forms, finding extemporaneous words to suit the occasion, and the Quaker, the Presbyterian, the Episcopalian, and the Rationalist—some kneeling, some standing, but all praying, and looking to Heaven for wisdom and counsel in this hour of doubt, anxiety, and responsibility. Adams and Sherman, the Puritans, standing erect—Thomson, the Quaker, finding the movement of the Spirit in the words of a consecrated priest—with Washington, Henry, and other Episcopalians, kneeling, according to their creed, and all invoking wisdom from above, would make a touching and instructive picture. Its moral would be, that the greatest minds, in moments of difficulty and danger, acknowledge their dependence upon God, and feel the necessity of elevating and purifying their hearts by prayer; and that the differences of sect, the distinctions of form, all vanish when emergency presses upon the consciences of men and forces them to a sincere and open avowal of their convictions."

Webster described, in the Senate, the same scene as follows—

"At the meeting of the first Congress, there was a doubt in the minds of many about the propriety of opening the sessions with prayer; and the reason assigned was, as here, the great diversity of opinion and religious belief; until at last Mr. Samuel Adams, with his gray hairs hanging about his shoulders, and with an impressive venerableness now seldom to be met with (I suppose owing to different habits), rose, in that assembly, and, with the air of a perfect

Puritan, said, 'it did not become men professing to be Christian men, who had come together for solemn deliberation in the hour of their extremity, to say there was so wide a difference in their religious belief that they could not, as one man, bow the knee in prayer to the Almighty, whose advice and assistance they hoped to obtain; and, Independent as he was, and an enemy to all prelacy as he was known to be, he moved that Rev. Mr. Duché, of the Episcopal Church, should address the Throne of Grace in prayer.' Mr. Duché read the Episcopal service of the Church of England; and then, as if moved by the occasion, he broke out into extemporaneous prayer; and those men who were about to resort to force to obtain their rights were moved to tears; and 'floods of tears,' he says, 'ran down the cheeks of pacific Quakers, who formed a part of that interesting assembly;' and depend upon it, that *where there is a spirit of Christianity there is a spirit which rises above form, above ceremonies, independent of sect or creed and the controversies of clashing doctrines."*

That Congress of Christian statesmen appreciated the services rendered by their first chaplain, and unanimously

"Voted, That the thanks of Congress be given to Mr. Duché, by Mr. Cushing and Mr. Ward, for performing divine service, and for the excellent prayer which he composed and delivered on the occasion."

The public worship of Almighty God was personally and officially observed by the statesmen of the Revolution. The records of the Continental Congress present this fact—

"*Saturday, July* 15*th*, 1775—On motion, *Resolved*, That the Congress will, on Thursday next, attend divine service in a *body*, both morning and *afternoon."*

On the 3d of October, 1776, on the occasion of the sudden demise of Peyton Randolph, Congress resolved to attend his funeral as mourners, and appointed a committee "to wait on the Rev. Mr. Duché and request him to prepare a proper discourse to be delivered at the funeral."

Legislation of the Bible

The legislation of Congress on the Bible is a suggestive Christian fact, and one which evinces the faith of the statesmen of that period in its divinity, as well as their purpose to place it as the corner-stone in our republican institutions.

Congress Appropriates Money to Purchase Bibles

The breaking out of the Revolution cut off the supply of "books printed in London." The scarcity of Bibles also came soon to be felt. Dr. PATRICK ALLISON, one of the chaplains to Congress, and other gentlemen, brought the subject before that body in a memorial, in which they urged the printing of an edition of the Scriptures.

On the 11th of September, 1777, the committee to whom the memorial was referred reported as follows—

> *Thursday, September* 11, 1777—The committee to whom the memorial of Dr. Allison and others was referred, report, That they have conferred fully with the printers, &c., in this city, and are of opinion that the proper types for printing the Bible are not to be had in this country, and that the paper cannot be procured, but with such difficulties, and subject to such casualties, as render any dependence on it altogether improper; that to import types for the purpose of setting up an entire edition of the Bible, and to strike off 30,000 copies, with paper, binding, &c., will cost £10,272, 10, which must be advanced by Congress, to be reimbursed by the sale of the books; that, in the opinion of the committee, considerable difficulties will attend the procuring the types and paper; that, afterwards, the risk of importing them will considerably enhance the cost, and that the calculations are subject to such uncertainty in the present state of affairs, that Congress cannot much rely on them; that the use of the Bible is so universal, and its importance so great, that your committee refer the above to the consideration of Congress, and if Congress shall not think it expedient to order the importation of types and paper, the committee recommend that Congress will order the Committee of Commerce to import 20,000 Bibles from Holland, Scotland, or elsewhere, into the different ports of the States of the Union.

Whereupon it was moved, That the Committee of Commerce be directed to import 20,000 copies of the Bible.

On this motion New Hampshire, Massachusetts, Rhode Island, Connecticut, New Jersey, Pennsylvania, and Georgia, voted in the affirmative; New York, Delaware, Maryland, Virginia, North Carolina, and South Carolina, voted in the negative.

So it was resolved in the affirmative.

Congress Superintends the Printing of an Edition of the Entire Bible

In 1781 Rev. Mr. Aitken memorialized Congress to aid him in printing an American edition of the Bible. Congress appointed a committee, who submitted a report on the subject as follows—

> By the United States Congress assembled:
> *September 12, 1782*
> The committee to whom was referred a memorial of Robert Aitken, Printer, dated 21st January, 1781, respecting an edition of the Holy Scriptures, report, That Mr. Aitken has, at great expense, now finished an American edition of the Holy Scriptures in English; that the committee have from time to time attended to his progress in the work; that they also recommended it to the, two chaplains of Congress to examine and give their opinion of the execution, who have accordingly reported thereon; the recommendation and report being as follows—
> Philadelphia, 1st Sept., 1782

> Reverend Gentlemen—
> Our knowledge of your piety and public spirit leads us, without apology, to recommend to your particular attention the edition of the Holy Scriptures published by Mr. Aitken. He undertook this expensive work at a time when, from the circumstances of the war, an English edition of the Bible could not be imported, nor any opinion formed how long the obstruction might continue. On this account, particularly, he deserves applause and encouragement. We therefore wish

you, reverend gentlemen, to examine the execution of the work, and, if approved, to give it the sanction of your judgment and the weight of your recommendation.

We are, with very great respect,

Your most obedient, humble servants,

(Signed)   James Duane, *Chairman,*

In behalf of a committee of Congress on Mr. Aitken's memorial.

Reverend Dr. White and Rev. Mr. Duffield, Chaplains of the United States in Congress assembled, report—

Gentlemen—

Agreeably to your desire, we have paid attention to Mr. Robert Aitken's impression of the Holy Scriptures of the Old and New Testaments. Having selected and examined a variety of passages throughout the work, we are of opinion that it is executed with great accuracy as to the sense, and with as few grammatical and typographical errors as could have been expected in an undertaking of such magnitude. Being ourselves witnesses of the demand for this invaluable work, we rejoice in the present prospect of a surplus—hoping that it will prove as advantageous as it is honorable to the gentleman who has exerted himself to furnish it, at the evident risk of private fortune.

We are, gentlemen,

Your very respectful and humble servants,

(Signed)   William White,

George Duffield

Philadelphia, Sept. 10, 1782.

Hon. James Duane, Esq., *Chairman*, and the other honorable gentlemen of the committee of Congress on Mr. Aitken's memorial.

Whereupon, *Resolved*, That the United States, in Congress assembled, highly approve of the pious and laudable undertaking of Mr. Aitken, as subservient to the interests of religion, as well as an instance of the progress of the fine arts in this country; and, being satisfied from the above report of his care and accuracy in the execution of the work, they recommend this edition of the Bible to the inhabitants of the United States, and hereby authorize him to publish this recommendation in the manner he shall think proper.

Charles Thomson, *Secretary*

Bibles Presented to Congress

The American Bible Society published, in 1856, the following statement in connection with the presentation of a Bible to each House of Congress—

THE BIBLE IN CONGRESS.

A joint note was received in May last from the two chaplains of Congress, suggesting that our Board present a copy of the pulpit Bible for use in public worship at the Capitol. The suggestion was cheerfully complied with, and the following response received, showing, with a thousand other incidents, that, while we have no state-established religion, we are correctly styled a Christian nation—

Washington, May 19, 1856

Letter of the Vice President and Speaker

To the Board of Managers of the American Bible Society.
GENTLEMEN—We have the pleasure to acknowledge the receipt of an imperial quarto Bible for the use of Congress at the hands of your Secretary.

In behalf of Congress, we beg to tender to you our grateful thanks for this appropriate present, and to express the hope that the great truths contained in that sacred record may be impressed upon all our minds and hearts.

With sentiments of the highest respect and consideration, we have the honor to be

Your obedient servants,
John C. Breckinridge, *Pres. Sen.*
Wm. Pennington, *Speaker H. R.*

THE BIBLE AND THE FIRST CONGRESS.

The above article, coming from the officers of the present Congress, leads us to subjoin a brief account of the doings of the first Congress in regard to the same divine book, as given in Rev. Dr. Strickland's History of the American Bible Society—

"As early as the beginning of the last century, laws existed in some of the colonies requiring every family to be furnished with a Bible. This supply continued to be kept up by individual exertion until the meeting of the first Congress in 1777, one year after the Declaration of Independence. In the early formation of our government, those who looked upon the experiment with jealous eyes anticipated a speedy dissolution, from the fact that it made no provision for the establishment of religion. Although the legislative power of our country is prohibited from making laws prescribing and enforcing the observance of any particular faith or form of worship, yet it is equally powerless in prohibiting the free exercise thereof; while at the same time it extends its protecting ægis over the rights of conscience. The Government has never been unmindful of the great interests of religion, but has from the beginning adhered to and carried out the language of Washington, that religion and morality are indispensable supports of political existence and prosperity.'

"The Congress of 1777 answered a memorial on the subject of Bible-distribution in this country, by appointing a committee to advise as to the printing an edition of thirty thousand Bibles. The population of the country then was only about three millions, and all the Bibles in the entire world at that period did not exceed four millions. Thus it will be seen that its circulation in this and all other countries at that time was exceedingly limited.

"The report of the committee appointed by Congress forms one of the brightest epochs in the history of our republic, and sheds a clear and steady light over every subsequent eventful period. The public recognition of God in that act was of infinitely greater importance in giving stability to the times, securing the permanency of our institutions, than all the imposing and formidable array of legal enactments ever made for the establishment of religion.

"The committee, finding it difficult to procure the necessary material, such as paper and types, recommended Congress, 'the use of the Bible being so universal, and its importance so great,' to direct the Committee on Commerce to import, at the expense of Congress, twenty thousand English Bibles from Holland, Scotland, or elsewhere, into the different ports of the States of the Union. The report was adopted, and the importation ordered.

"In 1781, when, from the existence of the war, no English Bible could be imported, and no opinion could be formed how long the obstruction might continue, the subject of printing the Bible was again presented to Congress, and it was on motion referred to a committee of three.

"The committee, after giving the subject a careful investigation, recommended to Congress an edition printed by Robert Aitken, of Philadelphia; whereupon it was

"'*Resolved*, That the United States, in Congress assembled, highly approve the pious and laudable undertaking of Mr. Aitken, as subservient to the interests of religion; and, being satisfied of the care and accuracy of the execution of the work, recommend this edition to the inhabitants of the United States.'"

How interesting is a history of the early circulation of the Bible in this country! What moral sublimity in the fact, as it stands imperishably recorded and filed in the national archives! Who, in view of this fact, will call in question the assertion that this is a Bible nation? Who will charge the Government with indifference to religion, when the first Congress of the States assumed all the rights and performed all the duties of a Bible society long before such an institution had an existence?

This was the first Bible published in the English language having an American imprint. It was a small duodecimo, in two volumes, in a brevier type. The report of the committee and the resolution of Congress (sometimes called the Bible Congress) are reprinted on a leaf immediately following the title-page. The recommendation of Congress bore no fruit. Immediately after the publication of the work, peace was proclaimed—when it was found that Bibles could be imported from Great Britain cheaper than it was possible to print them here. Mr. Aitken, therefore, not obtaining a ready sale for his edition, which he had carried on with great difficulty, was nearly ruined by the undertaking. Previous to the Revolution and the publication of the edition of the Bible by Mr. Aitken, this country was supplied with Bibles in the English language chiefly from Great Britain.

Chancellor Kent, of New York, states the results and influence of the Bible on society as follows—

"The general diffusion of the Bible is the most effectual way to civilize and humanize mankind; to purify and exalt the general system of public morals; to give efficacy to the just precepts of international and municipal law; to enforce the observance of prudence, temperance, justice, and fortitude, and to improve all the relations of domestic and social life."

Chief-Justice Hornblower, of New Jersey, remarks as follows—

"Let this precious volume have its due influence on the hearts of men, and our liberties are safe, our country blessed, and the world happy. There is not a tie that unites us to our families, not a virtue that endears us to our country, not a hope that thrills our bosoms in the prospect of future happiness, that has not its foundation in this sacred book. It is the charter or charters—the palladium of liberty, —the standard of righteousness. Its divine influence can soften the heart of the tyrant—can break the rod of the oppressor, and exalt the humblest peasant to the dignified rank of an immortal being—an heir of eternal glory."

Resolutions of Congress to Prevent Officers of the Government from Attending Theatres, etc.

The following record, found in the Journals of Congress, October 12, 1778, shows their high appreciation of the morality of the Bible as a necessary qualification for the discharge of official public duties—

> Whereas true religion and good morals are the only solid foundations of public liberty and happiness:

Resolved, That it be, and it hereby is, earnestly recommended to the several States to take the most effectual measures for the encouragement thereof, and for the suppressing theatrical entertainments, horse-racing, gaming, and such other diversions as are productive of idleness, dissipation, and a general depravity of principles and manners.

Resolved, That all officers in the army of the United States be, and hereby are, strictly enjoined to see that the good and wholesome rules provided for the discountenancing of profaneness and vice, and the preservation of morals among the soldiers, are duly and punctually observed.

On the 16th of October, 1778, Congress passed the following act, as may be seen on their official journal of that date—

Whereas frequenting playhouses and theatrical entertainments has a fatal tendency to divert the minds of the people from a due attention to the means necessary for the defence of their country and the preservation of their liberties:

Resolved, That any person holding an office under the United States who shall act, promote, encourage, or attend such plays, be deemed unworthy to hold such office, and shall be accordingly dismissed.

In this place it is appropriate to notice, as a patriotic and Christian memorial, Independence Hall, in Philadelphia, where the patriots and statesmen sat in solemn council, and passed the Declaration of Independence and previous Christian acts, and made their solemn appeals to God. That old State-House still stands as a relic of the Revolution, and its associations and inspirations attract the American people to look upon its venerable form, to tread its rooms and halls, and to gaze upon the portraits of many of the men who acted a distinguished part in achieving our independence and in forming our civil institutions. It was from the steps of this temple of freedom that John Nixon, on the 8th of July, 1776, in the hearing of thousands, read the Declaration of Independence; and from the same spot Samuel Adams pronounced an oration on the great event, in which he said—

"Brethren and fellow-countrymen! If it was ever granted to mortals to trace the designs of Providence and to interpret its manifestations in favor of their cause, we may, with humility of soul, cry out, 'Not unto us, not unto us, but to thy name be praise.'"

The American people, as they look upon this consecrated temple of freedom, will re-echo the words of an American poet—

> "This is the sacred fane wherein assembled
>   The fearless champions on the side of right—
> Men at whose declaration empires trembled,
>   Moved by the truth's immortal might.
>
> "Here stood the patriot—one Union folding
>   The Eastern, Northern, Southern sage and seer,
> Within that living band which, truth upholding,
>   Proclaims each man his fellow's peer.
>
> "Here rose the anthem which all nations, hearing,
>   In loud response the echoes backward hurl'd:
> Reverberating still the ceaseless cheering,
>   Our continent repeats it to the world.
>
> "This is the hallow'd spot where, first unfurling,
>   Fair Freedom spread her blazing scroll of light;
> Here, from oppression's throne the tyrant hurling,
>   She stood supreme in majesty and might."

The most interesting and suggestive memorial in Independence Hall is the old State-House bell. "This bell," says Watson, in his "Annals of Philadelphia," "was imported from England in 1753, for the State-House; but, having met with some accident in the trial ringing after it was landed, it lost its tone received in the fatherland, and had to be conformed to ours by recasting. This was done under the direction of Isaac Norris, Esq., the then Speaker of the Colonial Assembly; and to him we are probably indebted, for the remarkable motto, so indicative of its future use, 'PROCLAIM LIBERTY THROUGHOUT ALL THE LAND UNTO ALL THE INHABITANTS THEREOF.' That it was adopted from the Scriptures (Lev. xxv. 10) may to many be still more impressive, as being also the voice of God, that great Arbiter by whose signal providences we afterwards attained to that 'liberty' and self-government which bid fair to emancipate our whole continent, and, in time, to influence and ameliorate the condition of the subjects of arbitrary government throughout the civilized world."

The ringing of this bell first announced to the citizens, who were anxiously waiting the result of the deliberations of Congress (which were at that time held with closed doors), that the Declaration of Independence had been decided upon; and then it was that the bell proclaimed the realization of the divine motto inscribed upon it some fifteen years previous.

> "That old bell is still seen by the patriot's eye,
> And he blesses it ever when journeying by;
> Long years have pass'd o'er it, and yet every soul
> Will thrill, in the night, to its wonderful roll;
> For it speaks in its belfry, when kiss'd by the blast,
> Like a glory-breathed tone from the mystical past.
> Long years shall roll o'er it, and yet every chime
> Shall unceasingly tell of an era sublime;
> Oh, yes! if the flame on our altars should pale,
>   Let its voice but be heard, and the freeman shall start
> To rekindle the fire, while he sees on the gale
>   All the stars and the stripes of the flag of his heart."
>
> William Ross Wallace

Address of Congress to the People

In an address to the inhabitants of the United States of America, by Congress, are found the following Christian sentiments and principles—

"America, without arms, ammunition, discipline, revenue, government, or ally, almost stripped of commerce, and in the weakness of youth as it were, with a 'staff and a sling' only, dared, 'in the name of the LORD OF HOSTS,' to engage a gigantic adversary, prepared at all points, boasting of his strength, and of whom even mighty warriors 'were greatly afraid.'

"As to inferior officers employed in the public service, we ANX-IOUSLY desire to call your most *vigilant* attention to their conduct with respect to every species of misbehavior, whether proceeding from ignorance, negligence, or fraud, and to the making of laws for inflicting exemplary punishment on all offenders of this kind.

"Your government being now established, and your ability to contend with your invaders ascertained, we have, on most mature deliberation, judged it indispensably necessary to call upon you for forty millions of dollars, &c.

"We are persuaded you will use all possible care to make the promotion of the general welfare interfere as little as may be with the care and comfort of individuals; but though the raising of these sums should press heavily on some of your constituents, yet the obligations we feel to your *venerable* CLERGY, the truly helpless widows and orphans, your most gallant, generous, meritorious officers and soldiers, the public faith, and the common weal, so irresistibly urge us to attempt the appreciation of your clemency, that we cannot withhold obedience to these authoritative declarations.

"On this subject we will only add, that, as the *rules of justice are most pleasing to our infinitely good and gracious Creator, and an adherence to them most likely to obtain his favor, so they will ever be found to be the best and safest maxims of human policy.*

"What nation ever engaged in such a contest, under such a complication of disadvantages, so soon surmounted many of them, and in so short a period of time had so certain a prospect of a speedy and happy conclusion? We will venture to pronounce that so remarkable an instance exists not in the annals of mankind. Encouraged by favors already received from Infinite Goodness, gratefully acknowledging them, earnestly imploring their continuance, constantly endeavoring to draw them down on your heads by an amendment of your lives and a conformity to the Divine will, humbly confiding in the protection so often and wonderfully experienced, vigorously employ the means placed by Providence in your hands for completing your labors.

"Effectually superintend the behavior of public officers, *diligently promote piety*, virtue, brotherly love, learning, frugality, and moderation; and may you be approved before Almighty God, worthy of these blessings we devoutly wish you to enjoy.

"Done in Congress, by unanimous consent, this twenty-sixth day of May, one thousand seven hundred and seventy-nine.

"John Jay, *President*

"Attest, Charles Thomson, *Secretary*."

Legislation on the Sabbath

The Sabbath, in its moral and political influences, was regarded by the Puritans and the Christian statesmen of the Revolution as an essential pillar of support to the civil edifice.

The Provincial Congress of Massachusetts, on the 15th of June, 1775, adopted the following, on the Sabbath—

"As it has pleased *Almighty God*, in his providence, to suffer the calamities of an unnatural war to take place among us, in consequence of our sinful declensions from him, and our great abuse of those invaluable blessings bestowed upon us; and as we have reason to fear, unless we become a penitent and reformed people, we shall feel still severer tokens of the Divine displeasure; and as the most effectual way to escape those desolating judgments which so evidently hang over us, and, if it may be, obtain the restoration of our former tranquillity, will be that we repent and return every one from his iniquities unto Him that correcteth us, which if we do in sincerity and truth, we have no reason to doubt but he will remove his judgments, cause our enemies to be at peace with us, and prosper the work of our hands.

Discourage All Dissipation

"And as among the prevailing sins of this day, which threaten the destruction of this land, we have reason to lament the frequent profanations of the *Lord's* day, or Christian *Sabbath*; many spending their time in idleness or sloth, others in diversions, and others in journeying, or business which is not necessary on that day; and, as we earnestly desire that a stop may be put to this great and prevailing evil, it is, therefore,

"*Resolved*, That it be recommended by this Congress to the people of all ranks and denominations throughout this colony, that they not only pay a religious regard to that day, and to the public worship of *God thereon, but that they also use their influence to discountenance and suppress any profanation thereof in others.*

"And it is further Resolved, That it be recommended to the ministers of the gospel to read this resolve to their several congregations, accompanied with such exhortations as they shall think proper.

"And whereas there is great danger that the profanation of the *Lord's* day will prevail in the camp, we earnestly recommend to all the officers not only to set a good example, but that they strictly require of their soldiers to keep up a religious regard to that day, and attend upon the public worship of *God* there, so far as may be consistent with other duties."

The Provincial Congress of Georgia, Thursday, July 6, 1775, adopted the following resolution—

10. That we will, in our several stations, encourage frugality, economy, and industry, and promote agriculture, arts, and the manufactures of *British* America. especially that of wool, and will discountenance and discourage every species of extravagance and dissipation, especially horse-racing, and every kind of gaming, cock-fighting, exhibition of shows, plays, and other expensive diversions and entertainments; and on the death of any relation or friend, none of us, or any of our families, shall go into any farther mourning dress than a black crape or ribbon on the arm or hat for gentlemen, and a black ribbon or necklace for ladies; and we will discontinue the giving of gloves and scarfs at funerals.

Continental Congress a Christian Body

These facts show the religious sentiments and make us acquainted with the religious feelings of the members of the Continental Congress. That body of statesmen paid respect to religion by system, on principle, and in their official acts. Their state papers do not merely contain general references to a superintending Providence and a supreme Creator and Governor of the world, but they usually contain sentiments unequivocally Christian. Their journals disclose various circumstances which indicate the personal interest taken by the members in the stated and occasional religious services.

"Thus our republic," said Mr. Giddings, in Congress, "was founded on religious truth, and it was thus far emphatically a religious government. It has ever been sustained by the religious sentiment of the nation, and it will only fail when this element shall be discarded by the people. The Philadelphia Convention (the Continental Congress) will be remembered in coming time as the first, in the history of political parties of our nation, to make religious truths the basis of its political action, and first to proclaim the rights of mankind as universal, to be enjoyed equally by princes and people, by rulers and the most humble. It was the first to proclaim the fatherhood of God and the brotherhood of man."

The Moral Ends of Government

The Continental Congress, in the foregoing acts, kept in view the true aims and ends of a civil government, as expressed by Rev. E. D. McMaster, D.D., in his inaugural address as President of the Miami University of Ohio. He says—

"According to the notions that perhaps generally prevail, the end of civil society and its governmental institutions is an end purely secular, and this even not the highest of that class of ends. Its object, as is supposed, is to prevent men from the invasion of each other's persons and estates, and, after that, according to the various theories of different political schools, more or less to regulate and promote the industrial pursuits and interests of the members of the community. Nothing can be more unworthy the dignity of the subject, or more untrue, than these low conceptions of the object of civil institutions. The highest end of a state and of its whole order is a moral end—that is, a religious end. It is that by a scrupulous respect in all its own legislation and administration at home, and in all its relations and intercourse with other nations abroad, to do right, by the equitable and vindicatory punishment of crime and the establishment of justice, it may inspire and cherish in its citizens *the love of righteousness*. It is thus a great moral institution, of high dignity and of mighty power, whose highest end is the development of man's moral nature and the forming of him to virtue in this respect, and ultimately in all the glory of God, whose ordinance it is."

11

State Constitutions During the Revolution—Christian Doctrines Incorporated in them as Fundamental Law

The State Constitutions of the Era of the Revolution

When a people assume the condition and dignity of a civil state, their first want and effort is a just Constitution of government. This accomplished, it affords the highest evidence of their progress in intelligence, liberty, and social order. But the constitution of every nation, if it secures great moral and political prosperity, must be enforced by sanctions which are higher and more authoritative than human parchments and laws. Their practical force and value must be derived from faith in God and the sanctions of the Divine law. Hence the men who have founded states on written constitutions have always resorted to religious sanctions to give practical power to their constitutions and to enforce the laws of the government. This great principle is coexistent in all governments, whether pagan or Christian. Every oath that is taken to support a constitution acknowledges the power and necessity of the sanctions of religion. It is an appeal to God in behalf of constitutional government—to give it authority, by making the legislation of conscience and accountability to God support and uphold the laws of the land.

View of De Witt Clinton

"The sanctions of the Divine law," says De Witt Clinton, in an address delivered before the American Bible Society, May, 1823, "supply all deficiencies, cover the whole area of human action, reach every case, punish every sin, and recompense every virtue. Its rewards and punishments are graduated with perfect justice, and its appeals to the hopes and fears of men are of the most potential character and transcendent influence. The codes of men and the laws of opinion and government derive a great portion of their weight from the influence of a future world. Justice cannot be administered without the sanction of truth; and the great security against perjury is the amenability of another state. The sanctions of religion compose the foundations of good government; and the ethics, doctrines, and examples furnished by Christ exhibit the best models for the laws of opinion."

View of Winthrop

"All societies of men," says Winthrop, a member of Congress, and Speaker of the House of Representatives in 1848, "must be governed in some way or other. The less they may have of stringent state government, the more they must have of individual self-government. The less they rely on public law or physical force, the more they must rely on private moral restraint. Men, in a word, must necessarily be controlled, either by a power within them or by a power without them; either by the word of God or by the strong arm of man; either by the Bible or by the bayonet. It may do for other countries and other governments to talk about the state supporting religion: here, under our free institutions, it is religion which must support the state."

Lord Bacon, in enumerating what he calls the four pillars of government, three of which are justice, counsel, and treasure, places religion as the first in order and importance, says—

"The reason why religion is universally and justly represented as essential to the prosperity of states, is not less obvious than the fact.

The object of government is to enforce among individuals the observance of the moral law, and states are prosperous in proportion as this object is attained. But the only effectual sanction to this law is the Christian religion. Hence a government which neglects the care of religion is guilty of the folly of promulgating laws unaccompanied with any adequate sanction of requiring the community to obey without presenting to their minds the motives that generally induce to a prompt and cheerful obedience. Under these circumstances, the only resource left to the public authorities is mere physical force; and experience has abundantly shown that this is wholly ineffectual, excepting as an aid and supplement, in particular cases, to the moral influences, which alone can be depended on for the preservation of the tranquillity and good order of society. There are persons, and even parties, who, at the very moment when the use of physical force as an engine of government is discredited and abandoned, seem to be laboring with a sort of frantic energy to destroy the influence of all the moral motives that can be substituted for it—more especially religion. I have said, and I repeat, that if while we abandon the use of physical force as an engine of maintaining order we should also discard the only valuable and effectual moral influence, and leave the individual to the undirected guidance of his own selfish passions, our institutions will be found to be impracticable, and society will fall into a state of dissolution."

Doctrines of Christianity
Incorporated Into All the State Constitutions

Such views were radical in the faith of the Puritans and of the statesmen of the Revolution, and they incorporated the fundamental doctrines of Christianity into their systems of government. The following facts found in the State Constitutions of the Revolution demonstrate the Christian life and character of our civil institutions.

The Constitution of Massachusetts

In 1780, inserted the following organic law on the subject of the Christian religion—

That as the happiness of a people, and the good order and preservation of civil government, *essentially depend upon piety, religion, and morality*, and as these cannot be generally diffused through a community *but by the institutions of the public worship of God*, and *of public instruction in piety, religion, and morality*: therefore, to promote their happiness and to secure the good order and preservation of their government, the people of this commonwealth have a right to invest their legislature with power to authorize and require, and *the legislature shall, from time to time, authorize and require,* the several towns, parishes, precincts, and other bodies politic, or religious societies, *to make suitable provision, at their own expense, for the institution of the public worship, and for the support and maintenance of public Protestant teachers of piety, religion, and morality,* in all cases where such provision shall not be made voluntarily; and the people of this commonwealth have also a right to, and do, invest their legislature with authority *to enjoin upon all their subjects an attendance upon the instructions of the public teachers aforesaid at stated times and seasons,* if there be any on whose instructions they can conscientiously attend."

And that "because a frequent recurrence to the fundamental principles of the Constitution, and a constant adherence to those of *piety, justice,* moderation, *temperance, industry,* and frugality, are *absolutely* necessary to preserve the advantage of liberty and to maintain a free government, the people ought consequently *to have a particular regard to all those principles in the choice of their officers and representatives; and they have a right to require of their lawgiver, and magistrates an exact and constant observance of them* in the formation and execution of all laws necessary for the good of the commonwealth." And that every person "chosen governor, lieutenant-governor, senator, or representative, and accepting the trust, *shall subscribe a solemn profession* THAT HE BELIEVES IN THE CHRISTIAN RELIGION, AND HAS A FIRM PERSUASION OF ITS TRUTH."

"I am clearly of opinion," said Mr. Webster, in the Convention of Massachusetts, in 1820, met to revise the Constitution, "that we should not strike out of the Constitution all recognition of the Christian religion. I am desirous, in so solemn a transaction as the establishment of a Constitution, that we should keep in it an expression of our respect and attachment to Christianity—not, indeed, to any of its peculiar forms, but to its general principles." Another part of the Constitution recognizes in the fullest manner the benefits which civil society derives from those Christian institutions which cherish piety, morality, and religion.

The Constitution of South Carolina

Adopted in 1778, declares Christianity to be the fundamental law of the State, in the following language—

> That all persons and religious societies who acknowledge that there is one God, and a future state of rewards and punishments, and that God is to be publicly worshipped, shall be tolerated. The Christian Protestant religion shall be deemed, and is hereby constituted and declared to be, the established religion of the State. That all denominations of Christian Protestants in this State, demeaning themselves peaceably and faithfully, shall enjoy equal religious and civil privileges.
>
> To accomplish this desirable purpose without injury to the religious property of those societies of Christians which are by law already incorporated for the purpose of religious worship, and to put it fully into the power of every other society of Christian Protestants, either already formed or hereafter to be formed, to obtain the like incorporation, it is hereby constituted, appointed, and declared that the respective societies of the Church of England, that are already formed in this State for the purpose of religious worship, shall continue incorporate and hold the religious property now in their possession. And that whenever fifteen or more male persons not under twenty-one years of age, professing the Christian Protestant religion, and agreeing to unite themselves in a society

for the purposes of religious worship, they shall (on complying with the terms hereinafter mentioned) be and be constituted a Church, and be esteemed and regarded in law as of the established religion of the State, and on a petition to the legislature shall be entitled to be incorporated and to enjoy equal privileges. That every society of Christians so formed shall give themselves a name or denomination, by which they shall be called and known in law, and all that associate with them for the purpose of worship shall be esteemed as belonging to the society so called; but that previous to the establishment and incorporation of the respective societies of every denomination as aforesaid, and in order to entitle them thereto, each society so petitioning shall have agreed to and subscribed in a book the five following articles—without which no agreement or union of men upon pretence of religion shall entitle them to be incorporated and esteemed as a church of the established religion of the State. (See Locke's Const., Arts. 97—100).

I. That there is one Eternal God, a future state of rewards and punishments.

II. That God is to be publicly worshipped.

III. That the Christian religion is the true religion.

IV. That the Holy Scriptures of the Old and New Testaments are of divine inspiration, and are the rule of faith and practice.

V. That it is lawful, and the duty of every man being thereunto called by those that govern, to bear witness to truth. That every inhabitant of this State, when called to make an appeal to God as a witness to truth, shall be permitted to do it in that way which is most agreeable to the dictates of his own conscience. And that the people of this State may forever enjoy the right of electing their own pastors or clergy, and, at the same time, that the State may have sufficient security for the due discharge of the pastoral office by those who shall be admitted to be clergymen, no person shall officiate as minister of any established church who shall not have been chosen by a majority of the society to which he shall minister, or by

persons appointed by the said majority to choose and procure a minister for them, nor until the minister so chosen
and appointed shall have made and subscribed the following
declaration, over and above the aforesaid five articles, *viz.*—

That he is determined, by God's grace, OUT OF THE HOLY
SCRIPTURES, to instruct the people committed to his charge,
and to teach nothing (as required of necessity to eternal salvation) but that which he shall be persuaded may be concluded
and proved from the Scriptures; that he will use both public
and private admonitions, as well to the sick as to the whole
within his cure, as need shall require and occasion shall be
given; and that he will be diligent in prayers, and in reading of
the Holy Scriptures, and in such studies as help to the knowledge of the same; that he will be diligent to frame and fashion
his own self and his family according to the doctrine of Christ,
and to make both himself and them, as much as in him lieth,
wholesome examples and patterns to the flock of Christ; that
he will maintain and set forward, as much as he can, quietness,
peace, and love among all the people, and especially among
those who are or shall be committed to his charge.

No person shall disturb or molest any religious assembly,
nor shall use any reproachful, railing, or abusive language
against any Church, that being the certain way of disturbing
the peace, and of hindering the conversion of any to the truth,
by engaging them in quarrels and animosities, to the hatred
of the professors, and that profession which otherwise they
might be brought to assent to. No person whatsoever shall
speak any thing in their religious assembly irreverently or se-
ditiously of the government of the State. No person shall by
law be obliged to pay towards the maintenance and support
of a religious worship that he does not freely join in or has not
voluntarily engaged to support; but the churches, chapels,
parsonages, glebes, and all other property now belonging to
any societies of the Church of England, or any other religious
societies, shall remain and be secured to them forever.

They should choose by ballot from among themselves,
or from the people at large, a governor and commander-in-

chief, a lieutenant-governor, and privy council, *all of the Protestant religion*; that no person should be eligible to a seat in the Senate *unless he be of the Protestant religion*; that no person should be eligible to sit in the House of Representatives *unless he be of the Protestant religion*.

Virginia

In her organic charter and legislative acts, affirms the truth of the Christian system in terms an follows—

By an act of the Assembly in 1705, it was declared, that if any person brought up in the Christian religion denies the being of a God or the Trinity, or asserts that there are more Gods than one, or denies the Christian religion to be true, or the Scriptures to be of divine authority, he is punishable, on the first offence by incapacity to hold office or employment, ecclesiastical, civil, or military; on the second, by disability to sue, to take any gift or legacy, to be guardian, executor, or administrator, and by three years' imprisonment without bail.

This act may be found in Jefferson's Works, vol. viii. p. 399. This law, opposed to the spirit of Christianity while affirming its divinity, was abolished in 1786 by the following—

> ACT FOR ESTABLISHING RELIGIOUS FREEDOM
> Well aware that Almighty God hath created the mind free; that all attempts to influence it by temporal punishments or burdens, or by civil incapacitations, tend not only to beget habits of hypocrisy and meanness, and are a departure from the plan of the Author of our Religion, who, being Lord both of the body and mind, yet chose not to propagate it by coercion on either, as was in his almighty power to do:
> Be it, therefore, enacted by the General Assembly, That no man shall be compelled to frequent or support any religious worship, place, or ministry, whatsoever, nor shall be enforced, restrained, molested, or burthened in his body or goods, nor shall otherwise suffer, on account of his religious opinions or belief; but that all men shall be free to profess and

by argument to maintain their opinions in matters of religion, and that the same shall in no wise diminish, enlarge, or affect their civil capacities.

This act, passed under the auspices of Mr. Jefferson, he regarded as one of the best works of his life.

The Declaration of Rights, which passed unanimously the Virginia Legislature, June 12, 1776, affirmed that—

> Its free government could be preserved but by a firm adherence to justice, moderation, benevolence, frugality, and virtue, and by frequent recurrence to fundamental principles and the manner of discharging it. Religion is the duty we owe our Creator, and can be directed only by reason, not by force and violence; and therefore all men are equally entitled to the free exercise of it according to the dictates of conscience; and it is the mutual duty of all to practise Christian forbearance, love and charity towards each other.

The following ancient laws of Virginia show the historic fact of the incorporation of the Christian religion and its ordinances into the civil government of that Commonwealth. In 1662 it was enacted that—

> Every person who should refuse to have his child baptized by a lawful minister shall be amerced two thousand pounds of tobacco, half to be paid to the parish, half to the informer.
>
> The whole liturgy of the Church of England shall be thoroughly read at church, or chapel, every Sunday; and the canons for divine service duly observed.
>
> Church-wardens shall present at the county court, twice every year, in December and April, such misdemeanors of swearing, drunkenness, fornication, &c. as by their own knowledge, or common fame, have been committed during their being church-wardens.
>
> Enacted that the Lord's Day be kept holy, and no journeys be made on that day, unless upon necessity. And all persons inhabiting in this country, having no lawful excuse, shall, ev-

ery Sunday, resort to the parish church or chapel, and there abide orderly during the common prayer, preaching, and divine service, upon the penalty of being fined fifty pounds of tobacco by the county court.

The 27th of August 1668 appointed for a day of humiliation, fasting, and prayer, to implore God's mercy: if any person be found upon that day gaming, drinking, or working (works of necessity excepted), upon presentment by church-wardens and proof, he shall be fined one hundred pounds of tobacco, half to the informer, and half to the poor of the parish.

The Constitution of Pennsylvania

Adopted in 1776, declares that the Legislature shall consist of "persons most noted for wisdom and virtue," and that every member should subscribe the following declaration—

I do believe in one God, the Creator and Governor of the universe, the Rewarder of the good, and the Punisher of the wicked; and I acknowledge the Scriptures of the Old and New Testaments to be given by inspiration.

The Constitution of North Carolina

Bearing date 1776, declares—

That no person who should deny the being of a God, or the truth of the Protestant religion, or the divine authority of either the Old or New Testaments, or who should hold religious principles incompatible with the freedom and safety of the State, should be capable of holding any office or place of trust in the civil government of this State.

Delaware

In her first Constitution, formed during the Revolution, made the following declaration—

That every citizen who should be chosen a member of either house of the Legislature, or appointed to any other office, should be required to subscribe to the following declaration—"I do profess faith in God the Father, and in the Lord Jesus Christ his only Son, and in the Holy Ghost, one God and blessed for evermore; and I do acknowledge the Holy Scriptures of the Old and New Testaments to be given by divine inspiration."

Maryland

Formed a State Constitution in 1776, and the Declaration of Rights (Art. XIX) says—

> That as it is the duty of every man to worship God in such manner as he thinks most acceptable to him, all persons professing the Christian religion are equally entitled to protection in their religious liberty.
> And (in Art. XXXV) "That no other qualification ought to be required on admission to any office of trust or profit than such oath of support and fidelity to this State, and such oath of office, as shall be directed by this Constitution or the Legislature of this State, *and a declaration of belief in the Christian religion.*"

The Constitution also authorized the Legislature "to lay a general tax for the support of the Christian religion."

New Jersey

In her Constitution formed in 1776, declares—

> That there shall be no establishment of any one religious sect in this province in preference to another, and that no Protestant inhabitant of this colony shall be denied the enjoyment of any civil right on account of his religious principles; but that all persons professing a belief in the faith of any Protes-

tant sect, and who should demean himself peaceably under the government, should be capable of being elected unto any office of profit or trust, or of being a member of either branch of the Legislature.

The following instructions from the Legislature of New Jersey to its delegates in Congress in 1777 will exhibit the high Christian sentiments of the men who directed the civil and military concerns of the Revolution. Among the delegates were John Witherspoon and Elias Boudinot. The Legislature instructs as follows—

> 1. We hope you will habitually bear in mind that the success of the great cause in which the United States are engaged depends upon the favor and blessing of Almighty God; and therefore you will neglect nothing which is competent to the Assembly of the States for promoting *piety* and *good morals* among the people at large. But especially we desire that you may give attention to this circumstance in the government of the army, taking care that such of the articles of war as forbid profaneness, riot, and debauchery be observed and enforced with all due strictness and severity. This, we apprehend, is absolutely necessary for the encouragement and maintenance of good discipline, and will be the means of recruiting the army with men of credit and principle—an object ardently to be wished, but not to be expected if the warmest friends of their country should be deterred from sending their sons and connections into the service, lest they should be tainted with impious and immoral notions and contract vicious habits.

New Hampshire

Formed a State Constitution in 1776, and in it declares—

> That morality and piety, rightly grounded on evangelical principles, would give the best and greatest security to government, and would lay in the hearts of men the strongest obligation to due subjection; and that the knowledge of these was most

likely to be propagated by the institution of the public worship of the Deity and instruction in morality and religion.

The Constitution of the same State in 1792 empowered the Legislature to adopt measures "for the support and maintenance of public Protestant teachers of piety, religion, and morality."

The province of New Hampshire, in a convention composed of one hundred and forty-four deputies appointed by the various towns in the province aforesaid, after resolving "that we heartily approve of the proceedings of the late grand Continental Congress," passed the following—

> Lastly, we earnestly entreat you, at this time of tribulation and distress, when your enemies are urging you to despair, when every scene around is full of gloom and horror, that, in imitation of your pious forefathers, you implore the divine Being, who alone is able to deliver you from your present unhappy and distressing situation, to espouse your righteous cause, secure your liberties, and fix them on a firm and lasting basis.

The Constitution of Georgia,

Adopted in 1777, declares that "all the members of the Legislature shall be of the Protestant religion."

The Constitution of Vermont

Declares that—

> Every sect or denomination of Christians ought to observe the Sabbath or Lord's Day, and keep up some sort of religious worship, which to them shall seem most agreeable to the revealed will of God.

Connecticut

In Part 7, sec. 1 of her Constitution, declared that—

It being the duty of all men to worship the Supreme Being, the great Creator and Preserver of the Universe, and their right to render that worship in the mode most consistent with the dictates of their consciences, no person shall, by law, be compelled to join or support, nor be classed with or associated to, any congregation, church, or religious association. But every person now belonging to such congregation, church, or religious association shall remain a member thereof, until he shall have separated himself therefrom, in the manner hereinafter provided. And each and every society or denomination of Christians in this State shall have and enjoy the same and equal powers, rights, and privileges, and shall have power and authority to support and maintain the ministers or teachers of their respective denominations, and to build and repair houses for public worship, by a tax on the members of any such society only, to be laid by a major vote of the legal voters assembled at any society meeting, warned and held according to law, or in any other manner.

The Charter of Rhode Island

Granted by Charles II., in 1682—83, and which continued to be the Constitution of that Commonwealth till 1843, says—

The object of the colonists is to pursue, with peace and loyal minds, their sober, serious, and religious intentions of godly edifying themselves and one another in the holy Christian faith and worship, together with the gaining over and conversion of the poor ignorant Indian natives to the sincere profession and obedience of the same faith and worship.

The Constitution of New York

Though less full and explicit on the subject than those of other States, yet contains an organic act recognizing the Christian religion. The Constitution of 1777 has the following articles, the same as those inserted in the Constitution formed in 1821—

And *Whereas* we are required, by the benevolent principles of rational liberty, not only to expel civil tyranny, but also to guard against that spiritual oppression and intolerance wherewith the bigotry and ambition of weak and wicked priests and princes have scourged mankind: this Convention doth further, in the name and by the authority of the good people of this State, ORDAIN, DETERMINE, and DECLARE that the free exercise and enjoyment of religious profession and worship, without discrimination or preference, shall forever hereafter be allowed within this State to all mankind: *Provided*, That the liberty of conscience hereby granted shall not be so construed as to excuse acts of licentiousness or justify practices inconsistent with the peace or safety of this State.

And *Whereas* the ministers of the gospel are, by their profession, dedicated to the service of God and the cure of souls, and ought not to be diverted from the great duties of their functions: therefore, no minister of the gospel, or priest of any denomination whatsoever, shall, at any time hereafter, under any pretence or description whatever, be eligible to or capable of holding any civil or military office or place within this State.

The Present State Constitutions Christian

An examination of the present Constitutions of the various States, now existing, will show that the Christian religion and its institutions are recognized as the religion of the Government and the nation.

The recognitions of Christianity in the State Constitutions are of three kinds. 1. These instruments are usually dated in the *year of our Lord*. 2. Nearly all of them refer to the observance of Sunday by the Chief Executive Magistrate, in the same way in which such observance is referred to in the Constitution of the United States. 3. All the State Constitutions, or legislation under them, guard with vigilance the religious observance of the Christian Sabbath, and punish, with greater or less severity, all unlawful violation of the day. 4. Definite constitutional provisions not only recognizing the Christian religion, but affording it countenance, encouragements and protection.

"In perusing the thirty-four Constitutions of the United States, we find all of them recognizing Christianity as the well-known and well-established religion of the communities whose legal, civil, and political foundations they are. The terms of this recognition are more or less distinct in the Constitutions of the different States; but they exist in all of them. The reason why any degree of indistinctness exists in any of them, unquestionably, is that at their formation it never came into the minds of the framers to suppose that the existence of Christianity as the religion of their communities could ever admit of a question. Nearly all these Constitutions recognize the customary observance of Sunday; and a suitable observance of this day includes a performance of all the peculiar duties of the Christian faith. The Constitution of Vermont declares that 'every sect or denomination of Christians ought to observe the Sabbath or Lord's Day, and keep up some sort of religious worship, which to them shall seem most agreeable to the revealed will of God.' The Constitutions of Massachusetts and Maryland are among those which do not prescribe the observance of Sunday: yet the former declares it to be 'the right, as well as the duty, of all men in society, publicly and at stated seasons to worship the Supreme Being, the great Creator and Preserver of the universe;' and the latter requires every person appointed to any office of profit or trust to 'subscribe a declaration of his belief in the Christian religion.' Two of them concur in the sentiment that 'morality and piety, rightly grounded on evangelical principles, will be the best and greatest security to government; and that the knowledge of these is most likely to be propagated through a society by the institution of the public worship of the Deity, and of public instruction in morality and religion.' Only a small part of what the Constitutions of the States contain in regard to the Christian religion is here cited. At the same time, they all grant the free exercise and enjoyment of religious profession and worship, with some slight discriminations, to all mankind. The principle obtained by the foregoing inductive examination of our State Constitutions is this —THE PEOPLE OF THE UNITED STATES HAVE RETAINED THE CHRISTIAN RELIGION AS THE FOUNDATION OF THEIR CIVIL, LEGAL, AND POLITICAL INSTITUTIONS; WHILE THEY HAVE REFUSED TO CONTINUE A LEGAL PREFERENCE TO ANY ONE OF ITS FORMS OVER ANY OTHER."

Legislation of New York on the Sabbath

In 1838, the Legislature of New York, in a report from the Committee on Petitions, "praying a repeal of the laws for the observance of the Sabbath," by a vote nearly unanimous rejected the petition, and declared that—

> In all countries, some kind of religion or other has existed in all ages. No people on the face of the globe are without a prevailing national religion. Magistrates have sought in many countries to strengthen civil government by an alliance with some particular religion and an intolerant exclusion of all others. But those who have wielded this formidable power have rendered it a rival instead of an auxiliary to the public welfare—a fetter instead of a protection to the rights of conscience. With us it is wisely ordered that no one religion shall be established by law, but that all persons shall be left free in their choice and in their mode of worship. Still, *this is a Christian nation.* Ninety-nine hundredths, if not a larger proportion, of our whole population, believe in the general doctrines of the Christian religion. Our Government depends for its being on the virtue of the people—on that virtue that has its foundation in the morality of the Christian religion; and that religion is the common and prevailing faith of the people. There are, it is true, exceptions to this belief; but general laws are not made for excepted cases. There are to be found, here and there, the world over, individuals who entertain opinions hostile to the common sense of mankind on subjects of honesty, humanity, and decency; but it would be a kind of republicanism with which we are not acquainted in this country, which would require the great mass of mankind to yield to and be governed by this few.
>
> It is quite unnecessary to enter into a detailed review of all the evidences that Christianity is the common creed of this nation. We know it, and we feel it, as we know and feel any other unquestioned and admitted truth; the evidence is all around us, and before us, and with us. We know, too, that the

exceptions to this general belief are rare—so very rare that they are sufficient only, like other exceptions, to prove a general rule.

Provincial Congress of New York

The following papers reflect the Christian tone of the civil government and people of New York during the era of the Revolution—

DIE SATURNII, 9 HO. A.M., JULY 8, 1775.
The Continental congress having recommended it to the inhabitants of the Colonies to keep the twentieth day of *July* instant, 1775, as a day of fasting and prayer, this Congress does strictly enjoin all persons in this colony religiously to observe the said recommendation. And we, being taught by that holy religion, declared by the merciful *Jesus* and sealed by his blood, that we ought to acknowledge the hand of *God* in all public calamities, and being thoroughly convinced that the Great Disposer of events regardeth the hearts of his creatures, do most earnestly recommend it to all men to conform themselves to the pure dictates of Christianity, and by deep repentance, and sincere amendment of their lives, implore of our heavenly Father that favor and protection which he alone can give.

Its Proclamation

COMMITTEE-CHAMBER, NEW YORK, MAY, 1776.
Whereas the honorable Continental Congress have appointed and earnestly recommend "that the 17th inst. (being to-morrow) be observed by the United Colonies as a day of humiliation, fasting, and prayer, that we may with united hearts confess and bewail our manifold sins and transgressions against *God*, and, by a sincere repentance and amendment of life, as a people, appease his righteous displeasure against us, humbly imploring his assistance to frustrate the

cruel purposes of our unnatural enemies, and, by inclining their hearts to justice and peace, prevent the further effusion of human blood; but if, continuing deaf to the voice of reason and humanity, and inflexibly bent on desolation and war, they constrain us to repel their hostile invasions by open resistance, that it may please the Lord of hosts, the God of armies, to animate our officers and soldiers with invincible fortitude, to guard and protect them in the day of battle, and to crown the Continental armies, by sea and land, with victory and success; that he may bless all our representatives in General Congress, Provincial Congress, Conventions, and Committees; preserve and strengthen their union, give wisdom and stability to their councils, and direct the most efficient measures for establishing the rights of *America* on the most honorable and permanent basis; that he would be graciously pleased to bless all the people in these colonies with health and plenty, and grant that a spirit of incorruptible patriotism and of pure and undefiled religion may universally prevail, and that this continent may be speedily restored to the blessings of peace and liberty, and enabled to transmit them inviolate to the latest posterity." It is therefore expected that all the inhabitants of this city and county do, on the morrow, abstain from all and every kind of servile labor, business, and employment, and attend upon divine service in public, which will be performed in all churches in this city; that no persons (but such as are in the Continental service, whose business may require it) will be permitted to cross the ferries, ride or walk out of town, or about the streets, for amusement or diversion; and that all parents and masters will be careful to restrain their children from playing and straggling about this city on the ensuing day, which ought to be, and we trust will be, regarded as the most solemn day this devoted continent has ever yet beheld.

A true copy from the minutes. Published by order of the Committee,

Joseph Winter, *Secretary.*

General Court of Massachusetts

The following extracts from a proclamation issued by the Great and General Court of Massachusetts Bay in January, 1776, exhibit the high Christian character of the government of that Commonwealth—

> As the happiness of the people is the sole end of government, so the consent of the people is the only foundation of it, in reason, morality, and the natural fitness of things. And therefore every act of government, every exercise of sovereignty, against or without the consent of the people, is injustice, usurpation, and tyranny.
>
> It is a maxim of every government that there must exist somewhere a supreme, sovereign, absolute, and uncontrollable power; but this power resides always in the body of the people, and it never was or can be delegated to one man or a few—the great Creator having never given to men a right to invest authority over them unlimited either in duration or degree.
>
> When kings, ministers, governors, or legislators, therefore, instead of exercising the powers intrusted to them according to the principles, forms, and propositions stated by the constitution and established by the original compact, prostitute those powers to the purposes of oppression—to subvert instead of supporting a free constitution—to destroy instead of preserving the lives, liberties, and properties of the people—they are no longer to be deemed magistrates vested with a sacred character, but become public enemies, and ought to be resisted.
>
> The present generation may be congratulated on the acquisition of a form of government more immediately, in all its branches, under the influence and control of the people, and therefore more free and happy than was enjoyed by their ancestors. But, as a government so popular can be supported only by universal knowledge and virtue in the body of the people, it is the duty of all ranks to promote the means of education for the rising generation, as well as true religion, purity of manners, and integrity of life, among all orders and degrees.

That piety and virtue; which alone can secure the freedom of any people, may be encouraged, and vice and immorality suppressed, the Great and General Court have thought fit to issue this proclamation, commanding and enjoining it upon the good people of this colony that they lead sober, religious, and peaceable lives, avoiding all blasphemies, contempt of the Holy Scriptures and of the Lord's Day, and all other crimes and misdeameanors, all debauchery, profaneness, corruption, revelry, all riotous and tumultuous proceedings, and all immoralities whatsoever; and that they decently and reverently attend the public worship of God, at all times acknowledging with gratitude his merciful interposition in their behalf, devoutly confiding in him as the God of armies, by whose favor and protection alone they may hope for success in their present conflict.

And all judges, justices, sheriffs, grand jurors, tithing-men, and all other civil officers within this colony, are hereby strictly enjoined and commanded that they contribute all in their power, by their example, towards a general reformation of manners, and that they bring to condign punishment every person who shall commit any of the crimes or misdemeanors aforesaid, or that shall be guilty of any immoralities whatsoever; and that they use their utmost endeavors to have the resolves of the Congress and the good and wholesome laws of this colony duly carried into execution.

And as ministers of the gospel within this colony have, during the late relaxation of the powers of civil government, exerted themselves for our safety, it is hereby recommended to them still to continue their virtuous labors for the good of the people, inculcating by their public ministry and private example the necessity of religion, morality, and good order.

Ordered, That the foregoing proclamation be read at the opening of every superior court of judicature, &c. and inferior court of common pleas and court of general sessions for the peace within this colony, by their respective clerks, and at the annual town meetings, in March, in each town. And it is hereby recommended to the several ministers of the gospel throughout this colony to read the same in their respective assemblies, on the Lord's Day next after receiving, immediately after divine service.

By order of the General Court.

In Council, January 19, 1776.

In the House of Representatives, January 23, 1776.

Address to the People
GOD SAVE THE PEOPLE!

In January, 1777, the Legislature of the State of Massachusetts Bay addressed to the people, through civil officers and Christian ministers, a paper on the great conflict then in progress, which, after presenting the condition of the country, closes in these words—

> We, therefore, for the sake of religion, for the enjoyment. whereof your ancestors fled to this country, for the sake of your laws and future felicity, entreat you to act vigorously and firmly in this critical condition of your country. And we doubt not but that your humble exertions, under the smiles of Heaven, will insure that success and freedom due to the wise man and patriot.
>
> Above all, we earnestly exhort you to contribute all within your power to the encouragement of those virtues for which the Supreme Being has declared that he will bestow his blessing upon a nation, and to the discouragement of those vices for which he overturns kingdoms in his wrath; and that at all proper times and seasons you seek to him, by prayer and supplication, for deliverance from the calamities of war, duly considering that, without his powerful aid and gracious interposition, all your endeavors must prove abortive and vain.

Proclamation

The Christian views of the people and government of the colony of Massachusetts are further disclosed by the following proclamations—

PROVINCIAL CONGRESS, CONCORD, MASS.,
SATURDAY, APRIL 15, 1775, A.D.

Whereas it hath pleased the righteous Sovereign of the universe, in just indignation against the sins of a people long blessed with inestimable privileges, civil and religious, to suffer the plots of wicked men on both sides of the Atlantic, who for many years have incessantly labored to sap the foundation of our public liberties, so far to succeed that we see the New England colonies reduced to the ungracious alternative of a tame submission to a state of absolute vassalage to the will of a despotic minister, or of preparing themselves to defend at the hazard of their lives the inalienable rights of themselves and posterity against the avowed hostilities of their parent state, who openly threaten to wrest them from their hands by fire and sword.

In circumstances dark as these, it becomes us, as men and Christians, to reflect that, whilst every prudent measure should be taken to ward off the impending judgment, or to prepare to act in a proper manner under them when they come, at the same time, all confidence must be withheld from the means we use, and repose only on *that God* who rules in the armies of heaven, and without whose blessing the best human counsels are but foolishness, and all created power vanity.

It is the happiness of the church, that when the powers of earth and hell are combined against it, and those who should be nursing fathers become its persecutors, then the Throne of Grace is of the easiest access, and its appeal thither is graciously invited by that Father of Mercies who has assured it that "when his children ask bread, he will not give them a stone." Therefore, in compliance with the laudable practice of the people of God in all ages, with humble regard to the steps of Divine Providence towards this oppressed, threatened, and endangered people, and especially in obedience to the command of Heaven, that binds us to call on him in the day of trouble:

Resolved, That it be, and hereby is, recommended to the good people of this colony, of all denominations, that *Thursday*, the eleventh day of *May* next, be set apart as a day of public humiliation, fasting, and prayer; that a total abstinence from servile labor and recreation be observed, and all their religious assemblies solemnly convened, to humble themselves before *God* under the heavy judgments felt and feared; to confess the sins they have committed; to implore the forgiveness of all our transgressions; a spirit of repentance and reformation; and a blessing on the husbandry, manufactures, and other lawful employments of this people; and especially that the union of the *American colonies*, in defence of their rights (for which hitherto we desire to thank *Almighty God*) may be preserved and confirmed; that the Provincial, and especially the Continental, Congresses, may be directed to such measures as *God* will countenance; that the people of *Great Britain* and their rulers may have their eyes opened to discern the things that make for the peace of the nation and all its connections; and that *America* may soon behold a gracious interposition of Heaven for the redress of her many grievances, the restoration of all her invaded liberties, and their security to the latest generations.

Ordered, That the foregoing be copied, authenticated, and sent to all the religious assemblies in this colony.

Watertown, Nov. 20.

A Proclamation for a Public Thanksgiving

Although, in consequence of the unnatural, cruel, and barbarous measures adopted and pursued by the British administration, great and distressing calamities are brought upon our distressed country, and in this colony in particular we feel the dreadful effects of a *civil war*, by which America is stained with the blood of her valiant sons, who have bravely fallen in the laudable defence of our rights and privileges; our capital, once the seat of justice, opulence, and virtue, is unjustly wrested from its proper owners, who are obliged to flee from the iron hand of tyranny, or held in the unrelenting arms of oppression; our seaports greatly distressed, and towns burnt by the foes who have acted the part of barbarous incendiaries;

and although the wise and holy Governor of the world has, in his righteous providence, sent droughts into this colony, and wasting sickness into many of our towns; yet we have the greatest reasons to adore and praise the Supreme Disposer of all events, who deals infinitely better with us than we deserve, and amidst all his judgments hath remembered mercy, by causing the voice of health again to be heard amongst us; instead of famine, affording to an ungrateful people a competency of the necessaries and comforts of life; in remarkably protecting and preserving our troops when in apparent danger, while our *enemies*, with all their boasted skill and strength, have met with *loss*, *disappointment*, and *defeat*; and, in the course of his good providence, the Father of all Mercies hath bestowed upon us many other favors which call for our grateful acknowledgments:

Therefore, We have thought fit, with the advice of the Council and House of Representatives, to appoint Thursday, the 23d of November instant, to be observed throughout this colony as a day of public *thanksgiving*; hereby calling upon ministers and people to meet for religious worship on the said day, and *devoutly* to offer up their unfeigned praise to Almighty God, the source and benevolent bestower of all good, for his affording the necessary means of subsistence, though our commerce has been prevented and the supplies from the fishery denied us; that the lives of our officers and soldiers have been so remarkably preserved, while our enemies have fallen before them; that the vigorous efforts which have been made to excite the savage vengeance of the wilderness and to rouse the Indians in arms, that an unavoidable destruction might come upon our frontier, have been almost miraculously defeated; that our unnatural enemies, instead of ravaging the country with uncontrolled sway, are confined within such narrow limits, to their own mortification and distress, environed by an *American* army, *brave* and *determined*; and that our rights and privileges, both civil and religious, are so far preserved to us, notwithstanding all efforts to deprive us of them.

And to offer up humble and fervent prayers to Almighty God for the whole British empire, especially for the United

American Colonies; that he would bless our civil rulers, and lead them into wise and prudent measures at this dark and difficult day; that he would endow our General Court with all that wisdom which is profitable to direct; that he would graciously smile upon our endeavors to restore peace, preserve our rights and privileges and hand them down to posterity; that he would grant wisdom to the American Congress equal to their important station; that he would direct the generals and the American armies, wherever employed, and give them success and victory; that he would preserve and strengthen the hands of the *United Colonies*; that he would pour his spirit upon all orders of men through the land, and bring us to a hearty repentance and reformation, and purify and sanctify all his churches, and make ours Emanuel's land; that he would spread the knowledge of the Redeemer throughout the whole earth, and fill the world with his glory. And all servile labor is forbidden on this day.

Given under our hands, at the Council-Chamber at Watertown, the fourth day of November, in the year of our Lord one thousand seven hundred and seventy-five.

By their Honors' command.

James Otis.   Percy Morton, *Dep. Secy.*

God Save the People!

12

The Federal Constitution a Christian Instrument

Federal Constitution

By a Constitution," says Rawle, "we mean the principles on which the government is formed and conducted.

"On the voluntary association of men in sufficient numbers to form a political community, the first step to be taken for their own security and happiness is to agree on the terms on which they are to be united and to act. They form a Constitution, or plan of government, suited to their character, their exigencies, and their future prospects. They agree that it shall be the supreme rule of obligation among them. This is the pure and genuine source of a Constitution in the republican form.

"Vattel justly observes that the perfection of a state and its aptitude to fulfil the ends proposed by society depend on its Constitution. The first duty to itself is to form the best Constitution possible, and one most suited to its circumstances, and thus it lays the foundation of its safety, permanency, and happiness.

"The history of man does not present a more illustrious monument of human invention, sound political principles, and judicious combinations, than the Constitution of the United States. It is deemed to approach as near to perfection as any that have ever been formed."

The framers of the Constitution of the United States profoundly felt the magnitude and solemnity of their work. The Revolution had been won, with all its splendid results and animating hopes. The Articles of the old Confederation had proven too weak for the ends of a strong government, and fears pervaded the minds of public men and the people that the objects for which they had labored would be lost. Under these circumstances, "it is the duty," said Hamilton, "of all those who have the welfare of the community at heart, to unite their efforts to direct the attention of the people to the true source of the public disorders—the want of an EFFICIENT GENERAL GOVERNMENT—and to impress upon them this conviction, that these States, to be happy, must have a stronger bond of union, and a CONFEDERATION capable of drawing forth the resources of the country." Accordingly, on the 30th of June, 1783, Congress passed a series of resolutions setting forth the defects of the old Confederate Government, and concluded with the following—

His Resolution in Congress to Call a Convention

Whereas, it is essential to the happiness and security of these States that their union should be established on the most solid foundations; and it is manifest that this desirable object cannot be effected but by a government capable, both in peace and war, of making every member of the Union contribute in just proportion to the common necessities, and of combining and directing the forces and wills of the several parts to a general end; to which purposes, in the opinion of Congress, the present Confederation is altogether inadequate;

And Whereas, on the spirit which may direct the councils and measures of these States, at the present juncture, may depend their future safety and welfare; Congress conceive it to be their duty freely to state to their constituents the defects which, by experience, have been discovered in the present plan of the Federal Union, and solemnly to call their attention to a revisal and amendment of the same;

Therefore, *Resolved*, That it be earnestly recommended to the several States to appoint a convention to meet at on the

_____ day of _____, with full powers to revise the Confederation, and to adjust and propose such alterations as to them may appear necessary, to be finally approved or rejected by the States respectively, and that a committee of _____ be appointed to prepare an address upon the subject.

Recommendation of Virginia

The foregoing action of Congress was based on the recommendation of the Legislature of Virginia, who "proposed a convention of commissioners from all the States, for the purpose of taking into consideration the state of trade, and the propriety of a uniform system of commercial relations, for their permanent harmony and common interest. Pursuant to this proposal, commissioners were appointed by five States, who met at Annapolis in September, 1786. They framed a report to be laid before the Continental Congress, advising the latter to call a general convention of commissioners from all the States, to meet in Philadelphia in May, 1787, for a more effectual revision of the Articles of Confederation. Congress adopted the recommendation of the report, and in February, 1787, passed a resolution for the assembling a convention accordingly."

Virginia, in an act of her Assembly appointing her delegates and urging the other States to meet in general convention, says—

Convention Called

The crisis has arrived at which the good people of America are to decide the solemn question whether they will, by wise and magnanimous efforts, reap the just fruits which they have so gloriously acquired, and of that Union which they have cemented with so much of their common blood, or whether, by giving way to unmanly jealousies and prejudices, or to partial and transitory interests, they will renounce the auspicious blessings prepared for them by the Revolution, and furnish to its enemies an eventual triumph over those by whose virtue and valor it has been accomplished.

The convention accordingly met in Philadelphia, on May 14, 1787, and, after four months of solemn deliberation, the Federal Constitution was formed, and sent to the States and the people for ratification. After very thorough discussion before the people, it was adopted, and went into practical operation.

Character of Its Members

"It was a most fortunate thing for America," says Curtis, in his "History of the Constitution," "that the Revolutionary age, with its hardships, its trials, and its mistakes, had formed a body of statesmen capable of framing for it a durable Constitution. The leading persons in the convention which formed the Constitution had been actors, in civil or military life, in the scenes of the Revolution. In these scenes their characters as American statesmen had been formed. When the condition of the country had fully revealed the incapacity of the government to provide for its wants, these men were naturally looked to to construct a system to save it from anarchy; and their great capacities, their high disinterested purposes, their freedom from all fanaticism and illiberality, and their earnest, unconquerable faith in the destiny of the country, enabled them to found that government which now upholds and protects the whole fabric of liberties in the States of this Union."

"Of this convention," says a writer, "considering the character of the men, the work in which they were engaged, and the results of their labor, I think them the most remarkable body ever assembled."

No Recognition of the Christian Religion

This Constitution, formed by such a body of able and wise statesmen, contains no recognition of the Christian religion, nor even an acknowledgment of the providence of God in national affairs. This omission was greatly regretted by the Christian public at the time of the adoption of the Constitution, as it has been by the Christian sentiment of the nation ever since.

It is said that, after the convention had adjourned, Rev. Dr. Miller, a distinguished professor in Princeton College, met Alexander

Hamilton in the streets of Philadelphia, and said, "Mr. Hamilton, we are greatly grieved that the Constitution has no recognition of God or the Christian religion." "I declare," said Hamilton, "we forgot it!"

The attention of Washington was called to this omission. After he was inaugurated, in 1789, as the first President under the Constitution, the Presbytery Eastward, in Massachusetts and New Hampshire, sent a Christian address to Washington, in which they say, "We should not have been alone in rejoicing to have seen some explicit acknowledgment of the only true God, and Jesus Christ whom He has sent, inserted somewhere in the Magna Charta of our country."

To this Washington replies, "I am persuaded you will permit me to observe that the path of true piety is so plain as to require but little political direction. To this consideration we ought to ascribe the absence of any regulation respecting religion from the Magna Charta of our country. To the guidance of the ministers of the gospel this important object is, perhaps, more properly committed. And in the progress of morality and science, to which our Government will give every furtherance, we may confidently expect the advancement of true religion and the completion of our happiness."

The Constitution a Christian State Paper

Notwithstanding this omission, the record of facts now to pass before the reader will demonstrate that the Constitution was formed under Christian influences and is, in its purposes and spirit, a Christian instrument.

The Christian faith and character of the men who formed the Constitution forbid the idea that they designed not to place the Constitution and its government under the providence and protection of God and the principles of the Christian religion. In all their previous state papers they had declared Christianity to be fundamental to the well-being of society and government, and in every form of official authority had stated this fact. The Declaration of Independence contained a solemn "appeal to the Supreme Judge of the world," and expressed "a firm reliance on the protection of Divine Providence." An article in the old Confederation had declared that "it had pleased the great Governor of the world to incline the hearts of the legislatures we severally represent in Congress to approve of, and to authorize us to ratify, the said articles of confederation and perpetual union." The various States who had sent these good and great men to the convention to form a Constitution had, in all their civil charters, expressed, as States and as a people, their faith in God and the Christian religion. Most of the statesmen themselves were Christian men; and the convention had for its president George Washington, who everywhere paid a public homage to the Christian religion.

These statesmen, met to form a Constitution for a free and growing republic, were at times baffled in reaching desirable and harmonious results.

"I can well recollect," says Judge Wilson, a member, "though I cannot, I believe, convey to others, the impression which on many occasions was made by the difficulties which surrounded and pressed the convention. The great undertaking, at some times, seemed to be at a stand; at other times, its motions seemed to be retrograde. At the conclusion, however, of our work, the members expressed their astonishment at the success with which it terminated."

It was in the midst of these difficulties that Dr. Franklin, on the morning of the 28th of June, 1787, rose, and delivered the following address—

Franklin's Christian Address to the Convention

Mr. President—The slow progress we have made, after four or five weeks' close attendance and continual reasoning with each other—our different sentiments on almost every question, several of the last producing as many nays as yeas—is, methinks, a melancholy proof of the imperfection of human understanding. We indeed seem to feel our own want of political wisdom, since we have been running about in search of it. We have gone back to ancient history for models of government, and examined the different forms of those republics which, having been formed with the seeds of their own dissolution, now no longer exist. And we have viewed modern states all round Europe, but find none of their constitutions suitable to our circumstances.

In this situation of this assembly, groping as it were in the dark to find political truth, and scarce able to distinguish it when presented to us, how has it happened, sir, that we have not hitherto once thought of humbly applying to the Father of lights to illuminate our understanding? In the beginning of the contest with Great Britain, when we were sensible of danger, we had daily prayers in this room for the Divine protection. Our prayers, sir, were heard, and they were graciously answered. All of us who were engaged in the struggle must have observed frequent instances of a superintending Providence in our favor. To that kind Providence we owe this happy opportunity of consulting in peace on the means of establishing our future national felicity. And have we now forgotten that powerful Friend? Or do we imagine we no longer need his assistance?

I have lived, sir, a long time, and the longer I live, the more convincing proofs I see of this truth—*that God governs in the affairs of men.* And if a sparrow cannot fall to the ground without his notice, is it probable that an empire can rise without his aid? We have been assured, sir, in the sacred writings, that 'Except the Lord build the house they labor in vain that build it.' I firmly believe this; and I also believe that without his concurring aid we shall succeed in this political building no better than the builders of Babel. We shall be divided by our little, partial, local interests; our projects will be confounded, and we ourselves become a reproach and by-word down to future ages. And, what is worse, mankind may hereafter, from this unfortunate circumstance, despair of establishing governments by human wisdom, and leave it to chance, war, and conquest.

I therefore beg leave to move that henceforth prayers imploring the assistance of Heaven, and its blessings on our deliberations, be held in this assembly every morning before we proceed to business, and that one or more of the clergy of this city be requested to officiate in that service.

Madison says that—

"Mr. Sherman seconded the motion.

"Mr. Hamilton and several others expressed their apprehensions that, however proper such a resolution might have been at the beginning of the convention, it might at this late day, in the first place, bring on it some disagreeable animadversions, and, in the second, lead the public to believe that the embarrassments and dissensions within the convention had suggested this measure.

"It was answered by Dr. Franklin, Mr. Sherman, and others, that the past omission of a duty could not justify a further omission; that the rejection of such a proposition would expose the convention to more unpleasant animadversions than the adoption of it; and that the alarm out of doors, that might be excited for *the state of things within, would at least be as likely to do good as ill.*

"Mr. Williamson observed that the true cause of the omission could not be mistaken. The convention had no funds.

"Mr. Randolph proposed, in order to give a favorable aspect to the measure, that a sermon be preached, at the request of the convention, on the Fourth of July, the anniversary of Independence, and thenceforward prayers, &c. to be read in the convention every morning."

The Influence of Franklin's Speech Described by a Friend of a Member of the Convention

The following authentic account of the scene connected with Dr. Franklin's speech in reference to the need of Divine aid in forming the Constitution was written in 1825 by an intimate friend of the youngest member of the convention, and may be found in McGuire's "Religious Opinions and Character of Washington." It relates to the reconsideration of the provision which had been made for the representation of the States in the Senate. It had been determined that representation should be according to population. To this principle the representatives from the four smaller States objected. They moved a reconsideration, and expressed their purpose of withdrawing from the convention unless the Constitution was so modified as to give them an equal representation.

"A rupture," says the writer, "appeared almost inevitable, and the bosom of Washington seemed to labor with the most anxious solicitude for its issue. Happily for the United States, the convention contained many individuals possessed of talents and virtues of the highest order, whose hearts were deeply interested in the establishment of a new and efficient form of government, and whose penetrating minds had already deplored the evils which would spring up in our newly-established republic should the present attempt to consolidate it prove abortive. Among those personages the most prominent was Dr. Franklin. He was esteemed the Mentor of our body. To a mind naturally strong and capacious, enriched by much reading and the experience of many years, he added a manner of communicating his thoughts peculiarly his own, in which simplicity, beauty, and strength were equally conspicuous. As soon as the angry orators who had preceded him had left him an opening, the doctor rose, impressed with the weight of the subject before them, and the difficulty of managing it successfully.

"In a speech, the doctor urged the consideration of the great interests involved in the issue of their deliberations, and proposed a recess for three days, for cool reflection and impartial conversation among the members respecting their conflicting views and opinions, that they might return to the subject before them with more tranquil and amicable feelings. He then concluded in the following words—

"'Before I sit down, Mr. President, I will suggest another matter; and I am really surprised that it has not been proposed by some other member at an earlier period of our deliberations. I will suggest, Mr. President, the propriety of nominating and appointing, before we separate, a chaplain to this convention, whose duty it shall be uniformly to assemble with us, and introduce the business of each day by an address to the Creator of the universe and the Governor of all nations, beseeching him to preside in our council, enlighten our minds with a portion of heavenly wisdom, influence our hearts with a love of truth and justice, and crown our labors with complete and abundant success.'

Washington's Delight

"The doctor sat down; and never did I behold a countenance at once so dignified and delighted as was that of Washington, at the close of this address; nor were the members of the convention generally less affected. The words of the venerable Franklin fell upon our ears with a weight and authority even greater than we may suppose an oracle to have had in a Roman Senate. A silent admiration superseded for a moment the expression of that assent and approbation which was strongly marked on almost every countenance. The motion for appointing a chaplain was instantly put, and carried, with a solitary negative. The motion for an adjournment was then put, and carried unanimously; and the convention adjourned accordingly.

Its Effect on the Results of the Convention

"The three days of recess were spent in the manner advised by Dr. Franklin: the opposite parties mixed with each other, and a free and frank interchange of sentiments took place. On the fourth day we assembled again; and, if great additional *light* had not been thrown on the subject, every *unfriendly feeling* had been expelled, and a spirit of conciliation had been cultivated which promised at least a *calm* and *dispassionate reconsideration* of the subject.

"As soon as the chaplain had closed his prayer, and the minutes of the last sitting were read, all eyes were turned to the doctor. He rose, and said, in a few words, that during the recess he had listened attentively to all the arguments, *pro* and *con,* which had been urged by both sides of the House; that he had himself read much, and thought more, on the subject; he saw difficulties and objections which might be urged by individual States against every scheme which had been proposed, and he now more than ever was convinced that the Constitution which they were about to form, in order to be *just* and *equal,* must be founded on the basis of compromise and mutual concession. With such views and feelings, he would move a reconsideration of the vote last taken on the organization of the Senate. The motion was seconded, the vote carried, the former vote rescinded, and, by a successful motion and resolution, the Senate was organized on the present plan."

During the deliberations of the convention to form the Constitution, the 4th of July, 1787, was celebrated in Philadelphia with great enthusiasm. The oration was delivered in the Reformed Calvinistic Church, and Rev. William Rogers offered up a prayer, of which the following is an extract—

"As this is a period, O Lord, big with events impenetrable by any human scrutiny, we fervently recommend to thy fatherly notice that August body, assembled in this city, who compose our federal convention. Will it please thee, O thou Eternal I Am! to favor them, from day to day, with thy inspiring presence; be their wisdom and strength; enable them to devise such measures as may prove happy instruments in healing all divisions and prove the good of the great whole; incline the hearts of all the people to receive with pleasure, combined with a determination to carry into execution, whatever these thy servants may wisely recommend; that the United States of America may form one example of a free and virtuous government, which shall be the result of human mutual deliberation, and which shall not, like other governments, whether ancient or modern, spring out of mere chance or be established by force. May we trust in the cheering prospect of being a country delivered from anarchy, and continue, under the influence of republican virtue, to partake of all blessings of cultivated and Christian society."

His Closing Speech

In Dr. Franklin's closing speech in the convention, he said—

"It astonishes me, sir, to find this system approaching so near to perfection as it does; and I think it will astonish our enemies, who are waiting with confidence to hear that our councils are confounded, like those of the builders of Babel."

Franklin Declares the Constitution Formed Under the Direction of God

After the convention had closed its labors, and the Constitution had been adopted, Dr. Franklin acknowledged a divine intervention, as follows—

"I am not to be understood to infer that our General Convention was divinely inspired when it formed the new Federal Constitution; yet I must own that I have so much faith in the general government of the world by Providence, that I can hardly conceive a transaction of so much importance to the welfare of millions now in existence, and to exist in the posterity of a great nation, should be suffered to pass without being in some degree influenced, guided, and governed by that omnipotent and beneficent Ruler in whom all inferior spirits live, and move, and have their being."

This Constitution, freighted with such rich blessings, and tested by eighty-three years' trial, met at its formation with great opposition. Dr. Franklin wrote a paper comparing the conduct of the ancient Jews with that of the opponents of the Constitution of the United States, in which he says that "A zealous advocate for the proposed Federal Constitution, in a certain public assembly, said that the repugnance of a great part of mankind to good government was such, that he believed that if an angel from heaven was to bring down a Constitution from there for our use, it would nevertheless meet with violent opposition. He was reproved for the supposed extravagance of the sentiment.

"Probably," says Dr. Franklin, "it might not have immediately occurred to him that the experiment had been tried, and that the event was recorded in the most faithful of all histories, the Holy Bible; otherwise he might, as it seems to me, have supported his opinion by that unexceptionable authority.

"On the whole, it appears that the Israelites were a people jealous of their newly-acquired liberty, which jealousy was in itself no fault; but when they suffered it to be worked upon by artful men pretending public good, with nothing really in view but private interest, they were led to oppose the establishment of the new Constitution, whereby they brought upon themselves much inconvenience and misfortune. From all which we may gather that popular opposition to a public measure is no proof of its impropriety, even though the opposition be excited and headed by men of distinction."

Washington's Views

"It appears to me," writes Washington to Lafayette, February 8, 1788, "little short of a miracle that the delegates from so many States, differing from each other, as you know, in their manners, circumstances, and prejudices, should unite in forming a system of national government so little liable to well-founded objections. It will at least be a recommendation to the proposed Constitution that it is provided with more checks and barriers against the introduction of tyranny, and those of a nature less liable to be surmounted, than any government hitherto instituted among mortals. We are not to expect perfection in this world; but mankind in modern times have apparently made some progress in the science of government."

"We may with a kind of pious and grateful exultation," writes Washington to Governor Trumbull, of Connecticut, July 20, 1788, "trace the finger of Providence through those dark and mysterious events which first induced the States to appoint a general convention, and then led them one after another, by such steps as were best calculated to effect the object, into an adoption of the system recommended by the general convention, thereby, in all human probability, laying a lasting foundation for tranquillity and happiness, when we had too much reason to fear that confusion and misery were coming upon us."

His Address on the Adoption of the Constitution to the People of Philadelphia

On his way to New York, after its adoption, to assume the administration of the new government, processions and ovations were frequent in honor of the adoption of the Constitution and as a tribute to the good and great man who had presided over the convention that formed it. At Philadelphia twenty thousand people met and welcomed Washington with cries of, "Long live George Washington! Long live the father of his country!" Washington, in addressing the people of that city, spoke as follows—

"When I contemplate the interposition of Providence, as it has been visibly manifested in guiding us through the Revolution, in preparing us for the General Government, and in conciliating the good will of the people of America towards one another in its adoption, I feel myself oppressed and overwhelmed with a sense of the Divine munificence."

In that procession at Philadelphia, to honor the new Constitution, "the clergy formed a conspicuous part, manifesting by their attendance a sense of the connection between good government and religion. They marched arm in arm, to illustrate the General Union.

Care was taken to associate ministers of the most dissimilar opinions with each other, to display the promotion of Christian charity by free institutions. 'The rabbi of the Jews, with a minister of the gospel on each side, was a most delightful sight.' It exhibited the political equality, not only of Christian denominations, but of worthy men of every belief."

"It has sometimes been concluded," says a writer, "that Christianity cannot have any direct connection with the Constitution of the United States, on the ground that the instrument contains no express declaration to that effect. But the error of such a conclusion becomes manifest when we reflect that the same is the case with regard to several other truths, which are, notwithstanding, fundamental in our constitutional system. The Declaration of Independence says that 'governments are instituted among men to secure the rights of life, liberty, and the pursuit of happiness;' and that 'whenever any form of government becomes destructive of these ends, it is the right of the people to alter or to abolish it, and to institute a new government.' These principles lie at the foundation of the Constitution of the United States. No principles in the Constitution are more fundamental than these. But the instrument contains no declaration to this effect; these principles are nowhere mentioned in it, and the references to them are equally slight and indirect with those which are made to the Christian religion. The same may be said of the great republican truth that political sovereignty resides in the people of the United States. If, then, any one may rightfully conclude that Christianity has no connection with the Constitution of the United States because this is nowhere expressly declared in the instrument, he ought, in reason, to be equally convinced that the same Constitution is not built upon and does not recognize the sovereignty of the people, and the great republican truths above quoted from the Declaration of Independence. This argument receives additional strength when we consider that the Constitution of the United States was formed directly for political and not for religious objects. The truth is, they are all equally fundamental, though neither of them is expressly mentioned in the Constitution.

"Besides, the Constitution of the United States contemplates, and is fitted for; such a state of society as Christianity alone can form. It contemplates a state of society in which strict integrity, simplicity, and purity of manners, wide diffusion of knowledge, well-disciplined passions, and wise moderation, are the general characteristics of the people. These virtues, in our nation, are the offspring of Christianity, and without the continued general belief of its doctrines and practice of its precepts they will gradually decline and eventually perish."

The Constitution declares that "no religious test shall ever be required as a qualification to any office or public trust under the United States."

Judge Story on the Religious Features of the Constitution

On this article Judge Story says—

"The clause requiring no religious test for office is recommended by its tendency to satisfy the minds of many delicate and scrupulous persons, who entertain great repugnance to religious tests as a qualification for civil power or honor. But it has a higher aim in the Constitution. It is designed to cut off every pretence of an alliance between the Church and the State in the administration of the National Government. The American people were too well read in the history of other countries, and had suffered too much in their colonial state, not to dread the abuses of authority resulting from religious bigotry, intolerance, and persecution."

The first amendment to the Constitution is, "That Congress shall make no law respecting an establishment of religion, or prohibiting the free exercise thereof."

"The same policy," says Judge Story, "which introduced into the Constitution the prohibition of any religious test, led to this more extended prohibition of the interference of Congress in religious concerns. We are not to attribute this prohibition of a national religious establishment to an indifference to religion in general, and especially to Christianity (which none could hold in more reverence than the framers of the Constitution), but to a dread by the people of the influence of ecclesiastical power in matters of government—a dread which their ancestors brought with them from the parent country, and which, unhappily for human infirmity, their own conduct, after their emigration, had not in any just degree tended to diminish. It was also obvious, from the numerous and powerful sects in the United States, that there would be perpetual temptations to struggles for ascendency in the national councils, if any one might thereby hope to found a permanent and exclusive national establishment of its own; and religious persecutions might thus be introduced, to an extent utterly subversive of the true interests and good order of the republic. The most effectual mode of suppressing the evil, in the view of the people, was to strike down the temptations to its introduction. How far any government has a right to interfere in matters touching religion, has been a matter much discussed by writers upon public and political law. ... The right of a society or government to interfere in matters of religion will hardly be contested by any persons who believe that piety, religion, and morality are intimately connected with the well-being of the state and indispensable to the administration of civil justice.

"The promulgation of the great doctrines of religion—the being and attributes and providence of one Almighty God, the responsibility to him for all our actions, founded upon moral accountability, a future state of rewards and punishments, the cultivation of all the personal, social, and benevolent virtues—these never can be a matter of indifference in a well-ordered community. It is, indeed, difficult to conceive how any civilized society can exist without them. And, at all events, it is impossible for those who believe in the truth of Christianity as a divine revelation to doubt that it is the special duty of Government to foster and encourage it among all the citizens and subjects. This is a point wholly distinct from that of the right of private judgment in matters of religion, and of the freedom of public worship according to the dictates of one's conscience.

"The real difficulty lies in ascertaining the limits to which Government may rightfully go in fostering and encouraging religion. Three cases may easily be supposed. One, where a government affords aid to a particular religion, leaving all persons free to adopt any other; another, where it creates an ecclesiastical establishment for the propagation of the doctrines of a particular sect of that religion, leaving a like freedom to all others; and a third, where it creates such an establishment, and excludes all persons not belonging to it, either wholly or in part, from any participation in the public honors, trusts, emoluments, privileges, and immunities of the state. For instance, a government may simply declare that the Christian religion shall be the religion of the state, and shall be aided and encouraged in aft the varieties of sects belonging to it; or it may declare that the Roman Catholic or Protestant religion shall be the religion of the state, leaving every man to the free enjoyment of his own religious opinions; or it may establish the doctrines of a particular sect, as of Episcopalians, as the religion of the state, with a like freedom; or it may establish the doctrines of a particular sect as exclusively the religion of the state, tolerating others to a limited extent, or excluding all not belonging to it from all public honors, trusts, emoluments, privileges, and immunities.

"Probably at the time of the adoption of the Constitution and of the Amendments to it, the general, if not universal, sentiment in America was that Christianity ought to receive encouragement from the state, so far as such encouragement was not incompatible with the private rights of conscience and the freedom of religious worship. An attempt to level all religions, and to make it a matter of state policy to hold all in utter indifference, would have created universal disapprobation, if not universal indignation."

Judge Bayard's Views

In a work on the Constitution, by James Bayard, of Delaware, and which received the warm commendations of Chief-Justice Marshall, Judge Story, Chancellor Kent, and other distinguished civilians and jurists, the writer speaks on this fundamental law of the Constitution thus—

"The people of the United States were so fully aware of the evils which arise from the union of Church and State, and so thoroughly convinced of its corrupting influence upon both religion and government, that they introduced this prohibition into the fundamental law.

"It has been made an objection to the Constitution, by some, that it makes no mention of religion, contains no recognition of the existence and providence of God—as though his authority were slighted or disregarded. But such is not the reason of the omission.

The convention which framed the Constitution comprised some of the wisest and best men of the nation—men *who were firmly persuaded not only of the divine origin of the Christian religion,* but also of its importance to the temporal and eternal welfare of men. The people, too, of this country were generally impressed with religious feelings, and felt and acknowledged the superintendence of God, who had protected them through the perils of war and blessed their exertions to obtain civil and religious freedom. But there were reasons why the introduction of religion into the Constitution would have been unseasonable, if not improper.

"In the first place, it was intended exclusively for civil purposes, and religion could not be regularly mentioned, because it made no part of the agreement between the parties. They were about to surrender a portion of their civil rights for the security of the remainder; but each retained his religious freedom, entire and untouched, as a matter between himself and his God, with which government could not interfere. But, even if this reason had not existed, it would have been difficult, if not impossible, to use any expression on the subject which would have given general satisfaction. The difference between the various sects of Christians is such, that, while all have much in common, there are many points of variance: so that in an instrument where all are entitled to equal consideration it would be difficult to use terms in which all could cordially join.

"Besides, the whole Constitution was a compromise, and it was foreseen that it would meet with great opposition before it would be finally adopted. It was, therefore, important to restrict its provisions to things absolutely necessary, so as to give as little room as possible to cavil. Moreover, it was impossible to introduce into it even an expression of gratitude to the Almighty for the formation of the present government; for, when the Constitution was framed and submitted to the people, it was entirely uncertain whether it would ever be ratified, and the government might, therefore, never be established.

"The prohibition of any religious test for office was wise, because its admission would lead to hypocrisy and corruption. The purity of religion is best preserved by keeping it separate from government; and the surest means of giving to it its proper influence in society is the dissemination of correct principles through education. The experience of this country has proved that religion may flourish in all its vigor and purity without the aid of a national establishment; and the religious feeling of the community is the best guarantee for the religious administration of the government."

"Just and liberal sentiments on this subject," says Rawle, in his "View of the Constitution of the United States," "throw a lustre round the Constitution in which they are found, and, while they dignify the nation, promote its internal peace and harmony. No predominant religion overpowers another, the votaries of which are few and humble; no lordly hierarchy excites odium or terror; legal persecution is unknown; and freedom of discussion, while it tends to promote the knowledge, contributes to increase the fervor, of piety."

Speech in the Legislature of Massachusetts

The following extracts from a speech made in the convention in Massachusetts met to ratify the Constitution of the United States, are liberal and just. Rev. Mr. Shute, who presented these views, was a Congregational clergyman, and a member of the convention.

"To establish," says he, "a religious test as a qualification for office in the proposed Federal Constitution, it appears to me, would be attended with injurious consequences to some individuals, and with no advantage to the whole.

"In this great and extensive empire, there is, and will be, a great variety of sects among its inhabitants. Upon a plan of a religious test, the question must be, who shall be excluded from national trust? Whatever bigotry might suggest, the dictates of conscience and equity, I conceive, will say, 'None.'

"Far from limiting my charity and confidence to men of my own denomination in religion, I suppose and believe, sir, there are worthy characters among men of every denomination— among the Quakers, the Baptists, the Church of England, Papists, and even among those who have no other guide in the way to virtue and to heaven than the dictates of natural religion.

"I must, therefore, think, sir, that the proposed plan of government in this particular is wisely constructed; and that as all have an equal claim to the blessings of the government under which they live and which they support, so none shall be excluded by being of any particular denomination of religion.

"The presumption is, that the eyes of the people will be upon the faithful in the land, and, from a regard to their own safety, will choose for their rulers men of known abilities, of known probity, and of good moral character. The Apostle Peter tells us that 'God is no respecter of persons, but in every nation he that feareth him and worketh righteousness is acceptable to him;' and I know of no reason why men of such a character in a community, of whatever denomination of religion, *cœteris paribus*, with suitable qualifications, should not be acceptable to the people, and why they may not be employed by them with safety and advantage in the important offices of government.

"The exclusion of a religious test in the proposed Constitution, therefore, clearly appears to me, sir, to be in favor of its adoption."

Harmony of the Constitution with the Principles and Institutes of Christianity

The Constitution itself affirms its Christian character and purpose.

The seventh article declares it to be framed and adopted "by the unanimous consent of the States, the seventeenth day of September in the year of our Lord 1787, and of the Independence of the United States of America the twelfth." The date of the Constitution is twofold: first it is dated from the birth of OUR Lord Jesus Christ, and then from the birth of our independence. Any argument which might be supposed to prove that the authority of Christianity is not recognized by the people of the United States, in the first mode, would equally prove that the independence of the United States is not recognized by them in the second mode. The fact is, that the advent of Christ and the independence of the country are the two events in which, of all others, we are most interested—the former in common with all mankind, the latter as the birth of our nation. This twofold mode, therefore, of dating so solemn an instrument, was singularly appropriate and becoming.

A second fact is the harmony of the purposes for which the Constitution was established with the purposes and results of Christianity as affecting nations and the temporal interests of men. The preamble states this political and moral harmony in these words—

> We, the people of the United States, in order to form a more perfect union, establish justice, insure domestic tranquillity, provide for the common defence, promote the general welfare, and secure the blessing; of liberty to ourselves and our posterity, do ordain and establish this Constitution for the United States of America.

These fundamental objects of the Constitution are in perfect harmony with the revealed objects of the Christian religion. Union, justice, peace, the general welfare, and the blessings of civil and religious liberty, are the objects of Christianity, and are always secured under its practical and beneficent reign. "Our National Constitution is fitted to quicken the growth of a real manhood, to discipline the virtuous citizen for an ampler reward in heaven than he would reach if he were not trained to think for himself, to govern himself, to develop his own powers, to worship his Maker according to his own conscience."

A third fact indicating the Christian character of the Constitution is, that in no less than four places it requires an oath.

"No person can hold an executive or judicial office under it, or derived from any State, who does not take an oath to support it."

An oath is defined to be "a solemn appeal to the Supreme Being for the truth of what is said, by a person who believes in the existence of a Supreme Being, and in a future state of rewards and punishments, according to that form which will bind his conscience most." Can it with propriety be said that a government which forbids the exercise of the slightest of its functions by any one who cannot make and has not made such an appeal to a supreme Being, in whom he believes, does not recognize the authority of God? It includes other sovereignties, and provides that even there no man shall be intrusted with any power that concerns the whole people, who fails to furnish this testimony of his religious character.

It was objected in several of the State conventions held for the adoption of the Federal Constitution, that it contained no religious test. It was argued that Mohammedans, pagans, or persons of no religion at all, might be chosen into the government. In North Carolina Mr. Iredell replied, "It was never to be supposed that the people of America will trust their dearest interests to persons who have no religion at all, or a religion materially different from their own. It would be happy for mankind if religion was permitted to take its own course and maintain itself by the excellency of its own doctrines. The Divine Author of our religion never wished for its support by worldly authority. Has he not said, 'The gates of hell shall not prevail against it'? It made much greater progress for itself than when supported by the greatest authority upon earth."

In the convention held in Massachusetts, Rev. Mr. Payson said, "The great object of religion being God supreme, and the seat of religion in man being the heart or conscience, *i.e.*, the reason God has given us, employed on our moral actions in their most important consequences, as related to the tribunal of God—hence I infer that God alone is the God of the conscience, and, consequently, attempts to erect human tribunals for the consciences of men are impious encroachments upon the prerogatives of God." Theophilus Parsons, afterwards Chief-Justice, said, "It has been objected that the Constitution provides no religious test by oath, and we may have in power unprincipled men, atheists, and pagans. No man can wish more ardently than I do that all our public offices may be filled by men who fear God and hate wickedness; but it must remain with the electors to give the government this security. An oath will not do it. Will an unprincipled man be entangled by an oath? Will an atheist or a pagan dread the vengeance of the Christian's God—a being, in his opinion, the creature of fancy and credulity? It is a solecism in expression. No man is so illiberal as to wish the confining of places of honor or profit to any one sect of Christians; but what security is it to government that every public officer shall swear that he is a Christian? For what will then be called Christianity? The only evidence we can have of the sincerity and excellence of a man's religion is a good life; and I trust that such evidence will be required of every candidate by every elector."

The theory on this point upon which the Constitution was formed was perfect. It secured the recognition of a Supreme Being and a future retribution, and excluded all tests founded upon distinctions of religion or sects. It found the Bible at large among the people for whom it provided a government, and it left among them the power of the gospel without restraint, free. It left it in the authority and made it the highest interest of the people to select the citizens to office who believed in the Bible and acknowledged that power by conforming their lives to its requirements.

More than sixty years of prosperity and domestic peace, under the practical working of this system, attest the wisdom of the scheme on which it was founded.

A fourth fact is its recognition of the Christian Sabbath.

Article 1, section 7, says, "If any bill shall not be returned by the President within ten days (Sundays excepted) after it shall have been presented to him, the same shall be a law in like manner as if he had signed it, unless the Congress by their adjournment prevent its return, in which case it shall not be a law."

Views of Dr. Adams

"In adopting this provision," says Dr. Adams, "it was clearly presumed by the people that the President of the United States would not employ himself in public business on Sunday. The people had been accustomed to pay special respect to Sunday from the first settlement of the country. They assumed that the President also would wish to respect the day. They did not think it suitable or becoming to require him by a constitutional provision to respect the day: they assumed that he would adhere to the customary observance without a requirement. To have enacted a constitutional provision would have left him no choice, and would have been placing no confidence in him. They have placed the highest possible confidence in him, by assuming, without requiring it, that his conduct in this respect would be according to their wishes. Every man who is capable of being influenced by the higher and more delicate motives of duty cannot fail to perceive that the obligation on the President to respect the observance of Sunday is greatly superior to any which could have been created by a constitutional enactment. The people, in adopting the Constitution, must have been convinced that the public business intrusted to the President would be greater in importance and variety than that which would fall to the share of any functionary employed in a subordinate station. The expectation and confidence, then, manifested by the people of the United States, that their President will respect *their* Sunday, by abstaining from public business on that day, must extend *a fortiori* to all employed in subordinate stations."

Senator Frelinghuysen on the Sabbath

Senator Frelinghuysen said in Congress, in 1830, "Our predecessors have acted upon a true republican principle—that the feelings and opinions of the majority were to be consulted. And when a collision might arise, inasmuch as only one day could be thus appropriated, they wisely determined, in accordance with the sentiments of at least nine-tenths of our people, that the first day of the week should be the Sabbath of our Government. This public recognition is accorded to the Sabbath in the Federal Constitution. The President of the United States, in the discharge of the high functions of his legislative department, is expressly relieved from all embarrassment on Sunday. Both Houses of Congress, the offices of the State, Treasury, War, and Navy Departments, are all closed on Sunday.

"Long before the American Revolution, it was decided that the desecration of the Sabbath was an offence at common law, which all admit recognizes Christianity. The Sabbath is recognized, both by the statute and common law, by the States which compose this Union, as a day upon which courts cannot sit or civil process issue; the servant, apprentice, and laborer are exempt from worldly avocations on that day, and protected in its enjoyment as a day of rest; and all entertainments, exhibitions, reviews, or other things calculated to disturb the religions observance of this day, are prohibited.

"The humanizing effect of the Sabbath, in promoting works of benevolence, charity, schools for the instruction of those who cannot obtain instruction elsewhere, and in strengthening the social relations of friends and neighbors, is among its most benign results. The principles which are then inculcated in churches of all denominations strengthen that public morality, good order, and obedience to the laws so essential to the security of the state.

"The framers of the Constitution, and those who for many years administered it, doubtless had in their eye the *first* day—the Sabbath of the Christian religion. They were legislating not for Jews, Mohammedans, infidels, pagans, atheists, but for Christians. And, believing the Christian religion the only one calculated to sustain and perpetuate the government about to be formed, they adopted it as the basis of the infant republic. This nation had a religion, and it was the Christian religion.

"That Christianity is the religion of this country, and as such is recognized in the whole structure of its government, and lies at the foundation of all our civil and political institutions—in other words, that Christianity, as really as republicanism, is part and parcel of our laws—is evident from the following—

"Such was the relation Of Christianity to civil government in the several States as they existed prior to the formation of the present Federal Constitution; and there is no evidence that in acceding to said Constitution they Surrendered such relation either to the general or to their own particular governments.

The Christian Faith of the American People

"The colonies from which our present States originated were planted by decidedly Christian people, to be Christian communities, and with such views of the relations between civil government and religion as were then universal in Christendom. The experiment of a nation without an established religion had not then been tried, nor did they think of instituting it: Christianity, therefore, was made part of their civil institutions, as well in their minuter branches as in their essential foundations.

"In Massachusetts and other Northern colonies, a membership in the Church established by law was necessary to citizenship in the commonwealth. In Virginia and other Southern colonies, the Church of England was by law established.

"By-and-by, when the colonial character had ceased, and that of States been assumed, the legal establishment of any one form of Christianity in preference to all other forms of the same was discontinued. In the adoption of the present Federal Constitution, it was declared, among the amendments of that instrument, that 'Congress shall make no law respecting an establishment of religion, or prohibiting the free exercise thereof.' This article in the general Constitution, and the similar alterations in the laws of the several States above mentioned, by which the legal precedence of one form of Christianity over another was done away, are all the ground on which it can be asserted that either our General or State Governments have disowned all connection with the Christian religion as having any more countenance in their legislation than infidelity or Mohammedanism. But is this a warrantable conclusion? Is it not perfectly conceivable that Christianity may be the religion of the people and of the people's government, so far as that her great principles shall be assumed as the basis of their institutions and the promotion of those principles distinctly countenanced in their laws and customs, at the same time that no religion is, in the technical sense, 'established,' and no one form of Christianity is distinguished above another? To call religion into connection with the government, so far as to employ ministers of the gospel as chaplains, at the public charge, in Congress and other public departments, is decided by long-established practice to be not unconstitutional. And thus it is decided that it was not intended, by the article quoted above from the Constitution of the United States, to prevent the Government of the United States from being connected with religion, with some religion in preference to all others, or to have its institutions based upon the principles of Christianity instead of those of Deism or the Koran.

"How unlikely were the several States, in acceding to the present Constitution, to lay aside all connection with Christianity in the general institutions to which they gave birth, may be inferred from the consideration that in their own respective legislation a close relation between religion and the Government had always subsisted; that, though a strong aversion had arisen to the *national establishment* of any one form of Christianity, none had grown up against a distinct recognition of Christianity itself as the religion of the nation; and that the representatives of the States in the convention that formed the present Constitution were, for the most part, men of decided Christian principles."

Picture of Prosperity Under the Constitution

Judge Wilson, a member of the convention that formed the Constitution, in an oration at Philadelphia, July, 1788, commemorative of the adoption of the Constitution by the people of the several States, depicts the future progress and glory of the American nation under the Constitution in these glowing words—words of prophecy which have been fully realized. He said—

"The commencement of our government has been eminently glorious: let our progress in every excellence be proportionally great. IT WILL—IT MUST BE SO. What an enrapturing prospect opens on the United States! Placid Husbandry walks in front, attended by the venerable plough. Lowing herds adorn our valleys; bleating flocks spread over our hills; verdant meadows, enamelled pastures, yellow harvests, bending orchards, rise in rapid succession from East to West. Plenty, with her copious horn, sits easy smiling, and, in conscious complacency, enjoys and presides over the scene. Commerce next advances, in all her splendid and embellished forms. The rivers and lakes and seas are crowded with ships; their shores are covered with cities; the cities are filled with inhabitants. The Arts, decked with elegance, yet with simplicity, appear in beautiful variety and well-adjusted arrangement. Around them are diffused, in rich abundance, the necessaries, the decencies, and the ornaments of life. With heartfelt contentment, Industry beholds her honest labors flourishing and secure. Peace walks serene and unalarmed over all the unmolested regions; while liberty, virtue, and religion go hand in hand, harmoniously, protecting, enlivening, and exalting all. Happy country! may thy happiness be perpetual!"

The Virtue of the People to Preserve the Constitution

The people who ordained such a noble constitution of government, and for whom it was made, are under the highest and most solemn obligations to preserve it for themselves, their children, and future generations.

"This constitution of government," says Justice Story, "must perish, if there be not that vital spirit in the people which alone can nourish, sustain, and direct all its movements. It is in vain that statesmen shall form plans of government in which the beauty and harmony of a republic shall be embodied in visible order, shall be built upon solid substructions, and adorned by every useful ornament, if the inhabitants suffer the silent power of time to dilapidate its walls or crumble its massy supporters into dust, if the assaults from without are never resisted and the rottenness and mining from within are never guarded against. Who can preserve the rights and liberties of a people when they shall be abandoned by themselves? Who shall keep watch in the temple when the watchmen sleep at their post? Who shall call upon the people to redeem their possessions and revive the republic, when their own hands have deliberately and corruptly surrendered them to the oppressor and have built the prisons or dug the graves of their own friends? This dark picture, it is to be hoped, will never be applicable to the republic of America. And yet it affords a warning, which, like all the lessons of past ex-perience, we are not permitted to disregard. America, free, happy, and enlightened as she is, must rest the preservation of her rights and liberties upon the virtue, independence, justice, and sagacity of the people. If either fail, the republic is gone. Its shadow may remain, with all the pomp and circumstance and trickery of government, but its vital power will have departed."

The following language fell from the lips of Alexander Hamilton, on his resignation of the office of Secretary of the Treasury, in 1795. Holding in his hand a small book containing a copy of the Federal Constitution, he said, "Now, mark my words! so long as we are a young and virtuous people, this instrument will bind us together in mutual interest, mutual welfare, and mutual happiness; but when we become old and corrupt it will bind us no longer."

This dark condition of the republic, which would be produced by the general corruption of the people and the government, can only be prevented by the universal belief and application of the principles stated in Webster's address before the New York Historical Society. He says—

"If we and our posterity shall be true to the Christian religion—if we and they shall live always in the fear of God and shall respect his commandments—if we and they shall maintain just moral sentiments, and such conscientious convictions of duty as shall control the heart and life—we may have the highest hopes of the future fortunes of our country; and if we maintain those institutions of government, and that political union exceeding all praise as much as it exceeds all former examples of political association, we may be sure of one thing, that, while our country furnishes materials for a thousand masters of the historic art, it will be no topic for a Gibbon—it will have no decline and fall. It will go on prospering and to prosper. But if we and our posterity neglect religious instruction and authority, violate the rules of eternal justice, trifle with the injunctions of morality, and recklessly destroy the political constitution which holds us together, no man can tell how sudden a catastrophe may overwhelm us that shall bury all our glory in profound obscurity.

"If that catastrophe," he continues, "shall happen, let it have no history! Let the horrible narrative never be written! Let its fate be like that of the lost books of Livy, which no human eye shall ever read, or the missing Pleiad, of which no man can know more than that it is lost, and lost forever."

13

Christian Scenes in the First Congress Under the Constitution

First Congress Under the Constitution

THE first session of Congress after the adoption of the Federal Constitution opened with distinct legislative recognitions of the Christian religion. Washington was inaugurated and took the oath of office on the 30th of April, 1789. Congress, the day before the inauguration, passed the following—

> *Resolved*, That, after the oath shall be administered to the President, the Vice-President, and members of the Senate, the Speaker and members of the House of Representatives, will accompany him to St. Paul's Chapel, to hear divine service performed by the Chaplains.

Christian Scenes Attending His Inauguration

Chancellor Livingston administered the oath of office, and Mr. Otis held up the Bible on its crimson cushion. The President, as he bowed to kiss its sacred page, at the same time laying his hand on the open Bible, said, audibly, "I swear," and added, with fervency, that his whole soul might be absorbed in the supplication, "So help me God." Then the Chancellor said, "It is done!" and, turning to the multitude, waved his hand, and, with a loud voice, exclaimed, "Long live George Washington!" This solemn scene concluded, he proceeded with the whole assembly, on foot, to St. Paul's Church, where prayers suited to the occasion were read by Dr. Provost, Bishop of the Protestant Episcopal Church in New York, who had been appointed one of the chaplains of Congress.

Prayer Meeting of All Denominations in New York

Previous to his inauguration, on the morning of the same day, a general prayer-meeting of the various denominations of Christians in New York was held for the special object of praying for God's blessing to rest on the President and the new Government. The notice of the prayer-meeting is among the old files of the "New York Daily Advertiser," dated Thursday, April 23, 1789, and is as follows—

> As we believe in an overruling Providence and feel our constant dependence upon God for every blessing, so it is undoubtedly our duty to acknowledge him in all our ways and commit our concerns to his protection and mercy. The ancient civilized heathen, from the mere dictates of reason, were uniformly excited to this; and we find from their writings that they engaged in no important business, especially what related to the welfare of a nation, without a solemn appeal to Heaven. How much more becoming and necessary is such a conduct in Christians, who believe not only in the light of nature, but are blessed with a divine revelation which has taught them more of God and of their obligations to worship him than by their reason they ever could have investigated!
>
> It has been the wish of many pious persons in our land that at the framing of our new Constitution a solemn and particular appeal to Heaven had been made; and they have no doubt but Congress will soon call upon the whole nation to set apart a day for fasting and prayer for the express purpose of invoking the blessing of Heaven on our new Government. But this, in consequence of the distance of some of the States, cannot

immediately take place: in the meanwhile, the inhabitants of this city are favored with the opportunity of being present on the very day on which the Constitution will be fully organized, and have it thus in their power to accommodate their devotions exactly to the important season.

In this view, it gave universal satisfaction to hear it announced last Sunday from the pulpits of our churches that, on the morning of the day on which our illustrious President will be invested with his office, the bells will ring at nine o'clock, when the people may go up and in a solemn manner commit the new Government, with its important train of consequences, to the holy protection and blessings of the Most High. An early hour is prudently fixed for this peculiar act of devotion, and it is designed wholly for prayer: it will not detain the citizens very long, or interfere with any of the other public business of the day.

It is supposed Congress will adopt religious solemnities by fervent prayer with their chaplains, in the Federal Hall, when the President takes his oath of office; but the people feel a Common interest in this great transaction, and whether they approve of the Constitution as it now stands, or wish that alterations may be made, it is equally their concern and duty to leave the cause with God and refer the issue to his gracious providence. In doing this, the inauguration of our President and the commencement of our national character will be introduced with the auspices of religion, and our enlightened rulers and people will bear a consistent part in a business which involves the weal or woe of themselves and posterity.

I have heard that the notification respecting this hour of prayer was made in almost all the churches of the city, and that some of those who omitted the publication intend, notwithstanding, to join in that duty; and, indeed, considering the singular circumstances of the day, which in many respects exceed any thing recorded in ancient or modern history, it cannot be supposed that the serious and pious of any denomination will hesitate in going up to their respective churches and uniting at the throne of grace with proper prayers and supplications on this occasion. *"I was glad when they said unto me, Let us go into the house of the Lord."*—(David)

The people came out from the churches where Mason, Livingston, Provost, Rodgers, and other clergymen had given passionately earnest and eloquent expression to that reverent and profound desire for God's blessing upon the President and Government which filled all hearts, so universal was a religious sense of the importance of the occasion.

"The scene," said one, "was solemn and awful beyond description. It would seem extraordinary that the administration of an oath—a ceremony so very common and familiar—should to so great a degree excite public curiosity; but the circumstances of the President's election, the importance of his past services, the concourse of the spectators, the devout fervency with which he repeated the oath, and the reverential manner in which he bowed down and kissed the sacred volume—all these conspired to render it one of the most august and interesting spectacles ever exhibited. It seemed, from the number of witnesses, to be a solemn appeal to heaven and earth at once. In regard to this great and good man I may be an enthusiast, but I confess I was under an awful and religious persuasion that the gracious Ruler of the universe was looking down at that moment with peculiar complacency on an act which to a part of his creatures was so very important."

Washington's Inaugural

After divine service had been performed, Washington and the officers of the new Government and the members of Congress returned to the Federal Hall, where his inaugural was delivered.

Its Christian Sentiments

That address contains the following Christian sentiments—

It would be peculiarly improper to omit in this first official act my fervent supplications to that Almighty Being who rules over the universe, who presides in the councils of nations, and whose providential aids can supply every human defect, that his benediction may consecrate to the liberties and happiness of the people of the United States A GOVERNMENT instituted by themselves for these essential purposes, and may enable every instrument employed in its administration to execute with success the functions allotted to his charge. In tendering this homage to the great Author of every public and private good, I assure myself that it expresses YOUR sentiments not less than my own, nor those of my *fellow-citizens at large less than either.*

No people can be bound to acknowledge and adore the invisible hand which conducts the affairs of men more than the people of the United States. EVERY STEP *by which they have been advanced to the character of an independent nation seems to have been distinguished by some token of his providential agency.*

And in the important revolution just accomplished in the system of their united government, the tranquil deliberations and voluntary consent of so many distinct communities, from which the event has resulted, cannot be compared with the means by which most governments have been established, without some return of pious gratitude, along with an humble anticipation of the future blessings which the past seems to presage. These reflections, arising out of the present crisis, have forced themselves on my mind too strongly to be suppressed. You will join with me, I trust, in thinking that there are none under the influences of which the proceedings of a new and a free government can more auspiciously commence.

There is no truth more thoroughly established than that there exists in the economy and course of nature an indissoluble union between virtue and happiness, between duty and advantage, between the genuine maxims of an honest and magnanimous policy and the solid rewards of public prosperity and felicity; since we ought to be no less persuaded that the propitious smiles of Heaven can never be expected on a nation that disregards the eternal rules of order and right, which Heaven itself has ordained; and since the preservation of the sacred fire of liberty, and the destiny of the republican model of government, are justly considered as *deeply,* perhaps as *finally*, staked on the experiment intrusted to the hands of the American people.

Having thus imparted to you my sentiments, as they have been awakened by the occasion which brings us together, I shall take my present leave, but not without resorting once more to the benign Parent of the human race, in humble supplication, that since he has been pleased to favor the American people with opportunities for deliberating in perfect tranquillity, and disposition, for deciding with unparalleled unanimity, on a form of government for the security of their union and the advancement of their happiness, so his divine blessing may be equally *conspicuous* in the enlarged views, the temperate consultations, and the wise measures on which the success of this government must depend.

The first session of the first Congress was not suffered to pass without a solemn act of legislation recognizing the Christian religion. It was a national thanksgiving, proclaimed by the authority of Congress. The Journals of Congress present the following record.

Sept. 25, 1789

Day of Thanksgiving

Mr. Boudinot said he could not think of letting the session pass without offering an opportunity to all the citizens of the United States of joining with one voice in returning to Almighty God their sincere thanks for the many blessings he had poured down upon them. With this view he would move the following resolution—

Resolved, That a joint committee of both Houses be directed to wait upon the President of the United States, to request that he recommend to the people of the United States a day of public thanksgiving and prayer, to be observed by acknowledging, with grateful hearts, the many signal favors of Almighty God, especially by affording them an opportunity peaceably to establish a constitution of government for their safety and happiness.

Mr. Sherman justified the practice of thanksgiving on any signal event, not only as a laudable one in itself, but as warranted by precedents in Holy Writ: for instance, the solemn thanksgiving and rejoicing which took place in the time of Solomon after the building of the temple was a case in point. This example he thought worthy of imitation on the present occasion.

Washington's Proclamation

The resolution was unanimously adopted, and in pursuance thereof Washington issued the following—

Proclamation for a National Thanksgiving.

Whereas it is the duty of all nations to acknowledge the providence of Almighty God, to obey his will, to be grateful for his benefits, and humbly to implore his protection and favor; and whereas both Houses of Congress, by their joint committee, requested me "to recommend to the people of the United States a day of public thanksgiving and prayer, to be observed by acknowledging with grateful hearts the many signal favors of Almighty God, especially by affording them an opportunity peaceably to establish a form of government for their safety and happiness:"—

Now, therefore, I do recommend and assign Thursday, the twenty-sixth day of November next, to be devoted by the people of these States to the service of that great and glorious Being who is the beneficent author of all the good that was, that is, or that will be; that we then may all unite unto him our sincere and humble thanks for his kind care and protection of the people of this country previous to their becoming a nation; for the signal and manifold mercies and the favorable interpositions of his providence in the course and conclusion of the late war; for the great degree of tranquillity, union, and plenty which we have since enjoyed; for the peaceable and rational manner in which we have been enabled to establish constitutions of government for our safety and happiness, and particularly the national one now lately instituted; for the civil and religious liberty with which we are blessed, and the means we have of acquiring and diffusing useful knowledge, and, in general, for all the great and various favors which he has been pleased to confer upon us.

And, also, that we may then unite in most humbly offering our prayers and supplications to the great Lord and Ruler of Nations, and beseech him to pardon our national and other transgressions; to enable us all, whether in public or in private stations, to perform our several relative duties properly and punctually; to render our national government a blessing to all the people, by constantly being a government of wise, just, and constitutional laws, discreetly executed and obeyed; to protect and guide all sovereigns and nations (especially such as have shown kindness to us) and to bless them with good governments, peace, and concord; to promote the knowledge and practice of TRUE RELIGION and virtue, and the increase of science, among them and us; and generally to grant unto all mankind such a degree of temporal prosperity as he alone knows to be best.

Given under my hand, at the city of New York, the third day of October, in the year of our Lord one thousand seven hundred and eighty-nine.

George Washington.

Christian Ordinance of 1787

A memorable act of freedom and religion was passed by Congress, two years previous to the adoption of the national Constitution, which is here recorded as belonging to the Christian legislation of those earlier days of the republic. It was passed on the 13th day of July, 1787, and is as follows ;—

Be it ordained by the United States in Congress assembled, that for extending the fundamental principles of civil and religious liberty which form the basis whereon these republics, their laws and constitutions, are erected, to fix and establish those principles as the basis of all laws, constitutions, and governments which forever hereafter shall be formed in the said territories, it is hereby ordained and declared, by the authority aforesaid, that—

Religion, morality, and knowledge being necessary to good government and the happiness of mankind, schools and the means of education shall forever be encouraged; and that "No person demeaning himself in a peaceable and orderly manner shall ever be molested on account of his mode of worship or religious sentiments;" and "There shall be neither slavery nor involuntary servitude in the said Territory (the Northwest), otherwise than in the punishment of crimes, whereof the parties shall be duly convicted."

Washington's Letter to Lafayette

Writing to Lafayette, Washington alludes to this ordinance as follows—

"I agree with you cordially in your views in regard to negro slavery. I have long considered it a most serious evil, both socially and politically, and I should rejoice in any feasible scheme to rid our States of such a burden. The Congress of 1787 adopted an ordinance prohibiting the existence of involuntary servitude in our Northwestern Territory forever. I consider it a wise measure. It met with the approval and assent of nearly every member of the States more immediately interested in slave labor. The prevailing opinion in Virginia is against the spread of slavery in the new Territory; and I trust we shall have a CONFEDERACY OF FREE STATES."

Judge Nash's View of the Moral Ends of Civil Government

The Christian sentiments and acts in this chapter confirm the views of Judge Nash, of Ohio, who, in his work on the Morality of the State, says—

"The mission of a civil state is no political expediency organized to create offices and furnish employments and salaries for the venal, and a field of action for the aspiring. The state is an institution of God, as much as the church and the family; and duties are laid upon it which it must fulfil. Its ends are man's mortal and immortal interests; it has to do with materials only so far as those subserve and advance the spiritual. The state is a part of God's machinery, of God's instrumentalities, which he has appointed for the education, instruction, moral culture, and perfection of the human soul. Man is enthralled to nature; God has organized this world with the view of emancipating him from nature, and restoring him to that spiritual freedom which he himself rejoices in—the freedom of acting in conformity to the Divine law, which is the law of man's own being. Truth is the great agent of this emancipation: it is this, acting in his own spirit, that alone can make man free and elevate him to the dignity of a son of God. The state has an important part to act in this great work of human elevation and purification; its aim must ever be in this direction, its action should be guided and shaped so as to bear onward and co-operate in this holy work."

"And let us remember," says Webster, "that it is only religion, and morals, and knowledge, that can make men respectable and happy under any form of government. Let us hold fast the great truth that communities are responsible, as well as individuals, and that without unspotted purity of public faith, without sacred public principle, fidelity, and honor, no mere forms of government, no machinery of laws, can give dignity to political society. In our day and generation let us seek to raise and improve the moral sentiment, so that we may look, not for a degraded, but for an elevated and improved, future."

14

The Christian Acts and Scenes of the Army of the Revolution

The Army of the Revolution

WAR," says Dr. Bacon, "has a place among the agencies through which God's providence is working from age to age in the interest of that Divine kingdom which is righteousness and peace. In the sacred books of the Old Testament we have not only the record of the wars in which the chosen people fulfilled their destiny, but the prayers in which holy men commended their country to the God of Hosts in time of peril, and the songs in which they acknowledged that his right hand had given them the victory.

"Under the providence of God, then, and in the methods by which he governs the world, war, with its dreadful train of evils, is sometimes an inevitable incident in the world's progress. Conflicts attendant on the birth or the attempted subjugation and extinction of nationalities—conflicts arising out of the growth and collision of irreconcilable systems of civilization, or the collision of civilization with barbarism—conflicts between right and wrong, between liberty and despotic power, or between progressive and repressive forces—sometimes involve the necessity of war.

Views of the Puritans

"It was well for the interests of civilization and of humanity that the men who had undertaken to enlarge the kingdom of Christ by planting themselves here in this wilderness were not embarrassed at such a crisis by any doubts about the lawfulness of bearing arms in a righteous cause. The sentimentalism which would surrender the whole earth to the dominion of lawless violence, rather than resist force by force, had not yet been born, and was not likely to be engendered in minds like theirs. Hence one of the moral maxima of the New England Puritans was that 'they may lawfully, under the New Testament, wage war upon just and necessary occasions.' For this end, they kept up, for generations, the most rigid military discipline, and were ready at all times to repel invaders. In the first age of Puritan history, their rigid Christian polity and progress had a military as well as a moral force to make it effective and certain. Freedom and expansion over the wild domains of the savage were secured by the successful wars which the Puritans waged to secure a foothold and a progress to Christianity. This union of the military and Christian spirit was transmitted to their descendants, and was ready for earnest action, when the great war of the Revolution broke out.

"Our fathers, when that question arose, did not initiate a rebellion against an established Constitution; they stood simply for their hereditary English rights, their legal and chartered rights; and when those rights were assailed with armed invasion, they stood in arms for the defence of their inheritance and their political existence. They did not begin the war, rushing to take up arms before any demonstration in arms had been made against them: they waited in the hope that justice would prevail in the councils of the king; they offered no resistance, but by remonstrance and petition, till their king made war on them. They did not commence with an act of secession from the British Empire, nor with renunciation of their allegiance to the British crown. Their declaration of independence was not made till after the king and Parliament had begun the attempt to establish, by military power, new methods of government over them.

"Then war had become to them an inevitable necessity; for they could not tamely surrender their own birthright and the lawful inheritance of their children. Then, in the spirit of the generations which had preceded them, they girded themselves for the struggle to which they were summoned."

Extract From a Speech in the Continental Congress

The following fragment of a speech made in the General Congress of America, by a member whose name is unknown, in 1775, presents a just view of the results of war as an agency of good to freedom and the final glory of a nation. The war of the Revolution, about to open when the speech was made, grandly illustrated its views.

"The great God, sir, who is the searcher of all things, will witness for me that I have spoken to you from the bottom and purity of my heart. The God to whom we appeal must judge us.

"There are some people who tremble at the approach of war. They feel that it must put an inevitable step to the further progress of these colonies, and ruin irretrievably those benefits which the industry of centuries has called forth from this once savage land. I may commend the anxiety of these, without praising their judgment.

"War, like other evils, is often wholesome. The waters that stagnate corrupt; the storm that works the ocean into rage renders it salutary; heaven has given us nothing unmixed; the rose is not without its thorn. War calls forth the great virtues and efforts which would sleep in the gentle bosom of Peace. *'Paullum sepultœ distat inertiœ celata virtus.'* It opens resources which would be concealed under the inactivity of tranquil times; it produces a people of animation, energy, adventure, and greatness. Let us consult history. Did not the Grecian republics prosper amid continual warfare? Their prosperity, their power, their splendor, grew from the all-animating spirit of war. Did not the cottages of shepherds rise into imperial Rome, the mistress of the world, the nurse of heroes, the delight of gods, through the invigorating operation of unceasing wars? *'Per damna, per cœdes, ab ipso ducit opes animumque ferro.'*

"How often has Flanders been the theatre of contending powers, conflicting hosts, and blood! Yet what country is more fertile and flourishing? Trace back the history of our parent state. Whether you view her arraying Angles against Danes, Danes against Saxons, Saxons against Normans, the barons against usurping princes, or in the civil wars of the Red and White Roses, or that between the people and the tyrant Stuart, you see her in a state of almost continual warfare. In almost every reign to the commencement of that of Henry VII. her peaceful bosom (in her poet's phrase) was gored with war. It was in the peaceful reigns of Henry VII., Henry VIII., and Charles II. that she suffered the severest extremities of tyranny and oppression. But, amid her civil contentions, she flourished and grew strong: trained in them, she sent her hardy legions forth, which planted the standard of England upon the battlements of Paris, extending her commerce and her dominion.

"The beautiful fabric of her constitutional liberty was reared and cemented in blood. From this fulness of her strength those scions issued which, taking deep root in this delightful land, have reared their heads and spread abroad their branches like the cedars of Lebanon.

"Why fear we, then, to pursue, through apparent evil, real good? The war upon which we are about to enter is just and necessary. '*Justum est bellum, ubi necessarium; et pia arma, quibus nulla, nisis in armis, relinquiter spes.*' It is to protect these regions, brought to such beauty through the infinite toil and hazard of our fathers and ourselves, from becoming a prey of that more desolating and more cruel spoiler than war, pestilence, or famine—absolute *rule and endless extortion.*

"Our sufferings have been great, our endurance long. Every effort of patience, complaint, and supplication has been exhausted. They seem only to have hardened the hearts of ministers who oppress us and double our distresses. Let us therefore consult only how we shall defend our liberties with dignity and success. Our parent state will then think us worthy of her, when she sees that with her liberty we inherit her rigid resolution of maintaining it against all invaders. Let us give her reason to pride herself in the relationship.

> "'And thou, great Liberty! inspire our souls:
> Make our lives happy in thy pure embrace,
> Or our deaths glorious in thy just defence.'"

Religion Sanctions a Just War

"Religion supports valor by inspiring faith in the providence of God. Every Christian believes that the purposes and plans of God include, either directly or permissively, all the events of time, and that such are the resources of Divine power, wisdom, and goodness, that all things will be overruled to the final triumph of right. This is one of the reasons why those Christians whose theology lays great stress on the Divine purposes appear in history as such sturdy soldiers; in Switzerland, France, Scotland, England, and America. The Huguenots, the Covenanters, the Puritans—who have dared or sacrificed more than these? They felt that they were in God's hands, with the place of their lives and the hour and mode of their death marked out, and they had no other concern than to go forward under the guidance and protection of Divine Providence. The saint is bold in war because he has faith in God as pledged to sustain the right. He strikes hard, he takes aim coolly and accurately, because his strength has been summoned forth and his nerves steadied by fervent prayer and a conviction that God is with him. He kneels before he fires; he deals no blow without faith that God will make it effectual; he carries a rifle in his hand and a Bible in his pocket; and, like Cromwell's army, he 'trusts in God and keeps his powder dry.' Fighting in a good cause being part of his religion, he scruples not, but is zealous, rather, to do it well, that it may not need to be done again.

"This trust in God as the defender of right is conspicuous in the conduct and words of the warriors mentioned in the Bible. The general of the forces of Israel, in the battle with the Ammonites, made this address to the troops —'Be of good courage, and let us play the men for our people and for the cities of our God; and the Lord do that which seemeth him right.'"

The appointment of Washington as commander-in-chief of the American armies was, as John Adams beautifully said, "a providential inspiration;" and his Christian character and principles, in harmony with the righteousness of the cause at stake, gave the happiest auspices of final victory.

Washington's Views

He had no taste for war or desire for military glory. "My first wish," said he, "is to see the whole world in peace, and the inhabitants of it as one band of brothers, striving who should contribute most to the happiness of mankind. For the sake of humanity, it is devoutly to be wished that the manly employments of agriculture and the humanizing benefits of commerce should suspend the wastes of war and the rage of conquest, and that the sword may be turned into the plough-share."

But peace, the desire of all good men and the gift of Christianity, comes through conflict and war. Freedom and truth, in a world where wrong and tyranny reign, must win their way by the sword and conquer peace from the enemies of liberty and right. In these great conflicts the armies of freedom and righteousness receive an invincible spirit through the practical adoption of Christianity. Christian soldiers in a good cause are the most reliable and the most ardent. They go into battle with deep convictions that God is with them and will lead them to final victory. Hence the duty of a Christian nation to infuse and educate its armies into the spirit of Christianity. They should be girded with its power, clothed with its armor, and so be the warriors of God and liberty. This was the desire and effort of Washington and Congress during the Revolutionary War, as the following official facts will show.

Christian Legislation of the Colonial Congress on the War

The Colonial Congress incorporated Christianity in the organization of the Revolutionary army, where from the beginning of the Government till now it has been maintained. In the Act "for establishing rules and articles for the government of the armies of the United States," we have these articles—

Christian Rules for the Army

> Art. 2.—It is earnestly recommended to all officers and soldiers diligently to attend divine service; and all officers who shall behave indecently at any place of divine worship shall,

if commissioned officers, be brought before a general court-martial, there to be publicly and severely reprimanded by the president; if non-commissioned officers or soldiers, every person so offending shall, for the first offence, forfeit one-sixth of a dollar, to be deducted out of his next pay; for the second offence, he shall not only forfeit a like sum, but be confined twenty-four hours, and for every like offence shall suffer and pay in like manner.

ART. 3.—Any non-commissioned officer or soldier who shall use any profane oath or execration shall incur the penalties expressed in the foregoing article; and a commissioned officer shall forfeit and pay, for each and every such offence, one dollar. In both cases the money to go to the sick soldiers of the company or troop to which the offender may belong.

ART. 4.—Every chaplain commissioned in the army or armies of the United States who shall absent himself from the duties assigned (except in cases of sickness or leave of absence) shall, on conviction thereof before a court-martial, be fined not exceeding one month's pay, besides the loss of his pay during his absence, or be discharged, as the said court shall adjudge proper.

The Act "for the better government of the navy of the United States" is of similar tone—

ART. 1.—The commanders of all ships and vessels of war belonging to the navy are strictly enjoined and required to show in themselves a good example of virtue, honor, patriotism, and subordination; and to be vigilant in inspecting the conduct of all such as are placed under their command, and to guard against and suppress all dissolute and immoral practices, and to correct all such as are guilty of them according to the usages of the sea-service.

ART. 2.—The commanders of all ships and vessels in the navy, having chaplains on board, shall take care that divine service be performed in a solemn and reverent manner twice a day, and a sermon preached on Sunday, unless bad weather or other extraordinary accidents prevent it; and that they come all, or as many of the ship's company as can be spared from duty, to attend every performance of the worship of Almighty God.

ART. 3.—Any officer or other persons in the navy who shall be guilty of oppression, cruelty, fraud, profane swearing, or any other scandalous conduct tending to the destruction of good morals, shall, if an officer, be cashiered, or suffer such other punishment as a court-martial shall adjudge; if a private, shall be put in irons or flogged, at the discretion of the captain, not exceeding twelve lashes; but if the offence require severer punishment, he shall be tried by a court-martial and suffer such punishment as said court-martial shall inflict.

The proper discipline for those who are to be intrusted with the safety and honor of the country, the greatest of all trusts, is thus adjudged to be a discipline not only of good morals, but of regular, pious observance and instruction, of daily worship, of reverence for God's name and institutions, of Sabbath-keeping, hearing the gospel preached, learning and practising the whole lesson of the cross.

Washington a Christian Commander

Washington, in his first campaign as a military officer during the war of Great Britain against France, in our colonial history, developed his character as a Christian commander. The following is one of his earliest orders—

Colonel Washington has observed that the men of his regiment are very profane and reprobate. He takes this opportunity to inform them of his great displeasure at such practices, and assures them that, if they do not leave them off, they shall be severely punished.

A most affecting instance of Washington's early Christian feelings, as a military man, was displayed at the death and burial of Braddock, in 1766. After that unfortunate battle, Washington bore the body of the fallen hero, after night, to his final place of burial. In a slow and solemn march the spot was reached, and, around the open grave, the young chieftain, by the light of blazing torches, read the beautiful burial-service of the Episcopal Church, and, having committed "ashes to ashes," returned to his camp. How prophetic this of his future career as a Christian commander of the American army!

When Washington proceeded to Cambridge after his appointment as commander-in-chief, the Provincial Congress of Massachusetts appointed a committee to meet the general and escort him to Boston. That committee was Rev. Dr. Benjamin Church and Moses Gill, who, at Waterton, presented to Washington a formal congratulatory address, in which they said—

> The Congress of the Massachusetts colony, impressed with every sentiment of gratitude and respect, beg leave to congratulate you on your safe arrival, and to wish you all imaginable happiness and success in the execution of the important duties of your elevated station.
>
> While we applaud the attention to the public good manifested in your appointment, we equally admire that disinterested virtue and distinguished patriotism which alone could call you from those enjoyments of domestic life which a sublime and manly taste joined with a most affluent fortune can afford, to hazard your life and to endure the fatigues of war in the defence of the rights of mankind and the good of your country.
>
> We most fervently implore Almighty God that the blessings of Divine Providence may rest on you; that your head may be covered in the day of battle; that every necessary assistance may be afforded, and that you may be long continued in life and health, a blessing to mankind.

A graphic description of the American camp is given by Rev. William Emerson, a chaplain in the army, written a few days after the arrival of the commander-in-chief. He says—

"There is great overturning in the camp, as to order and regularity. New lords, new laws. The generals, Washington and Lee, are up and down the lines every day. New orders from his Excellency are read to the respective regiments every morning after *prayers*. The strictest government is taking place. Every one is made to know his place and keep in it."

The following extract from the journal of a chaplain in the American army presents an interesting and instructive view of Washington's appearance and religious character at the opening of the Revolutionary War, when, in obedience to Congress, he took command of the armies—

"*July 4th*, 1775.—I have seen the new general appointed by Congress to command the armies of the colonies. On seeing him I am not surprised at the choice. I expected to see an ardent, heroic-looking man; but such a mingled sweetness, dignity, firmness, and self-possession I never before saw in any man. The expression 'born to command' is peculiarly applicable to him. Day before yesterday, when under the great elm in Cambridge he drew his sword and formally took command of the army of seventeen thousand men, his look and bearing impressed every one, and I could not but feel that he was reserved for some great destiny.

"I have heard much of his religious character, and hence looked with a great deal of anxiety for his first order to see if there was any thing more than a mere formal recognition of the Supreme Being. To-day he issued it; and it was with a heart overflowing with gratitude to God that I read the following passage in it—

"'The general most earnestly requires and expects the due observance of those articles of war established for the government of the army which forbid cursing, swearing, and drunkenness, and in like manner he requires and expects of all officers and soldiers, not engaged on actual duties, a punctual attendance on divine service to implore the blessing of Heaven upon the means used for safety and defence.'

His Christian Orders

"Truly God is with us, and, though the way be dark and dreary, I will believe he will carry us through safely at last."

In a general order, July, 1776, Washington says—

> The fate of unborn millions will now depend, under God, on the courage and conduct of the army. Our cruel and unrelenting enemy leaves us only the choice of brave resistance or the most abject submission. Let us, then, rely on the goodness of

our cause and the aid of the Supreme Being in whose hands victory is, to animate and encourage us to noble action.

An army order, July 9, 1776, from Washington, says—

> The Honorable Continental Congress having been pleased to allow a chaplain to each regiment, the colonels or command-ing officers of each regiment are directed to procure chap-lains, persons of good character and exemplary lives, and to see that all inferior officers and soldiers pay them suitable re-spect. The blessing and protection of Heaven are at all times necessary, but especially so in time of public distress and danger. The general hopes and trusts that every officer and man will endeavor to live and act as a CHRISTIAN SOLDIER defending the dearest rights and liberties of his country.

The following order is eminently Christian—

> HEAD-QUARTERS, NEW YORK, MAY 15, 1776.
> The Continental Congress having ordered Friday, the 17th instant, to be observed as a day of "Fasting, Humiliation, and Prayer, humbly to supplicate the mercy of Almighty God, that it would please him to pardon all our manifold sins and trans-gressions, and to prosper the arms of the United Colonies, and finally establish the peace and freedom of America upon a solid and lasting foundation," the general commands all of-ficers and soldiers to pay strict attention to the orders of the Continental Congress, and, by the unfeigned and pious ob-servance of their religious duties, incline the Lord and Giver of victory to prosper our arms.

The following is a letter to the ministers, elders, and deacons of the Dutch Reformed Church at Raritan—

> CAMP MIDDLEBROOK, 2 JUNE, 1779.
> In quartering an army, and in supplying its wants, distress and inconvenience will often occur to the citizens. These have

been strictly limited by necessity, and regard to the rights of my fellow-citizens. I thank you for the sense you entertain of the conduct of the army. I trust the goodness of the cause and the exertions of the people, under Divine protection, will give us that honorable peace for which we are contending. Suffer me to wish the Reformed Dutch Church at Raritan all the blessings which flow from piety and religion.

Congress appointed the 18th of December, 1777, as a day of public thanksgiving and praise. Washington, with his army, were on the march from Whitemarsh to Valley Forge, where they were to go into winter quarters. They paused that day to wait upon God in prayer and praise, as the following order of December 17, 1777, shows—

> To-morrow being the day set apart by the Honorable Congress for public thanksgiving and praise, and duty calling us all devoutly to express our grateful acknowledgments to God for his manifold blessings he has granted to us, the general directs that the army remain in its present quarters, and that the chaplains perform divine service with their several regiments and brigades, and earnestly exhorts all officers and soldiers, whose absence is not indispensably necessary, to attend with reverence the solemnities of the day.

How sublime and suggestive this Christian scene! A patriot army, led by a Christian commander, stopping amid the snows and cold of winter, to worship God before going into winter quarters! These services were wisely preparatory to the hardships of that long and dreary winter at Valley Forge.

Profaneness is a common vice of an army. Congress and Washington labored hard to correct this shameful habit. Congress passed the following resolutions on the subject.

> THURSDAY, FEBRUARY 25, 1777
> It being represented to Congress that profaneness in general, and particularly cursing and swearing, shamefully prevail in the army of the United States:

> *Resolved*, That General Washington be informed of this; and that he be requested to take the most proper measures, in concert with his general officers, for reforming this abuse.

Washington issued the following order in 1776—

> *That the troops may have an opportunity of attending public worship, as well as to take some rest after the great fatigue they have gone through, the general, in future, excuses them from fatigue duty on Sundays*, except at the shipyards or on special occasions, until further orders. The general is sorry to be informed that the foolish and wicked practice of profane cursing and swearing, a vice hitherto little known in an American army, is growing into fashion. He hopes the officers will, by example as well as influence, endeavor to check it, and that both they and the men will reflect that we can have little hope of the blessing of Heaven on our arms if we insult it by our impiety and folly. Added to this, it is a vice so mean and low, without any temptation, that every man of sense and character detests and despises it.

In May, 1777, Washington sent to the brigadier-generals of the army the following instructions—

> Let vice and immorality of every kind be discouraged as much as possible in your brigade; and, as a chaplain is allowed to each regiment, see that the men regularly attend during worship. Gaming of every kind is expressly forbidden, as being the foundation of evil, and the cause of many a brave and gallant officer's and soldier's ruin.

The following order presents the character of a Christian superior to that of a patriot or soldier—

> HEAD-QUARTERS, VALLEY FORGE, MAY 2, 1778
> The commander-in-chief directs that divine service be performed every Sunday at ten o'clock in each brigade with a

chaplain. Those brigades which have none will attend the places of worship nearest them. It is expected that officers of all ranks will, by their attendance, set an example to their men. While we are duly performing the duty of good soldiers, we certainly ought not to be inattentive to the higher duties of religion. To the distinguished character of a patriot it should be our highest glory to add the more distinguished character of a Christian.

The signal instances of providential goodness which we have experienced, and which have almost crowned our arms with complete success, demand from us, in a peculiar manner, the warmest returns of gratitude and piety to the Supreme Author of all good.

Congress, on the 17th of March, appointed the 22d of April, 1778, as a day of religious solemnities. Washington, in pursuance thereof, issued to his army the following order—

HEAD-QUARTERS, VALLEY FORGE, APRIL 12, 1778. The Honorable the Congress having thought proper to recommend to the United States of America to set apart Wednesday, the 22d instant, to be observed as a day of fasting, humiliation, and prayer, that at one time, and with one voice, the righteous dispensations of Providence may be acknowledged, and his goodness and mercy towards our arms be supplicated and implored,

The general directs that the day shall be most religiously observed in the army; that no work shall be done thereon; and that the several chaplains do prepare discourses suitable to the occasion.

In 1778, the independence of the United States was acknowledged by France, and a treaty of friendship formed at Paris. Washington and his army were at Valley Forge when the news reached him. On the 7th of May, shortly after the news reached him, he issued the following order—

It having pleased the Almighty Ruler of the universe to defend the cause of the United American States, and finally to raise up a powerful friend among the princes of the earth, to establish our liberty and independence upon a lasting foundation, it becomes us to set apart a day for gratefully acknowledging the Divine goodness and celebrating the important event which we owe to his Divine interposition. The several brigades are to be assembled for this purpose at nine o'clock to-morrow morning, when their chaplains will communicate the intelligence, and offer up thanksgiving, and deliver a discourse suitable to the occasion.

The surrender of Cornwallis, at Yorktown, on the 21st of October, 1781, closed the war of liberty and revolution. General Washington immediately ordered religious ceremonies commemorative of the joyful event—

Divine service is to be performed to-morrow in the several brigades and divisions. The commander-in-chief earnestly recommends that the troops not on duty should universally attend, with that seriousness of deportment and gratitude of heart which the recognition of such reiterated and astonishing interpositions of Providence demands of us.

The following general order was issued by General Washington on the restoration of peace—

Head-Quarters, Chatham, April 18, 1783

The commander-in-chief orders the cessation of hostilities between the United States of America and the King of Great Britain to be publicly proclaimed to-morrow at twelve o'clock at the new buildings; and that the proclamation which will be communicated herewith be read to-morrow evening at the head of every regiment and corps of the army; after which, the chaplains, with the brigades, will render thanks to Almighty God for all his mercies, particularly for his overruling the wrath of man to his own glory, and causing the rage of war to cease among the nations.

Signed, April 18, 1783

At twelve o'clock, the large log temple which had been erected on the camp-ground for the meeting of the officers was thronged, and the joyful intelligence communicated amid deafening plaudits. At evening, the chaplains, in accordance with the orders of the commander-in-chief, offered up thanksgiving and prayer at the head of the several brigades.

As a military commander, Washington constantly and devoutly acknowledged the special interposition of a Divine Providence throughout the entire war, and habitually ascribed the victories and the final results to God's intervention and goodness. This fundamental doctrine of the Christian religion is the key of all historic events, giving confidence in auspicious, final results, and had a firm and deep hold on the faith and life of Washington. In the midst of disasters, defeats, and the darkness which sometimes clouded the prospects of the struggling colonies, his soul, in serene and sublime trust, rested on this great doctrine with hope and assurance, and it animated his courage and efforts in the great cause to which he was devoted. His thankful and reverential acknowledgments of the providence and presence of God are full of instruction, and present the brightest evidences of his Christian faith and piety. The following allusions to this great doctrine, in connection with himself and the events of the war, are here recorded.

When but twenty-three years of age, in a letter to Governor Dinwiddie, June 10, 1754, he acknowledges a striking interposition of a special Providence in reference to a supply of provisions for his troops. "If Providence," says he, "had not sent a trader from the Ohio to our relief; we should have been four days without provisions."

After the defeat of Braddock he wrote, "By the all-powerful dispensations of Providence, I have been protected beyond all human probability or expectation." His perfect preservation, during the eight years of the Revolutionary War, though often exposed and in danger, confirms his own declarations in reference to his providential protection.

Writing to Governor Trumbull, from Cambridge, 18th of July, 1775, he says—

"As the cause of our common country calls us both to an active and dangerous duty, I trust that Divine Providence will enable us to discharge it with fidelity and success."

He wrote to General Gage, of the British army, in the same year, and said—

"May that God to whom you appeal judge between America and you. Under his providence, those who influence the councils of America, and all the other united colonies, at the hazard of their lives, are determined to hand down to posterity those just and invaluable privileges which they received from their ancestors."

In a circular to his officers, September 8, 1775, in reference to an attack on the British at Boston, he said—

"The success of such an enterprise depends, I well know, upon the all-wise Disposer of events."

After the evacuation of Boston by the British troops, March 17, 1776, Washington, in answer to an address of the General Assembly of Massachusetts, wrote as follows—

"It must be ascribed to the interposition of that Providence which has manifestly appeared in our behalf through the whole of this important struggle."

In May, 1776, referring to expected battles in New York, and the feeble preparations for them, he said—

"However, it is to be hoped that if our cause is just, as I do most religiously believe it to be, the same Providence which has in many instances appeared for us will still go on to afford us aid."

On the 2d of July of the same year, in an order to his army, on the eve of an expected attack, he said, "The fate of unborn millions will now depend, *under God*, on the courage and conduct of this army. Let us rely upon the goodness of our cause and the *aid of that Supreme Being in whose hands victory is*, to animate and encourage us to great and noble actions."

To the officers and soldiers of the Pennsylvania Association he writes, the 8th of August, 1776, "We must now determine to be enslaved or free. If we make freedom our choice, we must obtain it by the *blessing of Heaven* on our united and vigorous exertions. I beg leave to remind you that liberty, honor, and safety are all at stake; and I trust Providence will smile upon our efforts, and establish us once more the inhabitants of a free and happy country."

In writing to General Armstrong, from Morristown, New Jersey, 4th July, 1777, he says—

"The evacuation of Jersey by the British troops, at *this time*, is a peculiar mark of the favor of Providence, as the inhabitants have an opportunity of securing their harvests of hay and grain."

When Washington received from Governor Clinton a despatch announcing the surrender of Burgoyne's army at Saratoga, in 1777, his first words were, "I most devoutly congratulate my country and every well-wisher to the cause on this signal stroke of Providence. Should Providence be pleased to crown our arms in the course of the campaign with one more fortunate stroke, I think we shall have no great cause for anxiety inspecting the future designs of Great Britain. I trust all will be well in his good time."

Alluding to the prisoners taken by the Northern armies, "including tories in arms against us," Washington wrote—

"This signal instance of Providence, and of our good fortune under it, exhibits a striking proof of the advantages which result from unanimity and a spirited conduct in the militia."

In reference to the disaffection of a portion of the people of New York to the cause, and the embarrassments thereby caused to his campaign in that State, Washington said, "I do not mean to complain. I flatter myself that a superintending Providence is ordering every thing for the best, and that, in due time, all will end well."

From Valley Forge, May 30, 1778, he wrote as follows—

"Providence has a just claim to my humble and grateful thanks for its protection and direction of me through the many difficult and intricate scenes which this contest has produced, and for its constant interposition in our behalf when the clouds were heaviest and seemed ready to burst upon us."

Referring to the distresses of the army at Valley Forge, and its sufferings during the previous eventful winter, he said, "Since our prospects have miraculously brightened, shall I attempt the des-cription of the condition of the army, or even bear it in remembrance, further than as a memento of what is due to the great Author of all, the care and good that have been extended in relieving us in difficulties and distresses?"

The battle of Monmouth, 28th of June, 1778, which threatened to prove disastrous from the mismanagement of General Lee, affords the occasion to Washington to say, "Had not that bountiful Providence which has never failed us in the hour of distress enabled me to form a regiment or two (of those who were retreating) in the face of the enemy, and under their fire, by which means a stand was made long enough to form the troops that were advancing upon an advantageous piece of ground in the rear, where our affairs took a favorable turn."

From Newport, Rhode Island, in March, 1781, Washington wrote to William Gordon, and said, "We have, as you very justly observe, abundant reasons to thank Providence for its many favorable interpositions in our behalf. It has at times been my only dependence, for all other resources seemed to have failed us."

To General Armstrong, in 1781, Washington expressed his faith in Providence as follows—

"Our affairs are brought to a perilous crisis, that the band of Providence, I trust, may be more conspicuous in our deliverance. The many remarkable interpositions of the Divine government, in the hours of our deepest distress and darkness, have been too luminous to suffer us to doubt the issue of the present contest."

To the President of Congress, in November, 1781, referring to "the success of the combined armies against our enemies at Yorktown and Gloucester," and the "proclamation for a day of public prayer and thanksgiving," Washington wrote—

"I take a particular pleasure in acknowledging that the interposing hand of Heaven, in the various instances of our extensive preparations for this operation, have been most conspicuous and remarkable."

"The great Director of events," he addressed in 1781 the citizens of Alexandria, "has carried us through a variety of scenes, during this long and bloody contest in which we have been for seven campaigns most nobly struggling."

In a circular to the States, dated Philadelphia, January 31, 1782, Washington said—

"Although we cannot, by the best-concerted plans, absolutely command success; although the race is not always to the swift, nor the battle to the strong; yet, without presumptuously waiting for miracles to be wrought in our favor, it is our indispensable duty, with the deepest gratitude to Heaven for the past, and humble confidence in its smiles on our future operations, to make use of all the means in our power for our defence and security."

At the close of the war he said, "I must be permitted to consider the wisdom and unanimity of our national councils, the firmness of our citizens, and the patience and bravery of our troops, which have produced so happy a termination of the war, as the most conspicuous effects of the Divine interposition and the surest presage of our future happiness. To the great Ruler of events—not to any exertions of mine—is to be ascribed the favorable termination of our late contest for liberty. I never considered the fortunate issue of any event in another light than the ordering of a kind Providence."

In his farewell address to the armies of the United States, he says—

"The singular interpositions of Providence, in our feeble condition, were such as could scarcely escape the attention of the most unobserving; while the unparalleled perseverance of the armies of the United States, through almost every possible suffering and discouragement, for the space of eight long years, was little short of a standing miracle. And being now about to bid a final adieu to the armies he has so long had the honor to command, he can only again offer, in their behalf; his recommendations to their grateful country, and his prayers to the God of armies. May ample justice be done them here, and may the choicest of Heaven's favors, both here and hereafter, attend those who, under the Divine auspices, have secured innumerable blessings for others. With these wishes, and this benediction, the commander-in-chief is about to retire from the service."

To General Nelson, of Virginia, in August, 1778, Washington wrote—

"It is not a little pleasing, nor less wonderful, to contemplate, that after two years' manoeuvring and undergoing the strangest vicissitudes that ever attended any one contest since the creation, both armies are brought back to the very point they set out from, and that the offending party at the beginning is now reduced to the use of the spade and pickaxe for defence. *The hand of Providence has been so conspicuous in all this, that he must be worse than an infidel that lacks faith, and more than wicked that has not gratitude enough to acknowledge his obligations.* I shall add no more on the doctrine of Providence."

In December, 1778, Washington was in Philadelphia, at the request of Congress, for a personal conference respecting the next campaign. From that city he wrote to Benjamin Harrison, of Virginia, and, after giving a gloomy picture of the times and the financial condition of the country, and the "idleness, dissipation, extravagance, speculation, peculation, and insatiable thirst for riches, and the party disputes and personal quarrels, which seem to have got the better of every other consideration," Washington closed as follows—

"I feel more real distress on account of the present appearance of things than I have done at any one time since the commencement of the dispute. Providence has heretofore taken us up when all other means and hopes seemed to be departing from us. *In this will I confide.*"

To Joseph Reed, President of Congress, referring to the condition of the currency and the smallness of the army, Washington, in July, 1779, wrote, "And yet, Providence having so often taken us up when bereft of every other hope, I trust we shall not fail even in this."

Washington, in his instructions to Colonel Arnold, in September, 1775, when that officer was about to march against Quebec, shows the spirit of a Christian commander, and the scrupulous regard he had to the rights of conscience. His instructions were as follows—

"As the contempt of the religion of a country by ridiculing any of its ceremonies, or affronting *its ministers* or votaries, has ever been deeply resented, you are to be particularly careful to restrain every officer and soldier from such imprudence and folly, and to punish every instance of it. On the other hand, you are to protect and support the free exercise of the religion of the country, and the unobstructed enjoyment of rights in religious matters, with your utmost influence and authority."

In a private communication to the same officer and of the same date, Washington says—

"I also give it in charge to you to avoid all disrespect of the religion of the country and its ceremonies. Prudence, policy, and a true Christian spirit will lead us to look with compassion on their errors, without insulting them. While we are contending for our own liberty, we should be very cautious not to violate the rights of conscience in others, ever considering that God alone is the judge of the hearts of men, and to him only in this case they are answerable."

General Washington, having triumphantly led the armies of the Revolution to victory, and closed the war with glory and honor to his country and himself, repaired, on the 23d of December, 1783, to

Annapolis, Maryland, where Congress was in session, and surrendered his military command in the following address—

> The great event on which my resignation depended having at length taken place, I now have the opportunity of offering my sincere congratulations to Congress, and of presenting myself before them to surrender into their hands the trust committed to me, and to claim the indulgence of retiring from the service of my country. Happy in the confirmation of our independence and sovereignty, and pleased with the opportunity afforded the United States of becoming a respectable nation, I resign with satisfaction the appointment I accepted with diffidence—a diffidence in my abilities to accomplish so arduous a task, which, however, was superseded by a confidence in the rectitude of our cause, the support of the supreme power of the Union, and the patronage of Heaven.
>
> The successful termination of the war has verified the most sanguine expectations. My gratitude for the interpositions of Providence and the assistance I have received from my countrymen increases with every review of the momentous crisis. While I repeat my obligations to the army, I should do injustice to my own feelings not to acknowledge in this place the peculiar services and the distinguished merits of the gentlemen who have been attached to my person during the war. It was impossible that the choice of confidential officers to compose my family should have been more fortunate. Permit me, sir, to recommend in particular those who have continued in the service to the present moment as worthy of the favorable notice and patronage of Congress.
>
> I consider it an indispensable duty to close this last act of my official life by commending the interests of our dearest country to the protection and care of Almighty God. Having now finished the work assigned me, I retire from the great theatre of action, and, bidding an affectionate farewell to this august body, under whose orders I have so long acted, I here offer my commission and take my leave of all the employments of public life.

President Mufflin replied as follows—

> Sɪʀ—The United States, in Congress assembled, receive with
> emotions too affecting for utterance the solemn resignation
> of the authorities under which you have led their troops with
> success through a perilous and a doubtful war. Called upon
> by your country to defend its invaded rights, you accepted
> the sacred charge before it had formed alliances, and while
> it was without friends or a government to support you. You
> have conducted the great military contest with wisdom and
> fortitude, invariably regarding the rights of the civil power
> through all disasters and changes. You have, by the love and
> confidence of your fellow-citizens, enabled them to display
> their military genius and transmit their fame to poster-
> ity. You have persevered until the United States, aided by a
> magnanimous king and nation, have been enabled, under a
> just Providence, to close the war in freedom, safety, and in-
> dependence—in which happy event we sincerely join you in
> congratulations. Having defended the standard of liberty in
> this new world— having taught a lesson useful to those af-
> flicted and to those who felt oppression—you retire from the
> great theatre of action with the blessings of your fellow-citi-
> zens. But the glory of your virtue will not terminate with your
> military command: it will continue to animate remotest ages.
> We feel with you our obligations to the army in general, and
> will particularly charge ourselves with the interests of those
> confidential officers who have attended your person to this
> affecting moment.
>
> We join you in commending the interests of our dearest
> country to the protection of Almighty God, beseeching him
> to dispose the hearts and minds of its citizens to improve
> the opportunity afforded them of becoming a happy and a
> respectable nation; and for you, we address to him our ear-
> nest prayers that a life so beloved may be fostered with all
> his care, that your days may be as happy as they have been
> illustrious, and that he will give you that reward which the
> world cannot give.

Scene At Valley Forge

One of the most hopeful and inspiring scenes of the Revolution was to see this great hero, with the interests of a nation on his soul, retire for prayer unto the God in whom he trusted.

The winter at Valley Forge witnessed the retirement of Washington daily to some secluded glen in the surrounding forest for prayer. Though gloom covered his desponding country and army, yet "a cloud of doubt seldom darkened the serene atmosphere of his hopes. He knew that the cause was just and holy, and his faith and confidence in God, as a defender and helper of right, steady in their ministrations of divine vigor to his soul."

While the American army was at Valley Forge, Isaac Potts strolled up a creek that ran through his farm, and, walking quietly through the woods, he heard the tones of a solemn voice, and, looking round, saw Washington's horse tied to a sapling. In a thicket near by was Washington, on his knees, in earnest prayer. Like Moses, Mr. Potts felt he was on holy ground, and retired unobserved. He returned home, and, on entering the room of his wife, burst into tears, and informed her what he had seen and heard, and exclaimed, "If there is any one on earth whom the Lord will hearken to, it is George Washington; and I feel a presentiment that under such a commander there can be no doubt of our eventually establishing our independence, and that God in his providence has willed it so."

> "Oh, who shall know the might
> Of the words he utter'd there?
> The fate of nations there was turn'd
> By the fervor of his prayer.
> "But wouldst thou know his name
> Who wander'd there alone?
> Go read enroll'd in Heaven's archives
> The prayer of Washington."
>
> Chester.

The following note from an octogenarian who had seen Washington when a boy is an incident illustrating Washington's habit of prayer—
"New Haven, February 18, 1860

"To the Editors of the Evening Post."

"Mr. Printer—In 1796, I heard the farmer referred to narrate the following incident. Said he, 'When the British troops held possession of New York, and the American army lay in the neighborhood of West Point, one morning at sunrise I went forth to bring home the cows. On passing a clump of brushwood, I heard a moaning sound, like a person in distress. On nearing the spot, I heard the words of a man at prayer. I stood behind a tree. The man came forth: it was George Washington, the captain of the Lord's host in North America.'

"This farmer belonged to the Society of Friends, who, being opposed to war on any pretext, were lukewarm, and, in some cases, opposed to the cause of the country. However, having seen the general enter the camp, he returned to his own house. 'Martha,' said he to his wife, 'we must not oppose this war any longer. This morning I heard the man George Washington send up a prayer to Heaven for his country, and I know it will be heard.'

"This farmer dwelt between the lines, and sent Washington many items concerning the movements of the enemy, which did good service to the good cause.

"From this incident we may infer that Washington rose with the sun to pray for his country, he fought for her at meridian, and watched for her in the silent hours of night.

"Every editor of a newspaper, magazine, or journal between Montauk Point and Oregon, if he has three drops of American blood in his veins, should publish this anecdote on the 22d of February (Washington's birthday) while woods grow and waters run. This day I enter on my eighty-eighth year.

"Grant Thorburn, Sr."

Prayer Recorded

In the summer of 1779, Washington, exploring alone one day the position of the British forces on the banks of the Hudson, ventured too far from his own camp, and was compelled by a sudden storm and the fatigue of his horse to seek shelter for the night in the cottage of a pious American farmer, who, greatly struck with the manners and language of his guest, after he retired to rest, listened at the door of Washington's chamber, and overheard the following prayer from the father of his country—

> Almighty Father, if it is thy holy will that we should obtain a place and a name among the nations of the earth, grant that we may be enabled to show our gratitude for thy goodness by our endeavors to fear and obey thee. Bless us with wisdom in our councils and success in battle, and let all our victories be tempered with humility. Endow also our enemies with enlightened minds, that they may become sensible of their injustice and willing to restore our liberties and peace. Grant the petition of thy servant for the sake of Him whom thou hast called thy beloved Son. Nevertheless, not my will, but thine, be done. Amen.

An officer who served under General Washington through the eight years of the Revolution says that on every practicable occasion he sought God's blessing upon the contest; and, when no chaplain was present, he often called his staff-officers around him and reverently lifted his heart and voice in prayer. He described the scenes as of unusual solemnity, and he carried the vivid impressions of them to the grave. Just before the battle of Monmouth, Washington was seen by one of his officers alone beneath a tree, supplicating the throne of grace. He knew that God was his "refuge and strength."

His Recognition and Dependence On God During the War

The God of the Bible and his providential presence and power during the whole Revolutionary War are gratefully recognized by Washington on various occasions.

No one could express more fully his sense of the Providence of God and the dependence of man. His faith in Providence was the anchor of his soul at all times.

"Ours is a kind of struggle," said he, "designed by Providence, I dare say, to try the patience, fortitude, and virtue of men. None, therefore, who is engaged in it will suffer himself, I trust, to sink under difficulties or be discouraged by hardships."

"Providence having so often taken us up when bereft of every other hope, I trust we shall not fail even in this."

"To that good Providence which has so remarkably aided us in all our difficulties, the rest is committed."

"We have abundant reasons to thank Providence for its many favorable interpositions in our behalf. It has at times been my only dependence, for all other resources seemed to have failed us. ... Our affairs are brought to a perilous crisis that the hand of Providence, I trust, may be more conspicuous in our deliverance. The remarkable interpositions of the Divine government in the hours of our deepest distress and darkness have been too luminous to suffer me to doubt the happy issue of the present contest."

The same sentiments were expressed on many occasions after the war. In a letter to General Armstrong, March 11, 1792, he wrote—

"I am sure there never was a people who had more reason to acknowledge a Divine interposition in their affairs, than those of the United States; and I should be pained to believe that they had forgotten that agency which was so often manifested during our Revolution, or that they failed to consider the omnipotence of that God who is alone able to protect them."

The following extracts are from his circular letter to the Governors of the several States on the disbanding of the army, June 8, 1783. They are full of the sentiment and spirit of Christianity which he had developed during the war.

"I now make my earnest prayer that God would have you and the States over which you preside in his holy protection; that he would incline the hearts of the citizens to cultivate the spirit of subordination and obedience to government, to entertain a brotherly affection and love for one another, for their fellow-citizens of the United States at large, and particularly for their brethren who have served in the field; and, finally, that he would be most graciously pleased to dispose us all to do justice, to love mercy, and to demean ourselves with that charity, humility, and pacific temper of mind which were *the characteristics of the divine Author of our blessed religion*, and without an humble imitation of whose example in these things we can never hope to be a happy nation.

"We have all been encouraged to feel the guardianship and guidance of that Almighty Being whose power regulates the destiny of nations, whose blessings have been so conspicuously displayed to this rising republic, and to whom we are bound to address our devout gratitude for the past, as well as our fervent supplications and best hopes for the future."

A very suggestive instance of the prevailing Christian spirit and habits of the American people and the American army was the universal and explicit recognition of God's providence in every event and battle of the Revolution. The following passage will illustrate this point.

Views of Dr. Stiles of the Presence and Guidance of God in the Revolutionary War

"A variety of success and defeat," said Dr. Stiles, in 1783, "hath attended our warfare both by sea and land. In our lowest and most dangerous estate, in 1776 and 1777, we sustained ourselves against the British army of sixty thousand troops, commanded by Howe, Burgoyne, and Clinton, and other of the ablest generals Britain could procure throughout Europe, with a naval force of twenty-two thousand seamen in above eighty British men-of-war. These generals we sent home, one after another, conquered, defeated, and convinced of the impossibility of conquering America. While oppressed by the heavy weight of this combined force, Heaven inspired us with resolution to cut the Gordian knot when the die was cast irrevocably in the glorious Act of Independence. This was sealed and confirmed by God Almighty in the victory of General Washington at Trenton, and in the surprising movement and battle of Princeton, by which astonishing efforts of generalship, General Howe, and the whole British army, in elated confidence and in open-mouthed march for Philadelphia, were instantly stopped, remanded back, and cooped up for a shivering winter in the little borough of Brunswick. Thus God 'turned the battle to the gate,' and this gave a finishing to the foundation of the American republic.

"This, with the Burgoynade at Saratoga by General Gates, and the glorious victory over the Earl of Cornwallis in Virginia, together with the memorable victory at Eutaw Springs and the triumphant recovery of the Southern States by General Greene, are among the most heroic acts and brilliant achievements which have decided the fate of America. *And who does not see the indubitable interposition and energetic influence of Divine Providence in these great and illustrious events?* Who but a Washington, inspired by Heaven, could have struck out the great movement and manœuvre at Princeton? To whom but to the Ruler of the winds shall we ascribe it that the British reinforcement in the summer of 1777 was delayed on the ocean three months by contrary winds, until it was too late for the conflagrating General Clinton to raise the siege at Saratoga?

"What but a providential miracle detected the conspiracy of Arnold, even in the critical moment of that infernal plot, in which the body of the American army then at West Point, with his Excellency General Washington himself, were to have been rendered into the hands of the enemy? Doubtless inspired by the Supreme Illuminator of great minds were the joint councils of a Washington and a Rochambeau in that grand effort of generalship with which they deceived and astonished a Clinton and eluded his vigilance, in their transit by New York and rapid marches for Virginia. Was it not of God that both the navy and army should enter the Chesapeake at the same time? Who but God could have ordained the critical arrival of the Gallic fleet, So as to prevent and defeat the British, and assist and co-operate with the combined armies in the siege and reduction of Yorktown?

"Should we not ever admire and ascribe to a Supreme energy the wise and firm generalship displayed by General Greene, when, leaving the active and roving Cornwallis to pursue his helter-skelter, ill-fated march into Virginia, he coolly and steadily went onwards, and deliberately, judiciously, and heroically recovered the Carolinas and the Southern States?

"How rare have been the defections and apostasies of our capital characters, though tempted with all the charms of gold, titles, and nobility! Whence is it that so few men of our armies have deserted to the enemy? Whence that our brave sailors have chosen the horrors of prison-ships and death, rather than to fight against their country? Whence that men of every rank have so generally felt and spoken alike, as if the cords of life struck unison through the continent? What but a miracle has preserved the union of the States, the purity of Congress, and the unshaken patriotism of every General Assembly? It is God who has raised up for us a great and powerful ally—an ally which sent us a chosen army and a naval force. It is God who so ordered the balancing interests of nations as to produce an irresistible motive in the European maritime Powers to take our part.

"So wonderfully does Providence order the time and coincidence of the public national motives co-operating in effecting great public events and revolutions. But time would fail me to recount the wonder-working providences of God in the events of this war. Let these serve as specimens, and lead us to hope that God will not forsake this people, for whom he has done such marvellous things, whereof we are glad and rejoice this day, having at length brought us to the dawn of peace.

"O Peace, thou welcome guest, all hail! Thou heavenly visitant, calm the tumult of nations, and wave thy balmy wing perpetually over this region of liberty. Let there be a tranquil period for the unmolested accomplishment of the *magnalia Dei*—the great events in God's moral government designed from eternal ages to be displayed in these ends of the earth.

"May this great event excite and elevate our first and highest acknowledgments to the Sovereign Monarch of universal nature, to the Supreme Disposer and Controller of all events! Let this our pious, sincere, and devout gratitude ascend in one general effusion of heartfelt praise and hallelujah, in one united cloud of incense, even the incense of universal joy and thanksgiving, to God, from the collective body of the United States."

"The special interposition of Providence," said Dr. Ramsey, of South Carolina, July, 1777, in an oration on the advantages of American independence, "in our behalf makes it impious to disbelieve the final establishment of our Heaven-protected independence. Can any one seriously review the beginning, progress, and present state of the war, and not see indisputable evidence of an overruling influence on the minds of men, preparing the way for the accomplishment of this great event?

"As all the tops of corn in a waving field are inclined in one direction by a gust of wind, in like manner the Governor of the world has given one and the same universal bent of inclination to the whole body of our people. Is it the work of man that thirteen States, frequently quarrelling about boundaries, clashing in interests, differing in politics, manners, customs, forms of government, and religion, scattered over an extensive continent, under the influence of a variety of local prejudices, jealousies, and aversions, should all harmoniously agree as if one mighty mind inspired the whole?

"Our enemies seemed confident of the impossibility of our union; our friends doubted it; and all indifferent persons, who judged of things present by what has heretofore happened, considered the expectation thereof as romantic. But He who sitteth at the helm of the universe, and who boweth the hearts of a whole nation as the heart of one man, for the accomplishment of his own purpose, has effected that which to human wisdom and foresight seemed impossible."

"When I trace," said Henry Lee, of Virginia, "the heroes of Seventy-Six through all their countless difficulties and hardships— when I behold all the dangers and plots which encompassed them, their 'hair-breadth escapes,' and final glorious triumphs—I am as strongly impressed with the belief that our cause was guided by Heaven as that Moses and the Israelites were directed by the finger of God through the wilderness."

Dr. Ladd's Address Before the Governor of South Carolina in 1785

The following extract, from an address by Dr. Ladd, of Charleston, South Carolina, delivered before the Governor of the State, and a large number of other gentlemen, on the 4th of July, 1785, being the anniversary of American independence, will present the views of the patriots of that day in reference to the special presence of Almighty God through the scenes and triumphs of the Revolution, and their desire to enthrone God as the Governor of the nation. The motto of his oration was—

> "'Tell ye your children of it, and let your children tell
> Their children, and their children another generation.'

"A prophet divinely inspired, and deeply impressed with the importance of the event which had just taken place, breaks into this exclamation—an exclamation happily adapted to the present occasion, tending to perpetuate the remembrance of an event written upon the heart of every true American, of every friend to his country.

"The eventful history of our great Revolution is pregnant with many a source of sublime astonishment. Succeeding ages shall turn to the historic page and catch inspiration from the era of 1776: they shall bow to the rising glory of America; and Rome, once mistress of the world, shall fade on their remembrance.

"The commencement of our struggles, their progress and their periods, will furnish a useful lesson to posterity: they will teach them that men desperate for freedom, united in virtue, and assisted by the God of armies, can never be subdued. The youthful warrior, the rising politician, will tremble at the retrospect and turn pale at the amazing story. America—the infant America—all defenceless as she is, is invaded by a most powerful nation, her plains covered by disciplined armies, her harbors crowded with hostile fleets. Destitute of arms, destitute of ammunition, with no discipline but their virtue, and no general but their GOD—threatened with the loss of their liberties (liberties which were coeval with their existence and dearer than their lives), they arose in resistance and were nerved in desperation. What was the consequence? The invaders were repulsed, their armies captured, their strong works demolished, and their fleets driven back. Behold, the terrible flag of the glory of Great Britain, dropping all tarnished from the mast, bewails its sullied honors.

"This, my countrymen, by assistance superhuman have we at length accomplished—I say superhuman assistance, for one of us has '*chased a thousand, and two put ten thousand to flight. The Lord of hosts was on our side, the God of the armies of Israel;*' and at every blow we were ready to exclaim, with glorious exultation, '*The sword of the Lord and of Washington!*'

"Yet how did even America despair when the protecting hand of our GREAT LEADER (GOD) was for one moment withheld! Witness our veteran army retreating through the Jerseys; an almost total withering to our hopes, while America trembled with expectation—trembled! though shielded and protected by the KING OF KINGS and her beloved WASHINGTON.

"And now, having in some measure paid our debt of acknowledgment to the visible authors of our independence, let us lay our hands on our hearts in humble adoration of that MONARCH who (in place of George the Third) was this day chosen to reign over us; let us venerate the great generalissimo of our armies, from whom all triumph flows; and be it our glory, not that George the Third, but JE-HOVAH, *the first and the last, is* KING *of America—he who dwelleth in the clouds, and whose palace is the heaven of heavens; for, independent as we are with respect to the political systems of this world, we are still a province of the* GREAT KINGDOM, *and fellow-subjects with the inhabitants of* HEAVEN."

Form of an Oath of Loyalty

The following form of an oath, exacted by General Lee of the people of Rhode Island in December, 1775, illustrates the Christian tone of the military orders and requirements of the Revolutionary era—

> I, _____, here, in the presence of Almighty God, as I hope for ease, honor, and comfort in this world and happiness in the world to come, most earnestly and devoutly and religiously swear that I will neither directly nor indirectly assist the wicked instruments of ministerial tyranny and villany, commonly called the king's troops and navy, by furnishing them provisions and refreshments of any kind, unless authorized by the Continental Congress, or Legislature at present established in this particular colony of Rhode Island: I do also swear, by the Tremendous and Almighty God, that I will not directly or indirectly convey any intelligence, nor give any advice, to the aforesaid enemies described, and that I pledge myself, if I should by any accident get knowledge of such treasons, to inform immediately the Committee of safety; and, as it is justly allowed that when the rights and sacred liberties of a nation or community are invaded, neutrality is not less criminal than open and avowed hostility, I do further swear and pledge myself, as I hope for eternal salvation, that I will, whenever called upon by the voice of the Continental Con-

gress, or by that of this particular colony under their authority, to take arms and subject myself to military discipline in
defence of the common rights and liberties of America. So
help me God.

15

Government Chaplains

History of the Office of Chaplains

T HE appointment of clergymen to official positions," says Headley, "in the army and navy, under the designation of chaplains,
is a custom of long standing, and at the present day, among Christian nations, is considered necessary to their complete organization.
It would have been natural, therefore, for Congress, as a mere matter of custom, and in imitation of the mother-country, to appoint
chaplains in the American army. They did so; and chaplains, at the
present time, form a part of our military organization, and rank as
officers and draw pay like them. The propriety of this custom is recognized by all; for the sick, the suffering and dying need spiritual
advisers as much as they do hospitals and surgeons."

The chaplains of the army of the Revolution, as well as those of
the civil service, were eminent for their talents, learning, eloquence,
and piety. All were ardent and active patriots, and many of them became distinguished in the pulpit, in theological literature, and in the
departments of education and science. Their influence and labors
are thus stated by Headley—"It is difficult in these days, when chaplains in the army are looked upon simply as a necessary part of its
methodical arrangement—a set of half-officers, half-civilians, who
are not allowed to fight, and often cannot preach—to get a proper
conception of those times when their (the chaplains of the Revolu-

tion) appeals thrilled the ranks and made the hand clutch its weapon with a firmer grasp, and when their prayers filled each heart with a lofty enthusiasm. Then the people composed the army, and when the man of God addressed the crowding battalion he addressed the young men, and old men of his flock, who looked up to him with love and reverence and believed him almost as they did the Bible. The enthusiasm kindled by the pastor's address, the courage imparted by his solemn parting blessing and assurance that God smiled on them, would be a revolutionary page that would thrill the heart.

Early History of Chaplains

"The history of our chaplaincy is, to religious men at least, a subject of no inconsiderable interest. Going back thirty years before the American Revolution, to that memorable event in our colonial history, 'the siege of Louisburg,' we shall see that the selection of a chaplain to accompany the army in their hazardous expedition was a matter of no small importance. No sooner was Mr. Pepperell appointed commander of the land-forces than he applied to the renowned George Whitefield, then on his third visit to America, and at that time preaching in New England, not only for his sanction of the expedition, but with a request that he would accept the position of chaplain. Although Whitefield declined that offer, he favored the undertaking. In order, therefore, to give it the air of a religious crusade, Mr. Whitefield selected for their banners the motto 'Nothing is to be despaired of with Christ for our leader.'

A clergyman distinguished for piety and learning—qualities at that time deemed necessary for so important a station—received the appointment.

The history of Braddock's defeat furnishes another striking illustration of the importance then given to the service of a chaplain. In that disastrous battle, the chaplain, as well as the brave general himself, were wounded. Three days after, when General Braddock died, a young American colonel, then about twenty-five years of age, would not suffer his deceased commander to be buried like a savage in the wilderness, but acted the part of a chaplain himself, by reading the solemn and impressive burial-service of the Church of England at the interment. This young officer was George Washington.

Washington's Views

After this event, when Washington was appointed commander of the Virginia forces, whose great work was to protect the frontier settlements from the incursions of the French and Indians, in what was called the "French War," he wrote to Governor Dinwiddie of Virginia as follows —"The want of a chaplain, I humbly conceive, reflects dishonor on the regiment. The gentlemen of the corps are sensible of this, and propose to support one at their own expense. But I think it would have a more graceful appearance were he appointed as other officers are." At another date, Washington wrote, "As to a chaplain, if the Government will grant a subsistence, we can readily get a person of merit to accept the place, without giving the commissary any trouble on that point."

In the Governor's reply to this letter, he thus writes—"In regard to a chaplain, you should know that his qualifications, and the bishop's letter of license, should be produced to the commissary and myself."

No chaplain was then appointed. About two years after this correspondence, Washington wrote to the President of the Virginia Council as follows—"The last Assembly, in their 'Supply Bill,' provided for a chaplain to our regiment. I now flatter myself that your Honor will be pleased to appoint a sober, serious man, of piety and merit, to this duty."

Chaplains of the Continental Congress

When Washington assumed command of the army at Cambridge, in 1775, he found chaplains attached to the different regiments sent from various colonies—some of them volunteers without pay, and others regularly appointed by the Provincial Congress. As the organization of the army was perfected, measures were adopted for their provision by the General Congress, and their number and the regiments to which they belonged formed a part of the regular army returns of Washington.

At first they were not numerous, as the Government had taken no action on the subject; but its attention was soon called to it, and on May 25, 1775, a committee of the Provincial Congress of Massachusetts reported—

> *Whereas* It has been represented to this Congress that several ministers of the religious assemblies within this colony have expressed their willingness to attend the army in the capacity of chaplains, as they may be directed by Congress: therefore,
>
> *Resolved*, That it be, and is hereby, recommended to the ministers of the several religious assemblies within the colony, that, with the leave of their congregations, they attend said army in their several towns, to the number of thirteen at one time, during the time the army shall be encamped; and that they make known their resolution to the Congress thereon, or to the Committee of Safety, as soon as may be.

Washington, who in the French and Indian War had more than once requested the Governor of Virginia to allow him a chaplain for his regiment, saw with the deepest gratification this early determination of the New England colonies to supply their regiments with regular chaplains, and encouraged it in every way he could. In the month of December, 1775, he wrote to the Continental Congress as follows—

> I have had it in my mind to mention it to Congress that frequent applications have been made to me respecting the chaplains' pay, which is too small to encourage men of abilities. Some of them who have left their flocks are obliged to pay the parson acting for them more than they receive. I need not point out the great utility of gentlemen whose lives and conversation are unexceptionable, being employed in that service in this army. There are two ways of making it worthy the attention of such. One is an advancement of their pay; the other, that one chaplain be appointed to two regiments. This last, I think, can be done without inconvenience. I beg leave to recommend this matter to Congress, whose sentiments hereon I shall impatiently expect.

The policy of having one chaplain for two regiments did not seem to work well; and on the 1st of July, 1776, Washington wrote to Congress on the subject as follows—

I beg leave to mention to Congress the necessity there is of some new regulation being entered into respecting the chaplains of the army. They will remember that applications were made to increase their pay, which was conceived to be too low for their support, and that it was proposed, if it could not be done for the whole, that the number should be lessened, and one be appointed to two regiments, with an additional allowance. This latter expedient was adopted, and, while the army continued all together at one encampment, answered well, or at least did not produce many inconveniences; but the army being now differently circumstanced from what it then was, part here, part in Boston, and a third part detached to Canada, has introduced much confusion and disorder in this instance; nor do I know that it is possible to remedy the evil but by affixing one to each regiment, with salaries competent to their support. No shifting, no changing from one to the other, can answer the purpose; and in many cases it could not be done although the regiments would consent, as when detachments are composed of unequal numbers or ordered from different posts. Many more inconveniences might be pointed out, but these, it is presumed, will sufficiently show the defects of the present establishment and the propriety of an alteration. What that alteration shall be, Congress will please to determine.

Congress immediately adopted his views, and Washington, having received a despatch to that effect, eight days after issued the following general order—

NEW YORK, JULY 9, 1776.

The Honorable Continental Congress having been pleased to allow a chaplain to each regiment, with the pay of thirty-three and one-third dollars per month, the colonels or commanding officers of each regiment are directed to procure chaplains accordingly—persons of good character and exemplary lives—and to see that all inferior officers and soldiers pay them a suitable respect and attend carefully upon religious exercises. *The blessing and protection of Heaven are at all times* necessary, but especially is it in times of public distress and danger. The general hopes and trusts that every officer and man will endeavor to live and act as becomes a *Christian* soldier defending the dearest rights and liberties of his country.

In 1776, Washington gave the following order to the chaplains—

The situation of the army frequently not admitting of the regular performance of divine service on Sundays, the chaplains of the army are forthwith to meet together and agree on some method of performing it at other times, which method they will make known to the commander-in-chief.

Washington deemed the services of religion so important in the army that, in the absence of a chaplain, he would perform divine service himself. "He has been frequently known," says Weems, "on the Sabbath to read the Scriptures and pray with the regiment in the absence of a chaplain."

On the 27th of May, 1777, Congress passed the following order—

Resolved, That for the future there be only one chaplain for each brigade of the army, and that such be appointed by Congress; that each brigade chaplain be allowed the same pay, rations, and forage allowed to a colonel in the said corps; that each general be requested to nominate and recommend a proper person for chaplain to his brigade; and that they recommend none but such as are men of experience and established character for piety, virtue, and learning.

The chaplains of the army of the Revolution were, in general, not only distinguished for "piety, virtue, and learning, but were," says Headley, "bold and active patriots, stirring up rebellion, encouraging the weak and timid by their example as well as by their teachings, and inspiring the brave and true with confidence by their heroism and lofty trust in the righteousness of the cause they vindicated."

Chaplains were also appointed for the hospitals, as the following record of Congress shows—

September 18, 1777

Resolved, That chaplains be appointed to the hospitals in the several departments, and that their pay be sixty dollars a month and three rations a day, and forage for one horse.

Congress was also mindful that chaplains were faithful in the discharge of their duties. The following is on the records of Congress—

Every chaplain commissioned in the army or armies of the United States who shall absent himself from the duties assigned him, excepting in case of sickness or on leave of absence, shall, on conviction thereof before a court-martial, be fined not exceeding one month's pay, besides the loss of his pay during his absence, or be discharged, as the said court-martial shall judge proper.

The commission of chaplains varied somewhat in the different colonies, but the following form, adopted in Connecticut, will answer as a sample of all—

To Rev._____, greeting:

Reposing special trust and confidence in your piety, ability, fidelity, and good conduct, I do hereby appoint you, the said _____, a chaplain of the _____ regiment, and do hereby authorize and empower you to exercise the several acts and duties of your office and station as chaplain of the said regiment, which you are faithfully to perform in a due and religious discharge thereof, according to the important trust reposed in you, for which this is your warrant.

Given under my hand and seal-at-arms, in the colony aforesaid, this _____day of _____, 1776.

Correspondence of Washington with a Church in Connecticut

The following correspondence between the Congregational Church of Woodstock, Connecticut, and Generals Washington and Putnam, is instructive and interesting—

WOODSTOCK, CONNECTICUT, April 22, 1776.
Whereas the inhabitants of the United Colonies of America are now engaged in the most important of causes or controversies with the greatest human Power upon earth—contending with Great Britain for the continuance and enjoyment of all their rights, privileges, and liberties, both civil and sacred;

And whereas it has been judged to be greatly advantageous to the camp, by the commander-in-chief of the forces of the United Colonies, and others in general command, that the Rev. Abiel Leonard, minister of the First Society in Woodstock, should still continue in the army as chaplain, as by their letters to the church and congregation in said society signified, now under consideration, which letter is in the words following—

"To the Church and Congregation at Woodstock.
"Mr. Abiel Leonard is a man whose exemplary life and conversation must make him highly esteemed by every person who has the pleasure of being acquainted with him. The congregation of Woodstock know him well. It therefore can be no surprise to us to hear that they are loath to part with him. His usefulness in the army is great. He is employed in the glorious work of attending to the morals of a brave people who are fighting for their liberties—the liberties of the people of Woodstock, the liberties of all America. We therefore hope that, knowing how nobly he is employed, the congregation of Woodstock will cheerfully give up to the public a gentleman so very useful. And when, by the blessing of a kind Providence, the glorious and unparalleled struggle for our liberties is at an end, we have not the least doubt but Mr. Leonard will, with redoubled joy, be received in the open arms of a congregation so very dear to him as the good people of Woodstock are. This is what is hoped for, this is what is expected, by the congregation of Woodstock's sincere well-wishers and very humble servants.

"Signed {George Washington
{Israel Putnam.
"Head-Quarters, Cambridge, March 24, 1776."

At a meeting of the inhabitants of the First Society in Woodstock, regularly warned and assembled, on the 22d day of April,
1776, Dr. William Skinner was chosen Moderator for said meeting. After some consultation upon the foregoing letter, and also
with the Rev. Mr. Leonard respecting his continuance in the
army for a longer time, the following vote was put, namely—

"Considering that it is desired by some gentlemen of distinction in the Continental army that the Rev. Mr. Leonard, minister of the society, should still continue in said army, and he apprehending it to be his duty, we hereby manifest our consent to
his being absent from this society from the 9th of May next to
the 1st day of January, 1777, with the expectation, if God spares
his life (which we earnestly and humbly implore of His great
goodness), that he then return to us and go on in the discharge
of the duties of his ministerial connections with us; and doing
this we act solely with the view to the public good."

Jedidah Morse, *Society Clerk.*

Notice, therefore, is hereby given to all the inhabitants of the First
Society of Woodstock, qualified by law to vote in society meeting,
to meet at the meeting-house in said First Society on Monday, the
22d of April instant, at two of the clock, after noon, there to consult and come unto some agreement with the Rev. Mr. Leonard
respecting the pulpit's being supplied in his absence.

William Skinner,}
Jedidah Morse,} *Soc. Com.*
Benjamin Lyon,}

Woodstock, April 12, 1776.

The policy of the Government, in securing the services of chaplains,
has always been the same in the civil as in the military departments
of the Government.

The first meeting of the Continental Congress took place in Philadelphia, September 5, 1774. The record for the 6th of September
contains the following—

Resolved, That Rev. Mr. Duché be desired to open Congress
to-morrow morning with prayers.

Sept. 7, 1774.—The meeting was opened with prayer by Rev. Mr. Duché. Voted that the thanks of Congress be given to Mr. Duché for performing divine service.

This Congress adjourned on the 26th of October, 1774, and reassembled the 10th of May, 1775. The Journal of that day shows the following—

Agreed, that the Rev. Mr. Duché be requested to open the Congress with prayers to-morrow morning.

May 11, 1775.—Agreeable to the order of yesterday, the Congress was opened with prayers by Rev. Mr. Duché.

July 9, 1776.—*Resolved*, That Rev. Mr. Duché be appointed chaplain to Congress, and that he be desired to attend every morning at nine o'clock.

Oct. 17, 1776.—Mr. Duché, having by letter informed the President that the state of his health and his parochial duties were such as obliged him to decline the honor of continuing chaplain to Congress—*Resolved*, That the President return the thanks of this House to the Rev. Mr. Duché for the devout and acceptable manner in which he discharged his duty during the time he officiated as chaplain to it; and that one hundred and fifty dollars be presented to him as an acknowledgment from the House for his services.

Oct. 30, 1776.—Mr. Duché writes to Congress, and requests that, as he became their chaplain from motives perfectly disinterested, the one hundred and fifty dollars voted to him may be applied to the relief of the widows and children of such of the Pennsylvania officers as have fallen in battle in the service of their country. In consequence, Congress orders the money to be deposited with the Council of Safety of Pennsylvania, to be applied agreeably to his request.

Dec. 23, 1776.—Agreeable to the order of the day, Congress elected the Rev. P. Allison and the Rev. W. White chaplains.

The old Colonial and Confederate Congresses paid respect to religion by system and on principle. If they were ever without a chaplain performing daily religious services, it was but for a short time; and it may well be presumed that Mr. Witherspoon *then* performed the stated divine service.

In the first Congress, after the adoption of the Constitution (1789), soon after a quorum had come together, Oliver Ellsworth was appointed to confer with a committee of the House "on rules and the appointment of chaplains." The House chose five men— Boudinot, Bland, Madison, Sherman, and Tucker. The result was a recommendation to appoint two chaplains of different denominations, one by each House, to interchange weekly. The Senate appointed an Episcopal clergyman, and the House a distinguished Presbyterian minister, both of New York, the city in which Congress was then holding its session. Thus began the practice of appointing chaplains to our national legislature—a practice continued without interruption to the present time.

The first chaplain appointed under the Constitution was the Right Rev. Dr. Provost, Bishop of New York. The next was Bishop White, whose memory is cherished as the father of the Protestant Episcopal Church in America—the man who at the call of the Continental Congress took his life in his hand and followed it as their chaplain. The service of these two chaplains to the Senate extended through eleven years, from 1789 to 1800, at which time the seat of government was removed to Washington.

The House elected, as colleagues of Provost and White, three distinguished Presbyterian divines, William Linn, of New York, and Blair and Green, of Philadelphia, the latter of whom was subsequently president of Princeton College. We need only look over the list of the earlier chaplains to Congress, to find the names of men who were lights in their day, and who made their mark, which has not been obliterated by time.

On this list we find, besides those who have been mentioned, the names of Breckenridge, Campbell, and Post, from the Presbyterians; Claggett, McIlvaine, and Johns, from the Episcopalians. From among the Methodists, we meet with the names of Bascom, Stockton, and Cookman; from the Baptists, Allison, Staughton, and Cone; and from the Congregationalists, Dr. Dwight, Jared Sparks, and President Bates.

To hear some of these men preach in the Capitol, one had to go early to secure a place to stand, even, in the crowded hall. Most of these men were able representatives of the religion of Christ, men who could with a force of character as well as of argument set before members of Congress its claims to their consideration, in such a manner as to command respect, even when it was urged upon their individual acceptance.

Chaplains in the Army and Navy

The navy as well as the army of the United States has a Christian record, confirming the uniform policy of the Government in the appointment of chaplains. The establishment of a navy was recommended by Washington, the first President, but the recommendation was not carried out until the administration of his successor, John Adams, began. From the earliest history of the navy till the present, the Government has recognized the need of chaplains, and has always had them on Government ships.

Cruising on every ocean, our sailors pass through the extremes of heat and cold, and the unhealthy climates of every latitude, in which some sicken and die and are buried in the sea, and but for a chaplain they would hear no prayer when sick, nor hardly have a Christian burial when dead. Long months, yea, years even, would pass without their hearing a sermon in a language they could understand. Who will deny that the navy opens many an important field for the labors of a faithful Christian teacher? One who has an aptness to teach and a love for doing good might find in the American navy a great work to do.

Appointed by Congress

In view of this Christian work, Congress passed the following order—

The commanders of all ships and vessels in the navy having chaplains on board shall take care that divine service be performed in an orderly and reverent manner twice a day, and a sermon preached on Sunday, except bad weather or other extraordinary accident prevent it, and that they cause all, or as many of the ship's company as can be spared from duty, to attend every performance of the worship of Almighty God.

CHAP. 204—*An Act for the better government of the navy of the United States.*

Be it enacted by the Senate and House of Representatives of the United States of America in Congress assembled, That, from and after the first day of September next, the following articles be adopted and put in force for the government of the navy of the United States.

ART. 1. The commanders of all fleets, squadrons, naval stations, and vessels belonging to the navy are strictly enjoined and required to show in themselves a good example of virtue, honor, patriotism, and subordination; to be vigilant in inspecting the conduct of all who may be placed under their command; to guard against and suppress all dissolute and immoral practices, and to correct all who may be guilty of them, according to the laws and regulations of the navy, upon pain of such punishment as a general court-martial may think proper to inflict.

ART. 2. The commanders of vessels and naval stations to which chaplains are attached shall cause divine service to be performed on Sunday, whenever the weather and other circumstances will allow it to be done; and it is earnestly recommended to all officers, seamen, and others in the naval service diligently to attend at every performance of the worship of Almighty God. Any irreverent or unbecoming behavior during divine service shall be punished as a general or summary court-martial shall direct.

In 1838, Congress passed the following—

An Act to increase the present military establishment of the United States, and for other purposes.

SEC. 18. *And be it further enacted,* That it shall be lawful for the officers composing the council of administration at any post, from time to time, to employ such person as they may think proper to officiate as chaplain, who shall also perform the duties of a schoolmaster at such post; and the person so employed shall, on the certificate of the commanding officer of the post, be paid such sum for his services, not exceeding forty dollars per month, as may be determined by the said council of administration, with the approval of the Secretary of War. In addition to his pay, the said chaplain shall be allowed four rations per diem, with quarters and fuel.

Approved, July 5, 1838.

This Act was extended, in 1849, by—

An Act to provide for the increase of the Medical Staff, and for an additional number of Chaplains of the Army of the United States.

SEC. 3. *And be it further enacted,* That the provisions of the Act of eighteen hundred and thirty-eight be, and hereby are, extended so as to authorize the employment of ten additional chaplains for military posts of the United States.

Approved, March 2, 1849.

Petitions to Abolish the Chaplaincy

At different times within the last twenty years a very small portion of the American people have petitioned Congress to abolish the office of chaplain. The petitions were respectfully received, and referred to the Committees on the judiciary, in both Houses of Congress, who made very able reports against granting the request of the petitioners. The doctrines of these reports are in harmony with the entire Christian policy of the Government, and are official records to prove that the Christian religion is the basis of the civil institutions of the United States. They are placed in this chapter in full, and will amply repay a careful perusal.

Reports of Congress

CHAPLAINS IN CONGRESS AND IN THE ARMY AND NAVY

March 27, 1854. Mr. Meacham, from the Committee on the Judiciary, made the following report—

The Committee on the Judiciary, to whom were referred the memorials of the citizens of several States, praying that the office of chaplain in the army, navy, at West Point, at Indian stations, and in both houses of Congress, be abolished, respectfully report—

That they have had the subject under consideration, and, after careful examination, are not prepared to come to the conclusion desired by the memorialists. Having made that decision, it is due that the reason should be given. Two clauses of the Constitution are relied on by the memorialists to show that their prayer should be granted. One of these is in the sixth article, that "no religious test shall ever he required as a qualification to any office or public trust under the United States." If the whole section were quoted, we apprehend that no one could suppose it intended to apply to the appointment of chaplains.

"ART. 6, Sec. 3. The senators and representatives before mentioned, and the members of the several State Legislatures, and all executive and judicial officers, both of the United States and of the several States, shall be bound, by an oath or affirmation, to support this Constitution; but no religious test shall ever be required as a qualification to any office or public trust under the United States."

Every one must perceive that this refers to a class of persons entirely distinct from chaplains.

Another article supposed to be violated is Article 1st of Amendments— Congress shall make no law respecting an establishment of religion." Does our present practice violate that article? What is an establishment of religion? It must have a creed, defining what a man must believe; it must have rites and ordinances, which believers must observe; it must have ministers of defined qualifications, to teach the doctrines and administer the rites; it must have tests for the submissive and penalties for the non-conformist. There never was an established religion without all these. Is there now, or has there ever been, any thing of this in the appointment of chaplains in Congress, or army, or navy? The practice before the adoption of the Constitution is much the same as since: the adoption of that Constitution does not seem to have changed the principle in this respect. We ask the memorialists to look at the facts. First, in the army: chaplains were appointed for the Revolutionary army on its organization; rules for their regulation are found among the earliest of the articles of war. Congress ordered, on May 27, 1777, that there should be one chaplain to each brigade of the army, nominated by the brigadier-general, and appointed by Congress, with the same pay as colonel, and, on the 18th of September following, ordered chaplains to be appointed to the hospitals in the several departments, with the pay of $60 per month, three rations per day, and forage for one horse.

When the Constitution was formed, Congress had power to raise and support armies, and to provide for and support a navy, and to make rules and regulations for the government and regulation of land and naval forces. In the absence of all limitations, general or special, is it not fair to assume that they were to do these substantially in the same manner as had been done before? If so, then they were as truly empowered to appoint chaplains as to appoint generals or to enlist soldiers. Accordingly, we find provision for chaplains in the acts of 1791, of 1812, and of 1838. By the last there is to be one to each brigade in the army; the number is limited to thirty, and these in the most destitute places. The chaplain is also to discharge the duties of schoolmaster. The number in the navy is limited to twenty-four. Is there any violation of the Constitution in these laws for the appointment of chaplains in the army and navy? If not, let us look at the history of chaplains in Congress. Here, as before, we shall find that the same practice was in existence before and after the adoption of the Constitution. The American Congress began its session September 5, 1774. On the second day of the session, Mr. Samuel Adams proposed to open the session with prayer. I give Mr. Webster's account of it—"At the meeting of the first Congress there was a doubt in the minds of many about the propriety of opening the session with prayer; and the reason assigned was, as here, the great diversity of opinion and religious belief; until, at last, Mr. Samuel Adams, with his gray hairs hanging about his shoulders, and with an impressive venerableness now seldom to be met with (I suppose owing to different habits), rose in that assembly, and, with the air of a perfect Puritan, said it did not become men professing to be Christian men, who had come together for solemn deliberation in the hour of their extremity, to say there was so wide a difference in their religious belief that they could not, as one man, bow the knee in prayer to the Almighty, whose advice and assistance they hoped to obtain; and, Independent as he was, and an enemy to all prelacy as he was known to be, he moved that Rev. Mr. Duché, of the Episcopal Church, should address the throne of grace in prayer. John Adams, in his letter to his wife, says he never saw a more moving spectacle. Mr. Duché read the Episcopal service of the Church of England; and then, as if moved by the occasion, he broke out into extemporaneous prayer, and those men who were about to resort to force to obtain their rights were moved to tears; and floods of tears, he says, ran down the cheeks of pacific Quakers, who formed part of that interesting assembly; and, depend upon it, that where there is a spirit of Christianity, there is a spirit which rises above form, above ceremonies, independent of sect or creed and the controversies of clashing doctrines." That same clergyman was afterwards appointed chaplain of the American Congress. He had such an appointment five days after the declaration of independence.

On December 22, 1776, on December 13, 1784, and on February 29, 1788, it was resolved that two chaplains should be appointed. So far for the old American Congress. I do not deem it out of place to notice one act, of many, to show that Congress was not indifferent to the religious interests of the people; and they were not peculiarly afraid of the charge of uniting Church and State. On the 11th of September, 1777, a committee having consulted with Dr. Allison about printing an edition of thirty thousand Bibles, and finding that they would be compelled to send abroad for type and paper, with an advance of £10,272 10s., Congress voted to instruct the Committee on Commerce to import twenty thousand Bibles from Scotland and Holland into the different ports of the

Union. The reason assigned was that the use of the book was so universal and important. Now, what was passing on that day? The army of Washington was fighting the battle of Brandywine; the gallant soldiers of the Revolution were displaying their heroic though unavailing valor; twelve hundred soldiers were stretched in death on that battle-field; Lafayette was bleeding; the booming of the cannon was heard in the hall where Congress was sitting, in the hall from which Congress was soon to be a fugitive. At that important hour Congress was passing an order for importing twenty thousand Bibles: and yet we have never heard that they were charged by their generation of any attempt to unite Church and State, or surpassing their powers to legislate on religious matters.

There was a convention assembled between the old and new forms of government. Considering the character of the men, the work in which they were engaged, and the results of their labors, I think them the most remarkable body of men ever assembled. Benjamin Franklin addressed that body on the subject of employing chaplains; and certainly Franklin will not be accused of fanaticism in religion, or of a wish to unite Church and State.

[Franklin's speech is omitted here, as it is be found: pp. 249–250, 251–252.]

There certainly can be no doubt as to the practice of employing chaplains in deliberative bodies previous to the adoption of the Constitution. We are, then, prepared to see if any change was made in that respect in the new order of affairs.

The first Congress under the Constitution began on the 4th of March, 1789; but there was not a quorum for business till the 1st of April. On the 9th of that month, Oliver Ellsworth was appointed, on the part of the Senate, to confer with a committee of the House on rules, and on the *appointment of chaplains.* The House chose five men—Boudinot, Bland, Tucker, Sherman, and Madison. The result of their consultation was a recommendation to appoint two chaplains of different denominations, one by the Senate and one by the House, to interchange weekly. The Senate appointed Dr. Provost on the 25th of April.

On the 1st day of May, Washington's first speech was read to the House, and the *first* business after that speech was the appointment of Dr. Linn as chaplain. By whom was this plan made? Three out of six of that joint committee were members of the convention that framed the Constitution. Madison, Ellsworth, and Sherman passed directly from the hall of the convention to the hall of Congress. Did *they* not know what was constitutional? The law of 1789 was passed in compliance with their plan, giving chaplains a salary of $500. It was re-enacted in 1816, and continues to the present time. Chaplains have been appointed from all the leading denominations, Methodist, Baptist, Episcopalian, Presbyterian, Congregationalist, Catholic, Unitarian, and others.

I am aware that one of our petitioners might truly reply that the article was not in the body of the Constitution, but was one of two amendments recommended by Virginia. This does not weaken the argument in favor of chaplains. In the convention of Virginia, which proposed amendments, James Madison, James Monroe, and John Marshall were members. All these men were members closely connected with the Government. Madison and Monroe were members of Congress when the first amendment was adopted and became a part of the Constitution. Madison was a member of the convention framing the Constitution, of the convention proposing the amendment, and of Congress when adopted; and yet neither Madison nor Monroe ever uttered a word or gave a vote to indicate that the appointment of chaplains was unconstitutional. The Convention of Virginia elected on its first day a chaplain, Rev. Abner Waugh, who every morning read prayers immediately after the ringing of the bell for calling the convention. No one will suppose that convention so inconsistent as to appoint their chaplain for their own deliberative assembly in the State of Virginia, and then recommend that this should be denied to the deliberative bodies of the nation.

The reason more generally urged is the danger of a union of Church and State. If the danger were real, we should be disposed to take the most prompt and decided measures to forestall the evil, because one of the worst for the religious and political interests of this nation that could possibly overtake us. But we deem this apprehension entirely imaginary; and we think any one of the petitioners must be convinced of this on examination of the facts. Now look at that score of different denominations, and tell us, do you believe it possible to make a majority agree in forming a league to unite their religious interests with those of the State? If you take from the larger sects, you must select some three or four of the largest to make a majority of clergy, or laity, or worshippers. And these sects are widely separated in their doctrines, their religious rites, and in their church discipline. How do you expect them to unite for any such object? If you take the smaller sects, you must unite some fifteen to make a majority, and must take such discordant materials as the Quaker, the Jew, the Universalist, the Unitarian, the Tunker, and the Swedenborgian. Does any one suppose it possible to make these harmonize? If not, there can be no union of Church and State. Your committee know of no denomination of Christians who wish for such union. They have had their existence in the voluntary system, and wish it to continue. The sentiment of the whole body of American Christians is against a union with the State. A great change has been wrought in this respect. At the adoption of the Constitution, we believe every State—certainly ten of the thirteen—provided as regularly for the support of the Church as for the support of the Government: one, Virginia, had the system of tithes. Down to the Revolution, every colony did sustain religion in some form. It was deemed peculiarly proper that the religion of liberty should be upheld by a free people. Had the people, during the Revolution, had a suspicion of any attempt to war against Christianity, that Revolution would have been strangled in its cradle. At the time of the adoption of the Constitution and the amendments, the universal sentiment was that Christianity should be encouraged, not any one sect. Any attempt to level and discard all religion would have been viewed with universal indignation. The object was not to substitute Judaism, or Mohammedanism, or infidelity, but to prevent rivalry among sects to the exclusion of others. The result of the change above named is, that now there is not a single State that, as a State, supports the gospel. In 1816 Connecticut repealed her law which was passed to sustain the Church; and in 1833 Massachusetts wiped from her statute-book the last law on the subject that existed in the whole Union. Every one will notice that this is a very great change to be made in so short a period—greater than, we believe, was ever before made in ecclesiastical affairs in sixty-five years, without a revolution or some great convulsion. This change has been made silently and noiselessly, with the consent and wish of all parties, civil and religious. From this it will be seen that the tendency of the times is not to a union of Church and State, but is decidedly and strongly bearing in an opposite direction. Every tie is sundered; and there is no wish on either side to have the bond renewed. It seems to us that the men who would raise the cry of danger in this state of things would cry fire on the thirty-ninth day of a general deluge.

If there be no constitutional objection and no danger, why should not the office be continued? It is objected that we pay money from the treasury for this office. That is certainly true; and equally true in regard to the sergeant-at-arms and doorkeeper, who, with the chaplain, are appointed under the general authority to organize the House. Judge Thompson, chairman of this committee in the Thirty-First Congress, in a very able report on this subject, said, that if the cost of chaplains to Congress were equally divided among the people, it would not be annually more than the two-hundredth part of one cent to each person. That being true, a man who lives under the protection of this Government and pays taxes for fifty years will have to lay aside from his hard earnings two and a half mills during his half-century for the purpose of supporting chaplains in Congress! This is the weight of pecuniary burden which the committee are called to lift from off the neck of the people.

If there be a God who hears prayer—as we believe there is—we submit that there never was a deliberative body that so eminently needed the fervent prayers of righteous men as the Congress of the United States. There never was another representative assembly that had so many and so widely different interests to protect and to harmonize, and so many local passions to subdue. One member feels charged to defend the rights of the Atlantic, another of the Pacific, coast; one urges the claims of constituents on the borders of the torrid, another on the borders of the frigid, zone; while hundreds have the defence of local and varied interests stretching across an entire continent. If personal selfishness or ambition, if party or sectional views alone, bear rule, all attempts at legislation will be fruitless, or bear only bitter fruit. If wisdom from above, that is profitable to direct, be given in answer to the prayers of the pious, then Congress need those devotions, as they surely need to have their views of personal importance daily chastened by the reflection that they are under the government of a Supreme Power, that rules not for one locality or one time, but governs a world by general laws, subjecting all motives and acts to an omniscient scrutiny, and holds all agents to their just awards by an irresistible power.

In the provisions of the law for chaplains in the army, the number is limited, and these not to be granted unless for "most destitute places;" and then for a very small salary they are to perform the double service of clergymen and schoolmasters. While every political office under all administrations is filled to overflowing, while the ante-chambers of the departments are crowded and crammed with anxious applicants, waiting for additions, or resignations, or death, to make for them some vacant place, it is of recent occurrence that only fourteen of the twenty posts for chaplains were supplied.

We presume all will grant that it is proper to appoint physicians and surgeons in the army and navy. The power to appoint chaplains is just the same, because neither are expressly named, but are appointed under the general authority to organize the army and navy, and we deem the one as truly a matter of necessity as the other. Napoleon was obliged to establish chaplains for his army, in order to their quiet, while making his winter quarters in the heart of an enemy's country; and that army had been drenched in the infidelity of the French Revolution. The main portion of our troops, though not in a foreign land, are stationed on the extreme frontiers, the very outposts of civilization; and if the Government does not furnish them moral and religious instruction, we know, as a practical fact, that they will go without it.

It is said that they can contribute and hire their own chaplains. Certainly they can—and their own physicians and surgeons; but if we throw on them this additional burden, are we not bound to increase their pay to meet these personal expenses? We may supply them directly with more economy and effect than we can do it indirectly. We trust that the military force of the United States will never be engaged in a contest, unless in such a one that devout men can honestly invoke the God of battles to go with our armies. If so, it will inspire fortitude and courage in the soldier to know that the righteous man is invoking the Supreme Power to succeed his efforts. If our armies are exposed to pestilential climates or to the carnage of the battlefield, we believe it the duty of Government to send to the sick and wounded and dying that spiritual counsel and consolation demanded by the strongest cravings of our nature.

The navy have still stronger claims than the army for the supply of chaplains: a large portion of the time our ships-of-war are on service foreign from our own shore. If they are in the ports of other nations, the crews cannot be disbanded to worship with the people of those nations; and, if they could, the instances are rare in which the sailors could understand the language in which the devotions are conducted. If you do not afford them the means of religious service while at sea, the Sabbath is, to all intents and purposes, annihilated, and we do not allow the crews the free exercise of religion.

In that important branch of service the Government is educating a large number of youth who are hereafter to have the control of our navy. They are taken from their homes at a very early age, when their minds are not generally instructed or their opinions formed on religious affairs. If the mature men can be safely deprived of such privileges, is it wise or just to deprive the youth of all means of moral and religious culture? Naval commanders have often desired to have their crews unite in devotions before commencing action. They have sometimes done it when there was no chaplain on board. One striking instance of this was in the naval action on Lake Champlain. On Sunday morning, September 11, just as the sun rose over the eastern mountains, the American guard-boat on the watch was seen rowing swiftly into the harbor. It reported the enemy in sight. The drums immediately beat to quarters, and every vessel was cleared for action. The preparations being completed, young McDonough summoned his officers around him, and there, on the deck of the Saratoga, read the prayers of the ritual before entering into battle; and that voice, which soon after rang like a clarion amid the carnage, sent heavenward, in earnest tones, "Stir up thy strength, O Lord, and come and help us; for thou givest not always the battle to the strong, but canst save by many or by few." It was a solemn, thrilling sight, and one never before witnessed on a vessel-of-war cleared for action. A young commander who had the courage thus to brave the derision and sneers which such an act was sure to provoke would fight his vessel while there was a plank left to stand on. Of the deeds of daring done on that day of great achievements, none evinced so bold and firm a heart as this act of religious worship.

While your committee believe that neither Congress nor the army or navy should be deprived of the service of chaplains, they freely concede that the ecclesiastical and civil powers have been, and should continue to be, entirely divorced from each other. But we beg leave to rescue ourselves from the imputation of asserting that religion is not needed to the safety of civil society. It must be considered as the foundation on which the whole structure rests. Laws will not have permanence or power without the sanction of religious senti-ment— without a firm belief that there is a Power above us that will reward our virtues and punish our vices. In this age there can be no substitute for Christianity: that, in its gen-eral principles, is the great conservative element on which we must rely for the purity and permanence of free institutions. That was the religion of the founders of the republic, and they expected it to remain the religion of their descendants. There is a great and very prevalent error on this subject in the opin-ion that those who organized this Government did not legis-late on religion. They did legislate on it, by making it free to all, "to the Jew and the Greek, to the learned and unlearned." The error has arisen from the belief that there is no legisla-tion unless in permissive or restricting enactments. But mak-ing a thing free is as truly a part of legislation as confining it by limitations; and what the Government has made free it is bound to keep free.

Your committee recommend the following resolution—

Resolved, That the Committee be discharged from the further consideration of the subject.

The Senate of the United States adopted the following report—

In Senate of the United States, January 19, 1853, Mr. Bad-ger made the following report—

The Committee on the Judiciary, to whom were referred sundry petitions praying Congress to abolish the office of chaplain, have had the same under consideration, and submit the following report—

The ground on which the petitioners found their prayer is, that the provisions of law under which chaplains are ap-pointed for the army and navy, and for the two Houses of Congress, are in violation of the first amendment of the Con-stitution of the United States, which declares that "Congress shall make no law respecting an establishment of religion, or prohibiting the free exercise thereof."

If this position were correct—if these provisions of law do violate either the letter or the spirit of the constitutional prohibition—then, undoubtedly, they should be at once repealed, and the office of chaplain abolished. It thus becomes necessary to inquire whether the position of the petitioners be correct.

The clause speaks of "an establishment of religion." What is meant by that expression? It referred, without doubt, to that establishment which existed in the mother-country, and its meaning is to be ascertained by ascertaining what that establishment was. It was the connection, with the state, of a particular religious society, by its endowment at the public expense, in exclusion of, or in preference to, any other, by giving to its members exclusive political rights, and by compelling the attendance of those who rejected its communion upon its worship or religious observances. These three particulars constituted that union of Church and State of which our ancestors were so justly jealous and against which they so wisely and carefully provided. It is true that, at the time our Constitution was formed, the strictness of this establishment had been, in some respects, and to a certain extent, relaxed in favor of Protestant dissenters; but the main character of the establishment remained. It was still, in its spirit, inconsistent with religious freedom, as matter of natural right to be enjoyed in its full latitude, and not measured out by tolerance and concession from the civil rulers. If Congress has passed, or should pass, any law which, fairly construed, has in any degree introduced, or should attempt to introduce, in favor of any church, or ecclesiastical association, or system of religious faith, all or any one of these obnoxious particulars—endowment at the public expense, peculiar privileges to its members, or disadvantages or penalties upon those who should reject its doctrines or belong to other communions—such law would be a "law respecting an establishment of religion," and, therefore, in violation of the Constitution. But no law yet passed by Congress is justly liable to such an objection. Take, as an example, the chaplains to Congress. At every session two chaplains are elected—one by each House—whose duty is to offer prayers daily in the two Houses, and to conduct religious services weekly in the Hall of the House of Representatives. Now, in this no religion, no form of faith, no denomination of religious professors, is established in preference to any other, or has any peculiar privileges conferred upon it. The range of selection is absolutely free in each House among all existing professions of religious faith. There is no compulsion exercised or attempted upon any member or officer of either House to attend their prayers or religious solemnities. No member gains any advantage over another by attending, or incurs any penalty or loses any advantage by declining to attend. The chaplain is an officer of the House which chooses him, and nothing more. He owes his place not to his belonging to a particular religious society or holding a particular faith, but to the voluntary choice of the members of the House, and stands, in this respect, upon the same footing with any other officer so elected. It is not seen, therefore, how the institution of chaplains is justly obnoxious to the reproach of invading religious liberty in the widest sense of that term.

It is said, indeed, by the petitioners, that if members of Congress wish any one to pray for them, they should, out of their own means, furnish the funds wherewith to pay him, and that it is unjust to tax the petitioners with the expense of his compensation. It has been shown that there is no establishment of religion in creating the office of chaplain, and the present objection is to the injustice of putting upon the public this charge for the personal accommodation of members of Congress. Let it be seen, then, to what this objection leads. If carried out to its fair results, it will equally apply to many other accommodations furnished to members of Congress at the public expense. We have messengers who attend to our private business, take checks to the bank for us, receive the money, or procure bank drafts, and discharge various other offices for our personal ease and benefit, unconnected with the despatch of any public function. Why might it not be said that members, if they wish these services performed in their behalf, should employ and pay their own agents? Members of

Congress come here to attend upon the business of the public. Many of them are professed members of religious societies; more are men of religious sentiment: and these desire not only to have the blessing of God invoked upon them in their legislative capacities, but to attend the public worship of God. But how are all to be accommodated in the churches of the city? And of those who belong to either House of Congress some have not the means to procure such accommodations for themselves. Where, then, is the impropriety of having an officer to discharge these duties? And how is it more a subject of just complaint than to have officers who attend to the private secular business of the members? The petitioners say, "A *national chaplaincy*, no less than a *national Church*, is considered by us emphatically an *establishment of religion*." In no fair sense of the phrase have we a national chaplaincy; in no sense in which that phrase must be understood when connected, as it is by the petitioners, with a "national Church." A national Church implies a particular Church selected as the Church of the nation, endowed with peculiar privileges, or sustained or favored by the public in preference to other Churches or religious societies. Of such a Church we have no semblance, nor have we any such chaplaincy. We have chaplains in the army and navy, and in Congress; but these are officers chosen with the freest and widest range of selection—the law making no distinction whatever between any of the religions, Churches, or professions of faith known to the world. Of these, none by law is excluded, none has any priority of legal right. True, selections, in point of fact, are always made from some one of the denominations into which Christians are distributed; but that is not in consequence of any legal right or privilege, but by the voluntary choice of those who have the power of appointment.

This results from the fact that we are a Christian people—from the fact that almost our entire population belong to or sympathize with some one of the Christian denominations which compose the Christian world. And Christians will of course select, for the performance of religious services, one who professes the faith of Christ. This, however, it should be carefully noted, is not by virtue of provision, but voluntary choice. We are Christians, not because the law demands it, not to gain exclusive benefits or to avoid legal disabilities, but from choice and education; and in a land thus universally Christian, what is to be expected, what desired, but that we shall pay a due regard to Christianity, and have a reasonable respect for its ministers and religious solemnities?

The principle on which the petitioners ask for the abolition of the office of chaplain, if carried out to its just consequences, will lead us much further than they seem to suppose. How comes it that Sunday, the Christian Sabbath, is recognized and respected by all the departments of the Government? In the law, Sunday is a *"dies non;"* it cannot be used for the service of legal process, the return of writs, or other judicial purposes. The executive departments, the public establishments, are all closed on Sundays; on that day neither House of Congress sits.

Here is a nearer approach, according to the reasoning of the petitioners, to an establishment of religion than is furnished by the official corps to which they object. Here is a recognition by law, and by universal usage, not only of a Sabbath, but of the *Christian* Sabbath, in exclusion of the Jewish or Mohammedan Sabbath. Why, then, do not the petitioners exclaim against this invasion of their religious rights? Why do they not assert that a national Sabbath, no less than a national Church, is an establishment of religion? It is liable to all the obligations urged against the chaplaincy in at least an equal, if not in a greater, degree. The recognition of the Christian Sabbath is complete and perfect. The officers who receive salaries, or per-diem compensation, are discharged from duty on this day, because *it is the Christian Sabbath*, and yet suffer no loss or diminution of pay on that account. Why, then, do not these petitioners denounce this invasion of their religious rights, and violation of the Constitution, by which their money is applied to pay public officers while engaged in attending on their religious duties, and not in the discharge of any secular function?

The whole view of the petitioners seems founded upon mistaken conceptions of the meaning of the Constitution. This is evident—if not from what we have said—from this consideration, that from the beginning our Government has had chaplains in its employment. If this had been a violation of the Constitution—an establishment of religion—why was not its character seen by the great and good men who were coeval with the Government, were in Congress and in the Presidency when this constitutional amendment was adopted? They were wise to discover the true character of the measure; they, if any one did, understood the true purport of the amendment, and were bound, by their duty and their oaths, to resist the introduction or continuance of chaplains, if the views of the petitioners were correct. But they did no such thing; and therefore we have the strongest reason to suppose the notion of the petitioners to be unfounded. Unfounded it no doubt is. Our fathers were true lovers of liberty, and utterly opposed to any constraint upon the rights of conscience. They intended, by this amendment, to prohibit "an establishment of religion" such as the English Church presented, or any thing like it. But they had no fear or jealousy of religion itself, nor did they wish to see us an irreligious people; they did not intend to prohibit a just expression of religious devotion by the legislators of the nation, even in their public character as legislators; they did not intend to send our armies and navies forth to do battle for their country without any national recognition of that God on whom success or failure depends; they did not intend to spread over all the public authorities and the whole public action of the nation the dead and revolting spectacle of atheistical apathy. Not so had the battles of the Revolution been fought and the deliberations of the Revolutionary Congress been conducted. On the contrary, all had been done with a continual appeal to the Supreme Ruler of the world, and an habitual reliance upon his protection of the righteous cause which they commended to his care.

What has thus been done, with modifications, indeed, to suit external circumstances and particular exigencies, but in substance always the same from the beginning of our existence as a nation; what met the approval of our Washington, and of all the great men who have succeeded him; what commands the general commendation of the people; what is at once so venerable and so lovely, so respectable and respected—ought not, in the opinion of the committee, now to be discontinued.

The committee, therefore, pray to be discharged from the further consideration of the petitions.

The House of Representatives of the Thirty-Fourth Congress, 1854, were for two months unable to organize by the election of a Speaker. The contest was protracted and exciting, and resulted in the election of Nathaniel P. Banks, of Massachusetts. In the midst of that long and fierce struggle for political ascendency, the House paused and passed the following preamble and resolutions—

Whereas, The people of these United States, from their earliest history to the present time, have been led by the hand of a kind Providence, and are indebted for the countless blessings of the past and present, and dependent for continued prosperity in the future upon Almighty God; and whereas the great vital and conservative element in our system is the belief of our people in the pure doctrines and divine truths of the gospel of Jesus Christ, it eminently becomes the representatives of a people so highly favored to acknowledge in the most public manner their reverence for God: therefore,

1. *Resolved*, That the daily sessions of this body be opened with prayer.

2. *Resolved*, That the ministers of the gospel in this city are hereby requested to attend and alternately perform this solemn duty.

The pastors of various churches in Washington City sent to the Senate of the United States the following proposition—

Gentlemen—The undersigned, ministers of the different denominations of Christians in Washington, respectfully submit to you the following statements and consequent proposal.

During the long delay in the organization of the present House of Representatives, several of our number were invited to officiate in prayer at the opening of the daily sessions. The suggestion was then made that the various clergymen of the city might discharge this duty permanently, in the place of a single chaplain, but doubt was expressed as to the readiness of the ministers of Washington to render such service.

An expression on our part seeming therefore to be called for, we beg leave to state to you our conviction that the established election of a chaplain from abroad by your honorable bodies had its origin in a necessity now no longer existing; that the plan adopted by many of our State legislatures, of inviting neighboring pastors to act as their chaplains, thus removing all objection to the associating religious devotion with their deliberations, would reflect more credit on Christian ministers, would conduce more to their individual acceptableness and general usefulness among members of Congress and their families, and would in every way promote the end had in view in the election of chaplains.

We therefore respectfully tender our services, offering to alternate in the weekly service of opening the two Houses with morning prayer, and in conducting divine service on Sabbath morning, with the distinct understanding that we decline receiving any remuneration for these services.

GEORGE W. SAMSON, *Pastor of E Street Baptist Church.*
BRYON SUNDERLAND, *Pastor of First Presbyterian Church.*
JAS. R. ECKARD, *Pastor of Second Presbyterian Church.*
T. A. HASKELL, *Pastor of Western Presbyterian Church.*
P. D. GURLEY, *Pastor of F Street Presbyterian Church.*
GEO. HILDT, *Pastor of McKendree Chapel, M. E. Church.*
GEO. D. CUMMINS, *Rector of Trinity Church.*
J. GEORGE BUTLER, *St. Paul Lutheran Church.*
J. MORSELL, *Rector of Christ Church.*
SAMUEL D. FINKEL, *Pastor of G. E. Church.*
P. LIGHT WILSON, *Pastor of Methodist Protestant Church.*

Resolution of Congress

An act of Congress, passed and approved July, 1861, contains the following sections in relation to chaplains—

SEC. 8. *And be it further enacted,* That no person shall be appointed a chaplain in the United States army who is not a regularly ordained minister of some religious denomination, and who does not present testimonials of his present good standing as such minister, with a recommendation for his appointment as an army chaplain, from some authorized ecclesiastical body, or not less than five accredited ministers belonging to said religious denomination.

SEC. 9. *And be it further enacted,* That hereafter the compensation of all chaplains in the regular or volunteer service or army-hospitals shall be one hundred dollars per month and two rations a day when on duty; and the chaplains of the permanent hospitals, appointed under the authority of the second section of the act approved May twentieth, eighteen hundred and sixty-two, shall be nominated to the Senate for its advice and consent, and they shall, in all respects, fill the requirements of the preceding section of this act relative to the appointment of chaplains in the army and volunteers; and the appointments of chaplains to the army-hospitals, heretofore made by the President, are hereby confirmed; and it is hereby made the duty of each officer commanding a district or port containing hospitals, or a brigade of troops, within thirty days after the reception of the order promulgating this act, to inquire into the fitness, efficiency, and qualifications of the chaplains of hospitals or regiments, and to muster out of service such chaplains as were not appointed in conformity with the requirements of this act, and who have not faithfully discharged the duties of chaplain during the time they have been engaged as such. Chaplains employed at the military posts called "chaplain-posts" shall be required to reside at the posts, and all chaplains in the United States service shall be subject to such rules in relation to leave of absence from duty as are prescribed for commissioned officers of the United States army stationed at such posts.

At West Point

West Point, the military school of the nation, has from its organization had the services of a Government chaplain. Some of the most distinguished ministers of the nation have received appointments, among whom has been the venerable Bishop McIlvaine. The importance of religious instruction and of the public worship of God in that national military school is thus stated by the venerable Christian statesman Lewis Cass. In 1832, Mr. Cass, as Secretary of War, in his annual report to Congress, says—

> Especially am I impressed with the importance of a place of public worship, where all the persons attached to the institution, amounting, with their families, to more than eight hundred individuals, can assemble and unite in the performance of religious duties. In a Christian community the obligation upon this subject will not be questioned; and the expense of providing a suitable place of worship, especially as a chaplain is maintained there, cannot be put in competition with the permanent advantages of a course of religious instruction to such a number of persons, a large portion of whom are in that critical period which determines whether the future course of life shall be for evil or for good.

Extract from the Report of the Board of Visitors in 1862

The report of the Board of Visitors at West Point for the year 1862 urged the same views of religious instruction at the Academy. They say—

> The moral element of the nation, by far the most important of all, receives far less attention than it deserves at the Academy. Moral and religious teaching is of supreme importance at all times to the young. How much more important is it to

young men, associated as they are at the Academy, far from all the influences of domestic affections and the counsel and examples of parents and friends! We desire to see the moral and intellectual powers cultivated simultaneously, believing we should desire as much at least that the cadet should be a good man as a good officer.

Reports of Chaplains in the Army in 1862

The following remarks in reference to the history and labors of chaplains are taken from a report made at a meeting of the chaplains of the army held in Washington City, in the month of November, 1862—

The office of chaplain in the army and navy is one of the oldest in the Government of the United States. In the early stages of the American Revolution and through to its glorious close, in the convention that framed the Constitution of our Union, in the subsequent wars of this country, on the land and the sea, chaplains have ever been a necessary and useful class of men. When engaged in negotiating treaties abroad, when making discoveries by means of exploring expeditions, when sending out ships to convey provisions and arms to suffering and struggling nations, when promoting the high purposes of commerce and science by means of electric oceanic communication, when preparing the way for the establishment of distant colonies that have become powerful and profitable auxiliaries to civilization and good government, competent and truly Christian army and navy chaplains have taken a conspicuous part. Their books and reports on these subjects are with the country, while the record of their faithful Christian labors is on high.

On the breaking out of the present wicked and futile rebellion, ministers of the gospel of all the denominations of Christianity were at once found among the most devoted and active supporters of the Union and its flag. They caused that honored standard to be suspended over their pulpits and from the towers of their churches. They addressed their congregations in the stirring appeals of Christian patriotism. They gave their sons and grandsons, by thousands, to the ranks of the Union army and navy. Some of them, with gray hairs on their brows, were among the first to volunteer as privates and march to the field of battle. As opportunity offered, they have borne themselves bravely in the fight, rising from the ranks to be acting generals, colonels, majors, captains, and lieutenants. They have borne all the privations of camp-life, side by side with their comrades in arms. Not a few of them have been borne down by exposure and fatigue, until the hand of death has interposed to translate them from time weary march, the sickly camp, the dangerous battle-field, to the rest and victory and peace of heaven.

A wide and effectual door of usefulness has been opened to truly devoted chaplains in the military and naval hospitals of the United States. Never was there a more inviting field presented to self-denying and laborious men. Peculiar obstacles exist at times in the way of its successful cultivation, but this has always been and always will be the case in the prosecution of every good word and work. Right-minded chaplains have constantly endeavored to overcome these obstacles. Prejudice, sometimes more invincible than strong men armed, has to be conquered. Passion has to be subdued. The schemes of peculator's on public and private rights have to be ferreted out and thwarted. Facilities for holding public worship have frequently to be obtained under great difficulties.

Views of the Dignity and Position of Chaplains in Congress, by Dr. Stockton

The character and qualifications of a chaplain for Congress are presented in the following view, given by Rev. Thomas H. Stockton, himself having occupied that responsible position for several years. He says—

"The Congressional chaplaincy is not (or ought not to be) a sectarian ministry, but a great American representative of a pure Bible

Christianity, above all parties, all glowing with the divinest energies of Father, Son, and Holy Ghost—arresting and commanding attention and exerting saving influences by its heavenly loftiness and majesty— something worthy of the sublimest Christian position on the face of the earth. We want evangelical ministers who represent the immense majority of American Christians, noble witnesses for Christ, orators of the Spirit, worthy to challenge heaven and earth to hear their 'Thus saith the Lord.' It is a glorious thing rightly managed."

Thus explicit and uniform has been the course of our legislative councils on the subject of religion. Their enactments have all been on the side of Christianity—taking its truth for granted, acknowledging its obligations, magnifying its importance, treating it as in fact the religion of the Government, and as worthy to be made the rule of action for public bodies and for States no less than for individuals.

16

Christian Ministers
of the Revolution

Their Influence in Forming Our Civil Institutions

IN the civil and Christian institutions which the providence of God directed to be established on the North American continent, ministers of the gospel acted a distinguished and leading part. As teachers of religion, Christian educators, assistants and often leaders in the great work of framing civil governments, they were by our Puritan fathers regarded as essential. Every band of colonists, for a century or more, beginning with the settlement at Jamestown and Plymouth, brought in their company one or more ministers of the gospel. They were in many cases the leaders in the emigration from Europe to the New World, and pioneers in the colonization of this continent. The legislation of the colonies, their "godly frames" of government, and the whole structure of society received their moulding influence and finish from ministers. The people looked up to them for counsel, legislators sought the aid of their learning and piety, and in every crisis to the civil liberties of the colonies ministers stood firm to freedom and animated the people by their patriotic sermons and fervent prayers.

"The earliest constitution of government in New England was a theocracy; under it the clergy had peculiar powers and privileges, which, it is but fair to say, they turned to the advantage of the commonwealth more than has generally been the case with any privileged order. Religion was the deep, underlying stratum on which their whole life was built. Like the granite frame-work of the world, it sunk below all and rose above all else in their life. They were always governed by the most profound reverence for God and his word; and they constituted the strong mental and moral discipline needed by a people who were an absolute democracy."

"The Puritan preachers," says Lossing, "promulgated the doctrine of civil liberty, that the sovereign was amenable to the tribunal of public opinion and ought to conform in practice to the expressed will of the people. By degrees their pulpits became the tribunes of the common people, and on all occasions the Puritan ministers were the bold asserters of that freedom which the American Revolution established." They deduced from the Bible the true doctrine of popular sovereignty—that government is *from* the people as well as for the people. They proclaimed that God is the Supreme Ruler in government, and that the people are to exercise their power "not according to their humors, but according to the blessed will and law of God." And so influential and authoritative were their teachings, that it is said of one of the Puritan ministers, John Cotton, "that what he preached on the Lord's day was followed by the synod, and that what he preached in the Thursday lecture was followed by the General Court."

Views of Bancroft and Others

"From the sermons of memorable divines," says Bancroft, "who were gone to a heavenly country, leaving their names precious among the people of God on earth, a brief collection of testimonies to the cause of God and his New England people was circulated by the press, that the hearts of the rising generation might know what had been the great end of the plantations, and count it their duty and their glory to continue in those right ways of the Lord wherein their fathers walked before them. Their successors in the ministry, with the people and of the people and true ministers to the people, unsurpassed by the clergy of an equal population in any part of the globe for learning, ability, and virtue, and for metaphysical acuteness, familiarity with the principles of political freedom, devotedness, and practical good sense, were heard, as of old, with reverence by their congregations in their meeting-houses on every Lord's day, and on special occasions of fasts, thanksgiving, lectures, and military musters. Their exhaustless armory was the Bible, whose scriptures were stored with weapons for every occasion, furnishing sharp swords to point their appeals, apt examples of resistance, prophetic denunciations of the enemies of God's people, and promises of the Divine blessing on the defenders of his law."

The ministers of the Revolution were, like their Puritan predecessors, bold and fearless in the cause of their country. No class of men contributed more to carry forward the Revolution and to achieve our independence than did the ministers of that grand era of liberty. They esteemed the cause just and right, and by their prayers, patriotic sermons, and services rendered the highest assistance to the civil government, the army, and the country.

"Ministers nursed the flame of piety and the love of civil liberty. On Sundays they discoursed on them, and poured out their hearts in prayer for the preservation of their precious inheritance of liberty." "They harangued the people, during the Revolutionary struggle, ardently and patriotically. Many of them went into the armies as chaplains; some, more zealous, even took up temporal arms; while the greater number of them showered the enemy with sermons, tracts, and pamphlets."

"As a body of men the clergy were pre-eminent in their attachment to liberty. The pulpits of the land rang with the notes of freedom. The tongues of the hoary-headed servants of Jesus were eloquent upon the all-inspiring theme, while the youthful soldier of the cross girded on the whole armor of his country, and fought with weapons not carnal."

"The Christian ministers," said another, "did as much as the civilian or the soldier to prepare the way for the American Revolution, and to sustain its spirit. If Christian ministers had not preached and prayed, there might have been no revolution as yet; or had it broken out, it might have been crushed. The deep, dauntless, uncompromising, truthful, hopeful, religious spirit of our fathers, who revered and whose love gathered around their ministers, imparted to the Revolution its most striking characteristic."

Trumbull, the historian of Connecticut, bears this honorable testimony to the patriotism and labors of the clergy —"Many of the clergy had good estates, and assisted their poor brethren and parishioners. The clergy possessed a very great proportion of the literature of the colonies. They were the principal instructors of those who received an education for public life. For many years they were consulted by the legislature in all affairs of importance, civil or religious. They were appointed committees with the governor and magistrates to assist them in the most delicate concerns of the commonwealth. They taught their hearers to reject with abhorrence the divine right of kings, passive obedience and non-resistance, and to hold that all civil power is originally with the people."

"The clergymen of New England," said Thatcher, in his "Military Journal," May, 1775, "are, almost without exception, advocates of Whig principles; there are few instances only of the separation of a minister from his people in consequence of a disagreement in political sentiment. The tories censure, in a very illiberal manner, the preacher who speaks boldly for the liberties of the people, while they lavish their praises on him who dares to teach the absurd doctrine that magistrates have a divine right to do wrong, and are to be implicitly obeyed. It is recommended by our Provincial Congress that, on other occasions than the Sabbath, ministers of parishes adapt their discourses to the times, and explain the nature of civil and religious liberty, and the duties of magistrates and rulers. Accordingly, we have from our pulpits most fervent and pious effusions to the throne of grace in behalf of our bleeding and afflicted country."

"To the clergy," says Charles Francis Adams, "as the fountains of knowledge and possessing the gifts most prized in the community, all other ranks in society most cheerfully gave place. If a festive entertainment was meditated, the minister was sure to be the first on the list of those to be invited. If any assembly of citizens was held, he must be there to open the business with prayer. If a political question was in agitation, he was among the first whose opinion was to be consulted. Even the civil rights of the other citizens, for a long time, depended, in some degree, on his decision; and, after that rigid rule was laid aside, he yet continued, in the absence of technical law and lawyers, to be the arbiter and judge in the differences between his fellow-men.

"The vast body of the ministry of the country advocated the Revolution, in public and private, on Christian principles. They justified the war on religious grounds. They believed that human rights and liberties would be gainers by its success. Among the most faithful of religious men, modest and painstaking in their parishes, there was no concealment of their sympathy. Scarcely was there a battle-field in the Revolutionary War where the clergy were not present, as chaplains or surgeons, to cheer and bless. Their patriotism was a thing of general admiration. They reasoned themselves and the country out of all hesitancy and scruples, as they knew how to reason. They abounded in what Sir John Hawkins calls 'precatory eloquence,' calling down the blessings of the Almighty upon the country; and the depth and sway of their influence in achieving the independence of the colonies cannot be too highly extolled. Withal, it was with them a time of great personal privation and hardship. They shared in the largest measure the calamities of the country. They practised the extremes of frugality to eke out their scanty subsistence. They were exposed to violent opposition in their distracted parishes. But they were, as a body, brave, patient, meek, pious, patriotic, and learned—an honor to any land. Under God, we owe it to the ministry of that day that the morals of the country were not hopelessly wrecked in the convulsions of the Revolution."

"They extended the aegis of a Divine religion over the battered and exhausted form of the colonial confederation, and inspired fortitude in all who were faint. They were agitated with a lofty inspiration, as the earth is shaken with the convulsions of an earthquake, not by the assaults of external power, but by the irresistible fires of freedom and piety which burned within their patriotic hearts.

"Then the people assembled in their churches to invoke the blessing of God on their arms, while their pastors preached to them under the frowns of power and in prospect of martyrdom. This gave fervor to their thoughts, depth to their sympathies, earnestness and solemnity to their daring resolutions. They seemed more like prophets than priests, master-spirits raised up to mould the destinies of mankind. Each one of those moral heroes who glorified the era of 1776 was a colossus among ordinary men, and stood forth, in native majesty, indomitable, unmoved, sublime."

"It is manifest in the spirit of our history, in our annals, and by the general voice of the fathers of the republic, that in a very great degree to the pulpit—the Puritan pulpit—we owe the moral force that won our independence."

The clergy, in all the colonies, were bold and frequent in their pulpit enunciations of the great principles of civil and religious liberty, and in rebuking despotism and the evils of the time. John Adams, writing to his wife, from Philadelphia, at the first meeting of the Continental Congress, 1774, says—

"Does Mr. Willibrand [pastor at Quincy] preach and pray against oppression and the cardinal vices of the times? The clergy here, of all denominations, thunder and lighten every Sabbath. They pray for Boston and Massachusetts. They thank God explicitly and fervently for our remarkable successes. They pray for the American army: they seem to feel as if they were among you."

The clergy of New England, and of all the colonies, from Puritan times to the Revolutionary era, were men not only of eminent piety and of profound Biblical learning, but were ardent lovers of liberty and thoroughly versed in the history and science of civil government. The peculiar circumstances in which they were placed, and the great reverence in which they were held by all classes, qualified them to be leaders of liberty and government, as they were of religion. "The profound thought and unanswerable arguments," says Headley, in his work on the chaplains and clergy of the Revolution, "found in their sermons, show that the clergy were not a whit behind the ablest statesmen of the day in their knowledge of the great science of human government. In reading them, one gets at the true pulse of the people, and can trace the progress of the public sentiment."

The Pulpit the Medium of Reaching the People

The election sermons, preached by the special appointment of the civil authorities, were especially full of the grandest ideas of freedom, and of thorough and just views of the rights of men and the nature and workings of civil government. "The publication of these sermons," says Headley, "in a pamphlet form was a part of the regular proceedings of the Assembly, and, being scattered abroad over the land, clothed them with the double weight of their high authors and the endowment of the legislature, became the text-books of human rights in every parish. They were regarded as the political pamphlets of the day. The pulpit was the most direct and effectual way of reaching the masses. The House of Representatives of Massachusetts knew this, and passed resolutions requesting the clergy to make the question of the rights of the colonies, and the oppressive conduct of the mother-country, the topic of the pulpit on weekdays. They thus proclaimed to all future time their solemn convictions of their dependence on the pulpit for that patriotic feeling and unity of action which they knew to be indispensable to success. Here is the deep, solid substratum that underlaid the Revolution.

"The preachers did not confine themselves to a dissertation on doctrinal truths or mere exhortation to godly behavior. They grappled with the great questions of the rights of man, and especially the rights of colonists in their controversy with the mother-country. In reading their discourses one is struck with the thorough knowledge these divines possessed of the origin, nature, object, character, and end of all true government. They went to the very foundations of society, showed what the natural rights of man were, and how those rights became modified when men gathered into communities—how all laws and regulations were designed to be for the good of the governed—that the object of concentrated power was to protect, not invade, personal liberty, and when it failed to do this and oppressed instead of protected, assailed instead of defending rights, resistance became lawful, nay, obligatory. They also showed the nature of compacts and charters, and applied the whole subject to the case of the colonies."

A brief sketch of the character and labors of some of these patriotic preachers, who swept the great heart of the country with their electric eloquence and power, and caused it to respond to the calls of liberty and the Revolution, will give the reader the highest admiration of the preachers of those days of Christian ideas and heroic action.

Preaching of Mayhew

Rev. Dr. Mayhew gave the key-note, on the part of the clergy of New England, to the great cause of liberty and of revolution. Robert

Treat Paine called Mayhew "the father of civil and religious liberty in Massachusetts and America." On the 25th of August, 1766, he preached in his own church, in Boston, a sermon against the Stamp Act, from the text, *"I would they were even cut off which trouble you. For, brethren, ye have been called unto liberty; only use not liberty for an occasion to the flesh, but by love serve one another."* (Gal. v. 12, 13.) This sermon, full of the noblest sentiments and of thorough views of the nature of civil government, was by John Adams called "the morning gun of the Revolution." "He was," says Adams, "a clergyman equalled by very few of any denomination in piety, virtue, genius, and learning. This transcendent genius threw all the weight of his great fame into the scale of his country." "Whoever," says Bancroft, "repeats the story of the Revolution will rehearse the fame of Mayhew. He spent whole nights in prayer for the dangers of his country. Light dawned on his mind on a Sabbath morning of July, 1766, and he wrote to Otis, saying, 'You have heard of the communion of the churches: while I was thinking of this in my bed, the great use and importance of the communion of the colonies appeared to me in a striking light. Would it not be decorous in our Assembly to send circulars to all the rest, expressing a desire to cement a union among ourselves? A good foundation has been laid by the Congress of New York. It may be the only means of perpetuating our liberties.' This suggestion of a 'more perfect union' for the common defence, originating with Mayhew, was the first public expression of that future Union which has been the glory of the American republic; and it came from a clergyman, on a Sabbath morning, under the inspiration of Heaven."

"It is my fixed resolution," said Mayhew, as early as 1764, "to do all I can for the service of my country, that neither the republic nor the churches of New England may sustain injury." "Having," says he, "been initiated in youth in the doctrines of civil liberty, as they were taught by such men as Plato, Demosthenes, Cicero, and other renowned persons among the ancients, and such as Sidney and Milton, Locke and Hoadly, among the moderns, I liked them: they seemed rational. And having learned from the Holy Scriptures that wise, brave, and virtuous men were always friends to liberty; that God gave the Israelites a king in his anger, because they had not sense and virtue enough to like a free commonwealth; that where the Spirit of the Lord is, there is liberty: this made me conclude that freedom was a great blessing."

In the year 1766, Thomas Hollis, of a distinguished Baptist family, in England, wrote to the Rev. Dr. Mayhew, "More books, *especially on government*, are going to New England. Should those go safe, it is hoped that no principal book on that FIRST subject will be wanting in Harvard College, from the days of Moses to these times. Men of New England, brethren, use them for yourselves and for others; and God bless you.

Expressing most fervent feelings for the purity and liberties of New England, and that the "spirit of luxury which was consuming us to the very marrow may be kept from the people of New England," Hollis said, again—

"One likeliest means to that end will be, to watch well over their youth, by bestowing on them a reasonable, manly education, and selecting thereto the wisest, ablest, most accomplished of men that art or wealth can obtain; for nations rise and fall by individuals, not numbers—as I think all history proveth. With ideas of this kind have I worked for the public *library* at Cambridge, New England."

"The books he sent," says a writer, "were often political, and of a republican stamp. And it remains for the perspicacity of our historians to ascertain what influence his benefactions and correspondence had in kindling that spirit which emancipated these States from the shackles of colonial subserviency, by forming 'high-minded men,' 'who, under Providence, achieved our independence."

"There were extant American reprints of Locke, Hoadly, Sidney, Montesquieu, Priestley, Milton, Price, Gordon's Tacitus, or of portions of their works issued prior to and during the Revolution, in a cheap form, for popular circulation, addressing not passion, but reason, diffusing sound principles and begetting right feelings. There could hardly be found a more impressive, though silent, proof of the exalted nature of the contest on the part of the Americans, than a complete collection of their publications during that period.

"Who can limit the influence exerted over the common mind by these volumes of silent thought, eloquent for the rights of man and the blessings of liberty, fervid against wrong, the miseries of oppression and slavery—teaching that resistance to tyrants is obedience to God? These books and libraries were the nurseries of 'sedition;' they were as secret emissaries, propagating in every household, in every breast, at morning, in the noonday rest, by the evening light, in the pulpit, the forum, and the shop, principles, convictions, resolves, which sophistry could not overthrow nor force extinguish. This was the secret of the strength of our fathers. Let us cherish it, as worthy sons of noble sires."

Writings of Wise

John Wise, pastor of the Congregational church of Ipswich, Massachusetts, published in 1705 a work on the vindication of the government of the New England churches. This work, abounding in sentiments of freedom and liberal ideas and profound views on civil government, was studied by the statesmen and the people during the Revolution; and "some of the most glittering sentences in the immortal Declaration of Independence are almost literal quotations from this essay of John Wise. And it is a significant fact that in 1772, only four years before that declaration was made, a large edition of his works was published, by subscription, in one duodecimo volume. It was used as a political text-book in the great struggle for freedom then opening. Distinguished laymen in all parts of New England, who were soon to be heralded to the world as heroes in that great struggle, are on the list of subscribers for six, twelve, twenty-four, thirty-six, and two of them for a hundred, copies each."

This author, after discussing the various kinds of governments, and their principles and workings, says—

"A democracy.—This is a form of government which the light of nature does highly value, and directs to as most agreeable to the just and natural prerogatives of human beings. This was of great account in the early times of the world. And not only so, but, upon the experience of several thousand years, after the world had been troubled and tossed from one species of government to another, at a great expense of blood and treasure, many of the wise nations of the world have sheltered themselves under it again, or at least have blended and balanced their governments with it.

"It is certainly a great truth, namely, that man's original liberty, after it is resigned (yet under due restrictions), ought to be cherished in all wise governments; or, otherwise, a man in making himself a subject, alters himself from a freeman into a slave, which to do is repugnant to the laws of nature. Also the natural equality of men amongst men must be duly favored; in that government was never established by God or nature to give one a prerogative to insult over another: therefore, in a civil as well as in a natural state of being, a just equality is to be indulged so far as that every man is bound to honor every man, which is agreeable both to nature and religion, (1 Pet. ii. 17): Honor all men. The end of all good government is to cultivate humanity, and promote the happiness of all, and the good of every man, in all his rights, his life, liberty, estate, honor, &c., without injury or abuse done to any one.

Rev. Mr. Howard

A Puritan preacher and patriot, before the legislative council of Massachusetts, in 1780, presented the following views on the duties and influence of civil rulers—

"Our political fathers and civil rulers will not fail to do all they can to promote religion and virtue through the community, as the surest means of rendering their government easy and happy to themselves and the people. For this purpose they will watch over their morals with the same affectionate and tender care that a pious and prudent parent watches over his children, and, by all methods which love to God and man can inspire and wisdom point out, endeavor to check and suppress all impiety and vice, and lead the people to the practice of that righteousness which exalteth a nation. They will render themselves a terror to evil-doers, as well as an encouragement to such as do well. They will promote to places of trust men of piety, truth, and benevolence. Nor will they fail to exhibit in their own lives a fair example of that piety and virtue which they wish to see practised by the people. They will show that they are not ashamed of the gospel of Christ, by paying a due regard to his sacred institutions, and to all the laws of his kingdom. Magistrates may probably do more in this way than in any other, and perhaps more than any other order of men, to preserve or recover the morals of a people. The manners of a court are peculiarly catching, and, like the blood in the heart, quickly flow to the most distant members of the body. If, therefore, rulers desire to see religion and virtue flourish in a nation over which they preside, they must countenance and encourage them by their own examples."

Jonas Clark

The pastor of the Congregational Church of Lexington, Massachusetts, was among the foremost and ablest champions of liberty and the Revolution. His field of spiritual labor is immortalized in American history as the field where the first battle for independence was fought, and Lexington is as noble and memorable as Bunker Hill in the annals of freedom. The pastor of this Christian flock had early indoctrinated his people into an ardent love for civil and religious liberty.

"His congregation," says Headley, "were ripe for revolution, ready to die rather than to yield to arbitrary force." "The people had become so thoroughly indoctrinated in his views, and been so animated by his appeals from the pulpit and in public meetings, that the 'General Court' had them embodied in instructions to their delegate to the Provincial legislature, as the expression of their wishes and determination." "This document," says Edward Everett, "in which the principles and opinions of the town are embodied, has few equals, and no superiors, among the productions of that class. Mr. Clark was of a class of citizens who rendered services second to no others in enlightening and animating the popular mind on the great questions at issue: *I mean the patriotic clergy of New England.*"

"It was to a congregation educated by such a man," says Headley, "that Providence allowed to be intrusted the momentous events of the 19th of April—events which were to decide more than the fate of a continent—that of civil liberty the world over. In surveying the scenes of carnage after the battle of Lexington, Mr. Clark, who had been an active participator, exclaimed, 'From this day *will be dated the liberty of the world.*' He believed the war to be as just a one as ever was waged by the Israelites of old, and as much under the direction of God. *The teachings of the pulpit of Lexington caused the first blow to be struck for American Independence.*"

Judah Champion

Of Litchfield, Connecticut, was one of the most earnest and eloquent advocates of the Revolution, and during the whole of those eventful times was active and influential in the cause of his country. He was remarkable for the fervor and power of his prayers for the success of the great cause of liberty. On one occasion a regiment of cavalry reached Litchfield on Saturday night, and remained over the Sabbath. The presence of the military raised the devotions of the patriotic pastor to the highest ardor, and in his prayer he spoke of "the hostile invasion, the cruel purpose for which it was set on foot—of their enmity to the American Church, and the ruin to religion which their success would accomplish—of congregations scattered, churches burned to the ground, and the Lord's people made a hissing and a by-word among their foes," till his own feelings and those of his hearers were roused into intense excitement in view of the great wrongs and sufferings designed for them and the Church of God, and he burst forth as follows—

"O Lord, we view with terror and dismay the enemies of our holy religion: wilt thou send storm and tempest to toss them upon the sea, to overwhelm them in the mighty deep, or scatter them to the uttermost parts of the earth. But, peradventure should they escape thy vengeance, collect them together again, O Lord, as in the hollow of thy hand, and let thy lightnings play upon them. We beseech thee, moreover, that thou do gird up the loins of these thy servants who are going forth to fight thy battles. Make them strong men, that one shall chase a thousand, and two put ten thousand to flight. Hold before them the shield with which thou wast wont in the old time to protect thy people. Give them swift feet, that they may pursue their enemies, and swords terrible as that of thy destroying angel, that they may cleave them down. Preserve these servants of thine, Almighty God, and bring them once more to their homes and friends, if thou canst do so consistently with thy high purpose. If, on the other hand, thou hast decreed that they shall die in battle, let thy

Spirit be present with them, that they may go up as sweet sacrifices into the courts of thy temple, where habitations are prepared for them from the foundation of the world."

Samuel Webster

In the spring of 1777, preached the election sermon before the House of Representatives of Massachusetts. It was delivered "after the successive disasters that had overtaken the American army, the defeat on Long Island, the fall of New York and Fort Washington, and the flight of Washington and his disorganized army through the Jerseys—a year wrapped in gloom and fraught with sad fore-bodings, with only one gleam of sunshine—the battle of Prince-ton—to cheer the desponding hearts of the patriots." The sermon was full of the fire and patriotism of the times, and closed with the following remarkable prayer—

"Awake, O Lord, for our help, and come and save us. Awake, O Lord, as in ancient times. Do with them, O Lord, if it be thy will, as thou didst unto the Midianites and their confederates, and to Sisera, and to Jabin, when they invaded thy people, and make their lords and nobles and great commanders like Oreb and Zeeb, and like Zeba and Zalmunna. Though these angry brethren profess to worship the same God with us, yet because it is in a somewhat different mode they seem to have said, Come let us take the houses of God in possession. Accordingly they have vented a peculiar spite against the houses of God, defaced and defiled thy holy and beautiful sanctuaries where our fathers worshipped thee, turning them into houses of merchandise and receptacles of beasts, and some of them they have torn in pieces and burned with fire. Therefore we humbly pray that thou wilt hedge up their way, and not suffer them to proceed and prosper. Put them to flight speedily, if it be thy holy will, and make them run fast as a wheel downward, or as far as stubble and chaff is driven before the furious whirlwind. As the fire consumes the wood, and sometimes lays waste whole forests on the mountains, so let them be laid waste and consumed if they obstinately persist in their bloody designs against us. Lord, raise a dreadful tempest and affright them, and let thy tremendous storms make them quake with fear; and pursue them with thy arrows, till they are brought to see that God is with us of a truth, and fighteth for us, and so return unto their own land, covered with shame and confusion, and humble themselves before thee and seek to appease thine anger by a bitter repentance for their murderous designs. And let them have neither credit nor courage to come out any more against us. That so all nations, seeing thy mighty power and thy marvellous works, may no more call themselves supreme, but know and acknowledge that thou art God alone, the only supreme Governor among men, doing whatsoever pleaseth thee."

Address of the Provincial Congress of Masachusettes to the Clergy

In 1774 the Provincial Congress of Massachusetts acknowledged their public obligation to the ministry, as friends of civil and religious liberty, and invoked their aid, in the following address—

REVEREND SIRS—When we contemplate the friendship and assistance our ancestors, the first settlers of this province, while overwhelmed with distress, received from the pious pastors of the churches of Christ, who to enjoy the rights of conscience fled with them into this land, then a savage wilderness, we find ourselves filled with the most grateful sensations. And we cannot but acknowledge the goodness of Heaven in constantly supplying us with preachers of the gospel, whose concern has been the temporal and spiritual happiness of the people.

In a day like this, when all the friends of civil and religious liberty are exerting themselves to deliver this country from its present calamities, we cannot but place great hopes in an order of men who have ever distinguished themselves in their country's cause; and do, therefore, recommend to the ministers of the gospel in the several towns and other places in the colony, that they assist us in avoiding that dreadful slavery with which we are now threatened, by advising the people of their several congregations, as they wish their prosperity, to abide by and strictly to adhere to the resolutions of the Continental Congress, at Philadelphia, in October, 1774, as the most peaceable and probable method of preventing confusion and bloodshed, and of restoring that harmony between Great Britain and these colonies on which we wish might be established not only the rights and liberties of America, but the opulence and lasting happiness of the whole British empire.

Resolved, That the foregoing address be presented to all the ministers of the gospel in this province.

Dr. Langdon

Samuel Langdon, D.D., President of Harvard College, preached before the Honorable Congress of Massachusetts Bay, in May, 1775, on the theme "Government corrupted by vice and recovered by righteousness."

"Let us consider," says he, "that for the sins of a people God may suffer the best government to be corrupted or entirely dissolved, and that nothing but a general reformation can give good ground to hope that the public happiness will be restored by the recovery of the strength and perfection of the state, and that Divine Providence will interpose to fill every department with wise and good men.

"When a government is in its prime, the public good engages the attention of the whole; the strictest regard is paid to the qualifications of those who hold the offices of state; virtue prevails; every thing is managed with justice, prudence, and frugality; the laws are founded on principles of equity rather than mere policy, and all the people are happy. But vice will increase with the riches and glory of an empire; and this generally tends to corrupt the Constitution and in time bring on its dissolution. This may be considered not only as the natural effect of vice, but a righteous judgment from Heaven, especially upon a nation which has been favored with the blessings of religion and liberty and is guilty of undervaluing them and eagerly going into the gratification of every lust.

"We have rebelled against God. We have lost the true spirit of Christianity, though we retain the outward profession and form of it. We have neglected and set light by the glorious gospel of our Lord Jesus Christ and his holy commands and institutions. The worship of many is but mere compliment to the Deity, while their hearts are far from him. By many the gospel is corrupted into a superficial system of moral philosophy, little better than ancient Platonism; and, after all the pretended refinements of moderns in the theory of Christianity, very little of the pure practice of it is to be found among those who once stood foremost in the profession of the gospel.

"But, alas! have not the sins of America, and of New England in particular, had a hand in bringing down upon us the righteous judgments of Heaven? Wherefore is all this evil come upon us? Is it not because we have forsaken the Lord? Can we say we are innocent of crimes against God? No, surely. It becomes us to humble ourselves under his mighty hand, that he may exalt us in due time. However unjustly and cruelly we have been treated by man, we certainly deserve at the hand of God all the calamities in which we are now involved. Have we not lost much of that spirit of genuine Christianity which so remarkably appeared in our ancestors, for which God distinguished them by the signal favors of his providence when they fled from tyranny and persecution into Western deserts? Have we not departed from their virtues? Have we not made light of the gospel of salvation, and too much affected the *cold, formal, fashionable religion* of countries grown old in vice and overspread with infidelity? Do not our follies and iniquities testify against us? Have we not, especially in our seaports, gone much too far into the pride and luxuries of life? Is it not a fact, open to common observation, that profaneness, intemperance, unchastity, the love of pleasure, fraud, avarice, and other vices, are increasing among us from year to year? And have not even these young governments been in some measure infected with the corruptions of European courts? Has there been no *flattery*, no *bribery*, no *artifices practised to get into places of honor and profit or to carry a vote to secure a particular interest without regard to right or wrong? Have our statesmen always acted with integrity*, and every judge with impartiality, in the fear of God? In short, have all ranks of men showed regard to the Divine commands, and joined to promote the Redeemer's kingdom and the public welfare? I wish we could more fully justify ourselves in all these respects. We must remember that the sins of a people who have been remarkable for the profession of godliness are more aggravated by all the advantages and favors they have enjoyed, and will receive more speedy and signal judgments, as

God says of Israel —'You only have I known of all the families of the earth: therefore will I punish you for all your iniquities.'

"Let me address you in the words of the prophet—'O Israel, return unto the Lord thy God, for thou hast fallen by thine iniquity.' Let us repent, and implore the Divine mercy; let us amend our ways and our doings, REFORM EVERY THING which has been provoking to the Most High, and thus endeavor to obtain the gracious interposition of Providence for our deliverance.

"If true religion is revived by means of these public calamities, and again prevails among us—if it appears in our religious assemblies, in the CONDUCT OF OUR CIVIL AFFAIRS, IN OUR ARMIES, in our *families*, IN ALL OUR BUSINESS and conversation—we may hope for the direction and blessing of the Most High, while we are using our best endeavors to preserve the civil government of this colony and defend America from *slavery*.

"And may we not be confident that the Most High will vindicate his own honor, and plead our righteous cause against such enemies to his government as well as our liberties? Oh, may our camp be free from every accursed thing! May our land be purged from *all* its sins! May we be truly a holy people, and all our towns cities of righteousness! Then the Lord will be our refuge and strength, a very present help in trouble, and we shall have no reason to be afraid, though thousands of enemies set themselves against us round about, though all nature should be thrown into tumults and convulsions. He can command the stars in their courses to fight his and our battles, and all the elements to wage war with his and our enemies. He can destroy them with innumerable plagues, or send faintness into their hearts, so that the men of might shall not find their hands. In a variety of methods he can work salvation for us, as he did for his people in ancient days, and according to the many remarkable deliverances granted in former times to New England.

"May the Lord hear us in this day of trouble, and the name of the God of Jacob defend us, send us help from his sanctuary, and strengthen us out of Zion! We will rejoice in his salvation, and in the name of our God will we set up our banners. Let us look to him to fulfil our petitions."

The following is an interesting and solemn scene of the Revolution, published in a religious newspaper of 1858—

"*June* 10, 1775—This has been one of the most important and trying days of my life. I have taken leave of my people for the present, and shall at once proceed to the American camp at Boston and offer my services as chaplain in the army. Ever since the battle of Bunker Hill my mind has been turned to this subject." "God's servants are needed in the army to pray with and for it. This is God's work; and his ministers should set an example that will convince the people that they believe it to be such. But the scene in the house of God to-day has tried me sorely. How silent, how solemn, was the congregation! and when they sang the sixty-first Psalm, commencing—

'When, overwhelm'd with grief,
My heart within me dies,'—

sobs were heard in every part of the building. At the close, I was astonished to see Deacon S., now nearly sixty years of age, arise and address the congregation. 'Brethren,' said he, 'our minister has acted right. This is God's cause; and as in days of old the priests bore the ark into the midst of the battle, so must they do it now. We should be unworthy of the fathers and mothers who landed on Plymouth Rock, and suffered privations and dangers to secure freedom for us, if we did not cheerfully bear what Providence shall put upon us in the great conflict now before us. I had two sons at Bunker Hill, and one of them, you know, was slain. The other did his duty, and for the future God must do with him what seemeth him best. I offer him to liberty. I had thought I was getting too old to offer myself, and that I would stay here with the church. But my minister is going, and I will shoulder my musket and go too.' In this strain he continued for some time, till the whole congregation was bathed in tears. Oh, God must be with this people in this unequal struggle: else how could they enter upon it with such solemnity and prayer, with such strong reliance on his assistance, and such a profound sense of their need of it? Just before separating, the whole congregation joined in singing—

'O God, our help in ages past,
Our hope for years to come.'"

Rev. James Caldwell

Pastor of the Presbyterian church of Elizabethtown, New Jersey, was a martyr for liberty. His church was burned by the British, and he and his family were murdered, in 1780. Rev. Nicholas Murray, pastor of the same church for many years, in a memorial to Congress, in 1840, for payment of the church property destroyed by the British, said—

"When the glorious war of our Revolution commenced which resulted in our independence, the Rev. James Caldwell was then pastor of this church. His name and fame are interwoven with the history of his country, and are as dear to the State as to the Church. He became early and deeply interested in the conflict, and devoted all his powers no less to the freedom of his country than to the service of his God. Such was his influence over his people that, with few exceptions, they became one with him in sentiment and feeling; and thenceforward he and they were branded as the rebel parson and parish. To the enemies of his country he was an object of the deepest hatred; and such was their known thirst for his life, that, while preaching the gospel of peace to his people, he was compelled to lay his loaded pistols by his side in the pulpit."

"In the exciting scenes," says Headley, "that immediately preceded the Revolution, he bore a prominent and leading part. His congregation upheld him, almost to a man; and when we remember that such patriots as Elias Boudinot, William Livingston, Francis Barber, the Daytons and Ogdens, composed it, we cannot wonder that both pastor and people were looked upon as head rebels of the province, and became peculiarly obnoxious to the loyalists. In intelligence, ardor, and patriotism they had no superior, and formed a band of noble men of which New Jersey is justly proud.

"At the first call to arms, the State offered its brigade for the common defence, and Mr. Caldwell was elected its chaplain. His immense popularity gave him an influence that filled the tories with rage and made his name common as a household word among the British troops. They offered a large reward for his capture. For his personal safety, he went armed.

"So entire was the confidence of the people in his integrity that, when the army became greatly reduced, and both provisions and money were hard to be obtained, he was appointed Assistant Commissary-General. He not only was earnest and eloquent in his pulpit for the cause of his country, but was active and brave in battle. In one of the engagements near Springfield, New Jersey, Mr. Caldwell was in the hottest of the fight, and, seeing the fire of one of the companies slacken for want of wadding, he galloped to the Presbyterian meeting-house near by, and, rushing in, ran from pew to pew, filling his arms with hymn-books. Hastening back with these into battle, he scattered them about in every direction, saying, as he pitched one here and another there, '*Now, boys, put Watts into them.*'

"The unselfish and entire devotion of this gifted man to his country was of the Washington type—a devotion in which life itself and all its outward interests were forgotten, or remembered only as an offering ever ready to be made to her welfare. The cause of freedom, and especially the State of New Jersey, owe him a large debt of gratitude."

A monument to Dr. Caldwell stands in the burial-ground of the First Presbyterian Church of Elizabethtown, New Jersey, where sleep many of the heroes of the Revolution. The inscription is as follows—

> EAST SIDE—"This monument is erected to the memory of the Rev. James Caldwell, the pious and fervent Christian, the zealous and faithful minister, the eloquent preacher, and a prominent leader among the worthies who secured the independence of his country. His name will be cherished in the Church and in the State so long as virtue is esteemed and patriotism rewarded."

> WEST SIDE—"Hannah, wife of the Rev. James Caldwell, and daughter of Jonathan Ogden, of Newark, was killed at Connecticut Farms, by a shot from a British soldier, June 24th, 1780, cruelly sacrificed by the enemies of her husband and of her country."

NORTH SIDE—"'The memory of the just is blessed.' 'Be of good courage, and let us behave ourselves valiantly for our people, and for the cities of our God, and let the Lord do that which is good in his sight.' 'The glory of children are their fathers.'"

SOUTH SIDE—"James Caldwell, born in Charlotte County, in Virginia, April, 1734. Graduated at Princeton College, 1750. Ordained pastor of the First Presbyterian Church of Elizabethtown, 1762. After serving as chaplain in the army of the Revolution, and acting as commissary to the troops in New Jersey, he was killed by a shot from a sentinel at Elizabethtown Point, November 24th, 1781.

"THE MEMORY OF THE JUST IS BLESSED."

George Duffield

Of Philadelphia, was an eminent preacher and patriot of the Revolution, and devoted to the cause of his country. He was among the first chaplains to the Colonial Congress, and did good service to the civil council as well as to the armies of his country. Dr. Sprague, in his "Annals of the American Pulpit," says of this pious and patriotic preacher—

"He was a bold and zealous assertor of the rights of conscience, an earnest and powerful advocate of civil and religious liberty. During the pending of the measures which were maturing the Declaration of Independence, while the prospects of the colonies seemed most gloomy, his preaching contributed greatly to encourage and animate the friends of liberty. So much did he value prayer, and so important did he feel it to be to excite and encourage the men that had left their homes and perilled their lives in the cause of freedom, to look to God and put their trust in Him, that he would, occasionally, in the darkest hour of the Revolution, leave his charge, and repair to the camp, where the fathers and sons of many of his flock were gathered, and minister to them in the public preaching of the word and personal service." "He was with the army in their battles and retreats through Jersey, during that dark and nearly hopeless period of the Revolution."

The patriots of the first Congress attended his church; and John Adams and his compeers were often his hearers.

His soul could infuse courage in the hour of danger, and sheer the disheartened in disaster, by example, precept, and prayer. He was well known in camp; and his visits were always welcome, for the soldiers loved the eloquent, earnest, fearless patriot.

The following is a fine specimen of the eloquence and fervor of Dr. Duffield's piety and patriotism, and a precious relic of Revolutionary times, taken from a discourse preached—

> At Pine Street Presbyterian Church, Philadelphia, March 17, 1776, by Rev. George Duffield, D.D., Pastor. Isaiah xxi. 11,12—"The burden of Dumah. He calleth to me out of Seir, Watchman, what of the night? Watchman, what of the night? The watchman said, The morning cometh, and also the night: if ye will inquire, inquire ye: return, come."

❋ ❋ ❋ ❋ ❋ ❋ ❋

The instruction afforded in these words is as follows—

I. That it is the duty of a people, under a pressure of trouble and distress, to be earnest in applying to God respecting their affairs.

II. That such a people have encouragement to expect God will answer them, and with the affliction administer comfort to them.

I. What is implied in applying to God in such circumstances?

1. generous concern for the public good.

Idumea's watchman, representing all those of the inhabitants of that country suitably exercised in that day of trial (and every true patriot in our day), seems to have abandoned every meaner consideration, to have lost every thought of private concern for himself or his own peculiar interest, in an ardent glow of zeal for the good of the common cause, by which, while others indulge in repose, his eyes slumber not; he watches for his country's good; his thoughts are all on this; and his busy, laboring mind is consulting, planning, and inquiring for its good.

View him a moment on his watch-tower on Mount Seir: his looks are the picture of deep concern; anxious care dwells seated on his brow; painful study for his country's good has emaciated his frame, spread a solemn composure over his countenance, and hastened his age faster far than hurrying time itself would roll away his years!

Such a patriot was good Hezekiah, who lived only to serve his country, whose days were measured by diligence for its good and planning for its greatest benefit, and whose constitution was so enfeebled by unremitting care that ere he had reached his fortieth year he had sunk before the first attack of disease, had not a miracle interposed for his deliverance.

Such patriots of old were Samuel and Ezra, and, in the field, the brave Uriah. Such may thy councils, O America, and such thine armies, ever contain.

2. A sense of the overruling government of God determining the affairs of men.

Without this, the Idumean patriot had never called with such ardor to the watchman God had appointed to observe and declare his will. So intimately is a reverence for God connected with the proper discharge of every duty we owe to our fellow-men, as individuals, or the community at large—both proceeding from the same good principle within—that never can there be a proper and sincere discharge of the latter where the former is neglected. TRUE PATRIOTISM IS FOUNDED IN TRUE RELIGION; and where the latter is not, *there is great danger of the former being bought or bribed by an adequate price*, or in some way blasted, like the seed sown in stony ground, that perished through want of root.

3. A diligent attention to the use of means.

God has so determined, in the ordinary course of his providential dispensations, that the blessings he designs to bestow are yet to be sought after and obtained in the use of the proper means. Eden itself was not to nourish Adam without dressing. The same God that fed Elijah by the brook could have commanded the ravens to feed the family of Jacob, but they must travel to Egypt for bread. Canaan was given to Israel, but they must march and fight and toil to subdue and possess it. Paul was assured that the ship's crew would all be saved, but the mariners must stay aboard and ply their endeavors, or not a soul would be safe. And who that considers the engagedness of this earnest Edomite, "calling from Seir," can doubt his diligence in every measure adapted to obtain the end?

4. The true patriot must be earnestly engaged in prayer.

In the common affairs of life, as well as in religion, we may adopt the language of the apostle, and, whether Paul plant or Apollos water, it is God must give the increase. This is the Psalmist's idea (Ps. cxxvii. 1), "Except the Lord build the house, they labor in vain that build it," &c. It is this blessing that makes prosperous as well as rich, &c. To him, therefore, with great propriety does the pious Idumean look, and ardently pray, in our text; and it will generally be found that when God is about to bestow any remarkable favor on a person or people, he previously pours upon that people or person a spirit of earnest supplication to God for his favor.

That it is the incumbent duty of a people, and especially when involved in calamitous circumstances, thus to pray; consider—

1. God has commanded it, and to his injunction added great encouragement. Ps. 1. 15: "Call upon me in the day of trouble; I will deliver thee, and thou shalt glorify me." Ps. xxxviii. 5: "Commit thy way unto the Lord; trust also in him; and he shall bring it to pass." Joel ii. 32: "Whosoever shall call on the name of the Lord shall be delivered; for in Mount Zion and in Jerusalem shall be deliverance, as the Lord has said." Hence—

2. Prayer is one of the most probable means of obtaining deliverance from trouble.

As the calamities of a people are the chastening of God for their sins, and one end designed therein is to bring them back to Him from whom they have departed, the more they are brought to a sense of their dependence on God, and engaged in returning and making supplication to him, the greater is their prospect not only of being delivered, but of having their calamities converted into blessings. Micah iv. 6: And "I will gather her that is driven out, and her that I have afflicted, and I will make her that was cast off a strong nation."

3. Prayer brings down the perfections of God to the assistance of those who are thus exercised. Ps. xvi. 1: "Preserve me, O God; for in thee do I put my trust." Ps. cxviii. 5—12: "I called upon the Lord in distress: the Lord answered me, and set me in a large place. The Lord is on my side; I will not fear: what can man do unto me? The Lord taketh my part with them that help me: therefore shall I see my desire upon them that hate me. It is better to trust in the Lord than to put confidence in man. It is better to trust in the Lord than to put confidence in princes. All nations compassed me about: but in the name of the Lord will I destroy them. They compassed me about; yea, they compassed me about; but in the name of the Lord I will destroy them. They compassed me about like bees; they are quenched as the fire of thorns: for in the name of the Lord I will destroy them."

II. Let us now consider THE ANSWER, and point out some signs that promise a morning of deliverance to a people afflicted.

Known unto God are all his ways from the beginning; and from the perfections of Deity we may safely assert that all moral and natural evil will finally be rendered subservient to the perfection of the Divine plan; but *in what manner* this shall be done surpasses the contracted power of the feeble mind of man to determine, and rests perhaps among the mysteries of heaven that Gabriel himself has not explained, but waits for the finishing scene to explain the mysterious drama. Yet so it is. As day and night succeed each other in the natural, so both the natural and the moral world have their nights and their days in successive interesting periods, since the memorable hour when Adam forsook his God, and introduced moral evil, and its inseparable attendant, natural evil, into this small province of the Great Creator's kingdom. The whole world throughout is as of the Jews in our text. "The morning cometh, and also the night," and so shall continue until night and day be blended no more.

Eternal day and eternal night will possess their eternally-separated regions, and separate the inhabitants in endless happiness and joy, or everlasting horror and despair.

The particular time of the Jewish state, designed in our text by the morning and the night here mentioned, may be hard to determine; but it will with great propriety apply to various periods.

It was, at the time of the prophecy, *a night* of sore impending distress from Sennacherib the Assyrian king. A MORNING of deliverance came in the destruction of Rabshakeh's army. (2 Kings xix.)

The troubled state of affairs for a series of years before and through the Babylonish captivity was a season of night. A *morning* came in the return under Cyrus.

It was a long night, in respect of religion, through the whole of their ceremonial service: this was still darker before the coming of Christ, but in him arose a bright morning.

"A dayspring from on high visited them, to give light to those that were in darkness and in the shadow of death, and to guide their feet into the way of peace." (Luke I. 78, 79.)

Night came on them in the destruction of their city and nation, and has continued now 1700 years; but the prophets and the Apostle Paul (Rom. xi. 15, 26) promise them a glorious morning in the latter days of the world.

The Christian Church has had its nights and its mornings.

And the like has been the case with every nation in a measure.

But it more especially concerns us to attend to the improvement of this doctrine, both with respect to individuals and to the present state of our own public affairs.

Improvement.—1. In the way of comfort to the people of God: for—

(a.) All their affairs are ordered by God, who is their God, and to whom they have a right to go as their God and inquire.

(b.) Though they have a night, there is an eternal morning in reserve. But—

2. Our subject is full of gloom to sinners out of Christ. Now they have a night of spiritual darkness and death; an eternal night of dreadful misery and despair awaits you—very shortly—hereafter.

3. The improvement of our subject naturally leads our thoughts to the state of our public affairs.

It is at present a night scene over this vast northern part of the New World. God, to chastise us for our offences, and for wise and important purposes, has suffered dark clouds to envelope our sky. It becomes every one, who wishes his own or his country's good, to inquire, "Watchman, what of the night?" It is a time for earnest prayer, joined with diligent endeavor. There is in store an answer of mercy! There is a morning in reserve, though the night may continue some time.

REASONS TO EXPECT A MORNING.—1. God never has cast off and destroyed a nation so soon, as it would be to deliver America now to ruin. Look at the antediluvian world—the Amorites, and other nations of Canaan—the Jews, &c.

2. The western world appears to have been retained for that purpose, and designed by an ordinance of heaven as an ASYLUM for LIBERTY, civil and religious. Our forefathers, who first inhabited yonder eastern shores, fled from the iron rod and heavy hand of tyranny. This it was, and no love of earthly gain or prospect of temporal grandeur, that urged them, like Abraham of old, to leave their native soil and tender connections behind, to struggle through winds and waves, and seek a peaceful retreat, in a then howling wilderness, where they might rear the banner of liberty and dwell contented under its propitious shade, esteeming this more than all the treasures of a British Egypt, from whence they were driven forth. Methinks I see them on the inhospitable shore they were hastening to leave, and hear them adopt the sentiment of the Psalmist, lv. 6, 7, to give it in the expressive language of Watts, with as small variation—

> "Oh, were I like a feather'd dove,
> And innocence had wings;
> I'd fly, and make a far remove,
> From *persecuting kings.*"

Nor was it the fostering care of Britain produced the rapid populating of these colonies, but the tyranny and oppression, both civil and ecclesiastical, of that and other nations, constrained multitudes to resign every other earthly comfort, and leave their country and their friends, to enjoy in peace the fair possession of freedom in this western world. It is this has reared our cities, and turned the wilderness, so far and wide, into a fruitful field. *America's sons, very few excepted, were all refugees—the chosen spirits of various nations, that could not, like Issachar, bow down between the two burdens of the accursed cruelly of tyranny in Church and State.* And can it be supposed that the Lord has so far forgot to be gracious, or shut up his tender mercies in his wrath, to favor the arms of oppression and to deliver up this asylum to slavery and bondage? Can it be supposed that the God who made man free, and engraved in indefeasible characters the love of liberty in his mind, should forbid freedom, already exiled from Asia, Africa, and *under sentence of banishment* from Europe—that he should forbid her to erect her banner here, and constrain her to abandon the earth? As soon shall he reverse creation, and forbid yonder sun to shine! To the Jews he preserved their cities of refuge; and while sun and moon endure, America shall remain a CITY OF REFUGE FOR THE WHOLE EARTH, until she herself shall *play the tyrant, disgrace her freedom, and provoke her God!* When that day shall come, if ever, then, and not till then, shall she also fall, "slain with those that go down to the pit."

3. The spirit and ardent love of liberty that has possessed these colonies so wide and far, is a strong evidence of a *morning*, a bright morning, hastening on. It is the same spirit that inspired our forefathers' breasts when first they left their native shores and embarked for this then howling desert. Their mortal part has mingled with the dust, but the surviving spirit has triumphed over death and the grave, and descended to their sons; and it is this spirit, beating high in the veins of their offspring, has roused them so unanimous and determined in the present struggle. 'Tis this spirit has formed our extensive UNION, and inspired our councils with that magnanimity and lustre that astonishes half the world. 'Tis this spirit has enrolled your Congresses and conventions in the an-

nals of immortal fame. 'Tis this spirit has enabled your dear, suffering brethren in yonder once flourishing city [Boston], now almost a ruinous heap, to endure joyfully the spoiling of their goods, glorying to be accounted worthy to suffer in the honorable cause! 'Twas this spirit that ranked a Warren, a Montgomery, and others, upon the list of protomartyrs for American liberty. And this same spirit has led you forth, ye patriot bands, associated in your country's cause, and will, I trust, still urge you on to noble deeds, and bravely to prefer a glorious death to slavery and chains!

And this—what shall I call it less than a Divine Afflatus so generally prevailing through all ranks, in the cabinet and in the field—is an argument from heaven that America shall rise triumphant over the proud waves and raging billows that now threaten her ruin! When a nation is to be destroyed, she is, as described by Hosea vii. 11, "like a silly dove without heart;" but when this divine afflatus comes upon a nation, and it is refreshed like a giant with new wine, the omen is sure and the victory inevitable.

4. There is great reason to believe that the Church of Christ is yet to have a glorious day in America.

Religion, like the sun, rose in the east, and has continued its progress in a western direction. Once it flourished in Asia. Now it is almost total darkness there. From thence it came to Europe, and there shone bright for a season; but scenes of persecution harassed it, and the shadows of a dark evening have long been gathering round it. America seems to have been prepared as the wilderness to which the woman should fly from the face of the dragon and be nourished for a long series of time. (Rev. xii. 6.) God has here planted his Church; he has hedged it round, and made it to flourish; and though there have been some few, some very few remains of a mistaken zeal for piety, in attempting to fetter the minds of men with pains and penalties, yet it may with great justice be said, in no part of the earth does religious liberty equally prevail, and just sentiments of the rights of conscience obtain, as in this land. Here has pure and undefiled religion lengthened her cords and strengthened her stakes. Yonder today are the praises of God singing, and the word of his grace proclaimed, where but a few years back his name was not known, nor any thing heard but the yells of savage beasts, or poor indarkened Indian tribes, equally ignorant of the true God as the beasts themselves.

How large an addition to the kingdom of Christ has been made in this land! The King of glory has here indeed gone forth, with his sword on his thigh, riding prosperously in state, conquering and to conquer! The progress of this kingdom is still continued with a rapid career; and shall his foes tear the laurels from the brow of the great Redeemer, and deliver his victory and glorious prospects into slavery and thraldom? Forbid it, Jesus, from thy throne! It shall not take place! The Church shall flourish here and hold on her way triumphant in spite of kings, lords, Commons, and devils, until yonder vast unexplored western regions shall all resound the praises of God, and the unenlightened tribes of the wilderness shall know and adore our Immanuel. And as civil and religious liberty live or languish together, so shall the civil liberty of America hold pace with the triumphs of the gospel throughout this extensive land.

Though we are wicked enough, God knows, and have much need of repentance and returning to our God, as we would wish and hope for his favor, yet we are not arrived to that degree of impiety, or that so generally prevailing as is usually, and, I may say, always, the case before God gives up and delivers a land into the hand of their enemies; and this is an argument why we may yet hope for a morning and a further day.

5. The peculiar hand of Providence that has evidently led us hitherto, and the remarkable smiles of Heaven on our attempts thus far for our defence, and his frowns upon those that have risen up against us, afford also a pleasing prospect. "Had not the Lord," now may America say, "had not the Lord been on our side, ... the proud waters had gone over our soul." "Our help is in the name of the Lord, who made heaven and earth." (Psalm cxxiv.)

In all these things I have mentioned, to which more might be added, God speaks clearly in his providence, as on Sinai out of the cloud; and to us is the watchman's reply, The MORNING COMETH, though a space of night may intervene. How long before it may arise, or in what manner the clouds shall break before it, or what connection America then shall have with any other nation (Britain going down to the deep,) or whether with any at all, that God who directs her counsels will determine!

At the conclusion of the war, Dr. Duffield delivered a sermon in the Pine Street Presbyterian Church, on the thanksgiving-day appointed for the peace of 1783, in which he said—

"The establishment of America in the peaceable possession of her rights stands an instance of the Divine favor unexampled in the records of time. Who does not remember the general language when the war commenced, *cheerfully to pay one-half of our property to secure our rights?* But even half of this has not been required. Taken on a national scale, the price of our peace, when compared with the advantages gained, scarce deserves the name.

"In whatever point of light we view this great event, we are constrained to say, 'It is the doing of the Lord, and marvellous in our eyes. And to him be rendered thanks and praise. *Not unto us, not unto us, but to thy name, O Lord, be the glory.* Both success and safety come of thee. And thou reignest over all, and hast wrought all our works, in us and for us. *Praise, therefore, thy God, O America; praise the Lord, ye his highly favored United States.* Nor let it rest in the fleeting language of the lip, or the formal thanksgiving of a day. But let every heart glow with gratitude, and every life, by a devout regard to his holy law, proclaim his praise. It is this our God requires, as that wherein our personal and national good and the glory of his great name consist, and without which all our professions will be but an empty name. It is that we love the Lord our God, to walk in his ways and keep his commandments, to observe his statutes and judgments—that we do justice, love mercy, and walk humbly with our God. Then shall God delight to dwell amongst us, and these United States shall long remain a great, a glorious, and a happy people."

Rev. John Woodhull, D.D.

Pastor of the Freehold Presbyterian Church of New Jersey, was distinguished for his devotion to the cause of freedom. "He was one of the most active patriots of his day, and his zeal in the cause of his country was largely infused into his congregation. On one occasion every man in his parish went out to oppose the enemy, except one feeble old invalid, who bade them God-speed. The zealous minister went with them as pastor."

Rev. Dr. John H. Livingston

Was a distinguished patriot and preacher of the Dutch Reformed Church of New York. Shortly after the War of the Revolution began, the British gained possession of the city, and those who were favorable to the American cause, with their families, sought refuge and sojourned during the war in different places in the country. The congregation of the Dutch Reformed Church was strongly united in the cause of independence. During the occupation of the city by the British, several of the churches, especially where the congregations generally espoused the cause of freedom, were sadly desecrated and abused. Conspicuous among these were the Middle and North Reformed Dutch Churches, where Dr. Livingston preached. The Middle Church was used as a prison, and afterwards as a riding-school for the British officers and soldiers, and became the scene of habitual ribaldry, profanity, and dissipation. The whole of the interior, galleries and all, was destroyed, leaving the bare walls and roof.

The treaty of peace was concluded in 1783, and the British forces left the city on the 25th of November. On the 2d of December the Consistory of the Dutch churches met, and by resolution expressed their gratitude to God for his blessing, which had granted success in the struggle for independence and returned them in peace to their homes and to the house of God. Whilst they rejoiced in this long-desired reunion, they contemplated with sadness the desolations which had taken place, but at once arose unitedly, with prayer and in faith, to build again the waste places. The Middle Dutch Church was reopened for divine service on the 4th of July, 1790, when Dr. Livingston preached an eloquent and patriotic sermon. It closed as follows—

Livingston's Sermon

"To these great purposes this building was formerly devoted, and for these important ends it is now raised from its ruins. But the mention of ruins calls back our thoughts to past scenes, and presents disagreeable ideas to our minds. When destruction is caused by the immediate hand of Heaven, by earthquakes, storms, or fire, we are silent before God, and dare not reply. But when men have been the instruments, it is difficult, although proper, to look up to the overruling Power and to forget the interposition of the means. I dare not speak of the wanton cruelty of those who destroyed this temple, nor repeat the various indignities which have been perpetrated. It would be easy to mention facts which would chill your blood! A recollection of the groans of dying prisoners which pierced this ceiling, or the sacrilegious sports and rough feats of horsemanship exhibited within these walls, might raise sentiments in your mind that would, perhaps, not harmonize with those religious affections which I wish at present to promote and always to cherish.

"The Lord has sufficiently vindicated our cause and avenged us of those who rose up against us. He girded our Joshua (Washington) for the field, and led him, with his train of heroes, to victory. Heaven directed our councils and wrought deliverance. Our enemies themselves acknowledged an interposing Providence, and were obliged to say, The Lord bath done great things for them; while we repeat the shout of praise, The Lord hath done great things for us, whereof we are glad. Through the long avenue of danger and perplexity, while discouragements like dark clouds were hovering all around, who could penetrate the gloom and foresee that God would soon bring order out of confusion—so soon dismiss the horrors of war and grant an honorable peace—perfect revolution? Where was it ever seen, excepting only in Israel, that God took a nation out of the midst of another nation, with such a mighty hand and a stretched-out arm?

"Who could have predicted that from such indigested materials, with such short experience, and within so few years, an efficient, liberal, and pervading government would have been formed? A station and a rank are now obtained among the nations of the earth; and if the full enjoyment of civil and religious liberty is a constitutional part of social happiness, if the prospects of the rising importance, strength, and greatness of our new empire are of any weight in the scale, we may safely pronounce ourselves on this day to be the happiest nation in the world—a nation where all the rights of man are perfectly secured—without a monarchy, without hereditary nobility, and without an hierarchy.

"Hail, happy land! A land of liberty, of science and religion! Here an undisturbed freedom in worship forms the first principle of an equal government, and is claimed as a birthright which none of our rulers dare call in question or control. Here no sect is legally professed with exclusive prerogatives, the chief magistrate worships as a private citizen, and legislators by their influential example, not by penal laws, prove nursing fathers to the Church of Christ. In this happy and elevated situation, the ruins of our temples and all we have sustained appear a price too small to mention. We are more than compensated. We have forgiven, and we forget, past injuries. God has abundantly made up all our former griefs. When the Lord turned again the captivity of Zion, we were like them that dream. Then was our mouth filled with laughter, and our tongue with singing.

"We are a happy people; we feel and know that we are so. The labors of the husbandman prosper, and there is plenty in all our borders. Commerce is enlarged, and public credit established. The education of youth is universally patronized, and there is no complaining in our streets. In safety we sit every man under his own vine and fig-tree, and there are none to make us afraid. With sufficient room to accommodate nations, and a government adequate to all the important purposes of society, we are not only at ease ourselves, but extend our arms and cordially invite an oppressed world to come under our shade and share in our happiness. Happy is that people that is in such a case! Yea, happy is that people whose God is the Lord. Whether we shall continue thus happy will greatly depend upon our wisdom and justice, our industry and manners, but principally upon our faithfully remembering the name of the Lord. According to the measure in which the religion of the blessed Jesus is honored and prevails, our land will be truly happy and our liberty secure. This holy religion establishes the purest morality, and inculcates the reciprocal obligations which members of society are under to each other. It engages men of all ranks, by the highest sanctions, conscientiously to fulfil the duties of their stations, and it is, without controversy, the surest pledge of Divine protection.

"The maintenance of this in its purity will most effectually establish our invaluable blessings, and as this declines our ruin will hasten. See the rule of Providence with respect to nations (Jer. xviii. 9, 10): 'At what instant I shall speak concerning a nation, and concerning a kingdom, to build and to plant it. If it do evil in my sight, that it obey not my voice, then I will repent of the good wherewith I said I would benefit them.'

"While others, at our political anniversary, in their animated orations, employ all the powers of eloquence to confirm your title of liberty, and by enraptured views of civil blessings touch with transport all the springs of life, I desire, with plainness of speech, but with a zeal becoming a minister of the gospel, to raise your views to heaven and persuade you wisely to improve your present privileges. Seven years are not elapsed since we returned to this city in peace. And, lo! in less than seven years two ruined churches have been repaired. The Lord hath strengthened our hands, and given success to our efforts. Let an humble sense of our dependence upon him, and recollection of his numerous mercies, call forth lively gratitude upon this occasion. Bless the Lord, O my soul, and all that is within me bless his holy name! Bless the Lord, O my soul! and forget not all his benefits. It is, my brethren, a circumstance which upon our part is altogether fortuitous, but it deserves your notice, that, in the direction of Providence, you have more than one object upon this memorable Fourth of July that claims your attention.

"While you glow with patriotic ardor for your country, and pour out fervent prayers for its rising honor and happiness, you are also exulting that the gates of this house are opened to you. Enter into his gates with thanksgiving, and into his courts with praise; be thankful unto him, and bless his name."

Smith's Sermon in Philadelphia in 1775

William Smith, D.D., Provost of the College at Philadelphia, preached, June 23, 1775, at the request of the officers of the third battalion of that city, and the district of Southwark, a sermon on American affairs, from which the following are extracts—

> You are now engaged in one of the greatest struggles to which freemen can be called. You are contending for what you conceive to be your constitutional rights, and for a final settlement of the terms upon which this country may be perpetually united to the parent state.
>
> Look back, therefore, with reverence. Look back to the times of ancient virtue and renown. Look back to the mighty purposes which your fathers had in view when they traversed a vast ocean and planted this land. Recall to your minds their labors, their toils, their perseverance, and let a divine spirit animate you in all your actions.
>
> Look forward also to a distant posterity. Figure to yourselves millions and millions to spring from your loins, who may be born freemen or slaves, as Heaven shall now approve or reject our councils. Think that on you it may depend whether this great country, in ages hence, shall be filled and adorned with a virtuous and enlightened people, enjoying liberty and all its concomitant blessings, together with the religion of Jesus as it flows uncorrupted from his holy oracles, or covered with a race of men more contemptible than the savages that roam the wilderness, because they once knew the things which belong to their happiness and peace, but suffered them to be hid from their eyes.
>
> And, while you thus look back to the past and forward to the future, fail not, I beseech you, to look up to "the God of gods, the rock of your salvation." As "the clay in the potter's hands," so are the nations of the earth in the hands of him, the everlasting JEHOVAH. He lifteth up, and he casteth down. He resisteth the proud, and giveth grace to the humble. He will

keep the feet of his saints. The wicked shall be silent in darkness, and by strength shall no man prevail.

The bright prospects of the gospel, a thorough veneration of the Saviour of the world, a conscientious obedience to his divine laws, faith in his promises, and the steadfast hope of immortal life through him—these only can support a man in all times of adversity as well as prosperity. You might more easily "strike fire out of ice" than stability or magnanimity out of crimes. But the good man, he who is at peace with the God of all peace, will know no fear but that of offending him whose hand can cover the righteous, "so that he needs not fear the arrow that flieth by day, nor the destruction that wasteth at noonday: for a thousand shall fall beside him, and ten thousand at his right hand; but it shall not come nigh to him, for he shall give his angels charge over him to keep him in all his ways."

On the omnipotent God, therefore, through his blessed Son, let your strong confidence be placed; but do not vainly expect that every day will be to you a day of prosperity and triumph. The ways of Providence lie through mazes too intricate for human penetration. Mercies may often be held forth to us in the shape of sufferings; and the vicissitudes of our fortune, in building up the American fabric of happiness and glory, may be various and checkered.

But let not this discourage you. Yea, rather let it animate you with a holy *fervor*, a divine *enthusiasm*, ever persuading yourselves that the cause of *virtue* and *freedom* is the *cause* of God upon the earth, and that the whole theatre of human nature does not exhibit a more August spectacle than a number of freemen, in dependence upon Heaven, mutually binding themselves to encounter every difficulty and danger in support of their native and constitutional rights and for transmitting them holy and unviolated to their posterity.

It was this principle that inspired the heroes of ancient times—that raised their names to the summit of renown and filled all succeeding ages with their unspotted praise. It is this principle, too, that must animate your conduct if you wish your names to reach future generations, conspicuous in the roll of glory; and so far as this principle leads you, be prepared to follow—whether to life or to death.

While you profess yourselves contending for liberty, let it be with the temper and dignity of freemen, undaunted and firm, but without wrath or vengeance, so far as grace may be obtained to assist the weakness of nature. Consider it as a happy circumstance, if such a struggle must have happened, that God hath been pleased to postpone it to a period when our country is adorned with men of enlightened zeal—when the arts and sciences are planted among us to secure a succession of such men—when our morals are not much tainted by luxury, profusion, or dissipation—when the principles that withstood oppression, in the brightest era of the English history, are ours as it were by peculiar inheritance— and when we stand upon our own ground, with all that is dear around us, animating us to every patriotic exertion. Under such circumstances and upon such principles, what wonders, what achievements of true glory, have not been performed!

For my part, I have long been possessed with a strong and even enthusiastic persuasion that Heaven has great and gracious purposes towards this continent, which no human power or human device shall be able finally to frustrate. Illiberal or mistaken plans of policy may distress us for a while, and perhaps sorely check our growth: but if we maintain our own virtue, if we cultivate the spirit of liberty among our children, if we guard against the snares of luxury, venality, and corruption, the GENIUS of AMERICA will still rise triumphant, and that with a power at last too mighty for opposition. This country *will be free*—nay, for ages to come, a chosen seat of *freedom*, *arts*, and *heavenly* knowledge; which are now either drooping or dead in most countries of the Old World.

To conclude, since the *strength* of all public bodies, under God, consists in their UNION, bear with each other's infirmities, and even varities of sentiment, in things not essential to the main point. The tempers of men are cast in various moulds. Some are quick and *feelingly alive* in all their mental operations, especially those which relate to their country's weal, and therefore are ready to burst forth into flame upon every alarm. Others, again, with intentions alike pure, and a clear unquenchable love of their country, too steadfast to be damped by the mists of prejudice or worked up into conflagration by the rude blasts of passion, think it their duty to weigh consequences, and to deliberate fully upon the probable means of obtaining public ends. Both these kinds of men should bear with each other, for both are friends to their country.

One thing further let me add: that without *order* and just *subordination* there can be no *union* in public bodies, however much you may be equals on other occasions, yet all this must cease in a united and associated capacity, and every individual is bound to keep the place and duty assigned him, by ties far more powerful over a man of virtue and honor than all the other ties which human policy can contrive. It had been better never to have lifted a voice in your country's cause than to betray it by want of *union*, or to leave worthy men, who have embarked their all for the common good, to suffer or stand unassisted.

Lastly, by every method in your power, and in every possible case, support the LAWS of your country. In a contest for liberty think what a crime it would be to suffer one *freeman* to be insulted, or wantonly injured in his liberty, so far as by your means it may be prevented.

Thus animated and thus acting, we may then *sing*, with the prophet—

"Fear not, O land; be glad and rejoice: for the Lord will do great things. Be not afraid, ye beasts of the field, for the pastures of the wilderness do spring, for the tree beareth her fruit, the fig-tree and the vine do yield their strength."

Thus animated and thus acting, we may likewise PRAY, with the prophet—

"O Lord, be gracious unto us; we have waited for thee. Be thou our arm every morning, our salvation also in the time of trouble. Some trust in chariots, and some in horses; but we will remember the name of the Lord our God. O thou hope of Israel, the Saviour thereof in time of need, thou art in the midst of us, and we are called by thy name; LEAVE US NOT. Give us *one* heart and *one* way, that we may fear thee forever, for the good of ourselves and our children after us. We looked for peace, but no good came; and for a time of health, but behold we are in trouble. Yet will we trust in the Lord forever: for in the Lord Jehovah is everlasting strength. He will yet bind up the broken-hearted, and comfort those that mourn." Even so, O our God, do thou comfort and relieve them, that so the bones which thou hast broken may yet rejoice. Inspire us with a high and commanding sense of the value of our constitutional rights; may a spirit of wisdom and virtue be poured down upon us all, and may our representatives, those who are delegated to *devise* and appointed to *execute* public measures, be directed to such as thou in thy sovereign goodness shalt be pleased to render effectual for the salvation of a great empire and reuniting all its members in one sacred bond of harmony and public happiness! Grant this, O Father, for thy Son Jesus Christ's sake, to whom, with thee and the Holy Spirit, one God, be glory, honor, and power, now and forever. AMEN.

Rev. Jacob Green, D.D.

Was a distinguished Presbyterian divine, and among the earliest defenders of his country. "He was," says Dr. Sprague, "an earnest advocate for independence. He published a pamphlet to show its reasonableness and necessity at a period when such an opinion was very extensively branded as a political heresy. He was elected a member of the Provincial Congress of New Jersey, which set aside the royal Government of that province and formed the present Constitution of the State; and he was Chairman of the Committee that drafted the Constitution."

Rev. Dr. Beatty

Gave four sons to the Revolutionary army—men of learning and true courage, who served their country with patriotism and marked ability. Their father was an earnest and able friend to his country, and prayed and preached patriotism in his pulpit.

Rev. John Rogers, D.D.

For many years a Presbyterian pastor of the city of New York, was distinguished as a patriot in the Revolution. He and Drs. Mason and Laidlie, of the Associate Reformed Church, with others, instituted a weekly prayer-meeting, to invoke God's blessing on the country and to counsel the best means to aid it. Rogers was on intimate terms with Washington, and the commander-in-chief often consulted the patriot minister on subjects connected with the war. In 1776 he was appointed chaplain in General Heath's brigade, the duties of which he performed "with great zeal and fidelity, exhibiting at once a spirit of earnest piety and glowing patriotism." At the close of the war, on the day of national thanksgiving, he preached a sermon, which was published, on "The Divine Hand displayed in the American Revolution." In that sermon, alluding to the destruction of the churches by the British, he says—

"It is much to be lamented that the troops of a nation who have been considered one of the bulwarks of the Reformation should act as if they had waged war with the God whom Christians adore. They have, in the course of this war, utterly destroyed more than fifty places of worship in these states. Most of these they burned; others they levelled with the ground, and in some places left not a vestige of their former situation; while they have wantonly defaced, or rather destroyed, others, by converting them into barracks, jails, hospitals, riding schools, &c. Boston, Newport, Philadelphia, and Charleston all furnished melancholy instances of this prostitution and abuse of the houses of God; and of *nineteen* places of public worship in this city, when the war began, there were but *nine* fit for use when the British troops left it. It is true, Trinity Church, and the old Lutheran, were destroyed by fire, that laid waste to so great a part of the city, a few nights after the enemy took possession of it. The fire was occasioned by the carelessness of *their* people, and they prevented its extinguishment. But the ruinous situation in which they left two of the Low Dutch Reformed churches, the three Presbyterian churches, the

French Protestant church, the Anabaptist church, and the Friends' new meeting-house, was the effect of *design*, and strongly marks their enmity against those societies."

Rev. Timothy Dwight

An eloquent and learned minister, and for many years a distinguished and learned president of Yale College, was a fearless patriot and preacher. "He entered," says Goodrich, in his "Recollections of a Lifetime," "the American Revolutionary army as chaplain to General Putnam's regiment, with the ardor of a youthful Christian patriot—preached with energy to the troops in the camp, sometimes with a pile of the regiment's drums before him instead of a desk. One of his sermons, intended to raise the drooping courage of his country when Burgoyne had come down from Canada with his army and was carrying all before him, was published, and a copy read to the garrison in Fort Stanwix, on the Mohawk River, when Sir John Johnson had cut off their communication with Albany and threatened their destruction. The venerable Colonel Platt, many years after, affirmed that it was owing to this sermon that the garrison determined to hold out to the last extremity, and made the sally in which they routed and drove off their besiegers, delivered Albany from imminent danger, and contributed materially to the defeat of the British in their campaign of 1777."

Previous to the Declaration of Independence, Mr. Dwight urged that act before the public. He says, "I urged, in conversation with several gentlemen of great respectability, firm Whigs and my intimate friends, the importance, and even the necessity, of a declaration of independence on the part of the colonies. *For myself, I regarded the die as cast* and the hope of reconciliation as vanished, and believed that the colonists would never be able to defend themselves, unless they renounced their dependence on Great Britain."

In 1777 he was licensed as a minister of the gospel, and in the same year offered himself as a chaplain, and rendered important services to his country as a preacher and an active patriot. He became a great favorite with the army, and especially with General Putnam.

On the 7th of October, 1777, the surrender of Burgoyne took place, which thrilled the American army with new hope and joy. General Putnam, overjoyed at the news, immediately spread it through the army, and shouts and firing of cannon signalized the glorious event. The Rev. Timothy Dwight, a chaplain in the army, preached a sermon at head-quarters the next day, from the text, "I will remove far off from you the northern army." Never was a sermon so listened to before by the officers and troops. Putnam could not refrain from nodding, winking, and smiling during the discourse at the happy hits with which it was filled, and at its close was loud in his praises of Mr. Dwight and the sermon—though, to be sure, he said, there was no such text in the Bible, the chaplain having coined it to meet the occasion. When shown the passage, he exclaimed, "Well, there is every thing in that book; and Dwight knows just where to lay his finger on it."

The victory at Saratoga filled Dwight's mind with the brightest anticipations of the future glory of the country, and, under the inspiration of the memorable victory, he wrote the popular American song, commencing—

> Columbia, Columbia, to glory arise,
> The queen of the world, and child of the skies!
> Thy genius commands thee: with rapture behold,
> While ages on ages thy splendors unfold.
> Thy reign is the last and the noblest of time,
> Most fruitful thy soil, most inviting thy clime;
> Let the crimes of the East ne'er encrimson thy name,
> Be freedom, and science, and virtue thy fame.

Mr. Dwight also wrote several other patriotic songs, which became great favorites, not only in the army, but throughout the country. During the war he wrote an extended poem on "The Conquest of Canaan," reciting the patriotic scenes of the wars of Joshua, and by permission dedicated it to "George Washington, Esq., commander-in-chief of the American armies—the savior of his country, the supporter of freedom, and the benefactor of mankind."

Washington, in answer to Dwight's letter, wrote him as follows—

HEAD-QUARTERS, VALLEY FORGE, March 18, 1778.
DEAR SIR—Nothing can give me more pleasure than to patronize the essays of genius, and a laudable cultivation of the arts and sciences, which had begun to flourish in so eminent a degree before the hand of oppression was stretched over our devoted country; and I shall esteem myself happy if a poem which has employed the labors of years will derive an advantage, or bear more weight in the world, by making its appearance under a dedication to me.

G. Washington.

The fame of Dwight as a theologian, his eloquence as a preacher, his success as President of Yale College, and his excellence as a man and Christian, are known throughout the land. A devoted patriot and faithful preacher, his brilliant talents and best efforts were given to God and his country.

Bishop William White

The father of the Protestant Episcopal Church in the United States, was a fast and firm friend of liberty. He had carefully studied the reasons for the rebellion, espoused the American cause, and placed himself in the attitude of a rebel to his king; so that when the British army was advancing towards Philadelphia he deemed it prudent to retire with his family to the house of his brother-in-law, Mr. Aquila Hall, in Harford county, Maryland. "At this eventful crisis," he writes, "I received notice that Congress, which had fled to Yorktown, had chosen me their chaplain, and with me the Rev. Mr. Duffield, of the Presbyterian communion. Nothing could have induced me to accept the appointment at such a time, even had the emolument been an object—as it was not—but the determination to be consistent in my principles and in the part taken. Under this impression, I divided my time between Congress and my family, which the double chaplaincy permitted, until the evacuation of Philadelphia, the June following." "The acceptance of this chaplainship," writes his biographer, "was a few days before the arrival of the news of the surrender of Burgoyne. It was at one of the gloomiest periods of the American

Revolution that he entered upon this duty. Philadelphia was soon in possession of the British. Burgoyne was marching, without having received any serious check, so far as was then known, through the northern parts of New York, the success of whom would have cut off all intercourse between the Eastern and Southern States. Having removed his family to Maryland, he was on a journey between Harford county and Philadelphia, when he was met by a courier from Yorktown, informing him of his appointment and requesting his immediate attendance. The courier found him at a small village where he had stopped for refreshment. He thought of it only a short time, when, with all the ill-forebodings of the non-success of the American cause, but with confidence in the right, and with a trust in God, he turned his horses' heads and travelled immediately to Yorktown, to encourage by his presence that little Congress, which was then deliberating as to how they should against such fearful odds maintain their cause. Such, then, was the adherence to principle and decision of character in the chaplain who followed that Congress as it was driven a fugitive, from place to place, while directing the Revolutionary War. The services of those chaplains could not have been without their effect in strengthening the hearts of the men who marked out our American independence."

One of the most thrilling reminiscences in the annals of the American Revolution is related of General Peter Muhlenberg, whose ashes repose in the burying-ground of "The Old Trappe Church," in Montgomery county, Pennsylvania. When the war broke out, Muhlenberg was the rector of a Protestant Episcopal Church in Dunmore county, Virginia. On a Sunday morning he administered the communion of the Lord's Supper to his charge, stating that in the afternoon of that day he would preach a sermon on "the duties men owe to their country." At the appointed time the building was crowded with anxious listeners. The discourse was founded upon the text from Solomon— "There is a time for every purpose and for every work." The sermon burned with patriotic fire; every sentence and intonation told the speaker's deep earnestness in what he was saying. Pausing a moment at the close of his discourse, he repeated the words of his text, and then, in tones of thunder, exclaimed, "*The time to preach has passed; THE TIME TO FIGHT HAS COME!*" and, suiting the action to the word, he threw from his shoulders his episcopal robes and stood before his congregation arrayed in military uniform. Drumming for recruits was commenced on the spot; and it is said that almost every male of suitable age in the congregation enlisted forthwith.

In defending his course in leaving the pulpit for the army, he said, "I am a clergyman, it is true, but I am also a member of society as well as the poorest layman, and my liberty is as dear to me as to any man. Shall I then sit still, and enjoy myself at home, when the best blood of the continent is spilling? Heaven forbid it! *Do you think if America should be conquered I should be safe? Far from it. And would you not sooner fight like a man than die like a dog?* The cause is just and noble. Were I a bishop, even a Lutheran one, I should obey without hesitation; and, so far from thinking that I am wrong, I am convinced it is my duty so to do—a duty I owe to my God and to my country."

Rev. John Blair Smith

Was President of Hampden Sidney College, Virginia, and afterwards of Union College, New York, and for many years pastor of the Pine Street Presbyterian Church, Philadelphia.

"His influence was great in the cause of liberty. When the war of the Revolution spread terror and desolation through the regions in which he lived, and interrupted the regular exercises of the college, instead of finding an apology in his profession for remaining inactive at home, he raised a company of volunteers from among his students and marched at their head as captain; joined the army, and performed a tour of military duty in pursuit of the British legions who were carrying desolation through the seaports and lower counties of Virginia. He subsequently set out to join a company of volunteers to assist General Morgan in a probable encounter with Cornwallis; but when he overtook the company his feet were blistered by travelling, and he was, though not without great difficulty, persuaded by Colonel Martin, one of his elders, to abandon the expedition and return home.

"The Federal Constitution was warmly opposed by Patrick Henry. He appointed a day on which to meet the people of Prince Edward's county to show the defects of the Constitution and the reasons why it should not be adopted. Dr. Smith designed to meet the great orator and answer him, but was prevented by a providence. He sent a student, however, who took down Henry's speech in short-hand. Afterwards, before a numerous audience in college, among whom was Henry, one of the students delivered Henry's speech, and another followed with one prepared by Dr. Smith, in which he put forth all his energies in defence of the Constitution."

Rev. David Jones

Was an eminent minister of the Baptist denomination, and pastor of the church in Freehold, New Jersey. His life was threatened by the tories on account of his active services for his country, and he moved to Chester county, Pennsylvania, in 1776, and took charge of the Great Valley Baptist church. He preached a sermon on the Continental fast-day, before a division of the army, entitled "Defensive War in a Just Cause Sinless." It was printed and circulated through the colonies, producing a powerful influence.

In 1776 he was chaplain to a regiment under Colonel Arthur St. Clair. He was with St. Clair at Ticonderoga, October 20, 1776, when the enemy was hourly expected from Crown Point. He was in the battles of Brandywine and Germantown, was with Wayne in the battle of Monmouth, and in all his subsequent campaigns, until the surrender of Cornwallis. He was so active in the cause of freedom and independence that a reward was offered for him by General Howe, and a detachment was sent to the Great Valley to arrest him. He was a fearless patriot, and ardently devoted to his country. The following address is a noble illustration of his love of country, as well as of his views and eloquence as a minister of the gospel. He seems to have had the mantle of some old prophet, as he poured out his fiery words of truth.

Address to the Army

To General St. Clair's Brigade at Ticonderoga, when the Enemy was hourly expected, October 20, 1776.

My Countrymen, Fellow-Soldiers and Friends—

I am sorry that during this campaign I have been favored with so few opportunities of addressing you on subjects of the greatest importance both with respect to this life and that which is to come. But what is past cannot he recalled, and now time will not admit of enlargement, as we have the greatest reason to expect the advancement of our enemies as speedily as Heaven will permit. (The wind blew to the north strongly.) Therefore, at present, let it suffice to bring to your remembrance some necessary truths.

It is our *common faith,* and a very just one too, that all events are under the notice of that God in whom we live, move, and have our being; therefore we must believe that, in this important contest with the worst of enemies, he has assigned us our post here at Ticonderoga. Our situation is such, that, if properly defended, we shall give our enemies a fatal blow, and in a great measure prove the *means* of the *salvation of America.*

Such is our present case, that we are fighting for all that is near and dear to us, while our enemies are engaged in the worst of causes, their design being to subjugate, plunder, and enslave a flee people that have done them no harm. Their tyrannical views are so glaring, their cause so horribly bad, that there still remains too much goodness and humanity in Great Britain to engage unanimously against us: therefore they have been obliged (and at a most amazing expense, too) to hire the assistance of a barbarous, mercenary people, that would cut your throats for the small reward of sixpence. No doubt these have hopes of being our taskmasters, and would rejoice at our calamities.

Look, oh, look, therefore, at your respective States, and anticipate the consequences if these vassals are suffered to enter! It would fail the most fruitful imagination to represent, in a proper light, what anguish, what horror, what distress, would spread over the whole land! See, oh, see the dear wives of your bosoms forced from their peaceful habitations, and perhaps used with such indecency that modesty would forbid the description. Behold the fair virgins of your land, whose benevolent souls are now filled with a thousand good wishes and hopes of seeing their admirers return home crowned with victory, would not only meet with a doleful disappointment, but also with insults and abuses that would induce their tender hearts to pray for the shades of death. See your children exposed as vagabonds to all the calamities of this life. Then, oh, then, adieu to all felicity this side of the grave!

Now, all these calamities may be prevented, if our God be for us—and who can doubt this who observes the point in which the wind now blows?—if you will only acquit yourselves like men, and with firmness of mind go forth against your enemies, resolving either to return with victory or to die gloriously. Every one who may fall in this dispute will be justly esteemed a *martyr* to liberty, and his name will be had in precious *memory* while the love of freedom remains in the breasts of men. All whom God will favor to see a glorious victory will return to their respective States with every mark of honor, and be received with joy and gladness of heart by all friends to liberty and lovers of mankind.

As our present crisis is singular, I hope, therefore, that the candid will excuse me if I now conclude with an uncommon address, in substance principally extracted from the writings of the servants of God in the Old Testament; though, at the same time, it is freely acknowledged that I am not possessed of any similar power either of blessing or cursing.

1. Blessed be the man who is possessed of true love of liberty; and let all the people say, *Amen.*

2. Blessed be the man who is a friend to the common rights of mankind; and let all the people say, *Amen.*

3. Blessed be the man who is a friend to the United States of America; and let all the people say, *Amen.*

4. Blessed be the man who will use his utmost endeavor to oppose the tyranny of Great Britain, and to vanquish all her forces invading North America; and let all the people say, Amen.

5. Blessed be the man who resolves never to submit to Great Britain; and let all the people say, *Amen.*

6. Blessed be the man who in the present dispute esteems not his life too good to fall a sacrifice to his country: let his posterity, if he has any, be blessed with riches, honor, virtue, and true religion; and let all the people say, *Amen.*

Now, on the other hand, as far as is consistent with the Holy Scriptures, let all these blessings be turned into curses to him who deserts the noble cause in which we are engaged, and turns his back to the enemy before he receives proper orders to retreat; and let all the people say, *Amen.*

Let him be abhorred by all the United States of America.

Let faintness of heart and fear never forsake him.

Let him be a major miserable, a terror to himself and all around him.

Let him be accursed in his outgoing, and cursed in his incoming; cursed in lying down, and cursed in uprising; cursed in basket, and cursed in store.

Let him be accursed in all his *connections,* till his *wretched* head with dishonor is laid low in the dust; and let all the soldiers say, *Amen.*

And may the God of all grace, in whom we live, enable us, in defence of our country, to acquit ourselves like men, to his honor and praise. *Amen*, and *Amen.*

Sermon to the Army

Extract from a Discourse delivered by the Chaplain of General Poor's

Brigade, October 17, 1779.

The fashionable gentleman thinks it an affront to delicacy and refinement of taste to observe that day set apart by the law of God and man for religious worship. The sublime truths of Christianity, the pure and simple manner of the gospel, are despised and insulted even where decency and policy, reason and virtue apart, they ought to hold them in the most profound veneration. How, then, can liberty exist, when neither supported by purity of manners, the principles of honor, nor the influence of religion? From this unhappy prospect I am led in imagination to sympathize with America drowned in tears and overwhelmed with distress. Methinks I hear her pathetically addressing her sons, and venting the anguish of her heart in this mournful language —"Am I not the only friend to liberty on all this peopled globe? And have I not, when she was excluded from every other region of the earth, opened the arms of my protection and received the persecuted stranger to my friendly and virtuous shores? But when the tyrant of Britain, not satisfied with expelling her from his dominions, pursued her with hostile rage even to those shores, did I not rouse you, my sons, in her defence, and make you the honorable protectors of insulted Liberty? Inflamed with love of this friend of mankind, you armed in her defence, you made a brave and successful resistance to her persecutors, and have rescued her from the vindictive malice of all her foreign foes. Thus far have you merited the titles of guardians of liberty, and deserve to be enrolled the heroes of the present age. But ah, my sons and citizens of the United States, whither is fled that patriotic zeal which first warmed your disinterested breasts? Whither that public spirit which made you willing to sacrifice not only your fortunes, but also your lives, in defence of Liberty? Whither is fled that happy union of sentiment in the great service of your country? And whither is fled that honorable love and practice of virtue, and that divine and generous religion, which cherishes the spirit of liberty and elevates it to an immortal height?" She paused and wept, nor gained an answer; and then, in a suppliant posture, again renewed her address—"I entreat you to rekindle that public and generous zeal which first blazed forth in the defence of that liberty which you have now too long slighted. I beseech you to banish from your breasts that lust of gain which is the baneful murderer of a generous and public spirit. I entreat you to silence the demons of discord and animosity, and to banish them from the shores of America, and let them find no place to set their feet, but in the assemblies of the enemies of this country.

"I conjure you, by the spirit of heaven-born Liberty, that you invite her to your bosom and kindle your love for her in a never-dying flame. By the blessing of posterity I conjure you, by the precious blood of the heroes, who have nobly shed it in the cause of their country, I conjure you, to practise and encourage that private and public virtue which ennobles the soul and erects the temple of Liberty on an everlasting foundation, not to be shaken by the threatening storms of war nor the impotent rage of tyrants. I conjure you, by the toils and dangers, by the suffering and poverty, of my brave armies now in the field, not to desert them in their defence of freedom, but to support them with that assistance which will save you and yours from internal and public ruin. Serve your country according to your abilities, and with the same zeal with which my persevering soldiery serve you. Then will a happy conclusion crown the war, and your independence be established immovable as the everlasting mountains."

The following pithy and ironical discourse on duelling will be read with interest, as a relic of the Revolution. It is entitled a

Sermon on the Combat of the Duel

By the Rev. William Macfee, a chaplain in the army.
Preached at the camp at Valley Forge, February, 1778.
"Two men of the Hebrews strove together."—*Exodus I.*

The sacred books have several instances of duels. The first that we read of is that of Cain and Abel, where the elder brother sent a challenge to the younger because his sacrifice had been more acceptable to the Lord. They met, and Abel fell, having received the end of a club, as is generally supposed, somewhere above his right temple.

The second instance of which we read is that of the text, where two young Hebrews had met, with their seconds, to decide a small difference; but what it was, has perplexed all commentators. Moses, like a young man as he was, endeavored to quiet their resentment to each other, or to overcome it by putting them in mind that they were brethren. The conduct of the young man was indiscreet, and he received a proper check, by the rebuke of the two bricklayers.

The next instance we read of is that of a young officer of a bear who sent a challenge to young David, Who reported that he was fond of eating sheep; which calumny, true or false, it behooved him, as a bear of honor, to resent. David met him, and, having discharged their pistols, they took to the points, and in the scuffle, while the bear had thrown himself too far forward, in attempting a lunge, David caught him by the beard and smote him through the body.

Having given these few instances from the Scriptures, I shall go on to show the necessity of the duel, and then to press it a little on my audience.

It is necessary, for it is not every man that has command of his passions; and these, unless they are suffered to evaporate in some manner, will burst out into robberies and burglaries, and do damage to society. The passion of pride is one of the most troublesome among men, and to this there is nothing so powerful an antidote as fear, which never fails to be excited when the challenge comes to hand. The man who this moment was boiling hot with pride and every haughty passion is now calm and moderate; for somebody has sent him a challenge. It is the only misfortune that this very principle of fear prevents the certainty of execution, for, by giving a trembling to the hand, it comes to pass that very few are wounded, and still fewer fall, in the combat. To remedy this, I would propose that the duellists should stand nearer, and put their noses into each other's hands, while the pistols are discharged. Swift says "he should be sorry to see the legislatures make any more laws against duelling; for if villains and rascals will dispatch one another, it is for the good of the community." But the misfortune is, they will not dispatch one another; for this principle of fear, and the distance at which they stand, prevents any shot being effective.

The philosophers of the former times, and the ecclesiastics of the present, are against duelling, forsooth, because, by studying and thinking, their warm passions are rendered tame, and they have no need of blood-letting; but they do not consider that there are many others who, if they were not suffered to give themselves vent in this way, would rage and roar like mad bears, and set the world on fire.

Having now seen the necessity of this excessive passion, it remains that I press it a little on my audience. Who is there among you that did not praise the corporal the other day, who, having observed something like a smile on the countenance of his neighbor, and not being able to assign the cause of it, sent him a challenge? The corporal, it is true, received a ball through the rim of his belly, and was buried that evening; but it is his consolation that he is now with the angel Michael in Abraham's bosom.

When I mention the angel Michael, it brings to my mind the circumstance of the devil sending him a challenge. But, according to the Apostle Jude, he (that is, Michael) durst not accept of it, or, as it is in the translation, "bring a railing accusation," but said, "The Lord rebuke thee." I do not know what to say for Michael, for certainly it must be granted that in this instance he did not act like an angel of honor.

The only objection I know of against the practice of the duel, is that in the New Testament it is considerably discouraged, by the spirit of forbearance inculcated in these words— "If any smite thee on the right cheek, turn to him the other also." But to this it is to be said that the pilot of the Galilean lake," as Milton calls him (for I know my business better than to speak plainly out and to say "Christ" in an army), the pilot of the Galilean lake, I say, and his apostles, among whose discourses and writings sentiments like these are found, were not what we call men of honor. Bred up about the Sea of Tiberias, they had not the best opportunity, by travelling, to become acquainted with the world. Nay, our Saviour himself plainly tells you so—"Verily, I say unto you, my kingdom is not of this world." Now, as men of honor never propose to go into his kingdom, why should they frame themselves agreeably to its customs? It is absurd; and while they live in this world, let them live as becomes men that know the world; and when they go to the devil, let them send challenges, as he has done, and fight duels according to his dictates.

Rev. Jacob Troute

The following interesting document was recently found among the papers of Major John Shaefmyer, a deceased patriot of the Revolution. It is a discourse delivered on the eve of the battle of Brandywine, by Rev. Jacob Troute, to a large portion of the American soldiers, in presence of General Washington, General Wayne, and other officers of the army.

"They that take the sword shall perish by the sword."

Soldiers and Countrymen—

We have met this evening perhaps for the last time. We have shared the toils of the march, the peril of the fight, and the dismay of the retreat, alike. We have endured the cold and hunger, the contumely of the internal foe, and the scourge of the foreign oppressor. We have sat night after night by the camp-fire, we have together heard the roll of the reveillé which calls us to duty, or the beat of the tattoo which gave the signal for the hardy sleep of the soldier, with the earth for his bed and the knapsack for his pillow.

And now, soldiers and brethren, we have met in this peaceful valley, on the eve of battle, in the sunlight that to-morrow morn will glimmer on the scenes of blood. We have met amid the whitening tents of our encampments; in the time of terror and gloom we have gathered together. God grant that it may not be for the last time.

It is a solemn moment! Brethren, does not the solemn voice of nature seem to echo the sympathies of the hour? The flag of our country droops heavily from yonder staff; the breeze has died away along the green plain of Chadd's Ford; the plain that spreads before us glitters in the sunlight; the heights of Brandywine arise gloomy and grand beyond the waters of yonder stream; all nature holds a pause of solemn silence on the eve of the uproar and bloody strife of to-morrow.

"They that take the sword shall perish by the sword."

And have they not taken the sword?

Let the desolate plain, the blood-sodden valley, the burned farmhouses, blackening in the sun, the sacked village and the ravaged town, answer; let the withered bones of the butchered farmer, strewed along the fields of his homestead, answer; let the starving mother, with her babe clinging to the withered breast that can afford no sustenance, let her answer—with the death-rattle mingling with the murmuring tones that marked the last moment of her life; let the mother and the babe answer.

It was but a day past, and our land slept in the quiet of peace. War was not here. Fraud and woe and want dwelt not among us. From the eternal solitude of the green woods arose the blue smoke of the settler's cabin, and golden fields of corn looked from amid the waste of the wilderness, and the glad music of human voices awoke the silence of the forest.

Now, God of mercy, behold the change. Under the shadow of a pretext, under the sanctity of the name of God, invoking the Redeemer to their aid, do these foreign hirelings slay our people. They throng our towns, they darken our plains, and now they encompass our posts on the lonely plain of Chadd's Ford.

"They that take the sword shall perish by the sword."

Brethren, think me not unworthy of belief when I tell you the doom of the British is sealed. Think me not vain when I tell you that, beyond the cloud that now enshrouds us, I see gathering thick and fast the darker cloud and thicker storm of Divine retribution.

They may conquer to-morrow. Might and wrong may prevail, and we may be driven from the field; but the hour of God's own vengeance will come!

Ay, if in the vast solitudes of eternal space there throbs the being oh an awful God, quick to avenge and sure to punish guilt, then the man George Brunswick, called king, will feel in his brain and heart the vengeance of the eternal Jehovah. A blight will light upon his life—a withered and an accursed intellect; a blight will be upon his children and on his people. Great God, how dread the punishment! A crowded populace, peopling the dense towns where the men of money thrive, where the laborer starves; want striding among the people in all forms of terror; an ignorant and God-defying priesthood chuckling over the miseries of millions; a proud and merciless nobility adding wrong to wrong, and heaping insult upon robbery and fraud; royalty corrupt to the very heart, and aristocracy rotten to the core; crime and want linked hand in hand, and tempting men to deeds of woe and death—these are a part of the doom and retribution that shall come upon the English throne and English people.

Soldiers, I look around upon your familiar faces with strange interest! To-morrow morning we go forth to the battle—for need I tell you that your unworthy minister will march with you, invoking the blessing of God's aid in the fight?—we will march forth to the battle. Need I exhort you to fight the good fight—to fight for your homesteads, for your wives and your children?

My friends, I urge you to fight, by the galling memories of British wrong. Walton, I might tell you of your father, butchered in the silence of the night on the plains of Trenton; I might picture his gray hairs dabbled in blood; I might ring his death-shrieks in your ears. Shaefmyer, I might tell you of a butchered mother and sister outraged, the lonely farmhouse, the night assault, the roof in flames, the shouts of the troops as they dispatched their victims, the cries for mercy, and the pleadings of innocence for pity. I might paint this all again, in the vivid colors of the terrible reality, if I thought courage needed such wild excitement.

But I know you are strong in the might of the Lord. You will march forth to battle to-morrow with light hearts and determined spirits, though the solemn duty—the duty of avenging the dead—may rest heavy on your souls.

And in the hour of battle, when all around is darkness, lit by the lurid cannon-glare and the piercing musket-flash, when the wounded strew the ground and the dead litter your path, then remember, soldiers, that God is with you. The eternal God fights for you; he rides on the battle-cloud, he sweeps onward with the march of a hurricane charge. God, the awful and infinite, fights for you, and you will triumph.

"They that take the sword shall perish by the sword."

You have taken the sword, but not in the spirit of wrong or revenge: you have taken the sword for your homes, for your wives and your little ones. You have taken the sword for truth, justice, and right, and to you the promise is, be of good cheer, for your foes have taken the sword in defiance of all that men hold dear, in blasphemy of God: they shall perish by the sword.

And now, brethren and soldiers, I bid you all farewell. Many of us will fall in the battle of tomorrow, and in the memory of all will ever rest and linger the quiet scene of this autumnal eve.

Solemn twilight advances over the valley; the woods on the opposite height fling their long shadows over the green of the meadow; around us are the tents of the Continental host, the suppressed bustle of the camp, the hurried tramp of the soldiers to and fro, and among the tents the stillness and awe that mark the eve of battle.

When we meet again, may the shadows of twilight be flung over the peaceful land. God in heaven grant it! Let us pray.

Address of the Clergy of Newport to Washington

The following is the address of the clergy of the town of Newport, in the State of Rhode Island—

To George Washington, President of the United States.

Sir—

With salutations of the most cordial esteem and regard, permit us, the clergy of the town of Newport, to approach your person, entreating your acceptance of our voice, in conjunction with that of our fellow-citizens, to hail your welcome to Rhode Island.

Shielded by Omnipotence during a tedious and unnatural war, you were as a messenger sent from Heaven, in conducting the counsels of the cabinet, and under many embarrassments directing the operations of the field. Divine Providence crowned your temples with unfading laurels, and put into your hand the peacefully waving olive-branch.

Long may you live, sir, highly favored of God and beloved of men, to preside in the grand council of our nation, which we trust will not cease to supplicate Heaven that its select and Divine influences may descend and rest upon you, endowing you with grace, wisdom and understanding, to go out and in before this numerous and free people, to preside over whom Divine Providence has raised you up.

And therefore, before God, the Father of our Lord Jesus Christ, in whom all the families both in heaven and earth are named, according to the law of our office, and in bounden duty, we bow our knee, beseeching him to grant you every tempo-ral and spiritual blessing, and that, of the plenitude of his grace, all the families of these wide-extended realms may enjoy, under an equal and judicious adminis-tration of government, peace and prosperity, with all the blessings attendant on civil and religious liberty.

(Signed)   SAMUEL HOPKINS,
Pastor of the First Congregational Church,
and by other ministers.

His Reply

Gentlemen—

The salutations of the clergy of the town of Newport on my arrival in the State of Rhode Island are rendered the more acceptable on account of the liberal sentiments and just ideas which they are known to entertain respecting civil and religious liberty.

I am inexpressibly happy that, by the smiles of Divine Providence, my weak but honest endeavors to serve my country have hitherto been crowned with so much success, and apparently given such satisfaction to those in whose cause they were exerted. The same benignant influence, together with the concurrent support of all real friends to their country, will still be necessary to enable me to be in any degree useful to this numerous and free people over whom I am called to preside.

Wherefore I return yon, gentlemen, my hearty thanks for your solemn invocation of Almighty God that every temporal and spiritual blessing may be dispensed to me, and that under my administration the families of these States may enjoy peace and prosperity, with all the blessings attendant on civil and religious liberty. In the participation of which blessings may you have an ample share.

G. Washington.

Address of the Clergy of Philadelphia to Washington on His Retirement from the Presidency

Washington closed his public life, as President of the United States, on the 4th of March, 1797. The day before this event the ministers of the gospel, of all denominations, in and near Philadelphia, sent him the following paper—

To George Washington, President of the United States.
Sir—

On a day which becomes important in the annals of America, as marking the close of a splendid public life, devoted for near half a century to the service of your country, we the undersigned, clergy of different denominations in and near the city of Philadelphia, beg leave to join the voice of our fellow-citizens in expressing our deep sense of your public services in every department of trust and authority committed to you. But, in our special characters as ministers of the gospel of Christ, we are more immediately bound to acknowledge the countenance which you have universally given to his holy religion.

In your public character we have beheld the edifying example of a civil ruler always acknowledging the superintendence of Divine Providence in the affairs of men, and confirming that example by the powerful recommendation of religion and morality as the firmest basis of social happiness—more particularly in the following language of your affectionate parting address to your fellow-citizens—

"Of all the dispositions and habits which lead to political prosperity, religion and morality are indispensable supports. In vain would that man claim the tribute of patriotism who should labor to subvert these great pillars of human happiness—the firmest props of the duties of men and citizens. The mere politician, equally with the pious man, ought to respect and cherish them. A volume could not trace all their connections with private and public felicity. Let us with caution indulge the supposition that morality can be maintained without religion. Reason and experience forbid us to expect that national morality can prevail in exclusion of religious principles."

Should the importance of these just and pious sentiments be duly appreciated and regarded, we confidently trust that the prayers you have offered for the prosperity of our common country will be answered. In these prayers we most fervently unite, and with equal fervor in those which the numerous public bodies that represent the citizens of these States are offering for their beloved chief. We most devoutly implore the Divine blessing to attend you in your retirement, to render it in all respects comfortable to you, to satisfy you with length of days, and finally to receive you into happiness and glory infinitely greater than this world can bestow.

Philadelphia, March 3, 1797.

THOMAS USTICK,
ANDW. HUNTER,
JNO. DICKING,
JOSHUA JONES,
JOSEPH TURNER,
EZEKIEL COOPER,
ANDW. J. RHEES,
JAM. ABERCROMBIE,
WM. WHITE,
ASHBEL GREEN,
WILLIAM SMITH,
JOHN EWING,

SAMUEL JONES,
WM. FRENDEL,
NICHOLAS COLLIN,
ROBERT ANNAN,
WILLIAM MARSHALL,
JOHN MEDER,
JOHN ANDREWS,
F. HENRY CH. HELMITH,
SAM. MORGAN,
J. FREDERICK SCHMIDT,
ROBT. BLACKWELL,
WM. ROGERS.

Reply

Gentlemen—

Not to acknowledge with gratitude and sensibility the affectionate addresses and benevolent wishes of my fellow-citizens on my retirement from public life, would prove that I have been unworthy of the confidence which they have been pleased to repose in me. And among those public testimonials of attachment and approbation, none can be more grateful than that of so respectable a body as yours.

Believing as I do that religion and morality are the essential pillars of society, I view with unspeakable pleasure that harmony and brotherly love which characterizes the clergy of different denominations as well in this as in all parts of the United States, exhibiting to the world a new and interesting spectacle, at once the pride of our country and the surest basis of universal harmony. That your labors for the good of mankind may be crowned with success, that your temporal enjoyments may be commensurate with your merits, and that the future rewards of good and faithful servants may be yours, I shall not cease to supplicate the Divine Author of life and felicity.

George Washington.

Address of the Congressional Ministers of Massachusettes to John Adams

The following correspondence of the Congregational ministers of Massachusetts with John Adams, President of the United States, refers to a very critical era in the history of the Government, and finely illustrates the patriotism and piety of American ministers. The atheism of France in 1795 had engulfed that empire in anarchy and blood. It was the first experiment in the history of the world, of the national reign of infidelity, and its results shocked the civilized world with horror, and demonstrated its terrific nature and evils on civil government and society. "God permitted," said Robert Hall, of England, in his masterly sermon on Modern Infidelity Considered, "the trial to be made. In one country—and that the center of

Christendom—revelation underwent a total eclipse, while atheism, performing on a darkened theatre its strange and fearful tragedy, confounded the first elements of society, blended every age, rank, and sex in indiscriminate proscription and massacre, and convulsed all Europe to its center; that the imperishable memorial of these events might teach the last generations of mankind to consider religion as the pillar of society, the safeguard of nations, the parent of social order, which alone has power to curb the fiery passions and to secure to every one his rights.

"Those who prepared the minds of the people for that great change, and for the reign of atheism, were avowed enemies to revelation; in all their writings the diffusion of skepticism and revolutionary principles went hand in hand; the fury of the most sanguinary parties was especially pointed against the Christian priesthood and religious institutions, without once pretending, like other persecutors, to execute the vengeance of God (whose name they never mentioned) upon his enemies; their atrocities were committed with a wanton levity and brutal merriment; the reign of atheism was avowedly and expressly the reign of terror; in the full madness of their career, in the highest climax of their horrors, they shut up the temples of God, abolished his worship, and proclaimed death to be an eternal sleep—as if by pointing to the silence of the sepulchre and the sleep of the dead these ferocious barbarians meant to apologize for leaving neither sleep, quiet, nor repose to the living. No sooner were the speculations of atheistical philosophy matured than they gave birth to a ferocity which converted the most polished people in Europe into a horde of assassins—the seat of voluptuous refinement and of arts, into a theatre of blood. Atheism is an inhuman, bloody, ferocious system, equally hostile to every useful restraint and to every virtuous affection; that, leaving nothing above us to excite our awe, nor round us to awaken our tenderness, wages war with heaven and with earth. Its first object is to dethrone God, its next to destroy man."

The French rulers, under the reign of atheism, during the Administration of John Adams, plied every art to bring the Government of the United States into political alliance with the French nation, and we were on the eve of a war with our ancient ally and friend. So imminent was the danger that Washington was appointed again commander-in-chief of the American armies, and accepted the appointment, with the understanding that he was not to take the field till actual war had begun. The President, during this crisis of our nation, received, from all parts of the country, numerous addresses, urging him to resist all influences and machinations, either at home or abroad, which aimed to make the United States an ally with atheistical France, who was "grasping at universal domination, had abandoned every moral and religious principle, trampled on sacred faith, sported with national laws, and demanded pecuniary exactions which would bankrupt our nation and render us slaves instead of a free, sovereign, and independent people." Among other addresses was the following—

We, the Congregational ministers of Massachusetts, met in annual Convention, feel ourselves called upon, as men, as American citizens, and as public professors and teachers of Christianity, to address you at this solemn and eventful crisis.

While the benevolent spirit of our religion and office prompts our fervent wishes and prayers for the universal extension of rational liberty, social order, and Christian piety, we cannot but deeply lament and firmly resist those atheistical, licentious, and disorganizing principles which have been avowed and zealously propagated by the philosophers of France—which have produced the greatest crimes and miseries in that unhappy country, and, like a moral pestilence, are diffusing their baneful influence even to distant nations. From these principles, combined with boundless avarice and ambition, have originated, not only schemes of universal plunder and domination, but insidious attempts to divide the American people from their rulers and involve them in a needless, unjust, and ruinous war; arbitrary and cruel depredations on their unoffending commerce; contemptuous treatment of their respected messengers and generous overtures of peace; rapacious demands and insulting threats in answer to the most fair and condescending proposals.

In this connection, we offer to you, sir, our tribute of affectionate esteem and gratitude, and to Almighty God our devout praise, for the wise, temperate, and benevolent policy which has marked your conduct towards the offending Power, and which has given a new and splendid example of the beauty and dignity of the Christian spirit contrasted with the base and profligate spirit of infidelity. We also bless God for your firm, patriotic, and important services to your country from the dawn of its glorious Revolution, and for the conspicuous integrity and wisdom which have been constantly displayed both by you, sir, and your excellent and beloved predecessors.

As ministers of the Prince of peace, we feel it our duty both to inculcate and exemplify the pacific spirit which adorns his character and doctrine. We remember his injunction to forgive and love our most injurious enemies. But neither the law of Christianity nor of reason requires us to prostrate our national independence, freedom, prosperity, and honor at the feet of proud, insatiable oppressors—especially of a Government which has renounced the gospel and its sacred institutions and has transferred to imaginary heathen idols the homage due to the Creator and Redeemer of the world. Such a prostration would be treason against the Being who gave us our inestimable privileges, civil and religious, as a sacred deposit to be defended and transmitted to posterity. It would be criminal unfaithfulness and treachery to our country, our children, and the whole human race.

The fate of Venice, and other countries subdued by France, though held up to intimidate us to degrading submission, shall teach us a far different lesson: it shall instruct us to shun that insidious embrace which aims not only to reduce us to the condition of tributaries, but to strip us of the gospel, the Christian Sabbath, and every pious institution. These privileges we consider the chief glory of our country, the main pillars of its civil order, liberty, and happiness; as, on the other hand, we view its excellent political institutions as, under God, the guardians of our religious and ecclesiastical privileges. This intimate connection between our civil and Christian blessings is alone sufficient to justify the decided part which the clergy of America have uniformly taken in supporting the constituted authorities and political interests of their country. While we forgive the censure which our order has received from some persons on this account, we will still, by our prayers and examples, by our public and private discourses, continue the same tenor of conduct which has incurred this malevolent or misguided abuse.

Amidst the fashionable skepticism and impiety of the age, it is a matter of consolation and gratitude that we have a President who, both in word and action, avows his reverence for the Christian religion, his belief in the Redeemer and Sanctifier of the world, and his devout trust in the Providence of God. May that Being, whose important favor you recently led us to implore, graciously answer our united prayers in behalf of our common country. May he preserve your valuable life and health, your vigor, firmness, and integrity of mind, and your consequent public usefulness, and at length transfer you, full of days and honor, to the possession of an eminent and everlasting reward.

The President replied as follows

This respectful and affectionate address from the Convention of the clergy of Massachusetts, not less distinguished for science and learning, candor, moderation, liberality of sentiment and conduct, and for the most amiable urbanity of manners, than for unblemished morals and Christian piety, does me great honor, and must have the most beneficial effects upon the public mind at this solemn and eventful crisis.

To do justice to its sentiments and language, I could only repeat it sentence by sentence and word for word: I shall therefore confine myself to a mere return of my unfeigned thanks.   John Adams.

Webster's Statement of American Minister's

These facts, so honorable to the patriotism, piety, learning, and zealous labors of ministers of all denominations during the era of the Revolution, and subsequently, fully justify the declaration of Mr. Webster, in the Supreme Court of the United States, expressed in his celebrated argument on the Girard Will Case, in 1844—

"I take upon myself to say that in no country in the world, upon either continent, can there be found a body of ministers of the gospel who perform so much service to men, in such a free spirit of self-denial, under so little encouragement from Government of any kind, and under circumstances almost always much straitened and often distressed, as the ministers of the gospel in the United States, of all denominations. They form no part of an established order of religion; they constitute no hierarchy; they enjoy no peculiar privileges. And this body of clergymen has shown, to the honor of our country and the admiration of the hierarchies of the Old World, that it is practicable in free governments to raise and sustain, by voluntary contributions alone, a body of clergymen which, for devotedness to their calling, for purity of life and character, for learning, intelligence, piety, and that wisdom which cometh from above, is inferior to none, and superior to most others.

"I hope that our learned men have done something for the honor of our literature abroad. I hope that the courts of justice and members of the bar have done something to elevate the character of the profession of law. I hope that the discussions above [in Congress] have done something to ameliorate the condition of the human race, to secure and strengthen the great charter of human rights, and to strengthen and advance the great principles of human liberty. But I contend that no literary efforts, no adjudications, no constitutional discussions, nothing that has been done or said in favor of the great interests of universal man, have done this country more credit, at home and abroad, than the establishment of our body of clergymen, their support by voluntary contributions, and the general excellence of their character, their piety and learning."

These views of Mr. Webster are confirmed by Dr. Gardiner Spring, for more than forty years a Presbyterian pastor of the city of New York, and whose father, Dr. Samuel Spring, of Massachusetts, was an able and patriotic preacher of the Revolution. In his work on "The Power of the Pulpit," Dr. Gardiner Spring says—

"The office of religious teacher among the Jews was a noble office. Without them the Hebrew State had been an irreligious, ignorant disjointed community. The nation was exalted or debased as their religious teachers were honored or dishonored, and as they exerted or failed to exert their appropriate influence. So long as the nation was in its glory, its religious teachers were the glory and strength of the nation. ...

"The voice of the pulpit," Dr. Spring continues, "has been often heard on subjects of *public* interest. Its influence has been felt in scenes which 'tried men's souls.' That great event in the history of the world, the American Revolution, never would have been achieved without the influence of the pulpit. Political society 'moved on the axis of religion. The religious movement gave its character to the social movement.'"

The facts in this chapter fully vindicate the patriotism and piety of the American clergy, and reveal one of the great sources of the Christian life and character of the civil institutions of the United States. They prove the mighty and beneficent power of the pulpit on the progress, prosperity, and true glory of the republic, and their essential relations to its very life and perpetuity. The pulpit, in every age, and in the battles and conflicts of truth and liberty with error and despotism, has always been on the side of the right. It has stood forth as the champion of the oppressed, and has ever been, with all the darkness that has enveloped the nations, the educator of the world in all the arts, refinements, and charities which adorn Christian civilization, and has, during the course of these ages, diffused the spirit and precepts of the Christian religion into the science of politics and the government and legislation of nations.

17

Christian Women of the Revolution

Agency in Forming Our Civil Institutions

Among the Christian agencies that commenced and completed the work of American civilization and freedom, that of the influence of woman was pre-eminent and controlling. Her piety, home-culture, prayers, and personal labor and sacrifices, were among the chief causes that contributed to the progress and elevation of the nation, and which assisted largely in the triumphs of liberty and the results of the Revolution. They have ever been the most effective and polished workmen on the edifice of society and on the temple of human freedom. "All history, both sacred and profane, both ancient and modern, bears testimony to the efficacy of female influence and power in the cause of human liberty. From the time of the preservation by the hands of women of the great Jewish lawgiver in his infantile hours, and who was preserved for the purpose of freeing his countrymen from Egyptian bondage, has woman been made a powerful agent in breaking to pieces the rod of the oppressor. With a pure and uncontaminated mind, her actions spring from the deepest recesses of the human heart."

Origin of the Revolution in American Homes

In an address to the ladies of Richmond, at a public reception which they gave to Mr. Webster, on the 5th of October, 1840, he said—

"It is by the promulgation of sound morals in the community, and more especially by the training and instruction of the young, that woman performs her part towards the preservation of a free government. It is generally admitted that public liberty and the perpetuity of a free constitution rest on the virtue and intelligence of the community which enjoys it. How is that virtue to be inspired, and how is that intelligence to be communicated? Bonaparte once asked Madame de Staël in what manner he could best promote the happiness of France. Her reply is full of political wisdom. She said, 'Instruct the mothers of the French people.' Mothers are indeed the affectionate and effective teachers of the human race. The mother begins her process of training with the infant in her arms. It is she who directs, so to speak, its first mental and spiritual pulsations. She conducts it along the impressible years of childhood and youth, and hopes to deliver it to the stern conflicts and tumultuous scenes of life armed by those good principles which her child has received from maternal care and love.

"If we draw," says Mr. Webster, "within the circle of our contemplation the mothers of a civilized nation, what do we see? We behold so many artificers, working, not on frail and perishable materials, but on the immortal mind, moulding and fashioning beings who are to exist forever. We applaud the artist whose skill and genius present the mimic man upon the canvas; we admire and celebrate the sculptor who works out that same image in enduring marble; but how insignificant are these achievements, though the highest and fairest in all departments, in comparison with the great vocation of human mothers! They work, not upon the canvas that shall fail, or the marble that shall crumble into dust, but upon mind, spirit, which is to last forever, and which is to bear the impress of a mother's plastic hand.

"The attainment of knowledge does not comprise all which is contained in the larger term of education. The feelings are to be disciplined, the passions are to be restrained, true and worthy motives are to be inspired, a profound religious feeling is to be instilled, and pure morality inculcated, under all circumstances. All this is comprised in education. Mothers who are faithful to this great duty will tell their children that neither in political nor in any other concerns of life can man ever withdraw himself from the perpetual obligations of conscience and of duty; that in every act, whether public or private, he incurs a just responsibility; and that in no condition is he warranted in trifling with important rights and obligations. They will impress upon their children the truth that the exercise of the elective franchise is a social duty, of as solemn nature as man can he called to perform; that a man cannot innocently trifle with his vote; that every free elector is a trustee as well for others as himself; and that every man and every measure he supports has an important bearing on the interests, of others, as well as on his own. It is in the inculcation of high and pure morals, such as these, that in a free republic woman performs her sacred duty and fulfils her destiny."

Views of Adams

"It is of great importance," says Charles Francis Adams, "not only to understand the nature of the superiority of the individuals who have made themselves a name above their fellow-beings, but to estimate the degree in which the excellence for which they were distinguished was shared by these among whom they lived. Inattention to this duty might present Patrick Henry and James Otis, Washington, Jefferson, and Samuel Adams, as the *causes* of the American Revolution, which they were not. There was a moral principle in the field, to the power of which a great majority of the whole population of the colonies, whether male or female, old or young, had been long and habitually trained to do homage. The individuals named, with the rest of their celebrated associates, were not the originators, but the spokesmen, of the general opinion, and instruments for its adaptation to existing events. Whether fighting in the field or deliberating in the senate, their strength against Great Britain was not that of numbers, nor of wealth, nor of genius; but it drew its nourishment from the sentiments that pervaded the dwellings of the entire population.

"How much this home-sentiment did then, and does ever, depend on the character of the female portion of the people, will be too readily understood by all, to require explanation. The domestic hearth is the first of schools and the best of lecture-rooms; for there the heart will co-operate with the mind, the affections with the reasoning powers. And this is the scene for the almost exclusive sway of woman. Yet,

great as the influence thus exercised undoubtedly is, it escapes observation in a manner that history rarely takes much account of it.

"In every instance of domestic convulsions, when the prun-
ing-hook is deserted for the sword and the musket, the sacrifice of
feelings made by the female sex is unmixed with a hope of worldly
compensation. With them there is no ambition to gratify, no fame
to be gained by the simple negative virtue of privations suffered in
silence. The lot of woman in times of trouble is to be a passive spectator of events which she scarcely hopes to make subservient to her
own fame and control."

Heroism of the Women of the Revolution

"The heroism of the females of the Revolution has gone from the
memory with the generation that witnessed it, and but little remains
upon the ear of the young of the present day but the faint echo of an
expiring tradition." "Instances of patience, perseverance, fortitude,
magnanimity, courage, humanity, and tenderness," says the wife of
John Adams, which "would have graced the Roman character, were
known only to those who were themselves the actors, and whose
modesty could not suffer them to blazon abroad their own fame."

Their Piety and Faith

And yet enough of the noble deeds and influence of the women of
the Revolution remains to show their piety, their patriotism, and
their self-denying efforts in the cause of their country. Their piety
and labors are thus referred to by Mrs. Ellet, the historiographer in
this field of the Revolution. "I have been struck," says she, "by the
fact that almost all were noted for piety. The spirit that exhibited
itself in acts of humanity, courage, patriotism, and magnanimity
was a deeply religious one. May we not with reason deem this an
important source of the strength that gave success to the American
cause? To inflame the fires of freedom by mutual interchanges of
feelings, and to keep them burning in the hearts of all around, they
formed freedom-associations, and entered into written pledges to
make every sacrifice they could for their country."

In Edenton, North Carolina, on the 26th of October, 1774, the women made the following covenant—

> As we cannot be indifferent on any occasion that appears to affect the peace and happiness of our country, and it has been thought necessary for the public good to enter into secret particular resolves by a meeting of the members of the Deputies from the whole Province, it is a duty we owe not only to our near and dear connections, but to ourselves who are severally interested in their welfare, to do every thing, as far as lies in our power, to testify our sincere adherence to the same; and we do therefore accordingly subscribe this paper as a witness of our fixed intention and solemn determination to do so.
>
> (Signed by fifty-one ladies.)

Pledges Not to Drink Tea

This patriotism was displayed in the willing sacrifices they made in their favorite beverage, tea. A tax being laid upon tea for the purpose of revenue to the British Government, its use was generally abandoned.

Three hundred heads of families in Boston, in a written covenant, resolved that they "would totally abstain from the use of tea till the revenue acts were repealed." The young ladies of Boston followed the example of their mothers, as the following pledge indicates—

> BOSTON, FEBRUARY 12, 1770.
>
> We, the daughters of those patriots who have and do now appear for the public interest—and in that principally regard their posterity—as such do with pleasure engage with them in denying ourselves the drinking of foreign tea, in hopes to frustrate a plan which tends to deprive a whole community of all that is valuable in life.

This pledge was signed by women throughout New England.

In an afternoon's visit of ladies in Newport, Rhode Island, it was resolved that those who could spin should be employed in that way, and those who could not should sew. When the time arrived for drinking tea, bohea and hyperion were provided; and every one of the ladies patriotically rejected the bohea, and unanimously, to their great honor, preferred the balsamic hyperion—the dried leaves of raspberry-plants.

Meet to Spin for the Army

In Boston, some fifty young ladies, enrolled as "The Daughters of Liberty," met at a minister's house (Rev. Mr. Morehead) and in a single day spun "two hundred and thirty-two skeins of yarn. Numerous spectators came to admire them, and the whole was concluded with many stirring tunes, anthems, and liberty songs, which were animated in their several parts by a number of the Sons of Liberty."

At Mecklenburg and Rowan, North Carolina, the young ladies entered into a written pledge not to receive the attentions of young men who would not volunteer in defence of their country. They declared they "were of opinion that such persons who stay loitering at home when the important calls of their country demand their military service abroad, must certainly be destitute of that nobleness of sentiment, that brave and manly spirit, which would qualify them to be the defenders and guardians of the fair sex."

An interesting incident, illustrative of female patriotism and activity, is given by Mr. Headley as occurring in the church at Litchfield, Connecticut. The pastor, Judah Champion, was an ardent patriot, and on a certain Sabbath was earnestly preaching and praying for the success of the American arms. During the service a messenger arrived, announcing that St. Johns—which had been besieged six weeks, and was regarded as the key to Canada—was taken. "Thank God for the victory!" exclaimed the patriot preacher, and the chorister, clapping his hands, vigorously shouted, "Amen, and amen!"

Supply the Army with Clothing

The communication of the messenger announced that our army was in a suffering condition, destitute of clothing, without stockings or shoes. "Sorrow and pity took the place of exultation, and generous sympathetic eyes filled with tears on every side. There was scarcely a dry eye among the females of the congregation. As soon as the audience was dismissed, they were seen gathered together in excited groups, and it was evident that some scheme was on foot that would not admit of delay. The result was that, when the congregation assembled in the afternoon, *not a woman was to be seen.* The men had come to church, but their earnest, noble wives and daughters had taken down their hand-cards, drawn forth their spinning-wheels, set in motion their looms, while the knitting and sewing needles were plied as they never were before. It was a strange spectacle to see that Puritan Sabbath turned into a day of secular work. The pastor was at the meeting-house, performing those duties belonging to the house of God, and the voice of prayer and hymns of praise ascended as usual from devout and solemn hearts; but all through the usually quiet streets of Litchfield the humming sound of the spinning-wheel, the clash of the shuttle flying to and fro, were heard, making strange harmony with the worship of the sanctuary. But let it not be supposed that these noble women had gone to work without the knowledge of their pastor. They had consulted with him, and he had given them his sanction and blessing.

"Swimming eyes and heaving bosoms were over their work, and lips moved in prayer for the destitute and suffering soldier. The pastor's wife contributed eleven blankets from her own stores to the collection."

The women of the Revolution were active in their services of relief and comfort to the armies of the country. "The supply of domestic cloth designed for families was in a short time, by the labor of the females, converted into coats for the soldiers; sheets and blankets were fashioned into shirts; and even the flannels already made up were altered into men's habiliments. Such aid was rendered by many whose deeds of disinterested generosity were never known beyond their own immediate neighborhood." Weights of clocks, pans, dishes, pewter services of plate, then common, were melted by the women and given to the army to be used in defence of freedom.

Lafayette in Baltimore

In 1776, Lafayette passed through Baltimore, and was honored with a public reception. In the gayeties of the scene he was seen to be sad. "Why so sad?" said a gay belle. "I cannot enjoy these festivities," said

Lafayette, "while so many of the poor soldiers are without shirts and other necessaries." "They shall be supplied," responded the fair ladies; and the scenes of the festive hail were exchanged for the service of their needles. They immediately made up clothing for the suffering soldiers— one of the ladies cutting out five hundred pairs of pantaloons with her own hands and superintending their making.

Women of Philadelphia

In 1780, a cold and dreary winter, when the soldiers greatly suffered, the ladies of Philadelphia formed an Industrial Association for the relief of the American army. They solicited money, sacrificed their jewelry, and labored with their own hands. Mrs. Bache, daughter of Dr. Franklin, was a leading spirit in these patriotic efforts. "She conducted us," said a French nobleman, in describing the scene, "into a room filled with work lately finished by the ladies of Philadelphia. It was shirts for the soldiers of Pennsylvania. The ladies bought the cloth from their own private purses, and took a pleasure in cutting them out and sewing them together. On each shirt was the name of the married or unmarried lady who made it; and they amount to twenty-two hundred." "During the cold winter that followed, thousands of poor soldiers in Washington's camp had occasion to bless the women of Philadelphia for these labors of love."

Their Correspondence with Washington

Mr. Reed, President of Congress, wrote to Washington, saying—

> The ladies have caught the contagion, and in a few days Mrs. Reed will have the honor of writing you on the subject. It is expected she will have a sum equal to one hundred thousand pounds to be laid out according to your Excellency's direction, in such a way as may be thought most honorable and gratifying to the brave old soldiers who have borne so great a share of the burden of this war. I thought it best to mention it in this way to your Excellency for your consideration, as it may tend to forward the benevolent scheme of the donors with dispatch.

I must observe that the ladies have excepted such articles of necessity as clothing, which the States are bound to provide.

We have just heard that Mrs. Washington is on the road to this city, so that, we shall have the benefit of her advice and assistance here, and, if necessary, refer afterwards to your Excellency.

A further account of this contribution was communicated in a letter from Mrs. Reed to General Washington, in which she wrote as follows—

The subscription set on foot by the ladies of this city for the use of the soldiers is so far completed as to induce me to transmit to your Excellency an account of the money I have received, which, although it has answered our expectations, does not equal our wishes. But I am persuaded it will be received as a proof of our zeal for the great cause of America, and of our esteem and gratitude for those who so bravely defend it. The amount of the subscription is 200,580 dollars, and £625 6*s.* 8*d.* in specie, which make in the whole, in paper money, 300,634 dollars. The ladies are anxious for the soldiers to receive the benefit of it, and wait your directions how it can be best disposed of. We expect considerable additions from the country; and I have also written to the other States in hopes that the ladies there will adopt a similar plan to render it more general and beneficial.

Philadelphia, July 4.

His Tribute to Their Patriotism

The reply of General Washington is as follows—

HEAD-QUARTERS, WHIPPANY, 25 JULY, 1780.
I very much admire the patriotic spirit of the ladies of Philadelphia, and shall with great pleasure give them my advice as to the application of their benevolent and generous donation to the soldiers of the army. Although the terms of the Association seem in some measure to preclude the purchase of any article which the public is bound to find, I would nevertheless recommend a provision of shirts, in preference to any thing

else, in case the funds should amount to a sum equivalent to a supply of eight or ten thousand. The soldiery are exceedingly in want of them, and the public have never, for several years past, been able to procure a sufficient quantity to make them comfortable. They are, besides, more capable of an equal and satisfactory distribution than almost any other article. Should the sum fall short of a supply of the number of shirts I have mentioned, perhaps there could be no better application of the money than laying it out in the purchase of refreshments for the hospitals. These are my ideas at present.

This example was followed by the ladies in New Jersey. Miss Mary Dagwerthy wrote to the commander-in-chief—

By order of Mrs. Dickinson and the other ladies of the committee, I have transmitted to your Excellency fifteen thousand four hundred and eighty-eight dollars, being the subscription received at this place, to be disposed of in such manner as your Excellency shall think proper for the benefit of the Continental soldiers. As the other subscriptions come in, they will be forwarded without delay.

Trenton, July 7.

The ladies of Maryland emulated their sisters in Pennsylvania and New Jersey and the other colonies. Washington, in writing to the ladies of Maryland, says—

I cannot forbear taking the earliest moment to express the high sense I entertain of the patriotic exertions of the ladies of Maryland in favor of the army.

"Amid all the distress and sufferings of the army," said Washington, "from whatever source they have arisen, it must be a consolation to our virtuous countrywomen that they have never been accused of withholding their most zealous efforts to support the cause we are engaged in, and encourage those who are defending them in the field.

"It embellishes the American character with a new trait, by proving that the love of country is blended with those softer domestic virtues which have always been allowed to be more peculiarly your own. You have not acquired admiration in your own country only; it is paid to you abroad, and, you will learn with pleasure, by a part of your own sex, whose female accomplishments have attained their highest perfection, and who from the commencement have been the patronesses of American liberty."

The patriotic sacrifices of the women were made with deep enthusiasm. Their firmness and intrepidity supplied every persuasive that could animate to perseverance and secure fidelity. So ardent were they in the cause of liberty, that a British officer said to Mrs. Pinckney, wife of Charles Pinckney, a distinguished orator of the Revolution, "It is impossible not to admire the intrepid firmness of the ladies of your country. Had your men but half their resolution, we might give up the contest. America would be free."

Letter of a Philadelphia Lady to a British Officer

The following is a letter from a lady of Philadelphia to a British officer in Boston, written immediately after the battle of Lexington, and previous to the Declaration of Independence. It fully exhibits the feelings of those times. A finer spirit never animated the breasts of Roman matrons than the letter breathes—

Sir—

We received a letter from you, wherein you let Mr. S. know that you had written after the battle of Lexington particularly to me—knowing my martial spirit, that I would delight to read the exploits of heroes. Surely, my friend, you must mean the New England heroes, as they alone performed exploits worthy of fame, while the regulars, vastly superior in numbers, were obliged to retreat with a rapidity unequalled, except by the French at the battle at Minden. Indeed, General Gage gives them due praise in his letter home, where he says Lord Percy was remarkable for his activity. You will not, I hope, take offence at any expression that in the warmth of my heart should escape me, when I assure you that, while we consider you as a public enemy, we regard you as a private friend, and while we detest the cause you are fighting for, we wish well to your own personal interest and safety. Thus far by way of apology.

As to the martial spirit you suppose me to possess, you are greatly mistaken. I tremble at the thoughts of war, but of all wars a civil one. Our all is at stake, and we are called upon, by every tie that is dear and sacred, to exert the spirit that Heaven has given us in this righteous struggle for liberty. I will tell you what I have done. My only brother I have sent to the camp with my prayers and blessings. I hope he will not disgrace me. I am confident he will behave with honor, and emulate the great example he has before him. Had I twenty sons and brothers, they should go. I have retrenched every superfluous expense in my table and family. Tea I have not drunk since last Christmas, nor bought a new cap or gown since your defeat at Lexington, and, what I never did before, have learned to knit, and am now making stockings of American wool for my servants; and in this way do I throw in my mite to the public good. I have the pleasure to assure you that these are the sentiments of all my sister Americans. They have sacrificed assemblies, parties of pleasure, tea-drinking, and finery, to that great spirit of patriotism that actuates all degrees of people throughout this extensive continent.

If these are the sentiments of females, what must glow in the breasts of our husbands, brothers, and sons? They are as with one heart determined to die or be free. It is not a quibble in politics—a science which few understand—which we are contending for; it is this plain truth, which the most ignorant peasant knows, and is clear to the weakest capacity, that no man has a right to take their money without their consent. The supposition is ridiculous and absurd, as none but highwaymen and robbers attempt it. Can you, my friend, reconcile with your own good sense that a body of men in

Great Britain, who have little intercourse with America, and of course know nothing of us, nor are supposed to know or feel the misery they would inflict upon us, shall invest themselves with a power to command our lives and properties at all times and in all cases whatsoever?

You say you are no politician. Oh, sir, it requires no Machiavelian head to develop this and to discover this tyranny and oppression. It is written with a sunbeam. Every one will see and know it, because it will make them feel, and we shall be unworthy of the blessing of Heaven if we ever submit to it.

All ranks of men among us are in arms. Nothing is heard now in our streets but the trumpet and the drum; and the universal cry is, "Americans, to arms!" All your friends are officers; there are Captain S.D., Lieutenant B., and Captain J.S. We have five regiments in the city and county of Philadelphia, complete in arms and uniform, and very expert at their military manœuvres. We have companies of light horse, light infantry, grenadiers, riflemen, and Indians, several companies of artillery, and some excellent brass cannon and field-pieces. Add to this that every county in Pennsylvania and the Delaware government can send two thousand men to the field. Heaven seems to smile on us; for in the memory of man were never known such quantities of flax, and sheep without number. We are making powder fast, and do not want for ammunition. In short, we want for nothing but ships of war to defend us, which we could procure by making alliances; but such is our attachment to Great Britain that we sincerely wish for reconciliation, and cannot bear the thought of throwing off all dependence on her, which such a step would assuredly lead to. The God of mercy will, I hope, open the eyes of our king, that he may see, while seeking our destruction, he will go near to complete his own. It is my ardent prayer that the effusion of blood may be stopped. We hope yet to see you in this city, a friend to the liberties of America, which will give infinite satisfaction to　　　　　Your sincere friend,

C.S.

To Captain S., in Boston.

Mrs. Wilson, of North Carolina, was a noble illustration of the patriotism of the women of the Revolution. Cornwallis, in his march through that State, had encamped his army on her husband's plantation. He tried by flattery to win her over to the royal cause. Her heroic reply to Cornwallis was, "I have seven sons who are now, or have been, bearing arms: indeed, my seventh son, Zaccheus, who is only fifteen years old, I yesterday assisted to get ready to go and join his brothers in Sumter's army. Now, sooner than to see one of my family turn back from the glorious enterprise, I should take my boys (pointing to three small sons), and with them would enlist under Sumter's standard, and show my husband and sons how to fight and, if necessary, to die for their country."

Another Christian mother had also the sacred number of seven sons in the army of freedom. "She has seven sons in the rebel army," was the reason given by the British officer for plundering the farm and burning the house of Widow Brevard, in Centre Congregation, while Cornwallis was in pursuit of Morgan and Greene after the victory of the Cowpens. What a mother! seven sons in the army at one time! and for this glorious fact the house of the widow plundered and burned and her farm pillaged!

Everywhere fife and drum were heard, and the fathers and sons, inspired by the patriotic women, took lessons together in the art of war. Such was the prevalent and inspiring spirit of patriotism inspired by liberty-loving women, that General Gage, the British commander, wrote, "The very children here draw in liberty from the air they breathe."

Mrs. Ellet, in her "Domestic history of the Revolution," says, "Throughout the war, the influence and exertions of women in all parts of the country contributed to impart a spirit of patriotism. They animated the courage and confirmed the self-devotion of those who ventured all in the common cause. They frowned upon instances of coldness or backwardness, and in the period of deepest gloom cheered and urged on the desponding. They willingly shared inevitable dangers and privations, relinquished without regret prospects of advantage to themselves, and parted with those they loved better than life, not knowing when they were to meet again. It is almost impossible now to appreciate the vast influence of woman's patriotism upon the destinies of the infant republic. We have no means of showing the important part she bore in maintaining the struggle, and in laying the foundation on which so mighty and majestic a structure has arisen. To her we are not less indebted for national freedom than to the swords of the patriots who poured out their blood."

Address of the American Woman to the Females of the Country

The pen of woman was gracefully wielded for freedom, as the sword was by the patriots and heroes. The following address, signed "An American Woman," written, it was supposed, by Mrs. Washington, in 1780, will present a delightful proof of woman's patriotism and her intellectual culture. It was printed and scattered throughout the country.

> On the commencement of the actual war, the women of America manifested a firm resolution to contribute as much as could depend on them to the deliverance of their country. Animated by the purest patriotism, they are full of sorrow at this day in not offering more than barren wishes for the success of so glorious a revolution. They aspire to render themselves more really useful, and this sentiment is universal from the north to the south of the thirteen United States. Our ambition is kindled by the fame of those heroines of antiquity who have rendered their sex illustrious, and have proved to the world that, if the weakness of our constitution, if opinion and manners, did not forbid us to march to glory by the same path as the men, we should at least equal and sometimes surpass them in our love for the public good. I glory in all my sex have done that is great and commendable. I call to mind with enthusiasm and admiration all those acts of courage, of constancy, and of patriotism which history has transmitted to us: the people favored by Heaven preserved from destruction by the virtues, the zeal, and the resolution of Deborah, of Judith, of Esther; the fortitude of the mother of the Maccabees, in giving up her sons to die before her eyes; Rome saved from the fury of a victorious enemy by the efforts of Volumnia and other Ro-

man ladies; so many famous sieges where women have been seen, forgetting the weakness of their sex, building new walls, digging trenches with their feeble hands, furnishing arms to their defenders, they themselves darting the missile weapons on the enemy, resigning the ornaments of their apparel, and their fortune, to fill the public treasury and to hasten the deliverance of their country; burying themselves under its ruins, throwing them-selves into the flames, rather than submit to the disgrace of humiliation before a proud enemy.

Born for liberty, disdaining to bear the irons of a tyrannical government, we associate ourselves to the grandeur of those sovereigns, cherished and revered, who have held with so much splendor the sceptre of the greatest states—the Matildas, the Elisabeths, the Marys, the Catharines, who have extended the empire of liberty, and, contented to reign by sweetness and justice, have broken the chains of slavery, forged by tyrants in the times of ignorance and barbarity. The Spanish women, do they not make, at this moment, the most patriotic sacrifices to increase the means of victory in the hands of their sovereign? He is a friend to the French nation. They are our allies. We call to mind, doubly interested, that it was a French maid who kindled up amongst her fellow-citizens the flames of patriotism buried under long misfortunes. It was the maid of Orleans who drove from the kingdom of France the ancestors of those same British whose odious yoke we have just shaken off; and when it is necessary, we drive them from this continent.

But I must limit myself to the recollection of this small number of achievements, Who knows if persons disposed to censure, and sometimes too severely, with regard to us, may not disapprove our appearing acquainted even with the actions of which our sex boast?

We are at least certain he cannot be a good citizen who will not applaud our efforts for the relief of the armies which defend our lives, our possessions, our liberty. The situation of our soldiery has been represented to me; the evils inseparable from war, and the firm and generous spirit which has enabled them to support these. But it has been said that they may apprehend that in the course of a long war the view of their distresses may be lost, and their services forgotten. Forgotten! never; I can answer, in the name of all my sex. Brave Americans, your disinterestedness, your courage, and your constancy will always be dear to America, so long as she shall preserve her virtue.

We know that, at a distance from the theatre of war, if we enjoy any tranquillity, it is the fruit of your watchings, your labors, your dangers. If I live happy in the midst of my family—if my husband cultivate his fields and reap his harvest in peace—if surrounded by my children, I myself nourish the youngest and press it to my bosom without being afraid of seeing myself separated from it by a ferocious enemy—if the houses in which we dwell, if our barns, our orchards, are safe at the present time from the hands of the incendiary—it is to you that we owe it. And shall we hesitate to evince to you our gratitude? Shall we hesitate to wear a clothing more simple, hair dressed less elegantly, while at the price of this small privation we shall deserve your benedictions? Who among us will not renounce with the highest pleasure those vain ornaments, when she shall consider that the valiant defenders of America will be able to draw some advantage from the money which she may have laid out in these? that they will be better defended from the rigors of the season? that after their painful toils they will receive some extraordinary and unexpected relief? that these presents will perhaps be valued by them at a greater price when they will have it in their power to say, *This is the offering of the ladies!*

The time is arrived to display the same sentiments which animated us at the beginning of the Revolution; when we renounced the use of teas, however agreeable to our taste, rather than receive them from our Persecutors; when we made it appear to them that we placed former necessaries in the rank of superfluities when our liberty was interested; when our republican and laborious hands spun the flax and prepared the linen intended for the use of our soldiers; when, exiles and fugitives, we supported with courage all the evils which are the concomitants of war. Let us not lose a moment; let us be engaged to offer the homage of our gratitude at the altar of military valor; and you, our brave deliverers, while mercenary slaves combat to cause you to share with them the irons with which they are loaded, receive with a free hand our offering, the purest which can be presented to your virtue.

The piety and patriotism of the women of the Revolution had an appropriate development in the preparation and presentation of flags; and on them were inscribed Christian symbols and mottoes. The Moravian Sisters at Bethlehem, Maryland, presented to Pulaski, the Polish patriot who assisted our Revolutionary fathers in their struggle for independence, a beautiful banner of crimson silk.

This banner bore on one side the letters U.S., and on a circle round them the words, *Unitas virtue fortior*—"Union makes valor stronger." On the other side, in the centre, an emblem, representing the all-seeing eye, with the words, *Non alius regit*—"No other governs." This banner, symbolical of woman's faith in God and her devotion to the cause of liberty, was borne by the brave Polander, in all his battles, till he fell, in 1779, on the field, a martyr to liberty.

An Interesting Incident

A Pennsylvania paper of June, 1775, contains the following incident illustrative of the enthusiasm of the females in the cause of the Revolution—

"The ladies in Bristol township have evidenced a laudable regard to the interests of the country. At their own expense they have furnished the regiment of that county with a suite of Colors and drums, and are now making a collection to supply muskets to such of the men as are not able to supply themselves. The lady who was appointed to present the colors to the regiment gave in charge to the soldiers never to desert the colors of the ladies, if they ever wished that the ladies should enlist under their banners."

Concerts of Prayer

Another source of woman's influence during the Revolution was in her constant devotions and prayers. She had power with God, and made her influence felt through all hearts and over all interests. Prayer does avail with God; and the women of the Revolution were almost all praying women, and hence their powerful and beneficent influence during the scenes of the Revolution. One cheering fact during those trying times was the surprising union of feeling among all the colonies and people in reference to the common cause of liberty.

"All America," said John Adams, in 1775, "is united in sentiment. One understanding governs, one heart animates, the whole. This is as if it had been a revelation from above." "Call me an enthusiast," said Samuel Adams, "this union among the colonies, and warmth of affection, can be attributed to nothing less than the agency of the Supreme Being." "The surprising union of the colonies," said Congress, "affords encouragement. It is an inexhaustible source of comfort that the Lord God omnipotent reigneth." And who can doubt that this "surprising union was the result of prayer? In every family, almost, as in all the pulpits, prayer was going up to God for this union and harmony among the defenders of freedom.

Christian Work of the Women of the Revolution

"In every trying hour of the Revolution, women would hold conferences for prayer, that God would be with the armies and give them the victory. During the battle at Guilford Court-House, North Carolina, March 15, 1781, two companies of Christian women were gathered from Dr. Caldwell's congregation, for prayer. Whilst the two armies met, the British under Cornwallis and the American under General Greene, these pious women were in prayer to Almighty God for his protection and aid. In many places the solitary voice of a pious woman went up to the Divine ear, with the earnest pleadings of faith, for the success of the Americans. The battling hosts were surrounded by a cordon of praying women during those dreadful hours of contest." Mr. Caldwell, in reply to the taunts of a British officer, said, "Wait and see what the Lord will do for us." The results of the battle were "highly beneficial to the cause of the patriots."

A Christian mother in New Rochelle, after melting all the pewter she had for bullets for her two sons, sent them forth to join the Continental army. As she stood in the door to bid them farewell, one turned back, saying he had no gun; but she said, Go on, for he would find a gun to spare in the army. When she had lost sight of them both, she went back weeping into the house, to pray for their safety and her country.

In the struggles of the Revolution and in gaining our independence, "who can tell how much availed the prayers of those righteous women?" They had continual audience with Heaven, and blessings on civil councils and on the armies of freedom descended to inspire and to guide to the auspicious and glorious results that followed the Revolution and crowned it with a system of free government.

During the winter of 1777, when the British had possession of Philadelphia, and Washington was passing a gloomy winter at Valley Forge, with his soul still resting with hope in God, the ladies of Philadelphia formed an association for the purpose of conveying important information to Washington respecting the plans of the British. Many of the British officers were quartered with patriotic families in the city, and, in a free and familiar way, would unfold to each other their future campaigns to capture our armies and subdue the colonists. The ladies listened with eager attention and silence to their statements, and then would delegate one of their number to convey the intelligence to a certain point, where another patriotic woman would carry it to another point, and thus these female couriers went from point to point, until the information reached Washington at his head-quarters. These journeys were all performed on foot, and made under pretence of visits of friendship and affection. The valuable information thus conveyed puzzled the British officers to know how it was communicated, and baffled some of their best-concerted plans. Among the heroic women of that noble band of patriots was a Mrs. Redman, who for many years, with the enthusiasm of woman's heart in a good cause, was accustomed to narrate these incidents of the female patriotism of Revolutionary times.

The above incident was narrated to the compiler of this volume, in April, 1863, by Mrs. Lydia R. Bailey, a venerable Christian lady of Philadelphia, now eighty-five years of age, who often heard it from the lips of Mrs. Redman and other female friends. She also remarked, with tearful emotion, that the present generation did not seem to realize the sacrifices which the blessings of liberty and *good government* cost, and that in the pride of their hearts they had forgotten the God of their fathers, and acted as if all their prosperity had come, not from the goodness of God, but from their own hands and efforts. How full of faith and piety were the Christian women of the Revolution, and those who caught the flame of patriotism and piety from such noble Christian ancestors!

Abigail Adams

Pre-eminent among the patriotic women of the Revolution was Abigail Adams, wife of John Adams. She was the daughter of a New England minister, Rev. Mr. Smith, and as distinguished for her intellectual accomplishments as for piety and patriotism. Her influence and activity were great and unwearied during the Revolution and in the opening scenes of the civil administration of the new government. She was polished with her pen, and self-sacrificing in her devotion to her country.

Her Labors, Character, and Influence

In 1770, when her husband returned home from a town-meeting in Boston, in which he had been chosen a Representative, he said to his wife, "I have accepted a seat in the House of Representatives, and thereby have consented to my own ruin, to your ruin, and the ruin of our children. I give you this warning, that you may prepare yourself for your fate." She burst into tears, but instantly cried out, in a transport of magnanimity, "Well, I am willing in this cause to run all risks with you, and be ruined with you, if you are ruined." "These were times," said John Adams, "which tried women's souls as well as men's."

Bancroft says that when the king's proclamation reached this country, "Abigail Smith, the wife of John Adams, was at the time in their home near the foot of Penn Hill, charged with the sole care of their little brood of children, managing their farm, keeping house with frugality, though opening her doors to the houseless and giving with a good will a part of her scant portion to the poor; seeking work for her own hands, and ever busily occupied, now at the spinning-wheel, now making amends for having never been sent to school, by learning French, though with the aid of books alone. Since the departure of her husband for Congress, the arrow of death has sped near her by day, and the pestilence that walks in the darkness had entered her humble mansion. She herself was still weak after a violent illness. Her house was an hospital in every part; and, such was the distress of the neighborhood, she could hardly find a well person to assist in looking after the sick. Her youngest son had been rescued from the grave by her nursing. Her own mother had been taken away, and, after the austere manner of her forefathers, buried without prayer. Woe followed woe, and one affliction trod on the heels of another. Winter was hurrying on; during the day family affairs took off her attention, but her long evenings, broken by the sound of the ocean, and of the enemy's artillery at Boston, were lonesome and melancholy. Ever in the silent night ruminating on the love and tenderness of her departed parent, she needed the consolation of her husband's presence; but when, in November, she read the king's proclamation, she willingly gave up her nearest friend exclusively to his perilous duties, and sent him her cheering message, 'This intelligence will make a plain path for you, though a dangerous one. I could not join to-day in the petitions of our worthy pastor for a reconciliation between our no longer parent State, but tyrant State, and these colonies. Let us separate: they are unworthy to be our brethren. Let us renounce them, and instead of supplications, as formerly, for their prosperity and happiness, let us beseech the Almighty to blast their counsels and bring to naught all their devices.'

Mrs. Adams's correspondence with her husband during the Revolutionary War, and his absence from the country in Europe, forms one of the most interesting chapters in our history. The following, after the battle of Bunker Hill, is full of piety and patriotism—

SUNDAY, 18TH JUNE, 1775

DEAREST FRIEND—

The day—perhaps the decisive day—is come, on which the fate of America depends. My bursting heart must find vent at my pen. I have just heard that our dear friend Dr. Warren is no more, but fell gloriously fighting for his country, saying, "Better to die honorably in the field than ignominiously hang upon the gallows." Great is our loss. He has distinguished himself in every engagement by his courage and fortitude, by animating the soldiers and leading them on by his own example. A particular account of those dreadful but, I hope, glorious days, will be transmitted you, no doubt, in the exactest manner.

"The race is not to the swift, nor the battle to the strong; but the God of Israel is he that giveth strength and power unto his people. Trust in him at all times, ye people, pour out your hearts before him: God is a refuge for us." The battle began upon our intrenchments upon Bunker's Hill, Saturday morning about three o'clock, and has not yet ceased, and it is now three o'clock Sabbath afternoon.

It is expected they will come out over the Neck to-night, and a dreadful battle must ensue. Almighty God, cover the heads of our countrymen and be a shield to our dear friends! How many have fallen we know not. The constant roar of the cannon is so distressing that we cannot eat, drink, or sleep. May you be supported and sustained in this dreadful conflict! I shall tarry here till it is thought unsafe by my friends, and then I have secured myself a retreat at your brother's, who has kindly offered me a part of his home. I cannot compose myself to write any further at present. I will add more as I hear further.

Mrs. Adams was in London in 1787, and received a letter from her sister (Mrs. Cranch) in the United States, giving her an account of some insurrectionary movements in Massachusetts [Shay's Rebellion]. In reply she writes as follows—

London, 25th February, 1787

My Dear Sister—

The thoughts that naturally occurred to me were, "For what have we been contending against the tyranny of Britain, if we are to become the sacrifice of a lawless banditti?" Must our glory be thus shorn and our laurels thus blasted? *Is it a trifling thing to destroy a Government?* Will my countrymen justify the maxim of tyrants, that mankind are not made for freedom? I will, however, still hope that the majority of our fellow-citizens are too wise, virtuous, and enlightened to permit these outrages to gain ground and triumph. Solon, the wise lawgiver of Athens, published a manifesto rendering infamous all persons who in civil seditions should remain spectators of their country's danger by a *criminal neutrality. More energy in Government would have prevented the evil from spreading as far as it has done.*

> "Mercy but gives Sedition time to rally.
> Every soft, pliant, talking, busy rogue,
> Gathering a flock of hot-brained fools together,
> Can preach up new rebellion,
> Spread false reports of the Senate, working up
> Their madness to a fury quick and desperate,
> Till they run headlong into civil discords,
> And do our business with their own destruction."

This is a picture of the civil dissensions in Rome, and, to our mortification, we find that human nature is the same in all ages. Neither the dread of tyrants, the fall of empires, nor the more gloomy picture of civil discord, are sufficient to deter mankind from pursuing the same steps which have led others to ruin. Selfishness, and spite, and avarice, and ambition, pride, and a levelling principle, are very unfavorable to the existence of civil liberty.

It is a very just observation, that those who have raised an empire have always been grave and severe, *they who have ruined it have been uniformly distinguished for their dissipation.*

In this same letter she says—

Disagreeable as the situation of my native State appears, I shall quit Europe with more pleasure than I came into it, uncontaminated, I hope, with its manners and vices. I have learned to know the world and its value; I have seen high life; I have witnessed the luxury and pomp of state, the power of riches, and the influence of titles, and have beheld all ranks bow before them as the only shrine worthy of worship. Notwithstanding this, I feel that

I can return to my little cottage and be happier than here; and, if we have not wealth, we have what is better—integrity.

In the War of 1812, Mrs. Cushing, an intimate friend of Mrs. Adams, lost a brother on the field of battle. Mrs. Adams writes as follows—

QUINCY, 18TH FEBRUARY, 1813

MY DEAR MRS. CUSHING—

The voice of friendship bids me sympathize with the bereaved sisters and relatives over the brave youth who has fallen in defence of the injured rights and honor of his country.

"How beautiful is death when earn'd by virtue!
Who would not be that youth? What is it
That we can die but once to serve our country?"

So spoke the Roman from the mouth of Cato. So said the father over the dead body of his son. "It is," said Ossian, "when the foes fly before them that fathers delight in their sons. But their sighs burst forth in secret when their young warriors yield." In the agony of grief for the loss of those most dear, it is an alleviation to the wounded bosom to know that they died, covered with glory, in the arms of victory. Long will young Aylwin be remembered and regretted, "by all his country's wishes blest."

To all of you, my afflicted friends, I wish consolation and support from a higher source than the honor and fame which man can bestow,

And am your sympathizing friend,

Abigail Adams

The following views are wise, and always timely to American females—

QUINCY, 5TH JUNE, 1809

MY DEAR SISTER—

You know, if there be bread enough and to spare, unless a prudent attention manage that sufficiency, the fruits of diligence will be scattered by the hand of dissipation. No man ever prospered in the world without the consent and co-operation of his wife. It behooves us who are parents or grandparents, to give our daughters and grand-daughters, when their education devolves upon us, such an education as shall qualify them for the useful and domestic duties of life, that they should learn the proper use of time, since time "was given for use, not waste." The finer accomplishments, such as music, drawing, and painting, serve to set off and embellish the picture; but the ground-work must be formed of more durable colors.

I consider it as an indispensable requisite that every American wife should herself know how to order and regulate her family—how to govern her domestics and train up her children. For this purpose the all-wise Creator made woman an help-meet for man; and she who fails in these duties does not answer the end of her creation.

> "Life's cares are comforts—such by Heaven design'd;
> They that have none must make them, or be wretched.
> Cares are employments, and without employ
> The soul is on a rack, the rack of rest."

I have frequently said to my friends, when they have thought me overburdened with care, I would rather have too much than too little. Life stagnates without action. I could never bear merely to vegetate.

> "Waters stagnate when they cease to flow."

Mrs. Adams, like all the female patriots of that era of liberty, felt deeply on the subject of slavery. Writing to her husband on the 22d of September, 1774, who was in the first Congress of the United Colonies, at Philadelphia, she says—

I wish, most sincerely, that there was not a slave in the province: it always seems a most iniquitious scheme, to me, to fight ourselves for what we are daily robbing and plundering from those who have as good a right to freedom as ourselves. You know my mind on this subject.

In another letter to a friend, she says—

Is it not amazing, when the rights of humanity are defined with precision, in a country above all others fond of liberty, that in such an age and in such a country we find men professing a religion the most humane and gentle, adopting a principle as repugnant to humanity as it is inconsistent with the Bible and destructive to liberty? Believe me, I honor the Quakers for their noble efforts to abolish slavery. It is a debt we owe the purity of our religion, to show that it is at variance with that law which warrants slavery.

Her piety and patriotism have a beautiful development in the following letter which she addressed to her husband when he was elected President of the United States—

QUINCY, 8th February, 1797

"The sun is drest in brightest beams
To give thy honors to the day."

And may it prove an auspicious prelude to each ensuing season! You have this day to declare yourself head of a nation. "And now, O Lord my God, thou hast made thy servant ruler over the people. Give unto him an understanding heart, that he may know how to go out and come in before this great people; that he may discern between good and bad. For who is able to judge this thy so great a people?" were the words of a royal sovereign—and not less applicable to him who is invested with the chief magistracy of a nation, though he wear not the crown nor the robes of royalty.

My thoughts and my meditations are with you, though personally absent, and my petitions to Heaven are that the things which make for peace may not be hidden from your eyes. My feelings are not those of pride or ostentation upon the occasion: they are solemnized by a sense of the obligations, the important trusts and numerous duties, connected with it. That you may be enabled to discharge them with honor to yourself, with justice and impartiality to your country, and with satisfaction to this great people, shall be the daily prayer of your

A.A.

Mrs. Adams rendered an eminent service to the country in the maternal training of her son.

Edward Everett, in his eulogy on John Quincy Adams, before the Legislature of Massachusetts, in April, 1848, says, "I may be permitted to pause for a moment, to pay a well-deserved tribute of respect to the memory of the excellent mother to whose instructions so much of the subsequent eminence of the son is due. No brighter example exists of auspicious maternal influence in forming the character of a great and good man. Her letters to him might almost be called a Manual of Wise Mother's Advice. The counsels of the faithful and affectionate mother followed him beyond the sea."

The following are among the Christian counsels Mrs. Adams inculcated upon her son, and by which she formed his character and prepared him for his eminent usefulness.

"The only sure and permanent foundation of virtue," says she to her young son, "is religion. Let this important truth be engraven on your heart, and also that the foundation of religion is the belief of one only God, as a Being infinitely wise, just, and good, to whom you owe the highest reverence, gratitude, and adoration. Placed as we are in this transitory scene of probation, drawing nigher and still nigher, day after day, to that important crisis which must introduce us to a new system of things, it ought to be our principal concern to become qualified for our expected dignity. Great learning and superior abilities, should we even possess them, will be of little value and small estimation, unless virtue, honor, truth, and integrity are added to them. Adhere, then, to those religious sentiments which were early instilled into your mind, and remember that you are accountable to your Maker for all your words and actions.

"Dear as you are to me, I would much rather you should have found your grave in the ocean you have crossed, or that an untimely death should crop you in your infant years, than to see you an immoral, profligate, or graceless child."

Mr. Adams acknowledged his indebtedness to his mother, when Governor Briggs, of Massachusetts, meeting him on the streets of Washington, both being members of Congress, said, "I have just found out who made you, Mr. Adams. I have been reading the letters of your mother; and she made you what you are." "Yes," replied the old man: "all I have been, and all I am, I owe to my mother."

Mr. Adams said, only a short period before his death, that he never retired to rest without repeating the simple prayer which his mother taught him in childhood—

> Here I lay me down to sleep:
> I pray the Lord my soul to keep;
> If I should die before I wake,
> I pray the Lord my soul to take.

A beautiful and tender exhibition of Mrs. Adams's piety and sense of Christian propriety was displayed on the occasion of the death of Washington. His sudden departure, amidst the quiet scenes of Mount Vernon, on the 13th of December, 1799, touched with universal grief the national sensibilities, and every household and heart felt it as a deep personal bereavement.

Mrs. Adams, when Washington died, was the wife of the President of the United States, and presiding with dignity in the court-circles of Philadelphia. The evening subsequent to the death of Washington Mrs. Adams had appointed for a public reception; but as soon as the intelligence reached the city she published the following notice—

"In consequence of the afflictive intelligence of the death of General Washington, Mrs. Adams's drawing-room reception is deferred to Friday, the 27th, when the ladies are respectfully requested to wear white trimmed with black ribbon, black gloves and fans, as a token of respect to the memory of the late President of the United States. The ladies of the officers of the General Government will please wear black."

Mary, the Mother of Washington,

Has, through her son, exerted a larger and more beneficent influence on the American nation than any other woman. Her faith, piety, and good

sense gave to the nation and the race this peerless man. "She was eminently qualified, by nature and religion, to fulfil all her duties to her family. She
possessed a strong mind and sound judgment, united with great simplicity of manners, energy, honesty, and truthfulness. She was a strict discipli-
narian, and obtained over her children an uncompromising, but benign,
control. She was deeply interested in forming the minds and hearts of her
children according to the teachings of the gospel; and she daily taught
them select parts of Sir Matthew Hale"s 'Contemplations, Moral and Divine,' wonderfully plain and simple, but exquisitely Christian, abounding
in golden maxims of sound wisdom and pure piety. It was the lot of Washington to receive from his father, as well as his mother, the advantages of
a sound religions education; but, in common with the worthies who have
adorned our race, he points the world to the chief earthly source of his
successes—HOME INFLUENCE DIRECTED BY A MOTHER."

Washington regarded his mother as the source of all his fortunate success and exalted greatness, and paid her the most profound
and heartfelt veneration and obedience. The secret of his greatness,
as well as his mother's influence, are seen in the memorable reply
she made to Lafayette when he hastened to her home in Fredericksburg, Virginia, after the victory at Yorktown, to announce to her the
great achievement of her fortunate son. She listened to the words of
Lafayette, as he described the victory and spoke of the honor and
fame which would thereby accrue to her son. She simply replied, "It
is nothing more than I expected; as George was always a good boy."

His farewell visit to her, before he set out to assume the responsibilities of the Presidency, is one of the most beautiful scenes recorded in the annals of history. He said—

> The people, honored madam, have been pleased, with the
> most flattering unanimity, to elect me to the chief magistracy
> of the United States; but, before I can assume the functions
> of that office, I have come to bid you an affectionate farewell.
> So soon as the public business which must necessarily be en-
> countered in arranging a new government can be disposed
> of, I shall hasten to Virginia, and—

Here his mother interrupted him, with—

You will see me no more. My great age, and the disease which is fast approaching my vitals, warn me that I shall not be long in this world. I trust to God I am somewhat prepared for a better. But go, George, fulfil the destiny which Heaven appears to assign you. Go, my son; and may Heaven's and your mother's blessing be with you.

On the death of his mother, which took place at Fredericksburg, August 25, 1789, in the eighty-third year of her age, Washington wrote to his sister, Mrs. Lewis, as follows—

Awful and affecting as the death of a parent is, there is consolation in knowing that Heaven has spared ours to an age beyond which few attain, and favored her with the full enjoyment of her mental faculties, and as much bodily strength as usually falls to the lot of fourscore. Under these considerations, and a hope that she is translated to a happier place, it is the duty of her relatives to yield due submission to the decrees of the Creator. When I was last at Fredericksburg, I took a final leave of my mother, never expecting to see her more.

There is no fame in the world more pure than that of the mother of Washington, and no woman since the mother of Christ has a better claim to the affectionate reverence of mankind.

The Wife of Washington

Martha, the wife of Washington, was a woman of fine accomplishments, eminently qualified for the exalted station she was called, in the providence of God, to fill. Her piety and patriotism were equal to every trial, and were constantly exerted in behalf of her country. She often left the comforts and elegancies of Mount Vernon and spent months with Washington and his armies, cheering them by her presence and encouraging the soldiers by her words.

Mrs. Washington accompanied the general to the line before Boston, and witnessed its siege and evacuation. At the close of each campaign, an aide-de-camp repaired to Mount Vernon to escort her to the head-quarters. Her arrival at the camp was an event much anticipated, and was always the signal for the ladies of general officers to repair to the bosoms of their lords. The arrival of Mrs. Washington at Valley Forge, Morristown, and West Point diffused a cheering influence amid the gloom that hung over those scenes. She always remained at head-quarters till the opening of the campaign, and often remarked, in after-life, that it had been her good fortune to hear the first cannon at the opening and the last at the closing of every campaign of the Revolutionary War. During the whole of the period when we struggled for independence, Mrs. Washington preserved her equanimity, together with a degree of cheerfulness that inspired all around her with the brightest hopes of ultimate success.

A Model President's Wife

The love of the old soldiers for Mrs. Washington had a tinge of romantic tenderness. They were welcomed by her on all occasions, after the war, and, while she was at Philadelphia, as the wife of the President of the United States. "They came, they would say, to head-quarters, just to inquire after the health of his excellency and Lady Washington. They knew his excellency was, of course, much engaged, but they would like to see the good lady. All were 'kindly bid to stay,' and were conducted to the steward's apartments and refreshments set before them; and, after receiving some little token from the lady, with her best wishes for the health and happiness of an old soldier, they went their way, with blessings upon their revered commander and the good Lady Washington uttered by many a war-worn veteran of the Revolution.

"She had an inveterate habit of knitting. It had been acquired, or at least fostered, in the wintry encampments of the Revolution, where she used to set an example to her lady-visitors by diligently plying her needles, knitting stockings for the poor destitute soldiery."

Mrs. Washington presided with graceful dignity and Christian propriety over the republican court of the Government. As the wife of the President of the United States, her elegant manners, elevated example, and the charms of her social and Christian character, exerted an ennobling influence on society, and won for her universal admiration and praise. As Washington was a model President and a finished gentleman, so Providence had given him a model wife and a Christian woman, whose influence was genial, and whose example was worthy of universal imitation by her countrywomen, and especially by all who should succeed her in the high position she occupied.

The following letter, written to a friend after the President had returned from his tour to the North and East, is a fine development of her feelings, taste, and character—

New York, December 26, 178.

My dear Madam—

Your very friendly letter of the 27th of last month has afforded me much more satisfaction than all the formal compliments and empty ceremonies of mere etiquette could possibly have done. I am not apt to forget the feelings that have been inspired by my former society with good acquaintances, nor to be insensible to their expressions of gratitude to the President of the United States; for you know me well enough to do me the justice to believe that I am only fond of what comes from the heart. Under a conviction that the demonstrations of respect and affection which have been made to the President originate from that source, I cannot deny that I have taken some interest and pleasure in them. The difficulties which presented themselves to view upon entering upon the Presidency seem thus to be, in some measure, surmounted. It is owing to this kindness of our numerous friends, in all quarters, that my new and unwished-for situation is not indeed a burden to me.

When I was much younger, I should probably have enjoyed the innocent gayeties of life as much as most of my age. But I had long since placed all the prospects of my future worldly happiness in the still enjoyments of the fireside at Mount Vernon.

I little thought, when the war was finished, that any circumstance could possibly have happened which would call the general into public life again. I had anticipated that from that moment we should have been left to grow old, in solitude and tranquillity, together. That was, dear madam, the first and dearest wish of my heart; but in that I have been disappointed. I will not, however, contemplate with too much regret disappointments that are inevitable.

Though the general's feelings and my own were perfectly in unison with respect to our predilection for private life, yet I cannot blame him for having acted according to his ideas of duty in obeying the voice of his country. The consciousness of having attempted to do all the good in his power, and the pleasure of finding his fellow-citizens so well satisfied with the disinterestedness of his conduct, will doubtless be some compensation for the great sacrifices which I know he has made. Indeed, in his journey from Mount Vernon to this place, in his late tour through the Eastern States, by every public and by every private information which has come to him, I am persuaded he has experienced nothing to make him repent his having acted from what he conceived to be alone a sense of indispensable duty. On the contrary, all his sensibilities have been awakened in receiving such repeated and unequivocal proofs of sincere regard from all his countrymen.

With respect to myself, I sometimes think the arrangement is not quite as it ought to have been—that I, who had much rather be at home, should occupy a place with which a great many younger women would be prodigiously pleased. As my grandchildren and domestic connections make up a great portion of the felicity which I looked for in this world, I shall hardly be able to find any substitute that would indemnify me for the loss of a part of such endearing society. I do not say this because I am dissatisfied with my present station. No: God forbid! For everybody and every thing conspire to make me as contented as possible in it. Yet I have seen too much of the vanity of human affairs to expect felicity from the splendid scenes of public life. I am still determined to be cheerful and happy in whatever station I may be, for I have also learnt that the greater part of our happiness or misery depends upon our disposition, and not upon our circumstances. We carry the seeds of the one or the other about us, in our minds, whithersoever we go. I have two of my grandchildren with me, who enjoy advantages in point of education, and who, I trust, by the goodness of Providence, will continue to be a great blessing to me. My other two grandchildren are with their mother in Virginia.

The President's health is quite restored by his late journey. Mine is much better than it used to be. I am sorry to hear that General Warren has been ill; I hope before this time that he may be entirely recovered. We should rejoice to see you both. To both I wish the best of Heaven's blessings, and am, dear madam, with esteem and regard, your friend and humble servant.

M. Washington

"What chiefly won old and young was a bland cheerfulness— the silent history of the soul's happiness—and an expressive smile, inspiring every beholder with confidence, like a beam from the Temple of Truth. There was about her in youth a womanly dignity which chastened the most forward admiration into respect." Her public life was in beautiful correspondence with her youthful accomplishments and graceful conduct. In the first republican court of America she formed the social etiquette of the Government on the rules of Christian dignity and propriety, and the example was pure and ennobling in its national influences.

Piety gave the crowning finish to her character, and adorned her public and private life with its virtues. Her Christian resignation at the death of her illustrious husband has all the humility and beauty of submission to the Divine will. When the great man breathed his last, she said, "Tis well: all is now over. I soon shall follow him; I have no more trials to pass through." "That piety," says Mrs. Sigourney, "which had so long been her strength, continued its support, but her heart drooped. Cheerfulness did not forsake her; yet she discharged the habitual round of duties as one who felt that the 'glory had departed.'"

"In the life of this model woman," says a writer, "we perceive that it was neither the beauty with which she was endowed, nor the high station she attained, that gave enduring lustre to her character, but her Christian fidelity in those duties which devolve upon her sex. These fitted her to irradiate the home, to lighten the cares, to cheer the anxieties, to sublimate the enjoyments, of him who was her exalted and illustrious husband. Christian fidelity marked her whole public life; and her influence, like that of Washington, has been beneficent upon the interests of the nation."

"I had," said a female relative who was twenty years an inmate of the family, "the most perfect model of female excellence ever with me as my monitress, who acted the part of a tender and devoted parent, loving me as only a mother can love, and never extenuating or approving in me what she disapproved in others. She never omitted her private devotions or her public duties; and she and her husband were so perfectly united and happy, that they must have been Christians. She had no doubts, no fears, of him. After forty years of devoted affection and uninterrupted happiness, she resigned him, without a murmur, into the arms of his Saviour and his God, with the assured hope of his eternal felicity."

Her Christian duties, public and private, she never omitted. During the Presidency of Washington in Philadelphia, Bishop White testifies to her habitual and devout attendance, with her husband, on the public services of the sanctuary, and that she was a constant communicant at the table of the Lord, in his church.

Request of Congress for the Remains of Washington

Among the resolutions of Congress, in session at Philadelphia, on the death of General Washington, were the following—

DECEMBER 24, 1799

Resolved, by the Senate and House of Representatives of the United States of America, in Congress assembled, That a marble monument be erected by the United States, in the Capitol, in the city of Washington, and that the family of GENERAL WASHINGTON be requested to permit his body to be deposited under it; and that the monument be so designed as to commemorate the great events of his military and political life.

And be it further resolved, That the President of the United States be requested to direct a copy of these resolutions to be transmitted to MRS. WASHINGTON, assuring her of the profound respect Congress will ever bear to her person and character, of their condolence on the late afflictive dispensation of Providence, and entreating her assent to the interment of the remains of General GEORGE WASHINGTON in the manner expressed in the first resolution.

The following message was received from the PRESIDENT—

GENTLEMEN OF THE SENATE, and GENTLEMEN OF THE HOUSE OF REPRESENTATIVES—

In compliance with the request in one of the resolutions of Congress of the 21st of December last, I transmitted a copy of those resolutions, by my secretary, Mr. Shaw, to Mrs. Washington, assuring her of the Profound respect Congress will ever bear to her person and character, of their condolence in the late afflictive dispensation of Providence, and entreating her assent to the interment of the remains of General GEORGE WASHINGTON in the manner expressed in the first resolution. As the sentiment of that virtuous lady, not less beloved by this nation than she is at present greatly afflicted, can never be so well expressed as in her own words, I transmit to Congress her original letter.

It would be an attempt of too much delicacy to make any comment upon it; but there can be no doubt that the nation at large, as well as all the branches of the Government, will be highly gratified by any arrangement which may diminish the sacrifice she makes of her individual feelings.

John Adams.

Mrs. Washington's Letter

MOUNT VERNON, December 31, 1799

SIR—While I feel, with keenest anguish, the late dispensation of Divine Providence, I cannot be insensible to the mournful tributes of respect and veneration which are paid to the memory of my dear deceased husband; and, as his best services and most anxious wishes were always devoted to the welfare and happiness of his country, to know that they were truly appreciated and gratefully remembered affords no inconsiderable consolation.

Taught, by that great example which I have so long had before me, never to oppose my private wishes to the public will, I must consent to the request made by Congress, which you have had the goodness to transmit to me; and in doing this I need not—I cannot—say what a sacrifice of individual feeling I make to a sense of public duty.

With grateful acknowledgments and unfeigned thanks for the personal respect and evidences of condolence expressed by Congress and yourself, I remain, very respectfully, sir,

Your most obedient servant,

Martha Washington

The following historical scene is thus described by Chief Justice Marshall—"At Trenton, Washington was welcomed in a manner as new as it was pleasing. In addition to the usual demonstrations of respect and attachment which were given by the discharge of cannon, by military corps, and by private persons of distinction, the gentler sex prepared, in their own taste, a tribute of applause indicative of the grateful recollection in which they held their deliverance, twelve years before, from a formidable enemy. On the bridge over the creek which passes through the town was erected a triumphal arch, highly ornamented with laurels and flowers, and supported by thirteen pillars, each entwined with wreaths of evergreen. On the front arch was inscribed, in large gilt letters,

The Defenders of the Mothers will
be the Protectors of the Daughters.

"On the center of the arch, above the inscription, was a dome or cupola of flowers and evergreens, encircling the dates of the two memorable events which were peculiarly interesting to the people of New Jersey. The first was the battle of Trenton, and the second the bold and judicious stand taken by the American troops at the same creek, by which the march of the British army was arrested on the evening preceding the battle of Princeton. At this place

Washington was met by a party of matrons leading their daughters dressed in white, who carried baskets of flowers in their hands, and sang, with exquisite sweetness, an ode composed for the occasion. It is as follows—

> Welcome, mighty chief, once more
> Welcome to this grateful shore!
> Now no mercenary foe
> Aims again the fatal blow—
> Aims at thee the fatal blow.
> Virgins fair and matrons grave,
> Those thy conquering arm did save,
> Build for thee triumphal bowers;
> Strew, ye fair, his way with flowers—
> Strew your hero's way with flowers!

"The beauty of the scene, and its lovely exhibition of gratitude and patriotism, touched the heart of the great hero, and tears testified to his deep emotion. Before he left Trenton, he sent the following note to the ladies—

Tribute of Washington to the Females of Trenton

> "General Washington cannot leave this place without expressing his acknowledgments to the matrons and young ladies who received him in so novel and grateful a manner at the triumphal arch in Trenton, and for the exquisite sensation he experienced in that affecting moment. The astonishing contrast between his former and actual situation at the same spot, the elegant taste with which it was adorned for the present occasion, and the innocent appearance of the white-robed choir who met him with the congratulatory song, have made such an impression on his remembrance as he assures them will never be effaced.
>
> "Trenton, April 21, 1789"

Piety Her Crowning Excellence

"The merit of these appropriate and classical decorations is due," says Custis, "to the late Mrs. Stockton, of Princeton, a lady of superior literary acquirements and refined taste. She was familiarly called *duchess*, from her elegance and dignity of manners. She was a most ardent patriot during the War of the Revolution, and, with the Stockton family, was marked for persecution on the ruthless invasion of the Jerseys. Her husband was accustomed to call her 'the best of women.' Piety and patriotism, as in the life and character of her husband, were her crowning excellencies."

High Character and Usefulness of American Women

Female life and influence during the heroic age of the republic were in harmony with the precepts of religion, and gave grace and purity and dignity to their public and private character. "The domestic life of that period," says a writer, "revealed in all we know of its refinement and elegance, its dignified courtesy and inflexible morality, can be contemplated only with a respectful admiration. It was in keeping with the frankness and sincerity of ascendant politics. Women unhesitatingly evinced their sympathies with whatever was generous and honorable in public conduct, but rarely, if ever, in forgetfulness of feminine propriety. Though patriotic, they were content to be women still, and were anxious for the distinctions of delicacy and grace. They perceived it was their nobility not to be men, but to be women worthy of men. In possession of every right with which they were endowed by nature, they had no desire to usurp men's prerogatives."

18

Christian Churches of the Revolution—Congregational Churches

Form of Government

THE American Christian Church, in all its forms of government, has in its colonial and national history produced two great results. Each form, while it has represented the faith of those who have adopted it, has at the same time developed the sentiments of freedom and of a true civilization. The religious sentiment which colonized the American continent, and incorporated itself into the life and character of the American government and people, assumed such a church-organization as gave to it its fullest power in favor of freedom.

Views of Graham

"By giving a welcome to every religious sect," says Grahame, "America was safe from narrow bigotry. At the same time, the moral unity of the forming nation was not impaired. Of the various parties into which the Reformation divided the people, each, from the proudest to the most puny sect, rallied round a truth. But, as truth never contradicts itself the collision of sects could but eliminate error; and the American mind, in the best and largest sense eclectic, struggled for universality, whilst it asserted freedom." Each Church thus blended its spirit of liberty with that of every other Church, and all co-operated to sustain freedom and to build up free institutions.

"The United States," said Dr. Stiles, in 1783, "will embosom all religious sects or denominations in Christendom. Here they may all enjoy their whole respective systems of worship and church-government complete; and, having on account of religion no superiority as to secular powers and civil immunities, they will cohabit together in harmony and with a most generous catholicism and benevolence—the example of a friendly cohabitation of all sects in America proving that men may be good members of civil society and yet differ in religion. Religion may here receive its last, most liberal and impartial examination."

"In our nation," says Washington, "however different the sentiments of citizens on religious doctrines, they generally concur in one thing; for their political professions and practices are almost universally friendly to the order and happiness of our civil institutions."

"It seems," said Webster, "to be the American destiny, the mission which has been intrusted to us here on this shore of the Atlantic, the great conception and the great duty to which we were born, to show that all sects and all denominations, professing reverence for the authority of the Author of our being and belief in his revelations, may be safely tolerated without prejudice either to our religion or to our liberties."

In the work of creating civil institutions on a Christian basis, and in achieving the liberties and independence of the United States, history places pre-eminent

The Congregational Churches of New England

This form of church-government is democratic. It was of Puritan birth, and, like the faith of the Puritans, it came fresh and vigorous from the word of God. It is the embodiment and practice of the American doctrine of popular sovereignty, applied to church-government, as it is to all the civil affairs of the nation. Each Church is an independent Christian democracy, where all the members have a right to a voice in the government of the Church, and whose decisions are subject to no reversal by any other ecclesiastical tribunal. The Bible is regarded as the text-book in theology and politics, in Church and State, as it is in its form of church-government; and, holding the Bible as the standard of form as well as of faith, the Puritans and their descendants constituted their ecclesiastic form after the pattern set them in the Bible. The fruits of their faith and polity everywhere abound.

"The principles of their religious system have given birth and vigor to the republican habits and republican virtue and intelligence of the sons of New England." The Congregational churches were not only schools of Christian faith, but of freedom, in which the ministers were the teachers and the people the pupils, and whence came the men and women to fight and pray for freedom and the battles of the Revolution. During the Revolution there were in New England five hundred and seventy-five ministers and seven hundred Congregational churches, almost all of which were in active sympathy with the cause of liberty. In every possible way they gave manifold proofs of their patriotism. It is no violence to truth to affirm that without the devotion and earnest activity of these churches the Revolution never could have been effected. Their faith and form of church-government were in harmony with the reigning spirit of liberty, and energized all the efforts of patriots with piety and ardor, and infused into that great conflict those Christian ideas and principles which impart a divine dignity and grandeur to a people struggling to be free.

Jefferson's Idea of a Republican Form of Government Suggested by the Congressional Form of Government

The Congregational form of church-government suggested to the philosophic mind of Mr. Jefferson our present republican form of government. Near his residence, in Virginia, several years previous to the Revolution, there existed a Baptist church on a congregational basis of government, whose monthly meetings Jefferson often attended. Being asked how he was pleased with their church-government, he replied that it struck him with great force, and interested him very much; that he considered it the only form of pure democracy that then existed in the world, and had concluded that it would be the best plan of government for the American colonies.

If Jefferson confessed himself indebted to the business meetings of a church in his neighborhood, substantially Congregational in government, for his best ideas of a democracy, much more were John Adams and his New England compatriots beholden to their ecclesiastical surroundings for the republican tendencies of their politics.

The churches of New England had been for a century and a half educating their people, in their Christian and political democracies, to love liberty, so that when the trial of their faith came at the Revolution, they were ready to enter with soul and energy into the great conflict, and to carry it to a happy consummation.

Boston Port Closed

The act of the British Parliament, closing the port of Boston, the news of which reached the city on the 9th of May, 1774, was the tocsin of liberty to New England, and acted as a cord of sympathy that bound all the colonies more closely together. Three days after the news—on the 12th of May, 1774—a large number of the patriots of the Commonwealth of Massachusetts assembled to consider the crisis. "The lowly men who now met," says Bancroft, "were most of them accustomed to feed their own cattle, to fold their own sheep, to guide their own ploughs; all trained to public life in the little democracies of their towns some of them captains in the militia, and officers of the church according to the discipline of Congregationalists; nearly all of them communicants under a public covenant with God."

Correspondence of Congregational Associations

The Boston port bill became the telegraphic medium of liberty and of universal sympathy between the Congregational churches of New England and patriots throughout the colonies. The following paper will not only disclose this fact, but will show how sensitive and ready the churches were to respond to the calls of patriotism and humanity. It is but a specimen of the piety and patriotism of the New England churches.

LETTER FROM THE GENERAL ASSOCIATION OF
CONGREGATIONAL MINISTERS IN CONNECTICUT TO THE
CLERGYMEN IN BOSTON.

MANSFIELD, June 22, 1774

Reverend and Dear Sirs—

We, your brethren of the Colony of *Connecticut*, met by
delegation from the several counties in General Association
at our annual meeting, cannot but feel deeply impressed with
the present melancholy threatened situation of *America* in
general, and the distressed state of the town of *Boston* in particular, suffering the severe resentment of the British Parliament, by which the subsistence of thousands is taken away.
We readily embrace this opportunity to manifest our hearty
sympathy with you in your present distresses. We consider
that you are suffering in the common cause of *America*—the
cause of liberty; which, if taken away, we fear would involve
the ruin of religious liberty also. Gladly would we contribute
every thing in our power for your encouragement and relief:
however, our situation enables us to do little more than to express our sincere and affectionate concern, and with fervent
addresses to commend your cause, and the cause of *America*,
the cause of liberty, and, above all, the cause of religion, to the
Father of Mercies, who can easily afford effectual relief—who
has the hearts of all at his disposal, and can turn them as he
pleases. We feel deeply sensible what a heavy load must lie
upon the minds of the ministers of *Boston*—enough to sink
their spirits, unless armed with vigorous Christian fortitude
and resolution. In hopes it may afford you some consolation,
we assure you of our sincere condolence and unremitting
prayers in your behalf, and that we shall, in every way suitable to our character and station, use our influence with the
good people of this colony to concur in every proper measure
calculated to afford relief to America in general, and to the
distressed town of Boston in particular.

We pray that the ministers of the gospel may be inspired
by the great Head of the Church with wisdom sufficient for
direction in such a critical day as the present, and that *God*

would give them and their people firmness, unanimity, patience, prudence, and every virtue which they need to support them under their heavy trials, and enable them to stand firm in the glorious cause of liberty and express such a temper and exhibit such an example as shall be well pleasing to God and recommend them to the favor and compassion of their fellow-men. We earnestly pray that *God* would humble us all under a deep sense of our numerous transgressions and criminal declensions, show us the absolute necessity of repentance and reformation, humble us under his mighty hand, and pour out a spirit of fervent supplication upon you, on us, and all his people in this land; and we cannot but hope the united prayers of America may obtain that audience in heaven which will bring salvation to us.

Signed by order of the General Association.

Benjamin Throop, *Moderator*.

To the Reverend CHARLES CHAUNCY, D.D., and the other ministers of the town of Boston.

The answer was prepared, but not sent, through the confusion of the times, and is as follows—

Boston, 1774

REVEREND AND DEAR BRETHREN—

Your very affectionate and obliging letter of June 22, 1774, was communicated to us at a time when we greatly needed the encouragement of our Christian friends.

You justly suppose that when Boston is treated with such unprecedented cruelty, and involved in the deepest distress, a heavy load must be upon the ministers of religion in that unhappy town. We have consoled ourselves with the thought that we are suffering in the common cause of *America*—in the cause of civil liberty, with which religious liberty hath a very close connection. All circumstances seem to make it evident that we are not mistaken in this view of things. It gives us the highest satisfaction to find that the sentiments of others are conformable to our own; especially to know that this is the opinion of so wise and venerable a body as the General Association of *Connecticut*.

We sincerely thank you for your tender sympathy with us under our sufferings, and the very kind and obliging manner in which you express it.

We present our particular acknowledgments for the great consolation you afford in the assurance you give us of your sincere condolence and unremitting prayers in our behalf, and that you will, in every way suitable to your character and station, use your influence with the good people of your colony to concur in every proper measure calculated to afford relief to America in general, and to the distressed town of Boston in particular. We trust *God* hath heard your prayers and the prayers of other friends to religion and to America, and by his all powerful influence hath supported our brethren in this town under their heavy trials, enabled them to stand firm in the glorious cause of liberty, and hath given some degree of that firmness, unanimity, patience, and prudence which you so fervently implore for them in this critical day.

We owe much to our brethren in other colonies for the very generous assistance we have received. Such were the difficulties to which great numbers were reduced by the almost total stagnation of our trade, that it must have been impossible for this town to have subsisted to this day, if the inhabitants had not been favored with such kind and generous relief from abroad.

The colony of *Connecticut* distinguished themselves, not only by the largeness of their donations, but by the seasonableness of their supplies, which were received and applied for the purpose of supporting those who were suffering by means of the cruel bill that shut up our port, while the other colonies, by reason of their distance, were not able to afford such immediate relief.

We think ourselves obliged on this occasion to testify that your charities have been most faithfully applied to the purpose for which they were sent. The gentlemen who have undertaken this trust are of the first character for probity and universal goodness. They generously employ a very great part of their time in this benevolent work, without the prospect of any reward but what ariseth from the pleasure of doing good, and of the approbation of their great Master and Lord.

While we think we have a right to complain to Heaven and earth of the cruel oppression we are under, we ascribe righteousness to *God*. We deserve every thing from him, and he punishes us less than our iniquities deserve. We earnestly entreat the continuance of your addresses to Him who heareth prayer, that he would humble, pardon, and bless us.

Our own distresses by no means employ all our attention. We are more deeply affected with the general danger of our country than with our own difficulties. We encourage ourselves in that glorious Being who hath ever been the hope of his *Israel* and the Saviour thereof in time of trouble, and who hath so often and so wonderfully appeared for this people. We are sinful and degenerate, but we trust there are many who have not forsaken *God*, and for whose sake be will not forsake us. If there had been ten righteous found in *Sodom*, the city had not been destroyed. And will not *God* have regard to the many thousands in this land, who walk uprightly before him, and who continually implore his favor to their distressed country?

The surprising union of the colonies at this day affords the strongest grounds of encouragement; and their spirited measures cannot, according to a human view of things, fail of success sooner or later. We are sensible, at the same time, that all depends on Him who is the great Governor of the world. It is an inexhaustible source of comfort that the *Lord God* Omnipotent reigneth. To him we refer all, in full confidence that he will do all things well. We devoutly wish you the presence of the great Head of the Church in all your labors for the honor of God and the good of men, and are,

With the sincerest gratitude and respect, your brethren, &c.,

Signed   Andrew Elliot.

Offerings of Churches

The churches and congregations made the most liberal offerings and contributions to the cause of liberty. The "Connecticut Gazette," of January, 1778, published in New London, says, in reference to the churches—

"On the last Sabbath of December, 1777, a contribution was taken up in the several parishes of Norwich for the benefit of the officers and soldiers who belonged to said town, when they collected 386 pairs of stockings, 227 pairs of shoes, 118 shirts, 78 jackets, 48 pairs of overalls, 208 pairs of mittens, 11 buff caps, 15 pairs of breeches, 9 coats, 22 rifle frocks, 19 handkerchiefs, and £258 17*s*. 8*d*. (about $1295), which was forwarded to the army. Also collect-ed a quantity of pork, cheese, wheat, rye, Indian corn, sugar, rice, flax, wood, &c. &c., to be distributed to the needy families of the officers and soldiers. The whole amounted to the sum of £1400, or about $7000."

The key to the patriotism, offerings, and sacrifices of the New England churches and people is found in such sentiments as the following, uttered in Massachusetts, January, 1773—

"Death," said they, "is more eligible than slavery. A freeborn people are not required by the religion of Jesus Christ to submit to tyranny, but to make use of such power as God has given them to recover and support their laws and liberties. We implore the Ruler above the skies that he would make bare his arm in defence of his Church and people, and let Israel go."

Ode Sung in the New England Churches

The following ode, entitled "The American Hero," was written by Nathaniel Niles, of Norwich, Connecticut, on hearing of the battle of Bunker Hill and the burning of Charlestown. It first appeared in the "Connecticut Gazette and Universal Intelligencer," February 2, 1776. The words were set to music by Rev. Mr. Ripley, father of General Ripley, who preached patriotism in his pulpit, composed music for the heroic odes of the Revolution, and furnished sons to lead the armies of the Revolution to the field of battle. This ode "was almost universally sung in the churches and religious assemblies of the Eastern and Northern States, and became the war-song of the New England soldiery:"—

THE AMERICAN HERO

A SAPPHIC ODE

Why should vain mortals tremble at the sight of
Death and Destruction in the field of battle,
Where blood and carnage clothe the ground in crimson,
          Sounding with death-groans?

Death will invade us by the means appointed,
And we must all bow to the king of terrors;
Nor am I anxious, if I am prepared,
                    What shape he comes in.

Infinite Goodness teaches us submission,
Bids us be quiet under all his dealings,
Never repining, but forever praising
                    God our Creator.

Well may we praise him; all his ways are perfect;
Though a resplendence infinitely glowing
Dazzles in glory on the sight of mortals,
                    Struck blind by lustre!

Good is Jehovah in bestowing sunshine;
Nor less his goodness in the storm and thunder:
Mercies and judgment both proceed from kindness—
                    Infinite kindness!

Oh, then, exult, that God forever reigneth!
Clouds which, around him, hinder our perception,
Bind us the stronger to exalt his name, and
                    Shout louder praises!

Then to the wisdom of my Lord and Master
I will commit all that I have or wish for;
Sweetly as babes sleep will I give my life up
                    When call'd to yield it.

Now, *Mars*, I dare thee, clad in smoky pillars,
Bursting from bomb-shells, roaring from the cannon,
Rattling in grape-shot, like a storm of hail-stones,
                    Torturing Æther!

Up the bleak heavens let the spreading flames rise,
Breaking like Ætna through the smoky columns,

Lowering like Egypt o'er the falling city
                Wantonly burnt down.

While all their hearts quick palpitate for havoc,
Let slip your blood-hounds, named the British lions:
Dauntless as death stares, nimble as the whirlwind,
                Dreadful as demons!

Let oceans waft on all your floating castles,
Fraught with destruction, horrible to nature,
Then, with your sails fill'd by a storm of vengeance,
                Bear down to battle!

From the dire caverns made by ghostly miners,
Let the explosion, dreadful as volcanoes,
Heave the broad town, with all its wealth and people
                Quick to destruction!

Still shall the banner of the King of Heaven
Never advance where I'm afraid to follow:
While that precedes me, with an open bosom,
                War, I defy thee!

Fame and dear freedom lure me on to battle,
While a fell despot, grimmer than a death's head,
Stings me with serpents, fiercer than Medusa's,
                To the encounter.

Life for my country and the cause of freedom
Is but a trifle for a worm to part with;
And, if preserved in so great a contest,
                Life is redoubled.

Norwich, Conn., Oct. 1775.

Address of Ministers in New Haven to Washington

The following correspondence between President Washington and the Congregational ministers of New Haven and vicinity affords a fine illustration of the patriotism and piety of New England. At the time it transpired, Washington was on a tour of inspection through New England, to see for himself the fruits of that freedom which he and the people had so nobly won by the Revolution. The originals of the letters are preserved in the archives of Yale College—

To the President of the United States.

Sir—

The Congregational ministers of the city of New Haven beg leave to make their most respectful address to the President of the United States. We presume that we join with the whole collective body of the Congregational pastors and Presbyterian ministers throughout these States, in the most heartfelt joy and the most cordial congratulation, of themselves, of their country, and of mankind, on your elevation to the head of the combined American Republic. As ministers of the blessed Jesus, the Prince of Peace, we rejoice and have inexpressible pleasure in the demonstrations you have given of your sincere assertion toward that holy religion which is the glory of Christian States, and will become the glory of the world itself, as that happy period when liberty, public right, and the veneration of the Most High, who presides in the universe with a most holy and benevolent sovereignty, shall triumph among all the nations, kingdoms, empires, and republics on earth. We most sincerely rejoice in the kind and gracious providence of Almighty God, who hath been pleased to preserve your life during your late dangerous sickness, and to restore you to such a degree of health as gives us this opportunity to express our joy, and affords us the most pleasing hopes that your health may be firmly established. We pray the Lord of Hosts, by whose counsels and wisdom you have been carried triumphantly and gloriously through the late war, terminating in the establishment of American liberty, and perhaps in the liberty of all nations, that he would be pleased ever to have you under his holy protection, continue to render you a blessing to Church and State, support you under your arduous cares, and perpetuate that estimation and honor which you have justly acquired of your country. And may the new and rising republic become, under your auspices, the most glorious for population, perfection of policy, and happy administration of government, that ever appeared on earth; and may you, sir, having finished a course of distinguished usefulness, receive the rewards of public virtue in the kingdom of eternal glory.

(Signed)	Ezra Stiles,
	James Dana,
	Jonathan Edwards,
	Samuel Wales,
	Samuel Austin, Jr.

CITY OF NEW HAVEN, Oct. 17, 1789.

To the Congregational Ministers of the City of New Haven.
Gentlemen—

The kind congratulations contained in your address claim and receive my grateful and affectionate thanks. Respecting, as I do, the favorable opinions of men distinguished for science and piety, it would be false delicacy to disavow the satisfaction which I derive from their approbation of my public services and private conduct.

Regarding that deportment which consists with true religion as the best security of temporal peace and the surest means of attaining eternal felicity, it will be my earnest endeavor (as far as human frailty can resolve) to inculcate the belief and practice of opinions which lead to the consummation of those desirable objects.

The tender interest which you have taken in my personal happiness, and the obliging manner in which you express yourselves on the restoration of my health, are so forcibly impressed on my mind as to render language inadequate to the utterance of my feelings.

If it shall please the Great Disposer of events to listen to the pious supplication which you have preferred in my behalf, I trust that the remainder of my days will evince the gratitude of a heart devoted to the advancement of those objects which receive the approbation of Heaven and promote the happiness of our fellow-men.

My best prayers are offered to the Throne of Grace for your happiness and that of the congregations committed to your care.

(Signed)   G°. Washington.

City of New Haven, Oct. 17, 1789.

ADDRESS OF THE CONGREGATIONAL CHURCH AND SOCIETY AT MEDWAY (FORMERLY ST. JOHN'S PARISH), STATE OF GEORGIA.

To the President of the United States.

Sir—

We feel ourselves happy in the opportunity of expressing our attachment to your person, and our peculiar pleasure in your election, by the unanimous voice of your country, to the Presidency of the United States.

Though situated in the extreme part of the Union, we have gratefully to acknowledge that we already experience the propitious influence of your wise and parental administration. To the troops stationed on our frontiers by your order, and to the treaty lately concluded with the Creek nation under your auspices, we are indebted, under Providence, for our perfect tranquillity. The hatchet is now buried, and we smoke with our Indian neighbors the calumet of peace. This, while it affords us a happy presage of our future protection, gives us, at the same time, a recent proof how justly you have secured, in your civil as well as military capacity, the glorious title of Father of your country. With the laurel, then, be pleased to accept the civic wreath from a grateful people.

We can readily conceive how arduous must be the duties, how weighty and complicated the cares, of office in the government of so extensive a republic as that over which you preside. Impressed with a deep sense of this, we will not fail to implore the Divine blessing in your behalf. May you continue to be directed by that wisdom from above which is necessary to the successful discharge of the duties of your high and responsible position! and may you be preserved the favored instrument of Heaven to secure to a free people those invaluable rights which you so eminently contributed to rescue from the hand of oppression!

Distant as our situation is from the seat of government, permit us to assure you that our influence, however inconsiderable in the national scale, shall not be wanting in encouraging submission to the laws of the United States, and thus, under God, perpetuating the blessings of our efficient Federal Government, now so happily established.

James Maxwell,
Danl. Stewart,
Abiel Holmes,
Henry Wood,
Jno. P. Mann.

Committee of the Church and Society.
MEDWAY, LIBERTY COUNTY, May 12, 1791

His Reply

GENTLEMEN—

I learn with gratitude proportioned to the occasion your attachment to my person, and the pleasure you express on my election to the Presidency of the United States.

Your sentiments on the happy influence of our equal government impress me with the most sensible satisfaction. They vindicate the great interests of humanity, they reflect on the liberal minds that entertain them, and they promise the continuance and improvement of that tranquillity which is essential to the welfare of nations and the happiness of men.

You overrate my best exertions when you ascribe to them the blessings which our country so eminently enjoys. From the gallantry and fortitude of her citizens, under the auspices of Heaven, America has derived her independence. To their industry and the natural advantages of the country she is indebted for her prosperous situation. From their virtue she may expect long to share the protection of a free and equal government, which their wisdom has established and which experience justifies as admirably adapted to our social wants and individual felicity.

Continue, my fellow-citizens, to cultivate the peace and harmony which now subsist between you and your Indian neighbors: the happy consequence is immediate; the reflection which arises in justice and benevolence will be lastingly grateful. A knowledge of your happiness will lighten the cares of my station, and be among the most pleasing of their rewards.

G. Washington.

The Presbyterian Church

In the United States has a noble history in the annals of civil and religious liberty. Its American origin began in 1703. Its form of Church-government is that of a representative republican government. Each church has its representatives, clerical and lay, in all its ecclesiastical courts, and the members are the source of all power, from the lowest to the highest judicatory. It resembles in its Church-government the civil government of the nation; and it is supposed that the framers of the Federal Constitution had before them the written manual of the Presbyterian Church and consulted and studied its ecclesiastical structure.

Its Early Action in the Revolution

The first General Assembly of the Presbyterian Church met in 1789, in Philadelphia, the same year, and the same month but one, in which the Constitution went into operation; and both forms of government had a contemporaneous origin. George Washington was President of the civil government, and Rev. John Rodgers, a distinguished patriot, and an intimate friend and adviser of Washington, was Moderator of the General Assembly of the Presbyterian

Church. At the close of the war, there were one hundred and forty ministers and three hundred Presbyterian churches in the United States. The history of that grand era of freedom bears ample testimony to the patriotism of the Presbyterian Church and the distinguished part which it took in the cause of liberty and in achieving the independence of the nation.

"The first public voice in America," says Bancroft, "for dissolving all connection with Great Britain, came not from the Puritans of New England, the Dutch of New York, nor from the planters of Virginia, but from the Scotch-Irish Presbyterians." The Convention of Mecklenburg county, North Carolina, met in Charlotteville, May, 1775, and was composed mainly of Presbyterian ministers, elders, and members. A committee was appointed to draft a declaration of independence for North Carolina, which was prepared and adopted on the 31st of May, 1775, more than a year before that declared by the united colonies. The two following were the main resolutions of that convention of Christian patriots—

> *Resolved*, That we do hereby declare ourselves a free and independent people—are, and of right ought to be, a sovereign and self-governing association, under the control of no power other than that of our God and the General Government of the Congress, to the maintenance of which independence we solemnly pledge to each other our mutual co-operation, our lives, our fortunes, and our most sacred honor.
>
> *Resolved*, That every member present of this delegation shall be a "committee-man, to preserve peace and union and harmony and to use exertions to spread the love of country and fire of freedom throughout America, until a more general organized government be established in this province."

"To these men," says Dr. Riddle, "we are indebted for the germs of our civil liberties and institutions. The spark of liberty, afterwards fanned to a flame in the halls of Congress, came first from these altars. In origin it was a sacred fire, more sacred than the vestal fires of old. It is now shining as the guiding light of bewildered nations in their perilous pathway to their predestinated privileges."

The Presbyterians of North Carolina were valiant and devoted in the cause of freedom. Descended from the Covenanters of Scotland and Ireland, they possessed in their fulness and purity the principles of their noble ancestors, "and planted deeply in the interior of that province the acorns of civil freedom, which had grown to unyielding oaks, strong and defiant, when the Revolution broke out." Those noble Christian men, "having first learned the lessons of freedom from the Bible, had its life and power freshened from the pure mountain air, and learned lessons of independence from the works and creatures of God around them."

In the route traversed by General Greene and his army when retreating from Cornwallis in 1778, "there were above twenty organized churches, with large congregations, and a great many preaching-places. All of these congregations, where the principles of gospel independence had been faithfully preached by McAden, Patillo, Caldwell, McCorkle, Hall, Craighead, Batch, McCaule, Alexander, and Richardson, were famous, during the struggle of the Revolution, for skirmishes, battles, prowess, individual courage, and heroic women. In no part of our republic was purer patriotism displayed than here."

The Presbytery of Hanover, in a memorial presented to the Legislature of Virginia, in 1776, subsequent to the adoption of the Declaration of Independence, expressed their patriotism as follows—

"Your memorialists are governed by the same sentiments which have inspired the United States of America, and are determined that nothing in our power or influence shall be wanting to give success to the common cause. We would also represent that dissenters from the Church of England, in this country, have ever been desirous to conduct themselves as peaceable members of the civil government, for which reason they have hitherto submitted to several ecclesiastical burdens and restrictions that are inconsistent with equal liberty. But now, when the many and grievous oppressions of the mother-country, have laid this continent under the necessity of casting off the yoke of tyranny and of forming independent governments upon equitable and liberal foundations, we flatter ourselves we shall be freed from all the encumbrances which a spirit of domination, prejudice, or bigotry hath interwoven with our political systems. This we are the more strongly encouraged to expect by the Declaration of

Rights, so universally applauded for the dignity, firmness and precision with which it delineates and asserts the privileges of society and the prerogatives of human nature, and which we embrace as the magna charta of our commonwealth, that cannot be violated without endangering the grand superstructure it was destined to sustain."

Pastoral Letter of the Synod of New York and Philadelphia in 1775

The following pastoral letter from the Synod of New York and Philadelphia to the congregations under their care, read in every pulpit on the 20th of July, 1776, being the day appointed by the Honorable Congress for a general fast, presents the patriotism of the American Presbyterian Church in a noble attitude—

Very Dear Brethren—

The Synod of *New York* and *Philadelphia*, being met at a time when publick affairs wear a threatening aspect, and when (unless God in his sovereign providence speedily prevent it) all the horrours of a civil war throughout this great continent are to be apprehended, were of opinion that they could not discharge their duty to the numerous congregations under their care without addressing them at this important crisis.

As the firm belief and habitual recollection of the power and presence of the living *God* ought at all times to possess the minds of real Christians, so in seasons of public calamity, when the *Lord* is known by the judgements which he executeth, it would be an ignorance or an indifference highly criminal, not to look up to him with reverence, to implore his mercy by humble and fervent prayer and, if possible, to prevent his vengeance by unfeigned repentance.

We do, therefore, brethren, beseech you, in the most earnest manner, to look beyond the immediate authors either of your sufferings or fears, and to acknowledge the holiness and justice of the *Almighty* in the present visitation. He is righteous in all his ways, and holy in all his works. Affliction springeth not out of the dust. He doth not afflict willingly, nor grieve the children of men; and therefore it becometh every person, family, city, and province, to humble themselves before his throne, to confess their sins, by which they have provoked his indignation, and entreat him to pour out upon all ranks a spirit of repentance and prayer. Fly, also, for forgiveness to the atoning blood of the great Redeemer—the blood of sprinkling which speaketh better things than that of *Abel*. Remember and confess not only your sins in general, but those prevalent national offences which may justly be considered as the procuring causes of publick judgements, particularly profaneness and contempt of *God*, his name, sanctuary, sabbath—pride, luxury, uncleanness, and neglect of family religion and government, with the deplorable ignorance and security which certainly ought to be imputed to this as their principal cause. All these are among us highly aggravated by the inestimable privileges which we have hitherto enjoyed, without interruption, since the first settlement of this country. If in the present day of distress we expect that *God* will hear our supplications and interpose for our protection and deliverance, let us remember what he himself requires of us is, that our prayers should be attended with a sincere purpose and thorough endeavour after personal and family reformation. "If thou prepare thine heart, and stretch out thine hand towards him: if iniquity be in thy hand, put it far away, and let not wickedness dwell in thy tabernacles." Job xi. 13, 14.

The Synod cannot help thinking that this is a proper time for pressing all, of every rank, seriously to consider the things that belong to their eternal peace. Hostilities, long feared, have now taken place; the sword has been drawn in one province, and the whole continent, with hardly any exception, seem determined to defend their rights by force of arms. If, at the same time, the *British* ministry shall continue to enforce their claims by violence, a lasting and bloody contest must be expected. Surely, then, it becomes those who have taken up arms, and profess a willingness to hazard their lives in the cause of liberty, to be prepared for death, which to many must be the certain, and to every one is a possible or probable, event.

We have long seen with concern the circumstances which occasioned, and the gradual increase of, this unhappy difference. As ministers of the gospel of peace, we have ardently wished that it could, and often hoped that it would, have been more easily accommodated. It is well known to you (otherwise it would be imprudent, indeed, thus publickly to profess) that we have not been instrumental in inflaming the minds of the people or urging them to acts of violence and disorder. Perhaps no instance can be given on so interesting a subject, in which political sentiments have been so long and so fully kept from the pulpit; and even malice itself has not charged us with laboring from the press. But things are now come to such a state that we do not wish to conceal our opinions as men and citizens; so the relation we stand to you seemed to make the special improvement of it to your spiritual improvement an indispensable duty. Suffer us, then, to lay hold of your present temper of mind, and to exhort especially the young and vigorous, by assuring them *that there is no soldier so undaunted as the pious man, no army so formidable as those who are superior to the fear of death.* There is nothing more awful to think of than that those whose trade is war should be despisers of the name of the Lord of Hosts, and that they should expose themselves to the imminent danger of being immediately sent from cursing and cruelty on earth to the blaspheming rage and despairing horrour of the infernal pit. Let, therefore, every one who, from a generosity of spirit or benevolence of heart, offers himself as a champion in his country's cause, be persuaded to reverence the name and walk in the fear of the Prince of the kings of the earth; and then he may with the most unshaken firmness expect the issue either in victory or death.

Let it not be forgotten that though, for the wise ends of his providence, it may please *God* for a season to suffer his people to lie under unmerited oppression, yet, in general, we may expect that those who fear and serve him in sincerity and truth will be favored with his countenance and strength. It is both the character and the privilege of the children of

God that they call upon him in the day of trouble, and He, who keepeth covenant and truth forever, has said that his ears are always open to their cry. We need not mention to you in how many instances the event of battles, and success in war, have turned upon circumstances which were inconsiderable in themselves, as well as out of the power of human prudence to foresee or direct; because we suppose you firmly believe that, after all the counsels of men, and the most probable and promising means, the Lord will do that which seemeth him good. Nor hath his promise ever failed of its full accomplishment. "The Lord is with you while ye be with him; and if ye seek him, he will be found of you; but if ye forsake him, he will forsake you." 2 Chron. xv. 2.

After this exhortation, which we thought ourselves called upon to give you at this time, on your great interest—the one thing needful—we shall take the liberty to offer a few advices to the societies under our charge, as to their publick and general conduct. And, first, in carrying on this important struggle, let every opportunity be taken to express your attachment and respect to our Sovereign King George, and the Revolution principles by which his August family was seated on the *British* throne. We recommend, indeed, not only allegiance to him from duty and principle, as the first magistrate of the empire, but esteem and reverence for the person of the prince, who has merited well of his subjects on many accounts, and who has probably been misled into the late and present measures by those about him. Neither have we any doubt that they themselves have been in a great degree deceived by false information from interested persons residing in *America*. It gives us the greatest pleasure to say, from our own certain knowledge of all belonging to *our communion,* and from the best means of information of the *far greatest part of all denominations* in this country, that the present opposition to the measures of the Administration does not in the least arise from disaffection to the king, or a desire of separation from the parent State. We are happy in being able with truth to affirm that no part of *America* would either have approved or permitted such insults as have been offered to the sovereign of *Great Britain*. We exhort you, therefore, to continue in the same disposition, and not to suffer oppression or injury itself easily to provoke you to any thing which may seem to betray contrary sentiments. Let it ever appear that you only desire the preservation and security of those rights which belong to you as freemen and *Britons*, and that reconciliation upon these terms is your most ardent desire.

Secondly, Be careful to maintain the union which at present subsists through the colonies. Nothing can be more manifest than that the success of every measure depends on its being inviolably preserved; and therefore we hope that you will leave nothing undone that will promote that end. In particular, as the Continental Congress, now sitting in *Philadelphia*, consists of delegates, chosen in the most free and unbiased manner by the body of the people, let them not only be treated with respect, but encouraged in their difficult service; let not only your prayers be offered up to *God* for his direction in their proceedings, but adhere firmly to their resolutions, and let it be seen that they are able to bring out the whole strength of this vast country to carry them into execution. We would also advise, for the same purpose, that a spirit of candour, charity, and mutual esteem be preserved and promoted towards those of different religious denominations. Persons of probity and principle of every profession should he united together as servants of the same Master; and the experience of our happy concord hitherto in a state of liberty should engage all to unite together in support of the common interest; for there is no example in history in which civil liberty was destroyed, and the rights of conscience preserved entire.

Thirdly, We do earnestly exhort and beseech the societies under our care to be strict and vigilant in their private government, and to watch over the morals of their several members. It is with the utmost pleasure we remind you that the last Continental Congress determined to discourage luxury in living, public diversions, and gaming of all kinds, which have so fatal an influence on the morals of the people. If it is undeniable that unusual profligacy makes a nation ripe for divine judgments and is the national means of bringing them to ruin, reformation of manners is of the utmost necessity in our present distress. At the same time, as it has been observed by many eminent writers that the censorial power, which had for its object the manners of the publick in the ancient free states, was absolutely necessary to their continuance, we cannot help being of opinion that the only thing which we have now to supply the place of this is the religious discipline of the several sects with respect to their own members; so that the denomination or profession which shall take the most effectual care of the instruction of its members, and maintain its discipline in its fullest vigour, will do the most essential service to the whole body. For the very same reason, the greatest service which magistrates or persons in authority can do with respect to the religion or morals of the people, is to defend and secure the rights of conscience in the most equal and impartial manner.

Fourthly, We cannot but recommend, and urge in the warmest manner, a regard to order and public peace; and as, in many cases, during the confusions that prevail, legal proceedings have become difficult, it is hoped that all persons will conscientiously pay their just debts, and to the utmost of their power serve one another, so that the evils inseparable from a civil war may not be augmented by wantonness and irregularity.

Fifthly, We think it of importance at this time to recommend to all of every rank, but especially to those who may be called to action, a spirit of humanity and mercy. "Every battle of the warrior is with confused noise, and garments rolled in blood." It is impossible to appeal to the sword without being exposed to many scenes of cruelty, and slaughter; but it is often observed that civil wars are carried on with a rancour and spirit of revenge much greater than those between independent states. The injuries received or supposed in civil wars wound more deeply than those of foreign enemies; it is therefore the more necessary to guard against this abuse, and recommend that meekness and gentleness of spirit which is the noblest attendant of true valor. That man will fight most bravely who never fights until it is necessary, and who ceases to fight when the necessity is over.

Lastly, We would recommend to all the societies under our care, not to content themselves with attending devoutly on general fasts, but to continue habitually in the exercise of prayer, and to have frequent occasional voluntary meetings for solemn intercession with *God* on the important trial. Those who are immediately exposed to danger need your sympathy: and we learn from the Scriptures that fervency and importunity are the very characteristics of that prayer of the righteous man which availeth much.

We conclude with our most earnest prayer that the *God* of heaven may bless you in your temporal and spiritual concerns, and that the present unnatural dispute may be speedily terminated by an equitable and lasting settlement on constitutional principles.

Signed in the name, presence, and by appointment of the Synod.

Benjamin Hait, *Moderator.*

New York, May 12, 1775

Pastoral Letter in 1783

After peace was concluded, the Synod of New York and Philadelphia addressed a pastoral letter to the people under their charge, as follows—

Very Dear Brethren—

You will remember that in May, 1775, the Synod thought proper to address a pastoral letter to the people under their inspection, on the state of public affairs. At that interesting period, hostilities had just commenced between Great Britain and America, and a long and bloody conflict was to be expected. Now that conflict is over, and we have the best reason to suppose (the preliminaries being signed and ratified) that a happy and honorable peace will be speedily settled by a definite treaty. We could not, therefore, longer delay addressing to you the following letter, which will contain our sentiments on this happy occasion, and our advice as to the duty incumbent upon all ranks in return for so great a mercy.

We cannot help congratulating you on the general and almost universal attachment of the Presbyterian body to the cause of liberty and the rights of mankind. This has been visible in their conduct, and has been confessed by the complaints and resentments of the common enemy. Such a circumstance ought not only to afford us satisfaction in the review, as bringing credit to the body in general, but to increase our gratitude to God for the happy issue of the war. Had it been unsuccessful, we must have drank deeply of the cup of suffering. Our burnt and wasted churches and our plundered dwellings, in such places as fell under the power of our adversaries, are but an earnest of what we must have suffered had they finally prevailed.

The Synod, therefore, request you to render thanks to Almighty God for all his mercies, temporal and spiritual, and, in a particular manner, for establishing the independence of the United States of America. He is the Supreme disposer of all events, and to him belong the glory, the victory, and the majesty. We are persuaded you will easily recollect many circumstances in the course of the struggle which point out his special and signal interposition in our favor. Our most remarkable successes have generally been when things had just before worn the most unfavorable aspect; as at Trenton and Saratoga at the beginning, in South Carolina and Virginia toward the end, of the war. It pleased God to raise up for us a powerful ally in Europe; and when we consider the unwearied attempts of our enemies to raise dissensions by every topic that could be supposed inflammatory and popular, the harmony that has prevailed, not only between the allied powers, but the troops of different nations and languages, acting together, ought to be ascribed to the gracious influence of Divine Providence. Without mentioning many other instances, we only further put you in mind of the choice of the commander-in-chief of the armies of the United States, who is alike acceptable to the citizen and soldier, to the State in which he was born, and to every other on the continent; whose character and influence, after so long a service, are not only unimpaired, but augmented. Of what consequence this has been to the cause of America, every one may judge; or, if it needs any illustration, it receives it from the opposite situation of our enemies in this respect. On the whole, every pious person, on a review of the events of the war, will certainly be disposed to say, with the Psalmist, "The Lord hath done great things for us, whereof we are glad."

Suffer us to put you in mind of the duty you owe to God in return for this great national deliverance. You ought to testify your gratitude by living in his fear. This is the only way by which public prosperity can become a real mercy to you. It were to be wished, indeed, that, in our contests about the most important interests of a temporal nature, we could still remember not only that eternity is of greater moment than any thing that relates merely to the present life, but that all outward things, even civil liberty, ought to be considered as subordinate and subservient to everlasting happiness. It would not be an honor to us to be wholly unconcerned about the rights of ourselves and others, as men and as citizens; yet the great part of our duty, and we hope of our desires, is to watch for your souls as those that must give an account to God. We therefore earnestly besecch every one who is nominally of our communion, not to be satisfied with the form of godliness, denying the power thereof. The substance of religion is the same to all denominations; neither is there any preference due to one before another but in so far as it has superior advantages in leading men to the saving knowledge of the only living and true God, and Jesus Christ, whom he hath sent, whom "to know is life eternal."

There is no doubt that you look upon it as a happy circumstance in the late Revolution, that the rights of conscience are inalienably secured, and even interwoven with the very constitutions of the several States. The duty which you owe to the community at large for this inestimable blessing is to support civil authority, by being subject not only "for wrath, but also for conscience' sake," and by living "quiet and peaceable lives in all godliness and honesty." It is a truth of much moment, and particularly to be remembered at this time, not only that the virtue of the people in general is of more consequence to the stability of republics, or free states, than those of a different kind. In monarchies, a sense of honor, the subordination of rank in society, and the rigor of despotic authority, supply in some measure the place of virtue, in producing public order; but in free states, where the power is ultimately lodged in the body of the people, if there is a general corruption of the mass, the government itself must speedily be dissolved.

You cannot but have observed that the war has occasioned great irregularity and relaxation as to the observance of the Sabbath and attendance on public ordinances. In some places congregations are broken up; in some places, for a considerable time, attendance was difficult, dangerous, or impossible. The public service, also, which made some things really necessary, was often made a pretence for irregularity when no necessity existed. It is, therefore, your duty, now that peace and harmony have returned, to revive and restore the respect due to the Sabbath and the worship of God's sanctuary. The regular administration of divine ordinances is a blessing that cannot be too highly valued or purchased at too great a price. We hope, therefore, that you will in general exert yourselves and do every thing in your power that will serve to promote so noble a purpose.

Be cheerful and liberal in assisting to educate pious youth for the ministry. Let vacant congregations be active and diligent to supply themselves with fixed pastors, and let those who have fixed pastors strengthen their hands in their Master's work, not only by obedience in the Lord, but by making such provision for their comfortable subsistence as that their duty may be practicable. We make this demand clearly and explicitly, because it is founded upon the plainest reason—upon the word of God—upon general or common utility, and your own interest—and make no doubt that wherever there is true religion it will be heard and complied with.

We look upon it as a very happy circumstance in the political revolution that has happened in America, that neither in its rise nor progress was it intermixed with or directed by religious controversy. No denomination of Christians among us have any reason to fear oppression or restraint, or any power to oppress others. We therefore recommend charity, forbearance, and mutual service. Let the great and only strife be, who shall love the Redeemer most, and who shall serve him with the greatest zeal. We recommend the strict exercise of discipline to the societies under our care. Let us not seek to increase our numbers by relaxation, but to justify the excellence of our principles by the inoffensive example and holy conversation of those who embrace them. The ultimate trial of religious truth is by its moral influence: therefore, as he is undoubtedly the best husbandman who raises the richest crops, so those are the best principles which make the best men. This is the great rule laid down by our Saviour—"By their fruits ye shall know them." By order.

Philadelphia, May, 1783 John McCrery, *Moderator.*

ADDRESS OF THE GENERAL ASSEMBLY OF THE PRESBYTERIAN CHURCH IN THE UNITED STATES.

To the President of the United States.

Sir—

The General Assembly of the Presbyterian Church in the United States of America embrace the earliest opportunity in their power to testify the lively and unfeigned pleasure which they, with the rest of their fellow-citizens, felt on your appointment to the first office in the nation.

We adore Almighty God, the author of every perfect gift, who hath endued you with such a rare and happy assemblage of talents as hath rendered you equally necessary to your country in war and in peace. Your military achievements insured safety and glory to America in the late arduous conflict for freedom, whilst your disinterested conduct and uniformly just discernment of the public interests gained you the entire confidence of the people; and, in the present interesting period of public affairs, the influence of your personal character moderates the divisions of political parties and promises a permanent establishment of the civil government. From a retirement more glorious to you than thrones and sceptres, you have been called to your present elevated station by the voice of a great and free people, and with an unanimity of suffrages that has few, if any, examples in history. A man more ambitious of fame, or less devoted to his country, would have refused an office in which his honors could not be augmented and where they might possibly be subject to a reverse.

We are happy that God hath inclined your heart to give yourself once more to the public; and we derive a favorable presage of the event from the zeal of all classes of the people and their confidence in your virtues, as well as from the knowledge and dignity with which the sacred councils are filled. But we derive a presage even more flattering from the piety of your character. Public virtue is the most certain mean of public felicity, and religion is the surest basis of virtue. We therefore esteem it a peculiar happiness to behold in our Chief Magistrate a steady, uniform, avowed friend of the Christian religion, who has commenced his administration in rational and exalted sentiments of piety, and who in his private conduct adorns the doctrines of the gospel of Christ, and on the most public and solemn occasions devoutly acknowledges the government of Divine Providence.

The example of distinguished characters will ever possess a powerful and extensive influence on the public mind; and when we see in such a conspicuous station the amiable example of piety to God, of benevolence to men, and of a pure and virtuous patriotism, we naturally hope it will diffuse its influence, and that eventually the most happy consequences will result from it. To the force of imitation we will endeavor to add the wholesome instructions of religion. We shall consider ourselves as doing an acceptable service to God in our profession when we contribute to render men sober, honest, and industrious citizens, and the obedient subjects of a lawful government. In these pious labors we hope to imitate the most worthy of our brethren of other Christian denominations, and to be imitated by them, assured that, if we can, by mutual and generous emulation, promote truth and virtue, we shall render essential service to the republic, we shall receive encouragement from every wise and good citizen, and, above all, meet the approbation of our Divine Master.

We pray Almighty God to have you always in his holy keeping. May he prolong your valuable life an ornament and a blessing to your country, and at last bestow on you the glorious reward of a faithful servant.

By order of the General Assembly.

John Rogers, *Moderator.*

Philadelphia, May 26, 1789

His Reply

To the General Assembly of the Presbyterian Church in the United States.

GENTLEMEN—

I receive with great sensibility the testimonial given by the General Assembly of the Presbyterian Church in the United States of America of the lively and unfeigned pleasure experienced by them on my appointment to the first office of the nation.

Although it will be my endeavor to avoid being elated by the too favorable opinion which your kindness for me may have induced you to express of the importance of my former conduct and the effect of my future services, yet, conscious of the disinterestedness of my motives, it is not necessary for me to conceal the satisfaction I have felt upon finding that my compliance with the call of my country, and my dependence on the assistance of Heaven to support me in my arduous undertakings, have, so far as I can learn, met the universal approbation of my countrymen.

While I reiterate the professions of my dependence upon Heaven, as the source of all public and private blessings, I will observe that the general prevalence of piety, philanthropy, honesty, industry, and economy, seems, in the ordinary course of human affairs, particularly necessary for advancing and confirming the happiness of our country. While all men within our territories are protected in worshipping the Deity according to the dictates of their consciences, it is rational to be expected of them in return that they all will be emulous of evincing the sincerity of their professions by the innocence of their lives and the beneficence of their actions; for no man who is profligate in his morals, or a bad member of the civil commonwealth, can possibly be a true Christian or a credit to his own religious society.

I desire you to accept my acknowledgments for your laudable endeavors to render men sober, honest, and good citizens and the obedient subjects of a lawful government, as well as for your prayers to Almighty God for his blessing on our country and the humble instrument he has been pleased to make use of in the administration of its government.

G. Washington.

ADDRESS OF THE FIRST PRESBYTERY EASTWARD, IN MASSACHUSETTS AND NEW HAMPSHIRE.

To George Washington, President of the United States.

Sir—

We, the ministers and ruling elders delegated to represent the churches in Massachusetts and New Hampshire which compose the First Presbytery Eastward, now holding a stated session in this town, beg leave to approach your presence with genuine feelings of the deepest veneration and highest esteem.

In union with rejoicing millions, we felicitate our country and ourselves on your unanimous election to the highest office a nation can bestow, and on your acceptance of the trust with every evidence which a citizen can give of being actuated thereto by the purest principles of patriotism of piety, and of self-denial.

Great was the joy of our hearts to see the late tedious and destructive war at length terminated in a fair and honorable peace—to see the liberty and independence of our country happily secured—to see wise constitutions of civil government peaceably established in the several States—and especially to see a confederation of them all finally agreed on by the general voice.

But, amid all our joys, we ever contemplated with regret the want of efficiency in the Federal Government: we ardently wished for a form of NATIONAL UNION which should draw the cord of amity more closely around the several States—which should concentrate their interests, and reduce the freemen of America to *one* great body, ruled by *one* head and animated by *one soul.*

And now we devoutly offer our humble tribute of praise and thanksgiving to the *all-gracious* FATHER OF LIGHTS, who has inspired our public councils with a wisdom and firmness which have effected that desirable purpose in so great measure by the *National Constitution*, and who has fixed the eyes of all America on you, as the worthiest of their citizens to be in trusted with the execution of it.

Whatever any have supposed wanting in the original plan, we are happy to see so wisely provided in its amendments; and it is with peculiar satisfaction that we behold how easily the entire confidence of the people in the *man* who sits at the helm of government has eradicated every remaining objection to its form.

Among these we never considered the want of a religious test, that grand engine of persecution in every tyrant's hand; but we should not have been alone in rejoicing to have seen some *explicit* acknowledgment of THE ONLY TRUE GOD, AND JESUS CHRIST *whom he has sent*, inserted somewhere in the Magna Charta of our country.

Under the nurturing hand of a RULER of such virtues, and one so deservedly revered by all ranks, we joyfully indulge the hope that virtue and religion will revive and flourish, that infidelity and the vices ever attendant in its train will be banished every polite circle, and that national piety will soon become fashionable there, and from thence be diffused among all ranks in the community.

Newbury Port, Oct. 25, 1789

THE ANSWER

Gentlemen—

The affectionate welcome which you are pleased to give me to the Eastern parts of the Union would leave me without excuse did I fail to acknowledge the sensibility which it awakens, and to express the most sincere returns that a grateful sense of your goodness can suggest.

To be approved by the praiseworthy, is a wish as becoming to the ambitious as its consequence is flattering to our self-love.

I am, indeed, much indebted for the favorable sentiments which you entertain towards me, and it will be my study to deserve them.

The tribute of thanksgiving which you offer to the *gracious* Father of Lights, for his inspiration of our public councils with wisdom and firmness to complete the National Constitution, is worthy of men who, devoted to the pious purposes of religion, desire their accomplishment by such means as advance the *temporal* happiness of their fellow-men. And here, I am persuaded, you will permit me to observe that the path of true piety is so plain as to require but little *political* direction.

To this consideration we ought to ascribe the absence of any regulation respecting religion from the Magna Charta of our country. To the guidance of the ministers of the gospel this important object is, perhaps more properly, committed. It will be your care to instruct the ignorant and to reclaim the devious. And in the progress of morality and science, to which our Government will give every furtherance, we may confidently expect the advancement of true religion and the completion of our happiness.

I pray the munificent Rewarder of Virtue that *your* agency in this good work may receive its compensation here and hereafter.

G. Washington

The Protestant Episcopal Church

Shares honorably in the labors of liberty during the Revolution. Many of the earlier emigrants in various colonies were from the Church of

England; and in Virginia it had been the State religion. Being under the Episcopal jurisdiction of England, some of the ministers and churches in the colonies sympathized with the mother-country; yet the most distinguished ministers and influential Episcopal churches were loyal to freedom and aided in the work of achieving the independence of the nation.

Bishop White

Bishop William White, the father and founder of the Church, early espoused the cause of the country, and was prominent in national affairs. He was the first chaplain to Congress, and was fearless in his defence of freedom and independence. The civil councils of the country during the whole period of the great conflict were represented by eminent and able men from the Episcopal Church, among whom, as chief, was the pure-minded and patriotic John Jay. Washington, the great leader in the Revolution and in the civil councils of his country—of whose influence it has been justly said that "the tone and character of the Revolutionary struggle on the part of the Americans were elevated and dignified by the exalted virtue that Washington brought into association with it,"—was a member and a vestryman of the Episcopal Church. At the time of the Revolution there were two hundred and fifty ministers and three hundred Episcopal churches in the country. As a Protestant Church, their main influence was on the side of liberty.

The following correspondence gives pleasing evidence of this fact—

ADDRESS OF THE CONVENTION OF THE PROTESTANT EPIS-
COPAL CHURCH IN THE STATES OF NEW YORK, NEW JERSEY,
PENNSYLVANIA, DELAWARE, MARYLAND, VIRGINIA, AND
SOUTH CAROLINA, HELD AT PHILADELPHIA.
To the President of the United States.
Sir—

We, the bishops, clergy, and laity of the Protestant Episcopal Church in the States of New York, New Jersey, Pennsylvania, Delaware, Maryland, Virginia, and South Carolina, in General Convention assembled, beg leave, with the highest veneration and the most animating national considerations, at the earliest moment in our power to express our cordial joy on your election to the chief magistracy of the United States.

When we contemplate the short but eventful history of our nation— when we recollect the series of essential services rendered by you in the course of the Revolution, the temperate yet efficient exercise of the mighty powers with which the nature of the contest made it necessary to invest you—and especially when we remember the voluntary and magnanimous relinquishment of those high authorities at the moment of peace, we anticipate the happiness of our country under your future administration.

But it was not alone from a successful and virtuous use of those extraordinary powers that you were called from your honorable retirement to the first dignities of our government. An affectionate admiration of your private character, the impartiality, the persevering fortitude, and the energy with which your public duties have been performed, and the paternal solicitude for the happiness of the American people, together with the wisdom and consummate knowledge of our affairs. manifested in your last military communication, have directed to your name the universal wish, and have produced, for the first time in the history of mankind, an example of unanimous consent, in the appointment of a governor of a free and enlightened nation.

To these considerations, inspiring us with the most pleasing expectations as private citizens, permit us to add that, as the representatives of a numerous and extended Church, we most thankfully rejoice in the selection of a civil ruler deservedly beloved and eminently distinguished among the friends of genuine religion, who has happily united a tender regard for other Churches with an inviolable attachment to his own.

With unfeigned satisfaction we congratulate you on the establishment of the new constitution of government for the United States; the mild yet efficient operation of which we confidently trust will remove every remaining apprehension of those with whose opinions it may not entirely coincide, and will confirm the hopes of its numerous friends. Nor do these expectations appear too sanguine when the moderation, patriotism, and wisdom of the honorable members of the federal legislature are duly considered. From a body thus eminently qualified, harmoniously co-operating with the executive authority in constitutional concert, we confidently hope for time restoration of order and our ancient virtues, the extension of genuine religion, and the consequent advancement of our respectability abroad amid of our substantial happiness at home.

We devoutly implore the Supreme Ruler of the Universe to preserve you long in health and prosperity, an animating example of all public and private virtues, the friend and guardian of a free, enlightened, and grateful people, and that you may finally receive the reward which will be given to those whose lives have been spent in promoting the happiness of mankind.

William White,

Bishop of the Protestant Episcopal Church in the Commonwealth of Pennsylvania, and President of the Convention.

Samuel Provost, D.D., Bishop of the Protestant Episcopal Church in the State of New York.

(Though prevented by indisposition from attending the late General Convention, he concurs sincerely in this particular act, and subscribes the present address with the greatest pleasure.)

New York:

Benjamin Moore, D.D.,

Assistant Minister of Trinity Church, in the City of New York.

Abraham Beach, D.D.,

Assistant Minister of Trinity Church, in the City of New York.

Moses Rogers.

August 1, 1789

His Reply

Gentlemen—

I sincerely thank you for your affectionate congratulations on my election to the Chief Magistracy of the United States.

After having received from my fellow-citizens in general the most liberal treatment—after having found them disposed to contemplate in the most flattering point of view the performance of my services and the manner of my retirement at the close of the war—I feel that I have a right to console myself in my present arduous undertakings with a hope that they will still be inclined to put the most favorable construction on the motives which may influence me in my future public transactions. The satisfaction arising from the indulgent opinion entertained by the American people of my conduct will, I trust, be some security from preventing me from doing any thing which might justly incur the forfeiture of that opinion, and the consideration that human happiness amid moral duties are inseparably connected will always continue to prompt me to promote the progress of the former by inculcating the practice of the latter.

On this occasion it would ill become me to conceal the joy I have felt in perceiving the fraternal affection which appears to increase every day among the friends of genuine religion. It affords edifying prospects, indeed, to see Christians of different denominations dwell together in more charity, and conduct themselves, in respect to each other, with a more Christian-like spirit, than ever they have done in any former age or in any other nation.

I receive with the greater satisfaction your congratulations on the establishment of the new constitution of government, because I believe its mild yet efficient operations will tend to remove every remaining apprehension of those with whose opinions it may not entirely coincide, as well as to confirm the hopes of its numerous friends, and because the moderation, the patriotism, and the wisdom of the present federal legislature seem to promise the restoration of order and our ancient virtues, the extension of genuine religion, and the consequent advancement of our respectability abroad and of our subsequent happiness at home.

I request, most reverend and respectable gentlemen, that you will accept my cordial thanks for your devout supplications to the Supreme Ruler of the universe in behalf of me. May you and the people whom you represent be the happy subjects of the Divine benedictions both here and hereafter!

G. Washington

19

Christian Churches of the Revolution—The Baptist Churches— Methodist Episcopal Church

The Baptist Church

Has in its American and English history a noble record in favor of freedom and free institutions. The great conflicts of the Reformation under Luther brought them into existence as an ecclesiastical body, and at all times and in all nations they have been loyal to civil and religious liberty. In England, their faith and freedom-loving principles led them, with the Puritans and Independents, to separate from the Church of England, and to seal, as many did, their devotion to truth by a martyr's death.

American Baptist Church Founded by Roger Williams

Roger Williams, of Rhode Island, was the founder of the Baptist Church in America. In 1638 he formed a church in Providence: so that the labors of this denomination date from the first era of the Christian history of the country. He had the honor first in this country to enunciate and incorporate into a civil constitution the principle that "the civil power has no jurisdiction over the conscience. The civil magistrate should restrain crime, but never control opinion—should punish guilt, but never violate the soul." "It became his glory," says Bancroft, "to found a state on that principle; and its application has given religious peace to the American world." A writer in the "Baptist Review," January, 1856, says that "the great principle of freedom of conscience in religious matters did not, however, originate with the Baptists of Rhode Island. In the religious conflicts of the Old World, this denomination enunciated this fundamental law in civil and religious matters. Their Confession of Faith, in 1614, declares 'that the magistrate is not to meddle with religion or matters of conscience, nor compel men to this or that form of religion, because Christ is the King and Lawgiver of the Church.'"

Noble Record for Freedom

Educated in these first principles of Christianity and civil liberty, the Baptist churches were fully prepared to enter the arena of freedom and to maintain, in all their integrity, the great principles of the Revolution. There were at the time of the Revolution three hundred and fifty ministers and three hundred and eighty Baptist churches in this country, all of whom were loyal to the cause of freedom. Cotton Mather says of the Baptist churches in Massachusetts that they were "as holy, watchful, fruitful, and heavenly people as perhaps any in the world."

Address to the Convention of Virginia in 1775

The following address occurs in the annals of the Virginia Convention of August, 1775—

> Wednesday, August 16, 1775
>
> An address from the Baptists of this colony was presented the Convention, and read; setting forth that, however distinguished from the body of their countrymen by appelatives and sentiments of a religious nature, they nevertheless consider themselves as members of the same community in respect to matters of a civil nature, and embarked in the same com-

mon cause; that, alarmed at the oppression which hangs over America, they had considered what part it would be proper to take in the unhappy contest, and had determined that in some cases it was lawful to go to war, and that they ought to make a military resistance against *Great Britain* in her unjust invasions, tyrannical oppression, and repeated hostilities; that their brethren were left at discretion to enlist, without incurring the censure of their religious communities, and, under these circumstances, many of them had enlisted as soldiers, and many more were ready to do so, who had earnestly desired their ministers should preach to them during the campaign: they, therefore, had appointed four of their brethren to make application to the Convention for the liberty of preaching to the troops at convenient times, without molestation and abuse, and praying the same may be granted them.

Resolved, That it be an instruction to the commanding officers of the regiments or troops to be raised, that they permit Dissenting clergymen to celebrate divine worship, and to preach to the soldiers, or exhort, from time to time, as the various operations of the military service may permit, for the sake of such scrupulous consciences as may not choose to attend divine service as celebrated by the chaplains.—*American Archives*, vol. iii. p. 38.

Jefferson's Tribute to Their Patriotism

Jefferson pays the following tribute to the patriotism of the Baptist churches, in 1809, in a reply to an address from a Baptist church in Virginia ;—"We have acted together from the origin to the end of the memorable Revolution, and we have contributed, each in the line allotted us, our endeavors to render its issue a permanent blessing to our country."

Six Baptist Associations Address Jefferson

A general meeting of six Baptist Associations was held in Chesterfield, Virginia, October 7, 1808, who sent a congratulatory address to Jefferson. He replies, that, "in reviewing the history of the times through which we have passed, no portion of it gives greater sat-isfaction, on reflection, than that which presents the efforts of the friends of religious freedom and the success with which they have been crowned. We have solved the fair experi-ment, the great and interesting question, whether freedom of religion is compatible with order in government and obedience to the law." Reference is here made to Jefferson's efforts in abolishing State religion in Vir-ginia, and the co-operation of the Baptist churches—a Christian and patriotic work on the part of both.

THE ADDRESS OF THE UNITED BAPTIST CHURCHES IN
THE STATE OF VIRGINIA, ASSEMBLED IN THE CITY OF RICH-
MOND, AUGUST 8, 1789
To the President of the United States of America.
Sir,

Among the many shouts of congratulation that you receive from cities, societies, States, and the whole world, we wish to take an active part in the universal chorus, in expressing our satisfaction in your appointment to the first office in the na-tion. When America, on a former occasion, was reduced to the necessity of appealing to arms to defend her natural and civil rights, a Washington was found fully adequate to the exi-gencies of the dangerous attempt, who, by the philanthropy of his heart and the prudence of his head, led forth her untu-tored troops into the field of battle, and by the skilfulness of his hands baffled the projects of the insulting foe, and pointed out the road to independence, even at a time when the energy of the cabinet was not sufficient to bring into action the natural aid of the confederation from its respective sources.

The grand object being obtained, the independence of the States acknowledged, free from ambition, devoid of sanguine thirst for blood, our hero returned with those he command-ed, and laid down the sword at the feet of those who gave it him. Such an example to the world is new. Like other nations, we experience that it requires as great valor and wisdom to make an advantage of the conquest as to gain one.

The want of efficacy in the confederation, the redundancy of laws, and their partial administration in the States, called aloud for a new arrangement of our systems. The wisdom of the States, for that purpose, was collected in a grand convention, over which you, sir, had the honor to preside. A national Government in all its parts was recommended, as the only preservative of the Union—which plan of government is now in actual operation.

When the Constitution first made its appearance in Virginia, we, as a society, had unusual strugglings of mind, fearing that the liberty of conscience (dearer to us than property or life) was not sufficiently secured. Perhaps our jealousies were heightened on account of the usage we received in Virginia under the regal government, when mobs, bonds, fines, and prisons were our frequent repast—convinced, on the one hand, that without an effective national Government the States would fall into disunion and all the consequent evils, and, on the other hand, fearing we should be accessory to some religious oppression should any one society in the Union preponderate over all the rest. But, amidst all the inquietudes of mind, our consolation arose from this consideration—the plan must be good, for it bears the signature of a tried, trusty friend; and if religious liberty is rather insecure in the Constitution, the Administration will certainly prevent all oppression, for a *Washington* will preside. According to our wishes, the unanimous voice of the Union has called you, sir, from your beloved retreat, to launch forth again into the faithless sea of human affairs, to guide the helm of the States. May that Divine munificence which covered your head in battle make you a yet greater blessing to your admiring country in time of peace.

Should the horrid evils that have been so pestiferous in Asia and Europe—faction, ambition, war, perfidy, fraud, and persecution for conscience' sake—ever approach the borders of our happy nation, may the name and administration of our beloved President, like the radiant source of day, scatter all those dark clouds from the American hemisphere.

And, while we speak freely the language of our hearts, we are satisfied that we express the sentiments of our brethren that we represent. The very name of Washington is music in our ears; and although the great evil in the States is want of mutual confidence between rulers and people, yet we all have the utmost confidence in the President of the States; and it is our fervent prayer to Almighty God that the Federal Government, and the Governments of the respective States, without rivalship, may so co-operate together as to make the numerous people over whom you preside the happiest nation on earth, and you, sir, the happiest man, in seeing the people who, by the smiles of Providence, you saved from vassalage by your martial valor and made wise by your maxims, sitting securely under their vines and fig-trees, enjoying the perfection of human felicity. May God long preserve your life and health for a blessing to the world in general, and the United States in particular; and when, like the sun, you have finished your course of great and unparalleled services, and you go the way of all the earth, may the Divine Being, who will reward every man according to his works, grant unto you a glorious admission into his everlasting kingdom, through Jesus Christ. This, sir, is the prayer of your happy admirers.

By order of the Committee.   SAMUEL HARRIS, *Chairman.*
REUBEN FORD, *Clerk.*

His Answer

GENTLEMEN—

I request you will accept my best acknowledgments for your congratulation on my appointment to the first office of the nation. The kind manner in which you mention my past conduct equally claims the expression of my gratitude.

After we had, by the smiles of heaven on our exertions, obtained the object for which we contended, I retired, at the conclusion of the war, with an idea that my country could have no further occasion for my services, and with the intention of never again entering into public life; but, when the exigencies of my country seemed to require me once more to engage in public affairs, an honest conviction of duty superseded my former resolution, and became my apology for deviating from the happy plan which I had adopted.

If I could have entertained the slightest apprehension that the Constitution framed in the Convention, where I had the honor to preside, might possibly endanger the religious rights of any ecclesiastical society, certainly I should never have placed my signature to it; and, if I could now conceive that the General Government might ever be so administered as to render the liberty of conscience insecure, I beg you will be persuaded that no one would be more zealous than myself to establish effectual barriers against the horrors of spiritual tyranny and every species of religious persecution. For you doubtless remember that I have often expressed my sentiments that every man, conducting himself as a good citizen, and being accountable to God alone for his religious opinions, ought to be protected in worshipping the Deity according to the dictates of his own conscience.

While I recollect with satisfaction that the religious society of which you are members have been throughout America, uniformly and almost unanimously, the firm friends of civil liberty and the persevering promoters of our glorious Revolution, I cannot hesitate to believe that they will be the faithful supporters of a free yet efficient General Government. Under this pleasing expectation, I rejoice to assure them that they may rely on my best wishes and endeavors to advance their prosperity.

In the mean time, be assured, gentlemen, that I entertain a proper sense of your fervent supplications to God for my temporal and eternal happiness.

George Washington.

The Methodist Episcopal Church
Form of Church Government

Has an active, Christian economy, eminently adapted to the spirit and energy of the free institutions of a Christian republic. Its form of government, infused with the vital and earnest power of its evangelical doctrines, is efficient and practical in its administrative functions, and one of the most beneficent and powerful agencies for good in the nation. No denomination of Christians has exerted a more extensive and benign influence on all the interests of the American nation and Government than this numerous body. It has put into operation a system of intellectual, moral, and spiritual forces, which have worked mightily for freedom and all the interests which belong to a Christian republic. In England, where this denomination was first founded by John Wesley, it was said by John Newton, an eminently pious minister of the Established Church, that "before the rise of Methodists the doctrines of grace in England were seldom heard from the pulpit, and the life and power of religion but little known."

American Origin of the Methodist Church

The Methodist Episcopal Church in America dates its distinct organization during the Revolution. In 1784 the first official act towards its organization in the United States took place in England. Mr. Wesley's account of it is as follows. "In America," says he, "there are but few parish ministers; so that for some hundred miles together there is none either to baptize or administer the Lord's Supper. Here, therefore, I am at full liberty to appoint and send laborers into the harvest to feed and guide the poor sheep in the wilderness. Know all men, that I, John Wesley, therefore, under the protection of Almighty God and with a single eye to his glory, have set apart, by the inspiration of my hands and prayer, Thomas Coke, Doctor of Civil Law and a presbyter of the Church of England, for this great work."

Francis Asbury came with Dr. Coke to America, and in Baltimore, at a Conference of sixty ministers, the latter ordained Asbury as Bishop; and thus the Methodist Episcopal Church in the United States was formally and officially instituted. But the influence and fruits of this great denomination began their development in this country in 1736. John and Charles Wesley came that year from England to Georgia, and devoted themselves to building up the kingdom of Christ. "They returned to England in less than two years, and designed to return again, but were providentially prevented." They preached and established Sunday-schools in Savannah, and so began an organized influence which has spread over the nation and the world. The American

Methodist Church has now "a million of members, with thousands of churches and preachers, spreading from age to age and nation to nation, until the name of Wesley and the tenets of Methodism are known and cherished in every Christian land, and the earth has been almost girdled with the love-feasts of its disciples."

"The introduction of Sunday-schools into America, in an efficient form, is due to Francis Asbury, first Bishop of the Methodist Episcopal Church—a man whose labors for the evangelization and civilization of this country are among the marvels of Christian history. In 1786 he established a Sunday-school in Hanover, Virginia, which was the parent of a multitude. It is clear, from a statement in Bishop Asbury's Journal (vol. ii. p. 65), that he set up such schools in many other parts of the country about the same time. So far as we can learn, no other denomination of Christians shared the labors or the reproach of this enterprise at that early period. Reproach there was, and it often took the severe form of persecution. In 1787 George Daughaday, a Methodist preacher in Charleston, South Carolina, was drenched with water pumped from a public cistern 'for the crime of conducting a Sunday-school for the benefit of the African children of that vicinity.' Nothing daunted by such rebukes, the pioneers of Methodism went on with their work. The Minutes of 1790 contain the first of church legislation on the subject known, perhaps, either in Europe or America. ... The path opened by the Methodists was soon entered by other laborers. In December, 1790, a meeting was held in the city of Philadelphia, 'for the purpose of taking into consideration the establishment of Sunday-schools for that city.' On the 26th of that month a constitution was adopted for the 'First-Day or Sunday School Society.' On the 11th of January, 1791, the officers of the Society were elected, and in March of the same year their first school was opened for the admission of children. If we are rightly informed, these schools were taught by paid teachers, and were devoted exclusively to the instruction of poor children. It was not until 1816 that the system of unpaid teaching was introduced by the Philadelphia Society. This valuable organization was the parent of the American Sunday-School Union. In the mean time the Methodist schools were going on under the gratuitous system; and in the notes to the Discipline of 1796 the bishops urge the 'people in cities, towns, and villages to establish Sunday-schools, wherever practicable, for the benefit of the children of the poor.'"

First Conference in New York

A Conference of the Church met in New York, May 28, 1789, the same year, and almost at the same time, that the Constitution of the United States went into operation. Congress was in session during the sittings of that Conference, and, as Washington had just been inaugurated and the new Government gone into practical operation, the Conference gave expression to their loyalty and patriotism in an official act. Bishop Asbury, a few days after its sessions commenced, offered a proposition to Conference, "whether it would not be proper for us, as a Church, to present a congratulatory address to General Washington, who had been lately inaugurated President of the United States, in which should be embodied our approbation of the Constitution, and professing our allegiance to the Government." The Conference unanimously approved of the measure; and the bishops, Coke and Asbury, drew up the address on the same day. Rev. Thomas Morrell, a member of Conference, and who had been a commissioned officer in the American army, was appointed to wait on President Washington with a copy of the address, and to request him to designate a day when he would publicly receive the bishops. "This address was not intended," says a writer in the "National Magazine," "to court popular favor by a servile fawning at the feet of a great man, but was intended as a tribute to God for favoring the American people with such a noble monument of his wisdom and goodness in the person of the illustrious chief, and in that admirable Constitution which his hands helped to frame and which he was now called upon to administer and carry into effect. It was natural to rejoice in beholding the adoption of a Constitution which guaranteed to all denominations their rights and privileges equally, and to see this Constitution committed to the hands of men who had ever manifested an impartial regard for each religious sect and for the inalienable rights of all mankind."

ADDRESS OF THE BISHOPS OF THE METHODIST
EPISCOPAL CHURCH.
To the President of the United States.

Sir—

We, the Bishops of the Methodist Episcopal Church, humbly beg leave, in the name of our Society, collectively, in these

United States, to express to you the warm feelings of our hearts and our sincere congratulations on your appointment to the Presidentship of these States. We are conscious, from the signal proofs you have already given, that you are a friend of mankind, and under this established idea place as full confidence in your wisdom and integrity for the preservation of those civil and religious liberties which have been transmitted to us by the providence of God and the glorious Revolution, as we believe ought to be reposed in man.

We have received the most grateful satisfaction from the humble and entire dependence on the great Governor of the Universe which you have repeatedly expressed, acknowledging him the source of every blessing, and particularly of the most excellent Constitution of these States, which is at present the admiration of the world, and may in future become its great exemplar for imitation; and hence we enjoy a holy expectation that you will always prove a faithful and impartial patron of genuine, vital religion—the great end of our creation and present probationary existence. And we promise you our fervent prayers to the throne of grace that God Almighty may endue you with all the graces and gifts of his Holy Spirit—that he may enable you to fill your important station to his glory, the good of his Church, the happiness and prosperity of the United States, and the welfare of mankind.

Signed in behalf of the Methodist Episcopal Church.

Thomas Coke,
Francis Asbury.

New York, May 29, 1789.

His Answer

To the Bishops of the Methodist Episcopal Church in the United States of America.

Gentlemen—

I return to you individually, and through you to the Society collectively in the United States, my thanks for the demonstrations of affection and the expressions of joy offered in their behalf on my late appointment. It shall be my endeavor to manifest the purity of my inclinations for promoting the happiness of mankind, as well as the sincerity of my desire to contribute whatever may be in my power towards the civil and religious welfare of the American people. In pursuing this line of conduct, I hope, by the assistance of Divine Providence, not altogether to disappoint the confidence which you have been pleased to repose in me.

It always affords me satisfaction when I find a concurrence of sentiment and practice between all conscientious men, in acknowledgments of homage to the great Governor of the Universe and in professions of support to a just civil government. After mentioning that I trust the people of every denomination, who demean themselves as good citizens, will have occasion to be convinced that I shall always strive to prove a faithful and impartial patron of genuine, vital religion, I must assure you in particular that I take in the kindest part the promise you make of presenting your prayers at the Throne for me, and that I likewise implore the Divine benediction upon yourselves and your religious community.

George Washington.

Rule of Discipline Concerning Civil Government

The loyalty and patriotism of the Methodist Church are displayed in the following article in their Church Constitution, adopted at the first Conference in Philadelphia, in 1784—

> Article 33.—Of the Rulers of the United States of America.
>
> The Congress, the General Assemblies, the Governors, and councils of States, as the delegates of the people, are the rulers of the United States of America, according to the division of power made to them by the general Act of Confederation and by the Constitutions of their respective States. And the said States ought not to be subject to any foreign power.

Subsequently the following was added—

As far as it respects civil affairs, we believe it is the duty of Christians, and especially of Christian ministers, to be subject to the supreme authority of the country where they may reside, and to use all laudable means to enjoin obedience to the *powers that be*; and therefore it is expedient that all our preachers and people who may be under the British Government, or any other Government, will behave themselves as peaceable and orderly subjects.

"These declarations," says a Methodist author, "embrace the doctrine of the Church in regard to civil government; and whoever is not governed by this doctrine, and is not loyal to the Government where he may reside, cannot be a Methodist of the American stamp."

Methodist Men in the Convention that Formed the Constitution

In the Convention that formed the Constitution of the United States, the Methodist Church was represented by Richard Bassett, of Delaware, a distinguished lawyer, and a confidential friend of Bishop Asbury. He, with other influential Methodists of Delaware, George Read, John Dickinson, and their associates, urged the people of Delaware to adopt the Constitution, which they did in 1787.

The Quakers

As a Christian denomination, have exerted no unimportant influence on the religious character and sentiments of the nation. They took their rise in England about the middle of the seventeenth century, and called themselves at first *Seekers, from the fact that they professed to seek pure truth; afterwards, however, from their peace principles and conduct, they assumed the name of Friends.*

George Fox was the founder of the Friends' Society, in 1648. In 1669 he visited America, and, spending two years in this country, he formally organized the denomination on this continent. It was, however, left for Penn to give system and vigor to the Society. In March, 1681, he obtained from Charles II. a grant of all the territory which now bears the name of Pennsylvania, where he desired to "spread the principles and doctrines of the Quakers, and to build up a peaceful and virtuous empire in the new land, which should diffuse its examples far and wide to the remotest ages." In 1682 Penn set sail for this country, and in the following year founded Philadelphia, and laid the permanent basis of a civil and religious society in accordance with the principles of the Quakers.

Their Conduct in the Revolution

They rapidly rose to prominence, and their influence for good has been extended over the continent. During the Revolution, many of this denomination declined to take up arms against George III., because forbidden by a fundamental article of their faith. Stephen Hopkins, of Rhode Island, a signer of the Declaration of Independence, was a member of the Friends' Society and labored zealously for its prosperity. This body of Christians, by their principles and the example of their peaceful lives, have done much to give a higher moral tone to our national character. Their patriotism and attachment to the new Government were evinced in the following congratulatory address to Washington on his being inaugurated President of the United States.

> THE ADDRESS OF THE RELIGIOUS SOCIETY CALLED THE QUAKERS FROM THEIR YEARLY MEETING FOR PENNSYLVANIA, NEW JERSEY, DELAWARE, AND THE WESTERN PART OF MARYLAND AND VIRGINIA.
>
> *To the President of the United States.*
>
> Being met in this our annual assembly, for the well-ordering the affairs of our religious society and the promotion of universal righteousness, our minds have been drawn to consider that the Almighty, who ruleth in heaven and among the kingdoms of men, having permitted a great revolution to take place in the government of this country, we are fervently concerned that the rulers of the people may be favored with the counsels of God—the only sure means of enabling them to fulfil the important trusts committed to their charge, and

in an especial manner that Divine wisdom and grace vouchsafed from above may qualify thee to fill up the duties of the exalted station to which thou art appointed.

We are sensible thou hast obtained a great place in the esteem and affection of the people of all denominations over whom thou presidest; and, many eminent talents being committed to thy trust, we much desire they may be fully devoted to the Lord's honor and service, that thus thou mayest be an happy instrument in his hands for the suppression of vice, infidelity, and irreligion, and every species of oppression on the persons or concerns of men, so that righteousness and peace, which truly exalt a nation, may prevail throughout the land, as the only solid foundation that can be laid for prosperity and happiness.

The free toleration which the citizens of these States enjoy in the public worship of the Almighty agreeably to the dictates of their consciences, we esteem among the choicest of blessings; and we desire to be filled with fervent charity for those who differ from us in matters of faith and practice—believing that the general assembly of saints is composed of the sincere and upright-hearted of all nations, kingdoms, and people, so we trust we may justly claim it in others. In full persuasion that the divine principle we profess leads into harmony and concord, we can take no part in warlike measures on any occasion or under any power, but we are bound in conscience to lead quiet and peaceable lives in godliness and honesty among men, contributing freely our proportion to the indigencies of the poor and to the necessary support of the civil government; acknowledging those that rule to be worthy of double honor, having never been chargeable from our first establishment as a religious society with fomenting or countenancing tumult or conspiracies, or disrespect to those who are placed in authority over us.

We wish not improperly to intrude on thy time and patience; nor is it our practice to offer adulation to any. But, as we are a people whose principles and conduct have been misrepresented and traduced, we take the liberty to assure thee that we feel our hearts affectionately drawn towards thee, and those in authority over us, with prayers that thy Presidency may, under the blessing of Heaven, be happy to thyself and to the people, that through the increase of morality and true religion Divine Providence may condescend to look down upon our land with a propitious eye, and bless the inhabitants with the continuance of peace, the dew of Heaven, and the fatness of the earth, and enable us gratefully to acknowledge his manifold mercies.

And it is our earnest concern that he may be pleased to grant thee every necessary qualification to fill thy weighty and important station to his glory, and that finally, when all terrestrial honors shall pass away, thou and thy respectable consort may be found worthy to receive a crown of unfading righteousness in the mansions of peace and joy forever.

Signed in and on behalf of the said meeting, held at Philadelphia, by adjournment, from the 28th of the 9th month to the 3d of the 10th month inclusive, 1789.

Signed,   NICHOLAS WALN, *Clerk.*

Answer

TO THE RELIGIOUS SOCIETY CALLED QUAKERS, AT THEIR YEARLY MEETING FOR PENNSYLVANIA, NEW JERSEY, DELAWARE, AND THE WESTERN PART OF MARYLAND AND VIRGINIA.

GENTLEMEN—

I receive with pleasure your affectionate address, and thank you for the friendly sentiments and good wishes which you express for the success of my administration and for my personal happiness.

We have reason to rejoice in the prospect that the present national Government, which, by the favor of Divine Providence, was formed by the common counsels and peaceably established with the common consent of the people, will prove a blessing to every denomination of them. To render it such, my best endeavors shall not be wanting.

Government being, among other purposes, instituted to protect the persons and consciences of men from oppression, it certainly is the duty of rulers not only to abstain from it them-selves, but, according to their stations, to prevent it in others.

The liberty enjoyed by the people of these States of wor-shipping Almighty God agreeably to their consciences, is not only among the choicest of their *blessings*, but also of their *rights*. While men perform their social duties faithfully, they do all that society or the state can with propriety demand or expect, and remain responsible to their Maker for the reli-gion or modes of faith which they may prefer or profess.

Your principles and conduct are well known to me; and it is doing the people called Quakers no more than justice to say that (except their declining to share with others the burthen of the common defence) there is no denomination among us who are more exemplary and useful citizens.

I assure you, very explicitly, that, in my opinion, the con-scientious scruples of all men should be treated with great delicacy and tenderness; and it is my wish and desire that the laws may always be as extensively accommodated to them as a due regard to the protection and interests of the nation may justify and permit.

George Washington.

20

Christian Churches of the Revolution—The Reformed Dutch Church and Other Churches—German Lutheran Church—Universalist Convention

The Dutch Reformed Church

In the United states has an ancient and honorable origin, and a history replete with the achievements of piety and patriotism. It is the oldest branch of the great Presbyterian family in America, its ecclesiastical history beginning in New York as early as 1626—almost cotemporaneous with that of the Puritans. The state of New York and its great commercial metropolis were both colonized by emigrants from Holland of this Christian faith. The Dutch Reformed was the established Church of the colony until it passed under the jurisdiction of the British in 1664, when, by an act of Parliament, the Episcopal Church was established, to whose support the Dutch Reformed and English Presbyterians, and all others, were, for almost a century, compelled to contribute.

This Church has ever been the zealous promoter of learning and the champion of civil and religious liberty. Her history is adorned with some of the brightest and most honorable names in the Christian and civic annals of the country, who, in the persons of the Livingstons and others, largely shared in the work of building up a Christian empire and establishing a free government.

The Christian, catholic spirit of the Dutch Reformed Church, in all the works of piety and patriotism, is well expressed in the Church motto, *"Eendragt maakt Magt"* (Union creates Strength). "Let," said Dr. De Witt, "this motto handed down to us be inscribed on all our banners and lodged in our hearts, and then let us enlist under the common banner of the Captain of our salvation, with the tribes of Israel. The word *eemdragt*, which we translate *union*, is a compound one, literally signifying *one pull*. So let it be 'A LONG PULL, A STRONG PULL, AND A PULL ALL TOGETHER.'"

"The character of the Church," says Dr. De Witt, "has been, throughout her history, conservative and catholic, steadfastly adhering to her faith and order, and dwelling in quietness and kindness by the side of other evangelical denominations. The history of our State [New York] shows the pervading spirit of patriotism among her members, in adherence to popular rights and civil liberty, throughout the colonial annals and the Revolutionary contest."

Tribute of Chancellor Kent

The tribute paid by Chancellor Kent to the early Dutch settlers of the State, in his address before the New York Historical Society in 1828, will be found characteristic and just—"The Dutch discoverers of New Netherlands (New York) were grave, temperate, firm, persevering men, who brought with them the industry, the economy, the simplicity, the integrity, and the bravery of our Belgic sires; and with those virtues they also imported the lights of the Roman civil law and the purity of the Protestant faith. To that period we are to look with chastened awe and respect for the beginning of our city, and the works of our primitive fathers, our *Albani patres, atque altœ Mœnia Romœ*."

Address of Their Synod to Washington

After Washington's inauguration, the Synod of this Church presented to him the following address—

NEW YORK, October 9, 1789
To the President of the United States.

Sir—

The Synod of the Reformed Dutch Church in North America embrace the occasion of their annual session, being the first since your appointment, to present you their sincere congratulations, and to join in that great and general joy testified by all descriptions of citizens on your acceptance of the highest office in the nation.

We cannot forbear expressing our gratitude to God for preserving your valuable life amidst so many dangers till this time; for inspiring you with a large portion of the martial spirit, and forming you also for the milder and more agreeable arts of government and peace; for endowing you with great virtues, and calling them into exercise by great events; for distinguishing you with honors, and giving you remarkable prudence and moderation; and for making your extraordinary talents the more conspicuous, useful, and durable, by superinducing the noble ornament of humility. Your country has, with one voice, attested your excellency by inviting you again to public life, and you have confirmed its judgment by returning to fresh scenes and toils after you had retired to the shade from the burden and heat of a long day.

Among the many signal interpositions of Divine Providence, we remark the late important change in the General Government—a change neither effected by accident nor imposed by force, but adopted in the bosom of peace, after a free and mature deliberation, and in which a people widely extended, and various in their habits, are united beyond the most; raised expectations. In these respects the United States of America stand single among all the nations of the earth. Other revolutions may have been more diversified and splendid, but none more honorable to human nature, and none so likely to produce such happy effects. This government being now completely organized, and all its departments filled, we trust that God will give wisdom to its councils and justice to its administration, and that we shall at length realize those blessings which animated our hopes through a difficult and ruinous war.

To our constant prayers for the welfare of our country and of the whole human race, we shall esteem it our duty and happiness to unite our earnest endeavors to promote the pure and undefiled religion of Christ; for as this secures eternal felicity to men in a future state, so we are persuaded that good Christians will always be good citizens, and that where righteousness prevails among individuals the nation will be great and happy. Thus, while just government protects all in their religious rights, true religion affords to government its surest support.

We implore the Lord God to be your sun and shield. May your administration be prosperous. May the blessings of millions come upon you, and your name be grateful to all posterity. Above all, may you finish your course with joy, be numbered among the redeemed of the Lord, and enter into everlasting rest.

In the name and by the order of Synod.

John H. Livingston,	Dirck Lefferts,
William Linn,	Isaac Roverett,
Geradus A. Kuypers,	Richard Varick,
Peter Louw,	Henry Roome.

GENTLEMEN—

I receive with a grateful heart your pious and affectionate address, and with truth declare to you that no circumstance in my life has affected me more sensibly, or produced more pleasing emotions, than the friendly congratulations and strong assurances of support which I have received from my fellow-citizens of all descriptions upon my election to the Presidency of these United States.

I fear, gentlemen, your goodness has led you to form too exalted an opinion of my virtues and merits. If such talents as I possess have been called into action by great events, and those events have terminated happily for our country, the glory should be ascribed to the manifest interposition of an overruling Providence. My military services have been abundantly recompensed by the flattering approbation of a grateful people; and if a faithful discharge of my civil duties can insure a like reward, I shall feel myself richly compensated for any personal sacrifice I may have made by engaging again in public life.

The citizens of the United States of America have given as signal a proof of their wisdom and virtue, in framing and adopting a constitution of government without bloodshed or the intervention of force, as they on a former occasion exhibited to the world of their valor, fortitude, and perseverance; and it must be a pleasing circumstance to every friend of good order and social happiness to find that our new government is gaining strength and respectability among the citizens of this country in proportion as its operations are known and its effects felt.

You, gentlemen, act the part of pious Christians and good citizens by your prayers and exertions for that harmony and good will towards men which must be the basis of every political establishment; and I readily join with you, "that, while just government protects all in their religious rights, true religion affords to government its surest support."

I am deeply impressed with your good wishes for my present and future happiness, and I beseech Almighty God to take you and yours under his special care.

George Washington

The German Lutheran Church

Bearing the name of the great Reformer, was a zealous co-laborer in the cause of freedom during the Revolution. In Europe, particularly in Germany, they wield a commanding influence, and in Denmark, Norway, Sweden, Prussia, Belgium, and many of the smaller States of Germany, it is the established religion. This denomination has ever been distinguished for its zeal in learning and its devotion to the cause of civil and religious liberty. They have a greater number of colleges and universities under their care than any other Protestant denomination, and are devoted to Bible and missionary operations in every part of the world.

Early History

Among the first emigrants to Pennsylvania and the adjoining colonies, they took an active part in the great work of Christian colonization, and have since spread through almost all parts of our extending country; and wherever they have gone, schools, and all the vitalizing forces of a Christian civilization, have sprung into being. They now number a thousand congregations, with a hundred thousand members.

Address of the Ministers, Church-Wardens, and Vestrymen of the German Lutheran Congregations in and near the City of Phila-delphia, to his Excellency George Washington, President of the United States.

Sir—

It is with inexpressible satisfaction that we, the ministers, church-wardens, and vestrymen of the German Lutheran Congregations in and hear the city of Philadelphia, address your Excellency on the present occasion. The entire esteem, the exalted consideration, with which we view your character, delightfully combine with the duty we owe to this our country and the love we bear to every fellow-citizen throughout these States, in exciting us to announce the joy we entertain in your appointment to the station of President-in-Chief.

The affairs of America, in which your Excellency bore so illustrious a part from the very beginning of a most arduous contest, all along exhibited more than the symptoms of a great and general prosperity to be at length completed. The most clouded portions of our time were not without some ray of hope, and numerous occurrences, through the blessing of Divine Providence, were brilliant and eminently fortunate. The present happy crisis sheds a lustre on the past events of our *Union*, and it seems to be the presage of every thing desirable to come. Pleasingly do we anticipate the blessings of a wise, efficient government, equal freedom, perfect safety, a sweet contentment spreading through the whole land, irreproachable manners, with pure religion, and that righteousness which exalteth a nation.

Though as individuals we can be but very little known to you, yet as representatives, in some respect, of a numerous people in this city, and being so situated as to know well the minds of our German brethren nearly through this State, we can with some propriety come forward in this manner. It is, therefore, with assurance and pleasure we affirm that there is no body of people whatsoever that can, or ever shall, exceed those with whom we are connected, in affection for your person, confidence in your abilities, patriotism, and distinguished goodness. You are the MAN of their bosoms and veneration. On this ground may we be entitled to some excuse for what might seem to be intrusion in the midst of your numerous weighty engagements. And here permit us to subjoin that we shall never cease to address the throne of grace with the same warmth and sincerity of heart for your present and everlasting happiness as for our own.

His Answer

GENTLEMEN—

While I request you to accept my thanks for your kind address, I must profess myself highly gratified by the sentiments of esteem and consideration contained in it. The approbation my past conduct has received from so worthy a body of citizens as that whose joy for my appointment you announce, is a proof of the indulgence with which my future transactions will be judged.

I could not, however, avoid apprehending that the partiality of my countrymen in favor of the measures now pursued, had led them to expect too much from the present government, did not the same Providence which has been visible in every stage of our progress to this interesting crisis, from a combination of circumstances, give us cause to hope for the accomplishment of all our reasonable desires.

Thus partaking with you in the pleasing anticipation of the blessings of a wise and efficient government, I flatter myself that opportunities will not be wanting to show my disposition to encourage the domestic and public virtues of industry, economy, patriotism, philanthropy, and that righteousness which exalteth a nation.

I rejoice in having so suitable an occasion to testify the reciprocity of my esteem for the numerous people whom you represent. From the excellent character, the diligence, sobriety, and virtue, which the Germans in general who are settled in America have ever maintained, I cannot forbear felicitating myself on receiving from so respectable a number of them such strong assurances of their affection for my person, confidence in my integrity, and zeal to support me in my endeavors for promoting the welfare of our common country.

So long as my conduct shall merit the approbation of the wise and the good, I hope to hold the same place in your affections which your friendly declarations induce me to believe I possess at present; and, amidst all the vicissitudes that may await me in this mutable existence, I shall earnestly desire the continuance of an interest in your intercessions at the throne of grace.

George Washington

The Convention of the Universalist Church assembled in Philadelphia, in 1790, sent the following address to Washington—

To the President of the United States

SIR—

Permit us, in the name of the Society whom we represent, to concur in the numerous congratulations which have been offered to you since your accession to the government of the United States.

For an account of our principles we beg leave to refer you to the pamphlet we have now the honor to put into your hands.

In this publication it will appear that the peculiar doctrine which we hold is not less friendly to the order and happiness of society than it is essential to the perfection of the Deity.

It is a singular circumstance in the history of this doctrine, that it has been preached and defended in every age since the promulgation of the gospel; but we represent the first society professing this doctrine that have formed themselves into an independent Church. Posterity will hardly fail of connecting this memorable event with the auspicious years of peace, liberty, and free inquiry in the United States which distinguished the administration of General Washington.

We join thus publicly with our affectionate fellow-citizens in thanks to Almighty God for the last of his numerous signal acts of goodness to our country, in preserving your valuable life in a late dangerous indisposition; and we assure you, sir, that duty will not prompt us more than affection to pray that you may long continue the support and ornament of our country, and that you may hereafter fill a higher station, and enjoy the greater reward of being a king and priest to our God.

Signed in behalf and by order of the Convention.

John Murray

Wm. Eugene, Secretary.

His Answer

GENTLEMEN—

I thank you cordially for the congratulations which you offer on my appointment to the office I have the honor to hold in the Government of the United States.

It gives me the most sensible pleasure to find that in our nation, however different are the sentiments of citizens on religious doctrines, they generally concur in one thing; for their political professions and practices are almost universally friendly to the order and happiness of our civil institutions. I am also happy in finding this disposition particularly evinced by your Society. It is, moreover, my earnest desire that all the members of every association or community throughout the United States may make such use of the auspicious years of peace, liberty, and free inquiry with which they are now favored, as they shall hereafter find occasion to rejoice for having done.

With great satisfaction I embrace this opportunity to express my acknowledgments for the interest my affectionate fellow-citizens have taken in my recovery from a late dangerous indisposition; and I assure you, gentlemen, that, in mentioning my obligations for the effusions of your benevolent wishes in my behalf, I feel animated with new zeal that my conduct may ever be worthy of your favorable opinion, as well as such as shall in every respect beat comport with the character of an intelligent and accountable being.

George Washington.

Address from the Members of the New (Swendenborgian) Church at Baltimore.
To George Washington, Esq.

Sir—

While the nations of the earth, and the people of the United States especially, have in their various denominations paid the tribute of respectful deference to the illustrious President thereof, permit, sir, a Society, however small in numbers, yet sincere, they trust, in their attachment, to offer up, in the dawn of their institution, that mark of dutiful esteem which well becometh new associations, to the Chief Magistrate of America.

We presume not, sir, to enter into any reiterated panegyric of matchless virtues or exalted character, but, assuming causes with effects, we are led to believe that you were a chosen vessel for great and salutary purposes, and that both in your actions and in your conduct you justly stand one of the first disinterested and exemplary men upon the earth. Neither in this address can we, were it expected, enter into a detail of the profession of our faith; but we are free to declare that we feel ourselves among the number of those who have occasion to rejoice that the word literally is spiritually fulfilling; that a new and glorious dispensation, or fresh manifestation of Divine Love, hath commenced in our land, when, as there is but one Lord, so is his name becoming one throughout the earth; and that the power of Light, or truth and righteousness, is in an eminent degree universally prevailing, and even triumphing over the power of darkness; when priestcraft and kingcraft, those banes of human felicity, are hiding their diminished heads, and equality in State, as well as in Church, proportionably to merit, are considered the true criterion of the majesty of the people.

Oh, sir, could we, without being charged with adulation, pour out the fulness of our souls to the enlightened conduct of him who stands chief among the foremost of men, what a volume of truth might we deservedly offer to the name of Washington on the altar of liberty uncircumscribed! Allow us, by the first opportunity, to present to your Excellency, among other tracts, the Compendium of the New Church, signified by the New Jerusalem in the Revelation, as the readiest means to furnish you with a just idea of the heavenly doctrines.

That the Lord Jesus, whom alone we acknowledge as "the true God and eternal life," will preserve you long to reign in the hearts of the people, and lastingly to shine as a gem of the brightest lustre, a star of the first magnitude, in the unfading mansions above, is the fervent aspiration of your faithful citizens and affectionate brethren.

Done, in behalf of the members of the Lord's New Church, at Baltimore, the 22d day of January, 1793.

Teste, W. Y. Didier,
Sec'y pro tem.

His Answer

To the Members of the Swedenborgian Church, Baltimore.

GENTLEMEN—

It has ever been my pride to merit the approbation of my fellow-citizens by a faithful and honest discharge of the duties annexed to those stations in which they have been pleased to place me; and the dearest rewards of my services have been those testimonies of esteem and confidence with which they have honored me. But to the manifest interposition of an overruling Providence, and to the patriotic exertions of the citizens of United America, are to be ascribed those events which have given us a respectable rank among the nations of earth.

We have abundant reason to rejoice that in this land the light of truth and reason has triumphed over the power of bigotry and superstition, and that every person may here worship God according to the dictates of his own heart. In this enlightened age, and in this land of equal liberty, it is our boast that a man's religious tenets will not forfeit the protection of the laws, nor deprive him of the right of attaining and holding the highest offices that are known in the United States.

Your prayers for my present and future felicity are received with gratitude; and I sincerely wish, gentlemen, that you may, in your social and individual capacities, taste those blessings which a gracious God bestows upon the righteous.

George Washington

Address of the Hebrew Congregation in Newport, Rhode Island, to the President of the United States of America.

Sir—

Permit the children of the stock of Abraham to approach you with the most cordial affection and esteem for your person and merit, to join with our fellow-citizens in welcoming you to Newport.

With pleasure we reflect on those days of difficulty and danger when the God of Israel, who delivered David from the peril of the sword, shielded your head in the day of battle; and we rejoice to think that the same spirit that rested in the bosom of the greatly beloved Daniel, enabling him to preside over the provinces of the Babylonish empire, *rests*, and ever will rest, upon you, enabling you to discharge the arduous duties of CHIEF MAGISTRATE of these States.

Deprived as we have heretofore been of the invaluable rights of free citizens, we now (with a deep sense of gratitude to the Almighty Disposer of all events) behold a government erected by the MAJESTY OF THE PEOPLE—a government which to bigotry gives no sanction, to persecution no assistance, but generously affording to all liberty of conscience and immunities of citizenship, deeming every one, of whatever nation, tongue, or language, equal parts of the great governmental machine.

This so ample and so extensive federal union, whose base is philanthropy, mutual confidence, and public virtue, we cannot but acknowledge to be the work of the great God who ruleth in the armies of heaven and among the inhabitants of the earth, doing whatsoever seemeth him good.

For all the blessings of civil and religious liberty which we enjoy under a benign administration, we desire to send up our thanks to the Ancient of Days, the great preserver of men, beseeching him that the angel who conducted our forefathers through the wilderness into the promised land may graciously conduct you through all the difficulties and dangers of this mortal life. And when, like Joshua, full of days and full of honors, you are gathered to your fathers, may you be admitted into the heavenly paradise, to partake of the water of life and the tree of immortality.

Done and signed by the order of the Hebrew Congregation in Newport, Rhode Island.

Signed,   Moses Seixas, *Warden*

Newport, August 17, 1790

Answer

GENTLEMEN—

While I receive with much satisfaction your address, replete with expressions of affection and esteem, I rejoice in the opportunity of assuring you that I shall always retain a grateful remembrance of the cordial welcome I experienced in my visit to Newport, from all classes of citizens. The reflection on the days of diffi-culty and danger which are past is rendered the more sweet from a consciousness that they are succeeded by days of uncommon prosperity and security.

If we have wisdom to make the best use of the advantages with which we are now favored, we cannot fail, under the just administration of good government, to become a great and happy people.

The citizens of the United States of America have a right to applaud themselves for having given to mankind examples of an enlarged and liberal policy—a policy worthy of imitation. All possess alike liberty of conscience and immunities of citizenship. It is now no more that toleration is spoken of as if it was by the indulgence of one class of the people that another enjoyed the exercise of their inherent natural rights. For happily the Government of the United States, which gives to bigotry no sanction, to persecution no assistance, requires only that those who live under its protection should demean themselves as good citizens, in giving it on all occasions their effectual support.

It would be inconsistent with the frankness of my character not to avow that I am pleased with your favorable opinion of my administration and fervent wishes for my felicity. May the children of the stock of Abraham, who dwell in this land, continue to merit and to enjoy the good will of the other inhabitants, while every one shall sit in safety under his own vine and fig-tree, and there shall be none to make him afraid.

May the Father of all mercies scatter light, and not darkness, in our paths, and make us all in our several vocations useful here, and, in his own due time and way, everlastingly happy.

G. Washington

ADDRESS OF THE HEBREW CONGREGATION OF THE CITY OF SAVANNAH TO THE PRESIDENT OF THE UNITED STATES.
SIR—

We have long been anxious to congratulate you on your appointment by unanimous approbation to the Presidential dignity of this country, and of testifying our unbounded confidence in your integrity and unblemished virtue. Yet, however exalted the station you now fill, it is still not equal to the merit of your heroic services through an arduous and dangerous conflict, which has embosomed you in the hearts of her citizens.

Our eccentric situation, added to a diffidence bounded on the most profound respect, has thus long prevented our address; yet the delay has realized anticipa-tion, giving us an opportunity of presenting our most grateful acknowledgments for the benedictions of Heaven through the energy of federal influence and the equity of your administration.

Your unexampled liberality and extensive philanthropy have dispelled that cloud of bigotry and superstition which has long, as a veil, shaded religion, unriveted the fetters of enthusiasm, enfranchised us with all the privileges and immunities of free citizens, and initiated us into the grand mass of legislative mechanism. By example you have taught us to endure the ravages of war with manly fortitude, and to enjoy the blessings of peace with reverence to the Deity and benignity and love to our fellow-creatures.

May the great Author of worlds grant you all happiness, an uninterrupted series of health, addition of years to the number of your days, and a continuance of guardianship to that freedom which, under the auspices of Heaven, your magnanimity and wisdom have given these States.

Levi Sheftal, *President,*
In behalf of the Hebrew Congregation.

To the Hebrew congregation of the city of Savannah, May, 1790, Washington sent the following address—

Gentlemen—

I thank you with great sincerity for your congratulations on my appointment to the office which I have the honor to hold by the unanimous choice of my fellow-citizens, and especially for the expressions which you are pleased to use in testifying the confidence that is reposed in me by your congregation.

As the delay which has naturally intervened between my election and your address has afforded an opportunity for appreciating the merits of the Federal Government and for communicating your sentiments of its administration, I have rather to express my satisfaction than regret at a circumstance which demonstrates (upon experiment) your attachment to the former, as well as approbation of the latter.

I rejoice that a spirit of liberality and philanthropy is much more prevalent than it formerly was among the enlightened nations of the earth, and that your brethren will benefit thereby in proportion as it shall become still more extensive. Happily, the people of the United States of America have in many instances exhibited examples worthy of imitation, the salutary influence of which will doubtless extend much farther, if, gratefully enjoying those blessings of peace which, under the favor of Heaven, have been obtained by fortitude in war, they shall conduct themselves with reverence to the Deity and charity towards their fellow-creatures.

May the same wonder-working Deity who long since delivered the Hebrews from their Egyptian oppressors, and planted them in the promised land, whose providential agency has lately been conspicuous in establishing these United States as an independent nation, continue to water them with the dews of Heaven, and to make the inhabitants of every denomination participate in the temporal and spiritual blessings of that people whose God is Jehovah.

George Washington

The Moravian Church—Unitas Fratrum— United Brethren,

Deserve an honorable record in the story of the labors and achievements of American freedom. Rising into denominational existence at the time of the Reformation under Luther, and corresponding with him and Calvin, and other Reformers, the great apostles of religious liberty, the Moravian Church was as notable for its steadfast devotion to freedom as it has ever been for the simplicity of its Christian faith and the fervor of its piety. The various colonies, transplanted to America and principally settled in North Carolina, brought with them their ardent love of liberty, and bore an honorable part in praying and fighting for independence and freedom. They, "with other German Protestants, were firmly attached, from the commencement, to the principles which gave vitality to our Declaration of Independence" and formation to our free institutions. Evangelical and enlightened, their Church not only watered the tree of liberty with their tears, prayers, and blood, but, in their growing influence and importance as a spiritual and active body of Christians, they aided in the great work of preserving our free institutions and in perfecting our Christian civilization.

Address of the United Brethren to President Washington

To his Excellency George Washington, President of the United States of America. The Address of the Directors of the United Brethren for Propagating the Gospel among the Heathen.

Sir—

The Directors of the Society of the United Brethren for Propagating the Gospel among the Heathen, do, in the name of this Society, and in the name of all the Brethren's congregations in these United States, most cordially congratulate you on being appointed President of the United States of America.

Filled with gratitude towards God and our Saviour, unto whose goodness and kind interposition we ascribe this great and joyous event, we rely on his mercy and on the influence of his good Spirit, when we expect that your administration will prove salutary and a blessing to that nation whose unanimous voice has called you to preside over it.

We embrace this opportunity to present you a small treatise which contains an account of the manner in which the Protestant Church of the Unitas Fratrum, or United Brethren, preach the gospel and carry on their missions among the heathen. You will be pleased, sir, to accept it as a token of our affection and reverence, and of the confidence we repose in you to patronize all undertakings for propagating Christianity among the heathen. Permit us at the present time to recommend in a particular manner the Brethren's mission among the Indians in the territory of the United States, which is at present at Petquotting, on Lake Erie, and in a very dangerous situation, to your kind notice and protection, and to lay before you the ardent wish and anxious desire of seeing the light of the glorious gospel spread more and more over this country, and great multitudes of poor, benighted heathen brought by it to the saving knowledge of Christ our Saviour, who gave himself a ransom for all, and who will have all men to be saved and to come to the knowledge of the truth.

We fervently pray the Lord to strengthen your health, to support you daily by his Divine assistance, and to be himself your shield and great reward.

Signed in behalf of the Society of the United Brethren for Propagating the Gospel among the Heathen, and in behalf of all the Congregations in the United States.

John Abner Aubner,	Charles Gotthold Reichel,
Hans Chr^n Schweinin,	Paul Minster,
Frederick Peter,	David Zeirlerger, Junior.

Bethlehem, July 10, 1789.

TO THE DIRECTORS OF THE SOCIETY OF THE UNITED BRETHREN FOR PROPAGATING THE GOSPEL AMONG THE HEATHEN. GENTLEMEN—

I receive with satisfaction the congratulations of your Society, and of the Brethren's Congregations in the United States of America. For you may be persuaded that the approbation and good wishes of such a peaceable and virtuous community cannot be indifferent to me.

You will also be pleased to accept my thanks for the treatise [missionary paper] you presented, and be assured of my patronage in your laudable undertakings.

In proportion as the General Government of the United States shall acquire strength by duration, it is probable that they may have it in their power to extend a salutary influence to the aborigines in the extremities of their territory. In the mean time, it will be a desirable thing for the protection of the Union to co-operate, as far as circumstances may conveniently admit, with the disinterested endeavors of your Society to civilize and Christianize the savages of the wilderness.

Under these impressions, I pray Almighty God to have you always in his holy keeping.

George Washington

The Address of the Ministers and Elders of the German Reformed Congregations in the United States, at their General Meeting held at Philadelphia on the 10th Day of June, 1789.

To the President of the United States

Whilst the infinite goodness of Almighty God, in his gracious providence over the American people of the United States of America, calls for sincerest and most cordial gratitude to Him that ruleth supremely and ordereth all things in heaven and on earth in unerring wisdom and righteousness, the happy, the peaceful establishment of the new Government over which you so deservedly preside cannot fail but inspire our souls with new and most lively emotions of adoration, praise, and thanksgiving unto his holy name.

As it is our firm purpose to support in our persons a Government founded in justice and equity, so it shall be our constant duty to impress the minds of the people intrusted to our care with a due sense of the necessity of uniting reverence to such a Government and obedience to its laws with the duties and exercises of religion. Thus we hope, by the blessing of God, to be in some measure instrumental in alleviating the burden of that weighty and important charge to which you have been called by the unanimous voice of your fellow-citizens, and which your love to your country has constrained you to take upon you.

Deeply possessed of a sense of the goodness of God in the appointment of your person to the highest station in the national Government, we shall continue in our public worship. and in all devotions before the throne of grace, to pray that it may please God to bless you, in your person, your family, and your Government, with all temporal and spiritual blessings in Christ Jesus.

Signed by order of the meeting,

Th. Hendel, *p. t. Præs.*
F. Delliken, *p. t. Scriba.*

His Answer

Gentlemen—

I am happy in concurring with you in the sentiments of gratitude and piety towards Almighty God which are expressed with such fervency of devotion in your address, and in believing that I shall always find in you, and the German Reformed congregations of the United States, a conduct correspondent to such worthy and pious sentiments.

At the same time, I return you my thanks for the manifestation of your firm purpose to support in your persons a Government founded in justice and equity, and for the promise that it will be your constant study to impress the minds of the people intrusted to your care with a due sense of the necessity of uniting reverence to such a Government and obedience to its laws with the duties and exercises of religion. Be assured, gentlemen, it is by such conduct very much in the power of the virtuous members of the community to alleviate the burden of the important office which I have accepted, and to give me the occasion to rejoice in this world for having followed therein the dictates of my conscience.

Be pleased also to accept my acknowledgments for the interest you so kindly take in the prosperity of my person, family, and administration. May your devotions before the throne of grace be effectual in calling down the blessings of Heaven upon yourselves and your country.

George Washington

The Roman Catholic Church

Contributed largely to the success of the cause of liberty and the Revolution.

"It is a curious fact," says Headley, "that in our first struggle for liberty, and in all the wars that the republic has since waged, even till now, when the North is struggling against a monstrous rebellion, Roman Catholic chaplains have sent up their prayers side by side with Protestant ones." They have presented the delightful spectacle of working together to support free institutions. The following address, delivered in a Roman Catholic church in Philadelphia, July 4, 1779, is a fair illustration of the spirit they exhibited throughout. After a Te Deum was chanted, the chaplain spoke as follows—

GENTLEMEN—We are assembled to celebrate the anniversary of that day which Providence has marked in his eternal decrees to become the epocha of liberty and independence to the thirteen United States of America. That Being, whose almighty hand holds all existence beneath its dominion, undoubtedly produces in the depth of his wisdom those great events which astonish the universe, and of which the most presumptuous, though instrumental in accomplishing, dare not attribute to themselves the merit. But the finger of God is still more peculiarly evident in the happy, the glorious Revolution which calls forth this day's festivity.

He hath struck the oppressors of a free people—free and peaceable— with the spirit of delusion, which always renders the wicked the artificers of their own proper misfortunes.

Permit me, my dear brethren, citizens of the United States, to address you on this occasion. It is God, the all-powerful God, who hath directed your steps when you knew not where to apply for counsel; who, when you were without arms, fought for you with the sword of eternal justice; who, when you were in adversity, poured into your hearts the spirit of courage, of wisdom, and of fortitude; and who at length raised up for your support a youthful sovereign, whose virtues bless and adorn a sensible, a faithful, and a generous nation. This nation has blended her interests with your interests and her sentiments with yours. She participates in all your joys, and this day unites her voice to yours at the foot of the altars of the eternal God to celebrate that glorious Revolution which has placed the sons of America among the free and independent nations of the earth.

We have nothing to apprehend but the anger of Heaven, or that the measure of our guilt should exceed the measure of his mercy. Let us, then, prostrate ourselves at the feet of the immortal God, who holds the fate of empires in his hands, and raises them up at his pleasure or breaks them to the dust. Let us implore him to conduct us by the way which his providence has marked out for arriving at so desirable an end; let us offer unto him hearts imbued with sentiments of love, consecrated by religion, by humanity and patriotism. Never is the August ministry of his altars more acceptable to his Divine majesty than when it lays at his feet homages, offerings, and vows so pure, so worthy of the common Parent of mankind. God will not reject our joy, for he is the author of it, nor will he reject our prayers, for they ask but the full accomplishment of his decrees that he hath manifested. Filled with this spirit, let us, in concert with each other, raise our hearts to the Eternal; let us implore his infinite mercy to be pleased to inspire the rulers of both nations with the wisdom and force necessary to perfect what it hath begun. Let us, in a word, unite our voices to beseech him to dispense his blessings upon the councils and arms of the allies, that we may soon enjoy the sweets of a peace which will cement the union and establish the prosperity of the two empires. It is with this view we shall cause the canticle to be performed which the custom of the Catholic Church hath consecrated to be at once the testimonial of public joy, a thanksgiving for benefits received from Heaven, and a prayer for the continuance of its success.

Archbishop Carroll

Archbishop Carroll, brother of Charles Carroll, who signed the Declaration of Independence, was able and eloquent in defence of the American cause. Those who heard him say "that when he recited the terrors, the encouragements, the distresses, and the glories of the struggle for independence," he was moved with intense emotion, and swayed the feelings of his audience with the strains of his patriotic and pious eloquence.

November, 1781

Address Delivered by M. Paul Bardole to Congress, the Supreme Executive Council, and the Assembly of Pennsylvania, &c. &c., who were invited by his Excellency the Minister of France to attend in the

ROMAN CATHOLIC CHURCH IN PHILADELPHIA, DURING THE
CELEBRATION OF DIVINE SERVICE AND THANKSGIVING FOR
THE CAPTURE OF LORD CORNWALLIS

GENTLEMEN—

A numerous people assembled to render thanks to the Almighty for his mercies is one of the most affecting objects, and worthy the attention of the Supreme Being. While camps resound with triumphal acclamations, while nations rejoice in victory and glory, the most honorable office a minister of the altar can fill is to be the organ by which public gratitude is conveyed to the Omnipotent.

Those miracles which he once wrought for his chosen people are renewed in our favor; and it would be equally ungrateful and impious not to acknowledge that the event which lately confounded our enemies and frustrated their designs was the wonderful work of that God who guards our liberties.

And who but he could so combine the circumstances which led to success? We have seen our enemies push forward amid perils almost innumerable, amid obstacles almost insurmountable, to the spot that was destined to witness their disgrace; yet they eagerly sought it as the theatre of their triumph! Blind as they were, they bore hunger, thirst, and inclement skies, poured their blood in battle against brave republicans, and crossed immense regions to confine themselves in another Jericho, whose walls were fated to fall before another Joshua. It is He whose voice commands the winds, the seas, and the seasons, who formed a junction on the same day, in the same hour, between a formidable fleet from the south, and an army rushing from the north like an impetuous torrent. Who but He in whose hands are the hearts of men could inspire the allied troops with the friendship, the confidence, the tenderness, of brothers? How is it that two nations, once divided, jealous, inimical, and nursed in reciprocal prejudices, are now become so closely united as to form but one? Worldlings would say that it is the wisdom, the virtue and moderation of their chief, it is a great national interest, which has performed this prodigy. They will say, to the skill of the generals, to the courage of the troops, to the activity of the whole army, we must attribute this splendid success. Ah! they are ignorant that the combining of so many fortunate circumstances is an emanation from the All-perfect Mind—that courage, that skill, that activity, bear the sacred impression of Him who is divine.

For how many favors have we not to thank him during the course of the present year! Your union, which was at first supported by justice alone, has been consolidated by your courage, and the knot which ties you together is indissoluble by the accession of all the States and the unanimous voice of all the confederates. You present to the universe the noble sight of a society which, founded in equality and justice, secures to the individuals who compose it the most happiness which can be derived from human institutions. This advantage, which so many other nations have been unable to procure, even after ages of efforts and misery, is granted by Divine Providence to the United States; and his adorable decrees have marked the present moment for the completion of that memorable happy revolution which has taken place on this continent. While your councils were thus acquiring new energy, rapid and multiplied successes have crowned your arms in the Southern States.

On this solemn occasion we might renew our thanks to the God of battles for the success he has granted to the arms of your allies and your friends, by land and by sea, through the other parts of the globe. But let us not recall those events, which too clearly prove how much the hearts of our enemies have been hardened. Let us prostrate ourselves at the altar, and implore the God of mercy to suspend his vengeance, to spare them in his wrath, to inspire them with sentiments of justice and moderation, to terminate their obstinacy and error, and to ordain that your victories be followed by peace and tranquillity. Let us beseech him to shed on the councils of the king, your ally, that spirit of wisdom, of justice, and of courage which has rendered his reign so glorious. Let us entreat him to maintain in each of the States that intelligence by which the United States are inspired. Let us return him thanks that a faction whose rebellion he has corrected, now deprived of support, is annihilated. Let us offer him pure hearts, unsoiled by private hatred or public discussion; and let us with one will and one voice pour forth to the Lord that hymn of praise by which Christians celebrate their gratitude and his glory.

This eloquent address was followed by a solemn anthem of praise to God.

ADDRESS OF THE ROMAN CATHOLICS TO GEORGE WASHINGTON, PRESIDENT OF THE UNITED STATES

Sir—

We have been long impatient to testify our joy and unbounded confidence on your being called by a unanimous voice to the first station of a country in which that unanimity could not have been obtained without the previous merit of unexampled services, of eminent wisdom, and unblemished virtue. Our congratulations have not reached you sooner because our scattered situation prevented our communication, and the collecting of those sentiments which warmed every breast. But the delay has furnished us with the opportunity, not merely of presaging the happiness to be expected under your administration, but of hearing testimony to that which we experience already. It is your peculiar talent, in war and in peace, to afford security to those who commit their protection into your hands. In war you shield them from the ravages of armed hostility; in peace you establish public tranquillity by the justice and moderation, not less than by the vigor, of your government. By example, as well as by vigilance, you extend the influence of laws on the manners of our fellow-citizens. You encourage respect for religion, and inculcate, by words and actions, that principle on which the welfare of a nation so much depends—that a superintending Providence governs the events of the world and watches over the conduct of men. Your exalted maxims, and unwearied attention to the moral and physical improvement of our country, have produced already the happiest effects.

Under your administration, America is animated with zeal for the attainment and encouragement of useful literature; she improves her agriculture, extends her commerce, and acquires with foreign nations a dignity unknown to her before. From these happy events, in which none can feel a warmer interest than ourselves, we derive additional pleasure by recollecting that you, sir, have been the principal instrument to effect so rapid a change in our political situation. This prospect of national prosperity is peculiarly pleasing to us on another account—because whilst our country preserves her freedom and independence we shall have a well-founded title to claim from her justice *the equal rights of citizenship, as the price of our blood spilt under your eyes, and of our common exertions for her defence under your auspicious conduct*—rights rendered more dear to us by the remembrance of former hardships. When we pray for the preservation of them where they have been granted, and expect the full extension of them from the justice of those States which still restrict them—when we solicit the protection of Heaven over our common country—we neither omit, nor can omit, recommending your preservation to the singular care of Divine Providence; because we conceive that no human means are so available to promote the welfare of the United States as the prolongation of your health and life, in which are included the energy of your example, the wisdom of your councils, and the persuasive eloquence of your virtues.

John Carroll,
In behalf of the Roman Catholic Clergy.

Charles Carroll, of Carrollton,   *In behalf of the*
Daniel Carroll,   *Roman Catholic*
Dominick Lynch,   *Laity.*
Thomas Fitzsimons

His Answer

GENTLEMEN—

While I now receive with much satisfaction your congratulations on my being called by a unanimous vote to the first station of my country, I cannot but duly notice your politeness in offering an apology for the unavoidable delay. As that delay has given you an opportunity of realizing, instead of anticipating, the benefits of the General Government, you will do me the justice to believe that your testimony to the increase of the public prosperity enhances the pleasure which I should otherwise have experienced from your affectionate address.

I feel that my conduct in war and in peace has met with more general approbation than I could have reasonably expected; and I feel disposed to consider that fortunate circumstance as in a great degree resulting from the able support and extraordinary candor of my fellow-citizens of all denominations.

The prospect of national prosperity now before us is truly animating, and ought to excite the exertions of all good men to establish and secure the happiness of their country in the permanent duration of its freedom and independence. America, under the smiles of Divine Providence, the protection of a good Government, the cultivation of manners, morals, and piety, can hardly fail of attaining an uncommon degree of eminence in literature, commerce, agriculture, improvements at home, and respectability abroad.

As mankind become more liberal, they will be more apt to allow that those who conduct themselves as worthy members of the community are equally entitled to the protection of civil government. I hope ever to see America among the foremost nations in examples of justice and liberality. And I presume that your fellow-citizens will not forget your patriotic part in the accomplishment of their Revolution and the establishment of their Government, or the important assistance which they received from a nation in which the Roman Catholic religion is professed.

I thank you, gentlemen, for your kind concern for me. While my life and my health shall continue, in whatever situation I may be, it shall be my constant endeavor to justify the favorable sentiments you are pleased to express of my conduct. And may the members of your society in America, animated alone by the pure spirit of Christianity, and still conducting themselves as the faithful subjects of our free Government, enjoy every temporal and spiritual felicity.

George Washington

21

Christian Character of Washington

WASHINGTON gives to American annals and institutions their chief historic grandeur. His genius was impressed on the organic formation of the republic, and his spirit and principles are its highest political and moral power. In a model republic it was providentially ordained that he who was its founder and father should be a model character, worthy of universal imitation. Washington is that model. Like a finished and faultless piece of painting, the more his life is studied the more will he be admired and the brighter will his virtues shine. He is one of the few men whose fame and influence constitute the common inheritance of the race and will live through all time. The impersonation of every great and true virtue, he gathers around him the affections of the good and commands the admiration of the world. In the republic which he founded, and over which he presided with singular integrity and felicity, he has enthroned his influence and embalmed his memory. Its annals speak his praise, proclaim his illustrious labors, and enshrine his genius and his works. Whatever constitutes the true and lasting glory of the republic, or is excellent and exalted in human character, finds a happy exemplification in the life and character of Washington. The republic will die only when the principles and spirit impressed upon it by Washington shall have ceased to animate it; and it will live in replenished purity and vigor in proportion as they are applied and transfused through the civil institutions of the nation.

Webster's View of Washington

"The character of Washington," said Webster, "is a fixed star in the firmament of great names, shining without twinkling or obscurity, with clear, steady, beneficent light. It is associated and blended with all our reflections on those things which are near and dear to us. If we think of the independence of our country, we think of him who was so prominent in achieving it; if we think of the Constitution which is over us, we think of him who did so much to establish it, and whose administration of its powers is acknowledged to be a model for his successors. If we think of glory in the field, of wisdom in the cabinet, of the purest patriotism, of the highest integrity, public and private, of morals without a stain, of religious feelings without intolerance and without extravagance, the August figure of Washington presents itself as the personation of all these ideas."

Patrick Henry's

He adorned and dignified every station which he filled, and left the impress of his greatness upon all with whom he acted. As a member of the Continental Congress of 1774, Patrick Henry said, "If you speak of solid information and of sound judgment, Washington was unquestionably the greatest man of them all."

"There is something charming to me," said John Adams, "in the conduct of Washington—a gentleman of one of the first fortunes upon the continent, leaving his delicious retirement, his family and friends, sacrificing his ease, and hazarding all in the cause of his country. His views are noble and disinterested."

Thomas Jefferson's

"On the whole," said Jefferson, "it may be truly said that never did nature and fortune combine more perfectly to make a great man, and to place him in the same constellation with whatever worthies have merited from man an everlasting remembrance. His integrity was the most pure, his justice the most inflexible, I have ever known."

Charles James Fox's

"I cannot, indeed, help admiring," says Fox, in the British Parliament, January 31, 1794, "the wisdom and fortune of this great man. Notwithstanding his extraordinary talents and exalted integrity, it must be considered as singularly fortunate that he should have experienced a lot which so seldom falls to the portion of humanity, and have passed through such a variety of scenes without stain and without reproach. It must, indeed, create astonishment that, placed in circumstances so critical and filling for a series of years a station so conspicuous, his character should never once be called in question—that he should in no instance have been accused either of improper insolence or of mean submission in his transactions with foreign nations. For him it was reserved to run the race of glory without experiencing the smallest interruption to the brilliancy of his career. Illustrious man! deserving honor less from the splendor of his situation than from the dignity of his mind—before whom all borrowed greatness sinks into insignificance, and all the potentates of Europe become little and contemptible."

Lord Erskine's

Lord Erskine, in writing to Washington, expressed his reverence for him in these words—"I have a large acquaintance among the most valuable and exalted classes of men; but you are the only human being for whom I ever felt an awful reverence. I sincerely pray God to grant a long and serene evening to a life so gloriously devoted to the universal happiness of the world."

Lord Brougham's

Lord Brougham says, "In Washington we may contemplate every excellence, military and civil, applied to the service of his country and of mankind—a triumphant warrior, unshaken in confidence when the most sanguine had a right to despair; a successful ruler in all the difficulties of a course wholly untried, directing the formation of a new government for a great people, the first time so rash an experiment had ever been tried by man; voluntarily and unostentatiously retiring from supreme power, with the veneration of all parties, of all nations, of all mankind, that the rights of men might be conserved and that his example might never be appealed to by vulgar tyrants. *It will be the duty of the historian and the sage, in all ages, to omit no occasion of commemorating this illustrious man; and until time shall be no more will a test of the progress which our race has made in wisdom and in virtue be derived from the veneration paid to the immortal name of Washington."*

George Bancroft's

Bancroft draws the following true and beautiful portraiture of Washington—

"Courage was so natural to him that it was hardly spoken of to his praise. No one ever at any moment of his life discovered in him the least shrinking in danger; and he had a hardihood of daring which escaped notice because it was so enveloped by superior calmness and wisdom. He was as cheerful as he was spirited, frank and communicative in the society of friends, fond of the fox-chase and the dance, often sportive in his letters, and liked a hearty laugh. This joyousness of disposition remained to the last, though the vastness of his responsibilities was soon to take from him the right of displaying the impulsive qualities of his nature, and the weight which he was to bear up was to overlay and repress his gayety and openness.

"His hand was liberal, giving quietly and without observation, as though he was ashamed of nothing but being discovered in doing good. He was kindly and compassionate, and of lively sensibility to the sorrows of others; so that if his country had only needed a victim for its relief; he would willingly have offered himself as a sacrifice. But, while he was prodigal of himself he was considerate for others—ever parsimonious of the blood of his countrymen.

"He was prudent in the management of his private affairs, purchased rich lands from the Mohawk valley to the flats of the Kanawha, and improved his fortune by the correctness of his judgment; but as a public man he knew no other aim than the good of his country, and in the hour of his country's poverty he refused personal emolument for service.

"His faculties were so well balanced and combined, that his constitution, free from excess, was tempered evenly with all the elements of activity, and his mind resembled a well-ordered commonwealth; his passions, which had the intensest vigor, owned allegiance to reason; and, with all the fiery quickness of his spirit, his impetuous and massive will was held in check by consummate judgment.

"He had in his composition a calm which gave him in moments of highest excitement the power of self-control, and enabled him to excel in patience even when he had most cause for disgust. Washington was offered a command when there was little to bring out the unorganized resources of the continent but his own influence, and authority was connected with the people by the most frail, most attenuated, scarcely discernible, threads; yet, vehement as was his nature, impassioned as was his courage, he so restrained his ardor that he never failed continuously to exert the attracting power of that influence, and never exerted it so sharply as to break its force.

"In secrecy he was unsurpassed; but his secrecy had the character of prudent reserve, not of cunning or concealment.

"His understanding was lucid, and his judgment accurate: so that his conduct never betrayed hurry or confusion. No detail was too minute for his personal inquiry and continued supervision; and, at the same time, he comprehended events in their widest aspects and relations. He never seemed above the object which engaged his attention, and he was always equal without an effort to the solution of the highest questions, even when there existed no precedents to guide his decision.

"In this way he never drew to himself admiration for the possession of any one quality in excess, never made in council any one suggestion that was sublime but impracticable, never in action took to himself the praise or the blame of undertakings astonishing in conception but beyond his means of execution. It was the most wonderful accomplishment of this man, that, placed upon the largest theatre of events, at the head of the greatest revolution in human affairs, he never failed to observe all that was possible, and at the same time to bound his aspirations by that which was possible.

"A slight tinge in his character, perceptible only to the observer, revealed the region from which he sprung; and he might be described as the best specimen of manhood as developed in the south;

but his qualities were so faultlessly proportioned that his whole country rather claimed him as its choicest representative, the most complete expression of all its attainments and aspirations. He studied his country, and conformed to it. His countrymen felt that he was the best type of America, and rejoiced in it and were proud of it. They lived in his life, and made his success and his praise their own.

"Profoundly impressed with confidence in God's providence, and exemplary in his respect for the forms of public worship, no philosopher of the eighteenth century was more firm in the support of freedom of religious opinion, none more tolerant or more remote from bigotry; but belief in God and trust in his overruling power formed the essence of his character. Divine wisdom not only illumines the spirit, it inspires the will.

"Washington was a man of action, and not of theory or words; his creed appears in his life, not in his professions, which burst from him very rarely, and only at those great moments of crisis in the fortunes of his country when earth and heaven seemed actually to meet, and his emotions became too intense for suppression; but his whole being was one continued act of faith in the eternal, intelligent, moral order of the universe. Integrity was so completely the law of his nature that a planet would sooner have shot from its sphere than he have departed from his uprightness, which was so constant that it often seemed to be almost impersonal.

"They say of Giotto that he introduced goodness into the art of painting. Washington carried it with him to the camp and the cabinet, and established a new criterion of human greatness. The purity of his will confirmed his fortitude, and, as he never faltered in his faith in virtue, he stood fast by that which he knew to be just, free from illusions, never dejected by the apprehension of the difficulties and perils that went before him, and drawing the promise of success from the justice of his cause. Hence he was persevering, leaving nothing unfinished—free from all taint of obstinacy in his firmness, seeking and gladly receiving advice, but immovable in his devotedness to right.

"Of a 'retiring modesty and habitual reserve,' his ambition was no more than the consciousness of his power, and was subordinate to his sense of duty; he took the foremost place, for he knew from inborn magnanimity that it belonged to him, and he dared not withhold the service required of him so that, with all his humility, he was by necessity the first, though never for himself or for private ends. He loved fame, the approval of coming generations, the good opinion of his fellow-men of his own time, and he desired to make his conduct coincide with their wishes; but not fear of censure, not the prospect of applause, could tempt him to swerve from rectitude; and the praise which he coveted was the sympathy of that moral sentiment which exists in every human breast and goes forth only to the welcome of virtue.

"There have been soldiers who have achieved mightier victories in the field and made conquests more nearly corresponding to the boundlessness of selfish ambition; statesmen who have been connected with more startling upheavals of society; but it is the greatness of Washington that in public trusts he used power solely for the public good; that he was the life and moderator and stay of the most momentous revolution in human affairs, its moving impulse and its restraining power. Combining the centripetal and the centrifugal forces in their utmost strength and in perfect relations, with creative grandeur of instinct he held ruin in check and renewed and perfected the institutions of his country. Finding the colonies disconnected and dependent, he left them such a united and well-ordered commonwealth as no visionary had believed to be possible. So that it has been truly said, 'he was as fortunate as great and good.'"

"It is the harmonious union of the intellectual and moral powers, rather than the splendor of any one trait," says Sparks, "which constitutes the grandeur of Washington's character. If the title of a great man ought to be reserved for him who cannot be charged with an indiscretion or a vice, who spent his life in establishing the independence, the glory and durable prosperity of his country, who succeeded in all he undertook, and whose successes were never won at the expense of honor, justice, integrity, or by the sacrifice of a single principle, this title will not be denied to Washington."

Washington Irving's

"The character of Washington," says Irving, "may want some of those poetical elements which dazzle and delight the multitude, but it possessed fewer inequalities and a rarer union of virtue than perhaps ever fell to the lot of one man. Prudence, firmness, sagacity, moderation, an overruling judgment, an immovable justice, courage that never faltered, patience that never wearied, truth that disdained all artifices, magnanimity without alloy. It seems as if Providence had endowed him in a pre-eminent degree with the qualities requisite to fit him for the high destiny he was called upon to fulfil—to conduct a momentous revolution which was to form an era in the history of the world, and to inaugurate a new and untried government, which, to use his own words, was to lay the foundation 'for the enjoyment of much purer civil liberty and greater public happiness than have hitherto been the portion of mankind.'

"The fame of Washington stands apart from every other in history—shining with a truer lustre and a more benignant glory. With us his name remains a national property, where all sympathies throughout our widely-extended and diversified empire meet in unison. Under all dissensions and amid all the storms of party, his precepts and example speak to us from the grave with a perpetual appeal; and his name, by all revered, forms a universal tie of brotherhood—a watchword of our Union."

"In what," says Winthrop, "did the power of Washington consist? I hazard nothing in saying that it was the high moral elements of his character which imparted to it its preponderating force. His incorruptible honesty, his uncompromising truth, his devout reliance on God, the purity of his life, the scrupulousness of his conscience, the disinterestedness of his purpose, his humanity, generosity, justice— these were the ingredients which, blended harmoniously with solid information and sound judgment and a valor only equalled by his modesty, made up a character for which the world may be fearlessly challenged for a parallel.

"Of him we feel it to be no exaggeration to say,

'All the ends he aimed at
Were his country's, his God's, and Truth's.'"

"The splendor of his character," said Professor Tappan, in 1800, "arose not so much from the striking predominance of any one virtue, as from the singular union and culture of all, and the wonderful adaptation of his leading moral qualities to his peculiar and arduous situations.

Christian Principles the Basis of Washington's Life and Character

"This bright assemblage of virtues strikes us with less astonishment when we add that their possessor was, both in *faith and practice, a Christian.* Whatever influence we ascribe to the peculiar structure of his mind and his polished education, yet, as *Christian principles* were early interwoven with this structure and education, they must, under the Divine blessing, have principally contributed to his excellent character."

Washington received the rudiments and foundation of his great life and character in a Christian household and training. He was blessed with pious parents, who were members of the Episcopal Church, under the ecclesiastical establishment of the Church of England, which was then almost the only denomination of Christians known in the colony of Virginia. He was consecrated to God in faith and prayer, and in the rite of baptism according to the creed of that Church. The record of this religious act is found in the family Bible of his parents.

His father not only instructed his son in the obligations of morality, but that "the fear of the Lord is the beginning of wisdom." Piety, as the source of all goodness and the elementary basis of all true greatness, was the cherished aim and the chief effort of Washington's father; and from him and his mother he received the inestimable blessing of a sound religious education; but, in common with most illustrious men who have adorned our race, Washington points, as the chief earthly source of his successes and greatness, to *home influence directed by a Christian mother.*

"Tradition," says Irving, "gives an interesting picture of the widow, with her flock gathered round her, as was her daily wont, reading to them lessons of religion and morality out of some standard work. Her favorite volume was Sir Matthew Hale's 'Contemplations, Moral and Divine.' The admirable maxims therein contained for outward actions, as well as self-government, sank deep into the mind of George, and doubtless had a great influence in forming his character. They certainly were exemplified in his conduct throughout life."

Early Christian Training by His Mother

His mother, being an eminently Christian woman, constantly inculcated the fear of God and the strict observance of the moral virtues. It was her habit not only to pray for her children, but to urge this duty upon them with maternal earnestness. "My son, neglect not the duty of secret prayer," was the injunction she was accustomed to give to her children and grandchildren as they surrounded her domestic altar or left the maternal mansion.

Her Library

A volume entitled "Contemplations, Moral and Divine, by Sir Matthew Hale, Knight, late Chief-Justice of the King's Bench," and which his mother so frequently read to him, passed into the hands of General Washington, and was found, after his death, in the library at Mount Vernon. It bears marks of frequent use, and the tradition in the family is that "it was a counsellor of past days." As this book had doubtless a large influence in forming the character and guiding the conduct of Washington, some of its leading truths are transcribed.

Chief-Justice Hale's Religious Work

In this work Chief-Justice Hale represents the good steward as giving his account to God as follows—

"As to all the *blessings and talents* wherewith thou hast intrusted me, I have looked up to thee with a thankful heart, as the only Author and Giver of them. I have looked upon myself as unworthy of them. I have looked upon them as committed to my trust and stewardship to manage them for the ends that they were given—the honor of my Lord and Master. I have therefore been watchful and sober in the use and exercise of them, lest I should be unfaithful in them. If I have at any time, through weakness, or inadvertence, or temptation, misemployed any of them, I have been restless till I have in some measure rectified my miscarriage by repentance and amendment.

"As touching my CONSCIENCE and the light thou hast given me in it, it hath been my care to improve that natural light and to furnish it with the best principles I could. Before I had the knowledge of thy word, I got as much furniture as I could from the writings of the best moralists and the examples of the best men; after I had the light of thy word, I furnished it with those pure and unerring principles that I found in it.

"Concerning my SPEECH, I have always been careful that I offend not with my tongue: my words have been few, unless necessity or thine honor required more speech than ordinary. My words have been true, representing things as they were, and sincere, bearing conformity to my heart and mind.

"I have esteemed it the most natural and excellent use of my tongue to set forth thy glory, goodness, power, wisdom, and truth; to instruct others, as I had opportunity, in the knowledge of thee, in their duty to thee, to themselves and others; to reprove vice and sin, to encourage virtue and good living; to convince errors; to maintain the truth; to call upon thy name, and by vocal prayers to sanctify my tongue and to fix my thoughts to the duty about which I was; to persuade to peace and charity and good works.

"I have always observed that honesty and plain dealing in transactions, as well public as private, is the best and soundest prudence and policy, and commonly, at the long run, over-matcheth craft and subtlety (Job xii. 16); for the deceived and deceiver are thine, and thou art privy to the subtlety of the one and the simplicity of the other; and thou, as the great Moderator and Observer of men, dost dispense success and disappointment accordingly.

"Touching my eminence of place or power in this world, this is my account. I never sought or desired it, and that for these reasons.

1. Because I easily saw that it was rather a burden than a privilege. It made my charge and my accounts the greater, my contentment and rest the less. I found enough in it to make me decline it in respect of myself, but not any thing that could invite me to seek or desire it.

"The external glory and splendor that attended it I esteemed as vain and frivolous in itself, a bait to allure vain and inconsiderate persons to affect and delight—not valuable enough to invite a considerate judgment to desire or undertake it. I esteemed them as the gilt that covers a bitter pill, and I looked through this dress and outside, and easily saw that it covered a state obnoxious to danger, solicitude, care, trouble, envy, discontent, unquietness, temptation, and vexation.

"When I undertook any place of power or eminence—*First*, I looked to my call thereunto to be such as I might discern to be thy call, not my own ambition. *Second*, that the place were such as might be answered by suitable abilities in some measure to perform. *Third*, that my end in it might not be the satisfaction of any pride, ambition, or vanity in myself, but to serve thy providence and my generation honestly and faithfully. In all which, my undertaking was not an act of my choice, but of my duty.

"In the holding or exercising of these places, I kept *my heart humble*: I valued not myself one rush the more for it. *First*, because I easily found that that base affection of pride, which commonly is the fly that haunts such employments, would render me dishonorable to thy Majesty and disserviceable in thy employment. *Second*, because I easily saw, great places were slippery places, the mark of envy. It was, therefore, always my care so to behave myself in it as I might be in a capacity to leave it, and so to leave it as that when I had left it I might have no scars or blemishes stick upon me. I carried, therefore, the same evenness of temper in holding it as might become me if I were without it. *Third*, I found enough, in great employments, to make me sensible of the danger, troubles, and cares of it; enough to make me humble, but not enough to make me proud and haughty.

"I never made use of my power or greatness to *serve my own turns*, either to heap up riches, or to oppress my neighbor, or to revenge injuries, or to uphold or bolster out injustice. For, though others thought me great, I knew myself to be still the same; and, in all things besides the due execution of my place, my deportment was just the same as if I had been no such man. For, first, I knew that I was but thy steward and minister, and placed there to serve thee and those ends which thou proposedst in my preferment, and not to serve myself, much less my passions or corruptions. And, further, I very well and practically knew that place and honor and preferment are things extrinsical, and have no ingredience into the man. His value and estimate before, and under, and after his greatness, is still the same in itself; as the counter that now stands for a penny, anon for six-pence, anon for twelve-pence, is still the same counter, though its place and extrinsical denomination be changed.

"I improved the opportunity of my place, eminence, and greatness to *serve thee and my country* in it, with all vigilance, diligence, and fidelity. I protected, countenanced, and encouraged thy worship, name, day, and people. I did faithfully execute justice, according to that station I had. I rescued the oppressed from the cruelty, malice, and insolence of their oppressors. I cleared the innocent from unjust calumnies and reproaches. I was instrumental to place those in offices, places, and employments of trust and consequence, that were honest and faithful. I removed those that were dishonest, irreligious, false, or unjust.

"Touching my REPUTATION and CREDIT. 1. I never affected the reputation of being rich, great, crafty, or politic; but I esteemed much a deserved reputation of *justice, honesty, integrity, virtue, and piety.*

"2. I never thought that reputation was the thing primarily to be looked after in the exercise of virtue; for that were to affect the substance for the sake of the shadow, which had been a kind of levity and impotence of mind; but I looked at virtue and the worth of it as that which was the first desirable, and reputation as a handsome and useful accession to it.

"3. The reputation of justice and honesty I was always careful to keep untainted, upon these grounds. *First,* because a blemish in my reputation would be dishonorable to thee. *Second,* it would be an abuse of a talent which thou hadst committed to me. *Third,* it would be a weakening of an instrument which thou hadst put into my hands, upon the strength whereof much good might be done by me.

"I will use all fidelity and honesty, and take care that it shall not be lost by any default of mine; *and if notwithstanding all this, my reputation be soiled by evil or envious men or angels, I will patiently bear it, and content myself with the serenity of my own conscience. Hic murus abenius esto.*

"When thy honor or the good of my country was concerned, I then thought it was a seasonable time to lay out my reputation for the advantage of either; and to act it, and by and upon it, to the highest, in the use of all lawful means. And upon such an occasion the counsel of Mordecai to Esther was my encouragement (Esther iv. 14)—'Who knoweth whether God hath given thee this reputation and esteem for such a time as this?'"

The treatise on "Redeeming Time" contains the following admirable maxims—

"How time is to be redeemed. The particular methods of husbanding time, *viz*, in relation to opportunity, and in relation to our time of life, shall be promiscuously set down. Now, the actions of our lives may be distinguished into several kinds; and in relation to those several actions will the employments of our times be diversified. 1. There are *actions natural*, such as are eating, drinking, sleep, motion, rest. 2. Actions *civil*, as provision for families, bearing of public offices in times of peace or war, moderate recreations and divertisements, employments in civil vocations, as agriculture, mechanical trades, liberal professions. 3. Actions *moral*, ... whether relating to ourselves, as sobriety, temperance, moderation, or relating to others, as acts of justice, charity, compassion, liberality. 4. Or, lastly, actions religious, relating to Almighty God, as invocation, thanksgiving, inquiring into his works, will, obedience to his law and commands, observing the solemn seasons of his worship and service, and—which *must go through and give a tincture to all the rest*—a habit of fear of him, love to him, humility and integrity of heart and soul before him; and, in sum, a habit of religion towards God in his Son Jesus Christ, which is the *magnum oportet*, the one thing necessary, and overweighs all the rest.

"Be obstinately constant to your devotions at certain set times, and be sure to spend the Lord's day entirely in those religious duties proper to it; and let nothing but an inevitable necessity divert you from it.

"Whatever you do, be very careful to retain in your heart a *habit of religion*, that may be always about you, and keep your heart and life always as in his presence and tending towards him. This will be continually with you, and put itself into acts, even though you are not in a solemn posture of religious worship, and will lend you multitudes of religious applications to God, upon all occasions and interventions, which will not at all hinder you in any measure in your secular occasions, but better and further you. It will make you faithful in your calling, through reflection on the presence and command of Him you fear and love. It will make you thankful for all successes and supplies; temperate and sober in all your natural actions; just and faithful in all your dealings; patient and contented in all your disappointments and crosses; and actually consider and intend his honor in all you do; and will give a tincture of religion and devotion upon all your secular employments, and turn those very actions which are materially civil or natural, into the very true and formal nature of religion, and make your whole life to be an unintermitted life of religion, and duty to God. For this habit of piety in your soul will not only not lie sleeping and inactive, but almost in every hour of the day will put forth actual exertings of itself in applications of short occasional prayers, thanksgivings, dependence, resort unto that God that is always near you and lodgeth in a manner in your heart by his fear and love, and habitual religion towards him. And by this means you do effectually and in the best and readiest manner imaginable doubly redeem your time.

"Now, the fear of God, being actually present upon the soul, and exerting itself, is the greatest motive and obligation in the world to consideration and attention touching things to be done or said. It mightily advanceth and improveth the worth and excellency of the most humane actions in the world, and makes them a nobler kind of thing than otherwise without it they would be.

"Take a man that is employed as a statesman or politician: though he have much wisdom and prudence, it commonly degenerates into craft and cunning and pitiful shuffling, without the fear of God; but mingle the fear of Almighty God with that kind of wisdom, it renders it noble, and generous, and staid, and honest, and stable. Again, take a man that is much acquainted with the subtler kind of learning, as philosophy, for instance; without the fear of God upon his heart, it will carry him over to pride, arrogance, self-conceit, curiosity, presumption; but mingle it with the fear of God, it will ennoble that knowledge, carry it up to the honor and glory of that God who is the Author of nature, to the admiration of his power, wisdom, and goodness; it will keep him humble, modest, sober, and yet rather with an advance than detriment to his knowledge."

The lessons of such a volume so early impressed upon the mind and heart of Washington laid the foundation of his future fame, and finished his finely-formed character in the mould of Christian virtues. When thirteen years of age, he wrote for his self-government and conduct many moral rules, from which the following are selections—

Washington's Maxims When a Boy

1. Every action in company ought to be with some sign of respect to those present.

2. Be no flatterer.

3. Let your countenance be pleasant, but in serious matters some-what grave.

4. Show not yourself glad at the misfortune of another, though he were your enemy.

5. Let your conversation with men of business be short and comprehensive.

6. Wherein you reprove another, be unblamable yourself; for example is more prevalent than precept.

7. Be not hasty to believe flying reports to the disparagement of any.

8. Associate yourself with men of good quality, if you esteem your own reputation; for it is better to be alone than in bad company.

9. Be not apt to relate news, if you know not the truth thereof.

10. Be not curious to know the affairs of others; neither approach to those that speak in private.

11. Undertake not what you cannot perform; but be careful to keep your promise.

12. Speak not evil of the absent; for it is unjust.

13. Be not angry at the table, whatever happens; and if you have reason to be, show it not. Put on a cheerful countenance, especially if there be strangers; for good humor makes one dish of meat a feast.

14. When you speak of God or his attributes, let it be seriously, in reverence.

15. Honor and obey your natural parents, though they be poor.

16. Let your recreations be manly, not sinful.

17. Labor to keep alive in your breast that little spark of celestial fire called "conscience."

18. Avoid gaming. This is a vice which is productive of every possible evil, equally injurious to morals and health.

19. Mock not nor jest at any thing of importance.

20. Use no reproachful language against any one, neither curse nor revile.

21. Be not forward, but friendly and courteous; the first to salute, hear, and answer.

22. Detract not from others, neither be excessive in commending.

23. A good moral character is the first essential in a man. It is, therefore, highly important to endeavor not only to be learned but to be virtuous.

24. Let your conversation be without envy, for it is a sign of a tractable and commendable nature; and in all causes of passion, admit reason to govern.

His Fillial Reverence

Among the most beautiful Christian elements of Washington's character was his filial love and reverence for his mother. He affectionately and conscientiously through all his life obeyed the Divine precept, *"Honor thy father and thy mother;"* and he realized the promised blessing—*"that it may be well with thee, and that thy days may be long in the land which the Lord thy God giveth thee."*

He cheerfully relinquished, at the age of fifteen, his purpose to enter the naval service of Great Britain, saying to his mother, with tears, "My dear mother, I did strongly desire to go, but I could not endure being on board the ship and knowing you were unhappy." His letter to his mother, in July, 1755, immediately after the defeat of Braddock, to relieve her anxiety about his safety, and giving her an account of the battle, closes with, "I am, honored madam, your dutiful son." In his letter to her, in August, 1755, commencing, "Honored Madam," he says, in reference to accepting the command to Ohio, "If the command is pressed upon me by the general voice of the country, it would reflect dishonor on me to refuse it; and that, I am sure, must or ought to give you greater uneasiness than my going into an honorable command." In his diary, in 1760, after his marriage, appears this record of his visit to his mother—"Reached my mother's, and then went to Fredericksburg. Returned in the evening to my mother's: all alone with her." After this, he was in the habit of regularly visiting his mother once or twice a year, as long as she lived, travelling about fifty miles to perform this filial duty. The last visit he paid his venerable mother was just preceding his departure from Mount Vernon to assume the Presidency at Philadelphia. The Fredericksburg newspaper of March 12, 1789, has the subjoined notice—"On Saturday evening last his Excellency General Washington arrived in town from Mount Vernon, and early on Monday morning he set out on his return. The object of his Excellency's visit was to take leave of *his aged mother*, previous to his departure for the new Congress, over the councils of which the united voice of America had called him to preside." That solemn and parting interview—the last they ever had—is one of the most affecting instances of filial affection recorded in history.

Washington a Model for Young Men

As a pattern to young men, Washington is worthy of constant study and imitation. His youthful character was moulded into the finest form of virtue, and at a very early age he attracted public notice and was called into active service. His disinterested devotedness to serve his country was early exemplified in his seeking an appointment in Braddock's expedition to the Ohio, which proved so disastrous to that British officer and so fortunate for the fame of Washington. "The solo motive," wrote Washington to the Speaker of the House of Delegates, under date of Mount Vernon, 20th April, 1755, "which invites me to the field, is the *laudable desire of serving my country, not the gratification of any ambitious or lucrative plans.*"

Having no sons of his own to educate, he adopted two grandchildren of his wife at the death of their father, one of whom was George Washington Parke Custis, in whose education and welfare he manifested a paternal solicitude. His counsels to him at college are full of practical wisdom and contain advice worthy the attention of all young men. Washington writes to him as follows—

"The assurances you give me of applying diligently to your studies, and fulfilling those obligations which are enjoined by your Creator and due to his creatures, are highly pleasing and satisfactory to me. I rejoice in it on two accounts: first, as it is the sure means of laying the foundation of your own happiness, and rendering you, if it should please God to spare your life, a useful member of society. You are now entering into that stage of life when good or bad habits will be formed—when the mind will be turned to things useful and praiseworthy, or to dissipation and vice. Fix on whichever it may, it will stick by you; for you know it has been said, and truly, that 'as the twig is bent, so it will grow.' This in a strong point of view shows the propriety of letting your inexperience be directed by mature advice, and of placing guard upon the avenues which lead to idleness and vice. The latter will approach like a thief, working upon your passions, encouraged, perhaps, by bad examples. Virtue and vice cannot be allied, nor can idleness and industry. It is the nature of idleness and vice to obtain as many votaries as they can.

"Endeavor to conciliate the good will of all your fellow-students, rendering them every act of kindness in your power. But, above all, be obedient to your tutors. Let it be your pride to demean yourself in such a manner as to obtain the good will of your superiors and the love of your fellow-students.

"I would guard you against imbibing hasty and unfavorable impressions of any one. Let your judgment always balance well before you decide, and even then, when there is no occasion for expressing an opinion, it is best to be silent, for there is nothing more certain than that it is at all times more easy to make enemies than friends. And, besides, to speak evil of any one, unless there is unquestionable proof of their deserving it, is an injury for which there is no adequate reparation. For, as Shakspeare says, 'He that robs me of my good name enriches not himself, but renders me poor indeed,' or words to that effect."

In Washington's counsels to his young ward in reference to reading, he remarked that he was particularly gratified to hear that the young man was about to commence a course of solid reading under the direction of the President of Princeton College, Dr. Samuel Stanhope Smith, and says, "Light reading (by this I mean books of little importance) may amuse for a moment, but leaves nothing solid behind."

His advice to young Custis on the early marriage of students is worthy of attention. On this point Washington wrote, "I have with much surprise been informed of your devoting much time and paying much attention to a certain young lady of that place [Annapolis]. Recollect the saying of the wise man, 'There is a time for all things;' and sure I am this is not a time for a *boy of your age* to enter into engagements which might end in sorrow and repentance."

"Enter upon the grand theatre of life with the advantages of a finished education, a highly-cultivated mind, and a proper sense of your duties to God and man."

In a letter to his nephew, Bushrod Washington, who was a student of law in Philadelphia, Washington, under date of "Newburgh, 15th Jan., 1783," wrote as follows—

"The last thing which I shall mention is first in importance; and that is, *to avoid gaming*. This is a vice productive of every possible evil, equally injurious to the morals and health of its votaries. It is the child of avarice, the brother of iniquity, and father of mischief. It has been the ruin of many worthy families, the loss of many a man's honor, and the cause of suicide."

These and all other vices were offensive to Washington's "sense of moral and religious propriety, and therefore discouraged from principle, through every period of his life. His example was in harmony with his precepts."

The obligations and duties of a Christian life had in Washington a conscientious and constant fulfilment in his private and public life.

He was a member of a Christian Church (the Episcopal), into which he was baptized, and under the influence of which he grew up to manhood, and of which he lived and died an active and consistent member. His mother was a member of the church at Fredericks-burg, where Washington's youth was spent, and the family Bible of his mother contains, in her own handwriting, the date of his birth, his baptism, and the names of his religious sponsors. After his location at Mount Vernon and marriage, he was a member and a vestryman of the Pohick church, in whose temporal and spiritual welfare he manifested a constant interest and care, and where he habitually worshipped till the commencement of the Revolutionary War. After the close of the war, and his return to Mount Vernon, in December, 1783, his place of worship was in Alexandria, where, in Christ's Church, he had a pew, and constantly attended. For the support of the ministry and the perpetual maintenance of religious institutions and services, he drew up a paper subjecting the pews of the church to an annual rent, the first clause of which is as follows—"We, the subscribers, do hereby agree that the pews we now hold in the Episcopal church at Alexandria shall be forever charged with an annual rent of five pounds, Virginia money, each. In witness whereof we have hereunto set our hands and seals, this 25th day of April, in the year of our Lord 1785." This pew-rent Washington when President, and resident a large portion of the year at Philadelphia, directed his steward regularly to pay.

Attends Constantly the Public Worship of God

He was through his whole life, private and public, a constant and reverential attendant on the public worship of God.

The Rev. Lee Massey, the rector of the parish in which Pohick Church was located, and who shared largely in the esteem of Washington, was heard often to say, "I never knew so constant an attendant on church as Washington; and his behavior in the house of God was ever so deeply reverential that it produced the happiest effects on my congregation, and greatly assisted me in my pulpit-labors. No company ever withheld him from church. I have often been at Mount Vernon on the Sabbath morning, when his breakfast-table was filled with guests; but to him they furnished no pretext for neglecting his God and losing the satisfaction of setting a good example; for, instead of staying at home out of false complaisance to them, he used constantly to invite them to accompany him."

The same habit was kept up during his military life. One of his secretaries, Judge Harrison, often said that "whenever the general could be spared from camp on the Sabbath, he never failed riding out to some neighboring church to join those who were publicly worshipping the great Creator." This was done when there was no public worship in the camp.

After Washington was chosen President, he chiefly resided at Philadelphia, and during the eight years of his administration he was punctual in his attendance on public worship. He had a pew in Christ Church, of which the venerable Bishop White was rector; and it was seldom vacant when the weather would permit him to attend. Mrs. Custis, of Arlington, bears this testimony to the habit of Washington in attending public worship at Philadelphia—

"On Sundays, unless the weather was uncommonly severe, the President and Mrs. Washington attended divine service at Christ

Church; and in the evenings the President read to Mrs. Washington, in her chamber, a sermon, or some portion of the sacred writings."

Bishop White, of the Episcopal Church, says, "The Father of his Country, as well during the Revolutionary War as in his Presidency, attended divine service in this city [Philadelphia]. During his Presidency our vestry provided him with a pew. It was habitually occupied by himself; by Mrs. Washington, who was a regular communicant, and by his secretaries. His behavior was always serious and attentive."

After he retired from the Presidency, he continued the same habit. The church in Alexandria was again his place of worship. The distance was nine miles; yet his pew was seldom unoccupied on the Lord's day. Neither in the parade of military life, nor in the cares of civil administration, nor in the retired circle of home, did Washington ever forget to worship God in a reverential and public manner.

His Reverence for the Sabbath

Washington obeyed the Divine injunction, "Thou shalt reverence my Sabbath," and "remember it to keep it holy."

The wisdom and piety of Washington combined to render him a strict observer of the Sabbath and a jealous advocate of its authority and sanctity. Of this his conscientious and habitual attendance on the services of the sanctuary would be sufficient testimony. There seemed to be, during his Presidency, an increased regard and reverence for the Sabbath, and the discipline of his house was strictly conformed to its obligations and proprieties. It was an established rule of his mansion, during the eight years of his administration, that visitors could not be admitted on Sundays. "No visitors," says Custis, "were admitted to the President's house on Sundays, with the exception of Mr. Speaker Trumbull," who was one of the most pious men of the age.

An incident while travelling in Connecticut will illustrate his regard for the Sabbath and the laws which protect its sacredness. Being unable, on account of the roughness of the roads, to reach the town on Saturday night where he designed to spend the Sabbath, on Sunday morning he proceeded on his journey to an inn near the place of worship which he proposed to attend. His coachman was accosted by a plain man from a cottage, who inquired if there was any urgent reason for his travelling on the Lord's day. General Washington explained the circumstances to the officer, and said "nothing was further from his intention than to treat with disrespect the laws and usages of Connecticut relative to the Sabbath, *which met with his most cordial approbation.*"

His Respect for Ministers

It is not known that he ever wantonly violated the Lord's day in a single instance. In no one duty of his life can a more fixed purpose of obedience be traced than in reference to this obligation.

Washington, at every period of his life, had a special respect for the office and persons of the ministers of the Christian religion.

"He honored the calling as one of Divine appointment, and him who filled it as the living representative of the Divine Author of Christianity. This was the combined result of his good sense, pious affections, and faith in the gospel of Christ." Through every stage of his illustrious career, the marks of this wise and patriotic course can be distinctly traced. He knew their piety and patriotism, and saw their auspicious and powerful influence on society, on the army, and on the affairs of government, and sought their counsels and entreated their prayers. Among his most cherished and confidential advisers during the war, and his civil administration, were ministers of the gospel. In his first youthful military campaign he earnestly labored for the appointment of chaplains, and frequently during the war of the Revolution he called the attention of Congress to their appointment, pay, and character, and wrote to churches requesting them to grant permission to their pastors to labor as chaplains in the army. His estimate of the influence and labors of pious and intelligent ministers of the Christian religion, and his high respect for them, may be found in the correspondence of Washington with the churches, in another chapter of this volume, to which the reader's attention is directed for further information on this point.

His Habits of Prayer

Washington was a man of prayer, and had faith in its divine efficacy.

He was no less punctual and constant in the duties of secret prayer than in those of the public sanctuary. In the French and Indian War, Colonel B. Temple testified to his habit of reading the Scriptures and praying with his troops on Sunday, in the absence of the chaplain, and "that on sudden and unexpected visits into Washington's marquee he has more than once found him on his knees at his devotions."

His private devotions during the gloomy winter of 1777, at Valley Forge, are a matter of authentic history. "He was frequently observed to visit a secluded grove," and General Knox and others were fully apprized that *prayer* was the object of his frequent visits to that consecrated spot. Other instances occurred during the war, in which Washington was heard, as he tarried for a night, engaged in his *private religious worship.*

During his residence at Philadelphia, as President of the United States, it was the habit of Washington to retire winter and summer, at nine o'clock, and he was seen "upon his knees at a small stand, with an open Bible upon it." This habit was conscientiously and constantly observed in the French and Indian War, and through the Revolutionary War, and during his Presidential terms, and no doubt till the end of his life.

It was in reference to this trait in the Christian character of Washington that Dr. Mason, of New York, on the occasion of his death, said, in a sermon, "That invisible hand which guided him at first continued to guard and guide him through the successive stages of the Revolution. Nor did he account it a weakness to bend the knee in homage to its supremacy, and prayer for its direction. This was the armor of Washington, this the salvation of his country.

"The example of Washington," continues Dr. Mason, "teaches a poignant reproof to those who think, or act as if they thought, that religion is incompatible with greatness. The majesty of his character forbids a suspicion that his reverence for the worship of God, and his solicitude for the prevalence of religious principles, were either a tribute to prejudice or a stratagem of state.

"But every possible doubt is removed by the fact that it was *his uniform practice to retire at a certain hour for the devotion of the closet.*"

"He was not one of those," said his adopted daughter, "who act and pray that they may be seen of men. He communed with God in secret. When my aunt, Miss Custis, died suddenly at Mount Vernon, before they could realize the event he knelt by her and prayed most fervently, most affectionately, for her recovery."

In the month of November, 1829, I was in Fredericksburg, Va., and in the family of the Rev. Mr. Wilson, pastor of the Presbyterian church in that place. He occupied the house in which the mother of Washington lived and died. Mr. Wilson informed me that a nephew of Washington, Captain Lewis, who had been his clerk, and had the charge of his books and papers, and was daily in his library until his decease, related to him the following occurrence. It was the custom of Washington to retire to his library every evening precisely at nine o'clock, and, although he had visitors, he invariably left at that hour, and did not return. He remained alone in his library till ten o'clock, and passed into his bedchamber by an inner door. Captain Lewis had long wondered how he spent that hour, knowing that he wrote nothing, and that the books and papers were as he himself left them the preceding day. During a violent storm of wind and rain, and when there were no visitors, he crept in his stocking-feet to the door, and through the key-hole he beheld him *on his knees*, with a large book open before him, which he had no doubt was a Bible—a large one being constantly in the room.

Nath. Hewit.

Bridgeport, January 10, 1859

"The commander-in-chief," says Rev. Albert Barnes, "of the American armies, was observed constantly to retire for the purpose of secret devotion. He went alone and sought guidance of the God of armies and of light."

"These incidents perfectly accord with that humble and devout spirit which steadily marked his visible conduct, and distinguished even his political addresses. His inaugural speech to Congress in 1789 is a signal display of this spirit. It strongly expresses his sense of his own deficiencies, his faith in Divine communications to the human mind, and his prayerful dependence upon them. Sound philosophy, as well as Christianity, justify a belief that his wisdom and virtue as a man, his conduct and success as a hero and statesman, were eminently indebted to his habitual devotion. If any admirers of our departed sage despise or neglect prayer and other offices of piety, they pour contempt on his past precepts and example on earth and his present employments in heaven."

Commemorates the Lord's Supper

Washington commemorated the love of the Saviour of the world, by frequently observing the sacrament.

This act of obedience to the Saviour was, according to the testimony of many residing in the neighborhood of Mount Vernon, frequently performed at Pohick Church previous to the Revolutionary War, of which he was a member and a communicant. "General Washington," said Mrs. Washington's grand-daughter, "always received the sacrament with my grandmother, before the Revolution."

Washington at the Communion-Table in the Presbyterian Church at Morristown, New Jersey

It is the Sabbath. The congregation are assembled in the house of worship; and among their number is the commander-in-chief of the American army. With a willing and devout spirit he unites with the people of God in the ordinances of religion. After a solemn sermon from a venerable minister, a hymn is sung, and the invitation given to the members of sister Churches to unite in the celebration of the Lord's Supper. A well-known military form rises in response to the invitation. With solemn dignity and Christian meekness he takes his seat with Christ's people and partakes of the bread and wine. It is Washington at the communion-table in a Presbyterian church.

The Rev. Dr. Cox, of Brooklyn, New York, first gave to the public the circumstances attending this interesting event, which he received from Dr. Hillyer, who had them from the lips of Rev. Dr. Timothy Johnes himself, the latter being the pastor of the church at Morristown at the time—

"While the American army, under the command of Washington, lay encamped in the environs of Morristown, New Jersey, it occurred that the service of the communion, then observed semi-annually only, was to be administered in the Presbyterian church of that village. On a morning of the previous week, the general, after his accustomed inspection of the camp, visited the house of the Rev. Dr. Johnes, then pastor of that church, and, after the usual preliminaries, thus accosted him—'Doctor, I understand that the Lord's Supper is to be celebrated with you next Sunday. I would learn if it accords with the canons of your Church to admit communicants of another denomination.' The doctor rejoined, 'Most certainly: ours is not the Presbyterian table, general, but THE LORD'S TABLE; and we hence give the Lord's invitation to all his followers, of whatever name.'

"The general replied, 'I am glad of it: that is as it ought to be: but, as I was not quite sure of the fact, I thought I would ascertain it from yourself; as I propose to join with you on that occasion. Though a member of the Church of England, I have no exclusive partialities.'

"The doctor reassured him of a cordial welcome, and the general was found seated with the communicants the next Sabbath."

This incident in the life of Washington shows, in the first place, his own impression that he was a *religious man*, entitled to the privileges of the household of faith; and, in the second place, that he understood the spirit and principles of the Thirty-Nine Articles, which recognize members of all evangelical Churches as belonging to the true Catholic Church. The anecdote in either aspect commends itself to thoughtful consideration.

"From the lips of a lady of undoubted veracity," says Rev. Dr. Chapman, "I received the interesting fact that soon after the close of the Revolutionary War she saw Washington partake of the consecrated symbols of the body and blood of Christ, in Trinity Church, New York."

Liberal to the Poor

Washington was liberal in his charities to the poor and in his Christian benefactions.

The traditions of Mount Vernon, still fresh in the memories of many in that region, rehearse the story of Washington's benevolence, and keep in remembrance his numerous and disinterested deeds of kindness. Almsgiving—a beautiful ornament and an excellent evidence of the presence of real piety—was not an impulse, but a principle, in the Christian character of Washington.

From his head-quarters at Cambridge, 26th of November, 1775, he wrote as follows to the manager of his estates, during the Revolutionary War—

"Let the hospitality of the house with respect to the poor be kept up. Let no one go hungry away. If any of this kind of people should be in want of corn, supply their necessities, provided it does not encourage them in idleness; and I have no objection to your giving my money in charity to the amount of forty or fifty pounds a year, when you think it is well bestowed. What I mean by having no objection is that it is my desire it should be done. You are to consider that neither myself nor wife is now in the way to do these kind offices."

"I had orders," said Mr. Peake, one of his managers after the war, "from General Washington to fill a corn-house every year for the sole use of the poor in my neighborhood, to whom it was a most seasonable and precious relief; saving numbers of poor women and children from extreme want, and blessing them with plenty."

He also provided for the poor around him in other ways. "He owned several fishing-stations on the Potomac, at which excellent herring were caught, which when salted proved an important article of food to the poor. For their accommodation he appropriated a station, one of the best he had, and furnished it with all the necessary apparatus for taking herring. By this means all the honest poor around him had the means of procuring, free of expense, a competent stock of this valuable food for their families."

His benefactions to persons in pecuniary embarrassments were timely and liberal, amounting sometimes to many thousands of dollars; and the recipients "never laid down their heads at night without presenting their prayers to Heaven for their 'beloved Washington.'"

In his will he bequeathed four thousand dollars "towards the support of a free school in Alexandria, for the purpose of educating orphan children, or the children of such other poor and indigent persons as are unable to accomplish it with their own means."

Besides this annuity secured by him to the Alexandria free school, he also endowed Washington College with ten thousand dollars, of which he was elected the honorary President.

This constant liberality, which he practised himself; he inculcated and urged upon others. In his paternal counsels to young Custis when at college, Washington writes from Philadelphia in 1793, "Never let an indigent person ask without receiving *something*, if you have the means—always recollecting in what light the widow's mite was viewed."

To his nephew Bushrod Washington, afterwards a distinguished Christian judge of the Supreme Court of the United States, when a student of law in Philadelphia, Washington, in 1783, wrote—

"Let your heart feel for the afflictions and distresses of every one, and let your hand give in proportion to your purse, remembering always the estimation of the widow's mite, but that it is not every one that asketh that deserveth charity: all, however, are worthy of the inquiry, or the deserving may suffer."

A Practical Emancipator

Washington was a practical lover of liberty for all men, and declared his faith by an act of emancipation to all his slaves.

In an interview with the two bishops of the Methodist Episcopal Church, Asbury and Coke, at Mount Vernon, on the 26th of May, 1785, Washington "gave them his opinion on that institution [slavery]; expressed his wishes for its abolition, and said that he had already delivered his sentiments upon the subject to some leading men of the State, and that in case any movement should be made for that purpose his suffrage should not be wanting."

His last will and testament, signed only a few days before his death, December, 1799, declares the emancipation of his slaves—

I, GEORGE WASHINGTON, of Mount Vernon, a citizen of the United States, and lately President of the same, do make, ordain, and declare that instrument, which is written with my own hand, and every page thereof subscribed by my own hand, to be my last WILL and TESTAMENT. ... Upon the decease of my wife, it is my will and desire that all the slaves whom I hold *in my own right* should receive their freedom. And I do most pointedly and most solemnly enjoin it upon my executors to see that this clause respecting slaves, and every part thereof, be religiously fulfilled.

"Read his *last will*," says Professor Tappan, of Cambridge University, "and see his anxious, tender, and effectual provision for the liberation of all his African servants, for the comfort of such of them as are aged or infirm or united by the sacred ties of marriage, and for the useful education of their infant offspring. This provision, added to his corresponding humanity while living, and the filial tears shed by his domestics on his tomb, erect one of the noblest monuments to his fame. These are monuments infinitely superior to those loud but hypocritical clamors for liberty and equality which distinguish many nominal Patriots and real tyrants of the present day."

His Liberal Christian Spirit

Washington constantly manifested a Christian spirit towards all religious denominations.

"A friend to our holy religion," said an officer in the United States army, January, 1800, "he was ever guided by its pious doctrines, and had embraced the tenets of the Episcopal Church; yet his charity, unbounded as his immortal mind, led him equally to respect every denomination of the followers of Jesus. Meek and distrustful of himself, he was liberal and candid to others. Superior to the little prejudices which subsist among different sects— prejudices which deform the beauty and destroy the harmony of the religious world—he loved and wept and prayed for all."

This spirit of Christian union and love was peculiarly pleasing to Washington, and on his final withdrawal from public life, in answer to an address of the ministers of various denominations in and around Philadelphia, he especially congratulated them and the country on its growing prevalence and happy influence.

His Accurate Business Habits

Washington was exact and thoroughly honest in all his business transactions.

"In the management of his private affairs," says Chief-Justice Marshall, "he exhibited an exact yet liberal economy. His accounts were all made in his own handwriting, and every entry made in the most particular manner." He kept his financial matters in such perfect order that, though his estate was large, little trouble was found by the executors, after his death, in settling it.

His pecuniary transactions with the Government were characterized by the same honesty and accuracy, and his original account, on file in the Treasury Department, is an honorable and suggestive memorial of his exact business habits and sterling integrity. In accepting the command of the American army, in June, 1775, Washington, in an address to Congress, said—

"As to pay, sir, I beg leave to assure the Congress that, as no pecuniary consideration could have tempted me to accept this arduous employment at the expense of my domestic ease and happiness, I do not wish to make any profit from it. I will keep an exact account of my expenses. These, I doubt not, they will discharge; and that is all I ask."

His integrity in business is exemplified by the incident that every barrel of flour which bore the brand "George Washington, Mount Vernon," was exempted from the customary inspection in the West India ports, that name being regarded as an ample guarantee of the quality and quantity of any article to which it was affixed. His vast business transactions illustrated the sentiment in his farewell address, that *"Honesty is always the best policy."*

"His exact and exemplary method of transacting all his business enabled him to accomplish more, and in a more perfect and advantageous manner, than perhaps any other man of the age."

Washington a Christian Hero, A Christian Statesman, A Christian Politician, A Christian Magistrate

The military life and character of Washington have an authentic record in the chapter in this volume on the Christianity of the American army. The splendor of his military campaigns, and that which crowned them with moral glory and final victory, consisted in the presiding and guiding presence of the Christian religion. He invoked constantly the blessing of the God of battles, profoundly and constantly recognized the providence of God in all the occurrences and conflicts of the war, discouraged and prohibited the vices so prevalent in an army, and enjoined his troops to act as *Christian* soldiers, and issued orders to his army declaring that it was in vain to hope for success in the glorious struggle for liberty and independence unless they received the guidance and blessing of Almighty God. As a Christian hero he stands in solitary grandeur, and in contrast to most of the leading warriors of the world.

"In Washington," says Lord Brougham, in his remarks on Napoleon and Washington, "we truly behold a marvellous contrast to almost every one of the endowments and the vices which we have been contemplating. This is the consummate glory of the great American: a triumphant warrior, but a warrior whose sword only left its sheath when the first law of our nature commanded it to be drawn; and, dying, he bequeathed to his heirs the sword he had worn in the war for liberty, charging them 'never to take it from the sheath but in self-defence, or in defence of their country and her freedom;' and commanding them that when it should be thus drawn they should never sheathe it, nor ever give it up, but prefer falling with it in their hands to the relinquishment thereof; words the majesty and simple eloquence of which are not surpassed in the oratory of Athens and Rome. To his latest breath did this great patriot maintain the noble character of a captain the patron of peace, and of a statesman the friend of justice."

The military character and conduct of Washington have a noble illustration in his tribute of praise to the patriotism of the soldiers of the army, and in his Christian sympathy for their sufferings. His cheeks were wet with manly tears at the hardships and trials they endured, and on every occasion he urged the justice of their claims upon the authorities of the land, and vindicated their valor and heroic labors.

The following passage from his general orders, issued at Newburgh, New York, April 18, 1783, on the cessation of hostilities, displays the admirable traits of a humane man and of a Christian military chieftain. He says—

> While the general recollects the almost infinite variety of scenes through which we have passed, with a mixture of pleasure, astonishment, and gratitude, and while he contemplates the prospects before us with rapture, he cannot help wishing that all the brave men, of whatever condition they may be, who have shared in the toils and dangers of effecting this glorious Revolution, of rescuing millions from the hand of oppression, and of laying the foundations of a great empire, might be impressed with a proper idea of the dignified part they have been called to act (under the smiles of Providence)

on the stage of human affairs; for happy, thrice happy, shall they be pronounced hereafter who have contributed any thing, who have performed the meanest office, in erecting this stupendous *fabric of Freedom and Empire* on the broad basis of independency; who have asserted, in protecting, the rights of human nature, and established an asylum for the poor and oppressed of all nations and religions.

The glorious task for which we flew to arms being thus accomplished, the liberties of our country being fully acknowledged and firmly secured by the smiles of Heaven on the purity of our cause and the honest exertions of a free people against a powerful nation disposed to oppress them, and the character of those who have persevered through every extremity of hardship, suffering, and danger being immortalized by the illustrious appellation of the *patriot army*, nothing now remains but for the actors of this mighty scene to preserve a perfect unvarying consistency of character through the very last act—to close the drama with applause, and to retire from the military theatre with the same approbation of angels and men which has crowned all their former virtuous actions.

The Statesmanship of Washington

Was pre-eminently Christian. This feature of his public life and character grew out of his inward religious life, and was impressed with the purity and immutability of the principles of piety. "In him religion was a steady principle of action. He was a firm believer in the Christian religion; and at his first entrance on the civic administration he made it known. He brought it with him into office, and he did not lose it there."

"To excel," says Dr. John M. Mason, of New York, February 22, 1800, "equally in military and political science, has been the praise of a few chosen spirits, among whom, with a proud preference, we enroll the Father of our country. When he entered on his first Presidency, all the interests of the continent were vibrating through the arch of political uncertainty. The departments of the new Government were to be marked out and filled up, foreign relations to be regulated, the physical and moral strength of the nation to be organized, and this at a time when skepticism in politics, no less than *in religion and morals*, was preparing throughout Europe to spring the mine of revolution and ruin."

In the midst of innumerable difficulties he began the administration of the new Government; and the sequel showed that he gave it a moral and Christian impress, and enunciated in his political principles and governmental acts the just and true ideas of a Christian Government.

As a statesman he at all times recognized God as the Ruler and Governor of nations. This ultimate fact in the science and wants of civil government Washington carried out in his whole civil career. The success of the Government, the harmony of political interests, the conciliation of party prejudices, the suppression of vices that tend to the destruction of republican institutions, the spread of the virtues that give strength and life and moral glory to a state, and the sources of lasting prosperity and greatness to the republic, as existing in the Christian religion, Washington uniformly and fully ascribed to God. He affirmed, in every variety of official enunciation, that the nation could not live and prosper without recognizing the presence and supremacy of God. "It is *impossible*," he said, "to govern the universe without God," and, "*a fortiori*, impossible to govern a nation without him."

This great Christian truth shines out in luminous brightness in his official state papers, which all have the moral impress of this great fact and are transparent with its purity and majesty. "It is the duty of all nations," said he, among his first official declarations, "to acknowledge the providence of Almighty God, *to obey his will*, to be grateful for his benefits, and humbly to implore his protection and favor."

His address to the Governors of the several States, in 1783, contains the following admirable thoughts on the same point. He says—

"I now make it my earnest prayer that God would have you, and the State over which you preside, in his holy protection; that he would incline the hearts of the citizens to cultivate a spirit of subordination and obedience to Government; to entertain a brotherly affection and love for one another, for their fellow-citizens of the United States at large, and particularly for their brethren who served in the field; and, finally, that he would most graciously be pleased to dispose us all to do justice, to love mercy, and to demean ourselves with that humility and pacific temper of mind which were the characteristics of the *Divine Author of our blessed religion*, and *without an humble imitation of whose example in these things we can never hope to be a happy nation."*

In the same address he refers to education, commerce, refinement of manners, and liberality of sentiment, as promising a favorable influence, and then adds, "But, *above all, the pure and benign light of revelation* has had a meliorating influence on mankind and increased the blessings of society."

During the close of his administration, and after his retirement from the Presidency, the atheistic convulsions of France were upheaving her foundations of state and society. The mind of Washington was at times saddened by the contemplation of the scenes of anarchy and blood which that unhappy country presented to the world, and by the knowledge that efforts were being made by misguided sympathizers in this country to entangle the American republic with France in her suicidal career. But, with a sublime moral courage, he stood firm, and, with his usual trust in God, said—"I cannot but hope and believe that the good sense of the people will ultimately get the better of their prejudices. I do not believe that Providence has done so much for nothing.

"The great Governor of the Universe has led us too long and too far on the road to happiness and glory to forsake us in the midst of it. By folly and improper conduct, proceeding from a variety of causes, we may now and then get bewildered; but I hope and trust that there is good sense and virtue enough left to recover the right path before we shall be entirely lost.

"The rapidity of national revolutions appears no less astonishing than their magnitude. In what they will terminate is known only to the great Ruler of events; and, confiding in his wisdom and goodness, we may safely trust the issue to him, without perplexing ourselves to seek for that which is beyond human ken—only taking care to perform the part assigned to us in a way that reason and our own consciences approve."

The following tribute to the administration and Christian principles of Washington, as displayed in his acts as a politician and a statesman, is extracted from the funeral oration delivered before Congress, by Richard Henry Lee, on the 26th of December, 1799—

"Commencing with his administration: what heart is not charmed with the recollection of the pure and wise principles announced by himself as the basis of his political life? He best understood the indissoluble union between virtue and happiness, between duty and advantage, between the genuine maxims of an honest and magnanimous policy and the solid rewards of public prosperity and individual felicity. Watching with an equal and comprehensive eye over this great assemblage of communities and interests, *he laid the foundation of our national policy in the unerring and immutable principles of* MORALITY *based* on RELIGION, exemplifying the pre-eminence of free government by all the attributes which win the affections of its citizens or command the respect of the world."

"We derive a presage," said a body of Christian ministers and laymen (Episcopalians), "from the piety of your character. Public virtue is the most certain means of public felicity, and religion is the surest basis of virtue. We therefore esteem it a peculiar happiness to behold in our Chief Magistrate a steady, uniform, avowed friend of the Christian religion, *who has commenced his administration in rational and exalted sentiments of piety*, and who in his private conduct adorns the doctrines of the gospel of Christ."

His Farewell Address contains among its Christian axioms and sentiments the following statements, which cannot be too often repeated, or too profoundly pondered by the American people. He says—

> The propitious smiles of Heaven can never be expected on a nation that disregards the eternal rules of right and order which Heaven itself has ordained.
>
> Observe good faith and justice towards all nations; cultivate peace and harmony with all. Religion and morality enjoin this conduct.
>
> Of all the dispositions and habits which lead to political prosperity, religion and morality are indispensable supports. In vain would that man claim the tribute of patriotism who should labor to subvert these great pillars of human happiness, these firmest props of the duties of men and citizens.

The mere politician equally with the pious man ought to respect and to cherish them. A volume could not trace out all their connections with private and public felicity.

Let us with caution indulge the supposition that morality can be maintained without religion. Whatever may be conceded to the influence of refined education on minds of peculiar structure, reason and experience both forbid us to expect that national morality can prevail in exclusion of *religious principles*. It is substantially true that virtue or morality is a necessary spring of popular government. The rule, indeed, extends with more or less force to every species of free government. Who that is a sincere friend to it can look with indifference upon attempts to shake the foundation of the fabric?

It will be worthy of a free, enlightened, and, at no distant period, a great, nation, to give to mankind the magnanimous and too novel example of a people always guided by an exalted justice and benevolence. Who can doubt that in the course of time and things the fruits of such a plan would richly repay any temporary advantages which might be lost by a steady adherence to it? Can it be that Providence has not connected the permanent felicity of a nation with its virtue? The experiment at least, is recommended by every sentiment which ennobles human nature. Alas! is it rendered impossible by its vices?

"The conduct of President Washington," says David Tappan, Professor of Divinity in Cambridge University, "was a humble and visible representation of the Divine government, in the uniform purity of its principles, measures, and objects. He approved himself the vice-gerent of God by his profound wisdom, impartial justice, unsuspected uprightness, and steady consistency—by his disinterested and universal love, his intense, unwearied, and successful exertions for the common good."

As a Christian Politician,

Washington, in his principles and action, is a model to public men. "He was the only man," says Jefferson, "in the United States that possessed the confidence of all: there was no other man who was considered any thing else than a party leader." His unselfish patriotism, the outgrowth of the Christian religion, comprehended all the great and true interests of the country, and harmonized with its permanent and progressive prosperity. No selfish interest ever prompted a single public act; and he was one of the few men in the world who rose above all party bias and prejudice and consecrated himself to the good of his country.

"No man," says Chief-Justice Marshall, "ever appeared upon the theatre of public action whose integrity was more incorruptible, or whose principles were more perfectly free from the contamination of those selfish and unworthy passions which find their nourishment in the conflicts of party. Having no views which required concealment, his real and avowed motives were the same; and his whole correspondence does not furnish a single case from which even an enemy would infer that he was capable, under any circumstances, of stooping to the employment of duplicity. No truth can be uttered with more confidence than that his ends were always upright and his means always pure. He exhibits the rare example of a politician to whom wiles were absolutely unknown, and whose professions to foreign Governments and to his own countrymen were always sincere. In him was fully exemplified the real distinction which forever exists between wisdom and cunning, and the importance as well as truth of the maxim that 'honesty is the best policy.'"

In reference to parties he said, "If we mean to support the liberty and independence which it has cost us so much blood and treasure to establish, we must drive far away the demon of party spirit.

"It is devoutly to be wished that faction was at an end, and that those to whom every thing dear and valuable is intrusted would lay aside *party* views and return to *first principles*. Happy, happy, thrice happy country, if such were the government of it! But, alas! we are not to expect that the path is to be strewed with flowers. That great, good Being who rules the universe has disposed matters otherwise, and for wise purposes, I am persuaded."

"There is an opinion that parties in free countries are useful checks upon the administration of the Government, and serve to keep alive the spirit of liberty.

"This, within certain limits, is probably true, and in Governments of a monarchical cast patriotism may look with indulgence, if not with favor, upon the spirit of party; but in those of the popular character—in Governments purely elective—it is a spirit not to be encouraged. From their natural tendency, it is certain there will always be enough of that spirit for every salutary purpose; and, there being constant danger of excess, the effort ought to be by force of public opinion to mitigate and assuage it. A fire not to be quenched, it demands a uniform vigilance to prevent its bursting into a flame, lest instead of warming it should consume."

The *political* character of Washington has its noblest illustration "in the pure and sublime maxims on which he founded his auspicious administration, and the steady magnanimity which marked his adherence to them. While such maxims and conduct reflected equal honor on his understanding and heart, while they illustrated the transcendent beauty and dignity of a *Christian policy*, they gave, at a critical period, the most salutary direction to our new political machine, and afforded a precious example to all succeeding patriots."

As a Christian Ruler

Washington was firm and inflexible in the administration of the Government. The rigid and impartial enforcement of the Constitution and the laws he regarded as vital to the very existence of the nation, and never for a moment did he relax the reins of government while he held them in his hands. On this point he says—

"The very idea of power, and the right of the people to establish government, presupposes the *duty of every individual* to *obey the established Government. All obstructions to the execution of its laws, all combinations and associations, under whatever plausible character, with the real design to direct, control, counteract, or awe the regular deliberations and action of the constituted authorities, are destructive of this fundamental principle, and of fatal tendency.*"

During the administration of Washington a practical test of these views and principles of the supreme power of the Government was applied. A portion of a sovereign State (Pennsylvania), in 1793, rebelled against the General Government, in resistance to an excise-law for revenue-purposes. Washington took immediate steps to vindicate the supremacy of law and to suppress the rebellion. He declared the insurrection to be "subversive of the just authority of the Government," and that the efforts of misguided or designing men were to substitute their misrepresentations in the place of truth, and their discontents in the place of stable government." He earnestly entreated, in an official form, all "to call to mind that, as the people of the United States have been permitted, under the *Divine favor*, in perfect freedom, after solemn deliberation, and in an enlightened age, to elect their own government, so will their gratitude for this inestimable blessing be best distinguished by firm exertion to *maintain the Constitution* and the laws."

> "When therefore," he continues, "*every form* of conciliation, not inconsistent with the being of the Government, has been adopted without effect—when, therefore, Government is set at defiance—the contest being whether a small portion of the United States shall *dictate to the whole Union*, and, at the expense of those who desire peace, indulge a desperate ambition;" "now, therefor, I, George Washington, President of the United States, in *obedience to that on high and irresistible duty consigned to me by the Constitution*, 'to take care that the laws be faithfully executed,' deploring that the *American name should be sullied by the outrages of citizens on their own Government*, but commiserating such as remain obstinate from delusion, have *Resolved*, in perfect reliance on that gracious Providence which so signally displays its goodness towards this country, to '*reduce the refractory to a due subordination to the law*;' and withal, the most solemn convictions of the essential *interests of the Union demand it, that the very existence of the Government and the fundamental principles of social order* are materially involved in the issue, and that the patriotism and firmness of all good citizens are seriously called upon, as occasion may require, to aid *in the effectual suppression* of so fatal a spirit."

The rebellion was effectually suppressed; and Washington, in view of the great triumph of constitutional government and the vindication and establishment of the supremacy of the laws, says, in his Message to Congress in 1794—

> It has been a spectacle displaying to the highest advantage the value of republican government, to behold the most and the least wealthy of our citizens standing in the same ranks as private soldiers, *pre-eminently distinguished by being the army of the Constitution.* ... To every description of citizens let praise be given; but *let them persevere in their affectionate vigilance over that precious deposit of American happiness—the Constitution of the United States.* Let them cherish it, too, for the sake of those who, from every clime, are daily seeking a dwelling in our land. And when, in the calm moments of reflection, they [the instigators of the rebellion] shall have retraced the origin and progress of the insurrection, let them determine whether it has not been fomented by combinations of men, who, careless of consequences, and disregarding the unerring truth that those who originate cannot always appease a civil convulsion, have disseminated, from an ignorance or perversion of facts, suspicions, jealousies, and accusations against the whole Government.

In 1786, a rebellion broke out in Massachusetts, headed by Daniel Shays, but was soon suppressed. In reference to this Washington expressed himself to Henry Lee as follows—

> You talk, my good sir, of employing influence to appease the present tumults in Massachusetts. (!) I know not where that influence is to be found, or, if attained, that it would be a proper remedy for the disorders. *Influence is not government.* Let us have a government, by which our lives, liberties, and properties will be secured, or let us know the worst at once—know precisely what the insurgents aim at. If they have real grievances, redress them, if possible; if they have not, *employ the force of Government against them at once.* These are my sentiments. Let the *reins of government, then, be braced with a steady hand, and every violation of the Constitution be reprehended.*

To the same import Washington wrote, March 31, 1787, to Madison—

> I have my doubts whether any system, without the means of coercion in the sovereign, will enforce due obedience to the ordinances of the General Government, without which every thing else fails.

Washington's Devotion to the Union

Grew out of his love for liberty and a strong government. He had a profound sense of the value of the Union to constitutional government and the blessings of freedom, and always felt that the destruction of the Union would be the destruction of the Government, the loss of liberty, and to establish the reign of civil anarchy. He says—

> The unity of government which constitutes you one people is also *now* dear to you. It is justly so; for it is a main pillar in the edifice of your real independence, the support of your tranquillity at home, your peace abroad—of your safety, of your prosperity, of that very liberty which you so highly prize. But as it is easy to foresee that, from different causes and from different quarters, much pains will be taken, many artifices employed, to weaken in your minds the conviction of this truth; as this is the point in your political fortress against which the batteries of internal and external enemies will be most constantly and actively (though often covertly and insidiously) directed, it is of infinite moment that you should properly estimate the immense value of your national union to your collective and individual happiness; that you should cherish a cordial, habitual, and immovable attachment to it; accustoming yourselves to think and speak of it as of the palladium of your political safety and prosperity, watching for its preservation with jealous anxiety, discountenancing whatever may suggest even a suspicion that it can in any event be abandoned, and indignantly frowning upon the first dawning of every attempt to alienate any portion of our country from the rest, or to enfeeble the sacred ties which now link together the various parts.

He consecrates and commits the Government, with all its precious interests, to God, in the following solemn and suggestive words—

> May that Almighty Being who rules over the universe, who presides in the councils of nations, and whose providential aid can supply every defect, consecrate to the liberties and happiness of the American people a Government instituted by themselves, for public and private security, upon the basis of law and equal administration of justice, preserving to every individual as much civil and political freedom as is consistent with the safety of the nation.
>
> While just government protects all in their rights, *true religion gives to government its surest support*.... The general prevalence of *piety*, philanthropy, honesty, industry, and economy seems, in the ordinary course of human affairs, particularly necessary for advancing and confirming the happiness of our country.... *Religion and morality are essential supports to society.*

As a Christian Patriot

Washington earnestly urged the Christian education of the people. He was a liberal patron of science and literature; and popular education under Christian auspices, he believed, was the only guardian of liberty and constitutional government.

In reply to an address from the President and Fellows of Harvard University, October 27, 1789, Washington says—

> It gives me sincere satisfaction to learn the flourishing state of your literary republic. Assured of its action in the past events of our political system, and of its further influence on those means which make the best support of good government, I rejoice that the direction of its measures is lodged with men whose approved knowledge, integrity. and patriotism give unquestionable assurances of their success.
>
> That the Muses may long enjoy a tranquil residence within the walls of your university, and that you, gentlemen, may be

happy in contemplating the progress of improvement through the various branches of your important departments, are among the most pleasing of my wishes and expectations. You will do me the justice of believing confidently in my disposition to promote the interests of science and true religion.

In answer to an address from the Corporation of Rhode Island College, August 17, 1790, Washington again gave his testimony to the influence of learning in the cause of liberty and the Revolution, in the following words—

In repeating thus publicly my sense of the zeal you displayed for the success of the cause of your country, I only add a single suffrage to the general testimony, which all who were acquainted with you in the most adverse and doubtful moments of our struggle for liberty and independence have constantly borne in your favor.

While I cannot remain insensible to the indulgence with which you regard the influence of my example and the tenor of my conduct, I rejoice in having so favorable an opportunity of felicitating the State of Rhode Island on the co-operation I am sure to find in the measures adopted by the guardians of literature in this place for improving the morals of the rising generation; and inculcating upon their minds principles peculiarly calculated for the preservation of our rights and liberties. You may rely on whatever Protection I may be able to afford in so important an object as the education of our youth.

The President and Faculty of the University of Pennsylvania, in April, 1789, presented an address of congratulation to Washington, to which he replied—

I am not a little flattered by being considered by the patrons of literature as one of their number. Fully apprized of the influence which sound learning has on religion and manners, on government, liberty, and laws, I shall only lament my want of abilities to make it still more extensive.

I conceive hopes, however, that we are at the eve of a very enlightened era. The same unremitting exertions which, under all the blasting storms of war, caused the arts and sciences to flourish in America, will doubtless bring them nearer to maturity, when they shall have been sufficiently invigorated by the milder rays of peace.

I return you my hearty thanks for your devout intercession at the throne of grace for my felicity both here and hereafter. May you also, gentlemen, after having been the happy instruments of diffusing the blessings of literature and the comforts of religion, receive the just compensation for your virtuous deeds.

George Washington

"Promote," he says, "as an object of primary importance, institutions for the general diffusion of knowledge. In proportion as the structure of a government gives force to public opinion, it is essential that public opinion should be enlightened."

The Pursuits of Agriculture

Had for Washington a delightful charm, and harmonized with his Christian taste and culture.

"The life of a husbandman," says he, "of all others is the most delightful. It is honorable, it is amusing, and, with judicious management, it is profitable." "For the sake of humanity, it is devoutly to be wished that the manly employment of agriculture and the humanizing benefit of commerce should supersede the waste of war and the rage of conquest; that the swords might be turned into ploughshares, the spears into pruning-hooks, and, as the Scriptures express it, 'the nations learn war no more.'"

"At the age of sixty-five," he writes, in 1797, "I am now recommencing my agricultural and rural pursuits, which were always more congenial to my temper and disposition than the noise and bustle of public employment."

A Christian Home

At Mount Vernon was the crowning glory and happiness of Washington's private life. He was blessed with one of the happiest homes on earth. Intelligence, taste, wealth, books, literature, friends, the picturesque scenes of surrounding nature, a wife who "was the most perfect model of female excellence," who never omitted her private devotions or domestic or public duties, and with whom Washington "was perfectly united and happy," these, crowned and beautified with the genial presence of piety, constituted the Christian home at Mount Vernon a model for loveliness and happiness. And such a home Washington most dearly loved. He says—

"I am now, I believe, fixed at this seat, with an agreeable partner, for life; and I hope to find more happiness in retirement than I ever experienced in the wide and bustling world!" "I can truly say, I had rather be at Mount Vernon, with a friend or two about me, than to be attended at the seat of government by the officers of state, and the representatives of every Power in Europe." "I should enjoy more real happiness," he writes to his wife, "in one month with you at home than I have the most distant prospect of finding abroad if my stay were to be seven times seven years." "The great Searcher of hearts is my witness that I have no wish but which aspires to the humble and happy lot of living and dying a private citizen on my own farm." "The scene is at last closed. I feel myself eased of a load of public care. I hope to spend the remainder of my days in cultivating the affections of good men, and in the practice of the domestic virtues." "Freed from the clangor of arms and the bustle of camp, from the cares of public employment and the responsibility of office, I am now enjoying domestic ease under the shadow of my own vine and my own fig-tree. And in a small villa, with the implements of husbandry and lambkins around me, I expect to glide down the stream of life till I am entombed in the mansions of my fathers."

The Death of Washington

Washington died December 14, 1799, aged sixty-eight years. "Great as he was in life, he was also great in death. He had fought the good fight, and death to him had no terrors." His death was worthy of his Christian faith and character. "I die hard," said he; "but I am *not afraid* to *die. I should have been glad, had it pleased God, to die a little easier; but I doubt not it is for my good. 'Tis well! Father of mer-*

cies, take me to thyself." On his dying bed lay an open Bible, the book of God, which he had read in the family circle and in his private devotions, and in the light of its heavenly truths his great soul passed, doubtless, into the light and immortality of heaven.

His Funeral

Presented a solemn scene of sorrow. "A multitude of persons," says an eye-witness, "assembled, from many miles around, at Mount Vernon, the choice abode and late residence of the illustrious chief. There were the groves, the spacious avenues, the beautiful and sublime scenes, the noble mansion; but, alas! the august inhabitant was now no more. That great soul was gone. In the long portico, where oft the hero walked in all his glory, now lay the shrouded corpse. The countenance, still composed and serene, seemed to express the dignity of the spirit which lately dwelt in that lifeless form."

The mortal remains were laid to rest at the bottom of the elevated lawn, on the banks of the Potomac, where the family vault was then placed. On the ornament at the head of the coffin was inscribed the Christian sentiment, SURGE AD JUDICIUM; about the middle of the coffin, GLORIA DEO; and on the silver plate, his name, age, and the day of his death. The vault, in which now rest his remains, bears the inscription of that glorious doctrine of the gospel—

"I am the Resurrection and the Life"

On the death of Washington, appropriate and solemn services were directed and observed by Congress, then in session at Philadelphia. The Senate presented the following address—

TO THE PRESIDENT OF THE UNITED STATES.

The Senate of the United States respectfully take leave, sir, to express to you their deep regret for the loss the country has sustained in the death of General GEORGE WASHINGTON.

This event, so distressing to all our fellow-citizens, must be peculiarly heavy to you, who have been long associated with him in deeds of patriotism. Permit us, sir, to mingle our tears with yours: on this occasion it is manly to weep. To lose such a man, at such a crisis, is no common calamity to the world. Our country mourns her father. The almighty Disposer of human events has taken from us our greatest benefactor and ornament. It becomes us to submit to Him who "maketh darkness his pavilion."

With patriotic pride we review the life of our Washington, and compare him with those of other countries who have been preeminent in fame. Ancient and modern times are diminished before him. Greatness and guilt have too often been allied; but his fame is whiter than it is brilliant. The destroyers of nations stood abashed at the majesty of his virtues. It reproved the intemperance of their ambition, and darkened the splendor of victory. The scene is closed; and we are no longer anxious lest misfortune should sully his glory: he has travelled on to the end of his journey, and carried with him an increasing weight of honor; he has deposited it safely where misfortune cannot tarnish it, where malice cannot blast it. Favored of heaven, he departed without exhibiting the weakness of humanity. Magnanimous in death, the darkness of the grave could not obscure his brightness.

Such was the man whom we deplore. Thanks to God, his glory is consummated. Washington yet lives on earth in his spotless example; his spirit is in heaven.

Let his countrymen consecrate the memory of the heroic general, the patriotic statesman, and the virtuous sage. Let them teach their children never to forget that the fruits of his labors and his example are their inheritance.

Samuel Livermore,
President of the Senate pro tempore.

The President of the United States made the following reply—

GENTLEMEN OF THE SENATE—

I receive with the most respectful and affectionate sentiments, in this impressive address, the obliging expressions of your regard for the loss our country has sustained in the death of her most esteemed, beloved, and admired citizen.

In the multitude of my thoughts and recollections on this melancholy event, you will permit me only to say that I have seen him in the days of adversity, in the scenes of his deepest distress and most trying perplexities, I have also attended him in his highest elevation and most prosperous felicity, with uniform admiration of his wisdom, moderation, and constancy.

Among all our original associates in that memorable League of the Continent, in 1774, which first expressed the sovereign will of a free nation in America, he was the only one remaining in the General Government. Although with a constitution more enfeebled than his, at an age when he thought it necessary to prepare for retirement, I feel myself alone, bereaved of my late brother, yet I derive a strong consolation from the unanimous disposition which appears in all ages and classes to mingle their sorrow with mine on this common calamity to the world.

The life of our WASHINGTON cannot suffer by a comparison with those of other countries who have been most celebrated and exalted in fame. The attributes and decorations of royalty could only have served to eclipse the majesty of those virtues which made him, from being a modest citizen, a more resplendent luminary. Misfortune, had he lived, could hereafter have sullied his glory only with those superficial minds who, believing that characters and actions are marked by success alone, rarely deserve to enjoy it. Malice could never blast his honor, and envy made him a singular exception to its universal rule. For himself, he had lived enough to life and to glory. For his fellow-citizens, if their prayers could have been answered, he would have been immortal. For me, his departure is at a most unfortunate moment. Trusting, however, in the wise and righteous dominion of Providence over the passions of men and the results of their councils and actions, as well as ever their lives, nothing remains for me but humble resignation.

His example is now complete; and it will teach wisdom and virtue to magistrates, citizens, and men, not only in the present age, but in future generations, as long as history shall be read. If a Trajan found a Pliny, a Marcus Aurelius can never want biographers, eulogists, or historians.

John Adams.

United States, December 23, 1799

Major-General Lee, at the request of Congress, prepared and delivered on the 26th of December, 1799, a funeral oration, of which the following are the closing sentences—

Methinks I see his august image, and hear falling from his venerable lips these deep-sinking words—

"Cease, sons of America, to lament our separation; go on and confirm by your wisdom the fruits of our joint councils, joint efforts, and common dangers; REVERENCE RELIGION; patronize the arts and sciences; let liberty and order be inseparable companions; control party spirit, the bane of free government; observe good faith to, and cultivate peace with, all nations; shut up every avenue to foreign influence; contract rather than extend national connection; rely on yourselves only; be American in thought, word and deed. Thus will you give immortality to that union which was the constant object of my terrestrial labors; thus will you preserve undisturbed to the latest posterity the felicity of a people to me most dear; and thus will you supply (if my happiness is aught to you) the only vacancy in the round of pure bliss high Heaven bestows."

The following comprehensive and eloquent apostrophe was written at Mount Vernon, by an English traveller, as is supposed, on the back of a mirror which hung in the public room of the mansion—

Washington

THE DEFENDER OF HIS COUNTRY, THE FOUNDER OF LIBERTY,
THE FRIEND OF MAN.
HISTORY AND TRADITION ARE EXPLORED IN VAIN
FOR A PARALLEL TO HIS CHARACTER.
IN THE ANNALS OF MODERN GREATNESS
HE STANDS ALONE,
AND THE NOBLEST NAMES OF ANTIQUITY
LOSE THEIR LUSTRE IN HIS PRESENCE.
BORN THE BENEFACTOR OF MANKIND,
HE UNITED ALL THE QUALITIES NECESSARY
TO AN ILLUSTRIOUS CAREER.
NATURE MADE HIM GREAT;
HE MADE HIMSELF VIRTUOUS.
CALLED BY HIS COUNTRY TO THE DEFENCE OF HER LIBERTIES,
HE TRIUMPHANTLY VINDICATED THE RIGHTS OF HUMANITY,
AND ON THE PILLARS OF NATIONAL INDEPENDENCE
LAID THE FOUNDATIONS OF A GREAT REPUBLIC.
TWICE INVESTED WITH SUPREME MAGISTRACY
BY THE UNANIMOUS VOICE OF A FREE PEOPLE,
HE SURPASSED IN THE CABINET
THE GLORIES OF THE FIELD,
AND, VOLUNTARILY RESIGNING THE SCEPTRE AND THE SWORD,
RETIRED TO THE SHADES OF PRIVATE LIFE.
A SPECTACLE SO NEW AND SO SUBLIME
WAS CONTEMPLATED WITH THE PROFOUNDEST ADMIRATION;
AND THE NAME OF WASHINGTON,
ADDING NEW LUSTRE TO HUMANITY,
RESOUNDED TO THE REMOTEST REGIONS OF THE EARTH.
MAGNANIMOUS IN YOUTH,
GLORIOUS THROUGH LIFE,
GREAT IN DEATH.
HIS HIGHEST AMBITION THE HAPPINESS OF MANKIND,
HIS NOBLEST VICTORY THE CONQUEST OF HIMSELF,
BEQUEATHING TO POSTERITY THE INHERITANCE OF HIS FAME,
AND BUILDING HIS MONUMENT IN THE HEARTS OF HIS COUNTRYMEN.
HE LIVED THE ORNAMENT OF THE EIGHTEENTH CENTURY,
HE DIED REGRETTED BY A MOURNING WORLD.

22

Fast and Thanksgiving Days

Divine in Their Origin

CIVIL Governments in all ages have consecrated special days to prayer and the public worship of God. This national custom has a Divine origin and sanction, and was designed, and is eminently adapted, to give religious culture to the national heart and conscience and to exert a beneficent influence on the civil and religious interests of a people. The Hebrew commonwealth had three great annual religious festivals, besides days of special prayer and worship, occasioned by national exigencies and the judgments and marked interventions of God.

The Practice of the Puritans

The Puritans of New England, from their earliest history, were distinguished for similar observances. Thanksgiving and fast days constitute an instructive and important part of their Christian history, and were observed with great solemnity and profit. They were seasons of special praise for the smiles or of prayer under the frowns of Providence, and became regular civil and religious ordinances of the colonies, which were universally observed. The custom extended to the other American colonists under the English Government; and thus it became a distinctive American Christian service, evincing the high and universal Christian tone of all the Colonies.

The fathers of the republic, in the earliest period of the Revolution, adopted the custom of consecrating, by acts of legislation, days of thanksgiving and prayer for special religious worship; and thus the public mind received a higher religious culture through the civil authorities of the country.

Fast-Day in Virginia in 1774

At the beginning of the great conflict for liberty and an independent nationality and government, Mr. Jefferson—who, whatever were his peculiar views of the Christian system, always acknowledged the government and providence of God in national affairs—recommended in Virginia the appointment and observance of a day of public prayer and humiliation. In June, 1774, when the news of the Boston Port Bill reached Virginia, the Colonial Legislature, then in session, appointed such a fast-day for that colony. Mr. Jefferson's account of it is as follows—

> We were under the conviction of the necessity of arousing our people from the lethargy into which they had fallen as to passing events, and thought that the appointment of a day of general fasting and prayer would be most likely to call up and alarm their attention. No example of such solemnities had existed since the days of our distresses in the war of '55— since which a new generation had grown up. With the help, therefore, of Rushworth, whom we rummaged over for the resolutionary precedents and forms of the Puritans of that day, preserved by him, we made up a resolution, somewhat modernizing their phrases, for appointing the 1st day of June, on which the Port Bill was to commence, for a day of fasting, humiliation, and prayer, to implore Heaven to avert from us the evils of civil war, to inspire us with firmness in support of our rights, and to turn the hearts of the king and Parliament to moderation and justice.

To give greater emphasis to our proposition, we agreed to wait the next morning on Mr. Nicholas, whose grave and religious character was more in unison with the tone of our resolution, and solicit him to move it. We accordingly went to him in the morning. He moved it the same day. The 1st of June was proposed, and it passed without opposition. The Governor dissolved us. We returned home, and in our several counties invited the clergy to meet the assemblies of the people on the 1st of June, to perform the ceremonies of the day and to address them in discourses suited to the occasion. The people met generally, with anxiety and alarm in their countenances; and the effect of the day through the whole colony was like a shock of electricity, arousing every man and placing him erect and solidly on his centre.

Washington, then a member of the House of Burgesses, sent a special message to his family and constituents to observe this day; and Mason, a distinguished patriot, also a member, "charged his household to keep the day strictly, and to attend church clad in mourning."

WILLIAMSBURG, MAY 30, 1774

The House of Burgesses of Virginia, on the 24th of May, adopted the following resolution, which was directed to he forthwith printed and published—

Tuesday, 25th of May, 14th George III., 1774. This House, being deeply impressed with apprehension of the great dangers to be derived to *British America* from the hostile invasion of the city of *Boston*, in our sister colony of *Massachusetts Bay*, whose commerce and harbor are on the 1st day of *June* next to be stopped by an armed force, deem it highly necessary that the said 1st day of *June* be set apart by the members of this House as a day of fasting, humiliation, and prayer, devoutly to implore the Divine interposition for averting the heavy calamity which threatens destruction to our civil rights, and the evils of civil war, to give us one heart and one mind firmly to oppose, by all just and proper means, every injury to *American* rights, and that the minds of his Majesty and his Parliament may be inspired from above with wisdom, moderation, and justice, to remove from the loyal people of *America* all cause of danger from a continual pursuit of measures pregnant to their ruin.

Ordered, therefore, That the members of this House do attend in their places, at the hour of ten in the forenoon, on the said 1st day of June next, in order to proceed, with the Speaker and mace, to the church in the city, for the purpose aforesaid; and that the Reverend Mr. Price be appointed to read prayers and to preach a sermon suitable to the occasion.

By the House of Burgesses,

George Wythe, C. H. B.

"The Journals of the Continental Congress contain numerous appointments of thanksgiving and fast days, and the resolutions expressing the wishes of Congress upon this subject were in the form of recommendations to the executive heads of the State Governments, reciting in appropriate terms the occasions which prompted the observance, and the favors which a benign Providence had conferred upon them as a people. With one exception, Congress suspended business upon the days it had appointed for thanksgiving;" and the army under Washington observed them with devout reverence. These official state papers are rich in Christian doctrines, and confirm the great truth that the religion of the fathers of the Revolution and the founders of our civil Governments was the religion of the Bible. The proclamations issued by Congress make known the religious sentiments and feelings of the members of Congress, and constitute a rich part of the political Christian literature of the republic. These papers, in their regular chronology and historical incidents, will form the contents of the present chapter, and may be found in the annals of the Continental Congress.

Monday, June 12, 1775

The committee appointed for preparing a resolve for a fast reported as follows—

As the great Governor of the world, by his supreme and universal providence, not only conducts the course of nations with unerring wisdom and rectitude, but frequently influences the minds of men to serve the wise and gracious purposes of his providential government, and it being at all times our indispensable duty devoutly to acknowledge his superintending providence, especially in times of impending danger and publick calamity, to reverence and adore his immutable justice, as well as to implore his merciful interposition for our deliverance:

This Congress, therefore, considering the present critical, alarming, and calamitous condition of these colonies, do earnestly recommend the twentieth day of *July* next to be observed by the inhabitants of all the *English* colonies on this continent as a day of publick humiliation, fasting, and prayer; that we may with united hearts and voices unfeignedly confess and deplore our many sins, and offer up our joint supplications to the all-wise, omnipotent, and merciful Disposer of all events; humbly beseeching him to forgive our iniquities, to remove our present calamities, to avert those desolating judgments with which we are threatened, and to bless our rightful sovereign *King George* the Third and inspire him with wisdom to discern and pursue the true interests of all his subjects; that a speedy end may be put to the civil discord between *Great Britain* and the *American Colonies*, without further effusion of blood; and that the *British* nation may be influenced to regard the things that belong to her peace, before they are hidden from her eyes; that these colonies may be ever under the care and protection of a kind Providence and be prospered in all their interests; that the Divine blessings may descend and rest upon all civil rulers and upon the representatives of the people, in their several assemblies and conventions; that they may be directed to wise and effectual measures for preserving the union and securing the just rights and privileges of the colonies; that virtue and true religion may revive and flourish throughout the land; and that America may soon behold a gracious interposition of Heaven for the redress of her many grievances, the restoration of her invaded rights, a reconciliation with the parent state, on terms constitutional and honorable to both, and that her civil and religious privileges may be secured to the latest posterity:

Ordered, That a copy of the above be signed by the President and attested by the Secretary, and published in the newspapers and in handbills.

In Massachusetts in 1776

In Massachusetts this proclamation was read in all the churches and distributed throughout the colony—

Saturday, March 16, 1776

Mr. W. Livingston, pursuant to leave granted, brought in a resolution for appointing a fast, which, being taken into consideration, was agreed to, as follows—

In times of impending calamity and distress, when the liberties of America are imminently endangered by the secret machinations and open assaults of an insidious and vindictive administration, it becomes the indispensable duty of these hitherto free and happy colonies, with true penitence of heart and the most reverent devotion, publicly to acknowledge the overruling providence of God, to confess and deplore our offences against him, and to supplicate his interposition for averting the threatened danger and prospering our strenuous efforts in the cause of freedom, virtue, and posterity.

The Congress, therefore, considering the warlike preparations of the British ministry to subvert our invaluable rights and privileges, and to reduce us by fire and sword, by the savages of the wilderness, and our own domestics, to the most abject and ignominious bondage—desirous, at the same time, to have people of all ranks and degrees duly impressed with a solemn sense of God's superintending providence, and of their duty devoutly to rely, in all their lawful enterprises, on his aid and direction—do earnestly recommend that Friday, the 17th day of May next, be observed by the said colonies as a day of humiliation, fasting, and prayer; that we may, with united hearts, confess and bewail our manifold sins and transgressions, and, by a sincere repentance and amendment of life, appease his righteous displeasure, and through the merits and mediation of Jesus Christ obtain his pardon and forgiveness; humbly imploring his assistance to frustrate the cruel purposes of our unnatural enemies, and, by inclining their hearts to justice and benevolence, prevent the further effusion of kindred blood. But if, continuing deaf to the voice of reason and inhumanity, and inflexibly bent on desolation and war, they constrain us to repel their hostile invasions by open resistance, that it may please the Lord of hosts, the God of armies, to animate our officers and soldiers with invincible fortitude, to guard and protect them in the day of battle, and to crown the Continental arms, by sea and land, with victory and success. Earnestly beseeching him to bless our civil rulers, and the representatives of the people, in their several assemblies and conventions; to preserve and strengthen their union; to inspire them with an ardent, disinterested love of their country; to give wisdom and stability to their councils, and direct them to the most efficacious measures for establishing the rights of America on the most honorable and permanent basis; that he would be graciously pleased to bless all his people in these colonies with health and plenty, and grant that a spirit of incorruptible patriotism and of pure, undefiled religion may universally prevail, and this continent be speedily restored to the blessings of peace and liberty, and enabled to transmit them inviolate to the latest posterity. And it is recommended to Christians of all denominations to assemble for public worship, and abstain from servile labor, on said day.

Monday, December 9, 1776

Resolved, That a committee of three be appointed to prepare an address to the inhabitants of America, and a recommendation to the several States to appoint a day of fasting, humiliation, and prayer.

The members chosen, Mr. Witherspoon, Mr. R. H. Lee, and Mr. Adams.

Wednesday, December 11, 1776

The committee appointed to prepare a resolution for appointing a day of fasting and humiliation brought in a report, which was read and agreed to, as follows;—

Whereas the war in which the United States are engaged with Great Britain has not only been prolonged, but is likely to be carried to the greatest extremity, and whereas it becomes all public bodies, as well as private persons, to reverence the providence of God, and look up to him as the Supreme Disposer of all events and the arbiter of the fate of nations: therefore,

Resolved, That it be recommended to all the United States, as soon as possible, to appoint a day of solemn fasting and humiliation, to implore of Almighty God the forgiveness of the many sins prevailing among all ranks, and to beg the countenance and assistance of his providence in the prosecution of the present just and necessary war.

The Congress do also, in the most earnest manner, recommend to all the members of the United States, and particularly the officers, civil and military, under them, the exercise of repentance and reformation; and, further, require of them the strict observation of the articles of war, and particularly that part of the said articles which forbids profane swearing and all immorality, of which all such officers are desired to take notice.

It is left to each State to issue out proclamations fixing the day that appears most proper within its bounds.

Ordered, That the above be published by the committee who brought in the report.

Thanksgiving-Days for Victory Over Burgoyne.

The Annals of Congress record the following—

Friday, October 31, 1777

Resolved, That a committee of three be appointed to prepare a recommendation to the several States to set apart a day for thanksgiving for the signal success lately obtained over the enemies of these United States. The members chosen were Mr. S. Adams, Mr. R. H. Lee, and Mr. Roberdeau.

Saturday, November 1, 1777

The committee appointed to prepare a recommendation to the several States to set apart a day of public thanksgiving, brought in a report, which was taken into consideration and agreed to, as follows—

Forasmuch as it is the indispensable duty of all men to adore the superintending providence of Almighty God, to acknowledge with gratitude their obligations to him for benefits received, and to implore such further blessings as they stand in need of; and it having pleased him in his abundant mercy not only to continue to us the innumerable bounties of his common providence, but also to smile upon us in the prosecution of a just and necessary war for the defence and establishment of our inalienable rights and liberties, particularly in that he hath been pleased in so great a measure to prosper the means used for the support of our troops and to crown our arms with most signal success: it is, therefore, recommended to the legislative or executive powers of these United States to set apart Thursday, the 18th day of December, for solemn thanksgiving and praise; that with one heart and one voice the good people may express the grateful feelings of their hearts and consecrate themselves to the service of their Divine Benefactor, and that together with their sincere acknowledgments of kind offerings they may join the penitent confession of their manifold sins, whereby they had forfeited every favor, and their humble and earnest supplication that it may please God, through the merits of Jesus Christ, mercifully to forgive and blot them out of remembrance; that it may please him graciously to afford his blessing on the Governments of these States respectively, and prosper the public councils of the whole; to inspire our commanders both by land and sea, and all under them, with that wisdom and fortitude which may render them fit instruments, under the providence of Almighty

God, to secure for these United States the greatest of all bless-ings—independence and peace; that it may please him to pros-per the trade and manufactures of the people and the labor of the husbandman, that our land may yield its increase; to take schools and seminaries of education, so necessary for cultivat-ing the principles of true liberty, virtue, and piety, under his nurturing hand, and to prosper the means of religion for the promotion and enlargement of that kingdom which consisteth in righteousness, peace, and joy in the holy Ghost.

And it is further recommended that servile labors and such, recreations as, though at other times innocent, may be unbecoming the purpose of this appointment, be omitted on so solemn an occasion.

Friday, November 7, 1777

Ordered, That a duplicate of the recommendation to the sev-eral States to set apart a day of thanksgiving, signed by the President, be sent to the several States and to General Wash-ington and General Gates.

The proceedings of Congress were sent to all the States by Henry Laurens, President in Congress, with an official request that each Governor would be pleased to take the necessary measures for car-rying the resolve into effect in the State over which he presided.

Washington, when the above proclamation reached him, was on his march to Valley Forge, and halted his whole army during the day, and the chaplains held religious services with their several corps and brigades, upon which the commander-in-chief exhorted all officers and soldiers to "attend with reverence the solemnities of the day."

The Proclamations of the Continental Congress

Saturday, November 7, 1779

Ordered, That the chaplains of Congress prepare and re-port a recommendation to the several States to set apart the 30th day of December next, as a day of general thanksgiving throughout the United States.

Tuesday, November 17, 1778

Congress resumed the consideration of the recommendation to the States for setting apart a day of thanksgiving, which, being amended, is as follows—

It having pleased Almighty God, through the course of the present year, to bestow many great and manifold mercies on the people of these United States, and it being the indispensable duty of all men gratefully to acknowledge their obligations to him for benefits received;

Resolved, That it be, and is hereby, recommended to the legislative or executive authority of each of the said States to appoint Wednesday, the 30th of December next, to be observed as a day of public thanksgiving and praise, that all the people may, with united hearts, on that day, express a just sense of his unmerited favors; particularly in that it hath pleased him, in his overruling providence, to support us in a just and necessary war for the defence of our rights and liberties, by affording us seasonable supplies for our armies, by disposing the heart of a powerful monarch to enter into an alliance with us and aid our cause, by defeating the councils and evil designs of our enemies and giving us victory over their troops, and by the continuance of that union among these States which, by his blessing, will be their future strength and glory.

And it is further recommended that together with devout thanksgivings may be joined a penitent confession of our sins, and humble supplication for pardon, through the merits of our Saviour; so that, under the smiles of Heaven, our public councils may be directed, our arms by land and sea prospered, our liberty and independence secured, our schools and seminaries of learning flourish, our trade be restored, our husbandry and manufactures be increased, and the hearts of all he impressed with undissembled piety, with benevolence and zeal for the public good.

And it is also recommended that recreations unsuitable to the purpose of such a solemnity may be omitted on that day.

Done in Congress, the 17th day of November, 1778, and in the third year of the independence of the United States of America.

Henry Laurens,
President in Congress.

Attest: Charles Thomson, *Secretary.*

Saturday, March 20, 1779

Whereas, Almighty God, in the righteous dispensation of his providence, hath permitted the continuation of a cruel and desolating war in our land: and it being at all times the duty of a people to acknowledge God in all his ways, and more especially to humble themselves before him when evident tokens of his displeasure are manifested, to acknowledge his righteous government, confess and forsake their evil ways, and implore his mercy;

Resolved, That it be recommended to the United States of America to set apart Wednesday, the 22d day of April next, to be observed as a day of fasting, humiliation, and prayer; that at one time and with one voice the inhabitants may acknowledge the righteous dispensations of Divine Providence, and confess their iniquities and transgressions, for which the land mourneth; that they may implore the mercy and forgiveness of God, and beseech him that vice, profaneness, extortion, and every evil may be done away, and that we may be a reformed and a happy people; that they may unite in humble and earnest supplication that it may please Almighty God to guard and defend us against our enemies, and give vigor and success to our military operations by sea and land; that it may please him to bless the rulers and people, strengthen and perpetuate our Union, and in his own good time establish us in the peaceable enjoyment of our rights and liberties; that it may please him to bless our schools and seminaries of learning, and make them nurseries of true piety, virtue, and useful knowledge; that it may please him to cause the earth to yield its increase and to crown the year with his goodness.

March 20, 1779

Whereas, in just punishment for our manifold transgressions, it hath pleased the Supreme Disposer of all events to visit these United States with a calamitous war, through which his Divine Providence hath hitherto in a wonderful manner conducted us, so that we might acknowledge that the race is not to the swift, nor the battle to the strong; and whereas, notwithstanding the chastisement received and benefits bestowed, too few have been sufficiently awakened to a sense of their guilt, or warmed with gratitude, or taught to amend their lives and turn from their sins, so be might turn from his wrath; and whereas, from a consciousness of what we have merited at his hands, and an apprehension that the malevolence of our disappointed enemies, like the incredulity of Pharaoh, may be used as the scourge of Omnipotence to vindicate his slighted majesty, there is reason to fear that he may permit much of our land to become a prey of the spoiler, our borders to be ravaged, and our habitations destroyed;

Resolved, That it be recommended to the several States to appoint the first Thursday in May next to be a day of fasting, humiliation, and prayer to Almighty God that he would be pleased to avert these impending calamities, which we have but too well deserved; that he will grant us his grace to repent of our sins and amend our lives according to *his holy word*; that he will continue that wonderful protection which hath led us through the paths of danger and distress; that he will be a husband to the widow and a father to the fatherless children who weep over the barbarities of a savage enemy; that he will grant us patience in suffering and fortitude in adversity; that he will inspire us with humility, moderation, and gratitude in prosperous circumstances; that he will give wisdom to our councils, firmness to our resolutions, and victory to our arms; that he will bless the labors of the husbandman, and pour forth abundance, so that we may enjoy the fruits of the earth in due season; that he will cause union, harmony, and mutual confidence to prevail throughout these States; that be will bestow on our great ally all those blessings which may enable him to be gloriously instrumental in protecting the rights of mankind and in promoting the happiness of his subjects; that he will bountifully continue his paternal care to the commander-in-chief and the officers and soldiers of the United States; that he will grant the blessings of peace to all contending nations, freedom to those who are in bondage, and comfort to those who are afflicted; that he will diffuse useful knowledge, extend *true religion*, and give us that peace of mind which the world cannot give; that he will be our shield in the day of battle, our comforter in the hour of death, and our kind parent and merciful judge through time and through eternity.

Done in Congress, this 20th day of March, in the year of our Lord one thousand seven hundred and seventy-nine, and in the third year of our independence.

John Jay, *President.*

Attest: Charles Thomson, *Secretary.*

Thursday, October 14, 1779

Resolved, That it will be proper to set apart the second Thursday of December next as a day of general thanksgiving in these United States, and that a committee of four be appointed to prepare a recommendation to the said States for this purpose.

The members chosen were Mr. Root, Mr. Holter, Mr. Muhlenberg, and Mr. Gouverneur Morris.

Wednesday, October 20, 1779

The committee reported as follows—

Whereas it becomes us humbly to approach the throne of Almighty God with gratitude and praise for the wonders which his goodness has wrought in conducting our forefathers to this Western world, for his protection to them and to their posterity amidst difficulties and dangers, for raising us, their children, from deep distress, to be numbered among the nations of the earth, and especially for that he hath been pleased to grant us the enjoyment of health, and so to order the revolving seasons that the earth hath produced her increase in abundance, blessing the labors of the husbandman and spreading plenty through the land; that he hath prospered our arms and those of our ally, been a shield to our troops in the hour of danger, pointed their swords to victory, and led them in triumph over the bulwark of the foe; that he has gone with those who went out into the wilderness against the savage tribes; that he hath stayed the hand of the spoiler, and turned back his meditated destruction; that he bath prospered our commerce, and given success to those who fought the enemy on the face of the deep; and, *above all, that he hath diffused the glorious light of the gospel, whereby, through the merits of our gracious Redeemer, we may become the heirs of his eternal glory*: therefore,

Resolved, That it be recommended to the several States to appoint Thursday, the 9th of December next, to be a day of public and solemn thanksgiving to Almighty God for his mercies, and of prayer for the continuance of his favor and protection to these United States; to beseech him that he would be graciously pleased to influence our public councils, and bless them with wisdom from on high, with unanimity, firmness, and success; that he would go forth with our hosts and crown our armies with victory; *that he would grant to his Church the plentiful effusions of Divine grace, and pour out his Holy Spirit on all ministers of the gospel*; that he would bless and prosper the means of education, and spread the *light of Christian knowledge through the remotest corners of the earth*; that he would smile upon the labors of his people, and cause the earth to bring forth her fruits in abundance; that we may with gratitude and gladness enjoy them; that he would take into his holy protection our illustrious ally, give him victory over his enemies, and render him signally great, as the father of his people, and the protector of the rights of mankind; that he would be graciously pleased to turn the hearts of our enemies, and to dispense the blessings of peace to contending nations; that he would in mercy look down upon us, pardon our sins, and receive us into his favor; and, finally, that he would establish the independence of these United States upon the basis of religion and virtue, and support and protect them in the enjoyment of peace, liberty, and safety.

Done in Congress, the 20th day of October, one thousand seven hundred and seventy-nine, and in the fourth year of the independence of the United States of America.

Samuel Huntington, *President.*

Attest: Charles Thomson, *Secretary.*

A Proclamation for a Fast.

Saturday, March 11, 1780

It having pleased the righteous Governor of the world, for the punishment of our manifold offences, to permit the sword of war still to harass our country, it becomes us to endeavor, by humbling ourselves before him and turning from every evil way, to avert his anger and obtain his favor and blessing: it is, therefore, recommended to the several States—

That Wednesday, the twenty-sixth day of April next, be set apart and observed as a day of fasting, humiliation, and prayer, that we may with one heart and one voice implore the sovereign Lord of heaven and earth to remember mercy in his judgments; to make us sincerely penitent for our transgressions; to prepare us for deliverance, and to remove the evil with which he bath been pleased to visit us; to banish vice and irreligion from among us, and establish virtue and piety by his Divine grace; to bless all public councils throughout the United States, giving them wisdom, firmness, and unanimity and directing them to the best measures for the public good; to bless the magistrates and people of every rank, and animate and unite the hearts of all to promote the interests of their country; to bless the public defence, inspiring all commanders and soldiers with magnanimity and perseverance, and giving vigor and success to the military operations by sea and land; to bless the illustrious sovereign and the nation in alliance with these States, and all who interest themselves in support of our rights and liberties; to make that alliance of extensive and perpetual usefulness to those immediately concerned, and mankind in general; to grant fruitful seasons, and to bless our industry, trade and manufactures; to bless all schools and seminaries of learning, and every means of instruction and education; to make wars to cease, and to establish peace among the nations.

Tuesday, March 20, 1780

The United States, in Congress assembled, agreed to the following—

PROCLAMATION

At all times it is our duty to acknowledge the overruling providence of the Great Governor of the universe, and devoutly to implore his Divine favor and protection. But in the hour of calamity and impending danger, when, by fire and the sword, by the savages of the wilderness, and by our own domestics, a vindictive enemy pursues a war of rapine and devastation with unrelenting fury, we are peculiarly excited with true penitence of heart to prostrate ourselves before our great Creator, and fervently to supplicate his gracious interposition for our deliverance.

The United States in Congress assembled, therefore, do earnestly recommend that Thursday, the third day of May next, may be observed as a day of humiliation, fasting, and prayer, that we may with united hearts confess and bewail our manifold sins and transgressions, and by sincere repentance and amendment of life appease his righteous displeasure, and, through the merits of our blessed Saviour, obtain pardon and forgiveness; that it may please him to inspire our rulers with incorruptible integrity, and to direct and prosper their councils; to inspire all our citizens with a fervent and a disinterested love of their country, and to preserve and strengthen their union; to turn the hearts of the disaffected, or to frustrate their devices; to regard with Divine compassion our friends in captivity, affliction, and distress, to comfort and relieve them under their sufferings, and to change their mourning into grateful songs of triumph; that it may please him to bless our ally, and to render the connection formed between these United States and his kingdom a mutual and a lasting benefit to both nations; to animate our officers and forces, by sea and land, with invincible fortitude, and to guard and protect them in the day of battle, and to crown our joint endeavors to terminate the calamities of war with victory and success; that the blessings of liberty and peace may be established on an honorable and permanent basis, and transmitted inviolate to the latest posterity; that it may please him to prosper our husbandry and commerce, and bless us with health and plenty; that it may please him to bless all schools and seminaries of learning, and to grant that truth, justice, and benevolence and pure and undefiled religion may universally prevail.

Wednesday, October 18, 1780

Congress took into consideration the resolution reported for setting apart a day of thanksgiving and prayer, and agreed to the following draft—

Whereas it hath pleased Almighty God, the Father of all mercies, amidst the vicissitudes and calamities of war, to bestow blessings on the people of these States, which call for their devout and thankful acknowledgments, more especially in the late remarkable interposition of his watchful providence in rescuing the person of our commander-in-chief and the army from imminent danger at a moment when treason was ripened for execution; in prospering the labors of the husbandman, and causing the earth to yield its increase in plentiful harvests; and, *above all,* in continuing to us the gospel of peace:

It is, therefore, recommended to the several States to set apart Thursday, the 7th day of December next, to be observed as a day of public thanksgiving and prayer; that all the people may assemble on that day to celebrate the praises of our Divine Benefactor, to confess our unworthiness of the least of his favors, and to offer our fervent supplications to the God of all grace, that it may please him to pardon our heinous transgressions and incline our hearts in the future to keep all his laws; to comfort and relieve our brethren who are anywise afflicted or distressed; to smile upon our husbandry and trade; to direct our public councils, and lead our forces, by land and sea, to victory; to take our illustrious ally under his special protection, and favor our joint councils and exertions for the establishment of speedy and permanent peace; to cherish all schools and seminaries of education, and to cause the knowledge of Christianity to spread over all the earth.

Done in Congress, this 15th day of October, 1780, and in the fifth year of the independence of the United States of America.

Friday, October 26, 1781

The committee, consisting of Mr. Witherspoon, Mr. Montgomery, Mr. Varnum, Mr. Sherman, appointed to prepare a recommendation for setting apart a day of public thanksgiving and prayer, reported the draft of a proclamation, which was agreed to, as follows—

PROCLAMATION

Whereas it hath pleased Almighty God, the Father of mercies, remarkably to assist and support the United States of America in their important struggle for liberty against the long-continued effort of a powerful nation, it is the duty of all ranks to observe and thankfully to acknowledge the interpositions of his providence in their behalf. Through the whole of the contest, from its first rise to this time, the influence of Divine Providence may be clearly perceived in many signal instances, of which we mention but a few.

In revealing the councils of our enemies, when the discoveries were seasonable and important and the means seemingly inadequate or fortuitous; in preserving, and even improving, the union of the several States, on the breach of which our enemies place their greatest dependence; in increasing the number and adding to the zeal and attachment of the friends of liberty; in granting remarkable deliverances, and blessing us with the most signal success, when affairs seemed to have the most discouraging appearance; in raising up for us a generous and most powerful ally in one of the first of European Powers; in confounding the councils of our enemies, and suffering them to pursue such measures as have most directly contributed to frustrate their own desires and expectations; above all, in making their extreme cruelty to the inhabitants of these States when in their power, and their savage devastation of property, the very means of cementing our union and adding vigor to every effort in opposition to them.

And as we cannot help leading the good people of these States to a retrospect on the events which have taken place since the beginning of the war, so we recommend in a particular manner to their observation the goodness of God in the year now drawing to a conclusion; in which the confederation of the United States has been completed; in which there have been so many instances of prowess and success in our armies, particularly in the Southern States, where, notwithstanding the difficulties with which they had to struggle, they have recovered the whole country which the enemy had overrun, leaving them only a port or two on or near the sea; in which we have been so powerfully and effectually assisted by our allies, while in all the conjunct operations the most perfect harmony has subsisted in the allied army; in which there has been so plentiful a harvest, and so great abundance of the fruits of the earth of every kind, as not only enables us easily to supply the wants of our army, but gives comfort and happiness to the whole people; and in which, after the success of our allies by sea, a general of the first rank, with his whole army, has been captured by the allied forces under the direction of our commander-in-chief.

It is therefore recommended to the several States to set apart the 13th day of December next, to be religiously observed as a day of thanksgiving and prayer; that all the people may assemble on that day, with grateful hearts, to celebrate the praises of our gracious Benefactor; to confess our manifold sins, to offer up our most fervent supplications to the God of all grace that it may please him to pardon our offences, and incline our hearts in the future to keep all his laws; to comfort and relieve all our brethren who are in distress or captivity; to prosper our husbandmen, and give success to all engaged in lawful commerce; to impart wisdom and integrity to our councillors, judgment and fortitude to our officers and soldiers; to protect and prosper our illustrious ally, and favor our united exertions for the speedy establishment of a safe, honorable, and lasting peace; to bless all seminaries of learning, and cause the knowledge of God to cover the earth as the waters cover the sea.

Done in Congress, this twenty-sixth day of October, 1781, and in the sixth year of the independence of the United States of America.

Thomas McKean, *President.*

Attest: Charles Thomson, *Secretary.*

General Washington, in reply to a letter from the President of Congress, enclosing this proclamation, thus wrote from Mount Vernon November 15, 1781—

> I have the honor to acknowledge the receipt of your favor of the 31st ult., covering the resolutions of Congress of the 26th, and a Proclamation for a day of public prayer and thanksgiving, and have to thank you, sir, for the very polite and affectionate manner in which these enclosures have been conveyed. The success of the combined arms against our enemies at York and Gloucester, as it affects the welfare and independence of the United States, I viewed as a most fortunate event.
>
> In performing my part towards its accomplishment, I consider myself to have done only my duty, and in the execution of that I ever feel myself happy; and at the same time, as it augurs well to our cause, I take a particular pleasure in acknowledging that the interposing hand of Heaven in the various instances of our extensive preparations for this operation has been most conspicuous and remarkable.

Tuesday, March 19, 1782

PROCLAMATION.

The goodness of the Supreme Being to all his rational creatures demands their acknowledgments of gratitude and love; his absolute government of this world dictates that it is the interest of every nation and people ardently to supplicate his favor and implore his protection.

When the lust of dominion or lawless ambition excites arbitrary power to invade rights or endeavor to wrest from a people their sacred and inalienable privileges, and compels them, in defence of the same, to encounter all the horrors and calamities of a bloody and vindictive war, then is that people loudly called upon to fly unto that God for protection who hears the cries of the distressed and will not turn a deaf ear to the supplications of the oppressed.

Great Britain, hitherto left to infatuated councils and to pursue measures repugnant to her own interest and distressing to this country, still persists in the design of subjugating these United States; which will compel us into another active and perhaps bloody campaign.

The United States in Congress assembled, therefore, taking into consideration our present situation, our multiplied transgressions of the holy laws of our God, and his past acts of kindness and goodness towards us, which we ought to record with the liveliest gratitude, think it their indispensable duty to call upon the several States to set apart the last Thursday in April next as a day of fasting, humiliation, and prayer, that our joint supplications may then ascend to the throne of the Ruler of the universe, beseeching him to diffuse a spirit of universal reformation among all ranks and degrees of our citizens, and make us a holy, that we may be a happy, people; that it would please him to impart wisdom, integrity, and unanimity to our counsellors; to bless and prosper the reign of our illustrious ally, and give success to his arms employed in the defence of the rights of human nature; that he would smile upon our military arrangements by land and sea, administer comfort and consolation to our prisoners in a cruel captivity, protect the health and life of our commander-in-chief, grant us victory over our enemies, establish peace in all our borders, and give happiness to all our inhabitants; that he would prosper the labor of the husbandman, making the earth yield its increase in abundance, and give a proper season for the ingathering of the fruits thereof; that he would grant success to all engaged in lawful trade and commerce, and take under his guardianship all schools and seminaries of learning, and make them nurseries of virtue and piety; that he would incline the hearts of all men to peace, and fill them with universal charity and benevolence, and that the religion of our Divine Redeemer, with all its benign influences, may cover the earth as the waters cover the seas.

Done by the United States in Congress assembled, &c. &c.

Friday, October 11, 1782

On the report of the committee, consisting of Mr. Witherspoon, Mr. Montgomery, and Mr. Williamson, appointed to prepare a recommendation to the States setting apart a day for thanksgiving and prayer, Congress agreed to the following act—

> It being the indispensable duty of all nations not only to offer up their supplications to Almighty God, the Giver of all good, for his gracious assistance in time of distress, but also in a solemn and public manner to give him praise for his goodness in general, and especially for great and signal interpositions of his providence in their behalf; therefore the United States in Congress assembled, taking into consideration the many instances of Divine goodness to these States in the course of the important conflict in which they have been so long engaged, the happy and promising state of public affairs, and the events of the war in the course of the year now drawing to a close, particularly the harmony of the public councils, which is so necessary to the success of time public cause; the perfect union and good understanding which has hitherto subsisted between them and their allies, notwithstanding the artful and unwearied attempts of the common enemy to divide them; the success of the armies of the United States and those of their allies, and the acknowledgment of their independence by another European Power, whose friendship and commerce must be of great and lasting advantage to these States; do hereby recommend it to the inhabitants of these States in general, to observe, and request the several States to interpose their authority in appointing and commanding the observation of, Thursday, the 28th day of November next, as a day of solemn thanksgiving to God for all his mercies; and they do further recommend to all ranks to testify their gratitude to God for his goodness, by a cheerful obedience to his laws, and by promoting, each in his station and by his influence, the practice of true and undefiled religion, which is the great foundation of public prosperity and national happiness.
>
> Done in Congress, &c. &c.
>
> Saturday, October 18, 1783

The committee, consisting of Mr. Duane, Mr. S. Huntington, and Mr. Holter, appointed to prepare a proclamation for a day of thanksgiving, reported a draft, which was agreed to as follows—

By the United States in Congress assembled.

A Proclamation

Whereas it has pleased the Supreme Ruler of all human events to dispose the hearts of the late belligerent Powers to put a period to the effusion of human blood, by proclaiming a cessation of all hostilities by sea and land, and these United States are not only happily rescued from the dangers and calamities to which they have been so long exposed, but their freedom, sovereignty, and independence are ultimately acknowledged; and whereas, in the progress of a contest on which the most essential rights of human nature depended, the interposition of Divine Providence in our favor hath been most abundantly and most graciously manifested, and the citizens of these United States have every reason for praise and gratitude to the God of their salvation: impressed, therefore, with an exalted sense of the blessings with which we are surrounded and of entire dependence on that Almighty Being from whose goodness and bounty they are derived, the United States in Congress assembled do recommend it to the several States to set apart the second Thursday in December next as a day of public thanksgiving, that all the people may then assemble to celebrate, with grateful hearts and united voices, the praises of their supreme and all-bountiful Benefactor for his numberless favors and mercies; that he hath been pleased to conduct us in safety through all the vicissitudes of the war; that he hath given us unanimity and resolution to adhere to our just rights; that he hath raised up a powerful ally to assist in supporting them, and hath so far crowned our united efforts with success that in the course of the present year hostilities have ceased, and we are left in the undisputed possession of our liberty and independence, and of the fruits of our land, and in the free participation of the treasures of the sea; that he hath prospered the labors of our husbandmen with plentiful harvests; and, *above all, that he hath been pleased to continue unto us the light of the blessed gospel,* and secured to us in the fullest extent the rights of conscience in faith and worship; and while our hearts overflow with gratitude, and our lips set forth the praises of our great Creator, that we also offer up fervent supplications that it may please him to pardon all our offences, to give wisdom and unanimity to our public councils, to cement all our citizens in the bond of affection, and to inspire them with an earnest regard for the national honor and interest, to enable us to improve the days of prosperity by every good work, and to be lovers of peace and tranquillity; that he may be pleased to bless us in our husbandry, our commerce and navigation; to smile upon our seminaries and means of education, to cause pure religion and virtue to flourish, to give peace to all nations, and to fill the world with his glory.

Done by the United States in Congress assembled. Witness his Excellency ELIAS BOUDINOT, our President, this 18th day of October, in the year of our Lord one thousand seven hundred and eighty-three, and of the sovereignty and independence of the United States of America the eighth.

Elias Boudinot, President.

Charles Williamson, *Secretary.*

Thanksgiving for Peace

A committee of the Committee of the States, consisting of Mr. Read, Mr. Dana, and Mr. Hand, to whom was referred the motion of Mr. Read of the 2d instant, "That a committee be appointed to prepare a proclamation for a day of solemn prayer and thanksgiving to Almighty God, to be observed throughout the United States of America, on the exchange of the instruments of ratification of the definite treaty of peace between the United States of America and his Britannic Majesty, and the happy completion of the great work of independency and peace to these United States," reported the following form of a proclamation—

By the United States of America in a
Committee of the States assembled.

A PROCLAMATION

Whereas it has pleased the Supreme Ruler of the universe, of his infinite goodness and mercy, so to calm the minds and do away with the resentment of the Powers lately engaged in a most bloody and destructive war, and to dispose their hearts towards amity and friendship, that a general pacification hath taken place, and particularly a definitive treaty of peace between the United States of America and his Britannic Majesty was signed at Paris, on the third day of September, in the year of our Lord one thousand seven hundred and eighty-three; the instruments of the final ratification of which, were exchanged at Passy, on the 12th day of May, in the year of our Lord one thousand seven hundred and eighty-four, whereby a finishing hand was put to the great work of peace, and the freedom, sovereignty, and independence of these States fully and completely established; and whereas, in pursuit of the great work of freedom and independence, and the progress of the contest in which the United States of America have been engaged, and on the success of which the dearest and most essential rights of human nature depended, the benign interposition of Divine Providence hath, on many occasions, been most MIRACULOUSLY and abundantly manifested; and the citizens of the United States have the greatest reason to return their most hearty and sincere praises and thanksgiving to the *God of their deliverance, whose name be praised*. Deeply impressed, therefore, with a sense of his mercies manifested to these United States, and of the blessings which it hath pleased God to shower down on us, of our future dependence at all times on his power and mercy, *as the only source* from which so great benefits can be derived—

We the United States of America, in the Committee of the States assembled, do earnestly recommend to the Supreme Executive of the several States to set apart Tuesday, the nineteenth day of October next, as a day of public prayer and thanksgiving, that all the people of the United States may then assemble in their respective churches and congregations, to celebrate with grateful hearts and joyful and united voices the mercies and praises of their all-bountiful Creator, most holy and most righteous, for his innumerable favors and mercies vouchsafed unto them—more especially that he hath been graciously pleased so to conduct us through the perils and dangers of the war as finally to establish the United States in freedom and independency, and to give them a name and a place among the princes and nations of the earth—that he hath raised great captains and men of war from amongst us to lead our armies, and in our greatest difficulties and distresses hath given us unanimity to adhere and to assert our just rights and privileges—and that he hath been most graciously pleased also to raise up a most powerful prince and magnanimous people as allies to assist us in effectually supporting and maintaining them; that he hath been pleased to prosper the labor of our husbandmen; that there is no famine or want seen throughout our land; and, *above all, that he hath been pleased to continue to us the light of gospel truth,* and secured to us in the fullest manner the rights of conscience in faith and worship.

And while our hearts overflow with gratitude and our lips pronounce the praises of our great and merciful Creator, that we may also offer up our joint and fervent supplications that it may please him of his infinite goodness and mercy to pardon all our sins and offences: to inspire with wisdom and a true sense of the public good all our public councils; to strengthen and cement the bonds of love and affection between all our citizens; to impress them with an earnest regard for the public good and national faith and honor, and to teach them to improve the days of peace by every good work; to pray that he will in a more especial manner shower down his blessings on Louis, the most Christian king, our ally, to prosper his house, that his son's sons may long sit on the throne of their ancestors a blessing to the people intrusted to his charge; to bless all mankind, and inspire the princes and nations of the earth with the love of peace, that the sound of war may be heard of no more; that he may be pleased to smile upon us and bless our husbandry, fishery, our commerce, and especially our schools and seminaries of learning: *and to raise up from among our youth men eminent for virtue, learning, and piety, to his service in Church and State; to cause virtue and true religion to flourish*; to give to all the nations amity, peace, and concord, and to fill the world with his glory.

Done by the United States in the Committee of the States assembled. Witness the Honorable Samuel Hardy, Chairman, this third day of August, in the year of our Lord one thousand seven hundred and eighty-seven, and in the ninth of the sovereignty and independence of the United States of America.

National Thanksgiving Under Washington's Administration

A resolution was adopted in the House of Representatives, September 25, 1789, in the following words—

On motion—

Resolved, That a joint committee of both Houses be directed to wait upon the President of the United States to request that he would recommend to the people of the United States a day of thanksgiving and prayer, to be observed by acknowledging with grateful hearts the many signal favors of Almighty God, especially by affording them an opportunity peaceably to establish a constitution of government for their safety and happiness.

Ordered, That Mr. Boudinot, Mr. Sherman, and Mr. Silvester be of the said committee on the part of this House.

Concurred in by the Senate the same day.

Washington, as President of the United States, on the 3d day of October, 1789, issued a proclamation, in pursuance of the above proceedings of Congress, which may be found on page 275 of this volume.

The following proclamation, by Washington, was made, without special authority from Congress, in view of the suppression of the rebellion in Western Pennsylvania in 1795, which for a time threatened the safety of the Union. It is invested with new and profound interest in view of the great Southern rebellion of 1863, and is a striking evidence of the prophetic vision of Washington, foreboding good or ill to the nation according to its adherence to, or departure from, the principles of order, morality, and piety.

A Proclamation

When we review the calamities which afflict so many other nations, the present condition of the United States affords much of consolation and satisfaction. Our exemption hitherto from foreign war, an increasing prospect of the continuance of that exemption, the great degree of internal tranquillity we have enjoyed, *the recent confirmation of that tranquillity by the suppression of an insurrection which so wantonly threatened it,* the happy course of our public affairs in general, the unexampled prosperity of all classes of our citizens, are circumstances which peculiarly mark our situation with indications of the Divine beneficence towards us. In such a state, it is in an especial manner our duty as a people, with devout reverence and affectionate gratitude, to acknowledge our many and great obligations to Almighty God, and to implore him to continue and confirm the blessings we experience.

Deeply penetrated with this sentiment, I, George Washington, President of the United States, do recommend to all religious societies and denominations, and to all persons whomsoever within the United States, to set apart and observe Thursday, the 19th day of February next, as a day of public thanksgiving and prayer, and on that day to meet together and render their sincere thanks to the Great Ruler of nations for the manifold and signal mercies which distinguish our lot as a nation, particularly for the possession of *constitutions of government* which unite, and by their union establish, liberty with order; for the preservation of our peace, foreign and domestic; for the *seasonable control which has been* given to a spirit of disorder in the suppression of the late insurrection; and, generally, for the prosperous course of our affairs, public and private; and at the same time humbly and fervently to beseech the kind Author of these blessings graciously to prolong them to us; to imprint on our hearts a deep and solemn sense of our obligations to him for them; to teach us rightly to estimate their immense value; *to preserve us from the arrogance of prosperity,* and from hazarding the advantage we enjoy by delusive pursuits; to dispose us to inherit the continuance of his favors by not abusing them, by our gratitude for them, and by a corresponding conduct as citizens and as men; to render this country more and more a safe and propitious asylum for the unfortunate of other countries; to extend among us true and useful knowledge; to diffuse and establish habits of sobriety, order, morality, and piety; and, finally, *to impart all the blessings we possess, or ask for ourselves, to the whole family of mankind.*

In testimony whereof, I have caused the seal of the United States of America to be affixed to these presents, and signed the same with my hand. Done at the city of Philadelphia, the first day of January, one thousand seven hundred and ninety-five, and of the independence of the United States of America the nineteenth.

G. Washington.

Proclamations Under Adams's Administration

PROCLAMATION FOR A NATIONAL FAST.

March 23, 1798

As the safety and prosperity of nations ultimately and essentially depend on the protection and blessing of Almighty God, and the national acknowledgment of this truth is not only an indispensable duty which the people owe to him, but a duty whose natural influence is favorable to the promotion of that morality and piety without which social happiness cannot exist nor the blessings of a free government be enjoyed; and as this duty, at all times incumbent, is so especially in seasons of difficulty and of danger, when existing or threatening calamities—the just judgments of God against prevalent iniquity—are a loud call to repentance and reformation; and as the United States of America are at present placed in a hazardous and afflictive situation by the unfriendly disposition, conduct, and demands of a foreign Power, evinced by repeated refusals to receive our messengers of reconciliation and peace, by depredations on our commerce, and the infliction of injuries on very many of our fellow-citizens while engaged in their lawful business on the seas; under these considerations, it has appeared to me that the duty of imploring the mercy and benediction of Heaven on our country demands at this time a special attention from its inhabitants.

I have, therefore, thought fit to recommend—and I do hereby recommend—that Wednesday, the 9th day of May next, be observed throughout the United States as a day of solemn humiliation, fasting, and prayer; that the citizens of these States, abstaining on that day from their customary worldly occupations, offer their devout addresses to the Father of mercies, agreeably to those forms or methods which they have severally adopted as the most suitable and becoming; that all religious congregations do, with the deepest humility, acknowledge before God the manifold sins and transgressions with which we are justly chargeable as individuals and as a nation; beseeching him at the same time, of his infinite grace, through the Redeemer of the world, freely to remit all our offences, and to incline us, by his Holy Spirit, to that sincere repentance and reformation which may afford us reason to hope for his inestimable favor and heavenly benediction; that it be made the subject of particular and earnest supplication that our country may be protected from all the dangers which threaten it; that our civil and religious privileges may be preserved inviolate and perpetuated to the latest generations; that our public councils and magistrates may be especially enlightened and directed at this critical period; that the American people may be united in those bonds of amity and mutual confidence and inspired with that vigor and fortitude by which they have in times past been so highly distinguished, and by which they have obtained such invaluable advantages; that the health of the inhabitants of our land may be preserved, and their agriculture, commerce, fisheries, arts, and manufactures be blessed and prospered; that the principles of genuine piety and sound morality may influence the minds and govern the lives of every description of our citizens; and that the blessings of peace, freedom, and pure religion may be speedily extended to all nations of the earth.

And, finally, I recommend that on the said day the duties of humiliation and prayer be accompanied by fervent thanksgiving to the Bestower of every good gift, not only for having hitherto protected and preserved the people of these United States in the independent enjoyment of their religious and civil freedom, but also for having prospered them in a wonderful progress of population, and for conferring on them many and great favors conducive to the happiness and prosperity of a nation.

Given, &c.   John Adams.

Proclamation for a National Fast.

March 6, 1799

As no truth is more clearly taught in the volume of inspiration, nor any more fully demonstrated by the experience of all ages, than that a deep sense and a due acknowledgment of the governing providence of a Supreme Being, and of the accountableness of men to him as the searcher of hearts and righteous distributor of rewards and punishments, are conducive equally to the happiness and rectitude of individuals and to the well-being of communities; as it is, also, most reasonable in itself that men who are made capable of social acts and relations, who owe their improvements to the social state, and who derive their enjoyments from it, should as a society make their acknowledgments of dependence and obligation to Him who hath endowed them with these capacities and elevated them in the scale of existence by these distinctions; as it is, likewise, a plain dictate of duty, and a strong sentiment of nature, that in circumstances of great urgency, and seasons of imminent danger, earnest and particular supplications should be made to Him who is able to defend or to destroy; as, moreover, the most precious interests of the people of the United States are still held in jeopardy by the hostile designs and insidious acts of a foreign nation, as well as by the dissemination among them of those principles, subversive to the foundations of all religious, moral, and social obligations, that have produced incalculable mischief and misery in other countries; and as, in fine, the observance of special seasons for public religious solemnities is happily calculated to avert the evils which we ought to deprecate, and to excite to the performance of the duties which we ought to discharge, by calling and fixing the attention of the people at large to the momentous truths already recited, by affording opportunity to teach and inculcate them, by animating devotion, and giving to it the character of a national act.

For these reasons, I have thought proper to recommend, and I do hereby recommend accordingly, that Thursday, the twenty-fifth day of April next, be observed throughout the United States of America as a day of solemn humiliation, fasting, and prayer; that the citizens on that day abstain, as far as may be, from their secular occupations, and devote the time to the sacred duties of religion, in public and in private; that they call to mind our numerous offences against the most high God, confess them before him with the sincerest penitence, implore his pardoning mercy, through the Great Mediator and Redeemer, for our past transgressions, and that, through the grace of his Holy Spirit, we may be disposed and enabled to yield a more suitable obedience to his righteous requisitions in time to come; that he would interpose to arrest the progress of that impiety and licentiousness in principle and practice so offensive to himself and so ruinous to mankind; that he would make us deeply sensible that "righteousness exalteth a nation; but that sin is the reproach of any people;" that he would turn us from our transgressions and turn his displeasure from us; that he would withhold us from unreasonable discontent, from disunion, faction, sedition, and insurrection; that he would preserve our country from the desolating sword; that he would save our cities and towns from a repetition of those awful pestilential visitations under which they have lately suffered so severely, and that the health of our inhabitants generally may be precious in his sight; that he would favor us with fruitful seasons, and so bless the labors of the husbandman as that there may be food in abundance for man and beast; that he would prosper our commerce, manufactures, and fisheries, and give success to the people in all their lawful industry and enterprise; that he would smile on our colleges, academies, schools, and seminaries of learning, and make them nurseries of sound science, morals, and religion; that he would bless all magistrates from the highest to the lowest, give them the true spirit of their station, make them a terror to evil-doers and a praise to them that do well; that he would preside over the councils of the nation at this critical period, enlighten them to a just discernment of the public interest, and save them from mistake, division, and discord; that he would make succeed our preparations for defence, and bless our armaments by land and by sea; that he would put an end to the effusion of human blood and the accumulation of human misery among the contending nations of the earth, by disposing them to justice, to equality, to benevolence, and to peace; and that he would extend the blessings of knowledge, of true liberty, and of pure and undefiled religion throughout the world.

And I do recommend that, with these acts of humiliation, penitence, and prayer, fervent thanksgiving to the Author of all good be united, for the countless favors which he is still continuing to the people of the United States, and which render their condition as a nation eminently happy when compared with the lot of others.

Given, &c.   John Adams.

Proclamations under Madison's Administration.

The second war with Great Britain was declared by the Government of the United States in 1812, and peace was restored in 1815. The calamities of war developed the Christian element of the Government and people in the following acts and proclamations—

In April, 1812, Congress passed the following resolution—

It being a duty peculiarly incumbent, in a time of public calamity and war, humbly and devoutly to acknowledge our dependence on Almighty God, and to implore his aid and protection; therefore,

Resolved, by the Senate and House of Representatives in Congress assembled, that they appoint a committee of both Houses of Congress to wait on the President of the United States and request that he recommend a day of public humiliation and prayer, to be observed by the people of the United States with religious solemnity and the offering of fervent supplications to Almighty God for the safety and welfare of these States, his blessing on their army, and a speedy restoration of peace.

President Madison immediately issued the following—

PROCLAMATION

Whereas the Congress of the United States, by a joint resolution of the two Houses, have signified a request that a day may be recommended to be observed by the people of the United States with religious solemnity, as a day of public humiliation and prayer; and whereas such a recommendation will enable the several religious denominations and societies so disposed to offer at one and the same time their common vows and adorations to Almighty God, on the solemn occasion produced by the war in which he has been pleased to permit the injustice of a foreign Power to involve these United States; I do therefore recommend the *third Thursday of August next,* as a convenient day, to be set apart for the devout purpose of rendering the Sovereign of the Universe and the Benefactor of mankind the public homage due to his holy attributes; of acknowledging the transgressions which might justly provoke the manifestations of his divine displeasure; of seeking his merciful forgiveness, and his assistance in the great duties of repentance and amendment; and especially of offering fervent supplications that in the present season of calamity and war he would take the American people under his peculiar care and protection; that he would guide their public councils, animate their patriotism, and bestow his blessing on their arms; that he would inspire all nations with a love of justice and of concord, and with a reverence for the unerring precept of our holy religion, to do to others as they would require that others should do to them; and, finally, that, turning the hearts of our enemies from the violence and injustice which sway their councils against us, he would hasten a restoration of the blessings of peace.

[L.S.] Given at Washington, the ninth day of July, in the year of our Lord one thousand eight hundred and twelve.

James Madison,

James Monroe,

By the President.   *Secretary of State.*

Thanksgiving at the Peace of 1815

The official notification of peace with Great Britain was communicated to the House of Representatives, by the President, February 18, 1815, and the same day the following resolution was introduced—

> It being a duty particularly humbly and devoutly to acknowledge our dependence on Almighty God, and to implore his aid and protection, and in times of deliverance and prosperity to manifest our deep and undissembled gratitude to the Almighty Sovereign of the Universe; therefore,
>
> *Resolved, by the Senate and House of Representatives of the United States of America, in Congress assembled,* That a joint committee of both Houses wait on the President of the United States, and request that he recommend a day of thanksgiving to be observed by the people of the United States, with religious solemnity, and the offering of devout acknowledgments to God for his mercies, and in prayer to him for the continuance of his blessings.

In accordance with this request, the President issued the following—

PROCLAMATION

The Senate and House of Representatives of the United States have, by a joint resolution, signified their desire that a day may be recommended to be observed by the people of the United States, with religious solemnity, as a day of thanksgiving, and of devout acknowledgments to Almighty God for his great goodness manifested in restoring to them the blessings of peace.

No people ought to feel greater obligations to celebrate the goodness of the Great Disposer of events and of the destiny of nations than the people of the United States. His kind providence originally conducted them to one of the best portions of the dwelling-place allowed for the great family of the human race. He protected and cherished them under all the difficulties and trials to which they were exposed in their early days. Under his fostering care, their habits, their sentiments, and their pursuits prepared them for a transition in due time to a state of independence and of self-government. In the arduous struggle by which it was attained, they were distinguished by multiplied tokens of his benign interposition. During the interval which succeeded, he reared them into strength, and endowed them with the resources which have enabled them to assert their national rights and to enhance their national character in another arduous conflict, which is now happily terminated by a peace and reconciliation with those who have been our enemies. And to the same Divine Author of every good and perfect gift we are indebted for all those privileges and advantages, religious as well as civil, which are so richly enjoyed in this favored land.

It is for blessings such as these, and more especially for the restoration of the blessings of peace, that I now recommend that the second Thursday in April next be set apart as a day on which the people of every religious denomination may, in their solemn assemblies, unite their hearts and their voices in a free-will offering to their heavenly Benefactor of their homage of thanksgiving and of their songs of praise.

Given at the city of Washington, on the fourth of March, in the year of our Lord one thousand eight hundred and fifteen, and of the independence of the United States the thirty-ninth.

James Madison.

Recommendation of a Fast-Day by President Tyler.

On the 7th day of April, 1841, William Henry Harrison, President of the United States, expired in the Presidential mansion. By this providential visitation upon the nation, John Tyler, of Virginia, Vice-President, became, by the Constitution, the acting President. After he entered upon his duties, he issued the following—

RECOMMENDATION

April 13, 1841

To the People of the United States.

When a *Christian* people feel themselves to be overtaken by a great public calamity, it becomes them to humble themselves under the dispensation of Divine Providence, to recognize his righteous government over the children of men, to acknowledge his goodness in times past, as well as their own unworthiness, and to supplicate his merciful protection for the future.

The death of William Henry Harrison, late President of the United States, so soon after his election to that high office, is a bereavement particularly calculated to be regarded as a heavy affliction, and to impress all minds with a sense of the uncertainty of human things, and of the dependence of nations, as well as individuals, upon our heavenly Parent.

I have thought, therefore, that I should be acting in conformity with the general expectations and feelings of the community in recommending, as I now do, to the people of the United States, of every religious denomination, that, according to their several modes and forms of worship, they observe a day of fasting and prayer, by such religious services as may be suitable on the occasion; and I recommend Friday, the fourteenth day of May next, for that purpose; to the end that on that day we may all, with one accord, join in humble and reverential approach to Him in whose hands we are, invoking him to inspire us with a proper spirit and temper of heart and mind under the frowns of his providence, and still to bestow his gracious benedictions upon our Government and our country.

John Tyler, *President.*

Recommendation by President Tyler in View of the Cholera

In the summer of 1849, a pestilence, in the form of the Asiatic cholera, visited a second time the United States. The President, in view of its general prevalence, and to seek its removal, issued the following—

RECOMMENDATION

At a season when the providence of God has manifested itself in the visitation of a fearful pestilence which is spreading itself throughout the land, it is fitting that a people whose reliance has ever been in his protection should humble themselves before his throne, and, while acknowledging past transgressions, ask a continuance of the Divine mercy.

It is therefore earnestly recommended that the first Friday in August be observed throughout the United States as a day of fasting, humiliation, and prayer. All business will be suspended in the various branches of the public service on that day; and it is recommended to persons of all religious denominations to abstain as far as practicable from secular occupation, and to assemble in their respective places of public worship, to acknowledge the infinite goodness which has watched over our existence as a nation and so long crowned us with manifold blessings, and to implore the Almighty, in his own good time, to stay the destroying hand now lifted against us.

Z. TAYLOR.

Washington, July 3, 1849

Death of President Taylor

Zachary Taylor, President of the United States, died on the 9th day of July, 1850. The proceedings in Congress on the event are as follows; but no proclamation was issued—

Washington, July 10, 1850
FELLOW-CITIZENS OF THE SENATE AND HOUSE
OF REPRESENTATIVES—

I have to perform the melancholy duty of announcing to you that it has pleased Almighty God to remove from this life

ZACHARY TAYLOR, late President of the United States. He deceased last evening, at the hour of half-past ten o'clock, in the midst of his family and surrounded by affectionate friends, calmly and in full possession of all his faculties. Among his last words were these—" I have always done my duty. I am ready to die. My only regret is for the friends I leave behind me."

A great man has fallen among us, and a whole country is called to an occasion of unexpected, deep, and general mourning.

To you, Senators and Representatives of a nation in tears, I can say nothing to alleviate the sorrow with which you are oppressed. I rely upon Him who holds in his hands the destinies of nations, to endow me with the requisite strength for the task, and to avert from our country the evils apprehended from the heavy calamity which has befallen us. I shall most readily concur in whatever measures the wisdom of the two Houses may suggest as befitting this deeply melancholy occasion.

Millard Fillmore.

Dr. Butler's Prayer

In the House of Representatives, before the session for the day began, the Rev. Dr. BUTLER, Chaplain of the Senate, made the following prayer—

Almighty God, King of kings and Lord of lords, who only hath immortality, dwelling in the light which no man can approach unto, thou doest according to thy will in the army of heaven and among the inhabitants of the earth. Just and true are thy ways, thou King of saints. Clouds and darkness are about thy throne; but righteousness and judgment are the habitation of thy seat!

Thou hast seen fit, Almighty God, to take out of this world our beloved and honored Chief Magistrate, the President of these United States. Thou didst cover his head in the day of battle; and thou hast given his life to the sickness that destroyeth at the noonday. We desire to bow in resignation to thy blessed will, and to realize that thou doest all things well. Now that thy judgments are abroad in the land, make us to learn and love and practise righteousness.

We ask thy special blessing for thy servant upon whom thy providence hath devolved the momentous duties of the Chief Magistracy of this republic. Thou hast seen fit to summon him to the great duties of his new position in a crisis of gloom and storm and danger. Let thy fatherly hand ever be over him. Let thy Holy Spirit ever be with him. Give him the spirit of wisdom and understanding, the spirit of counsel and ghostly strength, the spirit of knowledge and true godliness, and fill him with thy holy fear now and forever. Preserve him in health and prosperity, and so bless his administration that all the States of this vast republic, reconciled, happy, and fraternal, may be able unitedly to adore thee for thy goodness, and to declare that the Lord of Hosts is with us, the God of Jacob is our refuge!

Bless the deliberations of the Senate and Representatives in Congress assembled, to the advancement of thy glory, the good of thy Church, the safety, honor, and welfare of thy people; that peace and happiness, truth and justice, religion and piety, may be established among us for all generations.

Look with pity upon the sorrows of thy servants, the family of the departed Chief Magistrate of this land. Remember them, O Lord, in mercy; sanctify thy fatherly correction to them; endow their souls with patience under their afflictions, and with resignation to thy blessed will; comfort them with a sense of tiny goodness; lift up thy countenance upon them, and give them peace.

Grant, O Lord, that when we shall be summoned to go the way of all the earth, we may die in the communion of thy Church, in the confidence of a certain faith, in the comfort of a religious and holy hope, in favor with thee, our God, and in charity with the world.

All which we ask and offer in the name and for the sake of Jesus Christ, our Lord and Saviour. Amen.

The House, after the prayer, adopted the following—

Whereas it hath pleased Divine Providence to remove from this life ZACHARY TAYLOR, late President of the United

States, the House of Representatives, sharing in the general sorrow which this melancholy event must produce, is desirous of manifesting its sensibility on the occasion.

Remarks by Members on the Death of President Taylor

The death of the President of the United States was regarded by Congress and the nation as a providential national calamity, and Senators and Representatives, in their seats in Congress, gave expression to this truth in their remarks on the event.

Mr. Downs, of Louisiana, said, "The chief of a nation of more than twenty millions of freemen is suddenly withdrawn from the world by an act of God."

Mr. Webster, of Massachusetts, said, "It has pleased Divine Providence to visit the two Houses of Congress, and especially this House, with repeated occasions for mourning and lamentation. Great as this calamity is, we mourn, but not as those without hope. We have seen one eminent man, and another eminent man, and at last a man in the most eminent station, fall away from the midst of us. But I doubt not there is a Power exercising over us that parental care that has marked our progress for so many years. I have confidence still that the place of the departed will be supplied, that the kind, beneficent favor of Almighty God will still be with us, and that we shall he borne along, and borne onward and upward, on the wings of his sustaining providence."

Mr. Cass, of Michigan, said, "He has been called by Providence from his high functions with his mission unfulfilled. Let us humbly hope that this afflictive dispensation of Providence may not be without its salutary influence upon the American people and their representatives."

Mr. Underwood, of Kentucky, said, "The providence of God has terminated his earthly career. He was removed by the Ruler of the universe. Whatever purposes of the Deity the future may unfold, the present is a day of mourning."

Mr. King, of Alabama, said, "It depends essentially upon us, and the co-ordinate branch of the Government, to improve this afflictive dispensation of Almighty God to purposes at once salutary and beneficial to the great interests of the country."

In the House of Representatives, similar sentiments were uttered.

Mr. Winthrop, of Massachusetts, said, "As we now behold the late President borne away by the hand of God from our sight, in the very hour of peril, we can hardly repress the exclamation which was addressed to the departing prophet of old, 'My father, my father! the chariot of Israel, and the horsemen thereof!' Let us hope that this event may teach us all how vain is our reliance upon any arm of flesh. Let us hope that it may impress us with a solemn sense of our national as well as individual dependence on a higher than human power. Let us remember, sir, that 'the Lord is King, be the people never so impatient; that he sitteth between the cherubim, be the earth never so unquiet.' Let us, in language which is now hallowed to us all as having been the closing and crowning sentiment of his Inaugural Address, and in which he, 'being dead, yet speaketh,'—

"*Let us invoke a continuance of the same protecting care which has led us from small beginnings to the eminence which we this day occupy; and let us seek to deserve that continuance by prudence and moderation in our councils; by well-directed attempts to assuage the bitterness which, too often unavoidable, marks differences of opinion; by the promulgation and practice of just and liberal principles; and by an enlarged patriotism, which shall acknowledge no limits but those of our own wide-spread republic.'*"

Mr. Hilliard, of Alabama, said, "It is an interposition of Providence; and it comes to us in a trying hour. My trust in Providence is unshaken. Our country has been delivered, guided, and made glorious by a good Providence. It will be so still. I remember when the prophet referred to was surrounded by a hostile force, and all hope of escape seemed to be cut off, that a young man who was with him cried out in great fear; and the reply of the prophet was a prayer that the young man's eyes might be opened. He then saw that all within the hostile lines were 'chariots and horsemen of fire,' ready to succor and deliver the beleaguered city. So will it be with us. The very event which we deplore will be overruled for good; and HE that sitteth on high, mightier than the water-floods, will put forth his power and cause a great calm."

Proclaimation by President Buchanan on the Eve of the Rebellion

The following proclamation was issued by the President of the United States when the nation was imperilled by the opening scenes and acts of the great Southern rebellion—

To the People of the United States—

A Recommendation

Numerous appeals have been made to me by pious and patriotic associations and citizens, in view of the present distracted and dangerous condition of our country, to recommend that a day be set apart for humiliation, fasting, and prayer throughout the Union.

In compliance with their request and my own sense of duty, I designate Friday, the fourth day of January, 1861, for this purpose, and recommend that the people assemble on that day, according to their several forms of worship, to keep it as a solemn fast.

The union of the States is at the present moment threatened with alarming and immediate danger; panic and distress of a fearful character prevail throughout the land; our laboring population are without employment, and consequently deprived of the means of earning their bread. Indeed, hope seems to have deserted the minds of men. All classes are in a state of confusion and dismay, and the wisest counsels of our best and purest men are disregarded.

In this hour of our calamity and peril, to whom shall we resort for relief but to the God of our fathers? His omnipotent arm only can save us from the awful effects of our own crimes and follies—our own ingratitude and guilt towards our heavenly Father.

Let us, then, with deep contrition and penitent sorrow, unite in humbling ourselves before the Most High, in confessing our individual and national sins, and in acknowledging the justice of our punishment. Let us implore him to remove from our hearts that false pride of opinions which would impel us to persevere in wrong for the sake of consistency rather than yield a just submission to the unforeseen exigencies by which we are now surrounded. Let us, with deep reverence, beseech him to restore the friendship and good will which prevailed in former days among the people of the several States; and, above all, to save us from the horrors of civil war and "bloodguiltiness." Let our fervent prayers ascend to his throne, that he would not desert us in this hour of extreme peril, but remember us as he did our fathers in the darkest days of the Revolution, and preserve our Constitution and our Union, the work of their hands, for ages yet to come.

An Omnipotent Providence may overrule existing evils for permanent good. He can make the wrath of man to praise him, and the remainder of wrath he can restrain. Let me invoke every individual, in whatever sphere of life he may be placed, to feel a personal responsibility to God and his country for keeping that day holy, and by contributing all in his power to remove our actual and impending calamities.

James Buchanan.

Washington, Dec. 14, 1860

Act of Congress in 1861 Requesting President Lincoln to Appoint a Fast-Day

Several months after the civil war had commenced, and the Government had struggled unsuccessfully to subdue the rebellion in the Southern States, Congress passed the following resolution—

> *Resolved, by the Senate and House of Representatives of the United States of America in Congress assembled*; That a joint committee of both Houses wait on the President of the United States, and request that he recommend a day of public humiliation, prayer, and fasting, to be observed by the people of the United States with religious solemnity, and the offering of fervent supplications to Almighty God for the safety and welfare of these States, his blessings on their arms, and a speedy restoration of peace.
>
> Approved, August 5, 1861

The President's Proclamation

The President, seven days afterwards, issued the following—

PROCLAMATION

By the President of the United States of America.

Whereas a joint committee of both Houses of Congress has waited on the President of the United States, and requested him to recommend a day of public humiliation, prayer, and fasting, to be observed by the people of the United States with religious solemnities, and the offering of fervent supplications to Almighty God for the safety and welfare of these States, his blessing on their arms, and a speedy restoration of peace;

And whereas it is fitting and becoming in all people at all times to acknowledge and revere the supreme government of God, to bow in humble submission to his chastisements, to confess and deplore their sins and transgressions in the full conviction that the fear of the Lord is the beginning of wisdom, and to pray with all fervency and contrition for the pardon of their past offences, and for a blessing upon their present and prospective action;

And whereas when our beloved country—once, by the blessing of God, united, prosperous, and happy—is now afflicted with faction and civil war, it is peculiarly fit for us to recognize the hand of God in this visitation, and, in sorrowful remembrance of our own faults and crimes as a nation and as individuals, to humble ourselves before him, and to pray for his mercy—to pray that we may be spared further punishment, though justly deserved, that our arms may be blessed and made effectual for the re-establishment of law, order, and peace throughout our country, and that the inestimable boon of civil and religious liberty, earned, under his guidance and blessing, by the labors and sufferings of our fathers, may be restored in all its original excellence—

Therefore, I, ABRAHAM LINCOLN, President of the United States, do appoint the last Thursday in September next as a day of humiliation, prayer, and fasting for all the people of the nation; and I do earnestly recommend to all the people, and especially to all ministers and teachers of religion of all denominations, and to all heads of families, to observe and keep that day, according to their several creeds and modes of worship, in all humility, and with all religious solemnity, to the end that the united prayer of the nation may ascend to the throne of grace, and bring down plentiful blessings upon our own country.

In testimony whereof I have hereunto set my hand, and caused the great seal of the United States to be affixed, this twelfth day of August, A.D. 1861, and of the independence of the United States of America the eighty-sixth.

By the President: Abraham Lincoln.
William H. Seward, *Sec'y of State.*

Resolution of the Senate in 1863 Appointing a Day of Fasting and Prayer

At the close of the session of Congress, the Senate of the United States, March 2, 1863, passed the following resolution—

> *Resolved*, That, devoutly recognizing the supreme authority and just government of Almighty God in all the affairs of men and of nations, and sincerely believing that no people, however great in numbers and resources, or however strong in the justice of their cause, can prosper without his favor, and at the same time deploring the national offences which have provoked his righteous judgment, yet encouraged, in this day of trouble, by the assurances of his word, to seek him for succor according to his appointed way, through Jesus Christ, the Senate of the United States do hereby request the President of the United States, by his proclamation, to designate and set apart a day for national prayer and humiliation, requesting all the people of the land to suspend their secular pursuits and unite in keeping the day in solemn communion with the Lord of Hosts, supplicating him to enlighten the councils and direct the policy of the rulers of the nation, and to support all our soldiers, sailors,

and marines, and the whole people, in the firm discharge of duty, until the existing rebellion shall be overthrown and the blessings of peace restored to our bleeding country.

The President's Proclamation

In pursuance of this resolution and request, the President issued the following—

PROCLAMATION

Whereas the Senate of the United States, devoutly recognizing the supreme authority and just government of Almighty God in all the affairs of men and nations, has, by a resolution, requested the President to designate and set apart a day for national prayer and humiliation;

And whereas it is the duty of nations, as well as of men, to own their dependence upon the overruling power of God, to confess their sins and transgressions in humble sorrow, yet with assured hope that genuine repentance will lead to mercy and pardon, and to recognize the sublime truth announced in the Holy Scriptures, and proven by all history, that those nations only are blessed whose God is the Lord;

And insomuch as we know that, by his divine law, nations, like individuals, are subjected to punishments and chastisements in this world, may we not justly fear that the awful calamity of civil war, which now desolates the land, may be but a punishment inflicted upon us for our presumptuous sins, to the needful end of our national reformation as a whole people? We have been the recipients of the choicest bounties of Heaven. We have been preserved, these many years, in peace and prosperity. We have grown in numbers, wealth, and power as no other nation has ever grown. But we have forgotten God. We have forgotten the gracious hand which preserved us in peace, and multiplied and enriched and strengthened us; and we have vainly imagined, in the deceitfulness of our hearts, that all these blessings were produced by some superior wisdom and virtue of our own. Intoxicated with unbroken success, we have become too self-sufficient to feel the necessity of redeeming and preserving grace, too proud to pray to the God that made us!

It behooves us, then, to humble ourselves before the offended Power, to confess our national sins, and to pray for clemency and forgiveness.

Now, therefore, in compliance with the request and fully concurring in the views of the Senate, I do, by this my proclamation, designate and set apart Thursday, the 30th day of April, 1863, as a day of national humiliation, fasting, and prayer. And I do hereby request all the people to abstain on that day from their ordinary secular pursuits, and to unite, at their several places of public worship and their respective homes, in keeping the day holy to the Lord and devoted to the humble discharge of the religious duties proper to that solemn occasion.

All this being done in sincerity and truth, let us then rest humbly in the hope, authorized by the Divine teachings, that the united cry of the nation will be heard on high, and answered with blessings no less than the pardon of our national sins, and restoration of our now divided and suffering country to its former happy condition of unity and peace.

In witness whereof, I have hereunto set my hand, and caused the seal of the United States to be affixed.

Done at the city of Washington this thirtieth day of March, in the year of our Lord one thousand eight hundred and sixty-three, and of the independence of the United States the eighty-seventh.

Abraham Lincoln.

By the President:

William H. Seward, *Secretary of State.*

These State Papers Prove the Christianity of Our Civil Institution

The historical and official records presented in this chapter are cumulative and conclusive proofs of the Christian life and character of the civil institutions of the United States, and form a rich and an instructive part of the political Christian literature of the nation.

Their statements affirm, in unequivocal terms, that the whole fabric of the civil Governments and the social civilization of the nation had their origin and vigor from the Christian religion, and that the same Divine system alone can keep them pure and transmit them to future ages.

23

Thanksgiving Days Appointed by the States

Puritan Origin

THE annual festival of Thanksgiving originated in New England, and was the fruit of Puritan faith and pity. It has become national, and is commemorated with devout demonstrations of Christian worship and of social and family remembrances and reunions. It is a day canonized in the Christian and civil annals of the various State Governments, and carries with it the authority of legislative and executive action as well as the sanctions and solemnities of religion.

Their Influence on the Family, Church, and State

The influences of this festival are wide-spread and beneficent. It affords to the ministers of religion a favorable opportunity for the discussion of the great principles of civil and religious liberty which underlie our system of government, to review the Christian history which has marked the origin and progress of civilization and the civil and political Institutes of the nation, and to inculcate the fundamental fact that the Christian faith and principles of the founders

701

of the republic alone can preserve its life and perpetuity. Its social and family scenes and Christian services cultivate the best affections of human nature, and give fresher and purer tone and strength to the three great organic institutions of God—the Family, the Church, and the State.

These institutions are divinely united, and must live or perish together. The family, first in the order of its institution, is the source of growth and perpetuity to the Church, and of purity and moral strength and beauty to the State. The State covers with its shield of legislation the family and the Church, and this fosters and diffuses those Christian virtues and influences that are the only durable pillars of civil society and the only true and lasting glory of States. These three institutions, Divine in their origin and authority, are designed to be perpetual, and alone can work out the social, moral, political, and spiritual regeneration of nations and the race.

Relation of the Family to the State

As the family is the foundation of the civil state and the germ of its life a growth and source of its strength and glory, the republic of North America has not only been distinguished for the best types of the family organization, but the legislation of the national and State Governments has given the easiest facilities for the acquisition of family homesteads, out of which might flow the best and strongest influences to support and bless the State.

American Policy to Secure Homestead Similar to the Hebrew Policy

Congress, by an act "to secure Homesteads to actual settlers on the Public Domain," passed May 20, 1862, and approved by the President, secures a free homestead "to any person who is the head of a family, or who has arrived at the age of twenty-one years, and is a citizen of the United States, or who shall have filed his declaration of intention to become such, as required by the naturalization laws of the United States, and who has never borne arms against the United States Government or given aid and comfort to its enemies." It was also required in that Act that the person making application for such homestead must declare that "the said entry is made for the purpose of actual settlement and cultivation, and not, either directly or indirectly, for the use or benefit of any person or persons whomsoever."

This national policy in reference to securing a home and an ownership in the soil has a beneficent influence in the culture of all virtues, and gives to the people who support the Government a deeper and a stronger love of country. This feature of our Government and institutions has a striking analogy to the republican institutions of the Hebrew commonwealth, which were established under the immediate direction and authority of God.

Dr. Lyman Beecher's Statement

Dr. Lyman Beecher, an American divine of great eminence, eloquence, and piety, whose long life and talents were devoted to the defense and diffusion of the fundamental doctrines of Christianity and to the true welfare of the American republic, in his lecture on the republican elements of the Old Testament, says—

"The most admirable trait in the republican system of the Jews is the distribution of land, which made every adult male a land-holder—not a tenant, but the owner himself of the soil on which he lived. This is the great spring of civil liberty, industry, and virtue. By this simple arrangement the great body of the nation were elevated from the pastoral to the agricultural state, and were at once exempted from the two extremes most dangerous to liberty—an aristocracy of wealth and a sordid vicious poverty. It was the design of Heaven to secure a state of society eminently adapted to virtue and liberty; and, by this distribution of the soil to each individual and family, he made the whole nation agricultural. The single principle of universal ownership, in fee simple, of the soil, secured at once intense and universal patriotism, indomitable courage, untiring industry, and purity of morals: neither an hereditary nobility, nor a dependent peasantry, nor abject poverty, could exist. While the sun shone, or the streams flowed, or the hills remained, liberty and equality must exist among them. The whole land was kept in the line of family descent: no poverty or vice on the part of a man could deprive his family of the privilege of inheriting its portion of the soil—thus attaching them to the community as independent members, with all those inducements to freedom and intelligence and virtue which appertain to the owners and cultivators of the soil."

These results which were wrought out by the policy of the Hebrew commonwealth have been in some good measure gained under the republican institutions of the United States. The loyalty and love of country, and the settled and solemn purpose of the American people to maintain the unity of their nationality and the integrity of their civil institutions, which have had a new and sublime development in the great conflict arising out of the Southern rebellion, have their origin and fruitfulness in the fact that the Government, in its past and present policy, secures, on the easiest terms, ownership in the soil and a homestead for every family. It is a recognition of the vital need of the family, in its best estate, to the prosperity and perpetuity of the republic.

What, then, can make the families of this great nation happy, pure, moral, and orderly? Certainly nothing else but the power and resources of piety, and the cultivation of family religion. Here, in the sacred sanctuary of home, must virtue and piety exert their holy influences in the purification of these original fountains, and then every stream that flows from them on society and Government will be eminently healthy and saving. For the cultivation of family religion, and the Christian education and training of children, involve the whole issues of human happiness and the well-being of all civil Governments.

Let family religion flourish—let the children who are to occupy this glorious domain, and to wield the civil and political destinies of this great republic, be trained and educated under Christian influences—and all fear of danger to the integrity and perpetuation of our free institution will be removed. This will plant the fear of God in every heart, it will give right principles of moral action to every citizen, and send forth those pious and refreshing influences that will water the tree of American liberty, cause its roots to fix themselves deep in the rich soil, send the sap of a virtuous and a vigorous life through all its parts, and preserve in their purity and integrity the civil institutions of the country, and bless every interest of the nation.

View of the Early New England Families

"The family," says a modern divine, "is God's first institution. It was founded in Eden, and will last to the end of time. All other institutions come after it, cluster round it, grow out of it, and have the deepest roots both of their strength and weakness in it. The school is what the family makes it. The state is what the family makes it. So it is with communities and nations. So it is with universal human society, and with the whole race of man. They are all but so many streams of which the family is the fountain, circles of which it is the center, superstructures of which it is the foundation, branches of which it is the root. What it is they are and must be. Its spirit makes their life; its fibers shape their boughs; its juices feed their leaves and fill their fruits. All other institutions of society are to be formed and reformed, generated and regenerated, only through the family itself.

New England has ever been distinguished for its lovely pictures of home-life and the comforts and independence of its families. Before the century in which the Pilgrims settled at Plymouth had expired, it was said of New England, by Rev. John Wise, that "Religion is placed and exercised in its principles, virtues, and governments, through the families of the country, as so many little sanctuaries. There is no such spot of earth on the earthly globe so belabored with family devotion, reading God's word, catechizing and well-instructing youth, with neat and virtuous examples, and divine prayers, *non ex codice, sed ex corde*, not out of books, but out of hearts, the solemnizing Sabbaths and family attendance on public means, as in New England.

Bancroft's Picture of New England Families

Bancroft bears a similar testimony. "A lovely picture," says he, "of prosperity, piety, and domestic happiness was presented. Every family was taught to look up to God, as to the fountain of all good; yet life was not sombre. The spirit of frolic mingled with innocence; religion itself sometimes wore the garb of gayety, and the annual thanksgiving to God was, from primitive times, as joyous as it was sincere."

The festival of Thanksgiving—the symbol of family religion and love, and the fountain of beneficent and extensive good to the

Church and the State—mingles its songs of praise and joy from ocean to ocean, filling the continent with the incense of a Christian sacrifice precious to the American citizen and acceptable to God.

Thanksgiving Day of 1862

The annual Thanksgiving of 1862 in the loyal States, was observed with more than usual interest and attention. In the midst of a great rebellion, the people paused from worldly pursuits, went up to the temples of God, and "entered into his gates with thanksgiving, and into his courts with praise." Not a sanctuary, scarcely, in all the land but was vocal with praise and prayer, and in them the ministers of God reviewed the manifold blessings with which God had crowned the year, and especially dwelt upon the blessings of our civil institutions, and the duty of preserving the union and perpetuating the integrity of the Government against the rebellion of the Southern States. The capital of the nation—the city founded by Washington and bearing his name, the seat of civil power, and the home of the President of the United States, his Cabinet, and of Congress—observed with great unanimity and appropriateness the Thanksgiving of the year 1862.

A peculiar feature of the Thanksgiving of the year 1862 was its observance on the tented fields and in the numerous hospitals of the Government, in different parts of the country. The loyal States, in order to arrest and subdue the rebellion and to maintain the unity of the republic and vindicate the majesty and integrity of the Government, had, when the Thanksgiving of 1862 was observed, eight hundred thousand armed soldiers in the field. Thousands of these heroic men were accustomed to observe Thanksgiving-day in their own quiet homes; and now, amidst the scenes of war, in the camp, or in hospitals, they recalled the home-pictures of former days, and under the happy auspices of the day, and with loyal hearts, consecrated themselves anew to the cause of liberty and religion and to the salvation of the imperilled republic.

This chapter will be devoted to the official recognition of the Christian religion by the Governors of most of the States of the Union, in their annual proclamations for thanksgiving. Those of the year 1862, from all the loyal States except California, are given in full, as they are not only state papers of a high Christian tone, but relate also to the great rebellion of the Southern portion of the republic. The proclamation of Governor Andrew, of Massachusetts, for 1861, is inserted, as it is a noble Christian paper and a model of its kind. The proclamations of several of the Southern States for 1858 are also given. Other proclamations by the Governors of various States are given in brief. They will all be found interesting and cumulative in reference to the Christian life and character of the civil institutions of the United States.

Proclamations of the Various Governors

NEW YORK

The first appointment of a Thanksgiving day in the State of New York, after the General Government went into operation, was made by John Jay, Governor and commander-in-chief of the State. He was among the most eminent Christian statesmen of the Revolutionary and constitutional eras of the republic, and had largely contributed to give the civil and political institutions of New York and the nation a Christian impress; and among his first official acts when elected Governor was to appoint a day for thanksgiving unto God. In his proclamation for that year, 1794, he says—

> Whereas the great Creator and Preserver of the Universe is the Supreme Sovereign of nations, and does, when and as he pleases, reward or punish them by temporal blessings or calamities, according as their national conduct recommends them to his favor and beneficence or excites his displeasure and indignation;
>
> And whereas in the course of his government he hath graciously been pleased to show singular kindness to the people and nation of which this State is a constituent member, by protecting our ancestors in their first establishment in this then savage wilderness, by defending them against their enemies, by blessing them with an uncommon degree of peace, liberty, and safety, and with the civilizing light and

influence of his holy gospel, by leading us, as it were by the hand, through the various scenes of the late revolution, and crowning it with success, by giving a wisdom and opportunity to establish governments and institutions auspicious to order, security, and national liberty, by constantly favoring us with fruitful seasons, and, in general, by giving us a greater portion of public welfare and prosperity than to any other people; it appears to me to be the public duty of this State, collectively considered, to render unto God their sincere and humble thanks for all these his great and unmerited mercies and blessings, and also to offer to him their fervent petitions to continue to us his protection and favor; to preserve to us the undisturbed enjoyment of our civil ad religious rights and privileges, and the valuable life and usefulness of the President [Washington] of the United States; to enable all our rulers, councils, and people, to do the duties incumbent on them respectively, with wisdom and fidelity, to promote the *extension of true religion*, virtue, and learning, to give us grace to cultivate national unity, concord, and good will, and generally to bless our nation, and all other nations, in the manner and measure most conducive to our and their best interests and real welfare; being perfectly convinced that national prosperity depends, and ought to depend, on national gratitude and obedience to the Supreme Ruler of the Universe.

PROCLAMATION

By Daniel D. Tompkins, Governor of the State of New York, General and Commander-in-Chief of all the Militia, and Admiral of the Navy of the same, on the Restoration of Peace, in 1815.

In compliance with a resolution of the Senate and Assembly of this State, I do hereby set apart the second Thursday of April next, to be devoted to public prayer, thanksgiving, and praise; and I do most earnestly recommend to the good people of this State, of every denomination, to abstain from all kinds of labor and business on that day, to meet in their respective places of worship, and there unite their hearts in fervent prayer to the Most High, in humble acknowledgment of

his all-protecting influence, and in consideration of his goodness manifested to us, a nation, in that he has been pleased to
signalize our arms by so may splendid victories, to conduct
our country successfully through the perils of the late war,
to restore to us the blessings of peace, and to preserve unimpaired our civil and religious institutions.

In testimony whereof, I have caused the privy Seal of the
State of New York to be hereunto affixed [L.S.] at the city of
Albany, the seventeenth day of March, in the year of our Lord
one thousand eight hundred and fifteen.

Daniel D. Tompkins.

By his Excellency the Governor:

Robert Tillotson, *Private Secretary.*

De Witt Clinton, as the Governor of the State of New York, appointed Thanksgiving-day in 1817–1822, 1825, 1826, and 1827. In these
proclamations he declares it—

"An obvious and solemn duty to render the obligations of devout and grateful hearts to Almighty God for the manifold blessings conferred upon us at all times by the gracious dispensations
of his providence." In the enumeration of the blessings for which
"the State had been greatly distinguished by the dispensation of a
benign Providence" in the various years of his administration, the
Governor designates "an augmentation of the lights of religion and
know-ledge." He states as his "solemn conviction that private happiness and public prosperity are indissolubly connected with the
cultivation of religion, and a deep solicitude to endeavor to merit
the favor of Divine Providence;" and that, in view of the "Divine
pleasure in promoting the diffusion of religion, advancing the interests of knowledge, prospering internal improvements, and vouch-
safing the enjoyment of liberty, peace, and plenty," "demonstrations
of gratitude are enjoined by the most impressive considerations of
patriotism and the most solemn obligations of religion."

Joseph C. Yates, as Governor of New York, in his proclamations
of 1823–1824, says—

"The people of this State have been highly favored with unmerited blessing, from the protecting hand of the beneficent Creator and

Ruler of the Universe, signally manifested by continuing to promote the cause of religion in our land, the diffusion of it abroad, and the dissemination of useful knowledge among all classes of citizens;" and "by enabling the constituted authorities, under his superintending care and guidance, peacefully to organize a government according to a constitution formed and adopted by the people; securing to them the blessings of liberty, and the undisturbed fruition of their own labor and exertions."

New York, in 1821, formed a new Constitution, which was adopted by a popular vote in February, 1822, and went into full operation on the 1st day of January, 1823; and for this Divine blessing the Governor calls upon the people to render special thanksgiving to God.

Nathaniel Pitcher, the acting Governor of the State of New York after the death of De Witt Clinton, in his proclamation of 1828, calls upon the people to render thanksgiving unto Almighty God.

"In permitting us to enjoy the blessings of republican institutions, in the diffusion of moral instruction and science, by sustaining our colleges, academies, and Sabbath and common school institutions; in continuing to us the light of revelation and the consolation and toleration of religious profession and worship."

Enos T. Throop, acting as Governor after the resignation of Governor Van Buren, in his proclamations of 1829-30, says—

"It has pleased Almighty God to give us strength and wisdom, and by his guidance we have become members of a national and State Government which secures to each of us our due civil rights and freedom of religious opinion. By his great goodness our hearts have been disposed to cultivate the growth of knowledge and virtue by the instrumentality of public worship, of schools, and of benevolent and charitable institutions, and to consider them as means of individual happiness and national prosperity."

"Whereas," he continues, "the wisdom of man is but a small light shining around his footsteps, showing the things that are near, while all beyond is shrouded in darkness, manifesting our dependence upon a God of infinite wisdom, the Creator and Guide of all things, who directs our path through the dark and unseen places, and to ends which human wisdom foresees not, and evincing that our condition here, whether of good or evil, is according to his good pleasure, operating upon our hearts and minds, and not according to our own wills." "Deeply impressed with these truths," he recommends the people of Now York to render praise to Almighty God "for the general diffusion of knowledge and learning, to the enlightenment of our minds, and fitting us for the enjoyment of our social advantages, and the prosecution of our inestimable privileges as nation; for having cultivated in us a spirit of charity and an enlightened sense of religious and moral duties, and preserved to us an unrestrained religious worship.

"And in our aspirations let us beseech God to banish from among us superstition, contention, ignorance, and ill will, and hasten that era which we hope is within the plan of his providence, and now dawns upon us, when the human understanding shall be so enlarged, and the passions of men so chastened, that war shall cease, that civil institutions, founded on the principles of equality, shall be adopted by all nations, and that the love of man for his fellow-creatures shall be manifested in deeds of kindness and benevolence;" and with united hearts renew to God our acknowledgments of gratitude for his "remarkable interposition in staying the desolating moral pestilence of intemperate drinking."

William L Marcy, Governor of New York, issued thanksgiving proclamations for 1833–1838, in which he says—

> To acknowledge the bounties of the Giver of all good, and to cherish grateful recollections of his beneficence, is eminently worthy of an intelligent and highly favored people. In view of the numerous favors and blessings with which the past year has been crowned, our thoughts should be naturally directed to our munificent Benefactor, and our hearts moved to expressions of gratitude and thanksgiving. The same almighty arm which protected and sustained our forefathers has also been our shield of defence; the same bountiful hand which administered temporal and spiritual blessings to them has been more abundant in good gifts to us. Our civil and religious rights have been enjoyed without molestation; moral and intellectual improvement has rapidly advanced; the spirit of enterprise has been active in multiplying the means

of social happiness; and industry, in all its various branches, has received appropriate rewards. All things essential to our prosperity have been graciously offered for our acceptance. Surrounded as we are by numerous and signal manifestations of the Divine goodness towards us, as individuals, and in our social and political relations, it behooves us to render to our beneficent Benefactor the tribute of our love and gratitude.

William H. Seward, Secretary of State during the administration of President Lincoln, when Governor of the State of New York, issued his proclamation for a day of thanksgiving in 1839, in which he says—

Let us also beseech God to deliver the oppressed throughout the world, and vouchsafe to all mankind the privileges of civil and religious liberty, and the knowledge, influences, and blessed hopes of the gospel of his Son our Saviour.

In 1840, his proclamation said—

However much we may be separated by opinions or associations, all the citizens of the republic have equal political rights, and have the same motives to desire its peace, happiness, and perpetual prosperity. The Church of the living God is one, and embraces all those who in humility of spirit receive his holy faith and through Divine aid seek to keep his commandments. Let us, therefore, in perfect harmony and charity one with another, as patriots and Christians, implore him to sustain and bless all our civil and religious institutions, and to dispense to us abundantly that heavenly grace which, with faith in the Lord Jesus Christ, leads, through the ways of virtue here, to the blessed society of the redeemed in his everlasting kingdom.

Governor William C. Bouck, in his proclamation of 1844, declared that—

The blessed gospel has been gradually but surely extending its benign influence. Actuated by its diffusive benevolence,

Christian missionaries have not only labored among the waste and desolate places at home, but have gone forth to proclaim "Christ and him crucified" to the dark and benighted regions of the earth. With our thanksgiving let us mingle our prayers for a continence of the numerous blessings we enjoy, and especially that there may be an outpouring of the Spirit of God, to revive pure and undefiled religion among us—the best security of our civil and political institutions. We should always remember that "righteousness exalteth a nation."

Silas Wright as Governor of the State of New York, in his proclamation for 1845, make this official statement with respect to the Christian religion—

A Christian people should unite in a tribute of thanksgiving to Him who tempers the seasons and blesses the earth and makes it fruitful. Exercises such as these, entered into in the spirit and with the feelings which these considerations should excite, cannot fail to turn the mind to the lively remembrance of the immeasurably greater blessings of the redemption through a Saviour, and the revelation to fallen man of the way of salvation—blessings for which the human heart cannot be sufficiently thankful.

"The gift of a Saviour," he says, in his proclamation for 1846, "and the full light of Divine revelation, are spiritual blessings which should awaken to expressions of devout thankfulness the hearts and voices of a Christian people."

John Young, Governor of New York, in proclamations for 1847, 1848, says—

A day of public thanksgiving is due to Almighty God for blessings bestowed upon the people of this State. The State of New York presents a gladsome picture of universal happiness and prosperity. The blessings of free government, the means of universal education, and the supremacy of law and order have been vouchsafed to us in an eminent degree. As a Christian people, we are admonished that these blessings are the gifts of a beneficent God, and, while we thus rejoice in his bounty, we should not forget the homage due from grateful hearts.

Hamilton Fish, Governor of the State of New York, in proclamations for 1849, 1850, refers to Christianity in these words—

Civil and religious liberty continue to be vouchsafed to all within our borders, and the *blessings* of the gospel are extended to all who desire to enjoy its comforts and consolations.

And on this occasion we should not forget that, while an inscrutable Providence has seen fit to remove the Chief Magistrate of our Union [President Taylor died July 9, 1830], that same Providence has preserved us under the trial a free and a united people, has saved us from anarchy or civil commotion, and has continued to us the mild operation of a Government of our own adoption and rulers of our own choice.

Washington Hunt, Governor of New York, in his proclamations for 1851, 1852, says—

The maintenance of social order and free institutions, imparting fresh vigor to the cause of civil liberty, the diffusion of religion and learning, and the innumerable benefits which have been conferred upon our commonwealth, proclaim the infinite goodness and protecting care of the Creator and Supreme Ruler of the universe.

Horatio Seymour, Governor of New York, in proclamations for 1853, 1854, declares—

An acknowledgment of our dependence upon God and our obligations to him is at all times the duty of a Christian people. Let us mingle our prayers for a continuance of the numerous blessings we as a people enjoy, remembering that his wisdom alone can rightly direct, his power support, and his goodness give strength and security.

Governor Myron H. Clark, of New York, in his proclamations for 1855, 1856, made the following declaration—

> Every department of honorable human culture has advanced. The arts that adorn a republican state have not languished. The love of freedom has burned with a brighter flame. Our political rights have remained safe in the care of an enlightened and order-loving people. The public morals have not degenerated; and Religion has not failed to cheer us by her consolations, to warn us by her solemn admonitions, and to inspire us by her eternal hopes.
>
> And while we pray for forgiveness of our sins, as citizens of the State and subjects of the Divine government, let us consecrate ourselves anew on that [Thanksgiving] day to a religious life, which neglects no private or public obligation on earth, while it confides in the grace of God for the hope of an immortal life in heaven.

John A. King, Governor of New York, in his proclamations for 1857, 1858, says—

> The promise that seed-time and harvest shall never fail has been most signally manifested during the past season. The people of this State have been permitted to witness and enjoy during another year the noble works of God's hands—the fostering care of his goodness and mercy. We are called upon to acknowledge the power and goodness of our Almighty Father, the Lord and Giver of life, that we have received his merciful care, and beheld the wonderful works of his providence, and enjoyed the advantages and security which freedom, the public schools, and equal laws have established for ourselves and posterity.

PROCLAMATION BY EDWIN D. MORGAN, GOVERNOR OF THE STATE OF NEW YORK, 1862

From the depth of national affliction we come, with stricken hearts and chastened spirits, to own our dependence upon the Most High, and to render, with grateful sense, our thanks-givings for his mercies, countless in number and infinite in extent. A year fraught with the heaviest sorrows has yet, in the merciful plan of Providence, been distinguished by the most conspicuous blessings. Although it is numbered among the dark periods of history, and its sorrowful records graven on many hearth-stones, yet the precious blood shed in the cause of our country will hallow and strengthen our love and our reverence for it and its institutions, while the bitter sorrows of the year will discipline us into humility. Whatever was passionate in the earlier period of the war has given way to a deep and subdued conviction of duty in defending the integrity of the Union. Reflection has made clear our obligations, and the issues of the momentous struggle present themselves in more definite form. Our national aims have been elevated, and our sacrifices have made us less selfish; our Government and institutions placed in jeopardy have brought us to a more just appreciation of their value. Looking beyond the wicked leaders who have precipitated this terrible calamity of civil war upon us, we see that the people in arms against the Government possess the higher qualities of our national character; and though their minds have been perverted by passion and prejudice, yet on many occasions their prowess and devotion to their cause have been such as to win our respect. We are permitted to see that the war is developing the manhood of the nation; and, when peace shall return, we have faith that the American republic will be more powerful, the Government more permanent, the elements of society more perfectly blended, and the people more firmly united than ever.

We have other causes for gratitude. Disease has been averted at home; the unacclimated armies have been protected from pestilences which it was feared would follow them in distant latitudes. Earth's best fruits have been lavishly bestowed, the arts have prospered, the employments of peace have been rewarded, and the good order of society has been fully maintained. Reverses to our arms have been followed by successes on land and sea which specially call for thanksgiving, and justify the most sanguine expectations as to the final result of the contest.

That we may publicly signify our deep thankfulness for these, and countless other blessings of the past, and for the promise that his mercies endure forever; that we may fully acknowledge dependence upon the Supreme Being, and hear anew from his specially chosen servants that Judgments follow those nations wherein his prerogatives are usurped, and who give not God the glory in all things; and that, in proper spirit, we may ask that victory shall attend our armies and prosperity our dwellings, that peace may be restored, and that we may have strength to meet the trials of the future, I do appoint Thursday, the twenty-seventh day of November next, as a day of praise, thanksgiving, and prayer to Almighty God; and I do recommend that, suspending all ordinary business pursuits, the people of this State do meet together in their own chosen places of worship, and that the said day, throughout, be appropriately observed.

In witness whereof I have hereunto set my hand, and affixed the privy seal of the State, at the city of Albany, this first day of October, in the year of our Lord one thousand eight hundred and sixty-two.

Edwin D. Morgan.

By the Governor.

Lockwood L. Doty, Private Secretary.

MASSACHUSETTS

The proclamation of Governor Andrew, of Massachusetts, for 1861, is an important Christian state paper, and is a model of its kind for Christian rulers—

PROCLAMATION FOR A DAY OF PUBLIC THANKSGIVING AND PRAISE, NOVEMBER 21, 1861.

The example of the fathers, and the dictates of piety and gratitude, summon the people of Massachusetts at this, the harvest-season, crowning the year with the rich proofs of the wisdom and love of God, to join in a solemn and joyful act of united praise and thanksgiving to the bountiful Giver of every good and perfect gift.

I do, therefore, with the advice and consent of the Council, appoint Thursday, the twenty-first day of November next— the same being the anniversary of that day, in the year of our Lord sixteen hundred and twenty, on which the Pilgrims of Massachusetts, on board the Mayflower united themselves in a solemn and written compact of government—to be observed by the people of Massachusetts as a day of public thanksgiving and praise. And I invoke its observance by all the people with devout and religious joy.

"Sing aloud unto God our strength: make a Joyful noise unto the God of Jacob.

"Take a psalm, and bring hither the timbrel, the pleasant harp with the psaltery.

"Blow up the trumpet in the new moon, in the time appointed, on our solemn feast day.

"For this was a statute for Israel, and a law of the God of Jacob."

—Ps. lxxxi. 1–4.

"O bless our God, ye people, and make the voice of his praise to be heard:

"Which holdeth our soul in life, and suffereth not our feet to be moved.

"For thou, O God, hast proved us: thou hast tried us, as silver is tried."

—Ps. lxvi. 8–10.

Let us rejoice in God and be thankful—for the fulness with which he has blessed us in our basket and in our store, giving large reward to the toil of the husbandman, so that "our paths drop fatness;"

For the many and the gentle alleviations of the hardships which, in the present time of public disorder, have afflicted the various pursuits of agriculture;

For the early evidences of the reviving energies of the business of the people;

For the measure of success which has attended the enterprise of those who go down to the sea in ships, of those who search the depths of the ocean to add to the food of man, and of those whose busy skill and handicraft combine to prepare for various uses the crops of the earth and the sea;

For the advantages of sound learning, placed within the reach of all the children of the people, and the freedom and alacrity with which those advantages are embraced and improved;

For the opportunities of religious instruction and worship universally enjoyed by consciences untrammelled by any human authority;

For the "redemption of the world by Jesus Christ, for the means of grace, and the hope of glory."

And, with one accord, let us bless and praise God for the oneness of heart, mind, and purpose in which he has united the people of this ancient commonwealth for the defence of the rights, liberties, and honor of our beloved country.

May we stand forever in the same mind, remembering the devoted lives of our fathers, the precious inheritance of freedom received at their hands, the weight of glory which awaits the faithful, and the infinity of blessing which it is our privilege, if we will, to transmit to the countless generations of the future.

And while our tears flow in a stream of cordial sympathy with the daughters of our people, just now bereft, by the violence of the wicked and rebellious, of the fathers and husbands and brothers sons, whose heroic blood has made sacred the soil of Virginia, and, mingling with the waters of the Potomac, has made the river now and forever ours, let our souls arise to God, on the wings of praise, in thanksgiving that he has again granted us the privilege of living unselfishly and of dying nobly in a grand and righteous cause;

For the precious and rare possession of so much devoted valor and manly heroism;

For the sentiment of pious duty which distinguished our fallen in the camp and in the field;

And for the sweet and blessed consolations which accompany the memories of these dear sons of Massachusetts on to immortality.

And in our praise let us also be penitent. Let us "seek the truth and pursue it," and prepare our minds for whatever duty shall be manifested hereafter.

May the controversy in which we stand be found worthy, in its consummation, of the heroic sacrifices of the people and the precious blood of their sons, of the doctrine and the faith of the fathers, and consistent with the honor of God, and with justice to all men. And—

"Let God arise, let his enemies be scattered: let them also that hate him flee before him. As smoke is driven away, so drive them away." —Ps. lxviii. 1, 2.

"Scatter them by thy power; and bring them down, O Lord, our shield." —Ps. lix. 11.

Given at the Council-Chamber, this thirty-first day of October, in the year of our Lord one thousand eight hundred and sixty-one, and the eighty-sixth of the Independence of the United States of America.

John A. Andrew.

By his Excellency the Governor, with the advice and consent of the Council.

Oliver Warner, *Secretary.*

GOD SAVE THE COMMONWEALTH OF MASSACHUSETTS.
A PROCLAMATION FOR A DAY OF PUBLIC THANKSGIVING
AND PRAISE IN 1862.

By and with the advice and consent of the Council, I do hereby appoint Thursday, the twenty-seventh day of November current, to be observed throughout this Commonwealth as a day of public thanksgiving and praise. And I do earnestly invite and request all the people of Massachusetts to set apart that day for the grateful and happy remembrance of the boundless mercies and loving-kindness of Him in whose name our fathers planted our commonwealth, and to whose service they consecrated their lives and devoted their posterity.

"The Lord hath established his throne in the heavens, and his kingdom ruleth over all." He is the "Sovereign Commander of all the world, in whose hand is power and might, which none is able to withstand;" and to him only belong ascriptions of glory, who is "the only Giver of victory." Let our hearts, therefore, ascend higher than all the interests that entangle, all the doubts that bewilder, the passions that ensnare, and the prejudices that obscure—consenting to be led, illumined, and governed by his infinite intelligence and love.

In the meditations of the house of praise, let us take comfort and be thankful for the numberless manifestations of heroic and manly virtue which, amid the distractions of war, in the duties of the camp, and in the perils of battle, have illustrated the character of the sons of Massachusetts, and for the serene and beautiful devotion with which her daughters have given the dearest offerings of their hearts to the support of their country and for the defence of humanity.

Let us not forget the bountiful bestowments of the year, filling the granaries of the husbandman, and rewarding the toll of the laborer, the enterprise, thrift, and industry of all our people. No pestilence hath lurked in the darkness of night nor assailed us in the light of day. Calamity hath not overwhelmed us, nor hath any enemy destroyed.

Rising to the height of our great occasion, reinforced by courage, conviction, and faith, it has been the privilege of our country to perceive in the workings of Providence the opening ways of a sublime duty. And to Him who hath never deserted the faithful, unto Him "who gathereth together the outcasts of Israel, who healeth the broken in heart," we owe a new song of thanksgiving. "He showeth his word unto Jacob, his statutes and his judgments unto Israel. He hath not dealt so with any nation."

Putting aside all fear of man, which bringeth a snare, may this people put on the strength which is the Divine promise and gift to the faithful and obedient. "Let the high praises of God be in their mouth, and a two-edged sword in their hand." Not with malice and wickedness, but with sincerity and truth, let us keep this fast; and, while we "eat the fat and drink the sweet, forget not to send a portion to him for whom nothing is prepared." Let us remember on that day the claims of all who are poor or desolate or oppressed, and pledge the devotion of our lives to the rescue of our country from the evils of rebellion, oppression, and wrong; and may we all so order our conduct hereafter that we may neither be ashamed to live nor afraid to die.

Given at the Council-Chamber, in Boston, this twenty-seventh day of October, in the year one thousand eight hundred and sixty-two, and the eighty-seventh of the Independence of the United States of America.

John A. Andrew.

By his Excellency the Governor, with the advice and consent of the Council.

Oliver Warner, *Secretary*.

GOD SAVE THE COMMONWEALTH OF MASSACHUSETTS.

PENNSYLVANIA

In the name and by the authority of the Commonwealth of Pennsylvania, Andrew G. Curtin, Governor of the said Commonwealth.

A PROCLAMATION

Whereas it is a good thing to render thanks unto God for all his mercy and loving-kindness: therefore—

I, Andrew G. Curtin, Governor of the Commonwealth of Pennsylvania, do recommend that Thursday, the twenty-seventh day of November next, be set apart by the people of this Commonwealth as a day of solemn prayer and thanksgiving to the Almighty, giving him humble thanks that he has been graciously pleased to protect our free institutions and Government, and to keep us from sickness and pestilence, and to cause the earth to bring forth her increase, so that our garners are choked with the harvest, and to look so favorably on the soil of his children that industry has thriven among us and labor has its reward; and also that he has delivered us from the hands of our enemies, and filled our officers and men in the field with a loyal and intrepid spirit, and given them victory, and that he has poured out upon us (albeit unworthy) other great and manifold blessings.

Beseeching him to help and govern us in his steadfast fear and love, and to put into our minds good desires, so that by his continual help we may have a right judgment in all things, and especially praying him to give to Christian Churches grace to hate the thing which is evil, and to utter the teachings of truth and righteousness, declaring openly the whole counsel of God, and most heartily entreating him to bestow upon our civil rulers, wisdom and earnestness in council, and upon our military leaders zeal and vigor in action, that the fires of rebellion may be quenched; that we, being armed with his defence, may be preserved from all perils, and that hereafter our people, living in peace and quietness, may from generation to generation reap the abundant fruits of his mercy, and with joy and thankfulness praise and magnify his holy name.

Given under my hand and the great seal of the State, at Harrisburg, this twentieth day of October, in the year of our Lord one thousand eight hundred and sixty-two, and of the Commonwealth the eighty seventh.

Andrew G. Curtin.

By the Governor:
Eli Slifer, *Secretary of the Commonwealth.*

NEW JERSEY

PROCLAMATION

It being eminently right and proper that we, as a people, should at stated periods offer united thanks to Almighty God for his goodness to us as manifested by suffering us to lie down and rise up in safety even in these "troublous times," by the bestowal of health and plenty and innumerable temporal blessings, but, above all, by the inestimable gift of his dear Son Jesus Christ, for all the blessings of free salvation through him "for the means of grace and the hope of glory," I recommend that on Thursday, the twenty-seventh day of November instant, the people of this State do assemble in their wonted places for public worship, to acknowledge their entire dependence on him, to render hearty thanks for his loving-kindness during the bygone year, and humbly to supplicate a continuance of his favor.

Given under my hand and privy seal, this third day of November A.D. eighteen hundred and sixty-two.

Chas. S. Olden.

Attest: Chas. M. Herbert, *Private Secretary.*

OHIO

THANKSGIVING PROCLAMATION.

STATE OF OHIO, EXECUTIVE DEPARTMENT,

COLUMBUS, October 25, 1862

The time-honored custom, adopted by the fathers of our State, of setting apart one day in each year for praise, thanksgiving, and prayer to Almighty God for his goodness and mercy to us as a people, should be preserved. Especially at a time like the present should all good citizens unite in laying aside the ordinary business of life, at least for a day, and devote themselves to the teachings of their Maker.

The effort made by the legally constituted authorities of the land to put down the wicked rebellion against the Federal Government, the best ever enjoyed by any people, in which effort the gallant sons of Ohio have borne so conspicuous and proud a part, has filled every neighborhood with mourning. Our brave soldiers are yet exposed to the dangers of the field of battle and to the hardships and sickness of camp-life; and our system of government, in form after God's own laws, and so gentle that its reins were scarcely felt by the governed, is yet in peril.

Our heavenly Father can console the distressed, and heal the sorrows of the mother's and widow's heart; he can protect from danger our patriotic soldiers now in the field; he can paralyze the arm of the enemy our good Government.

Now, therefore, in obedience to the request of the General Assembly of the State of Ohio, and to the end that a simultaneous petition to him may ascend to heaven from all parts of our State, I do hereby fix upon, and set apart, Thursday, the twenty-seventh day of November next, as a day of praise, thanksgiving, and prayer to Almighty God. And I do recommend that abstaining from all business pursuits, the good and pure-minded people of our State meet tegether at their usual places of worship, and, with one voice, humbly ask the God of all nations to smile upon the distressed of our land; that he give wisdom and purity to those in authority; that he prostrate the enemies of our Government; and that in all things he give such wisdom to all the people of the earth as will enable them to conform to his laws, to the end that peace and good will shall prevail throughout the world.

In witness whereof I have hereunto set my hand and affixed the great seal of the State of Ohio, the day and year above written.

David Tod.

B. F. Hoffman, *Private Secretary.*

Salmon P. Chase, Secretary of the Treasury during the administration of President Lincoln, and Governor of the State of Ohio during the years 1856-59, presents in his proclamations for thanksgiving a clear and full statement of the Christian origin of all our social and family blessings, and that our civil and religious liberties and institutions, as well as our hopes of immortality, are derived from the Christian religion. In his proclamation for 1856 he uses the following language—

Assembling in our respective places of worship, or gathering around our domestic altars, let us devoutly acknowledge God as the gracious Author of every blessing and every benefit. Let us gratefully thank him especially for our prosperity and for our security; for our institutions of education, religion, and charity; for the products of our agriculture and of our arts; for the intercourse of commerce; for the preservation of health; for homes endeared by sweet family affections; for the mercies of redemption, and for the hopes of immortality. Adoring the Divine wisdom by which our fathers were guided in establishing the foundations of united empire in North America upon the solid basis of civil and religious freedom, and the Divine goodness by which the institutions of government which they founded have been transmitted to their children, let us give thanks for liberty guarded by law and defended by union. Confessing humbly our unworthiness of these inestimable benefits, let us fervently invoke our Father in heaven to continue them graciously to us and our posterity forever. Nor let us forget in our rejoicings or in our supplications our fellow-men less happy than ourselves. Of our abundance let us give liberally to those who need; nor let us fail to present before the throne of infinite justice our sincere prayers for the downfall of tyranny, for the deliverance of the oppressed, for the enfranchisement of the enslaved, and for the establishment everywhere of human rights and just governments.

His proclamation for 1857, after a specific enumeration of the common bounties of the Divine munificence, for which the people are to "present sincere offerings of humble adoration and grateful praise," and the distribution of their abundance to these who need, says—

And, invoking earnestly his gracious favor, that we may walk before him continually in the way of his commandments, to the end that his blessing may remain upon us, and upon our children, and upon the good land which he hath given us, forever.

His proclamation for 1858 recommends the people of the State to observe the day—

By public and private offerings of praise and gratitude for the multiform and manifold blessings and benefits, national, social, and personal, which God hath been graciously pleased to bestow upon us; and by fervent prayers that he will cause his goodness to abound yet more and more towards protecting our whole country front foreign enemies and domestic dissensions, distinguishing by his favor our State institutions of Government, education, and benevolence, and conducting each of us through the blessed ways of penitence and faith, to the glorious summation of earthly hopes in heavenly rest.

His proclamation for 1859 has the following Christian exhortations—

And offer unfeigned thanks to our heavenly Father for all the blessings wherewith he hath blessed us as a nation, as a State, and as individuals, and that they join to these offerings of gratitude and praise their fervent prayers that he will continue and multiply his grace and favor upon us and upon our land; that our institutions may be established in righteousness; that wisdom and knowledge may be the stability of our times; and that peace, prosperity, and freedom may be the portion of our people.

William Dennison, Governor of Ohio during the years 1860, 1861, in his proclamation for thanksgiving, ascribes all our blessings, temporal and social, civil and religious, to God, and declares us distinguished as a Christian people. His proclamation for 1860 recommends that the people—

Offer up their devout thanks to God for our institutions, national and State, civil and religious, educational and benevolent, for the peace that prevails throughout our borders, the health with which he hath blessed us, the abundant harvest wherewith he hath graciously rewarded the labors of the husbandman, the prosperity of our commerce and the mechanic arts, our social comforts and privileges, and for whatever contributes to our happiness as a community and as individuals.

And, while thus rendering to the Supreme Author of every blessing our grateful acknowledgments for his unbounded goodness, let us supplicate a continuance of the Divine protection and favor to this people, and to the people of all the States and territories of our National Confederacy, throughout all generations; and, fraternally remembering in our rejoicings our fellow-men of other nations who are less happy than ourselves, let us fervently implore him that in his benign providence he will confer upon them, and their posterity forever, like blessings of civil and religious liberty and social happiness which he hath been graciously pleased to bestow upon us.

His proclamation for 1861 recommends the people of Ohio to return praise to God "for the inestimable privileges of our civil and religious institutions, for protecting our homes from the ravages of war, and for the manifold blessings, individual and social, which surround and support us," and to "offer fervent prayer to our heavenly Father that he may continue to remember us in his mercy, remove the calamities of civil strife which afflict the nation, restore concord between the States, confirm and perpetuate our political union, and secure to us and to our posterity the privileges and advantages which distinguish a Christian people."

These views in the state papers of the Governors of Ohio are in harmony with the Constitution of the State, formed in 1802, and reaffirmed in the new Constitution of 1862, which state that—

"Religion, morality and knowledge, being essentially necessary to the government and the happiness of mankind, schools and the means of instruction shall forever he encouraged by legislative provisions not inconsistent with the rights of conscience."

KENTUCKY

PROCLAMATION

The acknowledgment of national as well as individual dependence upon the Supreme Ruler of the universe is the highest evidence of refined civilization; and no people ever prospered for any great length of time who did not admit and invoke his power and mercy; nor will any such ever rise to true greatness as a nation.

The spirit of the American people has been wellnigh crushed by the terrible realities of the intestine war into which the nation has been plunged by the disappointed ambition of maddened and reckless men; and it is the part alike of wisdom and of duty for us all to prostate ourselves in humiliation before the Author of all good, and supplicate his omnipotent arm to arrest this wicked and unjust rebellion and restore to a distracted people the blessings of peace, unity, and fraternal affection.

But while thus humiliating ourselves before the Almighty Disposer of events, we should remember that we have abundant cause to offer the homage of grateful hearts for the manifold blessings he has vouchsafed to us as a people. The seasons have bean propitious; the labor of the husbandman has been crowned with ample returns; we have not been called upon to mourn the ravages of extended disease in the country; the public health has never been more marked than during the year which is drawing to a close; and while, therefore, we have to lament the terrible consequences of the fratricidal war which afflicts and desolates the land, we yet have ample reason for returning thanks to him that we are free from those awful scourges—pestilence and famine—which so often afflict the human family, and not unfrequently add their horrors to those involved in war.

It is meet, therefore, that the time-honored custom of dedicating one day in the year to devotional exercises to Him who holds the destinies of nations and individuals alike in his hands, should be preserved, and, while pouring out our gratitude for the incalculable benefits we enjoy, bow ourselves in earnest supplication to Almighty God that he will, in his infinite mercy, interpose his omnipotent arm to stay the spirit of intestine strife which is sweeping over and desolating the land, restore peace and order to this hitherto Heaven-favored country, and make all to feel that a return to the government of our fathers, which has rendered us so powerful, prosperous, and happy, is at once the part of patriotism and religious duty.

I, therefore, as Governor of the Commonwealth, do hereby set apart Thursday, November 27th instant, as a day of thanksgiving and praise to Almighty God for all his mercies to us, and request a general observance of it, to the end that we may manifest, in a proper spirit, our dependence upon him, and supplicate his omnipotent power to protect and guard us from future misfortunes as a nation.

Done at the city of Frankfort, this twelfth day of November, 1862, and the seventy-first year of the Commonwealth.

By the Governor: J. F. ROBINSON.

D. C. WICKLIFFE, *Secretary of State.*

The Commonwealth of Kentucky, the first to enter the Union under the Constitution of the United States, began its civilization and organic life under the auspices of the Christian religion. Its opening scenes let in the light of Divine truth; and the pioneers, though unpolished in the manners of courtiers, carried with them a manly faith, which laid the foundation of the State on a Christian basis. The first Constitution secured "a perfect religions freedom and a general toleration."

"Thus," says Bancroft, "the pioneer lawgivers for the West provided for freedom of conscience. A little band of hunters put themselves at the head of the countless hosts of civilization in establishing the great principle of intellectual freedom. Long as the shadows of the Western mountains shall move round with the sun, long as the rivers that gush from those mountains shall flow towards the sea, long as seed-time and harvest shall return, that rule shall remain the law of the West.

"When Sunday dawned, the great tree which had been their council-chamber became their church. Penetrated with a sense of the Redeemer's love, they lifted up their hearts to God in prayer and thanksgiving, and the forest that was wont to echo only the low of the buffalo and the whoop of the savage was animated by the voice of their devotion. Thus began the Commonwealth of Kentucky: it never knew any other system than independence, and was incapable of any thing else."

INDIANA

EXECUTIVE DEPARTMENT, INDIANAPOLIS, NOV. 11.

To the people of Indiana.

The people of the State of Indiana are earnestly requested to assemble in their respective churches, and at their family altars, on Thursday, the twenty-seventh day of November, 1866, te return thanks to Almighty God for the manifold blessings he has bestowed upon them during the past year, and to pray him in his mercy to avert from our beloved country the evils by which it is now so deeply afflicted. It is their duty humbly to acknowledge the many favors bestowed by his hand, and their entire dependence upon his providence for deliverance from the evils by which they are suffering. It is their duty to pray for the success of our armies, for the suppression of this most wicked rebellion, and the preservation of our Government; that the lives of our brave soldiers may be spared, and that they be returned in safety to their homes; that the hearts of our people may he inspired with a perfect confidence in the ultimate success of a just came, and that the minds of all men may be awakened to a clear comprehension of the mighty interests for which we are struggling not only to ourselves, but to our posterity; and they should especially pray that the Divine will may put it into the hearts of the people to provide for and protect the families of our gallant soldiers and preserve them from all want and neglect; to cherish and comfort with sedulous care the orphans and broken-hearted widows and parents of such as have fallen in the field, or perished by disease in the camp.

In testimony whereof I have hereunto set my hand, and affixed the seal of the State, at Indianapolis, this eleventh day of November, 1862.

Signed, Oliver P. Morton, *Governor of Indiana.*

Attest: Wm. A. Peelle, *Secretary of State.*

NEW HAMPSHIRE

A PROCLAMATION FOR A DAY OF PUBLIC THANKSGIVING
AND PRAISE, BY HIS EXCELLENCY THE GOVERNOR.

The revolution of the seasons has brought again the period when it is the usage to set apart a day for public thanksgiving to Almighty God. In accordance with a time-honored custom, inaugurated by our forefathers, and so much in harmony with the convictions of all Christian people, I do, by the advice of the Council, appoint Thursday, the 27th of November next, to be observed as a day of thanksgiving and praise. And I hereby invite the people of this State to assemble in their usual places of public worship, to join in ascriptions of praise, and other devotional exercises so suitable for dependent beings, and of which the many mercies of our heavenly Father, at this time, are so eminently suggestive. Let us all meet to give him thanks for the bountiful harvest with which he has gladdened the heart of man; for peaceful homes, and the social, educational, and religious privileges vouchsafed to us; for the progress of civil liberty; for the general prevalence of health throughout our borders during the year approaching its close, and in which, notwithstanding the existence of great national calamities, there has been much to remind us of his never-failing mercy and goodness. Let us adore and bless his holy name for that Christian civilization which is our inheritance, and for the many and illustrious examples which came to us with that heavenly boon, of the patience, unfailing confidence, and heroic endurance of a holy ancestry in seasons of affliction and peril. Let us humbly and gratefully thank and praise the Disposer of Events that such examples of reliance upon his providential care have not been lost to succeeding generations, but are now abundantly developed among a great people, in a year the painful record of which will soon be closed; a year when the patriotism, courage and Christian faith of our fathers has been fully realized in their children, who disregarding the ties of affection, and the comfort of happy firesides, are bravely enduring the perils of camp and the storm of battle, that their country may live, and the cause of good government and free institutions be transmitted to succeeding generations. And, above all, let us praise him for that revelation which brings "life and immortality to light;" for the injunctions and promises of that Book which for our fathers was the source of reliance and consolation in seasons of disquietude and danger, and which may with equal certainty and efficacy be appropriated by ourselves in this season of doubt and peril. And, while we thank God for his mercies, let not a day so suggestive of good works be permitted to pass without the exercise of those offices of kindness for the needy which was an injunction of our Divine Redeemer, who published "peace on earth and good will to men."

Given at the Council-Chamber in Concord, this thirty-first day of October, in the year of our Lord one thousand eight hundred and sixty-two, and of the independence of the United States the eighty-seventh.

Nathaniel S. Berry.

By his Excellency the Governor, with advice of the Council:

Allen Tenny, *Secretary of State.*

CONNECTICUT

PROCLAMATION

In the midst of civil strife, and a rebellion which has arrayed the enemies of our Government in hostile and deadly conflict against the friends of national supremacy, it is wise and proper for us, as a people, to allow our minds to dwell upon the blessings by which we are still surrounded, and rest upon well-grounded hopes of future good: in view of which we should lift up our hearts and voices in thanksgiving and praise unto Him who healeth all our diseases, who redeemeth our lives from destruction, who crowneth us with loving-kindness and tender mercies, and "executeth righteousness and judgment for all that are oppressed."

I therefore recommend the people of this State to observe Thursday, the twenty-seventh day of November next, as a day of public thanksgiving and praise, and would urge them to such acts of benevolence and religious worship as will manifest their heartfelt gratitude to Almighty God.

Let us praise him for healthful seasons, for abundant harvests, for the means of knowledge, for social blessings, for religious liberty.

Let us be grateful for the labors unostentatiously performed, and the pecuniary offerings spontaneously bestowed, to relieve the necessities, to bind up the wounds, and to cheer the hearts of those who, with loyal devotion to their country's weal, are battling for national unity.

Let us also be grateful for the blessed memory of the honored dead, who in the camp and on the battle-field have cheerfully, heroically and religiously offered their lives upon the altar of patriotism.

Let us rejoice and praise God that he holds the destinies of this nation in his hands, that he confirms or changes the purposes of man at his pleasure, and overrules all human designs to establish righteousness, truth, and justice in the earth.

Given under my hand and the seal of the State, at the city of Hartford, this, the thirty-first day of October, in the year of our Lord one thousand eight hundred and sixty-two, and in the year of the independence of the United States of America the eighty-seventh.

William A. Buckingham.

By his Excellency's command:

J. Hammond Trumbull, *Secretary of State.*

Governor Buckingham, in his proclamation for 1858, after enumerating the general blessings vouchsafed to the State and nation, closes with this explicit acknowledgment of the Christian religion and its fundamental doctrines—

> And, above all, that "he hath not dealt with us after our sins, nor rewarded us according to our iniquities," but has magnified the riches of his grace in giving his Holy Spirit to revive his work and lead sinners to repentance, and that the door of mercy is yet open, through which the guilty and perishing may enter and obtain eternal life, by faith in the atonement of Jesus Christ his Son.

STATE OF RHODE ISLAND AND PROVIDENCE PLANTATIONS

A PROCLAMATION

In the midst of the greatest calamity that has ever befallen our country, we should not be unmindful of the blessings which are showered upon us by the all-wise Disposer of events and destinies. Our adversities should not tempt us to forget either our dependence upon a common Father or the multiplied mercies which accompany his chastenings. In the midst of war we are enjoying many of the blessings of peace. Our granaries are filled to overflowing; many departments of industry bring their usual rewards to the toiling masses; neither pestilence nor famine assails us in our households; order reigns in our cities and towns; our common schools prosper; domestic quiet rewards obedience to the laws of man and God, and the people worship securely in their temples.

Thus blest, it is fit that we should render thanks to the Supreme Ruler of the universe; and I therefore appoint Thursday, the twenty-seventh day of November instant, to be observed in this State as a day of public thanksgiving, prayer, and praise.

On that day let us assemble in our places of worship and in our family and social circles, and render to a beneficent Creator the adoration of grateful hearts, beseeching him, also, that he will continue to us the unnumbered mercies of the present, and especially that he will restore to us the national unity, peace, and prosperity of former years; that he will guide our rulers in the discharge of their duties; that he will reward patriotism in the soldier and in the citizen; that he will banish treason, corruption, and imbecility from high places; that he will preserve our Constitution and save us from anarchy; that he will restore to us hostile States and estranged hearts; that he will prosper all our worthy enterprises and labors; and that he will prompt those upon whom he has bestowed temporal blessings, to bind up the wounds and cheer the hearts of such as faint beneath the heavy burdens of adversity.

In testimony whereof I have hereto set my hand and affixed the seal of the State, at Providence, this sixth day of November, in the year of our Lord 1862 of independence the eighty-seventh, and of the founding of the State the two hundred and twenty-sixth.

William Sprague.

By his Excellency the Governor:

John R. Bartlett, *Secretary of State.*

The Governor of the State of Rhode Island and Providence Plantations, Elisha Dyer, in his proclamation of 1858, calls upon the people to return thanks to God for "the wide-spread manifestations and presence of the Holy Spirit," and the "means of grace and the hope of glory still offered us in the religion of Jesus Christ."

MAINE

PROCLAMATION

In times of calamity and trouble, our fathers did not neglect to celebrate their annual festival of Thanksgiving; and in this hour of the country's sorest trial, when bereavement and anguish have been brought to many hearts, their children will find strength and profit in its beautiful rites, its hallowed associations, and its gracious influences.

By advice of the Council, I appoint Thursday, the twenty-seventh day of November next, to be observed by the people of this State as a day of public thanksgiving and praise.

And may they all regard it as a day consecrated to emotions of gratitude and good will, to deeds of benevolence and love. Abstaining from all employments and pursuits inconsistent with a proper observance of the occasion, I invite them to repair to their temples of religious worship; and there, and in all places, may they be led to a devout and cheerful recognition of the many favors and privileges which have been lavished upon them during the year whose great, eventful history is so nearly made up. May they be unfeignedly thankful for the blessings of material prosperity and health which have been so largely vouchsafed to them; for the exhibitions of constancy, fidelity, and manly virtue in their countrymen, which have so often illustrated the dignity of human nature and the capacity of men for self-government; for the Christian charity and brotherly kindness which a better acquaintance with, and a more sensible dependence upon, each other, growing out of a common cause and a common danger, have developed and cultivated in their hearts; and especially may they be moved to praise and bless their heavenly father, the Lord of all things that he has put it into the heart of the chief magistrate of the nation to promulgate, in the fulness of time, a decree of wisdom and uprightness which shall make their beloved land strong, united, prosperous, peaceful, just, and forever free.

Given at the Council-Chamber at Augusta, this seventeenth day of October, in the year of our Lord one thousand eight hundred and sixty-two, and of the independence of the United States the eighty-seventh.

Israel Washburn, Jr.

By the Governor:

Joseph B. Hall, *Secretary of State.*

VERMONT

PROCLAMATION

Though the Almighty, in his providential dealings both with nations and individuals, mingles adversity with prosperity, discipline and sorrow with love and mercy, and his ultimate designs are often kept in a sacred reserve which we cannot penetrate, still enough is revealed to inspire a humble trust in his providence, and we are led to feel that even in times of trouble and calamity "it is a good thing to give thanks unto the Lord."

In obedience to custom and the universal sentiment of our people, I do, therefore, appoint Thursday, the fourth day of December next, to be observed by the people of this State as a day of public prayer, praise, and thanksgiving; and I invite them to lay aside the ordinary employments of life on that day, and to assemble in their usual places of public worship, to render thanks to Almighty God; for the fruitfulness of the year, and the plenty that everywhere abounds; for the prosperity of our material pursuits and interests; for the general prevalence of health; for our pleasant and comfortable homes, and the endearments and treasures of domestic life; for the pleasures and comforts of good neighborhood, and the advantages of intelligent, well-ordered society; for our institutions of education, benevolence, and religion; for our freedom from the desolations of war within our territory; for the fervent patriotism, nationality of sentiment, and unity of purpose and effort which have characterized the people of our State, leading thousands of its citizens to go forth voluntarily and cheerfully to fight the battles of the republic, and mothers and daughters to give up to country the dearest objects of their affection; for the devotion to country so generally manifested by the loyal people of the Union, and for the good order, the steadiness and faithfulness of purpose, and obedience to authority and law, which have universally prevailed and been a distinctive and striking feature in the character and conduct of free society in the loyal States, under a government so mild in its restraints as scarcely to be felt by the governed.

Let it be our special prayer to Almighty God that he will, in his good time, restore our beloved republic in peace and prosperity, in unity and power, and that therein the blessings of civil and religious liberty may be dispensed to mankind to the end of time; that he will dispose all men, everywhere, to accept the mild reign of the Redeemer, and will hasten the promised time when universally there shall be *"peace on earth, good will towards men."*

And though many of us, while gathered around the festive board or the domestic hearth, must inevitably observe the vacant chair, and direct our thoughts to him who is in the tented field, or lies in the soldier's grave, or, sick or wounded, is nursed by strange hands, yet let our sadness be tempered by the thought of his manly and heroic purpose to discharge the highest and last duty of the patriot to his country.

Given under my hand, and the seal of the State, in Executive Chamber, at Montpelier, this seventeenth day of November, in the year of our Lord one thousand eight hundred and sixty-two, and of the independence of the United States the eighty-seventh.

Frederick Holbrook.

By his Excellency the Governor:

Samuel Williams, *Secretary of Civil and Military Affairs.*

VIRGINIA

The following proclamation is from the Governor of the State of Western Virginia. An act of Congress, in 1863, admitted this portion of the "Ancient Dominion of Virginia" into a separate and independent State—

PROCLAMATION

In the midst of war and its afflictions, we are forcibly reminded of our dependence upon Divine Providence; and, while in all we suffer we should own his chastening hand, we should be ready to acknowledge that it is of his mercy that we are not destroyed, and that so many of the blessings of life are preserved to us. "Seed-time and harvest" have not failed, "the early and the latter rain" have fallen in their season, and the toil of the husbandman has been abundantly repaid. It is, therefore, becoming that, while we earnestly pray that the days of our affliction may he shortened, we should thankfully acknowledge the manifold mercies of which, nationally and individually, we are still the recipients.

Now, therefore, I, Francis H. Pierpoint, Governor of Virginia, do hereby recommend to the good people of the Commonwealth the observance of Thursday, the twenty-eighth instant, as a day of thanksgiving to Almighty God for the blessings of the year, and of humble and fervent prayer that he will, in more abundant mercy, bring to a speedy end the heart-burnings and civil strife which are now desolating our country, and restore to our Union its ancient foundation of brotherly love and just appreciation. And I do recommend that all secular business and pursuits be, as far as possible, suspended on that day.

In testimony whereof I have here set my hand, and caused the great seal of the Commonwealth to he affixed, at the city of Wheeling, this fourteenth day of November, in the year of our Lord one thousand eight hundred and sixty-one, and of the Commonwealth the eighty-sixth.

Francis H. Pierpoint.

By the Governor:

S. A. Hagans, *Secretary of Commonwealth.*

MARYLAND

Proclamation
To the People of the State

The return of the season in which, in obedience to a custom well becoming a Christian community, we have been taught to render annually to Almighty God our tribute of prayer and thanksgiving for the bounties received at his hand, naturally calls to mind the propriety of again designating a day for the discharge of that expected duty.

In conformity, therefore, with this established custom, I, Augustus W. Bradford, Governor of Maryland, do, by this my proclamation, designate and appoint Thursday, the twenty-seventh day of November next, to be observed by the people of the State as a day of general thanksgiving and prayer.

Although the copious stream of national blessings which has so long flowed in upon us has been at length interrupted, and the prosperity and peace that marked our career been arrested, by a war aimed at our national existence—a war all the more deplorable, waged as it is by those who have reaped with us the full share of these abundant bounties—still the blessings that yet remain demand profound acknowledgments.

We should thank God that a vast majority of our people still cherish the unfaltering purpose to preserve the integrity and indivisibility of our nation with an earnestness and zeal that spurn all other considerations. We should thank him that he has so lavishly supplied us with the means of accomplishing this cherished object; that our country has everywhere teemed with such an overflowing abundance that our own resources can feed and clothe our armies and still leave a surplus so ample that few yet feel the wants that follow in the train of war. We should thank him for the uninterrupted health which our whole country, with scarcely an exception, has throughout the year enjoyed. The pestilence that heretofore has habitually scourged certain portions of our land seem, in despite of heartless calculations to the contrary, to have suspended its annual visitation, as if by special providential interposition.

More especially should we in Maryland thank him that the attempt so recently made to invade our State and transfer to its soil the scene of the conflict has been so successfully resisted by our defenders and so impressively rebuked by our citizens; and that, whilst war in its most appalling aspects has for the past eighteen mouths raged within sight of our borders, our own people, with the exception of one memorable week, have all practically enjoyed most of the advantages of peace.

Let us, therefore, with grateful hearts, laying aside for the time all secular pursuits, as well as all partisan animosities, offer up, on the day above appointed, our united thanks for these and all the other blessings we still enjoy, accompanied with our prayers that they may be still continued. Let us implore Him who throughout our national career has so distinguished us with his favor, not to withdraw it now in the day of our severest trial, but that, inspiring our rulers with the wisdom to discern and strength to perform their responsible duties, he will cause our Union to be re-established in all its recent power, restore peace to our bleeding country, reunite its wrangling citizens, curb the mad ambition of those insanely attempting to dismember it, and the factious spirit that would divide those offering to defend it, and allow in it once more to resume among the nations of the earth the proud position which, through his unvarying goodness, it has been hitherto permitted to maintain.

Given under my hand, and the great seal of the State of Maryland, at the city of Annapolis, this twenty-seventh day of October, in the year of our Lord one thousand eight hundred and sixty-two, and of the independence of the United States the eighty-seventh.

A. W. Bradford.

By the Governor:

Wm. B. Hill, *Secretary of State.*

MISSOURI

A Proclamation

The affairs of states and of individuals are alike under the superintendence of Divine Providence, and it is becoming that, as people, we should render to the supreme Ruler suitable acknowledgments of our dependence upon him, and suitable expressions of thankfulness for the blessings he has conferred upon us during the year.

Although man's madness may have brought incalculable evils upon our State, we may contrast the evils thus produced with the beneficent results of a kind Providence acting for our good.

We have heard the "confused noise" of battle, and "seen the garments rolled in blood," while he has kept still the tempest, the whirlwind, and the earthquake—the ministers of his wrath.

We have seen the mother, the wife, the sister, clad in the garments of mourning, and we knew that man had brought the woe, while he held back the "pestilence that walketh in darkness," and tempered the atmosphere to the preservation of our lives and health.

We have seen man wasting and destroying, while he points us to the rich harvests which he has given, and calls us to praise him "for his goodness to the children of men."

Let us, then, praise him with thankful hearts, and express our joy that he reigns, and that he has been merciful to us amidst the calamities which a has brought upon us, and let us rejoice for the assurance that he will even "cause the wrath of man to praise him."

In view of the multiplied blessings conferred upon us as a people by Divine Providence, I, Hamilton R. Gamble, Governor of the State of Missouri, do appoint Thursday, the twenty-seventh day of this present month of November, as a day of thanksgiving to God for his goodness manifested to us during the year; and I do earnestly recommend to the good people of the State to assemble on that day in their respective places of worship, and present to God the homage of grateful hearts, in view of his abounding goodness, and invoke his protection for the future.

In testimony whereof I have hereto set my hand, and caused the great seal of the State to be affixed, this sixth day of November, in the year of our Lord one thousand eight hundred and sixty-two.

(Signed) H. R. GAMBLE.

MINNESOTA

PROCLAMATION

Whereas it is meet, and in accordance with a good and cherished custom of our fathers, worthy to be "a statute forever in all our dwellings," that the people, "when they have gathered the fruit of the land," should "keep a feast unto the Lord," in commemoration of his goodness, and by a public act of Christian worship acknowledge their dependence as a community upon Him in whose hands the kingdoms of the earth are but as dust in the balance;

Therefore I, Alexander Ramsey, Governor of the State of Minnesota, do hereby set apart the twenty-seventh day of the present month of November as a day of thanksgiving to Almighty God for his wonderful mercy towards us, for all the good gifts of his providence, for health and restored domestic peace, and the measure of general prosperity which we enjoy.

Especially let us recognize his mercy in that he has delivered our borders from the savage enemies who rose up against us, and cast them into the pit they had privily dug for us; that our friends have been rescued from the horrors of captivity, and that our homes and household treasures are now safe from the violence of Indian robbers and assassins.

And let us praise him for the continued preservation of the Government of our fathers from the assaults of traitors and rebels; for the sublime spirit of patriotism and courage and constancy with which he has filled the hearts of its defenders; for the victories won by the valor of our troops; for the glorious share of Minnesota in the struggles and triumphs of the Union cause; for the safety of her sons who have passed through the fire of battle unscathed, and the honorable fame of the gallant dead; for the alacrity and devotion with which our citizens have rushed from their unharvested fields to the standard of the nation; and, above all, for the assurance that their toils and perils and wounds and self-devotion are not in vain; for the tokens, now manifest, of his will that through the blood and sweat of suffering and sacrifice the nation is to be saved from its great calamity, and the great crime of which it is at once the effect and punishment; and that behind the thunders and lightnings and clouds of the tempest the awful form of Jehovah is visible, descending in fire upon the mount, to renew the broken tablets of the Constitution, and proclaim FREEDOM and the condition and the law of a restored and regenerated Union.

Given under my hand, and the great seal of the State, at the city of St. Paul, this third day of November, in the year of our Lord one thousand eight hundred and sixty-two.

Alexander Ramsey.

By the Governor:

James H. Baker, *Secretary of State.*

MICHIGAN

Proclamation

Another year has passed away into history. It has been a year of great events—a year of civil war, and all the bloody sacrifices, harassing doubts, and alternating triumphs and defeats which surely follow in its track. Vast armies, raised from the midst of the people, have gone forth to fight our country's battles. With a courage and constancy which will brighten the history of the republic forever, they have beaten back the hosts of rebellion and despotism from the loyal States and saved our homes from the horrors of invasion. Our liberties and laws are still preserved to us, and the power of the Government is gradually but surely being established over all the territory of the Union. Rebellion is being punished, and upon the wicked authors of this unseemly strife is falling the sure reward of their unparalleled sin. The war is carried into the midst of their country, and the victorious armies of the Union hasten on to strike them a final blow in the strongholds of the far South. There are solid grounds of hope for speedy victory and permanent peace.

While many of our homes are made desolate by the inevitable casualties of war, and all mourn the heroic dead, there is consolation in the faith that the blood of the true patriot is never shed in vain.

Our people, under all these trials, still cling with unflinching firmness and fidelity to the institutions and Government of our country. Trusting in God and the righteousness of our cause, they are ready to incur greater sacrifices and bear heavier burdens, in the confidence and hope that the future will more than compensate for the past, and that the blessing of liberty will be permanently scoured and greatly increased to our posterity.

The destinies of nations and individuals are in the hand of God. For bountiful harvests, for general health among the people, for civil and religious liberty and the diffusion of knowledge and education, for time continued existence of the republic and the triumphs of its arms, and for all the great and good gifts of a benign Providence, our acknowledgments and praises are due to him alone. That we may suitably acknowledge our dependence upon Almighty God, and with reverent thankfulness give glory to him, I do hereby set apart and appoint Thursday, the twenty-seventh instant, as a day of public thanksgiving and praise.

I request that upon that day the people may assemble in their places of public worship, and in their homes and keep this day in the spirit in which our fathers kept it, with pure, religious and patriotic hearts, full of faith and hope.

Given under my hand, and the great seal of the State, at the Capitol, in the city of Lansing, on the fifteenth day of November, in the year of our Lord one thousand eight hundred and sixty-two.

Austin Blair.

James B. Porter, *Secretary of State.*

ILLINOIS

Proclamation
To the People of the State of Illinois

It is the sacred duty of nations, as well a individuals, to acknowledge the manifestations of God's enduring mercy and loving-kindness.

The perils which surround us, the trials under which the nation is laboring, forcibly impress upon us the necessity and propriety of calling upon Him who is able to save, for deliverance.

Nevertheless, amid present evils and dangers, the Almighty has not left us without many signal evidences of his care and protection.

Our State has been blessed with an abundant harvest; the patriotism of our people is unparalleled in the history of nations; our soldiers have made as bright a record as that of the bravest of their brethren in arms and have been victorious on many hard-fought battle-fields; the munificence of our citizens in administering to the sufferings of our troops is worthy of a generous-hearted people; and above all, in the midst of an internecine war unparalleled in the history of the world, have the people of our State been allowed to pursue their peaceful avocations undisturbed.

In view, then, of these and all other evidences of his continued care and protection, and more particularly for the purpose of giving the people of the State an opportunity of uniting together and thanking God for his mercies, and beseeching him to deliver our nation from her present great afflictions, to grant victory to our arms, a speedy suppression of the rebellion, and a restoration of peace, I do hereby appoint Thursday, the twenty-seventh day of November next, as a day of thanksgiving and prayer, and recommend that the people on that day, laying aside ordinary avocations, meet in their several places of worship, to render up the tribute of grateful hearts to the Almighty Ruler of the universe.

In testimony whereof I have hereunto set my hand, adorned the great seal of the State of Illinois to be affixed, this twenty-seventh day of October, in the year of our Lord one thousand eight hundred and sixty-two.

Richard Yates.

DELAWARE

PROCLAMATION

The duty of a Christian people, and the observance of a long-established custom, alike demand that a day of thanksgiving and praise be set apart to Almighty God for his wonderful goodness and mercy extended to us during the past year.

Although our national calamities have been great and brethren of a once happy and united country have been arrayed in deadly strife against each other, whereby gloom and sorrow and mourning saddened many hearts and darkened many hearthstones, yet we of Delaware, through his Divine goodness, have been spared the dread ravages of war. While many of our sister States have experienced the terrible effect of his chastening hand in punishment of our manifold sins and wickedness, he has graciously shielded us from invasion from without and convulsions within. Visible and manifest are the blessings which he has lavishly bestowed upon us during the year now approaching its close. He has blessed us with sunshine and with rain. He has continued to us the inestimable enjoyments of good health and sound reason. He has spared us from disease, pestilence, and famine. He has bountifully rewarded the industry of the husbandman, and caused the earth to bring forth her richest fruits, storing our garners and filling the land with plenty. He has protected our institutions of learning and religion, prospered the arts and sciences, and repaid the labors of the mechanic and working-man.

In view of these and countless other manifestations of his loving-kindness so graciously vouchsafed unto us, and in grateful recognition thereof, I, William Burton, Governor of the State of Delaware, do hereby appoint Thursday, the twenty-seventh day of November next, as a day of public thanksgiving and praise to Almighty God, and do earnestly request that the people of this State will on that day abstain from their usual vocations, and, assembling in their accustomed places of public worship, unite in fervent prayers of thanksgiving and praise to the Giver of all good and perfect gifts, and especially that with humble and contrite hearts they devoutly beseech him to restore a speedy and honorable peace to our distracted country.

In testimony whereof I have hereto set my hand, and caused the great seal of the State of Delaware to be affixed.

Done at Dover, this twenty-ninth day of October, in the year of our Lord one thousand eight hundred and sixty-two and in the eighty-seventh year of the independence of said State.

William Burton.

By the Governor:

Edward Riggley, *Secretary of State.*

IOWA

Proclamation

Executive Office, Iowa, Iowa City, Nov. 3, 1862.

To the People of Iowa.

In token of our dependence upon the Supreme Ruler of the universe, the more especially in this the hour of peril to the nation; fervent thanksgiving to him that no pestilence has prevailed in our midst, that the labors of the husbandman have been measurably rewarded, and for the many blessings vouchsafed us as individuals and citizens; in devout acknowledgment of his sovereignty and overruling providence, and in heartfelt gratitude that our armies in the field have won such renown in the great cause of the Union, that our citizens at home have been inspired with such devoted loyalty and munificence in relieving our brave soldiers, and that we have been permitted to follow in a peaceable manner our usual pursuits while war is desolating the land;

I, Samuel J. Kirkwood, do hereby appoint Thursday, the twenty-seventh day of November next, as a day of thanksgiving, prayer, and praise, and do hereby entreat the people, abstaining from their usual pursuits, to assemble together on that day in their chosen places of worship, and offer up their earnest prayers to Almighty God, humbly acknowledging their short-comings and dependence upon him, thanking him for the manifold blessings on them by his hand, beseeching him to crown our arms and cause with signal triumph, to confer strength upon our gallant soldiery, to mitigate the sufferings of the sick, wounded, and imprisoned, and to succor and heal the anguish of the bereft, and Imploring a speedy extinction of the rebellion, a return of peace in his own good time to our distracted land, and that we may prove ourselves worthy of the institutions bequeathed us by the fathers of the republic, by becoming once more a united, fraternal, and happy people.

In testimony whereof I have hereunto set my hand, and caused the great seal of the State to be hereto affixed, this first day of November, in the year of our Lord one thousand eight hundred and sixty-two.

By the Governor: Samuel J. Kirkwood.

Elijah Sells, *Secretary of State.*

Ralph P. Lowe, Governor of Iowa, in his proclamation for 1858, uses this eminently Christian language—

Let us go into our temples of worship and fill them with thank-offerings to the God of our fathers;

Praise him for giving to this whole land so largely of his Spirit, by which the faces of multitudes have been turned heavenwards;

Praise him for the Christian's faith, the spread of our holy religion, the triumphs of science, and the progress making in the peaceful arts;

Praise him for the moral and social improvement of the race, by means of the intercommunication of telegraphs and railways.

Let the spirit of Divine truth be invoked to push forward all the great enterprises of the age, and that the outgoings of the morning and evening may still continue to rejoice over us.

KANSAS

Proclamation

The second year of our existence as a State is drawing to a close. The balance-sheet for 1862 will soon be struck. From the earliest settlement of our country the autumn months have been deemed the most appropriate for recounting the blessings of Providence and making public acknowledgment therefore in thanksgiving and praise.

As a State we have been highly favored during the year now closing. The earth has yielded abundantly, and health and general prosperity have been allotted to us. While deadly civil war has been waged upon our border and in many of the States, comparative peace and quiet have been our lot. While we mourn that civil war still spreads its desolation in our country, there is cause for the thankfulness that the immutable laws of God apply as well to nations as individuals, to war as well as peace, and that there is some reason to hope that our nation is beginning to understand the application of these laws to our present condition as a people.

In view of the numberless blessings showered upon our State and nation, I appoint Thursday, the twenty-seventh day of November next, as a day of thanksgiving and praise to Almighty God, and earnestly invite all good citizens to observe the same as becomes a Christian people, by abstaining from labor and business occupations, by attendance upon public worship, by deeds of charity to the poor and needy, and by a cultivation of the domestic and social virtues.

Given under my hand, and the seal of the State, at Topeka, this twenty-ninth day of October, 1862.   C. Robinson.

By the Governor:

S. R. Shepherd, *Secretary of State.*

WISCONSIN

PROCLAMATION

To the People of Wisconsin

Amidst the manifold vicissitudes and calamities that have befallen and surrounded us, threatening the life of our nation and the lives of so many of its heroic and noble sons, it peculiarly becomes us to turn with grateful hearts to the Supreme Being for the any blessings we have enjoyed and the afflictions we have been spared.

The horrors and devastations of war, so fiercely raging around us, have not touched the border of our State; excepting the brave men who have rallied around our country's flag in this time of peril, our citizens have been permitted to pursue their peaceful avocations; our harvest, though not as abundant as Providence sometimes has pleased to grant us, has yet well compensated the labor bestowed upon it, and well filled our houses and barns; the savage tribes upon our border settlements, so threatening at one time to our peace, have been quieted and kept under surveillance.

The great cause of our nation, it is true, has not triumphed yet over its enemies, but neither has it yet failed: the enemy has been driven from the soil of the loyal States; our army has been reinforced by hundreds of thousands of brave, patriotic, and noble men, ready to do battle, and, if necessary, to die, for the integrity of the Union; our resources and energies are unimpaired; we have reason to be hopeful for the future and, therefore, thankful for the past.

The loyalty, honor, and patriotism of the State of Wisconsin have been nobly sustained by her brave sons upon every field of battle where they have been called upon to vindicate our national flag. The just pride which we feel in the bravery of our noble soldiers should fill our hearts with gratitude to Almighty God, who has sustained them in their hour of trial.

For these and other uncounted blessings which the infinite goodness of God has vouchsafed to us during the past year, we should thank him from the depth of our hearts. And therefore, and in accordance with a time-honored custom, I do hereby appoint Thursday, the twenty-seventh day of November, 1862, as a day of thanksgiving and rest, and recommend to the people of this State on that day to abstain from secular labor, and to assemble at their usual places of worship, to show their grateful hearts to the beneficent Ruler of the universe, and pray for a speedy suppression of the rebellion, and for peace to a distracted country.

In testimony whereof I have hereunto subscribed my name, and caused the great seal of the State to be affixed, this thirty-first day of October, A.D. 1862.

Edward Salomon.

Edward Ilsley, *Assistant Secretary of State.*

GEORGIA, 1858

PROCLAMATION

Whereas it has pleased Almighty God to smile upon us as a people, in much mercy, another year, to crown our labors with rich blessings, to protect and preserve us from war, hunger, and pestilence, and to pour out his holy Spirit upon us in copious showers; and whereas these manifestations of his protecting care and loving-kindness admonish us of the debt of gratitude which we, as the people of a great State, owe to the Giver of every good and perfect gift, and of our duty to be humble and thankful, rendering praise to his great name "in psalms and hymns and spiritual songs, singing and making melody in our hearts to the Lord, giving thanks always for all things;"

I do therefore issue this my proclamation, setting apart Thursday the twenty-fifth day of the present month, as a day of thanksgiving and prayer. And I do earnestly invite the different congregations composing all the religious denominations of every name in this State, to meet at their respective places of worship on that day, and unite in returning thanks and singing praises to our God for his wondrous works in the past, and in fervent prayer for his protecting care in the future, remembering that the Psalmist has said, "Let the people praise thee; then shall the earth yield her increase, and God, even our God, shall bless us."

Given under my hand, and the seal of the Executive Department, at the Capitol, in Milledgeville, this fourth day of November, in the year of our Lord one thousand eight hundred and fifty-eight, and the independence of the United States of America the eighty-third.

By the Governor: Joseph E. Brown.

H. H. Waters, *Secretary Executive Department.*

NORTH CAROLINA, 1858

PROCLAMATION

Whereas by an act of the General Assembly it is made the duty of the Governor of the State for the time-being "to set apart a day in every year, and to give notice thereof by proclamation, as a day of solemn and public thanksgiving to Almighty God for past blessings, and of supplications for his continual kindness and care over us as a State and as a nation;"

Now, therefore, I do, by this my proclamation, appoint and set apart Thursday, the twenty-fifth day of November next, as such a day, and do most respectfully and earnestly recommend that it be observed accordingly by all the good people of this State.

Given under my hand, and attested by the great seal of the State. Done at the city of Raleigh, this fourth day of November, Anno Domino one thousand eight hundred and fifty-eight.

Thomas Bragg.

By the Governor:

Pulaski Cooper, *Private Secretary.*

SOUTH CAROLINA, 1858

PROCLAMATION

Whereas, whilst we humbly bow before the Almighty, in meek submission to the will of his inscrutable providence, chastening us with disappointment of some of our cherished hopes, with disease, with loss of faithful and valuable citizens, it becomes us as a people, now that the pestilence is stayed in the city, and the bright beams of the autumnal sun, with a bracing atmosphere, have dissipated the malaria of the fruitful country, now that the harvest-home is over, and the staple results of the seasons, wherever diminished, are still greater than we deserve at the hands of a bountiful Benefactor, "to assemble and meet together to render thanks for his great benefits that we have received at his hands, to set forth his most worthy praise, to hear his most holy word, and to ask those things which are requisite and necessary as well for the body as the soul;"

Now, therefore, I deem it meet to appoint and set apart Thursday, the twenty-fifth of November instant, as a day of thanksgiving and prayer. Accordingly, I do invite all persons on that day to assemble at their respective places of worship to return thanks for our numerous blessings, past and present, and to pray for the Divine guidance and blessing in our future life.

Given under my hand and seal of the State, at Columbia, this eleventh day of November, in the year of our Lord one thousand eight hundred and fifty-eight, and in the eighty-third year of American independence.

Robert W. Allston.

James Patterson, *Secretary of State.*

FLORIDA, 1858

PROCLAMATION

Whereas it is right and proper for States, as well as individuals, to return thanks to Almighty God for his manifold blessings and mercies; and whereas the fourth Thursday in November has been, by usage and custom, adopted by most of the States of the Union as a day of thanksgiving; and in order that said day may be observed with uniformity throughout the United States; therefore

I, Madison S. Perry, do, by this my public proclamation, set aside Thursday, the twenty-fifth day of November, as a day of public thanksgiving, and respectfully ask the clergy of all religious denominations to open their houses of worship, and deliver addresses suited to such an occasion, and request the good people of the State to lay aside their usual avocations and join in the religious exercises of the day.

In testimony whereof I have hereto set my hand, and caused to be affixed the great seal of the State of Florida. Done at the Capitol, in the city of Tallahassee, this third day of November, Anno Domini one thousand eight hundred and fifty-eight.

Madison S. Perry.

By the Governor:

Attest: F. L. VILLIPIGUE, *Secretary of State.*

TENNESSEE

PROCLAMATION

Isham G. Harris, Governor of the State of Tennessee,
To all the people of said State, greeting—

Whereas It has pleased an all-wise Providence to bestow upon our State peace, health, and prosperity, and to continue to us our civil and religious liberty under those free institutions vouchsafed to us by the same power, and in conformity to a commendable usage among Christian nations, I, Isham G. Harris, Governor aforesaid, do hereby appoint Thursday, the twenty-fifth instant, as a day of thanksgiving and praise, and earnestly invoke the people throughout the State to observe it as such.

In witness whereof I have hereunto set my hand, and caused the great seal of the State to be affixed, at the office in Nashville, on the eighth day of November, Anno Domini, one thousand eight hundred and fifty-eight.

By the Governor: Isham G. Harris.

J. E. R. Ray, *Secretary of State.*

MISSISSIPPI

PROCLAMATION

EXECUTIVE OFFICE, CITY OF JACKSON, October 12, 1858

Whereas it is a time-honored custom, and is of it self right and proper and becoming a Christian people, to observe annually a day of thanksgiving, I do hereby appoint Thursday, the twenty-fifth day of November next, for that purpose, and request its general observance throughout the State; for of all the people who have existed, none could so truly say, "The lines have fallen to us in pleasant places, and we have a goodly heritage." Then let us unite in one general thanksgiving, exclaiming, with the Psalmist, "Unto thee, O God, do we give thanks; yea, unto thee do we give thanks."

Wm. McWillie.

PROCLAMATION BY THE MAYOR OF WASHINGTON CITY
MAYOR'S OFFICE, WASHINGTON, NOVEMBER 20, 1862
Whilst another section of our country is famine-worn, and sister cities lie prostrate from evils dreadful to suffer and mournful to behold, results of a blind and lawless resistance to constitutional authority and the majesty of the law, an all-seeing Providence has averted from us this curse of treason, and with an unreluctant hand vouchsafed us numerous evidences of his grace.

For that manifestation and this benediction it behooves us to be thankful; and I therefore, and in compliance with the following joint resolution of the City Councils, request my fellow-citizens to abstain from secular employment, and, assembling in their respective places of worship, on Thursday, 27th instant, unite with reverent love in grateful expressions to Almighty God.

Richard Wallach, *Mayor*.

JOINT RESOLUTION APPOINTING A DAY OF THANKSGIVING.
Whereas it is becoming in a Christian people to return thanks to the Giver of all good for the manifold blessings he vouchsafes them as a community, and whereas it is peculiarly appropriate that the city of Washington should unite with her sister cities in the observance of a day of public thanksgiving and praise:

Be is therefore Resolved, &c., That his honor the mayor is hereby requested to set apart, by public proclamation, Thursday, 27th November instant, as a day of thanksgiving and praise to Almighty God for the mercies of the past year, and of prayer for the restoration of peace and of fraternal feeling throughout the Union, inviting all citizens to abstain from their usual secular employments and to unite in a proper observance of the day.

Alex. R. Shepherd,
President of Board of Common Council.
Joseph F. Brown,
President of Board of Aldermen.
Approved November 8, 1862.

Richard Wallach, *Mayor.*

These proclamations are the official papers of the sovereign States of the republic, and as such declare that the Christian religion is the religion of the Government and the people. They were authorized by special acts of legislation, and heartily approved and observed by the American people.

The Marriage Institution

Has always been a subject of careful legislation by all the States of the American Union. This institution was the first positive social organization constituted of God for the welfare of society and the purity and happiness of nations and the race. It is not only Divine in its origin, but it has received the solemn sanction of the constant legislation of God. Christ the Divine author of the Christian religion, restored it from its partial abrogation by the Jews to its original integrity and purpose, and shielded it by a new and solemn act of legislation. The Bible guards no one of its institutes with greater vigilance than that of the ordinance of marriage.

Civil states have uniformly protected with the shield of legislation the marriage institution. A Christian state recognizes marriage as a branch of public morality and a source of civil peace and strength. It gives dignity and harmony to a civil state, and secures to it its highest prosperity and purity, by the formation of families, out of which the state itself is formed, and which are its crowns of social and moral glory, as well as its sources of strength. The very safety and perpetuity of a nation in its civil government and in all its organic forms of society depend on the existence, purity, and power of the marriage institution. Hence is it that the Christian states of the American republic from their first civil organization and in all forms of legislation, have recognized marriage as a Divine institution, and have thus affirmed the indissoluble union of the civil state and the Christian religion.

The National Government

By a solemn act of legislation, has also protected the marriage institution from being corrupted and destroyed by polygamy. In the United States, a religious sect calling themselves "Latter-Day Saints," or Mormons, sprung up into a mongrel ecclesiastic and political system; and among the various fanatical and anti-christian rites introduced and established by the law of their Church was the practice of polygamy, or the "spiritual wife" system. The Territory in which they settled, and which they called Utah, belonged to the United States and was under its jurisdiction. Congress, in order to vindicate the civil and Christian integrity and sanctity of the marriage institution from this unlawful invasion by this antichristian sect, passed the following act, which was approved by the President—

> *An Act to punish and prevent the Practice of Polygamy in the Territories of the United States and other Places, and disapproving and annulling certain Acts of the Legislative Assembly of the Territory of Utah.*

> *Be it enacted by the Senate and House of Representatives of the United States of America in Congress assembled,* That every person having a husband or wife living, who shall marry any other person, whether married or single, in a Territory of the United States or other place over which the United States have exclusive jurisdiction, shall, except in the cases specified in the proviso to this section, be adjudged guilty of bigamy, and, upon conviction thereof, shall be punished by a fine not exceeding five hundred dollars, and by imprisonment for a

term not exceeding five years; *Provided, nevertheless,* That this section shall not extend to any person by reason of any former marriage whose husband or wife by such marriage shall have been absent for five successive years without being known to such person within that time to be living; nor to any person by reason of any former marriage which shall have been dissolved by the decree of a competent court; nor to any person by reason of any former marriage which shall have been annulled or pronounced void by the sentence or decree of a competent court on the ground of the nullity of the marriage contract.

Sec. 2. And be it further enacted, That the following ordinance of the provisional government of the State of Deseret, so called, namely: "An ordinance incorporating the Church of Jesus Christ of Latter-Day Saints," passed February eight, in the year eighteen hundred and fifty-one, and adopted, reenacted, and made valid by the Governor and Legislative Assembly of the Territory of Utah by an act passed January nineteen, in the year eighteen hundred and fifty-five, entitled "An act in relation to the compilation and revision of the laws and resolutions in force in Utah Territory, their publication and distribution," and all other acts and parts of acts heretofore passed by the said Legislative Assembly of the Territory of Utah, which establish, support, maintain, shield, or countenance polygamy, be, and the same hereby are, disapproved and annulled: *Provided,* That this act shall be so limited and construed as not to abet or interfere with the right of property legally acquired under the ordinance heretofore mentioned, nor with the right "to worship God according to the dictates of conscience," but only to annul all acts and laws which establish, maintain, protect, or countenance the practice of polygamy, evasively called spiritual marriage, however disguised by legal or ecclesiastical solemnities, sacraments, ceremonies, consecrations, or other contrivances.

Sec. 3. And be it further enacted, That it shall not be lawful for any corporation or association for religious or charitable purposes to acquire or hold real estate in any Territory of the United States, during the existence of the territorial government, of a greater value than fifty thousand dollars; and all real estate acquired or held by any such corporation or association contrary to the provisions of this act shall be forfeited and escheat to the United States: *Provided,* That existing vested rights in real estate shall not be impaired by the provisions of this section.

Approved, July 1, 1862.

When the Territorial Legislature of Utah convened, in December, 1862, Governor Harding, in his Inaugural Address, said—

> Much to my astonishment, I have not been able to find any law upon the statutes of this Territory regulating marriage. I earnestly recommend to your early consideration the passage of some law that will meet the exigencies of the people.
>
> I respectfully call your attention to an act of Congress, passed the first day of July, 1862, entitled "An act to punish and prevent the practice of polygamy in the Territories of the United States, and in other places, and disapproving and annulling certain acts of the Legislative Assembly of the Territory of Utah," chap. cxxvii., of the Statutes at Large of the last session of Congress, page 501. I am aware that there is a prevailing opinion here that said act is unconstitutional, and therefore it is recommended by those in high authority that no regard what ever should be paid to the same.
>
> And still more to be regretted, if I am rightly informed, in some instances it has been recommended that it be openly disregarded and defied, merely to defy the same.

The law was enforced by the authority of the United States, through the Governor of the Territory, who had the head of the Church, Brigham Young, arrested, and held amenable to the sovereign law of the Government for disannulling the marriage institution and for the practice of polygamy.

This vindication of the Divine integrity of the marriage institution in all the Territories over which the jurisdiction of the Government of the United States stands, tends to establish the Christian character of the American Government and is in harmony with the whole legislative history of the nation, as it stands related to the Christian religion.

The Presidents of the United States

As well as the Governors of nearly all the States, have been explicit, in their messages, in the recognition of the Christian religion. Washington, Adams, Jefferson, Madison, Monroe, John Quincy Adams, and Jackson, were more or less full in their official acknowledgments of our obligations to God and the Christian religion for national existence, preservation, and blessings. The more modern Presidents have united in the same acknowledgments.

President Van Buren

When entering upon the responsibilities of his office, said—

"I only look to the gracious protection of that Divine Being whom strengthening support I humbly solicit and whom I fervently pray to look down upon us all. May it be among the dispensations of his providence to bless our beloved country with honors and length of days; may her ways be ways of pleasantness, and all her paths peace."

Similar sentiments were officially announced in all his messages. Mr. Van Buren publicly testified to the value of the Christian religion by joining the Dutch Reformed Church in the autumn of 1860. He died inspired with the immortal hopes of the gospel, saying "the atonement of Christ was the only remedy and rest of the soul."

President Harrison

Said, in his inaugural—

"I deem the present occasion sufficiently important and solemn to justify me in expressing to my fellow-citizens a profound reverence for the Christian religion, and a thorough conviction that sound morals, religious liberty, and a just sense of religious responsibility, are essentially connected with all true and lasting happiness; and to that good Being who has blessed us with the gifts of civil and religious freedom, who watched over and prospered the labors of our fathers, and has hitherto preserved to us institutions far exceeding in excellence those of any other people, let us unite in fervently commending every interest of our beloved country in all future time."

When he entered upon his duties as President, he wrote to his Christian wife, saying, "I retired into the presence of my Maker, and implored his gracious guidance in the faithful discharge of the duties of my high station."

The Sabbath was observed during his brief occupancy of the Presidential mansion. He said to visitors, "We shall be happy to see you at any time except on the Sabbath." The absence of a Bible at the President's house, when he occupied it, was immediately supplied. Before his election to the Presidency, General Harrison, for years, was a warm and active friend of Sabbath-schools and Bible-classes (of which he was a teacher), and a constant attendant on the public worship of God. To his pastor—the pastor of the Presbyterian church near his home on the banks of the Ohio—he said, "I think I enjoy religion and delight in the duties of a child of God, and have concluded to unite with the Church of God as soon as my health will permit me to go out." This purpose he had resolved to carry out in Washington, after he had entered upon his duties as President, by joining the Episcopal Church on Easter Sunday; but his sudden death prevented. In a great revival in the Methodist Church in Cincinnati, just previous to his election, he said to the pastor, "I know there are some of my political opponents who will be ready to impugn my motives in attending this revival-meeting at this peculiar time; but I care not for the smiles or frowns of my fellow-countrymen. God knows my heart and understands my motives. A deep and an abiding sense of my inward spiritual necessities brings me to this hallowed place night after night."

President Tyler

In his Message of 1843, said—

"If any people ever had cause to render up thanks to the Supreme Being for parental care and protection extended to them in all tri-

als and difficulties to which they have been from time to time exposed, we certainly are that people. From the first settlement of our
forefathers on this continent—through the dangers attendant upon
the occupation of a savage wilderness—through a long period of
colonial dependence—through the War of the Revolution—in the
wisdom which led to the adoption of the existing form of republican
government—in the hazards incident to a war subsequently waged
with one of the most powerful nations of the earth—in the increase
of our population—in the spread of the arts and sciences—and in
the strength and durability conferred on our political institutions,
emanating from the people and sustained by their will—the superintendence of an overruling Providence has been plainly visible. As
preparatory, therefore, to entering once more upon the high duties
of legislation, it becomes us humbly to acknowledge our dependence
upon *him* as *our guide* and protector, and to implore a continuance
of his parental watchfulness over our beloved country."

President Polk

When inaugurated, in 1845, said—

"In assuming responsibilities so vast, I fervently invoke the aid of
the Almighty Ruler of the universe, in whose hands are the destinies
of nations and of men, to guard this Heaven-favored land against the
mischiefs which, without his guidance, might arise from an unwise
policy. I humbly supplicate that Divine Being who has watched over
and protected our beloved country from its infancy to the present
hour, to continue his gracious benedictions upon us, that we may
continue to be a prosperous and happy people."

"No country," he said, in his message of 1847, "has been so much
favored, or should acknowledge with deeper reverence the manifestations of the Divine protection. An all-wise Creator directed and
guarded us in our infant struggle for freedom, and has constantly
watched over our surprising progress, until we have become one of
the great nations of the earth."

"The gratitude of the nation," he says, in his annual message of
1848, "to the Sovereign Arbiter of all human events should be commensurate with the boundless blessings which we enjoy."

Mr. Polk, after his retirement from the cares of public life, was deeply impressed with the need of a personal interest in the Saviour. This conviction, indeed, was felt when in public life. He said, before his death, "that when in office he had several times seriously intended to be baptized; but the cares and perplexities of public life scarcely allowed time for the requisite solemn preparation; and so procrastination had ripened into inaction."

About a week before his death he sent for the Rev. Dr. Edgar, of Nashville, and said to him, with great solemnity, "Sir, if I had supposed, twenty years ago, that I should come to my death-bed unprepared, it would have made me an unhappy man; and yet I am about to die, and have not made preparation. I have not been baptized. Tell me, sir, can there be any ground for a man thus situated to hope? During his illness he evinced a thorough knowledge of the Scriptures, which he said "he had read a great deal, and deeply reverenced as Divine truth." A week before his death he was baptized, and received the sacrament of the Lord's Supper.

President Taylor

In his Inaugural Address, remarked—

"I congratulate you, my fellow-citizens, upon the high state of prosperity to which the goodness of Divine Providence has conducted our common country. Let us invoke a continuance of the same protecting care which has led us from small beginnings to the eminence we this day occupy; and let us seek to deserve that continuance by prudence and moderation in our councils, by well-directed attempts to assuage the bitterness which too often marks avoidable differences of opinion, by the promulgation and practice of just and liberal principles, and by an enlarged patriotism, which shall acknowledge no limits but those of our own widespread republic."

His first and only message, in 1849, says, "During the past year we have been blessed by a kind Providence with an abundance of the fruits of the earth; and although the destroying angel for a time visited extensive portions of our territory with the ravages of a dreadful pestilence, yet the Almighty has at length deigned to stay his hand, and to restore the inestimable blessings of general health to a people who have acknowledged his power, deprecated his wrath, and implored his merciful protection."

The cholera, in 1849, revisited the United States; and President Taylor issued a proclamation for a day of prayer and fasting; and his message alludes to that, in the passage quoted. God heard and answered prayer, in staying the march of the destroying angel.

President Taylor, on the Fourth of July, 1849, was present at the Sabbath-school celebration in the city of Washington, and made an address, in which he said, "The only ground of hope for the continuance of our free institutions is in the proper moral and religious training of the children, that they may be prepared to discharge aright the duties of men and citizens."

President Fillmore

Becoming such by the death of President Taylor, who died July 9, 1850, says, in his first message, "I cannot bring this communication to a close without invoking you to join me in humble and devout thanks to the Great Ruler of nations for the multiplied blessings which he has graciously bestowed upon us. His hand, so often visible in our preservation, has stayed the pestilence, saved us from foreign wars and domestic disturbances, and scattered plenty throughout the land. Our liberties, religious and civil, have been maintained; the fountains have all been kept open, and means of happiness widely spread and generally enjoyed, greater than have fallen to the lot of any other nation. And, while penetrated with gratitude for the past, let us hope that his all-wise providence will so guide our counsels as that they shall result in giving satisfaction to our constituents, securing the peace of the country, and adding new strength to the united Government under which we live."

His message of 1851 says, "None can look back on the dangers which are passed, or forward to the bright prospect before us, without feeling a thrill of gratification. At the time he must be inspired with a grateful sense of our profound obligation to a beneficent Providence, whose paternal care is so manifest in the happiness of this highly favored land." "We owe these blessings," he says, in his message of 1852, "under Heaven, to the happy Constitution and Government which were bequeathed to us by our fathers, and which it is our sacred duty to transmit in all their integrity to our children."

President Fillmore gives the following testimony to the value of the Sabbath—"I owe my uninterrupted bodily vigor to an originally strong constitution, to an education on a farm, and to life-long habits of regularity and temperance. Throughout all my public life I maintained the same regular and systematic habits of living to which I had previously been accustomed. I never allowed my usual hours for sleep to be interrupted. *The Sabbath I always kept as a day of rest.* Besides being a religious duty, it was essential to health. On commencing my Presidential career, I found that the Sabbath had frequently been employed by visitors for private interviews with the President. I determined to put an end to this custom, and ordered my doorkeeper to meet all Sunday visitors with an indiscriminate refusal."

President Pierce

In his Inaugural, 1853, says, "But let not the foundation of our hopes rest on man's wisdom. It will not be sufficient that sectional prejudices find no place in the public deliberations. It will not be sufficient that the rash counsels of human passions be rejected. It *must be felt* that there is no national security but in the *nation's humble,* acknowledged dependence upon God and his overruling Providence.

"Standing, as I do, almost within view of the green slopes of Monticello, and, as it were, within reach of the tomb of Washington, with all the cherished memories of the past gathering round me, like so many eloquent voices from heaven, I can express no better hope for my country than that the kind Providence which smiled upon our fathers may enable their children to preserve the blessings they have inherited."

His first annual message, 1853, declared that "We have still the most abundant cause for thankfulness to God, for an accumulation of signal mercies showered upon us as a nation. It is well that a consciousness of rapid advancement and increasing strength be habitually associated with an abiding sense of dependence on Him who holds in his hands the destiny of men and of nations.

"Recognizing the wisdom of the broad principle of absolute religious toleration proclaimed in our fundamental law, and rejoicing in the benign influence which it has exerted upon our social and political condition, I should shrink from a clear duty did I fail to express my deepest conviction that we can place no *secure reliance* upon any apparent progress *if a be not sustained by national integrity*, resting upon the GREAT TRUTHS affirmed and illustrated by DIVINE REVELATION."

"Public affairs ought to be so conducted that a settled conviction shall pervade the entire Union that nothing *short* of the HIGHEST tone and standard of PUBLIC MORALITY *marks* EVERY PART *of the administration and legislation of the Government.*"

President Buchanan

In his Inaugural, 1857, says, "In entering upon this great office, I must humbly invoke the God of our fathers for wisdom and firmness to execute its high and responsible duties in such a manner as to restore harmony and ancient friendship among the several States, and to preserve our free institutions throughout many generations."

In his first annual message, 1857, he says, "And, first of all, our thanks are due to Almighty God for the numerous benefits which he has bestowed upon this people; and our united prayers ought to ascend to him that he would continue to bless our great republic in time to come, *as he blessed it in times past.*"

In his message on Central American affairs, of January, 1858, President Buchanan declared the Divine law to be the basis of the law of nations. He said, "The avowed principle which lies at the foundation of the law of nations is the Divine command that 'all things whatsoever ye would that men should do to you, do ye even so unto them.' Tried by this unerring rule, we should be severely condemned if we shall not use our best exertions to arrest such expeditions against our feeble sister republic of Nicaragua."

President Lincoln

In his Inaugural Address delivered on the 4th of March, 1861, amidst the opening scenes of the great rebellion, refers as follows to the justice of God as displayed in the government of nations—

"Why should there not be a patient confidence in the ultimate justice of the people? Is there any better or equal hope in the world? In our present differences is either party without faith in being right? If the Almighty Ruler of nations, with his eternal truth and justice, be on your side of the North, or yours of the South, that truth and that justice will surely prevail, by the judgment of this great tribunal of the American people."

His message to Congress convened in extraordinary session, on the 4th of July, 1861, closes as follows—

"Having thus chosen our course, without guile, and with pure purpose, let us renew our trust in God, and go forward without fear and with manly hearts."

In his message to Congress at the opening of its session in December, 1861, President Lincoln used the following closing words—

"With a reliance on Providence all the more firm and earnest, let us proceed in the great task which events have devolved upon us."

The Statement of an American Jurist that the Gospel is the Glory of the State

This chapter will appropriately close with the following paragraphs from a work on the Institutes of International Law, by Daniel Gardner, an eminent jurist and lawyer of New York. He says—

"The permanent welfare and glory of every sovereign state demand a faithful obedience to the laws of nations, *founded on the precepts of the gospel.* Self-preservation calls for it; interest and duty require it. International and municipal law are based upon the gospel, and obedience to them is necessary to the happiness and prosperity of every state. The violation of those celestial doctrines has swept away the Assyrian, the Egyptian, the Greek, and the Roman Empires; and the ruins of Baalbec, Palmyra, and Thebes, the shattered Parthenon, and the remains of Roman grandeur, all attest the suicidal effect on empires of disobedience to God's law of nations. Spain, once great and powerful, has fallen by her atrocious national offences from her vast power in the reigns of Charles V. and Philip II. History teaches that national sins, by a fixed moral law, punish the states that commit them. Self-preservation, as well as the obligation of the Divine law, demands a voluntary obedience to the precepts of the gospel in all international transactions.

"The sanctions of that law cannot be disregarded, or its sure penalties avoided, as the King of kings enacted it. All nations before him are as the small dust of the balance; they are counted to him as less than nothing and vanity. He holdeth the seas in the hollow of his hand; he weigheth the mountains in scales; he sitteth on the circle of the earth; he ruleth the hosts of heaven and the inhabitants of the earth. His title is Jehovah in the highest.

"May our republic and all nations obey that law and enjoy its promised blessings.

"The precepts of the gospel are the basis of all law. It is a moral code of general principles, which, intelligently and honestly applied, will solve every question of international right said duty. In this age of civilization and improvement, a liberal code of public law, based upon the golden rule of the gospel, and assented to by the leading nations of Europe and America, is a great desideratum.

"Our American public and private international law is composed in part of a written code, enacted in the form of a national Constitution and State Constitutions and State laws, and in part of the law of national comity,

"This law seems to rest on the golden rule of the gospel, and, as the fruits of Christian civilization, to belong of necessity to American jurisprudence, as God's appointed regulator of the rights and duties of all national and State sovereignties. Treaties, constitutions, and laws merely recognize and regulate it in certain respects, but its true basis is in the command of Jehovah to nations and states, as well as to individuals, 'Do unto others as you would they should do unto you.' The observance of the principles of the gospel will insure the prosperity of every State and nation."

24

Christian Scenes in the Capitol
of the Republic

The Capital

T HE Capitol of the American republic, in its consecration to virtue, Christian civilization, and the purposes of Christian legislation, is in harmony with the genius and history of the nation.
Its foundations were laid with Christian services, and the blessing
of God invoked. Congress, on the 16th of July, 1790, set apart one
hundred square miles, on the banks of the Potomac, as the future
capitol. On the 15th day of April, 1791, the Hon. Daniel Carroll and
Dr. David Stewart superintended the fixing of the first corner-stone
of the District of Columbia, at Jones's Point, near Alexandria, where
it was laid with all the Masonic ceremonies usual at that time, and
a quaint address, almost all in scriptural language, delivered by the
Rev. James Muir. He said—

"Amiable it is for brethren to dwell together in unity: it is more
fragrant than the perfumes on Aaron's garment; it is more refreshing
than the dews on Hermon's hill! May this stone long commemorate
the goodness of God in those uncommon events which have given
America a name among nations. Under this stone may jealousy and
selfishness be forever buried. From this stone may a superstructure

arise whose glory, whose magnificence, stability, unequalled hitherto, shall astonish the world, and invite even the savage of the wilderness to take shelter under its wings."

Lay the Cornerstone of the Capital

On the 18th of September, 1793, the southeast corner-stone of the Capitol was laid by Washington, with Masonic and Christian services and military demonstrations. The commissioners delivered to the President, who deposited it in the stone, a silver plate, with the following inscription—

"This southeast corner-stone of the Capitol of the United States of America, in the city of Washington, was laid on the 18th day of September, 1793, in the eighteenth year of American Independence, in the first year of the second term of the Presidency of George Washington, whose virtues in the civil administration of his country have been as conspicuous and beneficial as his military valor and prudence have been useful in establishing her liberties, and in the year of Masonry 1793, by the President of the United States, in concert with the Grand Lodge of Maryland, several lodges under its jurisdiction, and Lodge No. 22 from Alexandria, Virginia.

"Thomas Johnson, David Stewart, and Daniel Carroll, Commissioners; Joseph Clarke, R.W.G.M.P.T.; James Hoban and Stephen Hallate, Architects."

Selected by Washington

The site was selected by Washington, and displays his usual taste and judgment. Mrs. Adams, the wife of the President, on the 25th of November, 1800—the month in which the President of the United States first went to Washington City—after an amusing description of the unfinished and unfurnished mansion which had been erected, and the inconveniences of opening it, says, "It is a beautiful spot, capable of any improvement; and the more I view it the more I am delighted with it."

John Cotton Smith, a distinguished member of Congress from Connecticut, on his arrival to attend the first session of Congress held in the city of Washington, says—

"I cannot sufficiently express my admiration of its local position. From the Capitol you have a distinct view of its fine undulating surface, situated at the confluence of the Potomac and its eastern branch, the wide expanse of that majestic river to the bend at Mount Vernon, the cities of Alexandria and Georgetown, and the cultivated fields and blue hills of Maryland and Virginia on either side of the river, the whole constitution a prospect of surpassing beauty and grandeur. The city has also the inestimable advantage of delightful water, in many instances flowing from copious springs, and always attainable by digging to a moderate depth; to which may be added the singular fact that such is the due admixture of loam and clay in the soil of a great portion of the city that a house may be built of brick made of the earth dug from the cellar: hence it was not unusual to see the remains of a brick-kiln near the newly-erected dwelling-house or other edifice. In short, when we consider not only these advantages, but, what is a national point of view is of superior importance, the location on a fine navigable river, accessible to the whole maritime frontier of the United States, and yet easily rendered defensible against foreign invasion, and that by the facilities of internal navigation and railways it may be approached by the population of the Western States—and, indeed, of the whole nation—with less inconvenience than any other conceivable situation, we must acknowledge that its selection by Washington as the permanent seat of the Federal Government affords a striking exhibition of the discernment, wisdom, and forecast which characterized that illustrious man."

Congress Meets in the Capital in 1800

In the month of June, 1800, the archives of the Government were removed from Philadelphia to Washington; and on the 25th of November of the same year the first Congress in the present Capitol opened its session.

President Adams, in his message, made the following address to the assembled legislators of the nation—

> I congratulate the people of the United States on the assembling of Congress at the permanent seat of their government;

and I congratulate you, gentlemen, on the prospect of a residence not to be exchanged. It would be unbecoming the representatives of this nation to assemble for the first time in this solemn temple without looking up to the Supreme Ruler of the universe and imploring his blessing. You will consider it as the capitol of a great nation, advancing with unexampled rapidity in arts, in commerce, in wealth, and in population, and possessing within itself those resources which, if not thrown away or lamentably misdirected, will secure to it a long course of prosperity and self-government. May this territory be the residence of virtue and happiness! In this city may that piety and virtue, that wisdom and magnanimity, that constancy and self-government, which adorned the great character whose name it bears, be forever held in veneration! Here, and throughout our country, may simple manners, pure morals, and true religion forever flourish.

The Senate, in their address to the President, responded as follows—

SIR—Impressed with the important truth that the hearts of rulers and people are in the hands of the Almighty, the Senate of the United States most cordially join in your invocations for appropriate blessings upon the government and people of this Union. We meet you, sir, and the other branch of the legislature, in the city which is honored with the name of our late hero and sage, the illustrious Washington, with sensations and emotions which exceed our power of description.

While we congratulate ourselves on the convention of the legislature at the permanent seat of government, and ardently hope that permanence and stability may be communicated as well to the Government itself as to its seat, our minds are irresistibly led to deplore the death of him who bore so honorable and efficient a part in the establishment of both. Great, indeed, would have been our gratification if his sum of earthly happiness had been completed by seeing the Government thus peaceably convened at this place; but we drive consolation from the belief that, in the moment we were destined to experience it, the loss we deplore was fixed by that Being whose counsels cannot err, and from a hope that, since in this seat of government which bears his name his earthly remains will be deposited, the members of Congress, and all who inhabit the city, with these memorials before them, will retain his virtues in lively recollection and make his patriotism, morals, and piety models for imitation.

We deprecate with you, sir, all spirit of innovation, from whatever source it may rise, which may impair the sacred bond that connects the different parts of this empire; and we trust that, under the protection of Divine Providence, the wisdom and virtue of the citizens of the United States will deliver our national compact unimpaired to a grateful posterity.

The President made the following reply—

With you, I ardently hope that permanence and stability may be communicated as well to the Government itself as to its beautiful and commodious seat. With you, I deplore the death of that hero and sage who bore so honorable and efficient a part in the establishment of both. Great, indeed, would have been my gratification if his sum of earthly happiness could have been completed by seeing the Government thus peaceably convened at his place, himself the head. But, while we submit to the decision of Heaven, whose counsels are inscrutable to us, we cannot but hope the members of Congress, the officers of Government , and all who inhabit the city or the country, will retain his virtues in lively recollection, and make his patriotism, morals, and piety models for imitation.

With you, gentlemen, I sincerely deprecate all spirit of innovation which may weaken the sacred bond that connects the different parts of this nation and Government; and with you I trust that, under the protection of Divine Providence, the wisdom and virtue of our citizens will deliver our national compact unimpaired to a free, prosperous, happy, and grateful posterity.

To this end it is my fervent prayer that in this city the fountains of wisdom may be always open and the streams of eloquence forever flow. Here may the youth of this extensive country forever look up, without disappointment, not only to the monuments and memorials of the dead, but to the examples of the living, in the members of Congress and officers of Government, for finished models of all those virtues, graces, talents, and accomplishments which constitute the dignity of human nature and lay the only foundation for the prosperity or duration of empires.

The House of Representatives addressed the President as follows—

The final establishment of the seat of national government, which has now taken place, within the District of Columbia, is an event of no small importance in the political transactions of the country; and we cordially unite our wishes with yours that this territory may be the residence of happiness and virtue.

Nor can we on this occasion omit to express a hope that the spirit which animated the great founder of this city may descend to future generations, and that the wisdom, magnanimity and steadiness which marked the events of his public life may be imitated in all succeeding ages.

Mr. Adams responded to these sentiments of the House of Representatives in a brief sentence corresponding to their form and import.

Extension of the Capitol in 1851

The Capitol was enlarged by an act of Congress; and on the Fourth of July, 1851, in the presence of an immense audience, President Fillmore laid the corner-stone, and Daniel Webster, Secretary of State, delivered the commemorative oration. Beneath the stone, among other things, is deposited, in Mr. Webster's own handwriting, the following record—

On the morning of the first day of the seventy-sixth year of the independence of the United States of America, in the city of Washington, being the Fourth of July, 1851, this stone, designed as a corner-stone of the extension of the Capitol, according to a plan approved by the President, in pursuance of an act of Congress, was laid by

MILLARD FILLMORE,
President of the United States,

assisted by the Grand Master of the Masonic Lodges, in the presence of many members of Congress, of officers of the Executive and Judiciary Departments—National, State and District—of officers of the army and navy, the corporate authorities of this and neighboring cities, many associations—civil, military, and masonic—members of the Smithsonian Institution and National Institute, professors of colleges and teachers of schools in the District of Columbia, with their students and pupils, and a vast concourse of people from places near and remote, including a few surviving gentlemen who witnessed the laying of the corner-stone of the Capitol by President Washington, on the 18th day of September, A.D. 1793.

If, therefore, it shall be hereafter the will of God that this structure shall fall from its base, that its foundation be upturned, and this deposit brought to the eyes of men, be it then known that on this day the union of the United States of America stands firm, that their Constitution still exists unimpaired and with all its original usefulness and glory, growing every day stronger and stronger in the affections of the great body of the American people, and attracting more and more the admiration of the world. And all here assembled, whether belonging to public life or to private life, with hearts devoutly thankful to Almighty God for the preservation of the liberty and happiness of the country, unite in sincere and fervent prayer that this deposit, and the walls and arches, the domes and towers, the columns and entablatures, now to be erected over it, may endure forever!

GOD SAVE THE UNITED STATES OF AMERICA!
DANIEL WEBSTER,
Secretary of State of the United States.

Mr. Webster, standing on the spot where Washington stood fifty-eight years before, in his address said, "This is the New World! This is America! This is Washington! And this the Capitol of the United States! And where else among the nations can the seat of government be surrounded, on any day of any year, by those who have more reason to rejoice in the blessings which they possess? To-day we are Americans, all, and are nothing but Americans. Every man's heart swells within him; every man's port and bearing become somewhat more proud and lofty as he remembers that seventy-five years have rolled away and that the great inheritance of liberty is still his—his, undiminished and unimpaired, his, in all its original glory, his to enjoy, his to protect, and his to transmit to future generations. This inheritance which he enjoys to-day is not only an inheritance of liberty, but of our own peculiar American liberty.

"And I now proceed to add that the strong and deep-settled conviction of all intelligent persons among us is that, in order to preserve this inheritance of liberty, and to support a useful and wise government, the general education of the people and the wide diffusion of pure morality and true religion are indispensable. Individual virtue is a part of public virtue. It is difficult to conceive how there can remain morality in the government when it shall cease to exist among the people, or how the aggregate of the political institutions, all the organs of which consist only of men, should be wise and beneficent and competent to inspire confidence, if the opposite qualities belong to the individuals who constitute those organs and make up that aggregate.

"If Washington actually were among us, and if he could draw around him the shades of the great public men of his own day, patriots and warriors, orators and statesmen, and were to address us in their presence, would he not say to us, 'Ye men of this generation, I rejoice and thank God for being able to see that our labors and toils and sacrifices were not in vain. You are prosperous, you are happy, you are grateful; the fire of liberty burns brightly and steadily in your heats, while DUTY and the LAW restrain it from bursting forth in wild and destructive conflagration. Cherish liberty, as you love it; cherish its securities, as you wish to preserve it. Maintain the Constitution which we labored so painfully to establish, and which has been to you such a source of inestimable blessings. Preserve the union of the States, cemented as it was by our prayers, our tears, and our blood. Be true to God, to your country, and to your whole duty. So shall the whole eastern world follow the morning sun to contemplate you as a nation; so shall all generations honor you as they honor us; and so shall that Almighty Power which so graciously protected us, and which now protects you, shower its everlasting blessings upon you and your posterity.'"

Decorations of the Capitol

Is a suggestive symbol of the political strength and growing greatness of the American republic. "Every form of noble architecture," says Ruskin, in his original and elaborate work on this subject, "is in some sort the embodiment of the polity, life, history, and religious faith of nations. In public buildings the historical purpose should be strikingly definite. There should not be a single ornament put upon great civic structures without some intellectual intention. Architecture is the art which so disposes and adorns the edifices raised by man, for whatever uses, that the sight of them should contribute to his mental health, power, pleasure," patriotism, and piety.

These ends are in a high degree attained in the magnificent structure of the Capitol of the republic and the works of art which adorn its surroundings and interior finish. The structure, costing already more than seventeen millions of dollars, is, in its gradual enlargement, stateliness, and strength, a noble symbol of the growth and greatness of the republic as developed in its past history.

The paintings and statuary which adorn the rotunda and the halls of Congress are all suggestive symbols of scenes in the history of our Christian civilization, and of the triumph of our principles of civil liberty and government. The nine large paintings in the rotunda represent De Soto's Discovery of the Mississippi, the Landing of Columbus, the Baptism of Pocahontas, the Embarkation of the Pilgrims at Delft, the Landing of the Pilgrims on Plymouth Rock, the Signing of the Declaration of Independence, the Surrender of Burgoyne at Saratoga, the Surrender of Cornwallis at Yorktown, and the Resignation of Washington at Annapolis. Groups of sculpture, representing scenes in our early Christian history and in the westward march of civilization, adorn the various parts of the Capitol, whilst similar symbols suggest Christian ideas and scenes on the eastern portico, in front of which is an area of ten acres or more, in the center of which is a statue of Washington, large as life, and on its pedestal inscribed "First in War; First in Peace; First in the Hearts of his Countrymen."

The Washington Monument is seen in its unfinished condition from the western portico, grouped with the romantic scenes of nature in Virginia and Maryland, Mount Vernon, and the cities of Washington and Alexandria, with their churches and the public buildings of the Government. The Washington Monument is a massive structure, the corner-stone of which was laid on the 4th of July, 1848, in the presence of the President of the United States and an immense concourse of citizens, and with masonic and Christian ceremonies. Robert C. Winthrop, Speaker of the House of Representatives, delivered a commemorative oration on Washington, in which he traced his exalted goodness and greatness to the educating influence of the Christian religion, which was followed by a consecrating prayer by Rev. J. McJilton, of which the following are the concluding sentences—

> And now, O Lord of all power and majesty, we humbly beseech thee to let the wing of thy protection be ever outspread over the land of Washington! May his people be thy people! May his God be their God! Never from beneath the strong arm of thy providence may they be removed; but, like their honored chief, may they acknowledge thee in peace and in war, and ever serve thee with a willing, faithful, acceptable service! Hear our prayer, we beseech thee, that the glory of this nation may never be obscured in the gloom of guilt; that its beauty may never be so marred by the foul impress of sin that the light of its religious character shall be dimmed. Open the eyes of the people, and let them see that it is their true interest to study thy laws, to seek thy favor, and to worship thee with a faithful worship. Teach them and deeply impress upon them the important political truth that opinions and

personal feelings, private advantages and sectional interests, are all as nothing when compared with the great interest that every American has in the union of the different States of the republic. Let them know and feel that as Americans they are a common brotherhood, a single family, and that any principle or proposition that would regard the interests or advantages of the few to the detriment of the many is not American in its character, but is hostile to American institutions and must be destructive of our peace. May the watchword of the nation ever be "UNION;" and let the prayer ascend from every American heart that it may ever be preserved! May this pile, sacred in memorial to the Father of his country, be the central point of union for the North and the South, the East and the West. And when the people of every section of the land shall look upon it, or think of it, may they feel that they are Americans, fellow-citizens with the venerated Washington, and strike hands and hearts together in the pledge that every thing shall fall before the federal union of the States shall be dissolved!

Direct us, O Lord, in all our doings with thy most gracious favor, and further us with thy continued help. While we acknowledge thee to be the Lord our God, and offer thee the services of our lips, may our hearts be devoted to thee, that we may bring forth the fruits of holiness in our lives and show by our deeds that we are thy faithful servants! Be pleased to perpetuate our free government, and continue its blessings to mankind. When the men of the present generation shall have passed away, may it be firmer and stronger than it was when committed to their hands, and so may it continue, in the succession of perpetual generations, the blessing of the American people, the envy and admiration of the world. Endue us with wisdom and innocency of life, and, when we shall have served thee in our generation, may we be fathered to our fathers having the testimony of a good conscience in communion with thy Church, in the confidence of a certain faith, in the comfort of a reasonable, religious, and holy hope, in favor with thee our God, and in perfect charity with all the world. All these mercies and blessings we ask in the name and mediation of Jesus Christ, our most blessed Lord and Saviour. Amen.

The flag of the union and nationality of the republic which waves over the Capitol during the sessions of Congress is a symbol of Christian liberty, and has a grand historic interest and significance. Mr. Jefferson, it is said, desired this emblem of the republic to bear on its folds a profession of our national faith in the Christian religion.

The following explanation of the colors and symbolic meaning of the "Stars and Stripes" was written by a member of the old Continental Congress, to whom (with others) was committed the duty of selecting a flag for the republic—

> The stars of the new flag represent the new constellation of States rising in the West. The idea was taken from the constellation Lyra, which in the hand of Orpheus signifies harmony. The blue in the field was taken from the edges of the Covenanters' banner in Scotland, significant of the league and covenant of the United Colonies against oppression, incidentally involving the virtues of vigilance, perseverance, and justice. The stars were in a circle, symbolizing the perpetuity of the Union—the ring, like the circling serpent of the Egyptians, signifying eternity. The thirteen stripes showed, with the stars, the number of the United Colonies, and denoted the subordination of the States of the Union, as well as equality among themselves. The whole was the blending of the various flags previous to the Union flag, *viz.*: the red flags of the army and the white of the floating batteries. The red color, which in Roman days was the signal of defiance, denotes daring; and the white, purity.

"That flag," says Henry Ward Beecher, "has ever been the symbol of liberty, and men rejoiced in it. It went everywhere upon sea and land, carrying the tidings and the hopes of freedom to the nations of the world. *Our* flag means liberty; it means all that our fathers meant in the Revolutionary War; it means all that the Declaration of Independence meant; it means all that the Constitution of our people, organizing for justice, for liberty, for happiness, meant. Our flag carries American ideas, American history, and American feeling. Beginning with the colonies and coming down to our times, it has gathered and stored chiefly this supreme idea—Divine right of liberty in man. Every color means liberty; every form of star and beam or stripe of light means liberty—organized, institutional liberty—liberty through law, and law through liberty.

"Under this flag rode Washington and his army. Before it Burgoyne laid down his arms. It cheered our armies driven from around New York, and in their solitary pilgrimage through New Jersey. This banner streamed in light over their heads at Valley Forge and at Morristown. And when the long years of war were drawing to a close, underneath the folds of that immortal banner sat Washington, while Yorktown surrendered its hosts, and our Revolutionary struggled ended in victory. It waved thus over that whole historic period, and over that period in which sat the immortal Convention that framed our Constitution. In the War of 1812 that flag still bade defiance to the imperial power of the British Empire, and waved in victory on land and sea. How glorious, then, has been its origin! How glorious has been its history! In all the world is there any other banner that carries such hope, such grandeur of spirit, such soul-inspiring truth, as our dear old American flag—made by liberty, made for liberty, nourished in its spirit, carried in its service, and never, not once, in all the earth, made to stoop to despotism?"

Historic Memories of the Capitol

The historic memories of the Capitol, the display of forensic eloquence, the great conflicts of opposing principles in politics and in the policy and views of the distinguished statesmen of the republic, living and dead, and the progress and final triumph of the principles of the fathers of the republic, constitute the chief glory of the American Capitol. The halls of Congress are associated with the most illustrious statesmen of the republic since the days of Washington, who have adorned its legislative history by their profound and masterly views of government and politics; whilst the decisions and written opinions of the judges of the Supreme Court constitute a proud memorial of the judicial learning of the nation. The archives in the Capitol are rich political treasures, worthy of a free, enlightened, Christian republic. No other nation in the history of the world, in so short a time, has elaborated such treasures of political thought, such profound views of the science of civil government, and such an amount of political and judicial learning, enunciating the truest ideas of political wisdom and of government, as are found in the archives of the Capitol. Though justice and the principles of universal freedom and of eternal right have had temporary checks and reactions, yet their progress and final triumph have been witnessed and maintained. These historic memories are the true glory of the American Capitol.

The Vice-President of the United States, when the Senate vacated its old Chamber, in 1858, for one more splendid and spacious, referred to the capitol in these well-chosen words—

Address of the Vice-President

"This capital is worthy of the republic. Noble public buildings meet the view on every hand; treasures of science and the arts begin to accumulate. The spot is sacred by a thousand memories, which are so many pledges that the city of Washington, founded by him and bearing his revered name, with its beautiful site, bounded by picturesque eminences and the broad Potomac, and lying within view of his home and tomb, shall remain forever the capital of the United States. Hereafter the American and stranger, as they wander through the Capitol, will turn with instinctive reverence to view the spot on which so many and so great materials have accumulated for history. They will recall the great and the good whose renown is the common property of the Union. All the States may point with gratified pride to the services in the Senate of their patriotic sons. Fortunate will be the American statesman who, in this age, or in succeeding times, shall contribute to invest the new hall to which we go with historic memories like those which cluster here.

"Let us devoutly trust that another Senate, in another age, shall bear to a new and larger chamber this Constitution vigorous and inviolate, and that the last generation of posterity shall witness the deliberations of the representatives of American States still united, prosperous, and free."

The attainment of the highest prosperity and true glory of the republic can be secured only by the choice of upright, moral, Christian men to administer the Government. Ours is a Christian nation, and all our civil institutions rest on the Christian religion; and hence duty demands, as does the very genius of our institutions, that all who administer the civil affairs of the nation should be men who will legislate and act in their official functions in harmony with the principles on which our institutions were founded by our Christian fathers.

Dr. Beecher's Parallel

"Our republic" says Dr. Lyman Beecher, "in its Constitution and laws, is of heavenly origin. It was not borrowed from Greece or Rome, but from the Bible. Where we borrowed a ray from Greece or Rome, stars and suns were borrowed from another source—the Bible. There is no position more susceptible of proof (the proof is in this volume) than that as the moon borrows from the sun her light, so our Constitution borrows from the Bible its elements, proportions, and power. It was God that gave these elementary principles to our forefathers as the 'pillar of fire by night and the cloud by day,' for their guidance. All the liberty the world ever knew is but a dim star to the noonday sun which is poured on man by these oracles of Heaven. It is truly testified by Hume that the Puritans introduced the elementary principles of republican liberty into the English Constitution; and when they came to form colonial constitution and laws, we all know with what veneration and implicit confidence they copied the principles of the constitution and laws of Moses. These elementary principles have gone into the Constitution of the Union and of every one of the States; and we have hence more consistent liberty than ever existed in all the world, in all time, out of the Mosaic code."

The Christian statesman and philosopher Thomas S. Grimké, of South Carolina, states the same fact of the harmony of our civil institutions with the Bible. "If ever," he says, "a political scheme resembled the Divine Government, it is ours, where each exists for the whole, and the whole for each. As in the planetary world, so in our system, each has its own peculiar laws; and the harmonious movement of the whole is but a natural emanation from the co-operative influence of the parts."

Character of Rulers Described by the Bible

A Christian nation whose civil institutions thus harmonize with the Divine government should have in its seat of legislation men whose faith and official acts and private lives harmonize with the purposes and principles of a Christian government. The Bible, out of which rose the forms as well as the spirit of our civil institutions, enjoins this policy on the part of the people.

"*The God of Israel said, the rock of Israel spake to me, He that ruleth over men must be just, ruling in the fear of God." "Thou shalt provide out of all the people able men, such as fear God, men of truth, hating covetousness, and place such over the people to be rulers."* And to designate the exalted character which civil rulers should possess, they are spoken of in the New Testament as "*ministers of God for good;" "for they are God's ministers, attending continually upon this very thing."* The influence of the administration of such rulers upon national virtue and prosperity is described under such emblems as these—

"*He* [a Christian ruler] *shall be as the light of the morning, when the sun riseth, even a morning without clouds; as the tender grass springing out of the earth, by clear shining after rain." "He shall come down like rain upon the mown grass; as showers that water the earth. In his days shall the righteous flourish, and abundance of peace so long as the moon endureth." "Then shall thy light break forth as the morning, and thy health shall spring forth speedily; and thy righteousness shall go before thee; the glory of the Lord shall be thy reward. Thou shalt be like a watered garden, and like a spring of water whose waters fail not. Then shall thy light rise in obscurity, and thy darkness be as noonday, and the Lord shall guide thee continually."*

Washington felt the importance of having all the offices filled with such men. Writing to Gouverneur Morris in 1797, he said, "The Executive branch of this Government never has suffered, nor will suffer while I preside, any improper conduct of its officers to escape with impunity." Himself one of the noblest types of a Christian ruler, he desired to see all the civil offices filled with upright, honest, able men. Each department of the Government has had those who have filled their offices as Christian men, acting in the fear of God; but a Christian people should be vigilant at all times to have the administration of their Government conducted by rulers who will rule in the fear of the Lord, and harmonize the legislation of the nation with the law of God.

The Capitol of the republic has witnessed the rites of religion in both branches of its legislature, and daily and Sabbath services have had a gracious influence in directing the deliberations of Congress and in calming the heated excitements of the hour.

Prayers of the Capitol

The following prayers of the chaplains during the Thirty-Seventh congress are recorded as illustrating the spirit of devotion and piety which daily was diffused through the halls of national legislation—

TUESDAY, JANUARY 7, 1862.
The Chaplain, Rev. Dr. Sunderland, offered up the following prayer—

O thou that seest from thy throne all the inhabitants of the earth, by whose favor the nations flourish, as by thy frown they fall, we pray thee for succor in this our time of need, as our fathers prayed before us. Give us the foresight and the discretion of thy wisdom, that we may know what to do and wherewithal to perform it. Imbue the whole heart of the nation with a religious faith, so that none among us may profane in any wise before thee. Fill us with the solemn spirit and the awful majesty of this crisis. Let every man forbear levity, that there be no trifling Nero in the midst of burning Rome, that each may be vitally in earnest, bearing his life in his hand, and moving gravely, as a living sacrifice upon the altar of God and of country, of freedom and of religion. O thou Sovereign of our hope, prepare thy servants and the whole people to vindicate in them thy sacred cause, thine honor, and thy name, in the sight of all the generations. Amen.

WEDNESDAY, JANUARY 8.
O, God, the most patient, we, thy servants, faint and weary with the business of the times, pray for strength and illumi-

nation to comprehend thy mighty providence. Make us not as the king which once of old bore the ark of thy covenant from among the profane to the place of its consecrated rest, the anxious instrument of thy purpose and of thy power. May we know what we are doing, and what we ought to do, in the present cause of constitutional Government and the predestined birthright of human nature. Spread out here, in the high halls of legislation, the glory of thy presence, as in the ancient Shekinah, the symbol of human faith and hope. May thy servants make despatch in their sublime and solemn duties; and we beseech thee that when they shall come to frame a law it may be as the besom to sweep from the land those vampires which come in the night of our country's woe, to such her life-blood at every monetary pore and fatten on her confusion and distress. From these and all other foes we pray thee to deliver us; and, if it please thee, may our soldiers, where they lie in camp, as once it was aforetime, hear the sound of thy coming in the tops of the forest trees, to prepare themselves for the battle. May every hour be a pulse of progress to waft them on to victory. O Lord of hosts, we pray thee succor them, and give them speedy triumph, for thy name's sake. Amen.

THURSDAY, JANUARY 9.

O God, who dost, as we have heard, make the very decay of nature to be but another name for her continued existence, who dost call light from the bosom of darkness, who dost make the very chaos of the universe to produce all forms of beauty and grandeur, brood, we beseech thee, by thine eternal Spirit, upon the tumultuous elements of this nation, and cause to spring from the present "winter of our discontent" a new and higher form of civilization in this land. And we beseech thee, O God, while the thunders of thy power are rocking through the mountain masses of human corruption, torn and wild with the old primordial fires of guilty passion, may the broader wing of thy salvation cover the face of the whole world, dropping its balm upon every bruised and scattered fragment of our nature. O God of truth and glory, the father and friend of our humanity, after so many rude and bloody revolutions, we pray that thy kingdom may fully come. Through Jesus Christ. Amen.

FRIDAY, JANUARY 10.

O God, most high, most holy, who dost visit our iniquities upon us, we confess to thee our unworthiness, and pray for thy compassion in this time of our nation's trouble and our own. Sorely pressed by insurrection and bloody war, yet hast thou not, though with all our faults, a ministry for this people, sacred as the soul of man, and lasting as his destiny? So will we believe, despite the hatred of rebellion at home, and the sudden bristling of that foreign arrogance which has so lately stirred the buried memories of a thousand wrongs in this ministry. We pray that we may ever keep the substance of justice, however changing may be its temporary forms. Give us that Divine instinct of equality, of equity, and of faith which clearly sees through the subtlety of eloquence and the menace of power and patiently waits the hour to strike down intrigue and oppression. Without thee we can do nothing. O God, this day inspire us afresh. For Christ's sake. Amen.

The following prayer was offered up by Dr. Sunderland, at the opening of the session of the Senate of the United States, on the first Monday of December, 1862—

Almighty and everlasting God, who art in heaven, while we, thy creatures, are upon earth, we come to thee in our prayers, to be directed aright this day before thee. We thank thee that thy servants are met again in the Capitol undisturbed. We thank thee that thou has graciously preserved them during the period of their separation, and hast brought them together in the high conclave of the nation to deliberate upon the affairs of a people greatly afflicted, but as yet not wholly destroyed, and, while we remember with the deepest reverence and humiliation that it has not pleased thee to fully answer all former supplications from this place, we yet implore thy blessing upon the Congress now convened together in their coming councils and labors. May they stand in more than Jewish reverence and in more than Roman virtue before the people. Remove far away from the body and members of the American Senate all levity of mind and of manners, all profanity and volubility of speech, and all unworthy motives and desires, to give to them influence with the people in their high avocation as conscript fathers and elders of the republic. We rejoice that the machinations of foreign intervention have been, thus far, postponed and defeated. We rejoice in that proclamation which, as we hope, has begun to inspire some salutary fear in the rebels of the South as well as also to outreach the false and lying prophets of the North. We rejoice in that terrible fiery furnace through which we are passing to test the true spirit of the people, and the real sentiments of those who have so long and so loudly cried out for the extinction of human bondage. We pray that thou wilt continue to uncover, on the one hand, the cruelties of mankind's oppressors, and, on the other, the insincerity of their philanthropy, and when our wounds and our wretchedness shall have been fully probed, we pray, gracious God, for thy cleansing and healing and sanctifying power, through Jesus Christ, our Lord. Amen.

The following prayer was offered up by Rev. Thomas H. Stockton, chaplain of the House of Representatives of the Congress of the United States, at its opening session on the first Monday of December, 1862—

O God, Father of our Lord Jesus Christ, giver of the Holy Spirit, maker of angels and of men, ruler of nations and of governments, have mercy upon us, and inspire us with all needful aid to the performance of the solemn duties which devolve upon us as a people and as legislators in this crisis of our nation. We thank thee for this reopening of Congress; that thy servants, having visited their homes, and seen and heard the state and feeling of the country, are now returning to these halls of supreme legislation to renew their deliberations and enactments in behalf of our noble and cherished Union. We thank thee that our Government still stands in full and pristine power; that nations abroad that might have taken advantage of any apparent weakness to aid in dividing our land and nation, so humbling our position and reducing our influence in the world, are restrained by the development and resources with which thou hast enriched and strengthened us, and which transcend our own former foolish boastings as much as they have proved to transcend the estimate of those nations and empires who have so jealously watched us from afar. We thank thee that the life of our beloved and honored President has been preserved; that the Cabinet and Judiciary are in full union, and in harmony with the Executive, and our Legislature with both; that our armies and navies are daily multiplying and extending their national energies and intensifying their moral aim, and that our people are becoming more convinced of the necessity of and more content with the management of our conservative and progressive war. Believing more profoundly that thou art superintending all its forms and all its issues, and bringing all things to thy own plans, and that thou wilt ultimately accomplish thy will in the promotion of the best interests of our country and of the whole world, we thank thee for the brightening prospects for the liberty of the slave, not the result of our own goodness and wisdom, but, as we trust, of thy gracious and urgent ordination. We pray for the entire abolition of the system which has involved us in so much sin and sorrow and shame, and which would be sure if continued to increase our guilt and grief forever. Yet, O Father, our common Father, we most earnestly beseech thee, of thy infinite mercy, to grant that this end may be secured, not by violence, with blood and tears and helpless cries of pain, but by repentance and faith and prudence, by forbearance and wisdom and love, with mutual concessions and consent and co-operation, followed by reconciliation and a restored Union, by perpetual peace and joy. So shall these United States by these blessings become the praise of the whole earth. We thank thee for the recent official and national recognition of the sanctity of the Sabbath. Bless, O Lord, in our land the seventh day of rest, and hallow it, and enable us, under all circumstances, to remember and keep it holy. We pray for a proclamation that will rebuke that covetousness which is idolatry and that profanity which is blasphemy and indignity to the glory of thy name. And as we are now brought in thy providence again to these halls, we pray that we may solemnly reaffirm with a whole heart thy whole law, not by the assent of hundreds of thousands, but by the amen and hosannas and hallelujahs of all our millions, shaking the continent and the heavens which are above us with the voice of praise and prayer. We pray, O Lord, that the time may soon come when the saints of the Most High shall take and convert and hold the land forever, even forever, that righteousness may spread like the morning upon the mountains, like the noon in our valleys, and like the evening upon our prairies, and when the whole circle of our Confederacy shall rejoice in the smile of Jehovah. We pray that in our conflicts just so far as thou seest right thou wilt give us victory and advancement. Be mindful, O Lord, of the havoc and desolation that is falling upon the land through this war. Remember the sick and the wounded and the dying. We pray for our brethren now in arms against us. We thank thee that it is so easy for us to obey the precepts of our Redeemer, Love your enemies. We cannot cease to love them. May they soon be induced to relinquish the evil that is amongst them, and place higher value on the great principles of the charter of our independence, and show that they regard "life, liberty, and the pursuit of happiness" as the right of all mankind, and as beyond all mere local advantages, so that there shall be a restored Union, with increased goodness, and love and glory and joy upon the earth for ever and ever.

Our Father who art in heaven, Hallowed be thy name. Thy kingdom come. Thy will be done on earth, as it is in heaven. Give us this day our daily bread. And forgive us our trespasses, as we forgive those who trespass against us. And lead us not into temptation; but deliver us from evil. For thine is the kingdom, and the power, and the glory, for ever and ever. Amen.

Union Meeting in the Capitol

As the Capitol was consecrated to union, liberty, and virtue, it is proper to record, in a work like this, the act of worship and the scenes and resolutions of a great Union meeting held in its halls on the 11th of April, 1863. The President of the United States, his Cabinet, many officers of the army and navy, and a vast multitude of citizens, were present, filling the House of Representatives, the Senate Chamber, the rotunda, and the halls. It was the largest political gathering ever held in the Capitol, and its object was sanctioned by the purest patriotism and piety. Its deliberations were opened by a solemn prayer offered by Dr. Sunderland, as follows—

> Thou everlasting and glorious Lord God, whom we are bound to acknowledge through Jesus Christ thy Son; the God of Abraham, and of Isaac, and of Jacob, and the God and Father of our Lord Jesus Christ; the God of thy people in all generations; the God of our fathers, and our God, and the God of our children after us: we implore thee to look down upon the hearts of this vast assemblage as now again we come unto thee for help in prayer; and we beseech thee to add thy blessing to the deliberations of this public assemblage on this occasion. We pray thee to bless thy servants, the President and rulers and lawgivers and magistrates and all the people of this land.
>
> We pray thee especially to bless the officers and men of our army and of our navy, and do thou grant to be the arm of their strength and the power of their inspiration and their defence in the fearful day of battle; and we beseech thee, O Lord, that thou wilt make all this people, from the highest to the lowest, of one spirit, of one mind; and may we never, no, never, no, never give it up, until the cause of civil and religious liberty shall be thoroughly established, not only in our own land, but through all the earth, that the honor of thy great name and the saving help of thy power may be known among all the nations of mankind, through Jesus Christ our Lord.

The following resolutions, prepared and presented by Ex-Governor Bell, of Ohio, were unanimously adopted—

We, the people of Washington, assembled in the National Capitol, do resolve and proclaim—

1. That in this hour of peril, abjuring every minor consideration, we swear allegiance to the Great Republic, one and indivisible, and rally around her constituted authorities—come life or come death—while one traitor or rebel North or South dare plot sedition, flaunt a flag, or fire a gun.

2. That we well remember and will never forget the day when, a previous Administration having given up half our priceless heritage as not to be fought for, Abraham Lincoln was inaugurated President of the United States; when armies and navies we had none; when open enemies were in our front, their allies in our midst, and traitors in our rear; when the Potomac was blockaded, and the railways cut off: when patriots rushing to our relief were slain in the streets of Baltimore; when our forts and armies were basely surrendered; and when not only the Gulf States, but Virginia, Kentucky, and Missouri, were lost. How changed is now the scene! We are deliberating in the Capitol. Maryland stands by the flag; Missouri and Kentucky are redeemed; Virginia, North Carolina, Tennessee, Arkansas, and Texas are soon to be added; New England is not "left out in the cold," but South Carolina and all the other Gulf States are to be "plucked as brands from the burning."

3. That more than half the battle is already fought and won. To the timid we say, Safety is in the front, and not in the rear. To advance is to save the republic, maintain our nationality, preserve our liberty, prove our manhood, challenge the respect of our enemies, and commend our institutions to all mankind. To retreat, to hesitate, to parley with treason, is to dismember the nation, trail our flag in the dust, assume the debts of traitors and repudiate our own, abandon our fathers, enslave our wives and children, and consign our names to eternal infamy.

4. That in this great struggle there is no middle ground for half-way men to stand upon. It is loyalty or treason, liberty or bondage, democracy or despotism—on one side free government, free homes, free schools, security, peace, and American progress—on the other the mongrel aristocrats who dream of empire, coronets, and titles of nobility, who sigh for the sympathy of the ruling classes of the Old World, to aid them to enslave the poor, oppress honest toil, and shut the light of knowledge out from the soul of man.

5. That, laying on the altar of our country all past political feuds, we here tender to the President and his Administration our confidence and admiration, for stemming the torrent of treason, allaying dissensions at home, holding at bay the enemies of freedom abroad, calling into being, as from nothing, great armies and navies, and money for their support, for striking boldly at slavery, the main-stay of the rebellion, and thus deserving and receiving the plaudits of the good and the brave of all lands, "the considerate judgment of mankind, and the gracious favor of Almighty God."

6. That the Congress just terminated will ever share this glory, for its unfaltering support of the President with men and money, for its foreign and internal revenue acts, for its great national currency, national loan, and national enrolment laws, and its determined and firm protest against all foreign intervention, interference, or counsel in the domestic affairs of our beloved country, for freedom in the District of Columbia, for the national homestead, Pacific railway, Agricultural Colleges, and other great measures beyond enumeration.

7. That we tender to our Union brethren of Kentucky, and to the fifteen thousand brave Union volunteers of East Tennessee now fighting in General Rosecrans's army, and to every loyal heart in all the South, our plighted faith that not one of them or their little ones shall ever be abandoned, but that, in the language of the Constitution, we "guarantee in every State of the Union a republican form of government," under the now dearer than ever flag of our fathers.

8. To our brethren in arms on land and sea we say, All hail! We will, "with our voices, our votes, and our treasure, sus-

tain you in the trials of the camp and the dangers of the field, console your families in their fears and their privations, and willingly prepare wreaths to crown, when your service ends, the returning soldiers of freedom, defenders of the republic, and saviors of the Union."

9. That we will never despair of the American republic. In the cheering language of our greatest living friend abroad, John Bright, "We cannot believe that civilization, in its journey with the sun, will sink into endless night to gratify the ambition of the leaders of this revolt, who seek to wade through slaughter to a throne, and 'shut the gates of mercy on mankind.' We have another and far brighter vision before our gaze. Through the thick gloom of the present we see the brightness of the future as the sun in heaven. We see one vast confederation stretching from the wild billows of the Atlantic to the calmer waters of the Pacific main; and we see one people, and one law, and one language, and one faith, and over all this wide continent the home of freedom and a refuge for the oppressed of every race."

Slavery Abolished in the District of Columbia

The District of Columbia, in which is located the Capitol of the nation, has become free territory by the abolition of slavery. On the 16th day of April, 1862, an act was passed by Congress and approved by the President, of which the following is the first section—

> Be it enacted by the Senate and House of Representatives in Congress assembled, That all persons held to service or labor within the District of Columbia by reason of African descent are hereby discharged and freed from all claim to such service and labor; and from and after the passage of this act neither slavery nor involuntary servitude, except for crime whereof the party shall be duly convicted, shall hereafter exist in said District.

This act was in harmony with the spirit and precepts of the Christian religion and with the genius and demands of the civil institutions of the nation, as well as with national justice, honor, and consistency. Lafayette expressed, in a letter published in the "Historical Magazine" of 1827, his earnest desire to see some measure of gradual emancipation in the District of Columbia adopted, and declared that "the state of slavery, particularly in that emporium of foreign visitors and European ministers, is a most lamentable drawback on the example of independence and freedom presented to the world by the United States." His wishes and those of many of his illustrious associates in the cause of universal emancipation, as well as those of all true lovers of their country at the present time, are at length consummated, and the Goddess of Liberty which crowns the magnificent dome of the Capitol overlooks a national territory forever consecrated to freedom. The influence of this act has inspired a new life into the enterprise of the city of Washington; and, if moral and Christian culture shall sanctify and direct the material prosperity and the political operations of all departments of the Government, the capital of the American republic will yet be the seat of virtue and religion, the center of beneficent influences to the nation, and realize the fondest hopes of Washington and the patriotic and Christian founders of this seat of civil empire.

25

Christianity of American Courts, and Christian Character of Eminent American Judges

Washington's View of Their Importance

THE Constitution, ordained to "establish justice," makes provision for the institution of courts and the appointment of judges. Washington, the first President, was called upon, among his first official duties, to organize the judicial department of the Government. He says, "Regarding the due administration of justice as the strongest cement of good government, I have considered the first organization of the judicial department as essential to the happiness of the people and to the stability of the political system. Under this impression it has been with me an invariable object of anxious solicitude to select the fittest characters to expound the laws and to dispense justice.

"I have always been persuaded that the stability and success of the national Government, and, consequently, the happiness of the people of the United States, would depend in a considerable degree on the interpretation and execution of its laws. In my opinion, it is important that the judiciary system should not only be independent in its operations, but as perfect as possible in its formation."

Under these convictions, Washington, by the appointment of judges, carried into practical execution the provision of the Constitution, and selected the most exalted characters to expound the laws and to dispense justice. In this he gave new evidence of his clear discrimination and sound judgment. They were men of rare judicial integrity and attainments, who, as Christian judges, ornamented the bench of a Christian nation and shed honor and glory on American jurisprudence. James Wilson, who signed the Declaration of Independence and was a member of the Convention that formed the Federal Constitution, was selected by Washington as one of the first judges of the Supreme Court of the United States. He said, in reference to a judge, that "in his heart should be written the words of the law, if the law says—and the law does say—that, in all its judgments, justice shall be executed in mercy. On the heart of a judge will this heavenly maxim be deeply engraven. He ought to be a terror to evil-doers, and a praise to them that do well. A judge is the blessing or he is the curse of society. His powers are important. His character and conduct cannot be objects of indifference."

Chief Justice Hale

The judiciary of England had an illustrious Christian judge in Matthew Hale. In entering upon his official duties he drew up, for the government of his official life, the following rules—

"1. That in the administration of justice I am intrusted for God, the king, and the country; and, therefore, 2. That it be upright. 3. Deliberate. 4. Resolutely. That I rest not upon my own understanding or strength, but implore and rest upon the direction and strength of God."

This eminent English judge was a strict observer of the Sabbath.

The incorruptible chief-justice of England, at the time of Cromwell and the Commonwealth, could not be seduced to desecrate the Sabbath by the example of crowned heads or by the influence of learned divines. Neither a Puritan nor a Cavalier, he was an honest Christian man, and an upright jurist. In his instruction to his children Sir Matthew Hale says—

"I have, by long and sound experience, found that the due observance of the Lord's day, and the duties of it, has been of singular comfort and advantage to me; and I doubt not it will prove so to you. God Almighty is the Lord of our time, and lends it to us; and as it is but just we should consecrate this part of that time to him, so I have found, by a strict and diligent observation, that a due attention to the duty of this day hath ever joined to it a blessing upon the rest of my time, and the week that hath so begun hath been blessed and prospered to me; and, on the other side, when I have been negligent of the duties of this day, the rest of the week hath been unsuccessful and unhappy to my own secular employments; so that I could early make an estimate of my success in my secular engagements the week following, by the manner of my passing of this day; and this I do not write lightly or inconsiderately, but upon a long observation and experience."

"Of all places," said Webster, "there is none which so imperatively demands that he who occupies it should be under the fear of God, and above all other fear, as the situation of a judge."

Christian Judges of American Courts

The judicial history of the American courts corresponds, in its Christian features, to the earlier ages of the republic, in the other departments of the Government. Before recording the decision of the courts of the United States in favor of the Christian religion being the religion of the Government as well as of the nation, it will be instructive to notice the eminent Christian characters of a number of the chief judges.

John Jay

Eminent on the roll of Christian judges is John Jay. He was the first Chief-Justice of the Supreme Court of the United States, and presided as such with unsurpassed integrity and wisdom. Webster, in alluding to him, said that "when the spotless ermine of the judicial robe fell on John Jay it touched nothing less spotless than itself."

Like Mansfield and Hale, of England, he ever sought "that wisdom that cometh down from above" to guide him in all his official investigations and decisions.

"If the character of this eminent man," says his biographer, "is beautiful in its simplicity and its moral purity, it becomes still more interesting when regarded as a bright example of Christian virtue. The tone of his mind was always serious. He regarded religious meditation and worship as no unimportant duties of life." He was a member of the Protestant Episcopal Church. "This," says Judge Story, "was the religion of his early education, and became afterwards that of his choice. But he was without the slightest touch of bigotry or intolerance. His benevolence was as wide as Christianity itself. It embraced the human race. He was not only liberal in his feelings and principles, but in his charities. His hands were open on all occasions to succor distress, to encourage enterprise, and to support good institutions."

Associated with Jay on the Supreme Bench were James Wilson, a Christian patriot and judge—"of great learning, patient industry, and uprightness of character,"—Cushing of Massachusetts, Blair of Virginia, Iredell of North Carolina, Paterson of New Jersey, and Bushrod Washington, a nephew of President Washington. These were all men distinguished for their legal accomplishments and Christian virtues. Of Judge Washington it was said that "the love of justice was a ruling passion, it was the master-spring of his conduct. He made justice itself, even the most severe, soften into the moderation of mercy."

"There was," said Judge Story, "a daily beauty in his life, which won every heart. He was benevolent, charitable, affectionate, and liberal, in the best sense of the terms. He was a Christian, full of religious sensibility and religious humility. Attached to the Episcopal Church by education and choice, he was one of its most sincere but unostentatious friends. He was as free from bigotry as any man, and, at the same time he claimed the right to think for himself, he admitted without reserve the same right in others. He was, therefore, indulgent even to what he deemed errors in doctrine, and abhorred all persecution for conscience' sake.

"But what made religion most attractive in him, and gave it occasionally even a sublime expression, was its tranquil, cheerful, unobtrusive, meek, and gentle character. There was a mingling of Christian graces in him, which showed that the habit of his thoughts was fashioned for another and a better world."

Chief Justice Marshall

Among the most eminent of American judges was Chief-Justice Marshall, of Virginia. He will ever be venerated as one of the brightest intellects of the country, and as having shed the most lucid light on the constitutional and legislative jurisprudence of the Government. His logical intellect, severe simplicity of character, legal knowledge, purity of life, and Christian faith, form one of the richest treasures of the American nation. He was, in public and private life, continued to a venerable age, loyal to his God, the Constitution of his country, his own conscience, and the Christian religion.

"He had," says one, "a pure and childlike religious faith. The hard, muscular intellect had not built up its strength on the ruins of the heart. It is related of him that he once chanced to be present at a discussion between two or three young men upon the evidences of the Christian religion. They indulged freely in sneers, and, at the end of their argument, turned indifferently to the chief-justice—whom they took, from his poor and plain costume, for some ignorant rustic—and asked him, jocularly, what he thought of the matter. If," said the narrator of the incident, "a streak of lightning had at that moment crossed the room, their amazement could not have been greater than it was at what followed. The most eloquent and unanswerable appeal was made for nearly an hour, by the old gentleman, that he ever heard. So perfect was his recollection that every argument used by the opponents of the Christian religion was met in the order in which it was presented. Hume's sophistry on the subject of miracles was, if possible, more perfectly answered than it had been done by Campbell. And in the whole lecture there was so much symmetry and energy, pathos and sublimity, that not another word was answered. An attempt to describe it would be an attempt to paint the sunbeam."

This deep-rooted religious faith never wavered. Marshall continued to repeat, night and morning, in his serene old age, the prayer which he had been taught at his mother's knees; and, at a period when skepticism was fashionable among cultivated men, he never uttered a word calculated to throw a doubt on the Divine origin of Christianity. A lesson of the deepest reverence for every thing holy was, on the contrary, taught by his daily life; and he died, as he had lived, trusting in the atonement of Jesus. This great jurist and eminent Christian man regarded it as among the highest honors of his life to be a teacher in the Sabbath-school. Here he was found, for many years of his life, on every Sabbath, with his class, expounding to them the law of God and the sublime truths of the gospel of Christ.

Judge Story

Judge Story, of Massachusetts, for many years Associate Justice on the Supreme Bench of the United States, was eminent for his judicial and literary attainments and his Christian virtues. He speaks thus of the Christian religion—

"One of the beautiful traits of our municipal jurisprudence is, that Christianity is a part of the common law, from which it seeks its sanction of its rights and by which it endeavors to regulate its doctrine. And, notwithstanding the specious objection of one of our distinguished statesmen, the boast is as true as it is beautiful. There has been a period in which the common law did not recognize Christianity as lying at its foundation. For many ages it was almost exclusively administered by those who held its ecclesiastical dignities. It now repudiates every act done in violation of its duties of perfect obligation. It pronounces illegal every contract offensive to its morals. It recognizes with profound humility its holydays and festivals, and obeys them as *dies non juridici*. It still attaches to persons believing in its Divine authority the highest degree of competency as witnesses."

John McLean

John McLean, of Ohio, adorned the judicial department of the Government, by his eminent talents, learning, and civic virtues, for more than a generation. He became in early life a sincere and humble Christian, and for more than half a century gave a most beautiful illustration of the pure and exalted virtues of the Christian religion both in public and in private life. Not one suspicious breath of corruption ever soiled his fair fame, or diminished the purity and power of his fame and influence. He was in the highest degree a Christian statesman and an upright judge. His views of the need and importance of Christianity to civil government are expressed in the following words—

"For many years my hope for the perpetuity of our institutions has rested upon Bible morality and the general dissemination of Christian principles. This is an element which did not exist in the ancient republics. It is a basis on which free governments may be maintained through all time.

"It is a truth experienced in all time, that a free government can have no other than a moral basis; and it requires a high degree of intelligence and virtue in the people to maintain it. Free government is not a self-moving machine. It can only act through agencies. And if its aims be low and selfish, if it addresses itself to the morbid feelings of humanity, its tendencies must be corrupt and weaken the great principles on which it is founded.

"Our mission of freedom is not carried out by brute force, by canon law, or any other law except the moral law and those Christian principles which are found in the Scriptures."

He was for many of the last years of his life President of the American Sunday-School Union, an institution whose beneficent influence has been felt in every department of Church and State.

In accepting the Presidency of the American Sunday-School Union, Judge McLean wrote the following letter—

Cincinnati. April 10, 1849.

Dear Sir—

Whilst I consider myself honored by the Board of Officers and Managers of the American Sunday-School Union in being placed nominally at their head, I cannot repress a fear that, in accepting the position, I may stand in the way of some one of higher merit and greater usefulness.

The more I reflect upon Sabbath-schools, the more deeply am I impressed with their importance. Education without moral training may increase national knowledge, but it will add nothing to national virtue. By a most intelligent and able report, made some years ago by Guizot, it appeared that in those departments of France where education had been most advanced, crime was most common. And, by later reports, it is shown that in Prussia, Scotland, and England, where the means of education has been greatly increased—especially in Prussia and Scotland—criminal offences have increased. Making due allowance for the growth of population and the aggregation of individuals in carrying on various useful enterprises, the principal cause of this is *a want of moral culture.*

Knowledge without moral restraint only increases the capacity of an individual for mischief. As a citizen, he is more dangerous to society, and does more to corrupt the public morals, than one without education. So selfish is our nature, and so prone to evil, that we require chains, moral or physical, to curb our propensities and passions.

Early impressions are always the most lasting. All experience conduces to establish this. Who has forgotten the scenes of his boyhood, or the pious instructions of his parents? Who does not carry these with him all along the journey of life? However they may be disregarded and contemned by an abandoned course, yet they cannot be consigned to oblivion. In the darkest hours of revelry, they will light up in the memory and cause remorse. And this feeling will generally, sooner or later, lead to reformation.

Whatever defect there may be of moral culture in our common schools, it is more than supplied in our Sabbath-schools. Here the whole training is of a moral and religious character, entirely free from sectarian influences. The child is instructed in his duty to God and to his fellow-beings, and for which he must answer in the great day of accounts. He becomes familiar with the Scriptures by his Bible lessons, which are fixed in his memory by his answer to questions propounded. In deed, the whole exercises of the school are eminently calculated to interest and elevate his mind.

Impressions thus made can never be eradicated. The associations of the school make the instruction more impressive than it could be under other circumstances. As a general rule, it may be assumed that the children who attend on Sunday-schools may be distinguished from others at all times, and especially in a regard for the Sabbath and the institutions of religion.

When we consider these schools as the nurseries of society, we cannot too highly appreciate them. The children are taken as tender plants; every noxious branch is cut off, and the ground is so prepared as to impart the utmost vigor and healthfulness. Under such care, the fruit must be good. The mind and heart of a child may be as certainly formed for good works by moral training as the plant may be improved by careful culture.

Who can estimate the influence on society of five millions of children thus educated? And it may not be an extravagant calculation to suppose that, every ten years, five millions of persons who had been Sabbath-school scholars enter into active society. More or less they may be supposed to be influenced by the principles inculcated at those schools. Restrained themselves by moral considerations, their example may have some influence on an equal number of their associates. Here, then, is an element of power which must be salutary on our social and political relations. The good thus done cannot be fully known and appreciated, as the amount of evil which it prevents cannot be measured.

It may be assumed as an axiom that free government can rest on no other basis than moral power. France has a republic which is maintained by bayonets. And there is reason to apprehend that in that country there is not a sufficient moral basis for the maintenance of a free government.

But are our own beloved institutions free from danger? Who has not seen the "yawning chasms" in our own beautiful edifice? Its pillars seem to be moved, its walls and its dome and the contour of the fabric have suffered; and nothing can restore it to its pristine beauty and strength but a united and a continued effort of the intelligent and virtuous citizens of our country. And we must increase the number of these by every possible means. Sabbath-schools must be relied on as a principal agent in this great work. Without their aid, I should look to the future with little hope. But having their co-operation I do not despair. Mere partyism should be discarded for principle; and moral power, founded as it must be on the justice and fitness of things, must be made the ground of action.

When I consider the mighty trust, moral and political, which has been committed to us; when I reflect upon the extent and fertility of our country, its diversified and healthful climates, and its capacity for human enjoyment, I am overwhelmed with the vastness of the subject. Rapidly as we have advanced for the last thirty years in the development of our physical resources and in the arts and sciences, the bow of promise still abides in the future. If faithful to our trust, we may expect to advance in the future more rapidly than we have done in time past.

But a nation may be great in its physical powers and in its mental attainments, without possessing the basis of moral power, which is the only foundation for practical liberty. I have no fears of the concentrated Powers of the world. We could drive them from our shores, without endangering our institutions. But, whilst I have no fear as to the permanency of our Government from influences and powers from without, I am not without apprehension from causes which arise among ourselves. This is, indeed, a strange paradox. Can we not trust ourselves? "Is thy servant a dog, that he should do this thing?"

There is no security against the enormities of our race, which have so often disgraced the history of the world, but a restraining influence, which sets bounds to human passions. The superior civilization, moderation, and justice of modern times is attributable to the benign influence of Christianity. The ancient republics were destitute of this power. They were united by military prowess—by the glory which arises from the butchery of our race, and from acts of injustice, rapine, and plunder. Physical force was the arbiter of right and the dispenser of justice. But now there is an element of moral power, which more or less pervades all civilized nations, and which has its foundation in the Bible. No nation can disregard this law with impunity. If it be not embodied in any published code, yet it is not the less powerful. It is written in the hearts and understandings of mankind. It shakes the thrones of despots, who, through a line of ancestry of many centuries, have governed with an absolute power.

To us, as a nation, are committed the great principles of free government; and we are responsible to those who shall come after us, for a faithful discharge of the trust. Now, we must continue to build upon the foundation of our fathers. They were equal to the crisis. Washington, and Hancock, and Adams, and their compatriots, were good men as well as great men. They looked to a superintending Providence, and to the precepts of the Bible. These they observed in their public and private acts, and thereby inculcated the same rule of action upon others.

To reform all abuses and perpetuate our institutions, we need only the force of such examples. There is enough of intelligence and virtue and of honest purpose in the nation, if embodied and made active, to free us from the prevailing corruptions of the day. And there is no agency more efficient to strengthen this state of the public mind than our Sabbath-schools. They are the nurseries of virtue, of an elevated patriotism, and of religion. I do not speak of a narrow or sectarian principle, which admits of no merit or virtue out of its own system, but of a principle which is as expansive, as benevolent, and as glorious as the doctrines of the Saviour.

Who will not sustain the uplifted hands and expanded hearts of those who are engaged in this work? It is connected with all that is lovely and of good report in this world, and all that is glorious in the world to come. It conduces to perpetuate an equality of human rights on the great principles of virtue and immutable justice. And what nobler motive could impel to human action? Compare it with the motives which lead to other lines of action and with their results. The aspiration of the mere politician begins and ends in himself. The benefits (if benefits they may be called) conferred on his supporters have no higher motive than this. The same remark will apply to many who are engaged in the pursuits of commerce, or in the prosecution of enterprises which ordinarily lead to the accumulation of individual and national wealth. They may become great in this respect, and advance the wealth of their country, without being exemplary themselves or increasing the public virtue. And so of professional renown. How empty is that bauble which entwines the brow of the orator in the senate, at the bar, or in the pulpit, whose heart is not full of the kindly feelings of humanity and who does not endeavor to mitigate the sufferings and increase the happiness of his race!

If we desire to make our nation truly great, and to transmit to posterity our institutions in their primitive simplicity and force, we must imbue the minds of our youth with a pure and an elevated morality, which shall influence their whole lives. And I know of no means so well calculated to produce this result as SABBATH-SCHOOLS. Whether we look to the good of our country, or to a future immortality, these schools are recommended by considerations of the deepest importance.

I regret that my public duties will prevent my being present at your annual meeting.

With the greatest respect, I am, dear sir, faithfully yours,

John McLean.

This eminent jurist and Christian died at a ripe and honored age, in 1861, and closed his long life in the same serene Christian hope which ennobled and embellished his whole private and public life. At his funeral, Dr. Clark, editor of the "Ladies' Repository," spoke of the life and character of Judge McLean as follows—

We come not to-day to utter words of eulogy, but to mourn: yet it is not too much to say that through the long period of his public life—extending over nearly half a century—his character as a public officer, as a man, and as a Christian, has stood out before the world untarnished—nay, I may say, unsuspected. With equal honesty and ability has he met and fulfilled every trust. The loss of such a man, at such a juncture, is a public calamity.

When humanity, with mighty throes, is yearning for higher developments and for the realization of a nobler destiny, well may we mourn the death of one whose own character was a living embodiment of whatever is noble in man, and whose influence was wide and powerful to benefit the race.

As fellow-citizens, well may we mourn the death of one whose history linked us to the heroic age of the republic, the purity of whose patriotism had been thoroughly tested, and whose very name was a talismanic charm for the preservation of the Union, and of the constitutional rights and liberties of our whole country, and of all our citizens, the lowest as well as the highest.

When the Christian character and virtues are so rarely illustrated in public life, well may we mourn the loss of the Christian statesman, the beauty of whose ermine was surpassed only by the spotlessness of his Christian life, whose devotion to his country was surpassed only by his fealty to Christ, and whose life and character will ever be pointed to as the means of inspiring the young men of our country with the conviction that there are nobler ends to be attained, even in this life, than the sordid gains of office or the selfishness of human ambition.

As members of the great Christian brotherhood, we have reason to mourn the death of one who has honored the Christian name. A little more than half a century ago, Judge McLean was led to Christ, through the instrumentality of that eminent minister of God, Rev. John Collins. He immediately identified himself with the Methodist Episcopal Church, through whose ministry he had been converted. A man of so noble a mind could not be otherwise than a man of broad views and catholic sympathies with all Christian denominations.

He was jealous of the honor of the Christian name; nor did he ever forget—even amid the fascinations of social or public life—that by character and act, if not by word, he was called to be a witness for Christ. He was faithful in the least of his Christian duties. In the closet and in the class, as well as in the more public services of the sanctuary, he obtained the spiritual nutriment which gave robustness to his Christian character. To the merely formal professor he could truly say, "I have meat to eat that ye know not of."

Others

Bellamy Storer, a Christian judge of Ohio, who illustrates the beauty and dignity of Christian virtues in union with high legal attainments and civic honors, and who was an intimate friend, at a meeting of the bar of Cincinnati, after the death of Judge McLean, paid the following tribute to his memory—

> A beautiful remark is made by one of the ancients, that we never begin to live until we are dead; and the remark applies with great propriety on the present occasion. For the lamented judge, whose memory we all cherish with so much sincerity, has now received his due; his many virtues are now justly estimated. The integrity of his character, the purity of his principles, the justice of his decisions, his deliberate judgment—all these are now not weighed in the balances of prejudice; but they are valued by their real worth; and when such a man dies, his memory ought to be cherished.
>
> Forty-four years ago in June next, he admitted me to the practice of this bar. He had just taken his seat as Judge of the Supreme Court of this State, and the moment he became acquainted with me he gave me the hand of friendship. To a young man that was an exceedingly cherished token of regard. But, more than that, he gave me his counsel, and although he lived not in our immediate neighborhood, yet I saw him often and knew him well. When, however, he sat as a judge of the United States, I was brought into intimate communion with him. He became my neighbor, and during the years that have followed we have had many delightful interviews. I know his generous nature; I know in private life he was all we could look for as a model, and in public life he justified the highest expectations of the public. There was one feature of his character that was pre-eminently great: it was that he always preserved an equanimity of temper—not as applied to his nervous temperament, but to his whole moral nature and all his intellectual powers; for he had so admirably composed them all, that each and every one had its influence upon the others,

so that, like a well-tuned instrument, his character was always in harmony. And the great secret of this was, that he did not abide in the strength of his intellect, in his power or genius, but he felt as a magistrate below he was responsible to Him who was King above. He knew that all the authority which be could possibly exert was but an emanation from the powers above, and he always so regulated himself. In the discharge of his duties in the court of justice, he asked himself the question whether he was performing his duty to his God. And this, brethren of the bar, is the great secret of all success—more especially upon the bench of justice. In the future time, although we may survive a few years, and may remember the prominent characteristics of that great man, yet this, in the history of the day, will stand out as a distinctive feature of his character—that he was a humble and sincere Christian.

Grimké's Tribute to the Supreme Judge of the United States

The Supreme Court of the United States, and the judges who sat upon its bench in 1827, received a just tribute from Thomas S. Grimké, in a speech he delivered in the Senate of South Carolina, December 17, 1827. He says—

> It is emphatically a court of the whole people and of every State, of the Government of the Union and of the Government of every State. It is as independent of the President and Congress as of the Governor and Legislature of South Carolina. Its members are selected from different States, and its bar gathers within its bounds the talents and learning, the courage, virtue, and patriotism, of the East and the West, of the North and the South. ... No one, indeed, can possibly read the judgments of this tribunal—equally beneficent and illustrious—and not be deeply impressed with its wisdom and learning, its moral courage and justice, its high sense of duty, its love of peace and order, its independence, dignity, and patriotism. I know not any body of men who are entitled to

more enlightened admiration, more sincere gratitude, more profound respect for their talents, learning, virtues, and services. Theirs is indeed a parental guardianship, full of moral dignity and beauty, sustained by the energy of wisdom and adorned by the simplicity of justice and truth.

The brief sketches contained in this volume of some of the eminent men who have adorned the judicial history of the republic and shed such light on the profound and important science of jurisprudence, and who in their private character illustrated so nobly the Christian virtues, were prepared, as they did in the administration of justice and law, to practically believe and carry out that true and admirable exposition of law, as given by the venerable and learned Hooker, of Puritan memory. He says—

"Of law there can be no less acknowledged than that her seat is the bosom of God, her voice the harmony of the world. All things in heaven and earth do her homage; the very least feel her care, and the greatest are not *exempt from her power. Both angels and men, and creatures of what condition soever, though each in a different sort and name, yet all with one uniform consent admire her as the mother of their peace and joy.*

In giving practical form to this sublime eulogy on law and its benignant power and results, the minds of many of the most eminent judges of the State and national Governments were illuminated, through prayer, with wisdom from heaven. They kneeled before the Infinite Judge of the Universe and humbly entreated that in the administration of earthly justice and law they might be inspired and guided of God. This fact is historic in the Christian lives of many American judges.

In the earlier history of the country, it was customary to open the colonial and State courts with prayer. South Carolina practiced this Christian usage for many years in her judicial history, as did also the other Southern colonies and States, as well as those of New England. The practice is still maintained by some of the State courts.

The judicial system of the State of Ohio, first-born into the Union under the Christian ordinance of freedom of 1787, was inaugurated, the next year after the enactment of this organic law of the nation, with the solemn service of prayer. The following is a historical description of the scene—

The first civil court ever held in the Northwest was that of the Court of Common Pleas of Washington county, at Marietta, September 2, 1788, by Rufus Putnam and Benjamin Tupper, presiding justices. The court was opened with pomp. A procession was formed, the sheriff, with a drawn sword, in advance, followed by the citizens, officers of the garrison at Fort Harmer, the members of the bar, the Judges of the Supreme Court, the Governor, and a clergyman, with the Judges of the Common Pleas, in the order in which they are named. Arriving at the hall of the Campus Martius, the whole of the procession was counter-marched into it, and the judges, Putnam and Tupper, took their seats upon the bench. The audience was seated, and after a Divine benediction was invoked by the Rev. Dr. Cutler, the High Sheriff, Ebenezer Sprout, advanced to the door and proclaimed aloud, "Oyez! Oyez! a court is opened for the administration of even-handed justice to the poor and the rich, to guilty and innocent, without respect of persons; none to be punished without a trial by their peers, and in pursuance of the laws and evidence in the case." Besides the crowds of emigrants and settlers, there were present at the ceremonies hundreds of Indians, who had their encampments in the vicinity for the purpose of entering into a treaty with the Federal Government.

The following opinions of judges in the courts of several of the largest and most influential States of the Union, affirming the great historic fact that the life and character of the civil institutions of the United States, as well as the whole fabric of our freedom and civilization, flow from the Christian religion, will present lucid and grateful views on this subject. They form a rich part of the Christian history of our civil governments, and are eminently worthy to be recorded and studied.

Decision of the Supreme Court of Pennsylvania in Favor of Christianity

In 1824, the Supreme Court of Pennsylvania reviewed the subject most thoroughly and extensively, and the decision of the court will repay a thoughtful perusal. The trial was on an indictment for blasphemy, founded on an act of Assembly passed in 1700. The decision may be found in Sergeant & Rawle's Reports, page 394, and is as follows—

> The court said that, even if Christianity was not part of the law of the land, it is the popular religion of the country, an insult on which would be indictable as directly tending to disturb the public peace. Christianity, general Christianity, is, and always has been, a part of the common law of Pennsylvania; not Christianity founded on particular religious tenets; not Christianity with an established Church, and tithes, and spiritual courts; but Christianity with liberty of conscience to all men. The first legislative act in the colony was the recognition of the Christian religion, and the establishment of liberty of conscience. It is called "the Great Law," and is as follows—
>
> "Whereas the glory of Almighty God and the good of mankind is the reason and end of government, and therefore government itself is a venerable ordinance of God, and forasmuch as it is principally devised and intended by the Proprietary and Governor and freemen of Pennsylvania and territories thereunto belonging, to make and establish such laws as shall best preserve true Christian and civil liberty, in opposition to all unchristian, licentious, and unjust practices, whereby God may have his due, Caesar his due, and the people their due;
>
> "*Resolved*, therefore, that all persons living in this Province, who confess and acknowledge the one Almighty and Eternal God to be the Creator, upholder, and ruler of the world, and who hold themselves obliged in conscience to live peaceably and justly in civil society, shall in no wise be molested," &c.

The court, after quoting the whole law at length, further says—

> Thus this wise legislature framed this great body of laws for a Christian country and a Christian people. Infidelity was then rare, and no infidels were among the first colonists. They fled from religious intolerance to a country where all were allowed to worship according to their own understanding. Every one

had the right of adopting for himself whatever opinion appeared to be the most rational concerning all matters of religious belief; thus securing by law this inestimable freedom of conscience, one of the highest privileges and greatest interests of the human race. Thus is the Christianity of the common law incorporated into the great law of Pennsylvania; and thus is it irrefragably proved that the laws and institutions of this State are built on the foundation of reverence for Christianity. On this the Constitution of the United States has made no alteration, nor in the great body of the laws, which was an incorporation of the common-law doctrine of Christianity, as suited to the condition of the colony, and without which no free government can long exist. Under the Constitution penalties against cursing and swearing have been enacted. If Christianity was abolished, all false oaths, all tests by oath in common form by the book, would cease to be indictable as perjury. The indictment must state the oath to be on the Holy Evangelists of Almighty God.

Opinion of the Court

After reviewing a series of decisions made in Pennsylvania and elsewhere, the court continues thus—"It has long been firmly settled that blasphemy against the Deity generally, or an attack on the Christian religion *indirectly*, for the purpose of exposing its doctrines to ridicule and contempt, is indictable and punishable as a temporal offence. The principles and actual decisions are that the publications, whether written or oral, must be malicious, and designed for that end and purpose." After stating that the law gave free permission for the serious and conscientious discussion of all theological and religious topics, the court said—

> A malicious and mischievous intention is, in such a case, the broad boundary between right and wrong, and that it is to be collected from the offensive levity, scurrilous and opprobrious language, and other circumstances, whether the act of the party was malicious; and, since the law has no means of

distinguishing between different degrees of evil tendency, if the matter published contains any such evil tendency it is a public wrong. An offence against the public peace may consist either of an actual breach of the peace, or doing that which tends to provoke and excite others to do it. Within the latter description fall all acts and all attempts to produce disorder, by written, printed, or oral communications for the purpose of generally weakening those religious and moral restraints without the aid of which mere legislative provisions would prove ineffectual.

No society can tolerate a wilful and despiteful attempt to subvert its religion any more than it would to break down its laws—a general, malicious, and deliberate attempt to over-throw Christianity, general Christianity. This is the line of in-dication where crime commences, and the offences become the subject of penal visitation. The species of offence may be classed under the following heads—

1. Denying the Being and Providence of God. 2. Contu-melious reproaches of Jesus Christ; profane and malevolent scoffing of the Scriptures, or exposing any part of them to contempt and ridicule. 3. Certain immoralities tending to subvert all religion and morality, which are the foundations of all governments. Without these restraints no free govern-ments could long exist. It is liberty run mad to declaim against the punishment of these offences, or to assert that their pun-ishment is hostile to the spirit and genius of our Government. They are far from being the friends to liberty who support this doctrine; and the promulgation of such opinions, and the general receipt of them among the people, would be the sure forerunner of anarchy, and, finally, of despotism. No free gov-ernment now exists in the world unless where Christianity is acknowledged and is the religion of the Country.

Christianity is part of the common law of this State. It is not proclaimed by the commanding voice of any human su-perior, but expressed in the calm and mild accents of cus-tomary law. Its foundations are broad and strong and deep; they are laid in the authority, the interest, the affections of the people. Waiving all questions of hereafter, it is the purest system of morality, the firmest auxiliary and only stable support of all human laws. It is impossible to administer the laws without taking the religion which the defendant in error has scoffed at, that Scripture which he has reviled, as their basis; to lay aside these is at least to weaken the confidence in human veracity, so essential to the purposes of society, and without which no question of property could be decided, and no criminal brought to justice; an oath in the common form on a discredited book would be a most idle ceremony. No preference is given by law to any *particular* religious persuasion. Protection is given to all by our laws. It is only the malicious reviler of Christianity who is punished.

While our own free Constitution secures liberty of conscience and freedom of religious worship to all, it is not necessary to maintain that any man should have the right publicly to vilify the religion of his neighbors and of the country. These two privileges are directly opposed. It is an open, public vilification of the religion of the country that is punished, not to force conscience by punishment, but to preserve the peace of the country by an outward respect to the religion of the country, and not as a restraint upon the liberty of conscience; but licentiousness, endangering the public peace, when tending to corrupt society, is considered as a breach of the peace, and punishable by indictment. Every immoral act is not indictable; but when it is destructive of morality generally it is, because it weakens the bonds by which society is held together, and government is nothing more than public order.

This is the Christianity which is the law of our land; and (continues the court) I do not think it will be an invasion of any man's right of private judgment, or of the most extended privilege of propagating his sentiments with regard to religion in the manner which he thinks most conclusive. If, from a regard to decency and the good order of society, profane swearing, breach of the Sabbath, and blasphemy, are punishable by civil magistrates, these are not punished as sins or offences against God, but crimes injurious to, and having a malignant influence on, society; for it is certain that by these practices no one pretends to prove any supposed truths, detect any supposed error, or advance any sentiment whatever.

Christianity presents to all men one Supreme Being, the only object of worship, unchangeable, infinite, omniscient, all-wise, all-good, all-powerful, all-merciful, the God of all, and the Father of all. It develops one complete system of duties, fit for all times and all stations—for the monarch on the throne and the peasant in the cottage. It brings all men to the same level, and measures all by the same standard. It humbles in the dust the proud and the arrogant; it gives no heed to the glory of princes, or conquerors, or nobles. It exalts the lowly virtues, the love of peace, charity, humility, forgiveness, resignation, patience, purity, holiness. It teaches a moral and final accountability for every action. It proposes and sanctions finite precepts of no earthly reach, but such as are infinite, unchangeable, and eternal. Its rewards are the promises of immortal bliss; its punishments, a fearful and overwhelming retribution. It excuses no compromises of principles, and no paltering with sin. It acknowledges no sacrifice but of a broken and contrite spirit; no pardon but by repentance of heart and amendment of life. In its view this life is but the entrance upon existence— a transitory state of probation and trial—and the grave is the portal to that better world, where "God shall wipe all tears from our eyes; and there shall be no more death, neither sorrow, nor crying, neither shall there be any more pain."

To minds engrossed with such thoughts, and fixed in such a belief, what could there be seducing or satisfying in the things of this world? It would be impossible for them, for a moment, to put in competition the affairs of time with the dazzling splendors and awful judgments of eternity.

Decision of Judge Parsons of Massachusetts

The Supreme Court of Massachusetts, Judge Parsons presiding, gave a similar decision in favor of Christianity. It was a case in which a Christian Church in Falmouth had occasion to vindicate the Third

Article of the Constitution of the State, respecting religion and its support. Judge Parsons, who delivered the opinion of the court, was regarded by men of legal learning as the equal of Hale, Holt, Mansfield, Marshall, Kent, and Story. His decision, so luminous and full, in reference to Christianity and its relations to civil government, is, therefore, of the highest authority. The article of the Constitution of Massachusetts, on which the decision is based, is as follows—

> ART. 3. As the happiness of a people and the good order and preservation of civil government essentially depend on piety, religion, and morality; and as these cannot be generally diffused throughout the community but by the institution of a public worship of God, and of public institutions in piety, religion, and morality; therefore, to promote their happiness, and to secure the good order and preservation of their Government, the people of this Commonwealth have a right to invest their Legislature with power to authorize and require, and the Legislature shall from time to time authorize and require, the several towns, parishes, precincts, and other bodies politic, or religious societies, to make suitable provision, at their own expense, for the institutions of the public worship of God, and for the support or maintenance of public Protestant teachers of piety, religion, and morality, in all cases where such provision shall not be made voluntarily.

The decision made by Judge Parsons is as follows—

> The object of a free government is the promotion and security of its citizens. These effects cannot be produced but by the knowledge and practice of our moral duties, which comprehend all the social and civil obligations of man to man, and the citizen to the state. If the civil magistrate in any state could procure by his regulations an uniform practice of these duties, the Government of that state would be perfect.
>
> To obtain that perfection, it is not enough for the magistrate to define the rights of the several citizens, as they are related to life, liberty, property, and reputation, and to punish

those by whom they may be invaded. Wise laws, made to this end, and faithfully executed, may leave the people strangers to many of the enjoyments of civil and social life, without which their happiness will be extremely imperfect. Human laws cannot oblige to the performance of the duties of imperfect obligation; as the duties of charity and hospitality, benevolence, and good neighborhood; as the duties resulting from the relation of husband and wife, parent and child, of man to man as children of a common parent; and of real patriotism, by influencing every citizen to love his country and to obey all its laws. These are moral duties, flowing from the disposition of the heart, and not subject to the control of human legislation.

Neither can the laws prevent by temporal punishment secret offences committed without witness, to gratify malice, revenge, or any other passion, by assailing the most important and most estimable rights of others. For human tribunals cannot proceed against any crimes unless ascertained by evidence; and they are destitute of all power to prevent the commission of offences, unless by the feeble examples exhibited in the punishment of those who may be detected.

Civil government, therefore, availing itself only of its own powers, is extremely defective; and unless it could derive assistance from some superior power, whose laws extend to the temper and disposition of the human heart, and before whom no offence is secret, wretched indeed would be the state of man under a civil constitution of any form.

This most manifest truth has been felt by legislators in all ages; and as man is born not only a social but a religious being, so in the pagan world, false and absurd systems of religion were adopted and patronized by the magistrates, to remedy the defects necessarily existing in a government merely civil.

On these principles, tested by the experience of mankind and by the reflections of reason, the people of Massachusetts, in the frame of their Government, adopted and patronized a religion which, by its benign and energetic influences, might co-operate with human institutions, to promote and secure the happiness of the citizens, so far as might be consistent with the imperfections of man.

In selecting a religion, the people were not exposed to the hazard of choosing a false and defective religious system. Christianity had long been promulgated, its pretensions and excellencies well known, and its Divine authority admitted. This religion was found to rest on the basis of immortal truth; to contain a system of morals adapted to man in all possible ranks and conditions, situations and circumstances, by conforming to which he would be ameliorated and improved in all the relations of human life; and to furnish the most efficacious sanctions, by bringing to light a future state of retribution. And this religion, as understood by Protestants, tending by its effects to make every man submitting to its influences a better husband, parent, child, neighbor, citizen, and magistrate, was, by the people, established as a fundamental and essential part of their Constitution.

The manner in which this establishment was made is liberal, and consistent with the rights of conscience on religious subjects. As religious opinions, and the time and manner of expressing the homage due to the Governor of the universe, are points depending on the sincerity and belief of each individual, and do not concern the public interest, care is taken in the second article of the Declaration of Rights to guard these points from the interference of the civil magistrate; and no man can be hurt, molested, or restrained in his person, liberty, or estate for worshipping God in the manner and season most agreeable to the dictates of his own conscience, or for his religious profession or sentiment, provided he does not disturb the public peace, or obstruct others in their religious worship; in which case he is punished, not for his religious opinions or worship, but because he interrupts others in the enjoyment of the rights he claims for himself, or because he has broken the public peace.

Having secured liberty of conscience on the subject of religious opinion and worship for every man, whether Protestant or Catholic, Jew, Mohammedan, or Pagan, the Constitution then provides for the public teaching of the precepts and maxims of the religion of Protestant Christians to all the people. And for this purpose it is made the right and duty of all corporate religious societies to elect and support a public Protestant teacher of piety, religion, and morality; and the election and support of the teacher depend exclusively on the will of a majority of each society incorporated for those purposes. As public instruction requires persons who may be taught, every citizen may be enjoined to attend on some one of those teachers, at times and seasons stated by law, if there be any on whose instructions he can conscientiously attend.

In the election and support of a teacher, every member of the corporation is bound by the will of the majority; but as the great object of this provision was to secure the election and support of public Protestant teachers by corporate societies, and some members of any corporation might be of a sect or denomination of Protestant Christians different from the majority of the members, and might choose to unite with other Protestant Christians of their own sect or denomination in maintaining a public teacher, who by law was entitled to support, and on whose instruction they usually attended, indulgence was granted, that persons thus situated might have the money they contributed to the support of public worship, and of the public teachers aforesaid, appropriated to the support of the teacher on whose instructions they should attend.

Several objections have at times been made to this establishment, which may be reduced to three: that when a man disapproves of any religion, or of any supposed doctrine of any religion, to compel him by law to contribute money for public instruction in such religion, or doctrine, is an infraction of his liberty of conscience; that to compel a man to pay for public religious instructions on which he does not attend, and from which he can, therefore, derive no benefit, is unreasonable and intolerant; and that it is antichristian for any state to avail itself of the precepts and maxims of Christianity to support civil government, because the founder of it has declared that his kingdom is not of this world.

These objections go to the authority of the people to make this Constitution, which is not proper nor competent for us to bring into question. And although we are not able, and have no inclination, to assume the character of theologians, yet it may not be improper to make a few short observations to defend our Constitution from the charges of persecution, intolerance, and impiety.

When it is remembered that no man is compellable to attend on any religious instruction which he conscientiously disapproves, and that he is absolutely protected in the most perfect freedom of conscience in his religious opinions and worship, the first objection seems to mistake a man's conscience for his money, and to deny the State a right of levying and of appropriating the money of the citizens, at the will of the legislature, in which they are all represented. But as every citizen derives the security of his property and the fruits of his industry from the power of the State, so, as the price of his protection, be is bound to contribute, in common with his fellow-citizens, for the public use, so much of his property and for such public uses as the State shall direct. And if any individual can lawfully withhold his contribution because he dislikes the appropriation, the authority of the State to levy taxes would be annihilated; and without money it would soon cease to have any authority. But all moneys raised and appropriated for public uses by any corporation, pursuant to powers derived from the State, are raised and appropriated substantially by the authority of the State. And the people in their Constitution, instead of devolving the support of public teachers on the corporations by whom they should be elected, might have directed their support to be defrayed out of the public treasury, to be reimbursed by the levying and collection of State taxes. And against this mode of support the objection of an individual disapproving of the object of the public taxes would have the same weight it can have against the mode of public support through the medium of corporate taxation. In either case, it can have no weight to maintain a charge of persecution for conscience' sake. The great error

lies in not distinguishing between liberty of conscience in religious opinions and worship and the right of appropriating
money by the State. The former is an unalienable right, the
latter is surrendered to the State as the price of protection.

The second objection is that it is intolerant to compel a
man to pay for religious instruction from which, as he does
not hear it, he can derive no benefit. This objection is founded
wholly in mistake. The object of public religious instruction is
to teach and to enforce by suitable arguments the practice of a
system of correct morals among the people, and to form and
cultivate reasonable and just habits and manners, by which
every man's person and property are protected from outrage
and his personal and social enjoyments promoted and multiplied. From these effects every man derives the most important benefits, and, whether he be or be not an auditor of any
public teacher, he receives more solid and permanent advantages from this public instruction than the administration of
justice in courts of law can give him. The like objection may be
made by any man to the support of public schools if he have
no family who attend; and any man who has no lawsuit may
object to the support of judges and jurors on the same ground;
when if there were no courts of law he would unfortunately
find that causes for lawsuits would sufficiently abound.

The last objection is founded upon the supposed anti-
christian conduct of the State in availing itself of the precepts
and maxims of Christianity for the purposes of a more excellent civil government. It is admitted that the Founder of
this religion did not intend to erect a temporal dominion,
agreeably to the prejudices of his countrymen, but to reign in
the hearts of men by subduing their irregular appetites and
propensities, and by moulding their passions to the noblest
purposes. And it is one great excellence of his religion, that,
not pretending to worldly pomp and power, it is calculated
and accommodated to ameliorate the conduct and condition
of man under any form of civil government.

The objection goes further, and complains that Christianity is not left for its promulgation and support to the means

designed by its author, who requires not the assistance of man to effect his purposes and intentions. Our Constitution certainly provides for the punishment of many breaches of the laws of Christianity; not for the purpose of propping up the Christian religion, but because those breaches are offences against the laws of the State; and it is a civil as well as religious duty of the magistrate not to bear the sword in vain. But there are many precepts of Christianity of which the violation cannot be punished by human laws; and as the obedience to them is beneficial to civil society, the State has wisely taken care that they should be taught and also enforced by explaining their moral and religious sanctions, as they cannot be enforced by temporal punishments. And from the genius and temper of this religion, and from the benevolent character of its Author, we must conclude that it is his intention that man should be benefited by it in his civil and political relations, as well as in his individual capacity. And it remains for the objector to prove that the patronage of Christianity by the civil magistrate, induced by the tendency of its precepts to form good citizens, is not one of the means by which the knowledge of its doctrines was intended to be disseminated and preserved among the human race.

The last branch of the objection rests on the very correct position that the faith and precepts of the Christian religion are so interwoven that they must be taught together; whence it is inferred that the State, by enjoining instruction in its precepts, interferes with its doctrines, and assumes a power not intrusted to any human authority.

If the State claimed the absurd power of directing or controlling the faith of the citizens, there might be some ground for the objection. But no such power is claimed. The authority derived from the Constitution extends no further than to submit to the understandings of the people the evidence of truths deemed of public utility, leaving the weight of the evidence and the tendency of those truths to the conscience of every man.

Indeed, this objection must come from a willing objector; for it extends in its consequences to prohibit the State from providing for public instruction in many branches of useful knowledge which naturally tend to defeat the arguments of infidelity, to illustrate the doctrines of the Christian religion, and to confirm the faith of its professors.

As Christianity has the promise not only of this but of a future life, it cannot be denied that public instruction in piety, religion, and morality by Protestant teachers may have a beneficial effect beyond the present state of existence. And the people are to be applauded, as well for their benevolence as for their wisdom, that in selecting a religion whose precepts and sanctions might supply the defects in civil government, necessarily limited in its power, and supported only by temporal penalties, they adopted a religion founded in truth; which in its tendency will protect our property here, and may secure to us an inheritance in another and a better country.

Decision of the Supreme Court of New York in 1811

In the Supreme Court of New York in 1811, in the case of the people against Ruggles for *blasphemy*, the subject was fully and ably discussed by that eminent and upright judge, Chief-Justice Kent. In delivering the opinion of the Supreme Court, Judge Kent declared that—

> The authorities show that blasphemy against God, and contumelious reproaches and profane ridicule of Christ or the Holy Scriptures, which are equally treated as blasphemy, are offences punishable at common law, whether uttered by words or writings. The consequences may be less extensively pernicious in the one case than in the other; but in both instances the reviling is still an offence, because it tends to corrupt the morals of the people and to destroy good order. Such offences have always been considered independent of any religious establishment or the right of the Church. There is nothing in our manners and institutions which has prevented the application or the necessity of this point of common law. We stand equally in need now as formerly of all that moral discipline

and of those principles of virtue which help to bind society together. The people of this State, in common with the people of this country, profess the general doctrines of Christianity as the rule of their faith and practice; and to scandalize the Author of these doctrines is not only in a religious point of view extremely impious, but even in respect to the obligations due to society is a gross violation of decency and good order. Nothing could be more offensive to the virtuous part of the community, or more injurious to the tender morals of the young, than to declare such profanity lawful. It would go to confound all distinction between things sacred and profane; for, to use the words of one of the greatest oracles of human wisdom, "profane scoffing doth by little and little deface the reverence of religion," and who adds, in another place, "two principal causes have I ever known of atheism—curious controversies and profane scoffing." The very idea of jurisprudence, with the ancient lawgivers and philosophers, embraced the religion of the country.

Though the Constitution has discarded religious establishments, it does not forbid judicial cognizance of those offences against religion and morality which have no reference to any such establishment or to any particular form of government, but are punishable, because they strike at the root of moral obligation and weaken the security of the social ties. The legislative exposition of the Constitution is conformable to this view of it, Christianity in its enlarged sense, as a religion revealed and taught in the Bible, is not unknown to our law. *The Statute for preventing immorality* (*Laws*, Vol. I. p. 224) consecrates the first day of the week as holy time, and considers the violation of it immoral. *The Act concerning Oaths* (*Laws*, Vol. I. p. 405) recognizes the common law mode of administering an oath, "by laying the hand on and kissing the Gospels." Surely, then, we are bound to conclude that wicked and malicious words, writings, and actions which go to vilify those Gospels continue, as at common law, to be an offence against the public peace and safety. They are inconsistent with the reverence due to the administration of an oath, and, among other evil consequences, they tend to lessen in the public mind its religious sanction.

This decision was concurred in by all the associate judges on the bench with Chief-Justice Kent.

In 1821, a Convention to revise the Constitution of New York met in Albany, and this decision of the Supreme Court of the State was unsparingly denounced by General Root, who said "he wished for freedom of conscience, and that if judges undertake to support religion by the arm of the law it will be brought into abhorrence and contempt."

Opinion Given by Chief Justice Kent

Chancellor James Kent, the eminent son of the eminent jurist who gave this decision, in defending it, said—

> Such blasphemy was an outrage on public decorum, and if sanctioned by our tribunals would shock the moral sense of the country and degrade our character as a Christian people. The authors of our Constitution never meant to extirpate Christianity, more than they meant to extirpate common decency. It is in a degree recognized by the statutes for the observance of the Lord's day, and for the mode of administering oaths. The court never intended to interfere with any religious creeds or sects, or with religious discussions. They meant to preserve, so far as it came within their cognizance, the morals of the country, which rested on Christianity as the foundation. They meant to apply the principles of common law against blasphemy, which they did not believe the Constitution ever meant to abolish. ARE WE NOT A CHRISTIAN PEOPLE? Do not ninety-nine hundredths of our fellow-citizens hold the general truths of the Bible to be dear and sacred? To attack them with ribaldry and malice, in the presence of these very believers, must and ought to be a serious public offence. It disturbs, and annoys, and offends, and shocks, and corrupts the public taste. The common law, as applied to correct such profanity, is the application of com-

mon reason and natural justice to the security of the peace
and good order of society.

Mr. Tompkins, who was President of the Convention and Vice-
President of the United States, said—

> The court had never undertaken to uphold by the authority of
> law any particular sect, but they had interposed, and rightfully
> interposed, as the guardians of the public morals, to suppress
> those outrages on public opinion and public feeling which
> would otherwise reduce the community to a state of barba-
> rism, corrupt its purity, and debase the mind. He was not on
> the bench at the time when the decision alluded to took place,
> but he fully accorded in the opinions that were advanced, and
> he could not hear the calumnies that had gone forth against
> the judiciary on that subject, without regret and reprobation.
> No man of generous mind, no man who regarded public senti-
> ment, or that delicacy of feeling that lies at the foundation of
> moral purity, could defend such an outrage on public morals,
> or say that the decision was unmerited or unjust.
>
> Chancellor Kent never intended to declare Christianity the
> legal religion of the State, because that would be considering
> Christianity as the established religion of the State, and mak-
> ing it a civil or political institution. The Constitution had de-
> clared that there was to be "no discrimination or preference
> in religious profession or worship." But Christianity was, *in
> fact*, the religion of the people of this State; and that fact was
> the principle of the decision. The Christian religion was the
> foundation of all belief and expectation of a future state, and
> the source and security of moral obligation. To blaspheme
> the Author of that religion, and to defame it with wantonness
> and malice, was an offence against public morals, and injured
> the social ties and moral sense of the country; and in that
> view it was indictable.
>
> The legislature had repeatedly recognized the Christian
> religion, not as the religion of the country established by law,
> but as being in fact the actual religion of the people of this

State. The statute directing the administration of an oath referred to the Bible as a sanction to it, and on the ground that the Bible was a volume of Divine inspiration, and the oracle of the most affecting truths that could command the assent or awaken the fears or exercise the hopes of mankind. So the act for the religious observance of the Lord's day equally recognizes the universal belief in Christianity, and the moral obligation and eminent utility of its precepts. In this sense, we may consider the duties and injunctions of the Christian religion as interwoven with the law of the land, and as part and parcel of the common law.

Views of Judge Spencer in the Convention of New York in 1821

Chief-Justice Spencer, also an eminent jurist, said he was in favor of striking out the words *"no particular religion shall ever be declared or adjudged to be the law of the land."*

> I am opposed to this provision in the Constitution, as it would go to prevent punishment for blasphemy, and thereby endanger the morals of the community. By *particular* religion he understood it was the Christian religion, distinct from Judaism, Mohammedanism, &c., without regard to any particular sect of the Christian religion. Are we prepared to send forth to the people a provision in our Constitution that shall suffer any man to blaspheme, in the most malicious manner, his God and the religion of the Redeemer of the world? If this provision be sanctioned, it will put it out of the power of any court to punish for the most infamous blasphemy.

Rufus King, a statesman of ripe attainments, and possessing a national reputation, on the same point said—

> I hesitate in agreeing to the legal doctrine now recommended to our acceptance, and which seems to deny to the Christian

religion the acknowledgment, protection, and authority to which I have believed it to be by law entitled. The laws of every nation in Christendom have for ages acknowledged the Christian religion, and in virtue of the laws and statutes of England the Christian religion for many centuries has been acknowledged and established in that nation.

While all mankind are by our Constitution tolerated, and free to enjoy religious profession and worship within this State, yet the religious professions of the Pagan, the Mohammedan, and the Christian are not, in the eye of the law, of equal truth and excellence. According to the Christian system, men pass into a future state of existence when the deeds of their life become the subjects of rewards and punishments. The moral law rests upon the truth of this doctrine, without which it has no sufficient sanction. Our laws constantly refer to this revelation, and, by the oath which they prescribe, we appeal to the Supreme Being so to deal with us hereafter as we observe the obligations of our oaths.

The pagan world were and are without the mighty influence of this principle, which is proclaimed in the Christian system; their morals were destitute of its powerful sanction, while their oaths neither awakened the hopes nor the fears which a belief in Christianity inspires.

While the Constitution tolerates the religious professions and worship of all men, it does more in behalf of the religion of the gospel, and by acknowledging, and in a certain sense incorporating its truths into the laws of the land, we are restrained from adopting the proposed amendment whereby the Christian religion may lose that security which every other Christian nation is anxious to afford it.

Decision of the Supreme Court of New York in 1861

In 1861, the Supreme Court of New York sustained and repeated the ancient decisions of the courts of that and other States in favor of Christianity.

Decision of the Supreme Court.

February Term, 1861—*Justices Clarke, Sutherland, and Allen.*

In the case of Gustav Lindenmuller, Plaintiff in Error, *vs.* The People, Defendants in Error, convicted under the act of April, 1860, of giving dramatic representations on Sunday, the opinion of the court was given May 29, 1861. As the test case, and as involving important principles, the following *abstract* of the views of the court will command deserved attention and general approbation. The full opinion is very elaborate and voluminous. Judge Allen is understood to be its author—

> Christianity is part of the common law of this State, in the qualified sense that it is entitled to respect and protection as the acknowledged religion of the people. The right of unconstrained religious belief, and the proper expression of it, is guaranteed to all; but it must be exercised with strict regard to the equal rights of others; and when belief or unbelief leads to acts which interfere with the rights of conscience of those who represent the religion of the country as established—not by law, but by immemorial consent and usage—their acts may be restrained by legislation. If Christianity were established by law, it would be a civil or political institution, which it is not. It is, in fact, the religion of the people, and ever has been, and has been so recognized from the first by Constitutional Conventions, legislatures, and courts of justice.
>
> It is not disputed that Christianity is a part of the common law of England. By the Constitution of 1777, the common law as it was then in force, subject to legislative changes, and with specified exceptions, was, and ever has been, a part of the law of this State. The claim that the constitutional guarantees of religious liberty are inconsistent with the recognition of Christianity as the religion of the people, is repelled by the known character and history of the framers of the Constitution. They would not sacrifice their freedom or their religion. They and their forefathers were the friends and champions of both.
>
> In the several Constitutions of 1777, 1821, and 1848, and in the proceedings of the Constitutional Conventions, there are

abundant provisions and recitals very clearly recognizing some of the fundamental principles of the Christian religion, embodying the common faith of the community with its ministers and ordinances, existing without the aid of or political connection with the State, but as intimately connected with a good government, and the only sure basis of sound morals. These conventions also opened their meetings with prayer, observed the Christian Sabbath, and excepted that day from the time allowed to the Governor for returning bills to the legislature.

The recognition of different denominations of Christians does not detract from the force of the recognition of Christianity as the religion of the people: but it was intended to prevent the unnatural connection between Church and State. It was believed that Christianity would be purer and more prosperous by leaving the individual conscience free and untrammelled: and "wisdom is justified of her children" in the experiment; which could hardly be said if blasphemy, Sabbath-breaking, and kindred vices were protected by the Constitution. They prohibited a Church establishment, and left every man free to worship God according to the dictates of his own conscience, or not to worship, as he pleases. But they did not suppose they had abolished the Sabbath as a day of rest for all, and of Christian worship for those who were disposed to engage in it, or deprived themselves of the power to protect religious worshippers from unseemly interruptions. Compulsory worship is prohibited; and religious opinion is beyond the reach of law; but this liberty of conscience is entirely consistent with the existence in fact of the Christian religion, entitled to and enjoying the protection of the law. The public peace and safety are greatly dependent upon the protection of the religion of the country, and the preventing and punishing of offences against it and acts subversive of it. The claim of the defence, carried to its necessary sequence, is that the Bible and religion with all its ordinances, including the Sabbath, are as effectually abolished as they were in the Revolution of France, and so effectually abolished that duties may not be enforced as duties to the State, because they have been heretofore associated with sets of religious worship or connected with religious duties.

The opinion proceeds to cite the decisions in our own and other State courts in support of the views expressed, and shows that in the Constitutional Convention of 1821 the question was intelligently discussed and settled by our most eminent jurists, so as to make the interpretation of Chancellor Kent, in the case of The People vs. Ruggles, that the Christian religion was the law of the land, in the sense that it was pre-ferred over all ether religions, and entitled to the recognition and protection of the temporal courts as the common law of the State, the fixed meaning of the Constitution. The Chris-tian Sabbath, as one of the institutions of that religion, may he protected from desecration by such laws as the legislature may deem necessary to secure to the community the privilege of undisturbed worship, and to the day itself that outward re-spect and observance which may be deemed essential to the peace and good order of society; and this not as a duty to God, but as a duty to society and to the State. Upon this ground the law in question could be sustained; for the legislature are the sole judges of the acts to be prohibited with a view to the public peace, and as obstructing religious worship or bringing into contempt the religious institutions of the people.

Civil Basis of Sunday Laws

As a civil and political institution, the establishment and regu-lation of a Sabbath is within the just power of the civil Gov-ernment. Older than our Government, the framers of the Constitution did not abolish, alter, or weaken its sanction, but recognized it, as they might otherwise have established it. It is a law of our nature that one day in seven should be observed as a time of relaxation, and experience proves a day of weekly rest to be "of admirable service to a State, considered merely as a civil institution." (4 Bl. Com. 63.) Physical laws accord with the Decalogue. All interests require national uniformity in the day observed, and that its observance should be so far compulsory as to protect those who desire and are entitled to the day.

As a civil institution the sanction of the day is at the option of the legislature; but it is fit that the Christian Sabbath should be observed by a Christian people, and it does not detract from the moral or legal sanction of a statute that it conforms to the law of God, as recognized by the great majority of the people. Existing here by common law, all that the legislature attempts to do is to regulate its observance. The common law recognizes the day; contracts, land-redemption, &c., maturing on Sunday, must be performed on Saturday or Monday. Judicial acts on the Sabbath are mostly illegal. Work done on Sunday cannot be recovered for, &c.

The Christian Sabbath is, then, one of the civil institutions of the State, to which the business and duties of life are by the common law made to conform and adapt themselves. Nor is it a violation of the rights of conscience of any that the Sabbath of the people, immemorially enjoyed, sanctioned by common law, and recognized in the Constitution, should be respected and protected by the law-making power.

The existence of the Sabbath as a civil institution being conceded, as it must be, the right of the legislature to control and regulate it and its observance is a necessary sequence. Precedents are found in the statutes of every Government really or nominally Christian, from the period of Athelstan to the present day. Even the "Book of Sports" of James I., to which our attention has been called, prohibited, as unlawful, certain games and sports on Sunday, "*interludes*" included: so that Lindenmuller's theater would have been proscribed even by the Royal "Book of Sports."

Nearly all the States of the Union have passed laws against Sabbath-breaking, and prohibiting secular pursuits on that day; and in none have they been held repugnant to the Constitution, with the exception of California; while in most States the legislature has been upheld by the courts and sustained by well-reasoned opinions. As the Sabbath is older than the Government, and has been legislated upon by colonial and early State authorities, if there were any doubt about the meaning of the Constitution securing freedom in religion, the cotemporaneous and continued acts of the legislature under it would be very good evidence of the intent of its framers, and of the people who adopted it as their fundamental law. From 1788 downward, various statutes have been in force to prevent Sabbath-desecration, and prohibiting acts upon that day which would have been lawful on other days. Early in the history of the State Government, the objections made to the act of 1860 were taken before the Council of Revision to an act which undertook to regulate Sabbath-observance. The Council overruled the objections, and held them not well taken. The act now complained of compels no religious observance, and offences against it are punishable not as sins against God, but as injurious to society. It rests upon the same foundation as a multitude of other statutes—such as those against gambling, lotteries, horse-racing, &c.—laws which do restrain the citizen and deprive him of some of his rights; but the legislature have the right to prohibit acts injurious to the public, subversive of the Government, and which tend to the destruction of the morals of the people and to disturb the peace and good order of society. It is exclusively for the legislature to determine what acts should be prohibited as dangerous to the community. Give every one what are claimed as natural rights, and the list of *mala prohibita* of every civilized state would disappear, and civil offences would be confined to those acts which are *mala in se*; and a man may go naked through the streets, establish houses of prostitution, and keep a faro-table on every street-corner. This would be repugnant to every idea of a civilized government. It is the right of the citizen to be protected from offences against decency, and against acts which tend to corrupt the morals and debase the moral sense of the community. It is the right of the citizen that the Sabbath, as a civil institution, should be kept in a way not inconsistent with its purpose and the necessity out of which it grew as a day of rest, rather than as a day of riot and disorder, which would be to overthrow it and render it a curse rather than a blessing.

But it is urged that it is the right of the citizen to regard the Sabbath as a day of innocent recreation and amusement.

Who, then, is to judge and decide what amusements and pastimes are innocent, as having no direct or indirect baneful influence upon the community—as not in any way disturbing the peace and quiet of the public—as not interfering with the equally sacred rights of conscience of others? May not the legislature, like James I. cited to us as a precedent, declare what recreations are lawful and what are not lawful, as tending to a breach of the peace or a corruption of the morals of the people? That is not innocent which may operate injuriously upon the morals of old or young, which tends to interrupt the quiet worship of the Sabbath, and which grievously offends the moral sense of the community, and thus tends to a breach of the peace. It may well be that the legislature thought that a Sunday theater, with its drinking-saloons and its usual inducements to licentiousness and other kindred vices, was not consistent with the peace, good order, and safety of the city. They might well be of the opinion that such a place would be "a nursery of vice, a school of preparation to qualify young men for the gallows and young women for the brothel." But, whatever the reason may have been, it was a matter within the legislative discretion and power, and their will must stand as the reason of the law.

We could not, if we would, declare that innocent which they have adjudged baneful and have so prohibited. The act, in substance, declares a Sunday theater to be a nuisance, and deals with it as such. The Constitution provides for this case, by declaring that the liberty of conscience secured by it "shall not be so construed as to excuse acts of licentiousness, or justify practices inconsistent with the peace and safety of the State." The legislature place Sunday theaters in this category, and they are the sole judges. The act is clearly constitutional as dealing with and having respect to the Sabbath as a civil and political institution, and not affecting to interfere with religious belief or worship, faith or practice.

It was conceded upon the argument that the legislature could entirely prohibit theatrical exhibitions. This, I think, yields the whole argument; for, as the whole includes all its parts, the power of total suppression includes the power of regulation and partial suppression.

The conviction was right, and the judgment must be affirmed.

As the solemnity of an oath and its administration more properly belongs to the judges of courts than to any other class of civil officers, we insert in this place the form of an oath prescribed by an act of Congress—

CHAP. CXXVIII.—*An Act to prescribe an Oath of Office, and for other purposes.*

Be it enacted by the Senate and House of Representatives of the United States of America in Congress assembled, That hereafter every person elected or appointed to any office of honor or profit under the Government of the United States, either in the civil, military, or naval departments of the public service, excepting the President of the United States, shall, before entering upon the duties of such office, and before being entitled to any of the salary or other emoluments thereof, take and subscribe the following oath or affirmation—"I, A B, do solemnly swear (or affirm) that I have never voluntarily borne arms against the United States since I have been a citizen thereof; that I have voluntarily given no aid, countenance, counsel, or encouragement to persons engaged in armed hostility thereto; that I have neither sought nor accepted nor attempted to exercise the functions of any office whatever, under any authority or pretended authority in hostility to the United States; that I have not yielded a voluntary support to any pretended Government, authority, power, or constitution within the United States, hostile or inimical thereto. And I do further swear (or affirm) that, to the best of my knowledge and ability, I will support and defend the Constitution of the United States against all enemies, foreign and domestic; that I will bear true faith and allegiance to the same; that I take this obligation freely, without any mental reservation or purpose of evasion, and that I will well and faithfully discharge the duties of the office on which I am about to enter, so help me God;" which said oath, so taken and signed, shall be preserved among the files of the court, House of Congress, or department to which the said office may appertain. And any person who shall falsely take the said oath shall be guilty of perjury, and, on conviction, in addition to the penalties now prescribed for that offence, shall be deprived of his office, and rendered incapable forever after of holding any office or place under the United States.

Approved, July 2, 1862.

26

The Christian Element in the Civil War of the United States

The Civil War of the United States

THE civil war of the United States, rising out of the Southern rebellion, is the most important event in modern history, and will constitute the most instructive chapter in the annals of the American republic. It produced new policies in political parties, new and extraordinary action in the civil and military departments of the Government, developed the unselfish patriotism of the people, and brought out, in purity and efficiency, the Christian element of the nation. The thirteen colonies had, by a common patriotism and costly sacrifices in a successful and sublime struggle for liberty, achieved their independence, and founded a system of constitutional government unequalled for wisdom and excellence. Under the beneficent influences of their political and civil institutions, the nation advanced rapidly in prosperity and greatness, and soon rose to be a first-class political Power among the empires of earth.

Agriculture, commerce, manufactures, all industrial pursuits, in auspicious harmony with education, the arts and sciences, social culture, and the blessings of liberty and religion, had for eighty-four years poured out their blessings upon the nation. The prosperity and happiness of the people were unexampled in the history of the world.

Rebellion of the Southern States

In the midst of this national culture and prosperity at home, and of the highest international prestige abroad, the States of South Carolina, North Carolina, Georgia, Alabama, Louisiana, Mississippi, Florida, Arkansas, Texas, Tennessee, and Virginia seceded from the Union and rebelled against the General Government.

The incipient stages of the rebellion, and its insidious progress and results, are summed up in the following statement made by Edwin M. Stanton, Secretary of War under President Lincoln's administration—

> War Department, Washington, Feb. 14, 1862.
> The breaking out of a formidable insurrection, based on a conflict of political ideas, being an event without precedent in the United States, was necessarily attended with great confusion and perplexity of the public mind.
>
> Disloyalty, before unsuspected, suddenly became bold, and treason astonished the whole world by bringing at once into the field military forces superior in numbers to the standing army of the United States.
>
> Every department of the Government was paralyzed by treason. Defection appeared in the Senate, in the House of Representatives, in the Cabinet, and in the Federal courts. Ministers and consuls returned from foreign countries to enter the insurrectionary councils or land or naval force. Commanding and other officers in the army and in the navy betrayed their councils or deserted their posts for commands in the insurgent forces. Treason was flagrant in the revenue and the post-office services, as well as in the Territorial Governments and in the Indian reserves.
>
> Not only Governors, judges, legislators, and ministerial officers in the States, but even whole States, rushed one after another, with apparent unanimity, into rebellion.
>
> The capital was beleaguered, and its connection with all the States cut off. Even in the portions of the country which were most loyal, political combinations and societies were found furthering the work of disunion; while, from motives of

disloyalty or cupidity, or from excited passions or perverted sympathies, individuals were found furnishing men, money, materials of war, and supplies to the insurgents' military and naval forces. Armies, ships, fortifications, navy-yards, arsenals, military posts and garrisons, one after another were betrayed or abandoned to the insurgents.

Congress had not anticipated, and so had not provided for, the emergency. The municipal authorities were powerless and inactive. The judicial machinery seemed as if it had been designed not to sustain the Government, but to embarrass and betray it.

Foreign intervention was openly invited and industriously instigated by the abettors of the insurrection; and it became imminent, and has only been prevented by the practice of strict and impartial justice, with the most perfect moderation, in our intercourse with other nations. The public mind was alarmed and apprehensive, though fortunately not distracted or disheartened. It seemed to be doubtful whether the Federal Government, which one year ago had been thought a model worthy of universal acceptance, had indeed the ability to defend and maintain itself. Some reverses, which perhaps were unavoidable, suffered by newly-levied and insufficient forces, discouraged the loyal, and gave new hopes to the insurgents. Voluntary enlistment seemed to cease, and desertions commenced. Parties speculated upon the question whether conscription had not become necessary to fill up the armies of the United States.

In this emergency, the President felt it his duty to employ with energy the extraordinary power which the Constitution confides to him in cases of insurrection. He called into the field such military and naval forces authorized by existing laws as seemed necessary. He directed measures to prevent the use of the post-office for treasonable correspondence. He subjected those going to and from foreign countries to a new passport regulation; and he instituted a blockade, suspended the *habeas corpus* in various places, and caused persons who were represented to him as being engaged, or about to engage, in disloyal and treasonable practices, to be arrested by special civil as well as military agencies, and detained in military custody, when necessary, to prevent them and deter others from such practices. Examinations of such cases were instituted, and some of the persons so arrested have been discharged from time to time, under circumstances or upon conditions compatible, as was thought, with the public safety. Meantime, a favorable change of public opinion has occurred. The line between loyalty and disloyalty is plainly defined. The whole structure of the Government is firm and stable. Apprehensions of public danger and facilities for treasonable practices have diminished with the passions which prompted the heedless persons to adopt them.

The Cause of the Rebellion

The *occasion* of the rebellion was alleged violations of the constitutional rights of the Southern States by Congress and the Northern States, and the election of Abraham Lincoln, of Illinois, as President of the United States, in 1860; but the *cause* of the rebellion was the long-cherished purpose of Southern politicians and statesmen to establish a Southern Confederacy on the basis of human bondage. This principle was announced by Alexander H. Stephens, the Vice-President of the Southern Confederacy, in these words— "*The foundations of the new Government are laid upon the great truth that slavery— subordination of an inferior race—is the negro's natural and moral condition; that it is the first Government in the history of the world based upon this great physical, philosophical, and moral truth; and that* THE STONE WHICH WAS REJECTED BY THE FIRST BUILDERS IS, IN THIS EDIFICE, BECOME THE CHIEF STONE OF THE CORNER."

On the 11th day of April, 1861, by the authority of the Southern Confederacy, Fort Sumter, the property of the United States, was fired upon, and surrendered; and this inaugurated the civil war. This fact thrilled the heart of the nation, and developed the patriotism and loyalty of the twenty millions of people in the Northern States. The sublime and universal uprising of the people to vindicate the insulted flag of the nation, to preserve the integrity of the Government and the unity of the republic, had no parallel in history, and was worthy of a free and Christian nation.

President Lincoln, who had been inaugurated on the 4th of March, 1861, convened Congress in extraordinary session on the Fourth of July, 1861. His message, after revealing the facts and causes connected with the rebellion, and recommending such measures as the imperilled condition of the Government and country required, closed with these words of Christian trust and courage— "Having chosen our course without guile and with pure purpose, let us renew our trust in God, and go forward without fear, and with manly hearts."

Congress Declares the Object of the War

Congress, soon after its meeting, declared the object of the war, on the part of the General Government, in the following resolution—

> *That the present deplorable civil war has been forced upon the country by the disunionists of the Southern States, now in arms against the constitutional Government and in arms around the capital; that, in this national emergency, Congress, banishing all feeling of mere passion or resentment, will recollect only its duty to the whole country; that this war is not waged on their part in any spirit of oppression, or for any purpose of conquest or subjugation or purpose of overthrowing or interfering with the rights or established institutions of those States, but to defend and maintain the supremacy of the Constitution, and to preserve the Union, with all the dignity, equality, and rights of the several States unimpaired; and that as soon as these objects are accomplished the war ought to cease.*

Providence of God in the Way

This great conflict, in its progress, impressed the public mind with the providence and presence of God, and developed largely and hopefully the Christian element of the nation. All devout and thoughtful minds felt that God, while he chastened and humbled the nation on account of its sins, would again interpose for the preservation and perpetuity of the nation.

"I do not forget," says Choate, "that a power above man's power, a wisdom above man's wisdom, a reason above man's reason, may be traced, without the presumptuousness of fanaticism, in the fortunes of America. I do not forget that God has been in our history. Beyond that dazzling progress of art, society, thought, which is of his ordaining, although it may seem to a false philosophy a fatal and inevitable flaw—beyond this, *there has been, and there may be again, interposition, providential, exceptional, and direct, of that Supreme Agency without which no sparrow falleth.*"

This great conflict assumed, on the part of the North, the moral grandeur of a religious war; "not in the old fanatical sense of that phrase; not a war of violent excitement and passionate enthusiasm; not a war in which the crimes of cruel bigots are laid to the charge of a Divine impulse; but a war by itself, waged with dignified and solemn strength, with clean bands and pure hearts—a war calm and inevitable in its processes as the judgments of God."

Christian Element on the Side of the Constitution

The Christian element had greatly aided in achieving the liberties of the republic and in forming our constitutions of government; and now, as these were threatened with subversion and destruction, the Christian element again came forth with fresh and earnest life and energy to shield and save the institutions of the nation. The rebellion aimed not only to exterminate the life of a great Christian nation, but it was an attack on the Christian religion and the institutions of a Christian civilization which had grown out of it and were cherished and sustained by it. It was in harmony, therefore, with the traditional history and genius of the Christian religion that it should array its whole force against the rebellion, and rally, in its spirit and principles, to defend and support the General Govern-ment. The Christian element developed itself in two prominent ways.

The first was the infusion into the loyal heart of the nation of a profound and universal conviction of right, thus giving to the conflict the devotion and heroism of a Christian war. This fact gave to the martial enthusiasm of the people a high moral tone, inspired the armies amid the navy with an indomitable and a Divine courage, impressed the acts of the national and State Governments with a religious dignity and authority, and elevated and strengthened the Christian piety and patriotism of the people. The pulpits, churches, and ecclesiastical denominations of the nation sent forth their voices to encourage and support the Government, and were the source of its hope and the right arm of its strength.

The second result of the Christian element was, and will be, to reinvigorate and recover the republic, its institutions and functions of civil government, and its political and social character, from the decay and degeneracy of national virtue, and to replenish the life of the nation with increased moral vigor and purity. This is the genius and the uniform fruits of the Christian religion. It is not only the life of a nation, but it is the only means to restore national life when impaired and enfeebled from national vices and degeneracy.

Moral Uses of Civil War Stated by Milton

Civil war has its moral uses and results. "For civil war," says Milton, "that it is an evil I dispute not. But that it is the greatest of evils, that I stoutly deny. It doth indeed appear to the misjudging to be a worse calamity than bad government, because its miseries are collected together within a short space and time and may easily at one view be taken in and perceived, ... When the devil of tyranny hath gone into the body politic, he departs not but with struggles, and foaming, and great convulsions. Shall he, therefore, vex it forever, lest in going out he for a moment tear and rend it?"

The civil war, though attended with many direful calamities. yet in its moral uses and result, through the prevalence and power of the Christian religion, will realize, in the future of a renovated and an ennobled nation, those other weighty words of Milton, that the American nation "has not degenerated, nor is drooping to a fatal decay, but destined, by casting off the old and wrinkled skin of corruption, to outlive these pangs and wax young again, *and, entering the glorious ways of truth and prosperous virtue, become great and honorable in these latter ages.* Methinks I see in my mind a great and puissant nation rousing herself like a strong man after sleep, and shaking her invincible locks. Methinks I see her as an eagle mewing her mighty youth, *and kindling her undazzled eyes at the full mid-day beam, purging and unscaling her long-abused sight at the fountain itself of heavenly radiance*, while the whole noise of timorous and flocking birds, with those also that love the twilight, flutter about, amazed at what she means, and in their envious gabble would prognosticate a year of sects and schisms."

Rev. Dr. Brainerd's Fast-Day Sermon

Pastor of the Pine Street Presbyterian Church, the historic remembrances of which are so honorable to the Christian patriotism of its Revolutionary pastor (Rev. Mr. Duffield) and people, preached a sermon on the day of fasting and prayer appointed by the President of the United States, April 30, 1863, on "PATRIOTISM AIDING PIETY." That sermon has the following just statements on the moral and ennobling results of the great civil war of the country—

> We are also to confess the sins of our people, as did Daniel. This admission of our national sinfulness as the just cause of our national judgments does not compel us to believe that we are more guilty than other nations, nor that we have backslidden from the virtues of our fathers. Each age has its own virtues and crimes; and every age has crimes to deserve God's judgments. "Say not that the former times were better than these; for thou dost not judge wisely concerning this thing."
>
> My impression is, that in Sabbath-keeping, and attention to the means of grace, in efforts to diffuse universal education and the circulation of religious truth, by Bibles, tracts, churches, preaching and Sabbath-school teaching, in efforts to establish institutions for the aged, the imbecile, and the unfortunate, in endeavors to help the sailor, the prisoner, the widow and the orphan, our own age and land have developed a piety and charity not common in the world.
>
> Indeed, I cannot avoid suspecting that this war is on our hands not because this age and people are worse than other times and men, but because we have risen to a higher principle, a holier aim, and more adhesive regard to justice and humanity.

* * * * * * *

Our war is the proper protest of justice and humanity against injustice, cruelty, and perfidy. It is the struggle of right and philanthropy against outrage, oppression, and bloody treason.

We have received from ages gone by the fruits of man's long struggles for civil and religious liberty and the right of self-government; we have received a broad, beautiful, and healthful country, to every foot of whose soil we have an equal claim as citizens; we received a civil constitution, which embraces the concentrated wisdom of the sages of the Revolution; and we have taken up arms to declare that no traitor hand shall cut the telegraphic wire on which these blessings are passing down to other generations. The cry of humanity from ages to come has called us to this bloody strife. It is simply a defence of our own institutions.

In such a contest we are not to interpret any defeats into an impeachment of our national virtue or our cause, but rather regard them as a moral discipline through which God purifies us from remaining corruptions, to make us "perfect" for our high national mission "through sufferings."

The war has certainly unveiled an appalling amount of individual selfishness, covetousness, fraud, cowardice, and perfidy. But it has also shown in our people a pure, unselfish patriotism, developed in the pecuniary sacrifices of the rich and poor, in the devotion of their lives by hundreds of thousands of our young men, in the rich, unfailing charities, especially of our ladies, for the suffering soldiers, in the patient suffering of our martyrs in the hospital or on the battle-field. War has ennobled as well as tried us; and I must thank God to-day for the grace he has given you, as well as exhort you to be penitent for your sins.

While I say this, I still believe that our sufferings are made necessary by our sins, and that the nearer we approach to holiness the fewer will be our disasters and the more certain our triumphs.

The present chapter will record the manifold and beneficent developments of the Christian element during the progress of the civil war, and show how the Christian religion is in earnest and practical sympathy with liberty, the rights of man, and our noble system of civil government, and how our Christian republic, struggling for its life and institutions, is aided by the Christian element, and the national virtues cultivated and the people ennobled in their efforts to preserve the civil institutions of the country.

President Lincoln's Address on Leaving His Home for Washington

Abraham Lincoln, of Illinois, anticipating the formidable scenes which were to open with his inauguration, felt sincerely and deeply the need of God's upholding and guiding hand in the grave responsibilities he was about to assume. When leaving his home in Springfield, Illinois, for Washington, he said—

> MY FRIENDS—One who has never been placed in a like position cannot understand my feelings at this hour, nor the oppressive sadness I feel at this parting. For more than twenty-five years I have lived among you, and during all that time I have received nothing but kindness at your hands. Here the most cherished ties of earth were assumed. Here my children were born, and here one of them lies buried.
>
> To you, my friends, I owe all that I have, all that I am. All the strange, checkered past seems to crowd now upon my mind. To-day I leave you. I go to assume a task more difficult than that which devolved upon General Washington. Unless the great God who assisted him shall be with and aid me, I cannot prevail; but, if the same Omniscient mind and the same Almighty arm that directed and protected him shall guide and support me, I shall not fail; I shall succeed. Let us pray that the God of our fathers may not forsake us now. To him I commend you all. Permit me to ask that with equal sincerity and faith you will all invoke his wisdom and guidance for me.
>
> With these few words I must leave you, for how long I know not. Friends, one and all, I must now wish you an affectionate farewell.

On his way to Washington he was encircled in an atmosphere of prayer; and, whilst the people everywhere met to welcome him, multitudes of Christians were in earnest prayer to God for his safe journey and successful inauguration. In some cities banners were thrown across the streets with the significant motto, "We will pray for you."

On the day of his inauguration, the Christian public, impressed with the imperilled condition of the nation and for the personal safety of the President, then to assume his solemn responsibilities, met, in many places in the North, for special prayer, and continued their intercessions till after the scenes of the inauguration had closed. The only parallel to this was that of Washington. On the day of his inauguration, seventy-three years previous, all denominations of Christians in New York met, and held a season of special prayer for the new President and the Government then to be put into practical operation. Both cases were full of Christian interest and hopeful for the nation. After Mr. Lincoln's inauguration, and when the rebellion had cropped out into frightful proportions, he said that nothing encouraged him so much as to know that Christians were praying for him.

Fort Sumter

The first war-scene in the great conflict was at Fort Sumter; and it was enveloped in an atmosphere of prayer. The flag of the Union, the symbol of the nationality of the republic, was to be unfurled over the fort. The flag-staff was planted, and the banner about to be run up. As Major Anderson, the commander of the fort, and his little band of loyal soldiers, gathered round the flag-staff, they all knelt with reverence, and the chaplain led in a fervent prayer to Almighty God to protect the flag and preserve the nation. After the prayer, the banner went up and floated over the fort; but in two days it was stricken down.

Major Anderson, in describing his course while in command of Fort Sumter, says—

> God has really seemed to bless us in every important step we have taken since I have been in command. My constant

appeal has been for wisdom and understanding of his Divine will, and for strength of purpose and resolution to perform my whole duty. We have been aided, too, by the prayers of our Christian friends. I humbly believe he has graciously listened to our prayers. I hope all Christians of our beloved country will continue in prayer, entreating God to have mercy on our people, to save us from our sins, and to unite us again as a people, not only in our civil Government, but one people in our love and adoration of his holy name.

I put my trust in God; and I firmly believe that God put it into my heart to do what I did. I believe, truly, that every act that was performed in that harbor from the 21st of November, when I took command, was ruled by that God whom we all should adore, and whom we must adore if we wish to do well both in this world and the next. I believe that every act done there was necessary in order to bring up the public heart to that sentiment of patriotism which now pervades throughout the North.

Prevalence of Prayer

The spirit and power of prayer became prevalent throughout the North as the great conflict progressed. The Christian public and all serious-minded men felt that the moral influence of prayer must guide and guard the national armaments and hover over and inspire our armies. Hence, in every closet, round every family altar, in every praying circle, in the Sabbath convocation, there was an outpouring of fervent prayer that God would vindicate the cause of the Government and suppress speedily the rebellion.

The various ministers of Providence, Rhode Island, met and issued, in June, 1861, the following circular—

To the Pastors, Churches, and Congregations of the State.
Christian Brethren and Fellow-Citizens—

We, who are of different denominations, and are resident together in this city, take a liberty, which you will not count assumption, to propose to you an observance of special prayer, now, for our country. We deem the exercises of such a service entirely appropriate to the Sabbath, and the Sabbath the day of the seven for the fullest attendance upon it, and for its highest influence for good. And, hoping that if it be a little deferred it may be the more extensively and effectually observed, we name for it the third Sabbath, occurring on the 19th day, of this month, May, 1861.

We make this proposal, because you and we all believe in a special Providence, and that its most special interpositions are granted to united, effectual, fervent prayer, and because, also, our precious country now urgently needs great Divine doings for us. Already have we, more or less, betaken ourselves to the mercy-seat for these great Divine movements on our behalf. And, when we had scarcely stammered the timid preface to our petition, a wonder answered that will long amaze the thoughtful to adoration. Up to that moment, doubtful in ourselves and distrustful of one another, in an instant our millions leaped to their feet, a giant unit of patriotism; life and property largely offered one readiest gift for our glorious land and its best, noblest Government on earth. This is the Lord's doing; it is marvellous in our eyes. For it let our glad thanksgivings mingle and vie with all the prayer we have yet to offer on this behalf. Indeed, let us daily hold our gratitude faithful before God for each new brightening omen.

Yet we have vast needs remaining, which he only can meet. Our first infinite need is, ever devoutly to feel that he is our all in all of help, and with all our heart to be delightedly jealous for his sole honor, as being all this to us. And to so great grace we can attain only as his Spirit shall steadily move us to it. We need to know that the battle is not to the strong, except as he shall fill the measure of their needed strength every moment of their conflict unto victory. Our brave patriotism, also, he only can hold steadfast, ever growing stronger. But all our great needs he will meet, if we but duly ask, and, duly asking, also duly act. "Ask," he says, "and ye shall receive." "If ye agree, it shall be done unto you."

And let us begin our requests where it so becomes sinners to begin, penitently co nfessing to God our own and our nation's sins, and imploring him most graciously to forgive them all, and by his Spirit most effectually to turn ourselves and our whole people from them all; we, while we so pray, turning ourselves "with full purpose of heart," in the Spirit's power, from all our Heaven-offending ways. And let us appeal to our infinite Helper that he will give complete and speedy success to the whole right in this struggle for it, and will do it in so clear lighting down of his own mighty arm that the praise shall rise from all hearts, as to him alone; and let us ask that he will so do it as chiefly to magnify peace while, if it must be, he also duly magnifies righteous war. Let us beseech him that he will ever guide and guard all our rulers, leaders, soldiers, and people; that he will greatly bless our own citizen soldiery and their homes; that he will signally, in highest mercy, revolutionize the whole mind of the South to repentance, to thorough Christian government and liberty, will also fix all minds in the North, from this time, complete and immovable in the principles of such government and liberty, and that he will wonderfully annihilate the power of Satan from this national scene of wicked, treacherous, bloody usurpation and oppression, and will issue it all in the most glorious salvation of souls by his Spirit: that all these things, and far more, he will do, for the sake of his dear Son.

For so great a rescue and blessing of our country, should not our whole State, on the day set a part, be one importunate concert of the prayerful, in the closet, the family, the prayer-meeting, and the house of prayer?

Yours, for Christ and onr country's cause.

Prayer Meeting in the Presbyterian General Assembly

In the month of May, 1861, the General Assembly of the Presbyterian Church (New School) met at Syracuse, New York. During their session special seasons of prayer were set apart, in which the piety and patriotism of the Assembly were delightfully developed. The following is an account of the second prayer-meeting of the Assembly—

The second prayer-meeting, held last evening by the General Assembly in Rev. Dr. Canfield's church, was remarkable for the number of persons present, the exciting character of the exercises, and the distinguished men who participated. Rev. Dr. Jenkins, of Philadelphia, presided, and various prayers were offered and numerous addresses made. The character of all the exercises was that of earnest Christian patriotism, and the warmest love for Christ and our country. Rev. Dr. Nelson, from St. Louis, said that the recent conflict in that city between the citizens and soldiers was almost within sight of his church. He had faith in the steadfastness of the State, and did not believe she would be faithless to her duty or the Constitution. It was his conviction that God designed it as a chastisement and as a means of grace to the country. He thought the camp was now one of the most interesting fields of Christian labor, and there, he thought, might be put forth the most successful religious efforts. Thousands were first giving themselves to their country, and then to their God. He saw no reason to doubt that there would yet be an extensive camp-revival.

Rev. Mr. Emerson, from the "Pea-Patch" in Delaware, said that he had recently visited the fort in his neighborhood. He found large numbers of pious young men among the soldiers, some of whom were very active as Christians. Some who never before had manifested any interest in religion were earnest readers of the Bible. Two or three young men had proposed a prayer-meeting and the study of the Scriptures. Some of their comrades objected, but offered to compromise by having the Bible read and omitting the prayers. This was done; but it resulted in the establishment of both exercises, and some conversions. They said they had given themselves to their country, and, as they might soon be called to die for her, they had resolved to die Christians. They were having the most common soldiers' fare, and sleeping upon straw, and yet they were happy and contented. He added that Delaware was loyal to the country and the Constitution, and always had been, and always would be; and, though small, she was the "Diamond" State. Delaware was the first to adopt the Constitution, and would be the last to desert it.

Rev. Dr. Darling, of Philadelphia, said he was delighted to hear from his brother Emerson such gratifying details from Fort Delaware. He had two of the most valued young men in his church in that fortress. Just before he left home, he saw them, and they united together in prayer. Not many days since, in Philadelphia, he stood by the bedside of the venerable Dr. Nott, who then was supposed to be on his dying bed. It was at that period when Washington City was in peril. Drums were heard, and the tramp and cheers of soldiers. The venerable man, stirred in his heart by the passing events, roused himself up, and said, "I don't know how you young men stand this, but it almost takes the heart out of me. I saw the Constitution adopted, but I don't want to live to see it destroyed." Dr. Darling said, I see no cause for despondency. The hour of trial has come. The peril is upon us. Yet I am more proud than ever of my country. Can we expect vigor without hardships, or manhood without perils? England has passed through fiery trials, been baptized in blood, and this has made her what she is— established her as the mistress of the world.

Rev. Asa Eaton said there was in the house, near him, a venerable man, who was nearly a century old, who had been a minister of the gospel over sixty years! He alluded to the Rev. Mr. Waldo. The venerable man, still hale and healthy, was led forward, and mounted the platform with ease and almost elasticity, although now ninety-nine years old! In a clear and almost powerful voice, with the vast audience almost hushed to stillness, he spoke a few words and then uttered a brief but most solemn, expressive prayer. He said he remembered well the battles of Lexington and Bunker Hill, being then thirteen years of age. He felt how important was the War, and he was only afraid then it would be over before he would be old enough to join in it. He never expected to live to see the Constitution destroyed. Nothing had ever grieved him so much as the present state of things. He knew there were lovely men at the South, good Christian men, but wicked people were now trying to ruin the country and destroy the Union. But he was glad there was unanimity North. This harmony was delightful. He was glad the Constitution was to be sustained; but one of the best ways to maintain it was through the prayers of the children of God.

Rev. Dr. Cox introduced Rev. Pastor Fische. He expressed great delight in having had his stay prolonged in this country so that he could visit this General Assembly and be present at the prayer-meeting. He arrived here in September, and had witnessed the canvass and saw all the war-movements. The Protestants of Europe are looking to your struggles with intense interest. Political and religious liberty is invoked in your efforts. If you succeed, it will be a day of rejoicing with us. You are remembered in our prayer-meetings. War is a great evil, but out of it in France has come much good. The army is the best part of the people, but yet they are all forced soldiers. They often cut off their fingers to escape enlistment. Among them the Bible is studied, and this book is freely circulated. We will pray for you, and you must pray for us. Your country is a blessed country. You are the hot current which carries religious liberty and civilization everywhere.

Rev. Mr. Canfield, the pastor of the church, said some surprise had been expressed that there was no flag floating from its steeple. It was hardly necessary. It was *here* (putting his hand upon his heart) with him and his people. The meeting had been in session over two hours, and no one seemed willing to have it terminate. But all things must have an end, and the presiding officer, Rev. Dr. Jenkins, said it had been proposed that another meeting would be held the succeeding (Saturday) evening. "I am not certain," said he, "that these are not the best days this country ever saw." After the benediction was pronounced, the choir, accompanied by the organ and the entire audience, sang superbly the "Star-Spangled Banner." The entire exercises of the evening were of the most exciting, but chastened, patriotic, Christian character.

Forms of Prayer for Episcopalian Churches

The Right Reverend Bishop Potter, of the Episcopal Church issued the following form of prayer, to be used in the churches in his diocese—

O Almighty God, who art a strong tower of defence to those who put their trust in thee, whose power no creature is able to resist, we make our humble cry to thee in this hour of our country's need. Thy property is always to have mercy. Deal not with us according to our sins, neither reward us according to our iniquities; but stretch forth the right hand of thy majesty, and be our defence for thy name's sake. Have pity upon our brethren who are in arms against the constituted authorities of the land, and show them the error of their way. Shed upon the counsels of our rulers the spirit of wisdom and moderation and firmness, and unite the hearts of our people as the heart of one man in upholding the supremacy of law and the cause of justice and peace. Abate the violence of passion; banish pride and prejudice from every heart, and incline us all to trust in thy righteous providence and to be ready for every duty. And oh that in thy great mercy thou wouldst hasten the return of unity and concord to our borders, and so order all things that peace and happiness, truth and justice, religion and piety, may be established among us for all generations. These things, and whatever else thou shalt see to be necessary and convenient for us, we humbly beg, through the merits and mediation of Jesus Cinrist our Lord and Saviour. Amen.

The Bishop of Minnesota issued the following pastoral letter and form of prayer—

FARIBAULT, April 17, 1861.

To the Clergy and Congregations of the Diocese of Minnesota.
DEAR BRETHREN:-Our beloved country is imperilled by civil war. Every tlning which the Christian and patriot holds dear is in jeopardy. Our country's flag is dishonored. Our Government is defied. Our laws are broken. Bitterest hatred is kindled between sections of a common country. Brother is arrayed against brother. Every thing seems to foreshadow the most awful strife which has ever darkened our land. The duty of the Christian is plain. He must be loyal to the Government. Our only hope in this day of peril, under the protection of Almighty God, is to stand firm as loyal and law-abiding citizens. Every tie of party, friendship, and kindred sinks into in-

significance before the impending danger. The lessons of our holy religion teach loyalty—first, loyalty to God, and second, loyalty to those whom the providence of God has made the guardians of our country.

The duty is no less plain, as followers of Jesus Christ, to seek and pray for peace. Let us, therefore, be careful that no word or deed of ours fans the flame of discord. Let us ever have the olive-branch in our hands and the love of God in our hearts. Let the memory of happier days tell us of the time when our fathers stood shoulder to shoulder in fighting the battles of freedom.

Disobedience to God, irreverence for his holy name and word, disloyalty to Government, and disregard of law, are the causes which have brought the nation to the verge of ruin, and of which no portion of the land is guiltless.

I earnestly beseech you, therefore, in this day of a common sorrow, to turn with all your hearts unto God. Let our churches be vocal with prayer; let our closets witness our devotions; let us not look to any arm of flesh, but to God, who alone can deliver us from our peril.

I hereby set forth the following prayer, to be used after the General Thanksgiving at daily morning and evening prayer. Praying God to bless you all, I am your friend and bishop,

HENRY B. WHIPPLE, *Bishop of Minnesota.*

PRAYER

Almighty and everlasting God, our only refuge in the hour of peril, look with pity upon the desolations of our beloved country. Our sins have called for thy righteous judgments. We confess our guilt and bewail our transgressions. O Lord, in thy judgment remember mercy. Take away from us all hatred and strife. Spare us, for thy Church's sake, for the sake of thy dear Son, from the calamities of civil war which have fallen upon us. Give thy Holy Spirit to our rulers, that they may, under thy protection, save this great nation from anarchy and ruin. Preserve them from all blindness, pride, prejudice, and enmity. Give unto the people unity, a love of justice, and an understanding heart. Restrain the wrath of man, and save the effusion of blood. Bring again the blessings of peace, and grant unto us a heart to serve thee and walk before thee in holiness all the days of our life. These things, which we are not worthy to ask, we humbly beg, for the sake of thy dear Son our Lord and Saviour, Jesus Christ. Amen.

The following prayer was recommended to be used by the congregations of the United Brethren—

To the Congregations of the United Brethren in the Northern District of the United States.
We recommend that during the continuance of the present civil war the subjoined petitions be substituted for the petitions in our Church Litany designated as "to be prayed in time of war."

YOUR BRETHREN OF THE PROVINCIAL
ELDERS' CONFERENCE.

Bethlehem, September 1, 1861.

O thou Almighty Lord God of Hosts, who rulest and commandest all things,
We call upon thee in this time of our trouble;
Take our cause into thine own hands:
O Lord, come and help us!
Save and defend our country;
Revive in all hearts a spirit of devotion to the public good;
Fill the President of the United States with the spirit of wisdom and understanding;
Let thy Divine protection and guidance be over all who serve in council or in the field; and so rule their hearts and strengthen their hands that they may preserve to us the goodly heritage which thou gavest to our fathers;
Forgive our adversaries, and turn again their hearts toward us;
Cause us to humble ourselves under thy mighty hand, and to confess and bewail the grievous sins which have drawn these thy judgments upon us;

Turn us, O God of our salvation, and cause thine anger toward us to cease;

Oh, bring this unhappy war to a speedy end, and let a just and lasting peace be soon again established, to the glory of thy name.

Hear us, gracious Lord and God.

Thou Helper of all who flee to thee for succor,

We commend to thy almighty care and protection all those who have gone forth in our defence ;

Guard them, we beseech thee, from the dangers that beset their way; from sickness, from the violence of enemies, and from every peril to which they may be exposed;

Give them comfort in every time of their need, and a sure confidence in thee; and of thy great goodness restore them to us, in due time, in health and safety.

Hear us, gracious Lord and God.

Bishop Purcell, of the Catholic Church, in the Diocese of Cincinnati, issued the following pastoral circular—

To the Right Reverend Prelates, the Very Reverend and Reverend Clergy and beloved Laity of the Province of Cincinnati.
BELOVED BRETHREN AND FELLOW-SERVANTS OF CHRIST—
The Ecclesiastical Council of the province convenes in this city tomorrow. It convenes under such circumstances as were never before witnessed in this glorious republic since the proud day when it won its high rank among the nations of the earth. The hearts of citizens and friends are alienated. The hands of brothers are raised to shed each others' life-blood. The iron bands of our highways, which we once fondly hoped would link us in indissoluble union, and the noble rivers which bear the rich products of our lands and the creations of our sciences and arts to our respective marts and homes, have failed to keep us, what God and our fathers intended we should be, one people.

In the midst of the most formidable preparations of our fellow-citizens for mutual destruction, the Church, in her peaceful meeting, gives us a glimpse of the peace of the heavenly Jerusalem. She renews the blessings of the "Truce of God." We pray God that hostilities may cease, that wiser and better counsels may prevail, and that the great heart of this magnificent land which our Council represents—the States of Ohio, Kentucky, Indiana, Michigan—may send its throbbing pulses of fraternal love to the most distant extremities of our common country. We ought to be one people. We are all the children of the same God, whom we should worship in peace; we pray for all and love all in spirit and in truth. May the Spirit of Peace, the Comforter, sent us by Jesus Christ, descend as the dove, to breathe holy desires and righteous counsels into every heart, and dispose the minds of Catholics and Protestants to see in each other not enemies, but brethren, and that all may work with willing hands and hearts for the tranquillity and glory of our common country.

J. B. Purcell, *Archbishop of Cincinnati.*

Statement of a Religious Paper on the Prevalence of Prayer

"There has probably been more prayer," said a religious paper, "offered for this country, within the last twelve months, than in all the years before since the war of the Revolution. And it is now being answered. In fact, our successes began at the point of our lowest humiliation; and have continued to advance ever since. In our darkest hour we had to fall back upon the moral convictions which lie at the foundation of our system, the Divine right of liberty and popular government, and the necessity of Providential protection for the triumph of the right. When we hardly believed that we any longer had a Government, when the nation was reeling with the public confusion and the fear that our whole system was collapsing, the conviction arose strong in the religious mind that God would not, could not, give it over to destruction; for, notwithstanding its great corruptions, it was full of churches and other institutions of faith and beneficence; it had millions of praying people; it had momentous connections with the foreign interests of religion and civilization. It appeared impossible that God could cast it away while thus intimately related to his general kingdom in the world. And, then, its history was apparently but begun; not only had its career been comparatively brief in time, but, great as had been its advances in industry, invention, commerce, education, it had evidently only begun to develop its vigor and resources.

"It became the general sense that we were passing through an ordeal of purification rather than destruction. A profound moral feeling began to pervade the sorrow-stricken mind of the country. Good men betook themselves to importunate prayer. Public fasts were observed; religious assemblies were held in behalf of the country. Almost every pulpit discussed public affairs from a religious stand-point; our social religious occasions soon became characterized by a profound sympathy with, and supplications for, the public interest; our family prayers were burdened with the same theme; and millions of devout men and women mourned in their closets of devotion over the national sins and perils.

"Never since the American Revolution have the masses of the American people entertained so general and impressive a conviction of God's overruling providence in human affairs as at the present time.

"Never before have so many earnest hearts been lifted in prayer, night and day, to the God of battles as now—mothers praying for their sons, sisters for their brothers, wives for their husbands. Never in the thousands of Christian pulpits of the free States has the gospel been more earnestly, broadly, and fervently preached than during the present moral crisis of the age. It is the testimony of many ministers that the exercise of public prayer in the sanctuary— prayer for the outpouring of God's Spirit upon the people, for victories to our armies, for the binding up of wounded hearts at home, for the sick languishing in hospitals, for the Divine guidance of the President and all others in authority—never has been more impressive, hearty, and touching than in these very Sabbath days whose quietude has been disturbed by the echoes of war.

"Can any one doubt that the prevailing moral tone of the public mind is constantly improving? Every day witnesses the cheering growth of a general sentiment favoring liberty and justice, prompting to individual self-sacrifice, inspiring a courageous spirit among the masses, kindling a general zeal of patriotism, and maintaining a cheerful faith that God will give final victory to the right.

"The religious spirit of the nation, instead of decaying, is daily making men's hearts more reverent, more humble, more courageous, and more worthy of our first national heritage of liberty, which God is now a second time purifying by fire!"

President Appoints a Day of Fasting and Prayer

The President of the United States, by a joint resolution of request from Congress, issued, on the 12th day of August, 1861, a proclamation appointing the last Thursday of September ensuing "as a day of humiliation, prayer, and fasting, ... to the end that the united prayers of the nation may ascend to the throne of grace and bring down plentiful blessings upon our own country." The proclamation will be found in a former chapter of this volume. The day was devoutly observed throughout the loyal States and in the capital of the nation, and exerted a healthful religious influence upon the people.

The Action of the Various Christian Denominations on the State of the Country.

The Methodist Episcopal New York Conference,
March, 1861.

Whereas an attack has been made on the flag of our country, in violation of the public peace, and threatening the existence of our Government—and whereas we love peace and are the ministers of the Prince of peace, yet hold it to be the duty of all men to love their country and to cherish freedom, and especially in times of peril to offer our civil rulers our aid and sympathy: therefore,

Resolved, That we do here and now declare our earnest and entire sympathy with the cause of our country in this conflict, and our purpose to use all means legitimate to our calling to sustain the Governnnent of the United States in defence and support of the Constitution and the nation's welfare.

Resolved, That, in duty bound, we will not cease to pray in public and in private for the Divine blessing upon our country, for the suppression of rebellion, and the speedy restoration of peace, especially beseeching Almighty God that, if in his justice he chastise us, his mercies may so temper his wrath that we may not be wholly destroyed.

ERIE ANNUAL CONFERENCE OF THE METHODIST EPISCOPAL CHURCH OF PENNSYLVANIA, APRIL, 1861.
Resolved, That, in its prompt and vigorous efforts to preserve the Union, and suppress rebellion and treason, the Government at Washington shall have our earnest sympathy and prayers, our hearty approval and co-operation.

Resolved, That we are opposed to all compromises with armed traitors, believing that unconditional submission to the Constitution and laws of our country is a duty which our Government has both the right and power to enforce.

Resolved, That we confidently trust the time has come when slavery shall no longer be the controlling power either in our domestic or foreign relations, but that its influence in the affairs of the nation shall grow less and less, until it shall please God to remove the great evil altogether.

Resolved, That, without intending any improper interference with the affairs of the army, we respectfully and earnestly recommend to all officers in command to respect the obligations of the holy Sabbath, and to carefully guard the morals of our soldiers against those evils which are but too common to a state of war. Our confidence in the justice of our cause inspires the belief that complete success will be all the more certain and speedy by the careful observance of Christian morals.

RHODE ISLAND EVANGELICAL ASSOCIATION, JUNE, 1861.
The Rhode Island Evangelical Consociation assembles in a day of grave events. Several States of this Union, bound to the national life, as all others, by all that is sacred in league and public compact, have joined in a revolt fomented and enacted by robbery, treason, and violence unparalleled in the history of nations.

We therefore declare our unqualified condemnation of this rebellion, begun in shameless treason, carried on in foulest corruption and remorseless violence. We judge it a scheme abhorred of God, and deserving the abhorrence of all good men to the end of time.

As Christian men and ministers of the gospel, we deplore with inexpressible grief the collusion, in this iniquitous and devastating usurpation, of Christian ministers and professed disciples of Him at whose blessed kingdom these crimes are destructive strokes; and while we deplore their participation in these "deeds of darkness," we sincerely pray, "Father, forgive: they know not what they do."

We also deeply sympathize with the numbers enforced by dominant terrorism into silence, flight, or position in which love of life and love of country distress their choice; and we remember them as bound with them.

We also would assure the Government of the United States of our unceasinng prayers to Heaven on their behalf; and we entreat all who direct affairs to continue to temper the retributions of justice with humane execution; to make full provision for the moral and religious wants of the army by chaplains, and by such regulations and dissemination of religious reading as shall shield our beloved friends engaged in the national service from the fatal contaminations of an otherwise debased camp.

We also recognize with thanks to God the numbers of pious men, both officers and privates, drawn from our churches and congregations; and we assure them of our constant and affectionate remembrance.

This Consociation would also record their special approval of the decisive, generous, and timely patriotism of his Excellency the Governor of this State, of the officers of the Government, and of the Assembly co-operating with him and them.

We therefore pledge to one another, and to all engaged in the support of our Government, our earnest supplications that the Divine blessing and continued sympathy may attend them in a complete success.

HUDSON RIVER BAPTIST ASSOCIATION OF NEW YORK,
JUNE, 1861.

The committee appointed to consider the duties that pertain to our relations as Christian citizens and churches to the nation at large and the Government that protects us, beg leave to report the following statement, preamble, and resolutions—

STATEMENT.

The letters from the churches that compose this association have expressed, in the most solemn manner, their sense of painful bereavement caused by the departure of their brethren, fellow-worshippers, and Sabbath-school teachers, from their various fields of labor, to the camp and the battle-field for the defence of our country against an armed rebellion that seeks the utter destruction of the Constitution that shelters us, and is aiming fatal blows at the foundation of all effective government, of all righteous law, of all social order, and of national prosperity. At the same time, these letters declare, without any exception, the fixed determination of our brethren, by means of every sacrifice that God may permit them to offer, to uphold our Federal Government in the deadly contest that has been ruthlessly forced upon it, until it shall have re-established its supreme authority over every part of its domain whence that authority has been defied, and shall have caused our desecrated banner to wave again over every spot of earth whence the hand of treason may have displaced it.

We hail with joy, with hope, and responsive devotion to a common cause the expression of these stern and sacred resolves as the expression of "sentiments proper to the present crisis."

Therefore, the Committee propose to this association the following preamble and resolutions for their consideration and adoption—

PREAMBLE.

Whereas the Government of the United States, which was bequeathed to us by our fathers, who established it by the sacrifice of blood and of treasure for the protection of their own inalienable rights and of the children that should come after them, is now engaged in a struggle with banded and armed traitors for its very existence; and

Whereas, These men, the leaders of this war, having recognized the supreme authority of what is called "The Confederate States of America," have proclaimed as the vital doctrine of their coalition that "All government begins with usurpation and is continued by force;

"That nature puts the ruling elements uppermost, and the masses below and subject to those elements;

"That less than this is not a government;

"That the right to govern resides with a very small minority; and the duty to obey is inherent in the great mass of mankind;

"And that man's right of property in man is the true cornerstone of a republic, and of all permanent social prosperity."

RESOLUTIONS.

Therefore, *Resolved*, That we solemnly abjure, denounce, and resist these doctrines, as being essentially antichristian, pagan, barbarous, inhuman.

Resolved, That we declare it to be our solemn conviction, as Christian men, who take the word of God as our rule of faith and practice, that the cause which the Government of the United States is now sustaining by its arms is the cause of righteousness, of freedom, and of humanity; and that for its support we pledge our toils, our prayers, "our lives, our fortunes, and our sacred honor."

Resolved, That in the spontaneous uprising of twenty millions of people for the support and honor of our country's flag we recognize not the working of a blind sentiment or unreasoning passion, but the out-gush of a stronger, holier love, carrying the whole force of our moral nature with it, because it is nourished by those lofty and eternal *ideas* which emanate from the mind of God, which were enshrined in the religion of our Messiah's cross, which are associated with the sacred rights, the elevation and the progress, of our redeemed humanity—*ideas* that are dear to the heart of our enthroned sovereign, to which we most devoutly pledge unalterable allegiance, while we adopt the words of the inspired Psalmist of Israel—"Thou hast given a banner to them that feared thee, that it may be displayed because of the truth."

Resolved, That, while we desire peace and pray for peace as being in its nature an inestimable blessing, nevertheless peace itself, or compromise of any sort, would be worse than all the ravages of war, if the enemies of our Government should so far prevail as to give the leading character to public opinion or to a national policy; because such a state of things would separate us from the sympathies of Christendom, and bring down upon us the curses of every civilized community in Europe, in Asia, in Australia, and in the "isles of the sea," because the course of events have brought us to a crisis that is *ultimate*, beyond which there is no issue for which any party can make a stand in behalf of any idea that enfolds a hopeful future; and therefore better for us to perish *now* in the struggle for the eternal right, than to experience the degradation of an inglorious life, or the pangs of a lingering death, under that reign of terror which the enemies of our banner would be sure to inaugurate.

Resolved, That, as Christian men, we recognize the truly righteous character of this conflict; that while it may be properly regarded as a war for our nationality, or a war for the life of a constitutional government, or for the maintenance of our flag, or as a war for the rights of the people against the usurpations of an oligarchy, nevertheless beyond all these aims we recognize the existence of a war waged for the absolute supremacy of a despotic earthly power on the one hand, against the rightful dominion of our Lord Jesus Christ, whose kingdom guarantees the inalienable and universal rights of our redeemed humanity, on the other.

Resolved, That, in view of the death of our Lord and Saviour for men of every rank and class, of every nation, tribe, "kith or kin," we regard the brotherhood of man, the moral and spiritual equality of all the races of men, as an essential doctrine of the Christian religion; that it rests like a sure corner-stone upon the foundation that God hath laid in Zion ; that whosoever falleth upon that stone shall he broken, but upon whomsoever it shall fall it will grind him to powder.

Resolved, That, in the patriotic devotion of the Christian women of our land, we hail a "sign of the times" propitious of success; and, while we remember that for many centuries in Europe the virtues of *Christian womanhood* have been a great barrier against the triumphs of antichristian barbarism, we commend the cause of our country in its day of peril to the prayers and co-operation of the mothers and daughters of Israel and to the cherished sympathies of every household.

Resolved, That we cherish a profound regard for the thousands of our brethren within the bounds of the Southern States who are loyal to the Government for which their fathers as well as ours sacrificed treasure and blood and transmitted to all as a common heritage; and while many of them may have been deceived by misrepresentation in respect to the sentiments we cherish towards them, and while all of them are prevented from realizing in action personal convictions of truth and duty, we extend to them the assurances of our fraternal confidence and of our continuance in prayer that God would soon appear for their deliverance, so that the bonds which have united us in former days may be strengthened by the fiery trials through which they shall have passed.

Resolved, That the churches connected with this Association be requested to set apart the last Friday of June as a day of solemn humiliation and prayer for the re-establishment of our national union in peace and prosperity.

DECLARATION AND RESOLUTIONS OF THE BAPTISTS, MET AT BROOKLYN, NEW YORK, MAY 29, 1861.

The Assembly of Baptists, gathered from the various Northern States of the Union, would, in the present solemn crisis of our national history, put on record some expression of their judgment as Christians, loving their country and seeking in the fear and from the grace of God its best interests. We are threatened to be rent, as a people, into two hostile camps:

several States of the Union have claimed to release themselves by their own act from the National Constitution and
Union, having formed what they designate as a confederacy.
They have seized the national forts, armaments, and ships.
Such proceedings on the part of a neighboring community
would be actual war. Yet there has been no precedent such
as in modern contests inaugurates ordinary hostilities. They
have bombarded a national garrison. The General Government at Washington have refused to recognize the right of
secession, and have proclaimed alike their own right and
their own purpose to occupy the national property and de-
fences now usurped. One of the foremost Statesmen in the
new movement, and himself the executive officer of the new
assumed Confederacy, had declared African slavery the immediate cause of the revolution thus attempted. He has alleged that the old—and, as the North deems it, the only
existing—Constitution regarded such slavery as wrong in
principle, and that the founders of this Constitution expected
the bondage, in some way and at some time, to *vanish*. He
declares of the new Confederate States that they assume as
their basis the fundamental erroneousness of such original
estimate and expectation on the part of the fathers of our
land. Accepting not only the propriety but the perpetuity of
such servitude, he places the new government on the alleged
inferiority of the negro race as its corner-stone. He claims for
the new confederacy that it is the first government in all history thus inaugurated on this new truth, as he would call it.
He invites the Northwestern States to enter the Confederacy.
But he anticipated the disintegration of the older States; and
he declares that, in case of these last, admission to the new
Confederacy must not be merely by reconstruction, but reorganization and assimilation. In other words, African bondage
seems required as the mortar that is to agglutinate and the
rock that is to sanction the recombined and rebuilt sovereignty that shall include even these last. Those high in position in the new organization of the South have proclaimed the
intent of seizing the national capital and flaunting their flag

on the seats of Northern State government. The President of
the United States has summoned a large and formidable force
to the metropolis of the Union, rallying to the defence of the
General Government. Remembering their own character
as the servants of the Prince of peace, this Assembly would
speak fraternally, not heedlessly exasperating strife, but also
with a frankness and decision as not endorsing injustice. The
Church is a kingdom not of the world. But the men of the
Church are not the less bound to recognize and loyally to uphold all rightful secular government.

The powers that be are ordained of God, and the magistracy is by his will to bear the sword not in vain. Christ, in
his Messiahship, would not be made a judge or a divider as
to the statutes and estates of this earth; but he did not therefore abrogate the tribunals of earthly judgment. To Caesar
he bade us render Caesar's dues. He cherished and exemplified patriotism when answering to the appeal made to him in
the behalf of that Gentile ruler, as far as one who loved "our"
(Jewish) nation. He showed it when weeping as he predicted
the coming woes of his own people and of their chief city. The
gospel of Christ, then, sanctions and consecrates true patriotism. Shall the Christians of the North accept the revolution
thus to be precipitated upon them, as warranted and necessary? or shall they acquiesce in it as inevitably dismissing the
question of its origin in the irrecoverable past? Shall they wait
hopefully the verdict of the nations and the sentence of Providence upon the new basis of this extemporized Confederacy?
Meanwhile, shall they submit passively to the predicted disintegration of their own North, pondering wistfully upon the
possibilities of their own reorganization to qualify them for
their admission on the novel platform, and for their initiation
into the new principles of this most summary revolution?
The memories of the past and the hopes of the future; history
and Scripture; the fear of God and regard to the well-being
of man; the best interests of their own estranged brethren at
the South, and their own rights and duties, not to themselves
and their children only, but as the stewards of constitutional

liberty in behalf of all other nations, encouraged by our success, as such remotest nations are baffled and misled, as by our failure such nations would necessarily be—all considerations unite in shutting up the Christians of the North to one course,

The following resolutions present correspondingly what, in our judgment, is the due course of our churches and people—

Resolved, That the doctrine of secession is foreign to our Constitution, revolutionary, suicidal—setting out in anarchy, and finding its ultimate issue in despotism.

Resolved, That the National Government deserves our loyal adhesion and unstinted support in its wise, forbearing, and yet firm maintenance of the national unity and life; and that, sore, long, and costly as the war may be, the North has not sought it, and the North does not shun it, if Southern aggressions press it; and that a surrender of the national Union and our ancestral principles would involve sorer evils, and longer continuance, and vaster costliness.

Resolved, That the wondrous uprising, in strongest harmony and largest self-sacrifice, of the whole North to assert and vindicate the national unity, is the cause of grateful amazement and devoutest acknowledgment to the God who sways all hearts and orders all events; and that this resurgent patriotism, wisely cherished and directed, may, in God's blessed discipline, correct evils that seemed chronic and irremediable in the national character.

Resolved, That, fearful as is the scourge of war even in the justest cause, we need, as a nation, to humble ourselves before God for the vain-glory, self-confidence, greed, venality, and corruption of manners too manifest in our land; that in its waste of property and life, its, invasion of the Sabbath, its demoralization, and its barbarism, we see the evils to which it strongly tends; but that, waged in a good cause and in the fear of God, it may be to a people, as it often in past times has been, a stern but salutary lesson for enduring good. In this struggle, the churches of the North should, by prayer for them, the distribution of Scripture and tract, and the encouragement of devout chaplains, seek the religious culture of their brave soldiers and mariners.

Resolved, That the North seek not, in any sense, the subjugation of the South, or the horrors of a servile war, or the devastation of their homes by reckless and imbruted mercenaries, but believe most firmly the rejection, were it feasible, of the Constitution and Union would annihilate the best safeguard of Southern peace.

Resolved, That the churches of our denomination be urged to set apart the last Friday in June as a day of solemn humiliation and prayer for the interposition of God's gracious care to hinder or to limit the conflict, to stay the wrath, and to sanctify the trial; and that one hour also in the Friday evening of each week be observed as a season of intercession, privately, for our country during this period of her gloom and peril.

Resolved, That, brought nearer as eternity and judgment are in such times of sharp trial and sudden change, it is the duty of all to redeem the fleeting hour—the duty of all Christ's people to see that the walls of Zion be built in troublous times, and to hope only and ever in that wonder-working God who made British missions to India and the South Seas to grow amid the Napoleon wars; who trained, in Serampore missions, Havelock, the Christian warrior, as, two centuries before, he had prepared in the wars of the Commonwealth the warrior Baxter, who wrote, as army chaplain, the "Saint's Everlasting Rest," and the Bunyan who described for all aftertime the "Pilgrim's Progress" and "The Holy War."

Resolved, That what was bought at Bunker Hill, Valley Forge, and Yorktown was not with our consent sold at Montgomery; that we dispute the legality of the bargain, and, in the strength of the Lord God of our fathers, shall hope to contest through this generation, if need be, the feasibility of the transfer.

Bishop Whittingham, of Maryland, issued the following circular to the Episcopal churches in his diocese, May, 1861—

Reverend and Dear Brethren—I have learned with extreme regret that in several instances the "Prayer for the President of the United States and all in civil authority" has been omitted, of late, in the performance of Divine service in the diocese.

Such omission in every case makes the clergyman liable for presentment for wilful violation of his ordination vow, by mutilation of the worship of the Church; and I shall hold myself bound to act on any evidence of such offence laid before me after the issue of this circular.

I beseech my brethren to remember that current events have settled any question that might have been started concerning citizenship and allegiance. Maryland is admitted and declared by the Legislature and Governor of the State to be at this time one of the United States of America. As resident in Maryland, the clergy of this diocese are citizens of the United States, and bound to the recognition and discharge of all duties appertaining to that condition. It is clearly such a duty, by the express word of God, to make supplication and prayer for the chief magistrate of the Union, and for all that are in authority, that we lead a quiet and peaceful life, in all godliness and honesty; and it is clearly my duty, by the same direction, to put those whom God has committed to my charge in mind to be subject to the principalities and powers, to obey magistrates, to speak evil of no man, to be no brawlers. To my deep distress and disquiet, I have too much reason to fear that in one instance a minister of Christ may have so far forgotten himself, his place, and his duty as actually to commit the canonical offence known as "brawling in the church," while resolving to do what an archangel durst not to do, and to defend transgression of an injunction of the word of God.

We of the clergy have no right to intrude our private views of the questions which are so terribly dividing those among whom we minister, into the place assigned us that we may speak for God and minister in his worship. Still less claim have we to assume to frame and fashion the devotions of the brethren by our private notions, and, to that end, interpolate and mutilate the service of the Church. In such times as these we are more strictly than ever bound to adhere to the precise letter of the prescribed form, and to deserve the praise of non-interference with others' rights by the closest seclusion within the limits of our plain duty.

It is not merely my advice, dear brethren, but it is the solemn injunction and caution of the word of God, to be reverenced and regarded accordingly as you believe it to be his— "My son, fear thou the Lord and the king, and meddle not with them that are given to change; for their calamity shall rise suddenly; and who knoweth of them both? These things belong unto the wise."

Your loving friend and brother,

Wm. R. Whittingham,

Bishop of Maryland.

Baltimore, May 15, 1861.

MASSACHUSETTS CONGREGATIONAL ASSOCIATION,
JULY, 1861.

Whereas our nation is at the present time engaged in a war for the suppression of treason and rebellion against the Government of the United States:

Resolved, That we, the General Association of Massachusetts, devoutly recognize and acknowledge our dependence upon the God of our fathers for the success of our arms and the establishment of the laws.

Resolved, That we cordially approve the vigorous measures of the Government for the maintenance of the Constitution, and that we are ready to devote our property, our influence, and, if need be, our lives, in its vindication and support.

Resolved, That, while we earnestly desire the speedy return of peace to our divided country, we deprecate any concession or compromise which shall not secure the loyalty and obedience to the Federal Government of all the States of the Union, or which shall be inconsistent with the nationality of freedom.

Resolved, That, believing the institution of Slavery to have been the fruitful source of the great trouble now upon us, we cannot but pray and hope that the present war may be overruled by Divine Providence for the ultimate removal of human bondage from our land.

General Congregational Association of Illinois, June, 1861.

Met in a time of national convulsion and civil war, we, the General Association of the Congregational ministers and churches of Illinois, deem it important to place on record our solemn convictions with regard to its origin and responsibility, and the duties which it devolves upon the people of God and the nation: therefore,

Resolved, 1. That American slavery is responsible, before God and man, for the present deplorable condition of our country; that the neglect to use appropriate measures in Church and State to secure the speedy and peaceful overthrow of oppression has involved the nation in civil war; that the slave-power has grown bolder and more rapacious in its demands with every passing year; and that its inability longer to control the Government has led to secret plots and open treasonable efforts to break up the Union and subvert our national Constitution.

Resolved, 2. That this rebellion is not only treason against the United States Government, but a revolt against the Divine scheme for the world's advance in civilization and religion, to which our land, with its free institutions, sustains so important a relation, and is, therefore, a high crime against universal humanity, and an impious defiance of Divine Providence.

Resolved, 3. That the Union instituted by our fathers fresh from the battles of liberty was intended to preserve and favor freedom and limit and discountenance slavery; that the Union constituted the several States one nation, with supreme political power in all the respects named in the Federal Constitution; and that the secession of any State can only be revolutionary in nature; while the present secession of slaveholding States is as destitute of moral justification as it is of constitutional validity.

Resolved, 4. That the present civil war is a heavy but just judgment from the hand of God for our national sins, and especially for the heaven—provoking sin of oppressing the poor; and that as the whole land has been involved in the guilt, so all its sections deserve and must expect to bear the retribution.

Resolved, 5. That, as the war is but the ripe and bitter fruit of slavery, we trust the American people will demand that it shall result in relieving our country entirely and forever of that sin and curse, that the future of our nation may never again be darkened by a similar night of treason.

Resolved, 6. That in the spirit of our Puritan ancestors, who preserved English liberty, and of our fathers, who fought in the battles of the American Revolution, we tender to the Federal authorities our cordial support to the very last, in the present life-and-death struggle for righteous laws and government, and assure them and the troops who have gone to the defence of freedom, that our prayers shall be continually offered to God that they may have the courage, wisdom, and success which the emergency demands and the nature of the conflict leads us to expect.

Resolved, 7. That the people of God should aim to give a high moral and religious tone to the war, as one means of obviating the evils attendant upon such a conflict; and that, to this end, pastors of churches, and chaplains in the army, should by their discourses purify public sentiment, direct the current of national purpose, and elevate military ardor, while the churches send forth their members, in the spirit of Christian patriotism, to fight the battles of their country, and supply the means of bringing religious truth to bear in every appropriate way upon the mind and heart of the army.

Resolved, 8. That we urge upon the Government the duty of making ample provision for the religious wants of the troops, as necessary alike to the spiritual welfare of the soldiers and the success of the war; and that we remind the civil and military authorities that no armies were ever more effective than those of the English Parliament, in which Richard Baxter was a chaplain, and that the invincible regiment of that army was "the Ironsides," led by Oliver Cromwell, and composed of godly men.

Resolved, 9. That we are gratified at the presence of so many religious men in the army, and at the efforts already made under official auspices to guard the troops against the demoralizing influences of war and to provide for their spiritual instruction upon the Sabbath; and we express the hope that all possible precautions will be taken not to encourage the desecration of the Sabbath by unnecessary parade or labor.

PROTESTANT EPISCOPAL CHURCH OF OHIO.

Resolved, By the Convention of Clergy and by Delegates of the Protestant Episcopal Church in the Diocese of Ohio, now here assembled in Cleveland, that we cordially approve the sentiment and appreciate the wise counsels expressed by the bishop and assistant bishop on the present condition of our beloved country, in their several addresses yesterday, delivered to the Convention, and desire hereby fully to recognize our obligations, as Christian men, in this crisis, to stand by the Government in its efforts to maintain the Constitution.

Resolved, That we fervently hope, and our earnest prayer to God is, that the delusion which has seized the minds of so many of our brethren in the Southern States of this Union, originating, as we are constrained to believe, in an erroneous estimate of State sovereignty and a corresponding depreciation of the superior power of the National Government, may be dispelled, and they be brought to unite with us in a holy endeavor that the Union may be preserved, the just authority of the Government maintained, and the blessings of peace again restored to our borders.

Resolved, That we have undiminished confidence in the piety and Christian spirit of the clergy and laity of the Protestant Episcopal Church in the Southern States. We cannot, and we do not, believe they would willingly do wrong. We earnestly invite them to retrace their steps—to reconsider their actions and their published opinions, and to join with us in an effort to preserve the unity of the Church of Christ in the United States of America. Brethren of the South, in a question touching the existence of the Government under which we live, should not Christian brethren in all parts of the country have a voice?

Resolved, That, whether these counsels be heeded or disregarded, we still hope that our Southern brethren will not fail to send their bishops and clerical and lay delegates to the next General Convention, in 1862, that by prayer and supplication to God, by unimpassioned consultations and friendly conferences, we may yet adopt measures to prevent the sundering of those ties which are so essential to the prosperity and integrity of the nation.

GENERAL CONFERENCE OF THE CONGREGATIONAL CHURCHES OF OHIO, JUNE, 1861.

Recognizing the present calamities of our country as the just judgment of God our heavenly Father sent upon us because of our sins and designed for our reformation, we are led to inquire for the causes which have thus brought his chastening hand upon us.

The brief enumeration of these calamities presents the spectacle of unjustifiable and wicked rebellion —a band of conspirators in the interest of a gigantic system of unrighteous oppression— condemned by the word of God and the Spirit of Christ—seizing by fraud and force upon the Government of States, trampling under foot the liberties of their people, treasonably arraying their power against the General Government and its principle of universal human freedom, and inaugurating civil war, with its train of fearful and demoralizing evils, to desolate the land; the spectacle of large bodies of professedly Christian ministers and Churches uniting with these conspirators in prostituting the word of God and debauching the public conscience to the service of this monstrous sin; the spectacle of national industry paralyzed and impoverished, the hard-earned wealth of years and generations destroyed in a moment, by an immoral and profligate repudiation of just obligations, and the consuming necessities of war; the spectacle of a united, prosperous, and Christian nation approaching conditions of unexampled power for the kingdom of Christ, evidently checked in mid-career, its integrity and greatness imperilled, and its good name and usefulness among the nations threatened with blasting and destruction.

Reviewing these calamities, we are compelled to behold in them signal tokens of Divine displeasure with us as a nation, foe that cupidity and pride which has led us to tolerate, or even maintain by direct or indirect means, that vast system of human chattelism for whose further aggrandizement this great nation is thus threatened with dismemberment and ruin, or the destruction of its free and Christian institutions.

As the Conference of the Congregational Churches of Ohio, engaged in establishing that kingdom whose foundations and spirit are righteousness, peace, and joy in the Holy Spirit, and the overthrow of every thing opposed to this, we are, therefore,

Resolved, That we see in the madness and wickedness of the conspirators against our Government a new proof of that disorganizing tendency of slavery which Christian statesmen and Christian philanthropists have ever asserted.

Resolved, That we acknowledge the Divine hand in our present troubles, and that we discover in them a sign of righteous indignation, on the one hand, at the iniquity which has so cruelly degraded the bondman, and, on the other, at the mercenary spirit which has persuaded this whole people to strike hands with oppression for the sake of gain.

Resolved, That with devout gratitude to our God we recognize the presence and power of the Christian element of this nation in the present conflict for the cause of truth and our national integrity, and that we regard this cheering fact as an assurance of ultimate and complete re-establishment of the Government's authority, throughout the whole extent of our country, upon purer and firmer foundations.

Resolved, That, with humble acknowledgment of our sins and unworthiness as a nation, we make our united supplications unto God that he will turn us away from our sins, giving all our people a heart to do justly, love mercy, and walk humbly before him; and that while we yield ourselves to maintain the cause of right and righteous Government at every cost, he will be graciously pleased to bestow upon our rulers, the President of the United States, and all in authority with him, a wise and understanding heart, that he will protect and strengthen our armies, and that he will at length bestow upon our nation that union and peace which shall be founded in righteousness, enduring forever.

Whereas a portion of the people of the United States of America have risen up against the rightful authority of the Government, have instituted what they call the "Confederate States of America," in the name and defence of which they have made war against the United States, have seized the property of the Federal Government, have assailed and over-powered its troops in the discharge of their duty, and are now in armed rebellion against it, the General Assembly of the Presbyterian Church of the United States of America cannot forbear to express their amazement at the wickedness of such proceedings, and at the bold advocacy and defence thereof, not only in those States in which ordinances of "secession" have been passed, but in several others; and

Whereas the General Assembly—in the language of the Synod of New York and Philadelphia on the occasion of the Revolutionary War— "being met at a time when public affairs wear so threatening an aspect, and when (unless God in his sovereign providence speedily prevent it) all the horrors of civil war are to be apprehended, are of opinion that they cannot discharge their duty to the numerous congregations under their care without addressing them at this important crisis; and as a firm belief and habitual recollection of the power and presence of the living God ought at all times to possess the minds of real Christians, so in seasons of public calamity, when the Lord is known by the judgments which he executeth, it would be an ignorance or indifference highly criminal not to look up to him with reverence, to implore his mercy by humble and fervent prayer, and, if possible, to prevent his vengeance by unfeigned repentance:"—therefore,

1. *Resolved*, That, inasmuch as the Presbyterian Church, in her past history, has frequently lifted up her voice against oppression, has shown herself a champion of constitutional liberty, as against both despotism and anarchy, throughout the civilized world, we should be recreant to our high trust were we to withhold our earnest protest against all such unlawful and treasonable acts.

2. *Resolved*, That this Assembly and the churches which it represents cherish an undiminished attachment to the great principles of civil and religious freedom on which our national Government is based, under the influence of which our fathers prayed and fought and bled, which issued in the establishment of our independence, and by the preservation of which we believe that the common interests of evangelical religion and civil liberty will be most effectively sustained.

3. *Resolved*, That inasmuch as we believe, according to our *Form of Government*, that "God, the Supreme Lord and King of all the world, hath ordained civil magistrates to be under him over the people for his own glory and the public good, and to this end hath armed them with the power of the sword for the defence and encouragement of them that are good, and for the punishment of evil-doers,"—there is, in the judgment of the Assembly, no blood or treasure too precious to be devoted to the defence and perpetuity of the Government in all its constitutional authority.

4. *Resolved*, That all those who are endeavoring to uphold the Constitution and maintain the Government of these United States in the exercise of its lawful prerogatives are entitled to the sympathy and support of all Christian and law-abiding citizens.

5. *Resolved*, That it be recommended to all our pastors and churches to be instant and fervent in prayer for the President of the United States and all in authority under him, that wisdom and strength may be given them in the discharge of their arduous duties; for the Congress of the United States; for the lieutenant-general commanding the army in chief, and all our soldiers, that God may shield them from danger in the hour of peril, and, by the outpouring of the Holy Spirit upon the army and navy, renew and sanctify them, so that, whether living or dying, they may be the servants of the Most High.

6. *Resolved*, That in the countenance which many ministers of the gospel and other professing Christians are now giving to treason and rebellion against the Government, we have great occasion to mourn for the injury thus done to the

kingdom of the Redeemer; and that, though we have nothing to add to our former significant and explicit testimonies on the subject of slavery, we yet recommend our people to pray more fervently than ever for the removal of this evil, and all others, both social and political, which lie at the foundation of our present national difficulties.

7. *Resolved*, That a copy of these resolutions, signed by the officers of the General Assembly, be forwarded to his Excellency Abraham Lincoln, President of the United States.

Old School General Assembly or the Presbyterian Church, May, 1861.

Gratefully acknowledging the distinguished bounty and care of Almighty God towards this favored land, and also recognizing our obligation to submit to every ordinance of man for the Lord's sake, this General Assembly adopt the following resolutions—

1. *Resolved*, That, in view of the present unhappy and agitated condition of this country, the first day of July next be set apart as a day of prayer throughout our bounds, and that on this day ministers and people are called on humbly to confess and bewail our national sins, to offer our thanks to the Father of Lights for his abundant and undeserved goodness towards us as a nation, to seek his guidance and blessings upon our rulers and their councils, as well as on the Congress of the United States about to assemble, and to implore him, in the name of Jesus Christ, the Great High-Priest of the Christian profession, to turn away his anger from us and speedily restore us the blessings of an honorable peace.

2. *Resolved*, That this General Assembly, in the spirit of that Christian patriotism which the Scriptures enjoin, and which has always characterized this Church, do hereby acknowledge and declare our obligation to promote and perpetuate, so far as in us lies, the integrity of these United States, and to strengthen, uphold, and encourage the Federal Government in the exercise of all its functions under our noble Constitution; and to this Constitution, in all its provisions, requirements, and principles, we profess our unabated loyalty. And,

to avoid all misconception, the Assembly declare that by the terms "Federal Government," as here used, is not meant any particular administration, or the peculiar opinions of any political party, but that central administration which, being at any time appointed and inaugurated according to the forms prescribed in the Constitution of the United States, is the visible representative of our national existence.

GENERAL CONGREGATIONAL ASSOCIATION OR CONNECTICUT, JULY, 1861.

Whereas the beneficent Government of these United States, the noble heritage which God gave to the toils, sacrifices, and prayers of our fathers, is put in jeopardy by an organized rebellion—a rebellion instigated mainly and deliberately to secure the extension and permanence of slavery—we, as ministers of God's word, in General Association convened, hereby record the sentiments we entertain in relation to this contest, and adopt the following resolutions —

Resolved, That we gratefully acknowledge the Divine goodness in uniting so generally the people of the free States for the suppression of this treason and the defence of the Federal Union.

Resolved, That the right of violent revolution can only exist in a case in which a Government, through neglect to fulfil its proper functions, or otherwise, becomes intolerably oppressive, and in which no possibility remains of reform by regular and peaceful methods—the Divine word requiring in all other cases obedience to human government as the ordinance of God.

Resolved, That it is the duty of all citizens, especially all ministers of the gospel and Christian people, to sustain at any and every sacrifice the Federal Government in suppressing this wicked rebellion; to repress, in the conduct of the war, all unhallowed passions and whatever is contrary to the will of God, and to exert all their influence against efforts, should any be made, to secure a peace by unreasonable concessions in the interest of slavery.

Resolved, That, regarding, as we do, the system of slavery in this country as mainly the cause of this treasonable war against the Federal Government, we wait reverently on the providence of God, in the earnest hope and prayer that he will so overrule this conflict and direct its issues that it may result sooner or later, and as soon as may be, in the peaceful and complete removal of this iniquitous and shameful system of oppression.

The Synod of New York and New Jersey (Old School) passed, unanimously, the following paper on the country, at their annual session in Newark, N.J., November, 1861—

Whereas the people of those United States, after the achievement of their independence, established a government based on constitutional liberty, giving to all just and equal rights; and

Whereas a portion of the people of these United States have taken up arms against the lawful Government and seized upon its property, and are endeavoring to overthrow it—a Government in which are centered our dearest hopes and interests pertaining to civil liberty and the advancement of civilization throughout the world; and

Whereas the Presbyterian Church in the United States has ever shown herself, in all her history, the advocate of civil liberty and freedom—that freedom the defence of which drove our fathers from the Old World, and for the security of which, in this land, they prayed and fought and bled, ever lifting their voice and hands against anarchy and tyranny and oppression in every form—and believing that the present solemn crisis in our national affairs calls upon us, as patriots and Christians, to lay upon the altar of our country our influence, our property, and our lives: therefore,

Resolved, That we pledge to the Government our individual support and confidence, and will use all lawful means and efforts in our power to aid it in maintaining its authority and in putting down this rebellion, in its very nature so utterly causeless and unjust.

Resolved, That we commend the President of the United States, his constitutional advisers, the American Congress, the commander-in-chief and soldiers of the army and navy, to the God of our fathers, humbly praying that he will impart to them wisdom and unity in councils and fidelity and courage in action, that the cause intrusted to their hands may be brought to a speedy and successful issue.

Resolved, That, while we do not feel called upon to add any thing to the repeated testimonials of our Church on the subject of slavery, nor to offer any advice to the Government on the subject, still, fully believing that it lies at the foundation of all our present national troubles, we recommend to all our people to pray more earnestly than ever for its removal, and that the time may speedily come when God, by his providence, shall in his own good time and way bring it to an end, that nothing may be left of it but the painful record of its past existence.

Resolved, That we recommend to all our people to humble themselves, and take a low place before God, in view of all our social and political sins, and each one remember and lament his own personal complicity with them all.

REPLY OF SECRETARY SEWARD.

Department or State, Washington, November 27, 1861.

To the Synod of New York and New Jersey.

REVEREND GENTLEMEN—The minute containing your resolutions on the condition of the country, which you directed to be sent to me, has been submitted to the President of the United States.

I am instructed to express to you his great satisfaction with those proceedings, which are distinguished equally by their patriotic sentiments and a purely Christian spirit. It is a just tribute to our system of government that it has enabled the American people to enjoy unmolested more of the blessings of Divine Providence, which affect the material conditions of human society, than any other people ever enjoyed, together with a more absolute degree of religious liberty than, before the institution of that great Government, had ever been hoped for among men. The overthrow of the Government, therefore, might justly be regarded as a calamity not only to this nation, but a misfortune to mankind. The President is assured of the public virtue and the public valor. But these are unavailing without the favor of God. The President thanks you for the invocation of that indispensable support, and he earnestly solicits the same invocations from all classes and conditions of men. Believing that these prayers will not be denied by the God of our fathers, he trusts and expects that the result of this most unhappy attempt at revolution will confirm and strengthen the Union of the republic, and ultimately secure the fraternal affections among its members, so essential to a restoration of the public welfare and happiness.

I am, very sincerely, your very humble servant,

William H. Seward.

THE CINCINNATI CONFERENCE OR THE METHODIST EPISCOPAL CHURCH, AUGUST, 1861.

State of the Country

The committee, through J. T. Mitchell, made a report, closing with the following resolutions—all adopted by a rising vote—

1. That civil government is of God, and the obligation to obey just human laws refers directly to Divine authority and sanction, as revealed in the Holy Scriptures.

2. That the Constitution of the United States, and the laws of Congress in conformity therewith, are the supreme law of this whole land, binding on the inhabitants of every State and Territory.

3. That armed resistance to this law is a most wicked and unwarrantable rebellion; and that it is the sacred duty of those charged with the administration of our national Government to put down this rebellion by every proper means required to that end.

4. That it is the religious duty of every citizen to lend all practicable support to the national Government, in the maintenance of its authority over the whole land.

5. That the Union of the States is as pressing a necessity now as when it was originally formed by our fathers, and it is our bounden duty to sympathize and co-operate with the

thousands of loyal Union men in the South, claiming their rights under the Constitution, and anxiously awaiting the opportunity successfully to assert them.

6. That we can but look on the calamities which so grievously afflict our country as the chastening of God for our national sins, by which he is teaching us our duty by terrible things in righteousness, and that it becomes us all to humble ourselves under his hand, to confess and forsake our personal and national offences, and to implore the Divine mercy in their forgiveness, that the work of righteousness may be peace.

7. That we recommend to all our teachers and people the sincere and devout observance of the National Fast appointed by the President of the United States for the 26th of the present month, and that public religious services be held in all our churches in town and country.

8. That we regard with deep interest the provision made by the Government for the religious instruction and comfort of our citizen soldiery, by the appointment of a chaplain to each regiment; and that we assure our brethren of other Churches who are appointed to that responsible and difficult position, of our heartfelt sympathy and of our earnest prayers for the success of their labors.

9. That we hail with unmingled satisfaction and gratitude to God the General Order of Major-General McClellan, commanding the Department of the Potomac, on the proper observance of the holy Sabbath by the army of the United States under his command, and assure him that this order has thrilled the hearts of Christians throughout the land, and especially of those who have husbands, sons, and brothers in the field of conflict.

Southeastern Indiana Conference, September, 1862. The Committee on the State of the Country submitted the following, which was adopted with a unanimous rising vote, and ordered to be published in the "Western Christian Advocate"—

Your committee see no reason in the acts of the administration to warrant the rebellion that now destroys the peace of the country; that it is the work of ambitious, bloody, and deceitful men, and if it should prove successful must utterly destroy the safeguards the fathers have so wisely thrown around the liberties of the people. We can see in the future no guarantee for the rights of conscience and free speech, save in the suppression of the rebellion, and the holding of its leaders to the penalty provided by the law of the land.

As the ministers of Christ, we deplore the existence of war. It is an evil always demoralizing; and yet we feel, terrible as war may be, it is not so blasting in its effects as anarchy. Therefore,

Resolved, That we do most heartily espouse the cause of the Constitution and the laws, and pledge our prayers, together with all the moral influence we may be able to exert, to the maintenance of the Government.

Resolved, That we find nothing in the acts of the administration of the Government to call for a change in the twenty-third Article of Religion, as found in our Book of Discipline, and that we esteem it as a violation of the law of God for the ministers or members of our Church to give aid and comfort to the rebellion.

Resolved, That we have read with pleasure the proclamation of the President setting apart a day of humiliation, fasting, and prayer to Almighty God for the success of our arms and the restoration of peace to the nation, and that we recommend to all our people a strict observance of the day.

Resolved, That we have read with pleasure and heartily approve of the order of Major-General McClellan in reference to the observance of the Christian Sabbath in the army.

James Havens, Chairman.

J. B. Lathrop, *Secretary.*

Northwestern Indiana Conference,
September, 1861.

Whereas a formidable rebellion against the Constitution and authority of the United States has been inaugurated by ambitious and intriguing men, whose course of procedure furnishes the clearest evidence that they are the enemies of this Government, thereby menacing the very existence of the nation, desolating the country, and deluging it with fraternal blood, threatening the safety of our homes and the lives of our families;

And whereas the Twenty-Third Article of Religion, in the Discipline of the Methodist Episcopal Church, holds the following language— "The President, the Congress, the General Assemblies, the Governors, and the Councils of State, *as the delegates of the people*, are the rulers of the United States of America, according to the division of power made to them by the Constitution of the United States and by the Constitutions of their respective States. And the said States are a sovereign and independent nation, and ought not to be subject to any foreign jurisdiction:" therefore,

Resolved, That we look upon this rebellion as wicked in the highest degree, and without any just excuse; and that it calls for the indignation and united opposition of all good citizens.

Resolved, That we, as ministers of the gospel, ignoring all partisan politics, will not cease to exert our influence in sustaining our Government, in this trying hour, by all proper means within the sphere of our calling.

Resolved, That the administration has our cordial sympathies, and shall have our prayers that its efforts to put down this rebellion and restore constitutional law and order may be successful.

Action has not yet been taken upon those of our number who have gone at our country's call, and there seems to be considerable perplexity connected with this new feature. All are favorably disposed, however; and, while the law of our Discipline will not be transcended, such relation to the Conference will be given these brethren as will doubtless give general satisfaction.

THE WISCONSIN CONVENTION OF CONGREGATIONAL AND PRESBYTERIAN CHURCHES ON THE STATE OF THE COUNTRY, AUGUST, 1861.

In view of the distracted and perilous state of our beloved country, recognizing as we heartily and sorrowfully do the justice of the Divine retribution now descending with terrible power upon the nation; believing that the favor of our righteous God can be secured only through a penitence that shall bear its legitimate fruits in our national life, reformed from its great iniquities believing moreover, that our national liberties can be perpetuated only in righteousness, justice, and truth, and that our Union and Constitution, as the bulwarks of universal human freedom and of the sacred rights of humanity throughout the world, ought to be maintained unbroken and inviolable at all hazards:

Resolved, 1. That we approve of the war now waged by this Government for the crushing of rebellion; that, by whatever means God furnishes us, we will maintain the Constitution and the Union; that we favor a decided, prompt, and unwavering policy in conducting the war, and a just and speedy punishment of the chief traitors for their enormous crimes, while we warmly sympathize with all who may be forced away from their allegiance to the Government by tyrannical leaders and merciless mobs, and will welcome them heartily to their active loyalty again.

2. That we regard it as indispensable to the best and most successful prosecution of the contest that the moral principles involved be practically recognized by the people and the Government.

3. That, in our opinion, the institution of African slavery, as it exists in a portion of our national domain, is the real cause of the present rebellion, and of the wicked endeavors of certain States to dissever and destroy this Federal Union; and that, with our eye upon this iniquitous fountain of our present calamities and perils, it becomes this people and Government to inquire diligently, reverently, and anxiously of God, what duties in this terrible exigency we owe to the negro held in unrighteous and cruel bondage in our land, and to ourselves also as the dominant and oppressing race.

4. That, while nations of the Old World are emerging from their tyrannies and ascending exultingly into higher states of civil and religious liberty, we, as a confessedly Christian

people, owe it to ourselves, our fathers, to posterity, humanity, and God, to be second to no nation in the sublime service of human freedom.

5. That to us, as a Christian people, the will of God, so far as we can ascertain it, should be the only rule of our action, and the sole guide of our national policy; that politics and religion have an indissoluble connection.

6. That we have observed with unspeakable regret the frequent and needless violations of the Sabbath on the part of military leaders; and that we hail with delight the order for the better observance of this holy day recently issued by Major-General McClellan, commanding the Army of the Potomac.

7. That we will do all in our power to render this national contest a war for justice, liberty, and humanity ; that we will give it, wherever we can, the moral and religious aspect which should characterize it.

8. That we desire and are willing to accept no peace based upon a timid compromise with treason and rebellion, but only such a peace as shall rear its firm and substantial structure of national glory and prosperity on the grave of this Confederate rebellion, when the Union and the Constitution shall be re-established forever upon the ashes of dead and buried secession.

9. That we regard this struggle as for our very national existence; and that, God helping us, praying for our brethren in arms, or fighting shoulder to shoulder with them, as our lot may be, we will maintain and defend what we here resolve to the uttermost of ability and life.

10. That all traitors against the Government of the United States—a Government the most beneficent and excellent under the sun—have forfeited their lives by their crimes, and that, therefore, it were mercy to try to save their lives by wresting from their wicked grasp their suicidal weapon of slavery.

11. That we recommend the members of our churches in their various localities throughout Wisconsin to engage actively and zealously in petitioning the Congress of the United States at its next session to enact a law which shall confiscate and endow with freedom all the slaves in the country in the legal ownership

of rebels against this nation, and to set at liberty all remaining slaves by compensation to all loyal slave-holders.

WELCH CONGREGATIONAL CONFERENCE OF NEW YORK, 1861.
In view of the present disturbed state of affairs in our country, when the Union of the States is endangered, the laws disregarded, and the property of the Government pilfered, by men of ambitious and corrupt minds:

Resolved, That we, as ministers and delegates of the New York Welch Association assembled, declare publicly our fullest and most steadfast adherence to the Constitution and the Union.

Resolved, That as citizens and Christians we fully approve and heartily co-operate with the President and his Cabinet in their measures to subdue rebellion in the seceded States and to restore order and peace in our land.

Resolved, That we feel gratified at the bold and uncompromising stand our ministers and churches have taken on the great principles of equity, liberty, and the rights of man; and we earnestly hope and pray that they will continue in their efforts and fidelity until the source of the present calamity be entirely removed.

Resolved, That we hope and pray that God, in his wise and beneficent providence, may overrule the present disturbances in our country to hasten the overthrow of slavery, which disgraces our land and threatens the existence of our Government.

MIAMI CONFERENCE OF THE CHRISTIAN DENOMINATION
OF OHIO, 1861.
Whereas our nation is now in the midst of one of the worst rebellions ever known in the history of the world, led on by reckless thirst for political power, and animated by a spirit drawn from a system of oppression and slavery "the vilest which the sun ever saw," bringing upon us all the calamities and horrors of civil war, threatening the overthrow of the Government whose institutions, under the blessing of God, have secured to us the privileges of civil and religious liberty and given us a career of prosperity unparalleled in the his-

tory of nations, and whereas the issues of this war involve also the issues of human and political liberty among the nations: therefore,

Resolved, That it is the duty of all loyal citizens, as Christian patriots, friends of human liberty, and brothers of the human family, to maintain and defend this Government, their institutions and liberties, by such means and measures as are necessary to disperse the traitors who threaten them.

Resolved, That while we receive the gospel we profess as the gospel of peace, forbidding us to take up arms in offensive operations, we believe that now, when war is waged upon us, when our forts, arsenals, mints, and other public property have been recklessly and violently taken by the plundering hand of treason, and immense hordes of armed traitors are threatening the destruction of our national capital and peaceful commercial cities, when piracy is systematized, armed, and sent abroad to plunder our commerce upon the high seas, the heaven-implanted instincts of self-preservation, our obligations to God, who has given us in sacred trust the blessings which are thus threatened, our obligations to coming generations to transmit to them the privileges we have received, to the nations of the world to hold up before them undimmed the beacon of liberty, our obligations to God to be true to the trusts he has committed to us, call an us to resist these attacks, even in the direful issues which are now presented.

The American Board of Commissioners for Foreign Missions, the largest missionary association in the world, at their annual session, October, 1861, passed the following—

Resolved, 1. That we sympathize with our national Government in its struggle with rebellion which threatens its very existence and imperils the success of this Missionary Board; and we fervently implore the God of nations so to overrule the conflict that the rebellion may be crushed, slavery, its prime cause, removed, and that peace, prosperity, and righteousness may be permanently established throughout our whole land.

Resolved, 2. That we not only thus pray for deliverance from our present national distress, but that the nation, having been purified in the furnace of affliction and made meet for the Master's service, shall hereafter render the same devotedness to the cause of Christ and Christian missions which is now put forth for the preservation of our beloved country.

The Presbytery of the Potomac (Old School), 1862. The following resolutions, presented by the Rev. Dr. Tustin, were unanimously adopted—

Whereas it is more than intimated in the Sacred Scriptures (see Romans xiii. from 1st to 7th verses inclusive) that all wise and wholesome Governments are the product of the power, wisdom, and goodness of Almighty God, and cannot, except for grossly abusing the trust committed to them, be resisted or overturned without incurring the fearful penalty of the Divine displeasure; and whereas the Government of these United States is eminently the offspring of the abounding grace of God to the people of this highly favored nation: therefore,

Resolved, That, in the opinion of this Presbytery, the causeless uprising of a portion of our countrymen, with the view of overturning the best human Government that the light of heaven ever shone upon—may God forgive them!— is an exhibition of folly and wickedness which has scarcely a parallel in the history of civilized nations.

Resolved, That we heartily approve the wise and vigorous measures adopted by the President and his constitutional advisers in order to preserve unimpaired, at all hazards, the precious and priceless legacy bequeathed to us by our forefathers, now sleeping in their honored graves.

Resolved, That our heartfelt thanks are due to the brave and patriotic officers and men who compose our army and navy, for their generous and voluntary offering of blood and treasure in order to rescue our beloved country from threatened dismemberment and consequent ruin.

Resolved, That, inasmuch as large and extraordinary expenditures have been necessarily made by the General Government in order to preserve the Federal Union from disintegration and overthrow, we cheerfully consent to bear our just proportion of the pecuniary responsibility incurred for that purpose.

Resolved, That our deepest gratitude is due to the Great Ruler of nations for his gracious assistance vouchsafed during this fearful contest, and especially for the manifestations of his grace and favor in the recent victories which have crowned our arms upon field and flood; and that we will continue to invoke his guidance and protection until peace and all its balmy influences shall again return to our weary and distracted country, and we become what we once were, a united, happy, and prosperous people.

Resolved, unanimously, That the proceedings of this meeting be published in the National "Intelligencer," "Baltimore American," "Presbyterian," "Standard and Expositor."

EVANGELICAL LUTHERAN SYNOD, MAY, 1862.
The Rev. Prof. L. Sternberg, of Hartwick Seminary, New York, the chairman of the committee, in presenting the resolutions, addressed the President as follows—

MR. PRESIDENT—We have the honor, as a committee of the General Synod of the Lutheran Church in the United States, to present to your excellency a copy of the preamble and resolutions in reference to the state of the country adopted by that body at its late session in the city of Lancaster, Pennsylvania.

We are further charged to assure you that our fervent prayers shall ascend to the God of nations that Divine guidance and support may be vouchsafed to you in the trying and responsible position to which a benignant Providence has called you.

With your permission, the Rev. Dr. Pohlman, of Albany, N.Y., will briefly express to you the sentiments which animated the committee and the Church they represent in view of the present crisis of our national affairs.

The Rev. Dr. Pohlman, of Albany, N.Y., in his speech, alluded to the fact that the late session of the General Synod of the Lutheran Church at Lancaster was the first that had been held since the troubles in our country commenced; that the General Synod represents twenty-six district Synods, scattered over the Middle, Western, and Southern States, from twenty-one of which delegates were in attendance; that from the States in rebellion no delegates were present, except one from Tennessee, who had, in praying for the President, avoided arrest only in consequence of the fact that he conducted Divine service in the German language, the vernacular of many in the Lutheran Church. He further expressed his deep conviction that we were greatly indebted for the degree of success that has crowned the efforts of the Government in quelling the rebellion to the prayers of Christians, and concluded by invoking the Divine benediction to rest on the President and on our beloved country.

Reply of the President.

Gentlemen—I welcome here the representatives of the Evangelical Lutherans of the United States. I accept with gratitude their assurances of the sympathy and support of that enlightened, influential, and loyal class of my fellow-citizens in an important crisis, which involves, in my judgment, not only the civil and religious liberties of our own dear land, but in a large degree the civil and religious liberties of mankind in many countries and through many ages. You well know, gentlemen, and the world knows, how reluctantly I accepted this issue of battle forced upon me, on my advent to this place, by the internal enemies of our country. You all know, the world knows, the forces and the resources the public agents have brought into employment to sustain a Government against which there has been brought not one complaint of real injury committed against society, at home or abroad. You all may recollect that, in taking up the sword thus forced into our hands, this Government appealed to the prayers of the pious and the good, and declared that it placed its whole dependence upon the favor of God. I now humbly and reverently, in your presence, reiterate the acknowledgment of that dependence, not doubting that if it shall please the Divine Being who determines the destinies of nations that this shall remain a united people, they will, humbly seeking the Divine guidance, make their prolonged national existence a source of new benefits to themselves and their successors and to all classes and conditions of mankind.

The Resolutions of the Synod.

Whereas our beloved country, after having long been favored with a degree of political and religious freedom, security, and prosperity unexampled in the history of the world, now finds itself involved in a bloody war to suppress an armed rebellion against its lawfully constituted Government; and

Whereas the word of God, which is the sole rule of our faith and practice, requires loyal subjection to "the powers that be," because they are "ordained of God" to be "a terror to evil-doers and a praise to those who do well," and at the same time declares that they who "resist the power" shall receive to themselves condemnation; and

Whereas we, the representatives of the Evangelical Lutheran Synod of the United States, connected with the several Synods assembled in Lancaster, Pennsylvania, recognize it as our duty to give public expression to our convictions of' truth on this subject, and in every proper way to co-operate with our fellow-citizens in sustaining the great interests of law and authority, of liberty and righteousness: Be it, therefore,

Resolved, That it is the deliberate judgment of this Synod that the rebellion against the constitutional Government of this land is most wicked in its inception, unjustifiable in its cause, unnatural in its character, inhuman in its prosecution, oppressive in its aims, and destructive in its results to the highest interests of morality and religion.

Resolved, That in the suppression of this rebellion, and in the maintenance of the Constitution and the Union by the sword, we recognize an unavoidable necessity and a sacred duty which the Government owes to the nation and the world; and that, therefore, we call upon our people to lift up holy hands in prayer to the God of battles, without personal wrath against the evil-doers on the one hand, and without doubting the righteousness of our cause on the other, that he would give wisdom to the President and his counsellors, and success to the army and navy, that our beloved land may speedily be delivered from treason and anarchy.

Resolved, That, whilst we regard this unhappy war as a righteous judgment of God visited upon us because of the individual and national sins of which we have been guilty, we nevertheless regard this rebellion as more immediately the natural result of the continuance and spread of domestic slavery in our land, and therefore hail with unmingled joy the proposition of our Chief Magistrate which has received the sanction of Congress, to extend aid from the General Government to any State in which slavery exists which shall deem fit to initiate a system of constitutional emancipation.

Resolved, That we deeply sympathize with all loyal citizens and Christian patriots in the rebellious portions of our country, and we cordially invite their co-operation in offering united supplications at a throne of grace, that God would restore peace to our distracted country, re-establish fraternal relations between all the States, and make our land, in all time to come, the asylum of the oppressed and the permanent abode of liberty and religion.

Resolved, That our devout thanks are due to Almighty God for the success which has crowned our arms; and whilst we praise and magnify his name for the help and succor he has graciously afforded to our land and naval forces, in enabling them to overcome our enemies, we regard these tokens of his Divine favor as cheering indications of the final triumph of our cause.

THE EAST BALTIMORE CONFERENCE OF THE METHODIST EPISCOPAL CHURCH, MARCH, 1862.

Whereas since the annual session of this body a fearful rebellion has broken out in several of the Southern States, threatening to overthrow the best and most benign Government the world ever saw; and

Whereas the Federal authority has been compelled to use force of arms to suppress said rebellion and to maintain its own supremacy; and

Whereas patriotism is a Christian virtue, taught in the word of God and enjoined upon us in our Twenty-Nine Articles of Religion: therefore,

1. *Resolved*, That, as a body of Christian ministers in Conference assembled, we hereby express our abhorrence of the rebellion now existing within our borders, as being treasonable in its origin, sanguinary in its progress, and as tending to retard the advancement of civil liberty through the world.

2. *Resolved*, That we hereby *approve* and *endorse* the present wise and patriotic administration of the Federal Government in its efforts to defeat the plans and to overcome the armed resistance of the so-called Confederate States, with a view of maintaining the unity and perpetuity of this Government.

3. *Resolved*, That, in our patriotic efforts in the past or present to sustain the Government of our country in her time of trial, we are not justly liable to the charge of political teaching, and in the inculcation of loyal principles and sentiments we regard the pulpit and the press as legitimate instrumentalities.

These resolutions were signed by Bishop Ames, and a committee appointed to present them to President Lincoln.

The committee proceeded to Washington for the purpose specified, and—accompanied by Senator Wright, of Indiana, Senator Willey, of Virginia, and Representative Leary, of Maryland—were formally presented to President Lincoln, by the Hon. Mr. Leary, in a brief but eloquent address. The address of the committee and the reading of the resolutions followed. During the reading of the document the President listened with much apparent interest, and made the following response—

GENTLEMEN—I am happy to see you; but, having no previous notice of your coming, I do not feel altogether prepared to reply to the paper and addresses you have presented me in such terms as they merit. Allow me to say, however, that I have the highest regard for the numerous and influential Christian body whom you represent. I am profoundly impressed with the influence you are exerting, as a Church, on the morals of the nation, as also with the loyalty of your people to the Government of the United States. I thank you, gentlemen, for your kind words and loyal expressions, and will, at the earliest moment I can command amid my pressing duties, reply to you in a more formal manner.

The President's Reply.

EXECUTIVE MANSION, WASHINGTON, MARCH 18, 1862.
REV. J. A. GERE, A. A. REESE, D.D., G. D. CHENOWETH—

GENTLEMEN—Allow me to tender to you, and through you to the East Baltimore Conference of the Methodist Episcopal Church, my grateful thanks for the preamble and resolutions of that body, copies of which you did me the honor to present yesterday. These kind words of approval, coming from so numerous a body of intelligent Christian people, and so free from all suspicion of sinister motives, are indeed encouraging to me. By the help of an all-wise Providence, I shall endeavor to do my duty; and I shall expect the continuance of your prayers for a right solution of our national difficulties, and the restoration of our country to peace and prosperity.

Your obliged and humble servant,

A. Lincoln.

BLACK RIVER METHODIST CONFERENCE,
NEW YORK, MAY, 1862.
On the State of the Country.

Whereas our beloved nation is distracted and torn by rebellion, and undergoing the peril of civil war, and has, in the order of God, a right to claim our deepest sympathies and most complete support, and even the sacrifice of the comfort, property, and the life of its citizens in its defence; and

Whereas Christianity inspires the truest and most earnest patriotism, and creates and develops those virtues in which it worthily consists, our own loved Church recognizing it in the Twenty-Third Article of Religion in our Book of Discipline, especially enjoining upon us obedience to the rulers of this nation; and

Whereas, while we declare that our patriotism and loyalty are not new virtues with us, and that we do not hold to or manifest them because the strong arm of power obliges us to do so, but that our hearts, our dearest earthly hopes and interests, together with our faith in the superiority of our national organization, impel us ever to pray and labor for our nation's welfare, yet in this time of its peril we feel that, more than ever before, God and humanity, gratitude and imperative duty, move us to exert ourselves to the utmost within our allotted sphere to uphold and support the Government of these United States in its noble and mighty efforts to save and preserve this nation. which is, in our opinion, more than any other nation the *people's* inheritance: therefore,

Resolved, 1. That, first of all, with profound reverence and chastened gratitude, we would render homage and thanksgiving to Almighty God for the manifestation of his presence, seen in the succession of events transpiring in our land, in which his righteousness has been mingled with mercy, not dealing with us according to our grievous national and social sins. but while chastening yet reforming and purifying us, teaching us impressively that "he reigneth, though clouds and darkness may be round about him," and that the prayers of the righteous are not offered to him in vain; for we recognize in the manifest tendency of these events that he answereth his people's prayers.

2. That we join with the loyal millions of our countrymen in rendering praise to God for the victories that have attended our arms in the navy and army, realizing, as expressed by our esteemed Secretary of War, that we cannot in ourselves alone organize victory, but that if we prevail our help must come from God, in whose hands is the destiny of nations; while we also remember with gratitude our brave and self-sacrificing citizens who have consecrated themselves upon the altar of our country, which so many of them have baptized with their blood, as did our fathers before them.

3. That we recognize slavery as the cause of the present rebellion and civil war, and are more than ever convinced that

either slavery or the nation must perish; and therefore we hail with joy the recent emancipation of the slaves in the District of Columbia by Congress.

4. That we believe it to be the duty of all good men to sustain our national administration by prayer to God for its guidance and support, by their influence, and, if necessary, by their arms, recognizing, as we do, the very great responsibilities of our Chief Magistrate, and we confide in his integrity and his ability.

5. That we sympathize with our soldiers in their toil and peril. and especially with the sick and wounded and those in the enemy's prisons, and also with the thousands of widows and orphans, fathers and mothers, who are bereft of their loved ones, sacrificed in their country's service, and that, so far as in us lies, we do offer, and will by God's grace carry, the consolations of our blessed Christianity to assuage the griefs and bless the hearts of those afflicted ones.

6. That we would urge upon all good citizens, what events so impressively teach us, the imperative obligation that rests upon every Christian to participate in the election of our lawmakers and rulers, especially to attend primary elections or caucuses, remembering that in this nation, where the people rule, God will hold every citizen responsible for civil privileges and duties, and that no man will be held excusable if he neglects to do all he can to elect good men to the places of trust and responsibility in the Government; and we would also remind Christian men that the cause of Jesus Christ is so involved in this as to demand that they should be untiring in vigilance and invincible in their purpose and action to control the very origin and source of civil power in this land.

7. That we renewedly pledge ourselves to our nation's welfare and perpetuity; and may our right hand forget her cunning, and our tongue cleave to the roof of our mouth, if we forget or cease to pray for her.

The New School General Assembly of the Presbyterian Church, May, 1862, adopted the following paper, prepared by Rev. Dr. N. S. Beman.

The State of the Country.

Whereas this General Assembly is called, in the providence of God, to hold its deliberations at a time when a wicked and fearful rebellion threatens to destroy the fair fabric of our Government, to lay waste our beloved country, and to blight and ruin, so far as the present life is concerned, all that is dear to us as Christians; and

Whereas, as a branch of the Christian Church, Presbyterians have ever been found loyal and the friends of good order, believing, as they do, that civil government is ordained of God, that the magistrate is the minister of God for good, that he beareth not the sword in vain, and they are, therefore, subject to this ordinance of God, "not only for wrath," or under the influence of fear, "but also for conscience' sake," or under the influence of moral and Christian principle; and

Whereas the particular Church whose representatives we are, and in whose behalf we are now and here called to act, have inscribed on our banner "THE CONSTITUTIONAL PRESBYTERIAN CHURCH," having never favored secession or nullification, either in Church or State, deem it quite becoming and proper in us to express ourselves with great Christian sincerity and frankness on those matters which now agitate our country: therefore,

Resolved, 1. That we deem the Government of these United States the most benign that has ever blessed our imperfect world; and should it be destroyed, after its brief career of good, another such, in the ordinary course of human events, can hardly be anticipated for a long time to come; and, for these reasons, we revere and love it as one of the great sources of hope, under God, for a lost world, and it is doubly dear to our hearts because it was procured and established by the toil, sacrifice, and blood of our fathers.

Resolved, 2. That rebellion against such a Government as ours, and especially by those who have ever enjoyed their full share of its protection, honors, rich blessings of every name, can have no excuse or palliation, and can be inspired by no other motives than those of ambition and avarice, and can find no parallel except in the first two great rebellions—that which assailed the throne of heaven directly, and that which peopled our world with miserable apostates.

Resolved, 3. That whatever diversity of sentiment may exist among us respecting international wars, or the appeal to the sword for the settlement of points of honor or interest between independent nations, we are all of one mind on the subject of rebellion, and especially against the best Government which God has yet given to the world; that our vast army now in the field is to be looked upon as a great police force, organized to carry into effect the Constitution and laws, which insurgents, in common with other citizens, have ordained by their own voluntary acts, and which they are bound by honor and oath and conscience to respect and obey, so that the strictest advocates of peace may bear a part in this deadly struggle for the life of the Government.

Resolved, 4, That while we have been utterly shocked at the deep depravity of the men who have framed and matured this rebellion, and who are now clad in arms, manifested in words and deeds, there is another class found in the loyal States who have excited a still deeper loathing—some in Congress, some in high civil life, and some in the ordinary walks of business—who never utter a manly thought or opinion in favor of the Government but they follow it, by way of comment, by two or three smooth apologies for Southern insurrectionists, presenting the difference between an open and avowed enemy in the field and a secret and insidious foe in the bosom of our own family.

Resolved, 5. That, in our opinion, this whole insurrectionary movement can be traced to one primordial root, and one only—African slavery, the love of it, and a determination to make it perpetual; and while we look upon this war as having one grand end in view, the restoration of the Union, by crushing out the last living and manifested fiber of rebellion, we hold that every thing—the institution of slavery, if need be—must be made to bend to this great purpose; and while, under the influence of humanity and Christian benevolence, we may commiserate the condition of the ruined rebels, once in fraternity with ourselves, but now, should the case occur, despoiled of all that makes the world dear to them, we must be, at the same time, constrained to feel that the retribution has been self-inflicted, and must add, *Fiat justitia, ruat coelum.*

Resolved, 6. That we have great confidence in Abraham Lincoln, President of the United States, and his Cabinet, and in the commanders of our armies and our navy, and the valiant men of this republic, prosecuting a holy warfare under their banners; and we bless God that he has stood by them and cheered them on in what we trust will ever stand as the darkest days of our country's humiliation, and crowned them with many signal victories. Knowing that ultimate success is with God alone, we will ever pray that the last sad note of anarchy and misrule may soon die away, and the *old flag of our country*, radiant with stripes and brilliant with stars, may again wave over a great, undivided, and happy people.

Resolved, 7. That we here, in deep humility for our sins and the sins of the nation, and in heartfelt devotion, lay ourselves, with all we are and have, on the altar of God and our country; and we hesitate not to pledge the churches and Christian people under our care as ready to join with us in the same fervent sympathies and united prayers that our rulers in the Cabinet, and our commanders in the field and on the waters, and the brave men under their leadership, may take courage, under the assurance that the Presbyterian Church of the United States are with them, in heart and hand, in life and effort, in this fearful existing conflict.

Resolved, finally, That a copy of these resolutions, signed by the officers of the General Assembly, be forwarded to his Excellency Abraham Lincoln, President of the United States, accompanied by the following respectful letter—

To the President of the United States.

The General Assembly of the Presbyterian Church, holding its annual session in the city of Cincinnati, Ohio, in transmitting the following resolutions, beg leave most respectfully to express in a more personal manner the sentiments of our Church in reference to yourself and the great issues with which you are called to deal. It is with no desire to bring a tribute of flattery when we assure you, honored sir, of the affection and confidence of our Church. Since the day of your inauguration, the thousands of our membership have followed you with unceasing prayer, beseeching the throne of Heaven on your behalf. In our great church courts, in our lesser judicatures, in our weekly assemblages in the house of God, at our family altars, in the inner place of prayer, you have been the burden of our petitions; and when we look at the history of your administration hitherto, and at the wonderful way in which this people have been led under your guidance, we glorify God on account of you. We give praise not to man, but to God. In your firmness, your integrity, challenging the admiration of even your enemies, your moderation, your wisdom, the timeliness of your acts exhitited at critical junctures, your paternal words, so eminently fitting the chosen head of a great people, we recognize the hand and power of God. We devoutly and humbly accept it as from Him in answer to the innumerable prayers which have gone up from our hearts. We desire, as a Church, to express to you our reverence, our love, our deep sympathy with you in the greatness of your trust, the depth of your personal bereavements, and to pledge to you, as in all the future, our perpetual remembrance of you before God, and all the support that loyal hearts can offer. We have given our sons to the army and navy; some of our ministers and many of our church-members have died in hospital and field. We are glad that we have given them, and we exult in that they were true to death. We gladly pledge as many more as the cause of our country may demand. We believe that there is but one path before this people: this gigantic and inexpressibly wicked rebellion must be destroyed. The interests of humanity, the cause of God and his Church, demand it at our hands. May God give to you his great support, preserve you, impart to you more than human wisdom, and permit you, ere long, to rejoice in the deliverance of our beloved country in peace and unity.

Signed,   George Duffield, D.D., *Moderator.*
                              Edwin F. Hatfield, D.D., *Stated Clerk.*

These resolutions and letter were solemnly adopted by a unanimous vote taken by rising. And, after this expression was taken, the congregation were requested to unite with the Assembly in this vote by also rising. The whole congregation arose, and while standing the Moderator lifted up his hands in devout and thankful prayer for the Divine blessing to accompany the letter. The prayer for the President was hearty and touching.

The President's Response to the General Assembly.
DEPARTMENT OF STATE, WASHINGTON, JUNE 9, 1862.
TO THE GENERAL ASSEMBLY OF THE PRESBYTERIAN CHURCH OF THE UNITED STATES, HOLDING ITS ANNUAL SESSION IN THE CITY OF CINCINNATI.

Reverend Gentlemen—I have had the honor of receiving your address to the President of the United States, and the proceedings of your venerable body on the subject of the existing insurrection, by which that address was accompanied.

These papers have been submitted to the President. I am instructed to convey to you his most profound and grateful acknowledgments for the fervent assurances of support and sympathy which they contain. For many years hereafter, one of the greatest subjects of felicitation among good men will be the signal success of the Government of the United States in preserving our Federal Union, which is the ark of civil and religious liberty on this continent and throughout the world. All the events of our generation which preceded this attempt at revolution, and all that shall happen after it will be deemed unimportant in consideration of that one indispensable and invaluable achievement. The men of our generation whose memory will be the longest and the most honored will be they who thought the most earnestly, prayed the most fervently, hoped the most confidently, fought the most heroically, and suffered the most patiently, in the sacred cause of freedom and humanity. The record of the action of the Presbyterian Church seems to the President worthy of its traditions and its aspirations as an important branch of the Church founded by the Saviour of men.

Commending our yet distracted country to the interposition and guardian care of the Ruler and Judge of nations, the President will persevere steadily and hopefully in the great work committed to his hands, relying upon the virtue and intelligence of the people of the United States and the candor and benevolence of all good men.

I have the honor to be, reverend gentlemen, your very obedient servant.

William H. Seward.

The Old School General Assembly of the Presbyterian Church, May, 1862, adopted the following paper, prepared by Dr. R. J. Breckinridge.

The General Assembly of the Presbyterian Church in the United States of America, in session at Columbus, in the State of Ohio, considering the unhappy condition of the country—in the midst of a bloody civil war—and of the Church—agitated everywhere, divided in sentiment in many places, and openly assailed by schism in a large section of it—considering also the duty which this chief tribunal, met in the name and by the authority of the glorified Saviour of sinners, who is also the Sovereign Ruler of all things, owes to him our Head and Lord, and to his flock committed to our charge, and to the people whom we are commissioned to evangelize, and to the civil authorities who exist by his appointment—do hereby in this deliverance give utterance to our solemn convictions and our deliberate judgment touching the matters herein set forth, that they may serve for the guidance of all over whom the Lord Christ has given us any office of instruction or any power of government.

1. Peace is among the very highest temporal blessings of the Church, as well as of all mankind; and public order is one of the first necessities of the spiritual as well as the civil commonwealth. Peace has been wickedly superseded by war, in its worst form, throughout the whole land; and public order has been wickedly superseded by rebellion, anarchy, and violence, in the whole Southern portion of the Union. All this

has been brought to pass in a disloyal and traitorous attempt to overthrow the national Government by military force, and to divide the nation contrary to the wishes of the immense majority of the people of the nation, and without satisfactory evidence that the majority of the people, in whom the local sovereignty resided, even in the States which revolted, ever authorized any such proceeding, or ever approved the fraud and violence by which this horrible treason has achieved whatever success it has had. This whole treason, rebellion, anarchy, fraud, and violence is utterly contrary to the dictates of natural religion and morality, and is plainly condemned by the revealed will of God. It is the clear and solemn duty of the national Government to preserve, at whatever cost, the national Union and Constitution, to maintain the laws in their supremacy, to crush force by force, and to restore the reign of public order and peace to the entire nation, by whatever lawful means that are necessary thereunto. And it is the bounden duty of the people who compose this great nation, each one in his several place and degree, to uphold the Federal Government, and every State Governtnent, and all persons in authority, whether civil or military, in all their lawful and proper acts, unto the ends hereinbefore set forth.

2. The Church of Christ has no authority from him to make rebellion, or to counsel treason, or to favor anarchy, in any case whatever. On the contrary, every follower of Christ has the personal liberty bestowed on him by Christ to submit, for the sake of Christ, according to his own conscientious sense of duty, to whatever government, however bad, under which his lot may be cast. But, while patient suffering for Christ's sake can never be sinful, treason, rebellion, and anarchy may be sinful, most generally, perhaps, are sinful, and probably are always and necessarily sinful in all free countries, where the power to change the Government by voting, in the place of force, exists as a common right constitutionally secured to the people who are sovereign. If in any case treason, rebellion, and anarchy can possibly be sinful, they are so in the case now desolating large portions of this nation and laying

waste great numbers of Christian congregations and fatally obstructing every good word and work in those regions.

To the Christian people scattered throughout those unfortunate regions, who have been left of God to have any hand in bringing on these terrible calamities, we earnestly address words of exhortation and rebuke, as unto brethren who have sinned exceedingly and whom God calls to repentance by fearful judgment. To those in like circumstances who are not chargeable with the sins which have brought such calamities upon the land, but who have chosen, in the exercise of their Christian liberty, to stand in their lot and suffer, we address words of affectionate sympathy, praying God to bring them off conquerors. To those in like circumstances who have taken their lives in their hands and risked all for their country and for conscience' sake, we say we love such with all our heart, and bless God such witnesses were found in the time of thick darkness. We fear, and we record it with great grief, that the Church of God and the Christian people, to a great extent, throughout all the revolted States, have done many things that ought not to have been done, in this time of trial, rebuke, and blasphemy; but concerning the wide-spread schism which is reported to have occurred in many Southern Synods this Assembly will take no action at this time. It declares, however, its fixed purpose, under all possible circumstances, to labor for the extension and permanent maintenance of the Church under its care in every part of the United States. Schism, so far as it may exist, we hope to see healed. If that cannot be, it will be disregarded.

3. We record our gratitude to God for the prevailing unity of sentiment, and general internal peace, which has characterized the Church in the States that have not revolted, embracing a great majority of the ministers, congregations, and people under our care. It may still be called, with emphasis, a loyal, orthodox, and pious Church; and all its acts and works indicate its right to a title so noble. Let it strive for Divine grace to maintain that good report. In some respects the interests of the Church of God are very different front those of civil institu-

tions. Whatever may befall this or any other nation, the Church of Christ must abide on earth triumphant even over the gates of hell. It is, therefore, of supreme importance that the Church should guard itself from internal alienations and divisions, founded upon questions and interests that are external as to her, and which ought not by their necessary working cause her fate to depend on the fate of things less important and less enduring than herself. Disturbers of the Church ought not to be allowed, especially disturbers of the Church in States that never revolted or that have been cleared of armed rebels—disturbers who, under many false pretexts, may promote discontent, disloyalty, and general alienation, tending to the unsettling of ministers, to local schisms, and to manifold trouble. Let a spirit of quietness, of mutual forbearance, and of ready obedience to authority, both civil and ecclesiastical, illustrate the loyalty, the orthodoxy, and the piety of the Church. It is more especially to ministers of the gospel, and among them particularly to any whose first impressions had been on any account favorable to the terrible military revolution which has been attempted, and which God's providence has hitherto so signally rebuked, that these decisive considerations ought to be addressed. And, in the name and by the authority of the Lord Jesus, we earnestly exhort all who love God and fear his wrath to turn a deaf ear to all counsels and suggestions that tend towards a reaction favorable to disloyalty, schism, or disturbance, either in the Church or in the country. There is hardly any thing more inexcusable connected with the frightful conspiracy against which we testify than the conduct of those office-bearers and members of the Church who, although citizens of loyal States and subject to the control of loyal Presbyteries and Synods, have been faithless to all authority, human and Divine, to which they owed subjection. Nor should any to whom this deliverance may come fail to bear in mind that it is not only their outward conduct concerning which they ought to take heed, but it is also, and especially, their heart, their temper, and their motives, in the sight of God, and towards the free and beneficent civil Government which he has blessed us withal, and towards the spiritual commonwealth to which they are subject in the Lord. In all these respects we must all give account to God in the great day. And it is in view of our own dread responsibility to the Judge of quick and dead that we now make this deliverance.

At the Yearly Meeting of the Quakers, May, 1862, they adopted the following address, which originated in the women's meeting, and which has been transmitted to the President of the United States—

> *To the President, Senate, and House of Representatives of the United States of America.*
> At the yearly meeting of Friends, held in Philadelphia for Pennsylvania, New Jersey, Delaware, and the Eastern Shore of Maryland, by adjournment from the twelfth day of the fifth month to the sixteenth of the same, inclusive, Anno Domini one thousand eight hundred and sixty-two,
>
> The following minute was read, united with, directed to be signed by the clerks, and forwarded—
>
> This meeting has been introduced into a deep concern relative to the present condition of our country. Our minds have been directed to those who preside over our national Government, and gratitude has been felt to the Great Ruler of nations that he has so far moved the hearts of these that they have decreed the District of Columbia free from slavery. We earnestly desire that the Chief Magistrate of the nation and our Congress may, in this season of deep trial, humbly seek Divine guidance, that under this influence they may act for the cause of justice and mercy, in that wisdom which is pure, peaceable, and profitable to direct, and that the effusion of blood may be stayed.
>
> Signed by direction and on behalf of the meeting aforesaid.
> Mary S. Lippincott, *Clerk of the Women's Meeting.*
> William Griscom, *Clerk of the Men's Meeting.*

UNITED PRESBYTERIAN ASSEMBLY, MAY, 1862.

The Committee recommend the appointment of the last Thursday of November as a day of thanksgiving, for the following reasons—the enjoyment of gospel ordinances, our civil and religious liberty, the supply of provisions so unusually cheap and abundant, that God has stirred up the people to give themselves and their substance for the defence of the country, and the abolition of slavery in the District of Columbia.

RESOLUTIONS ON THE STATE OF THE COUNTRY

The following resolutions on the state of the country were presented by the Committee—

Whereas our country suffers under a desolating civil war, and calamities not often equalled in the history of the world are now endured by our fellow-citizens; and whereas the ministers of the gospel, as witnesses for Christ and watchmen on the walls of Zion, are bound by their testimony to give the trumpet a certain and distinct sound in order to warn the people of their danger and direct them in the way of duty. Therefore,

Resolved, That we recognize in the defeats and disasters of our forces in the beginning of the conflict a deserved visitation of God's wrath upon us for our complicity in the sin of slavery, and while we have reason to fear further reverses to our arms, yet we feel and hereby express our gratitude to God for the recent victories and advantages obtained over the enemy, and cherish the hope and belief that God will continue his favor till rebellion shall be forever crushed and peace restored.

Resolved, That, believing that so long as slavery lives no permanent peace can he enjoyed, we express our highest gratification at the emancipation policy indicated in the President's recent proposition to aid the slave States in the "abolishment" of slavery. We thank God for the deliverance of the District of Columbia from the national curse and disgrace of slavery, and would hail with pleasure the proclamation of universal liberty; and we trust that our President and Congress will pursue the course of emancipation till liberty shall be proclaimed throughout all the land to all the inhabitants thereof.

Resolved. That, believing compromise with wrong to be the rock on which our Union has been in danger of splitting, we warn our fellow-citizens, politicians, and statesmen that a compromise with rebellion in behalf of slavery will be no less dangerous to the stability of our Government than to the cause of human freedom.

Resolved, That, believing it to be a duty specially incumbent on the Church to let her light shine, and that her ministry are particularly bound in the present perilous crisis of our country's history to declare the counsel of God regarding the sin and crime of slavery, we trust that all the preachers of that gospel which proclaims liberty to the captive of every denomination will hear and obey God's voice, now calling upon them louder than ever before to open their mouth in behalf of the dumb. And we would especially urge upon our brethren under our care to give a clear testimony on this subject in order to instruct our people and the nation in the great truth that righteousness exalteth a nation, whilst sin is a reproach to any people.

Resolved, That, as we can only succeed by depending entirely on Divine agency, we will call upon the Lord in our trouble, and ask him to so overrule the present war, inaugurated for the purpose of extending and perpetuating slavery, that it shall issue in its final and complete overthrow; and that we will bear on our spirits continually at a throne of grace, our President, his counsellors, the Congress, the army and navy, and pray especially that God would preserve those who have enlisted in the cause of their country from the perils of the camp and the field, and restore them to their families and friends in peace and safety, and prepare those who may have to die in the conflict for a victory over death and hell, and a triumphant entrance into heaven.

Adopted unanimously.

TESTIMONY OF THE GENERAL ASSOCIATION OF CONNECTICUT CONCERNING THE DUTY OF CHRISTIAN CITIZENS AT THE PRESENT CRISIS.

The General Association of Connecticut, being convened at Norwalk on the third Tuesday in June, A.D. 1862, when the loyal people of the United States are in the agony and crisis of a war for the Union and the Constitution and for the great principle of popular self-government, is called to put upon record and to publish to its constituency, the associated Congregational pastors and ministers in this Commonwealth, and to the churches, its testimony concerning the duty of all Christian citizens at such a time as this.

I. We rejoice that we have no need to inculcate on our brethren in the ministry, nor on our churches, the duty of sustaining our national Government in this conflict, by unceasing prayer to God in public and in private, by a cheerful submission to the burdens and sorrows inseparable from so great a war, and by voluntary contributions and sacrifices for the comfort, the encouragement, and the moral and religious welfare of our brethren and our sons who are in arms, as well as for the relief of those who are suffering with wounds received in battle, or with sickness induced by the hardships and exposures incident to military service. Yet it is not superfluous to insist distinctly on the duty of a large and generous confidence in the men whom God's providence has called to the administration of our Government at this time. When we bless God that the President of the United States has shown himself from the beginning of his administration to this time eminently sagacious and prudent as well as honest and patriotic, we express the deep conviction and feeling of thousands of our fellow-citizens whose voices were not given to make him President. If there be any thing in the proceedings or the policy of our Government which, seen from our point of view, seems doubtful, let it be remembered that, in the present peril, the first duty of every citizen is confidence in the constituted leadership till confidence shall be impossible.

II. While we acknowledge the justice of God in the present visitation of his displeasure against the many sins of this most favored nation, we record our conviction that the cause of this rebellion against popular self-government is nothing else than the institution of slavery, maintained in defiance of the first principles of natural justice, as well as of Christianity, and that no durable peace can be expected with the slaveholding States till that institution, so odious in the sight of God and so long the abhorrence of the civilized world, shall have ceased to be formidable as a power, and shall have received its death-wound. Nothing else than such an institution, reducing millions of human beings to the condition of merchandise, taking away from them by law the key of knowledge and thus forbidding them to read the Bible, robbing them of all domestic rights and sanctities, and relentlessly maintaining an infamous traffic in human beings for whom Christ died, could have bred in such a land as this a population so ignorant, so barbarous, so morally and socially degraded, though nominally free, as that which wicked conspirators, the leaders of the rebellion, have used at their pleasure in this infamous and ever-memorable war against the most beneficent Government which God has ever given to any people.

During all the progress of that great apostasy from the first principles of Christian morality which has characterized the history of Christianity in the slaveholding States for the last thirty years, the General Association of Connecticut, while studiously refusing to hold forth any other doctrine concerning the relations and mutual duties of masters and servants than that which was held forth by the apostles, has never ceased to testify "that to buy and sell human beings, and to hold them and treat them as merchandise, or to treat servants, bond or free, in any manner inconsistent with the fact that they are intelligent and voluntary beings, made in the image of God, is a violation of the word of God, and should be treated by all the churches as an immorality inconsistent with a profession of the Christian religion." It has never ceased to declare that it "regards the laws and usages in respect to slavery which exist in many of the States of this Union, as inconsistent with the character and responsibilities of a free and Christian people;" nor to proclaim "the duty of every Christian, and especially of every minister of the gospel, to use all prudent and lawful efforts for the peaceful abolition of slavery." We have no occasion now to give any other testimony on that point than what we have always given.

III. As we look forward in hope to the conclusion of this war, we anticipate the restoration of the Constitution of the

United States, and of the acts of Congress and treaties made in conformity therewith, as the supreme law of the land, in every one of the now revolted States. For the abolition of slavery in those States, we look not to the action of the Federal Government exercising any power inconsistent with the Constitution, but rather to the all-wise and almighty providence of God compelling those States to accept and to incorporate into their own laws those principles of natural justice which are liberty to every man unjustly held in bondage. We demand of our enemies that they shall accept, and we trust in God that when he has sufficiently humbled them by his power and scourged them in his justice he will give them the heart to accept with gladness, the priceless boon of freedom for all. Then shall the word of God be no longer bound, but have free course and be glorified, and our whole land shall be adorned with the beauty and the riches of a truly Christian civilization.

Meanwhile, we charge ourselves and we exhort our brethren of the ministry and in the churches to be instant in prayer and ready for all efforts and sacrifices.

THE CONGREGATIONAL ASSOCIATION OF RHODE ISLAND, JUNE, 1862.

Whereas the great conspiracy against our national Government, which, before the last annual meeting of this body, had ripened into open rebellion and revolt, though greatly crippled and weakened, remains yet unsubdued; and

Whereas, in the progress of the strife resulting therefrom, God in his providence has graciously smiled upon us, preserving our Chief Magistrate from the hands of bloody men who lay in wait for his life, our national capital from sacrilegious hands, our civil polity from being subverted, strengthening our hands to war and our fingers to fight, while he weakened our enemies in many an hour of decision; and

Whereas he has also touched the hearts of our civil rulers as with the finger of his love, moving them to undo the heavy burdens and break every yoke from the necks of those who could be directly reached by the arm of their authority, and also to propose a generous help in breaking others which they cannot directly reach: therefore,

Resolved, That this Consociation here makes devout acknowledgment to Almighty God for his mercies in these regards, and here also lifts up its voice in supplications that he will still be favorable unto us, that he will give wisdom and virtue to our civil rulers, that he will lead our armies to victory, that he will animate the hearts of all military governors and generals with the true spirit of liberty and humanity, so that the great power which they wield shall be so used as to secure his favor and the advancement of this whole people in knowledge and virtue, thus securing to us a righteous peace, purify our civil institutions from every stain of oppression, and enable us to transmit them with blessings and benedictions to the generations following.

THE IOWA STATE CONGREGATIONAL ASSOCIATION,
JUNE, 1862.

State of the country

Resolved, The history of our country since the outbreak of the present rebellion has furnished occasion for unceasing and most devout gratitude and praise to God, inasmuch as our defeats and disasters have, through his gracious overruling, contributed to the ultimate success of the national cause scarcely less than the many glorious victories which have been achieved.

Resolved, The wisdom, impartiality, tenacity of purpose, endurance, philanthropy, honesty, and honor exhibited by our Chief Magistrate in the administration of the Government, command our respect, confidence, admiration, and love, as for a man of extraordinary fitness for his high office in these times of unparalleled trial.

Resolved, We have observed with profound satisfaction the high ground taken by Messrs. Grimes and Harlan of the United States Senate, and Wilson of the House, from the State of Iowa, on the various questions of national concern which have recently been under consideration in the Federal legislature, and we rejoice in the great ability, the undoubted patriotism, the sturdy independence, and humane policy which have distinguished the course of these gentlemen in the discharge of their grave Congressional duties.

Resolved, While we rejoice in the great progress of anti-slavery sentiment throughout the loyal States, we deeply deplore before God the powerful pro-slavery sympathies and tendencies which are still manifest among the people, and regard it as the duty of all Christians to continue in labor and prayer for the deliverance of all the oppressed and for the proclamation of liberty throughout the land to all the inhabitants thereof.

GENERAL CONVENTION OF CONGREGATIONAL MINISTERS AND CHURCHES IN VERMONT, JUNE, 1862.

Whereas our country is now suffering under the dire calamities of civil war, as the result of a wicked rebellion; and whereas the Church of Christ in her membership is bound to bear witness to the truth, and against all wrong: therefore,

Resolved, 1. That we regard the war now being carried on by the Government to put down this unrighteous rebellion as an unavoidable necessity, sanctioned alike by all right-minded, patriotic men, and the principles of the word of God.

Resolved, 2. That we believe that, though other things may have had their measure of influence, yet that the *hitherto cherished institution of slavery* has been the principal and exciting *cause* and origin of this attempt to destroy the Constitution and break down the Government.

Resolved, 3. That we gratefully approve of the course the Government has taken in freeing itself from all complicity with slavery, that we sincerely hope that this institution may be done away, in the providence of God, speedily and effectively, and that we desire the President and Congress to use all their constitutional powers, in the present crisis, for its removal.

Resolved, 4. That we tender to the President of the United States, and his associates in the Government, our hearty confidence and support, and to the army and navy our sincere sympathy, with the assurance of our prayers that the same power which has been so visibly displayed in the past may guide to the complete re-establishment of the Union on the principles of justice and republican freedom.

Report was adopted, and ordered that a copy, signed by the Moderator and Scribe, be sent to the Secretary of State of the United States, to be laid before the President.

The Answer of the President through the Secretary of State.

DEPARTMENT OF STATE, WASHINGTON, JULY 11, 1862.

To Rev. CLAKE E. FERRIN, *Moderator, &c.*

SIR—I have the honor to acknowledge the reception of your note of the 23d of June, accompanied by a copy of resolutions which were unanimously adopted by the General Convention of Congregational ministers and churches recently assembled at Norwich.

In compliance with your request, these resolutions have been submitted to the President of the United States.

I am instructed to express his cordial thanks for the assurances of confidence and support thus tendered to him by a body so deservedly respected and so widely influential as the Congregational Church of Vermont.

The President is deeply impressed by the fervent and hopeful patriotism and benevolence which pervade the resolutions. It is the Union and the Constitution of this country which are at stake in the present unhappy strife; but that Union is not a mere strigent political band, nor is that Constitution a lifeless or spiritless political body. The Union is a guarantee of perpetual peace and prosperity to the American people, and the Constitution is the ark of civil and religious liberty for all classes and conditions of men.

Who that carefully reads the history of the nations for the period that this republic has existed under this Constitution and this Union can fail to see and appreciate the influence it has exerted in ameliorating the condition of mankind? Who that justly appreciates that influence will undertake to foretell the misfortunes and despondency which must occur on every continent should this republic desist all at once from its auspicious career and be resolved into a confused medley of small, discordant, and contentious States? The duty of the Christian coincides with that of the patriot, and the duty of the priest with that of the soldier, in averting so sad and fearful a consummation.

Be pleased, sir, to express these sentiments of the President to the reverend gentlemen in whose behalf you have addressed me, together with assurances of profound respect with which I have the honor to be their humble servant.

William H. Seward.

The Ohio Conference of the Methodist Episcopal Church, September, 1862.

Whereas the war now raging in our beloved country thickens with apparent disaster, which we cannot but regard as a chastisement from God for the sin of the nation; and

Whereas the interests of the Church, as well as the nation, are imperilled by the disasters of the times: therefore,

1. *Resolved,* That, as a Conference, we deeply deplore and humbly confess before Almighty God our manifold national sins, and do heartily implore his forgiveness and grace for reformation.

2. Resolved, That we have unwavering devotion to the cause of human freedom, and unshaken confidence in the God of battles and of nations.

3. *Resolved,* That, in our view, the Government should spare no vigor and know no *compromise* in treating *rebellion.*

4. *Resolved,* That we give all support consistent with our calling and within our power to sustain the arms of the Government.

5. *Resolved,* That we redouble our efforts in promoting vital godliness, both in the army and in civil life.

Presbytery of Elyria, Ohio, September, 1862.

Whereas the present session of this Presbytery occurs at a time of great danger and distress, when dark clouds lower upon us as a nation, and our minds are afflicted with fears and forebodings, if not for the ultimate success of the struggle of arms now progressing, at least for the lives of thousands, and for the multiplied interests of civilization and religion: therefore,

Resolved, 1. That, as a Presbytery and as individuals, we deeply sympathize with the great effort which loyal men of the nation are making to put down this wicked and causeless rebellion.

2. That we feel ourselves called upon and bound to support, in every legitimate way, by our influence, our prayers, and our efforts, our *national Executive* in the great leading purpose which he has declared to the world of preserving by every means within his reach, *the Union*, and of restoring and vindicating the outraged authority of our national Government throughout all that territory now in rebellion.

3. That, esteeming American slavery to be the primary and immediate cause of our present trouble, we believe that all protection and forbearance to it on the part of the nation has been forfeited, and that it is the duty of our national authorities, legislative and executive, to bring it to an end just as soon as may be consistent with the success of the present conflict of arms in which we are engaged.

4. That we recognize it as a time for being humbled before God, in view of the heavy judgments that have come upon us, and of discerning the cause not only in the sin of enslaving and perpetuating the bondage of the colored race, but in other national sins.

5. That the loyal men of the nation are, in our judgment, called upon to look to Almighty God for deliverance, and to use every means to propitiate his merciful favor, not only by putting away with a strong hand the crime of American slavery, but by every other proper means. Especially do we feel that intemperance, profanity, and Sabbath-breaking, now fearfully prevalent, since they alienate from us the favor of God, should be looked upon as offences against our nation's cause, disloyalties as well as sins.

6. That the Lord's day should not be broken in upon and diverted from its original purpose, as a day of rest unto him, so long as in the providence of God it is not rendered absolutely necessary, believing as we do that this course will best subserve not only the interests of religion, but the cause of our country.

THE SYNOD OF OHIO (NEW SCHOOL PRESBYTERIAN),
SEPTEMBER, 1862.

Resolved, That we cordially approve the patriotic action of our General Assembly, at its late sessions in Cincinnati, on the state of the country, and rejoice to know that our ministers and members with such unanimity sustain the Government in its great struggle for existence, and for the suppression of the vast and wicked rebellion now threatening its overthrow.

Resolved, That we regard the rebellion as permitted in the righteous providence of God as a chastisement for our sins as a nation, and especially for the sin of enslaving our fellow-men and holding them in cruel bondage; and we therefore rejoice in the recent proclamation of our worthy President, striking at the root of this evil by prohibiting our armies from returning slaves escaping from their masters and coming within our lines, by requiring the confiscation act to be enforced, and by proclaiming liberty to the slaves of all those States that shall be found in rebellion against our Government on the 1st day of January, 1863, and that we will exert our influence in all appropriate ways in our several spheres of labor to give practical effect to these principles.

Resolved, That we will remember and sustain in the future, as we have done in the past, by our prayers and sympathies and contributions, all those engaged in the praiseworthy and noble work of maintaining our free institutions intact, and preserving the integrity of our nation, and suppressing this rebellion and eradicating its bitter root, so that we may enjoy a righteous and honorable peace that shall be enduring as our mountains and deep and perpetual as the flow of our mighty rivers.

THE GENERAL ASSOCIATION OF NEW YORK
(CONGREGATIONAL), SEPTEMBER, 1862.
Resolutions on the State of the Country

1. *Resolved*, That, inasmuch as freedom to worship God according to the unrestricted dictate of conscience, and the inalienable equality in the rights and privileges of all, are the elemental and vitalizing principles of our Church polity, we, as

Congregationalists, are unalterably devoted to the holy cause of liberty, and always to the Government that maintains it.

2. That we regard as the basis of civil and religious freedom the eternal law of God, which requires that every man shall love his neighbor as himself, and we rejoice that the Constitution of the United States, in its article on the freedom of religious worship, recognizes the same Divine and unchangeable principle.

3. That so long as this nation is true to the principle of equality of civil and religious rights we can have no fear for the perpetuity of our Union, which was constructed to maintain that principle for ourselves, our posterity, and the world.

4. That we recognize with devout gratitude the unusual and continued spirit of prayer for the nation, and the repeated interpositions of Divine Providence in our behalf, as the evidence that God has set his seal of approbation on the efforts of the people and the Government to preserve and perpetuate the Constitution and the Union.

5. That in the steady progress toward unity of sentiment, from the day of the wanton attack on Fort Sumter, we see the educational process of God in preparing us to take our proper stand in the great struggle between Liberty and Despotism, on which the highest interests of our nation and humanity are staked.

6. That we hail with great joy the late proclamation of the President of the United States, in which he announces EMANCIPATION FOR THE ENSLAVED; regarding it as eminently wise and timely, and as a grand advance towards the desired consummation of our present conflict, in the establishment of enduring peace with freedom throughout the entire land.

7. That we confidently anticipate that when God shall have disciplined and thoroughly purified us as a people, and delivered us from the degradation and curse of slavery, he will make our example eminently effective for the education of the struggling nations of the world in the great principles of healthful civil and religious freedom, so fulfilling his manifest purpose in the formation of this Christian republic on

the basis of popular intelligence, of wholesome liberty, and of constitutional self-government.

8. That a delegation of this body be appointed to proceed to Washington City, personally to present the above resolutions to his Excellency the President of the United States, with the assurance of our profoundest sympathy with him in his present trying situation; and that we shall continue our earnest daily supplications to God, the great Ruler of Nations, that he would bestow upon him the wisdom and the fortitude necessary for the prompt and faithful discharge of his duties.

GENERAL CONFERENCE OF THE CONGREGATIONAL
MINISTERS OF MASSACHUSETTS, SEPTEMBER, 1862.

Resolved, With humility and shame we confess the sins that have brought the righteous judgments of God upon our nation. Our pride, ambition, and worldliness have led us to sin with a high hand. We have oppressed and enslaved the poor and needy. We have defiled the good land that the Lord has given us.

Resolved, We receive the fact tlaat an armed rebellion still rages unsuppressed and defiant against our Government not only as a proof that we are not yet as a nation sufficiently humbled before God and therefore not prepared for his deliverance, but also as an earnest call for our greatly increased humiliation and prayers, and our augmented energy and self-sacrifice for the defence of our liberties.

Resolved, While we acknowledge our entire dependence upon God for the triumph of our Government, we believe that God will secure this result through appropriate human agencies; and therefore we look for a *complete* and *permanent* restoration of union and peace to our country only from the removal of slavery—the chief source of this rebellion.

Resolved, We believe that we express the unanimous feeling of our churches in this State when we pledge our loyal support and sympathy to the President of these United States in the most vigorous measures for the suppression of this rebellion. We fervently implore for him, his cabinet, and all our civil and military authorities, the wisdom and guidance of Heaven, so necessary to the discharge of their present solemn responsibilities; upon our army and navy, the protection of God and the courage which comes from his presence and obedience to his holy commands; and the consolations of the gospel upon the sick and wounded, and the households mourning for the death of the slain.

Resolved, That since the first distracting novelty of the war has given place to deeper thoughtfulness in the public mind, and multitudes are called to the most solemn duty of laying themselves or their friends on the altar of their country—and we know not but that more fearful judgments of Heaven will yet take away one of every two in the field and by the fireside—it is the pressing duty of ministers and churches to labor as never before for the immediate conversion of all hearts to Christ.

United States Convention of Universalists, September, 1862.

Resolved, That while in our judgment we must accept the existing strife as the natural and inevitable penalty of our national infidelity to our republican principles and of an attempt to reconcile freedom and slavery (which are essentially irreconcilable), we renewedly profess our faith in the justice of our cause and in the certainty of our final triumph, and renewedly tender to the President and his constitutional advisers the assurance of our sympathy amid the great responsibilities of their position, and of our hearty support in all proper and efficient efforts to suppress this atrocious rebellion.

Resolved, That we have occasion in the midst of events through which we are passing to be deeply impressed with the reality of God's moral rule, and to learn anew the lesson that neither nations nor individuals can safely defy his law, nor hope to escape from the inexorable ordinance that sinners must eat the fruits of their doings.

THE OHIO PRESBYTERY OF THE REFORMED PRESBYTERIAN CHURCH, OCTOBER, 1862.

The proclamation of emancipation, bearing date September 22, 1862, by Abraham Lincoln, we regard—and no doubt enlightened and liberal men over all the earth will regard—as one of the greatest events and one of the best Signs of our extraordinary times. To have been destined to issue it is glory enough for one man. It will stand in future history in the same category with Magna Charta and the Declaration of American Independence. It is a living, hearty, and generous seed, which will produce through God much good—local and world-wide fruit. It will save our nation. It is, in the result, the death of slavery and the rebellion. This also cometh forth from the Lord of hosts, who is wonderful in counsel and excellent in working. Therefore,

Resolved, That this Presbytery recognizes the late proclamation of the President of the United States in reference to the emancipation of the slaves of those States now in rebellion against the Government as righteous and eminently proper; that we hail it as a favorable omen that this nation is at last disposed to be just to the oppressed of the land and place itself on the side of God and humanity.

That, in carrying out the principles of this proclamation, the President should receive the hearty support of all loyal citizens, and that now more than ever we and the people under our care should remember him in all his enlightened efforts to save the nation and in all his righteous measures for the emancipation of The oppressed.

NEW SCHOOL PRESBYTERIAN SYNOD OF WISCONSIN,
SEPTEMBER, 1862.

Whereas a fearful civil war still continues to rage with increasing intensity in these United States, and by its falling victims bringing grief and mourning to a multitude of homes; and

Whereas it comes like a withering blight over the fair heritage of God, taking away the standard-bearers from our churches, and making large drafts upon the young, who soon were expected to be the efficient laborers in the vineyard of the Lord, who, with hearts full of loyalty and patriotism, have gone forth to their country's call: therefore,

Resolved, 1. That we do penitently acknowledge the justice of God, who has laid on us the rod of his correction for the national sins and individual offences of which we have been guilty, though often rebuked and reproved, and heartily pray that the time may soon be at hand when his wrath may be averted, and peace be restored to our distracted and bleeding country.

2. That as a Church our testimony in the past has ever been against oppression and in favor of constitutional liberty: so we cannot now withhold an earnest expression of our deepening hostility to the infamous evil which is admitted as the guilty cause of what we are now suffering.

3. That we are anxiously waiting to hear authoritatively proclaimed from the seat of Government universal freedom to the oppressed, which presents the only hope that the Divine displeasure will be turned away and the blessings of peace and prosperity again restored.

4. That the Church is most impressively urged to withdraw her confidence from all human instrumentalities as adequate to overthrow this gigantic rebellion, and to fix her eye unswervingly on the God of nations and the God of battles in this day of our country's peril.

THE CONGREGATIONAL ASSOCIATION OF WESTERN PENNSYLVANIA, SEPTEMBER, 1862.

Inasmuch as God has permitted civil war to exist in this nation, and to spread and gain in intensity and power till it involves the entire energies of the nation and threatens the very existence of the Government, it becomes us who profess to fear God, to love our Government and the institutions which are sustained and cherished by it, to inquire into the causes of this dire calamity, and to help put them away, that peace may be restored and the blessing of God once more rest upon the nation.

We believe that while there are many violations of God's law, and much that is evil, and only evil, provoking continually the Almighty to jealousy and anger, yet still the great crowning evil, and that for which God has poured his judgments upon us in so terrible a manner, is our system of slavery. As a Christian and democratic nation, we have so far departed from our principles as to hold four millions of our fellow-beings as property. We have made the largest cities in the nation slave-marts, where the voice of the auctioneer offering for money "the souls and bodies of men" is almost continually heard. We have made whole States slave-breeding and slave-selling States, in consequence of which the sighs and tears caused by the separation of famalies and kindred ties have never ceased to be heard or to flow. We have prostituted our civil principles to this barbarous practice. We have denied the equality of men's natural rights. We have by judicial dicta thrown a whole race beyond the pale of Governmental protection. We have denied the sovereignty of God in the supremacy of his law, that this evil might be sustained. We have chased the poor fugitive, and delivered him to his inhuman master, in direct contravention of the word of God and the violation of every principle of civilization or feeling of humanity. We have built political parties on a prejudice of color, and have gained political influence by the crushing out of the African mind the last ray of hope of protection by the Government for a solitary right. The religious influence of the nation, as a great whole, has either participated in this inhuman work or stood by consenting.

For this great sin, deeply ingrained in the public character, God has permitted this war to come upon us. The hand of God has so directed it as to make it, from a trifling beginning, to assume gigantic proportions, already to have slain its hundreds of thousands, and is now wasting with a fury seldom known in any land. If the nation escapes an entire overthrow in all its material and moral interests, or even its existence, it will be through God's great mercy alone.

With these convictions upon our minds, and the fear of God before our eyes, we do now confess this great sin of ourselves and the nation, and we will continually pray for God's wrath to be averted, that the nation may be restored to such a peace as God shall ordain and establish. We will especially pray for our rulers and the leaders in the army and navy, that they may fear God, and be directed by Divine wisdom in overcoming this rebellion, by destroying slavery, the cause of it, and thereby secure again the favor and aid of the Almighty.

We will pray for the soldiers, every day, that they may be sustained in the great sacrifices they are making for their country's good and in accomplishing the Divine purpose. We will sympathize also with the friends of those who have fallen, or may fall, while fighting for their country.

As individuals, we pledge ourselves to go or stay, to give our substance or suffer, as God in his providence may seem to require for our country's good. And, acting under the conviction that the judgment of God is resting upon us as a nation, we will abstain from amusements and gratifications in which we may have indulged in other circumstances, and give ourselves up to self-denial, that God's wrath may be turned away, and freedom and peace without sinful compromise be restored to the nation, and vital godliness be revived and spread.

THE AMERICAN BOARD OF COMMISSIONERS FOR FOREIGN MISSIONS, OCTOBER, 1862.

The Board of Commissioners for Foreign Missions, in its last annual meeting, rendered its sympathy in the struggle of our national Government with rebellion, and its prayer to the God of nations so to overrule the conflict that the rebellion may be crushed, slavery, its prime cause, removed, and that peace, prosperity, and righteousness may be permanently established throughout our land.

Again assembled for the annual review of our work in its progress and in its hindrances, we are compelled to recognize again the relation between the great extension of Christian benevolence with which we are intrusted, and the conflict of our country with a huge and desperate rebellion; we are reminded that wherever our missionaries labor, their personal safety, their liberty to pursue their work, and their privilege of standing unawed before the rudest of barbarous nations, are partly dependent, under the providence of God, on the fact that they are citizens of the United States, protected in all parts of the earth by the influential power of the great republic, and we are compelled to see that what this rebellion aims at—the division of our country among two or more naturally independent confederacies, weak in themselves and jealous and hostile towards each other—would weaken the hands of American missionaries in every part of the world. We are reminded, too, that the entire moral influence of the American Churches upon the world is far more powerful and beneficent from the fact that they are the Churches of a great, united, sovereign, and self-governed people. Therefore it is impossible for us to entertain a thought of any termination of this war otherwise than in the perfect restoration of the Union under the Constitution, which, by the favor of God, has made this nation heretofore so great and prosperous in its freedom. We record again our loyal sympathy with the President of the United States in the struggle to vindicate and maintain "the supreme law of the land" according to his inaugural oath, and our confidence that, according to his proclaimed intention, he will not fail to employ for that purpose against the enemies of the United States all those powers with which he is invested by the Constitution of the United States, and all those means of subjugation which are warranted by the law of nations and the law of God. And with our renewed prayer to the God to whose displeasure at the wickedness which fills the earth with sadness and oppression all history has testified, and who so often wrought deliverance for our fathers in their perils, we record our grateful confidence that the rebellion will be crushed, that slavery, its prime cause, will be removed, and that peace, prosperity, and righteousness will be permanently established in our land.

New School Synod of Pennsylvania, October, 1862. Whereas the Synod is called once more to meet in the midst of a civil conflict which has carried desolation and suffering through a wide district of country: therefore,

Resolved, 1. That we render devout thanksgivings to Almighty God for that measure of success which has hitherto attended our arms; that we humble ourselves, and acknowledge the justice of our heavenly Father, wherein he has seen good to afflict us; that we rejoice in the integrity, the patriotism, and the firmness of our distinguished Chief Magistrate; that we record with lively satisfaction his avowal of a purpose to protect the unity of these States and the nationality of our Government, at every expense of treasure and of blood, and that he has recently, by his repeated proclamations, expressed his determination to subordinate every local interest and institution to the great cause of American freedom, of good government, and of the universal and permanent safety and prosperity of his native land.

2. That the Synod expresses its highest approbation of the brave, faithful, and true-hearted men who have volunteered for their country's protection; that we sympathize with them in all their hardships and sufferings; that we give them the assurance of our daily and fervent prayers for their triumph in the day of battle, for their consolation if cast down wounded, for their comfort in the hospital, and their support in sickness and in death.

3. That in the bloody martyrdoms of this wicked rebellion we recognize new motives to abhor the crime of treason against law, and new inducements to condemn and abrogate that system of oppression which has not only suggested treason, but the most cruel and bloody methods of putting it into practice; and we urge upon all loyal people to mark with their complete abhorrence all who resist the efforts of the Government for its suppression.

4. That in the labors of our ministers and people for the benefit of the sick and wounded soldiers, in the readiness of parents, wives, sisters, and friends to surrender their objects of dearest affection to the perils of war, in the large contributions of money and goods made to the Government to aid in suppressing the unholy rebellion, in the patient endurance with which our people have borne themselves in seasons of social bereavement and national disaster, we recognize a blessed revival of patriotism, humanity, and Christian devotion to the pure, the noble, the right.

HARRISBURG PRESBYTERY, 1862.

1. That, while the Presbytery deeply mourns the continuance of the unhappy war in which our country is involved, we see

no other path of duty for the Government and the loyal people of the land to walk in than a vigorous prosecution of it, with all the means that God has placed in our power and that humanity will approve, until the Union of the States is restored and the authority of the Constitution is everywhere acknowledged.

2. That, recognizing the good providence of God which has hitherto been with us to encourage us in the days of our country's deepest humiliation and to grant many signal victories, and realizing that ultimate success must come from God alone, we humbly pray that he would guide the councils and the armies of the Government to a speedy and happy issue of all our troubles.

3. That we regard the late proclamation of President Lincoln, which, after the 1st of January, 1863, confers emancipation upon the slaves of all who shall then be found in rebellion to the Government, as a most just and necessary measure in securing the speedy termination of the war, and as an auspicious providential opening for the final deliverance of the country from that system of iniquity which is the chief cause of our national wars.

4. That, recognizing the hand and the power of God in that Government which we have ordained over us, we view with abhorrence, and call upon all loyal people to mark with their complete disapprobation, all efforts, wherever made, to impair the confidence of the people in the Government, or to resist by word or deed the execution of the laws .

5. That we urge upon all Christian people, while confessing in deep humiliation their own sins and the sin of the nation, to cease not, in the weekly assemblages of the house of God, at their family altars, and in the place of secret prayer, to beseech God for his blessing upon the Government, the army and the navy, for the suppression of rebellion, and for the speedy restoration of a righteous and a permanent peace.

6. That, in view of the great demand which is laid upon the practical beneficence of the country in behalf of the sick and wounded soldiers of the army, we urge upon our congregations, and upon the patriot everywhere, to repay their debt of gratitude to these brave and noble men by all possible care for their health and comfort.

THE TRIENNIAL CONVENTION OF THE PROTESTANT
EPISCOPAL CHURCH OF THE UNITED STATES, IN SESSION
AT THE CITY OF NEW YORK, OCTOBER, 1862.

Resolved, By the House of Clerical and Lay Deputies of this stated Triennial Convention, that assembling, as we have been called to do, at a period of great national peril and deplorable civil convulsion, it is meet and proper that we should call to mind, distinctly and publicly, that the Protestant Episcopal Church in the United States hath ever held and taught, in the language of one of its articles of religion, that "it is the duty of all men who are professors of the gospel to pay respectful obedience to the civil authority regularly and legitimately constituted," and hath accordingly incorporated into its Liturgy "a prayer for the President of the United States and all in civil authority," and a "prayer for the Congress of the United States, to be used during their session," and hath bound all orders of its ministry to the faithful and constant observance, in letter and spirit, of these and all other parts of its prescribed ritual.

Resolved, That we cannot be wholly blind to the course which has been pursued, in their ecclesiastical as well as in their civil relations, since this Convention last met in perfect harmony and love, by great numbers of the ministers and members of this Church within certain States of our Union which have arrayed themselves in open and armed resistance to the regularly constituted Government of our country; and that while, in a spirit of Christian forbearance, we refrain from employing towards them any terms of condemnation and reproach, and would rather bow in humiliation before our common Father in heaven for the sins which have brought his judgment on our land, we yet feel bound to declare our solemn sense of the deep and grievous wrong which they will have inflicted on the great Christian communion which this Convention represents, as well as on the country within which it has been so happily and harmoniously established, should they persevere in striving to rend asunder those civil and religious bonds which have so long held us together in peace, unity, and concord.

Resolved, That while, as individuals and citizens, we acknowledge our whole duty in sustaining and defending our country in the great struggle in which it is engaged, we are only at liberty, as deputies to this council of a Church which hath ever renounced all political association and action, to pledge to the national Government—as we now do—the earnest and devout prayers of all, that its efforts may be so guided by wisdom and replenished with strength that they may be crowned with speedy and complete success, to the glory of God and the restoration of our beloved Union.

Resolved, That if, in the judgment of the bishops, any other forms of occasional prayer than those already set forth shall seem desirable and appropriate, whether for our Convention or Church or our country, for our rulers or our defenders, or for the sick and wounded and dying of our army and navy and volunteers, we shall gladly receive them and fervently use them.

During the sittings of the Convention, the House of Bishops, with a dignity worthy of themselves and the occasion, ordered a day of prayer and fasting in view of the great national crisis through which we are passing. The official resolution was worded as follows—

The House of Bishops, in consideration of the present afflicted condition of the country, propose to devote Wednesday, the 8th of October instant, as a day of fasting, humiliation, and prayer, and to hold in Trinity Church a solemn service appropriate to the occasion.

The Bishops affectionately request the House of Clerical and Lay Deputies to join with them in said observance.

In accordance with this resolution, the Convention adjourned for the day specified.

Long before eleven o'clock—the hour announced for the service—the church was crowded. At eleven precisely the bishops and clergy entered the church, and occupied the seats leading to the middle aisle.

The order of Morning Service was modified for the occasion. Instead of the Venite, the one hundred and thirtieth Psalm was chanted—

"Out of the deep have I called unto thee, O Lord; Lord, hear my voice,"—the proper Psalm for the day. The first lesson was the forty-ninth chapter of Isaiah, and the second from the sixth chapter of St. Luke, beginning at the twentieth verse.

To the suffrage in the Litany for "unity, peace, and concord" was added, "and especially to this nation, now afflicted by civil war.

Immediately after the general thanksgiving the following special prayers were read—

Almighty and most holy Lord our God, who dost command us to humble ourselves under thy mighty hand that thou mayest exalt us in due time, we, thine unworthy servants, desire most humbly to confess before thee, in this the time of sore affliction in our land, how deeply as a nation we deserve thy wrath. In the great calamities which have come upon us we acknowledge thy righteous visitation, and bow down our souls under the mighty hand of our holy and merciful God and Father. Manifold are our sins and transgressions, and the more sinful because of the abundance of our privileges and mercies under thy providence and grace. In pride and living unto ourselves; in covetousness and worldliness of mind; in self-sufficiency and self-dependence; in glorying in our own wisdom and richness and strength, instead of glorying only in thee; in making our boast of thy unmerited blessings, as if our own might and wisdom had gotten them, instead of acknowledging thee in all and seeking first thy kingdom and righteousness; in profaneness of speech and ungodliness of life; in polluting thy Sabbaths, and receiving in vain thy grace in the gospel of our Lord Jesus Christ, we acknowledge, O Lord, that as a nation and people we have grievously sinned against thy Divine Majesty, provoking most justly thy wrath and indignation against us. Righteousness belongeth unto thee, but unto us confusion of face. Because thy compassions have not failed, therefore we are not consumed. Make us earnestly to repent and heartily to be sorry for these our misdoings. May the remembrance of them be grievous unto us. Turn unto thee, O Lord, the hearts of all this people in humiliation and prayer, that thou mayest have compassion upon us and deliver us. When thy judgments are thus upon us, may the inhabitants of the land learn righteousness. Have mercy upon us, have mercy upon us, most merciful Father. For thy Son our Lord Jesus Christ's sake, forgive us all that is past, and grant that we may ever hereafter serve and please thee in newness of life, to the honor and glory of thy name. We beseech thee so to sanctify unto us our present distresses, and so to make haste to deliver us, that war shall be no more in all our borders, *and that all resistance to the lawful Government of the land shall utterly cease.* May our brethren who seek the dismemberment of our national Union, under which this people by thy providence have been so signally prospered and blest, be convinced of their error and restored to a better mind. Grant that all bitterness and wrath and anger and malice may be put away from them and us, and that brotherly love and fellowship may be established among us to all generations. Thus may the land bring forth her increase, under the blessings of peace, and thy people serve thee in all godly quietness, through Jesus Christ our Lord. Amen.

Grant, O Lord, we beseech thee, to all such as are intrusted with the government and defence of this nation, thy most gracious support and guidance. Graft in their hearts a deep sense of dependence on thy wisdom and power and favor, and incline them with all humility to seek the same. In all their ways may they dutifully acknowledge thee, that thou mayest direct their steps. Make thy word to be their light, thy service their glory, and thine arm their strength. Further them with thy continual help, that in all their works—begun, continued, and ended in thee—they may glorify thy holy name. Under their heavy burdens and trials be thou their refuge and consolation. By their counsels and measures, under thy blessing, may the wounds of the nation be speedily healed. For those our brethren who have gone forth for our defence, by land or water, we seek thy most gracious blessing and protection. In every duty and danger be thou their present help. In all privations and sufferings give them patience and resignation, and a heart to seek their comfort in thee. May they be strong in the Lord and in the power of his might, hating iniquity, fearing God, and obeying his word. Give them success in every enterprise that shall be pleasing to thee. Visit with the consolations of thy grace all sick and wounded persons, all prisoners, and all those bereaved of relatives and friends by reason of the present calamities. Prepare to meet thee all those who shall die in this conflict. Give them unfeigned repentance for all the errors of their lives past, and steadfast faith in thy Son Jesus, that they may be received unto thyself. And finally unite us all together in the blessedness of thy everlasting kingdom, through Him who liveth and reigneth, with thee and the Holy Ghost, ever one God, world without end. Amen.

Let thy continual pity, O Lord, cleanse and defend thy Church; and in these days of sore trial to thy people raise up thy power, and come among us, and with great might succor us. Grant that, by the operation of the Holy Ghost, all Christians may be so joined together in unity of spirit and in the bond of peace that they may be a holy temple acceptable unto thee. May all counsels of dissension and division be brought to naught. Increase our faith and love and zeal in thy service and for the coming of thy kingdom. Make the whole Church a light in the world; and the more her afflictions abound, so much the more may her consolations also abound by Christ, to the praise and glory of thy name. Amen.

After the liturgical service, the thirty-second selection of Psalms, beginning—

"Thy chastening wrath, O Lord, restrain,"

—was sung by the choir.

The eightieth hymn was sung. It begins thus—

"Almighty God, before thy throne
    Thy mourning people bend;
'Tis on thy pardoning grace alone
    Our prostrate hopes depend."

By special request the music was, in accordance with the sentiment of the occasion, as simple and unpretending as possible.

Before the benediction a short prayer was read, beseeching "Infinite Mercy" to appease the tumults among us, to bring to an end the dreadful strife which is now raging in our land, and to restore peace to our afflicted country.

The services were conducted by Bishops McCroskey, of Michigan, Kemper, of Wisconsin, Smith, of Kentucky, Whittingham, of Maryland, Hopkins, of Vermont, and McIlvaine, of Ohio.

Bishop McIlvaine prepared the following—

PASTORAL ADDRESS OF THE HOUSE OF BISHOPS TO THE CLERGY AND LAITY.

BRETHREN—We have been assembled together in our Triennial Convention under most afflicting circumstances. Hitherto, whatever our Church had to contend with from the fallen nature of man, from the power of this evil world, or the enmity of that mighty adversary who is called by St. Paul the '"god of this world," her chief council has been permitted to meet, amidst the blessings of peace, within our national boundaries and as representing a household of faith at unity in itself. Our last meeting was in the metropolis of a State which has long held a high place and influence in the affairs of our Church and country. Long shall we remember the affectionate hospitality which was there lavished on us, and the delightful harmony and brotherly love which seemed to reign, almost without alloy, in a Convention composed of representatives of all our dioceses. Never did the promise of a long continuance of brotherly union among all parts and sections of our whole Church appear more assuring; but, alas! what is man! how unstable our surest reliances, based on man's wisdom or will!

How unsearchable His counsel who hath "his way on the sea, and his path on the mighty waters," and whose footsteps are not known! What is now the change! We look in vain for the occupants of seats in the Convention belonging to the representatives of not less than ten of our dioceses, and to ten of our bishops. And whence comes such painful and injurious absence? The cause stands as a great cloud of darkness before us, of which, as we cannot help seeing it and thinking of it wherever we go and whatever we do, and that most sorrowfully, it is impossible not to speak when we address you in regard to the condition and wants of our Church. That cause is all concentrated in a stupendous rebellion against the organic law and the constitutional Government of the country, for the dismemberment of our national Union, under which, confessedly, all parts of the land have been signally prospered and blessed—a rebellion which is already too well known to you, brethren, in the vast armies that it has compelled our Government to maintain, and in the fearful expense of life and treasure, of suffering and sorrow, which it has cost on both sides, to need any further description here.

We are deeply grieved to think how many of our brethren, clergy and laity, of the regions over which that dark tide has spread, have been carried away by its flood—not only yielding to it, so as to place themselves, as far as in them lay, in severance from our ecclesiastical union, which has so long and so happily joined us together in one communion and fellowship, but to a sad extent sympathizing with the movement and giving it their active co-operation.

In this part of our letter we make no attempt to estimate the moral character of such doings. At present we are confined to the statement of notorious facts, except as to one matter of which this is the convenient place to speak.

When the ordained ministers of the gospel of Christ, whose mission is so emphatically one of peace and good will, of tenderness and consolation, do so depart from their sacred calling as to take the sword and engage in the fierce and bloody conflicts of war—when in so doing they are fighting against authorities which, as "the powers that be," the Scriptures declare "are ordained of God," so that in resisting them they are resisting the ordinance of God—when, especially, one comes out from the exalted spiritual duties of an overseer of the flock of Christ, to exercise high command in such awful work—we cannot, as ourselves overseers of the same flock, consistently with duty to Christ's Church, ministry, and people, refrain from placing on such examples our strong condemnation. We remember those words of our blessed Lord, uttered among his last words, and for the special admonition of his ministers, "they that take the sword shall perish with the sword."

Returning to this great rebellion, with all its retinue of costs and sacrifices, of tribulation and anguish, of darkness and death, there are two aspects in which we must contemplate it, namely, as it comes by the agency of man, and as it proceeds from the providence of God.

We desire, first, to call your attention thereto, as it proceeds *from the providence of God.* So comprehensive is that providence that it embraces all worlds and all nations, while it is so minute that not a sparrow falleth without the knowledge and will of our Father in heaven. In its vast counsels, this deep affliction has a place; God's hand is in it; his power rules it. It is his visitation and chastening for the sins of the nation. Who can doubt it? Just as the personal affliction of any of you is God's visitation to turn him from the world and sin unto himself, so is this national calamity most certainly his judgment on this nation for its good. And we trust, dear brethren, that we are in no danger of seeming, by such interpretation of our distresses, to excuse in any degree such agency as men have had in bringing them upon us. God's providence has no interference with man's responsibility. He works by man, but so that it is still man that wills as well as works. The captivities of God's chosen people were, as his word declares, his judgment upon them for their sins; while the nations that carried them captive were visited of God for heinous guilt in so doing. Saint Peter declares that our Lord was delivered unto death by the determinate counsel and foreknowledge of God, and that, nevertheless, it was by "wicked hands" that he was "crucified and slain." Thus, we need be under no temptation to diminish our estimate of the present dispensation of sorrow, as proceeding from the counsel of God, in punishment for our sins, whatever the agency of man therein. So to consider it is our duty, as Christians and as patriots, that it may do us the good for which it is sent and may be the sooner taken away.

It is not possible for us in this address to set before you in detail, or in their true proportions, all the national and other sins which make us as a people to deserve and need the chastisements of a holy God. It needs no Daniel, inspired from on high, to discover them. Surely you must all be painfully familiar with many of them in the profaneness of speech with which God's name and majesty are assailed; in the neglect of public worship, which so dishonors his holy day; in the ungodliness of life which erects its example so conspicuously; and especially in that great sin for which Jerusalem was given over to be trodden down by the heathen, and the people of Israel have ever since been made wanderers and a by-word among the nations—namely, the rejection—whether in positive infidelity or only in practical unbelief—of God's great gift of grace and mercy, his beloved Son, our Lord Jesus Christ, to be a sacrifice of propitiation for our sins and an all-glorious Saviour of our souls.

But there is a passage in the Scriptures which is of great use as a guide in the consideration of national sinfulness. It is a warning to the nations of Israel, and is found in the eighth chapter of the book of Deuteronomy, as follows—"Beware that thou forget not the Lord thy God, in not keeping his commandments, and his judgments, and his statutes, which I command thee this day; lest when thou hast eaten and art full, and hast built goodly houses, and hast dwelt therein, and when thy herds and thy flocks multiply, and thy silver and thy gold is multiplied, and all that thou hast is multiplied, then thy heart is lifted up, and thou forget the Lord thy God; and thou say in thy heart, My power and the might of my hand hath gotten me all this wealth. But thou shalt remember the Lord thy God; for it is he that giveth thee power to get wealth. And it shall be that if thou do at all forget the Lord thy God, as the nations which the Lord destroyed before your face, so shall ye perish, because ye would not be obedient to the voice of the Lord your God."

Now, it was because that nation was guilty of precisely such self-glorying and such forgetfulness of its indebtedness to God and dependence on his favor as this warning describes, that the grievous calamities which so fill its history before the advent of Christ were brought upon it. And it is because there is so much agreement between this description and the aspect which we, as a people, have presented before God, that we place the passage before you.

Marvellously have we been prospered in every thing pertaining to national prosperity, riches, and strength. God has loaded us with benefits, and with our benefits have grown our ingratitude, our self-dependence and self-sufficiency, our pride and vain-glory.

A synopsis of the residue of the address can only be given.

After exhorting the people to repent of the sins which have caused God's judgments on the nation, that they might be exalted in due time, as God's hand was not shortened that it could not save, the letter broached the second point—the agency of man in creating the troubles of the country. It was a subject which was approached with great diffidence, but one which the House of Bishops could not refrain from mentioning, especially as the clergy and laity desired their expression on it. They looked around and beheld the vacant seats of their absent brethren. It was the first time the Convention had met since the calamities of the nation commenced; and might the Almighty order that, when they should again convene, those calamities should have passed away and peace and union reign throughout the land. When they reviewed the state of the country, they found an immense force ready to effect its division: they beheld all the sad results of the war; they saw vast armies in the field, sharing the perils of battle; military hospitals were thronged with the wounded, and everywhere they witnessed the painful results of the conflict. The Church looked on the scene. What was her duty, and how should she accomplish it? Her duty in the emergency was to proclaim obedience to the Government, or, in the words of Scripture, the powers that be which are ordained of God, and to declare that whoever resisted them resisted the ordinance of God and was liable to damnation. That was the course of the Church. The obligations to remain in the Union were as legal and forcible on the States which had seceded as those which remained in it.

Allegiance was rightly due to their common Government, and refusing such allegiance was sin, which culminated in a great crime against the laws of God and man when it appeared in the form of rebellion. In cases where States should leave the Government without cause, or in the event of their suffering wrongs which provisions had been made to redress, they were guilty of the horrors of the war which they opened. The *homily* against rebellion denounced all attempts to subvert legally-constituted Government. The letter next noticed, in eloquent terms, the patriotism of the people in giving their substance and treasure and sending forth mighty armies to battle for the unity of the nation and the Government. After stating that the troubles of the country might lead many away from religion and draw others to God, it enjoined the people to be constant in prayer, and not let their love of country decrease their love of God. They should beseech the Almighty in mercy to take away the calamities which they all deplored, and which were caused by sin. They should, however, remember that to hate rebellion was a duty, but to hate rebels was the opposite of duty. Let them under no circumstances be unmindful of the words of the Saviour, who told them to love their enemies, and who, while they were themselves enemies, died on the cross for their salvation.

Reply of the President

RIGHT REVEREND AND DEAR SIR—The copy which you sent me of the "Pastoral Letter of the Bishops of the Protestant Episcopal Church in the United States of America" has been submitted to the President. He authorizes me to assure you that he receives with the most grateful satisfaction the evidences which that calm, candid, and earnest paper gives of the loyalty of the very extended religious communion over which you preside, to the Constitution and Government of the United States. I am further instructed to say that the exposition which the highest ecclesiastical authority of that communion has given in the Pastoral Letter, of the intimate connection which exists between fervent patriotism and true Christianity, seems to the President equally seasonable and unanswerable. Earnestly invoking the Divine blessing equally upon our religious and civil institutions, that they may altogether safely resist the storm of faction, and continue hereafter, as heretofore, to sustain and invigorate each other, and so promote the common welfare of mankind, I have the honor to be, right reverend and dear sir, faithfully yours,

William H. Seward.

THE GENERAL CONVENTION OF THE METHODIST PROTESTANT CHURCH, CINCINNATI, OHIO, NOVEMBER, 1862.

Whereas our country continues to be involved in all the horrors and dangers of a civil war unparalleled in the history of the world, alike in its gigantic proportions and in the vital interests which it shall affect for good or ill; and

Whereas we cannot be cold spectators of the scenes occurring around us, because they appeal to our sympathies and our principles as patriots, as Christians, and as philanthropists; and

Whereas we deem it our duty to our country, to the world at large, and to our God, to utter our sympathies and sentiments in this hour of danger to the country and to civil liberty: therefore,

1. *Resolved*, That we cling with fond affection to the institutions bequeathed to us by our Revolutionary sires, and that we infinitely prefer them to any other that ever have been, or that may be, proposed as a substitute for them.

2. *Resolved*, That we therefore sanction, with all our hearts, the prosecution of the current war for their maintenance, and we recommend that this war be pushed with the utmost energy and to the last extremity; because in its successful prosecution alone we see the prevention of anarchy and misrule, of wide-spread dissensions and mediaeval tyranny and vassalage, of universal distraction, contentions, and bloodshed, more

fearfully desolating and terrible than any thing that can now result from the course that we thus earnestly recommend.

3. *Resolved*, That we heartily endorse the Emancipation Proclamation of President Lincoln, because it strikes at that baleful cause of all our civil and ecclesiastical difficulties, American slavery," the sum of all villainies," the darling idol of villains, the central power of villainous secessionism, but now, by the wisdom of the President, about to be made the agent of retributive justice in punishing that culmination of villainous enterprises, the attempt to overthrow the most glorious civil Government that God's providence ever established upon earth.

4. *Resolved*, That we earnestly deprecate all dissensions and divisions among those who profess loyalty to the Government and attachment to our free institutions; and that we deem it suspicious at least, if not strong evidence of sympathy with our enemies, when men in our midst attempt to create such divisions or dissensions upon any pretext whatsoever.

5. *Resolved*, That a committee be appointed to address the President of the United States, and express to him, in the name of the Methodist Protestant Church, the sentiments of loyalty contained in these resolutions, and to assure him that our people endorse his Proclamation, sustain the war, and are ready to do and suffer all things necessary for the maintenance of our glorious Government intact.

These resolutions were unanimously adopted by a rising vote, followed by a solemn season of prayer for the President of the United States.

THE SYNOD OF NEW JERSEY (OLD SCHOOL PRESBYTERIAN), OCTOBER, 1862.

Whereas, being deeply impressed with the sinfulness before God of the present rebellion against our Government, with the widespread wickedness of our whole nation, which has brought upon us all the chastisement of civil war, with the necessity of that humiliation which the Divine judgments demand and are well fitted to induce, and with the duty of trusting sincerely in God alone for our national deliverance, and fearing that our people at large are not duly alive to the religious aspect of our public troubles: therefore,

Resolved, 1. That this Synod express to all the people under its care the deep and solemn conviction that the armed rebellion now in progress against our national Government cannot be viewed in any other light than as a grievous sin against God and his Church, and that in the present conflict of our Government with this rebellion there can be but two parties—the friends and the enemies of the Government; and therefore all who in any way sympathize with or uphold the rebellion are involved in the guilt of its great sin.

Resolved, 2. That we regard the continuance, the enlarged and calamitous proportions, of our civil war as a solemn token of God's righteous displeasure with our whole nation, and a most impressive admonition that we are not suitably humbled for the manifold heinous sins of corruption, pride, ambition, self-confidence, forgetfulness of God, covetousness, Sabbath-desecration, irreligion, both of rulers and people, and oppression, especially of the colored race.

Resolved, 3. That a committee be appointed to draft a memorial to the President of the United States, to be signed by the Moderator and Stated Clerk, requesting him to appoint an early day for humiliation, fasting, and prayer.

Resolved, 4. That, in case the President shall not have previously appointed such a day, this Synod hereby recommend to all its churches to observe the said Thursday in December as a day of fasting, with suitable public and private services of devout humiliation and prayer, that the Lord may turn away his anger from our country, save the Union from destruction, and restore peace and harmony to our whole land.

Resolved, 5. That these resolutions be read by the ministers of this Synod to their respective congregations from the pulpit.

The Synod of Wheeling, Virginia (Old School Presbyterian), October, 1862.

In view of the present condition of our Church and country, caused by the existing and terrible rebellion in the whole

Southern portion of this Union, calling forth the warmest sympathy of God's people in behalf of our land and nation, the Synod of Wheeling do reaffirm her attachment to our Federal Government and Constitution, and that it is the imperative duty of all our people to maintain the same by upholding all persons in authority in all their lawful and proper acts, whether civil or military; and, with profound humility and dependence on the grace of God, we would seek for Divine guidance and assistance in our national troubles, and be encouraged by the blessed truth that "the Lord reigneth." And

Whereas God has revealed himself the hearer of prayer, and it is the privilege and duty of Christians to cry earnestly to the Lord in the time of individual or national calamity; and

Whereas the united prayers of God's people might be prevalent with the Most High to remove from our beloved land and nation the chastening hand with which he is so severely afflicting us, and that he would make us sincere in confessing our sins and humbling ourselves before the Lord in consequence of his judgments, which rest so heavily upon us, and, moreover, that he would grant grace unto those in rebellion to change their hearts and make them willing to return to loyalty and obedience to the Federal Government, which the God of nations has so long upheld and so wonderfully blessed in years that are past: therefore,

Resolved, 1. That the Synod of Wheeling, of the Presbyterian Church (Old School), now in session at Washington, Pennsylvania, do respectfully, but earnestly, ask his Excellency the President of these United States to appoint a day of humiliation, fasting, and prayer, to be observed by all the people of this land in view of the distracted state of our country.

Resolved, 2. That if his Excellency the President should fail to appoint said day, then the Synod do appoint the first Thursday of December next a day of humiliation, fasting, and prayer within our bounds, on which our people are recommended to meet in their respective churches, and confess their individual and national sins, and pray to Almighty God in behalf of our beloved and bleeding country, its Government, its army and navy, and its people, that armed rebellion may be overthrown and cease, and that the constitutional authorities of the Government may be vindicated, and that we may obtain a speedy, honorable, and permanent peace.

Resolved, 3. That the Stated Clerk of Synod be directed to forward a copy of the first resolution to the President of the United States as soon as practicable.

THE SYNOD OF INDIANA (OLD SCHOOL PRESBYTERIAN), OCTOBER, 1862.

The Synod of Indiana, in session at Greensburgh, October 18, 1862, recognizing the manifold and grievous evils of the civil war by which the nation is convulsed and its very existence threatened, as the righteous judgment of God upon it for its national sins, and especially for its complicity with, and support of, the system of slavery existing in many of the States, for the instruction and guidance of the people under its own pastoral care, and all men to whom its voice may come, deems it its duty to declare:

That the nation has no right to expect that God will turn away from the nation his judgment, until the nation shall have, with sincere and godly repentance, turned from the sins by which the judgment has been provoked.

That it is, therefore, the imperative duty of the citizens of the nation, while humbling themselves under the mighty hand of God, and confessing their own sins and the sins of the nation, supplicating his mercy upon it, to urge upon the national Government the exertion of the whole power with which it is legitimately invested, whether under military law or otherwise, to withdraw the nation from all complicity with and support of slavery.

That it is the sacred duty of the whole people, by all the means in their possession and to the whole extent of their power, to sustain and support the Government in all lawful and just measures for the suppression of the traitorous rebellion which has been originated and sustained in the interest of slavery and slavery propagandism and domination.

The Philadelphia Baptist Association,
October, 1862.

Resolved, That, as members of the Philadelphia Baptist Association, we reaffirm our unswerving loyalty to the Government of these United States.

Resolved, That in the trials through which we are passing as a nation we recognize the guidance of the Almighty, and see, not dimly, the purpose of his love to purify the fountains of our national life and develop in righteousness the elements of our national prosperity.

Resolved, That, as Christian citizens of this republic, it is our bounden duty to renounce all sympathy with sin, to rebuke all complicity with evil, and cherish a simple, cheerful confidence in Him whose omnipotence flowed through a stripling's arm and sank into the forehead of the Philistine.

Resolved, That, in pursuance of this spirit, we hail with joy the recent proclamation of our Chief Magistrate, declaring freedom on the 1st day of January next to the slaves in all the then disloyal States, and say to him, as the people said to Ezra, "Arise, for the matter belongeth unto thee; we also will be with thee: be of good courage, and do it."

Resolved, That in the name of Liberty, which we love, in the name of Peace, which we would make enduring, in the name of humanity and of Religion, whose kindred hopes are blended, we protest against any compromise with rebellion; and for the maintenance of the war on such a basis, whether for a longer or a shorter period, we pledge, in addition to our prayers, our "lives, our fortunes, and our sacred honor."

Resolved, That a copy of these resolutions be forwarded to the President and his advisers, with assurances of the honor in which, as Christians, we hold them, and with our solemn entreaty that no one of them will, in the discharge of duties however faithful for his country, neglect the interests of his own personal salvation.

The following reply was received from Mr. Seward—

WASHINGTON, October 18, 1862.

TO THE PHILADELPHIA BAPTIST ASSOCIATION—

GENTLEMEN—I have the honor to acknowledge for the other heads of Departments, as well as in my own behalf, the reception of the resolutions which were adopted by your venerable Association during the last week, and to assure you of our high appreciation of the personal kindness, patriotic fervor, and religious devotion which pervade their important proceedings. You seem, gentlemen, to have wisely borne in mind, what is too often forgotten, that any Government—especially a republican one—cannot be expected to rise above the virtue of the people over whom it presides. Government is always dependent on the support of the nation from whom it derives all its powers and all its forces, and the inspiration which can give it courage, energy, and resolution can come only from the innermost heart of the country which it is required to lead or to save. It is indeed possible for an administration in this country to conceive and perfect policies which would he beneficent, but it could not carry them into effect without the public consent; for the first instruction which the statesman derives from experience is that he must do, in every case, not what he wishes, but what he can.

In reviewing the history of our country, we find many instances in which it is apparent that grave errors have been committed by the Government, but candor will oblige us to own that heretofore the people have always had substantially the very kind of administration which they at the time desired and preferred. Political, moral, and religious teachers exercise the greatest influence in forming and directing popular sentiments and resolutions. Do you, therefore, gentlemen, persevere in the inculcation of the principles and sentiments which you have expressed in your recent proceedings, and rest assured that, if the national magnanimity shall be found equal to the crisis through which the country is passing, no efforts on the part of the administration will be spared to bring about a peace without a loss of any part of the national territories or the sacrifice of any of the constitutional safeguards of civil or religious liberty. I need hardly say that the satisfaction which will attend that result will be immeasurably increased if it shall be found also that in the operations which shall have produced it humanity shall have gained new and important advantages. Commending ourselves to your prayers, and to the prayers of all who desire the welfare of our country and of mankind, I tender you the sincere thanks of my associates, with whom I have the honor to remain, gentlemen,

Your very obedient servant,

William H. Seward.

The State Baptist Convention of Ohio, October, 1862, passed the following resolutions, prepared by Rev. Dr. M. Stone—

"Whereas the powers that be are ordained of God, and he that resisteth the power resisteth the ordinance of God," and is threatened with damnation: therefore, be it

Resolved, 1. That it is our right and duty, as a body of Christian citizens, in these times of rebellion against our beneficent Government, to tender our hearty sympathy and support to those who are intrusted with it.

Resolved, 2. That we will accord a cheerful and earnest support to our rulers and our armies in their endeavors to crush the wicked rebellion, until that object shall be accomplished and peace and order restored; and that we will offer up our prayers and supplications daily to the sovereign Disposer of events for his interposition in this behalf.

Resolved, 3. That since the present terrible civil war was begun by our enemies, without any just cause or provocation, for the purpose of *extending, strengthening, and perpetuating* the wicked institution of slavery, against the moral sense of the civilized world, and though in the beginning we had no intention of interfering with the institutions of the rebellious States, yet the progress of the war clearly indicates the purpose of God to be the summary extinction of slavery, therefore we approve the late proclamation of liberty of our President, and we will sustain him in carrying out that proclamation till our beloved country shall be purged of the accursed blot, both the cause of the war and the chief means in our enemy's hands of carrying it on, and will stand by our country in the adoption of such further measures as may be necessary to put an end to this great rebellion.

SENECA BAPTIST ASSOCIATION OF NEW YORK, SEPTEMBER, 1862.

That, while we deplore the evils of the war, we still believe that the interests of humanity freedom, and religion require its prosecution until the rebellion is utterly crushed out.

That, as slavery has taken the sword, we should therefore let it perish by the sword, being absolved from whatever legal or moral obligations we may have been under to support it.

That we recognize in the scenes of blood now being enacted, the righteous judgments of God for our sins. It therefore becomes us to bow in humility and penitence, lest iniquity be our ruin.

That the recent proclamation of the President is but a step in the order of Providence, necessitated by the logic of events. We therefore accept it, praying that the same Providence will make it a sure proclamation for liberty.

That we cherish in our memories and prayers our brethren and friends upon the field, making incessant effort to promote their spiritual welfare, and trusting in God for their protection.

At the Baptist State Convention, October 7, 1862, in Ithaca, the Committee on the State of the Country made the following report, which was adopted unanimously—

Whereas the civil war which was in progress in our country at our last annual meeting is still in existence, threatening the destruction of our Government, with all the precious interests it involves: therefore,

Resolved, 1. That, as a religious body, we deem it our duty to cherish and manifest the deepest sympathy for the preservation and perpetuity of a Government which protects us in the great work of Christian civilization.

Resolved, 2. That, in our opinion, the history of civil governments furnishes no example of more audacious wickedness than is exhibited by the rebellion which has been inaugurated against the free government framed by our fathers and so eminently in harmony with the conscious and obvious rights of man.

Resolved, 3. That while we see, with the profoundest sorrow, thousands of husbands, fathers, brothers, and sons falling on the battle-field, considering the interests to be preserved and transmitted to future generations, we cannot regard the sacrifice of treasure and of life too much for the object to be secured.

Resolved, 4. That as human slavery in the Southern portion of our country is, in our judgment, the procuring cause of the rebellion now raging among us, having been proclaimed as the corner-stone of the rebellion and as the institution for which they are fighting, as Christian men and citizens we fully and heartily endorse the recent proclamation of the President of the United States, declaring forever free all slaves in the rebel States on the 1st of January, 1863.

Resolved, 5. That the spirit of the age, the safety of the country, and the laws of God require that among the results of the present bloody war shall be found the *entire* removal of that relic of barbarism, *that bane and shame* of the nation, *American slavery*, and that the banner of freedom float triumphantly and *truthfully* over all the land.

Resolved, 6. That the foregoing preamble and resolutions be signed by the officers of the Convention, and transmitted to the President of the United States.

THE PENNSYLVANIA STATE CONVENTION OF THE BAPTIST CHURCHES, NOVEMBER, 1862.

Resolved, That this Convention, representing forty thousand of the citizens of Pennsylvania, mindful, in the present national crisis, of our own solemn duties to our country and our God, hereby declare our profound conviction of the intimate relation there is between the cause of human liberty and the cause of pure religion, and also our set purpose, as citizens, as

Christians, and as Christian ministers, to employ our whole influence in supporting the supremacy of our national Constitution against all enemies whatever.

Resolved, That as the institution of slavery stands before the world as the confessed feeding source of the present mighty and wicked rebellion against our national Constitution, we most heartily approve of the President's proclamation of emancipation, without modification in substance and without change of time in its execution.

Resolved, That a copy of these resolutions, duly authenticated, be forwarded to the President of the United States.

The two following letters are in answer to resolutions which the author was not able to obtain.

DEPARTMENT OF STATE, September 29, 1862.
TO THE WEST NEW JERSEY BAPTIST ASSOCIATION.

REVEREND GENTLEMEN—The resolutions concerning the state of public affairs which you have transmitted to me have been communicated to the President of the United States. I am instructed by him to reply that he accepts with the most sincere and grateful emotions the pledges they offer of all the magnanimous endeavors and all the vigorous efforts which the emergencies of the country demand. The President desires, also, that you may be well assured that, so far as it belongs to him, no vigor and no perseverance shall be wanting to suppress the existing insurrection and to preserve and maintain the union of the States and the integrity of the country. You may further rest assured that the President is looking for a restoration of peace on no other basis than that of the unconditional acquiescence by the people of all the States in the constitutional authority of the Federal Government.

Whatever policy shall lead to that result will be pursued; whatever interest shall stand in the way of it will be disregarded.

The President is, moreover, especially sensible of the wisdom of your counsels in recommending the cultivation by the Government and people of the United States of a spirit of meekness, humiliation, and dependence on Almighty God, as an indispensable condition for obtaining that Divine aid and favor without which all human power, though directed to the wisest and most benevolent ends, is unavailing and worthless. In a time of public danger like this, a State, especially a republic, as you justly imply, ought to repress and expel all personal ambitions, jealousies, and asperities, and become one united, harmonious, loyal, and devotional people.

Your obedient servant,

William H. Seward.

DEPARTMENT OF STATE, WASHINGTON, October 6, 1862. TO THE CONGREGATIONAL WELSH ASSOCIATION OF PENNSYLVANIA.

REVEREND GENTLEMEN—I have had the honor to receive the resolutions which you have adopted; and, in compliance with your request, I have submitted them to the consideration of the President of the United States.

The President entertains a lively gratitude for the assurances you have given him of your loyalty to the United States and your solicitude for the safety of our free institutions, the confidence you have reposed in him, and your sympathy with him in the discharge of responsibilities which have devolved upon the Government. The President directs me to assure you that wherever the Constitution of the United States leads him, in that path he will move as steadily as shall be possible, rejoicing with yourselves whenever it opens the way to an amelioration of the condition of any portion of our fellow-men, while the country is escaping from the dangers of revolution. The President is deeply touched by your sympathies with those of our fellow-citizens who suffer captivity or disease, and the grief with which you lament those who fall in defence of the country and humanity; and he invokes the prayers of all devotional men that these precious sufferings may not be altogether lost, but may be overruled by our heavenly Father to the advancement of peace on earth and good will to all men.

I have the honor to be,

Reverend gentlemen,

Your obedient servant,

WILLIAM H. SEWARD.

BAPTIST CONVENTION OF THE STATE OF MASSACHUSETTS,
OCTOBER, 1862.

Resolved, That, in the present terrible national crisis in which we are involved by the unreasonable and wicked insurrection of disloyal men in the interest of a stupendous system of oppression, we hail with pleasure the proclamation of the President of the United States in favor of emancipation, and the acts of harmony therewith, as a favorable indication of Divine Providence and as an important instrumentality for the suppression of the rebellion.

Resolved, That in the fearful and wide-spread conflict now raging in our land we regard the interests of civil and religious liberty throughout the world for future ages as deeply involved, and therefore regard it as the solemn duty of every man to sustain the Government to the whole extent of his ability.

Resolved, That, for the speedy and complete suppression of the rebellion, we deem it eminently important that the loyal portion of the nation, holding in abeyance all minor issues, should remain united and present an unbroken front against the insurgents, and should therefore put forth all their energies to prevent any division of the people in the loyal States which shall weaken their support of the President in the execution of his avowed policy.

Resolved, That whilst we mourn over our individual and national sins. and acknowledge the justice of Almighty God in the severe affliction which has befallen us, we also recognize his Divine sovereignty, that as the race is not to the swift, nor the battle to the strong, so deliverance from our present troubles can be effected only through his mighty and beneficent agency, for which it becomes us to offer earnest and persevering prayer.

Resolved, That a copy of these resolutions, signed by the President and Secretary of this Convention, be forwarded to the President of the United States as expressive of our approval of his policy in the prosecution of the War, and as a pledge of our sympathy, prayers, and co-operation with him in his arduous efforts to restore the Union and bring back to us national peace and prosperity.

THE NEW SCHOOL SYNOD OF WABASH, INDIANA, OCTOBER, 1862.

Whereas a giant rebellion is still struggling to plunge its dagger into the heart of our beloved country, that it may establish an empire of slavery on the ruins of our freedom; and

Whereas our national Government is manfully struggling to crush this rebellion and annihilate its power: therefore,

Resolved, 1. That we do hereby express our unfaltering loyalty to the Government under which we live, and do pledge all our means of influence, and our personal resources, for the preservation of the national existence.

Resolved, 2. That we tender to the President of the United States our cordial esteem and sympathy, and we will not cease to pray that God may give to him wisdom and courage and faith adequate to the responsibilities of his position, and to the people patriotism equal to the exigencies of the national peril.

Resolved, 3. That while we bow in humble and sorrowful acknowledgment of our national sins that have provoked God's displeasure, and deeply sympathize with the bereaved who have lost life-treasures and heart-treasures for the salvation of the nation, we yet cherish an unwavering faith in God, confirmed by the orderings of his providence and the conquests of his truth in the progress of this struggle, that he is disciplining us for a nobler national life in order to a wider national usefulness and prosperity; and we give thanks to God for the Executive proclamation of freedom, which we trust may sound the death-knell of slavery to the whole human race.

WESTERN RESERVE SYNOD OF OHIO (NEW SCHOOL), OCTOBER, 1862.

While we are deliberating for the interests of that kingdom "which is peace," we are reminded that the war begun by a Wicked rebellion still rages in the land.

The Synod, at their last annual meeting, adopted a carefully prepared report upon the state of the country, in which they bore testimony against the prime cause of the war, and pledged their support of the Government in its efforts to reestablish its authority over the States in revolt. Since that time the conflict has assumed larger proportions, and gathered to itself greater moral interest. Battles have been fought; new armies have been sent into the field; and legislation, and the supreme military power, have made, and have foreshadowed, important changes in the political and social condition of the slave. These events have come to pass under the wise government of the Ruler of the nations. God has made himself known by acts of righteousness, and by that wonderful overruling which has wrought in thoughtful minds the belief that the exodus of the bondman is at hand.

It is fitting, then, that this body again give expression to their convictions in regard to the character of the war, and the duty of Christian citizens in the emergencies which the progress of events has forced upon the nation: therefore,

1. We reaffirm our unalterable belief that the cause of the Government and of the loyal States is a *just* one; we express our sympathy with the President of the United States in his position of peculiar trial and grave responsibility; and we exhort all Christians within the bounds of the Synod to pray without ceasing that God will give to him wisdom and strength for the right performance of his high duties.

2. Believing that Providence is shaping events for the extirpation of slavery from the land, we heartily welcome the proclamation of emancipation by the President. Receiving it as a measure of military necessity, we yet gratefully record our admiration of that Divine government which makes this measure harmonize with the demands of justice and the requirements of Christian love; and we pledge all our influence in support of a policy so eminently wise and just.

3. Inasmuch as we believe God is punishing the nation for its sins, and is seeking its reformation, we earnestly desire that the army and navy, the exponents and the arms

of the nation's strength, may be purified from all vices and crimes which may provoke the Divine displeasure and render them unfit instruments for the execution of the Divine purposes. Therefore, we lament that so much intemperance, and profanity, and neglect of the Sabbath, and indulgence of brutal and revengeful passions, exist in these branches of the public service, and especially that so many who are intrusted with places of command are chargeable with these grave offences. And we earnestly pray those who have the requisite authority to remove from such places all those who thus dishonor God and injure the national cause.

THE NEW SCHOOL PRESBYTERIAN SYNOD OF ILLINOIS, OCTOBER, 1862.

1. The Synod of Illinois continues to sympathize with the Government of the United States in its efforts to put down rebellion and restore the supremacy of the Constitution and laws.

2. We recognize the desolations of civil war as tokens of the displeasure of God kindled against us on account of our sins.

3. The principles of the word of God and the history of God's dealings with other nations forbid us to hope for the turning away of his wrath without national humiliation, confession, and repentance.

4. In this view, we rejoice and give thanks to the great God, in whose hands are the hearts of kings and presidents, that he has inspired the President of the United States to issue that grand proclamation which is at once (1) *a war measure* which strikes at the very life of the rebellion, and also (2) an act *of national justice* which will, we trust, go far to propitiate the wrath of God.

5. As slavery and its champions have forced this war upon the country, we shall regard it as a signal illustration of God's retributive justice if he shall cause the war to result in the utter extirpation of slavery and in the humiliation of all who have sought or helped to perpetuate or extend it. The prospect that we may become in truth *"the land of the free"*—one

people, from ocean to ocean, and from the lakes to the gulf—is a prospect grand enough to inspire the sublimest hopes and nerve us to heroic endurance of the horrors of war.

6. To our brave defenders in the field, to the sick and wounded in our camps and hospitals, to those who languish in the prisons of the enemy, to the loyal men and women whom war has driven from their sanctuaries and their homes, to all those among us who mourn the loss of dear ones fallen as martyrs in our holy cause, we extend assurances of our sympathy and of a constant remembrance in our prayers.

7. We believe it to be the duty of all good men to frown upon all attempts to weaken confidence in the Government or to divide and distract the loyal people of the country. The efforts of scheming politicians and selfish demagogues, and of an unprincipled or disloyal newspaper press, to give aid and comfort to the rebellion by dividing our people, and raising up a reactionary party that would *sell justice* and liberty and barter away all that is most sacred in our institutions for the sake of the *personal aggrandizement of a treacherous and short-lived peace*, ought to receive the indignant condemnation of all who fear God and love justice. None but a righteous peace can be permanent.

8. We solemnly declare it as our conviction that this war should be prosecuted with the utmost vigor until every traitor lays down his arms, until every State returns to its allegiance, and until all the rights guaranteed by the Constitution, and especially the rights of *free labor, free thought, free speech, free press, and free worship, shall be secured to every loyal citizen of the republic.*

9. We enjoin upon our ministers and elders the duty of instructing the people in the great first principles of the Bible concerning the *conditions of God's favor to nations,* and we exhort them to expound and enforce the teachings of the gospel concerning the brotherhood of men and the inalienable right of every man made in the image of God to *life, liberty,* and the *pursuit of happiness.* It is the disregard of these principles and teachings which has brought all our woes upon us; it is only

by a return to them and by their hearty observance that we can hope for enduring national peace and prosperity.

10. We exhort all our people to personal humiliation and repentance, to earnest prayer, to constant vigilance, and to a cheerful endurance of the burdens of taxation, and, if needs be, of the perils of the camp and the field.

11. Finally, we repeat, with the emphasis of convictions strengthened and emotions intensified by a year of conflict, the language with which we closed our action on this subject one year ago—*viz.*:

We urge all the members of our churches to sustain with a generous confidence the Government and all who do its bidding, and cherish such a view of the momentous importance and sacredness of our cause that they shall bear with cheerfulness all the sacrifices which the war imposes, and, whether it be long or short, cheerfully pour out., if needs be, *the last ounce of gold and the last drop of blood to bring it to a righteous issue.*

THE UPPER WABASH CONFERENCE OF THE UNITED
BRETHREN CHURCH, SEPTEMBER, 1862.

Whereas the Church of the United Brethren in Christ is antislavery in principle, as set forth in Sec. 22, Dis.; and whereas there are found among us members who, in this dark hour of our country's peril, are sympathizing with rebellion by opposing those who stand to advocate and defend the anti-slavery principles of the Church, by refusing them their support: therefore,

Resolved, That we earnestly admonish those who may be found among us operating against the *spirit, letter,* and *intent* of Discipline (Sec. 22) on slavery, to consider the duty they owe to God, their *country*, and the Church of their choice, to cease to manifest a spirit so contrary to the teaching of the Church on this subject.

Resolved, That it be enjoined on the circuit preachers to labor in the spirit of meekness with those who are found acting in opposition to the spirit of the gospel on this subject, and strive to bring them to a sense of their obligations, and, should they refuse to desist from such a course, to expel them from the Church.

Resolved, That we heartily sympathize with our Government in striving to maintain the principles of civil and religious liberty against slavery and rebellion, and pledge to it our prayers, our lives, out fortunes, and our sacred honor; and should there be found any among us who cannot respond to these sentiments, or who are found sympathizing with traitors in any respect whatever, we admonish them, in the spirit of brotherly love, to desist from such a course, or cease to remain in membership with us.

THE CENTRAL METHODIST CONFERENCE OF OHIO, APRIL, 1863.

Resolved, That, in the judgment of this Conference, the declaration of war, the marshalling of arms, the desolation and confiscation of property, the robbery on land and the piracy on sea, the loss of life, the blood that has already drenched the soil of Virginia and Missouri, are all attributable to *slavery* as a cause.

Resolved, That, as the secessionists have forfeited, by rebellion, all rights under the Constitution and laws, their slaves have a right to go free; and we hope the whole policy of the Government will be shaped to this result.

Resolved, That, in the judgment of this Conference, the Proclamation of General Fremont, declaring the emancipation of the slaves of all rebels against the Government, is of paramount importance in the present crisis, and meets the hearty approval of this body of ministers, and, we believe, of all undeluded friends of the Government.

Resolved, That we shall never cease to pray for our armies and navy now engaged in war in defence of our country; and we shall look forward with hope and faith, when our hills and valleys shall shout, and our mountains shall echo back the glad response, *Universal emancipation from slavery and rebellion!*

THE NEW YORK METHODIST EPISCOPAL CONFERENCE, APRIL, 1863.

Whereas the Southern rebellion, gigantic in its proportions and unparalleled in its wickedness, continues to imperil the existence of this republic; and

Whereas our national life is intimately identified not only with the cause of civil and religious liberty in the world, but also with the best interests of the kingdom of Christ—for, so far as we may judge, our nation is a choice and chosen instrument for the extension and establishment of that kingdom on the earth; and

Whereas in a crisis like the present it is the solemn duty of every citizen to rally to the support of a cause so unspeakably important and glorious: therefore,

Resolved, 1. That, as members and ministers of the Methodist Episcopal Church within the bounds of the New York Annual Conference, we cheerfully renew our vows of uncompromising and unconditional loyalty to the United States of America, a nationality we are proud to acknowledge, and resolved, with the blessing of Heaven, to maintain.

2. That it is our duty, enforced alike by the word of God and our Book of Discipline, to submit to and co-operate with the regularly constituted civil authorities, and to enjoin the same upon our people.

3. That while we do not deny, but rather recognize and defend, the right of our people to discuss the measures and policy of the Government, at the same time we would counsel that, in the present critical condition of public affairs, this right is to be exercised with great forbearance, caution, and prudence.

4. That the conduct of those who, influenced by political affinities or Southern sympathies, and under the pretext of discriminating between the Administration and the Government, throw themselves in the path of every warlike measure, is, in our view, a covert treason, which has the malignity, without the manliness, of those who have arrayed themselves in open hostility to our liberties, and is deserving of our sternest denunciations and our most determined opposition.

5. That slavery is an evil incompatible in its spirit and practice with the principles of Christianity, with republican institutions, with the peace and prosperity of the country, and with the traditions, doctrines, and discipline of our Church; and our long and anxious inquiry, What shall be done for its

extirpation? has been singularly answered by Divine Providence, which has given to Abraham Lincoln, President of the United States, the power and the disposition to issue a proclamation guaranteeing the boon of freedom to millions of Southern bond-men.

6. That we heartily concur in this proclamation, as indicating the righteousness of our cause, securing the sympathies of the liberty-loving the world over, and, above all, insuring the approbation of the Universal Father, who is invariably on the side of justice and freedom.

7. That we find abundant reason for gratitude and encouragement in the recent revival of the nation's patriotism, in the maintenance of the public credit, in the change of public opinion abroad, especially in England, and in the gradual, but we trust sure, progress of our arms.

8. That we cordially accept the President's recommendation to observe the 30th day of the present month as a season of solemn fasting and prayer, and that, assembling in our various places of worship, we will humble ourselves, and earnestly supplicate the great Ruler of Nations to forgive our national offences, to guide, sustain, and bless our public rulers, to look on our army and navy mercifully, giving success to our arms, so that this infamous rebellion may be speedily crushed, and peace, at once righteous and permanent, may return to smile on our American heritage.

9. That our interest and sympathy for those who represent us in the field continue unabated; and that to all those who are suffering in consequence of the havoc or desolation of this terrible war we offer our sincerest sympathies and our Christian condolence.

10. That a copy of these resolutions be transmitted to the President of the United States, and that they be published in "The Christian Advocate and Journal."

EAST BALTIMORE CONFERENCE, MARCH, 1863.
Whereas the war which has been devastating our beloved land for the past two years still continues, and whereas silence might be construed into indifference in such a crisis: therefore,

Resolved, By the East Baltimore Conference, in Conference assembled, that we reaffirm our loyalty to the Government, and our most unflinching devotion to our country in the hour of her peril.

THE BAPTIST ASSOCIATION OF ILLINOIS, JUNE, 1863.

In the midst of many dangers and reverses which have overtaken our arms during the past year, we yet have great reason for thankfulness, not only for important victories vouchsafed to us, but for a far juster conception, on the part of the masses of the people, of the great moral issues involved in the struggle. We bless God that he has taught us by the rod of disaster that there can be no peace until the claims of Him whose right it is to reign shall be recognized and obeyed.

We cordially support the administration in their efforts to put down the rebellion, and hail with joy the proclamation of emancipation, believing that when we as a nation shall "keep the fast which God hath chosen," "that our light shall break forth as the morning, and our health shall spring forth speedily."

We recognize human slavery now, as we have heretofore done, to be the cause of the war and its kindred evils, and we reiterate our convictions that there can be no peace and prosperity in the nation until it is destroyed.

We feel that the hope of our country in the suppression of treason in the revolted States, and in our midst, lies not merely in military successes or in military orders, but in the incorruptible virtue and the profound devotion of the people to the principles of the glorious gospel of the blessed God.

We deeply sympathize with our brethren who have gone to fight the battles of our country, with such as are sick and wounded in the hospitals, and with those who have been bereaved because their loved ones have been stricken by the hand of death while connected with the army. We pledge to our brave soldiers everywhere our sympathies, our prayers, and our utmost efforts that they may be sustained in all their troubles, and that they may be abundantly successful in the great task committed to their hands.

The Conference of the Western Unitarian Association, Held at Toledo, Ohio, June, 1863.

Whereas our allegiance to the kingdom of God requires of us loyalty to every righteous authority on earth: therefore,

Resolved, That we give to the President of the United States, and to all who are charged with the guidance and defence of our nation in its present terrible struggle for the preservation of liberty, public order, and Christian civilization, against the powerful wickedness of treason and rebellion, the assurance of our cordial sympathy and steady support, and that we will cheerfully continue to share any and all needful burdens and sacrifices in the holy cause of our country.

Resolved, That we hail with gratitude and hope the rapidly growing conviction among the loyal masses of our countrymen that the existence of human slavery is inconsistent with the national safety and honor, as it is inconsistent with natural right and justice, and that we ask of the Government a thorough and vigorous enforcement of the policy of emancipation, as necessary alike to military success, to lasting peace, and to the just supremacy of the Constitution over all the land.

Presbytery of St. Louis (Old School), June, 1863.

Whereas violent resistance to the authority of civil government, without adequate cause, is, by the teaching of Scripture and the standards of the Presbyterian Church, *a sin against God*; and whereas our fellow-citizens now in rebellion against our national and State Governments, among whom are found a number of our own church-members, have never experienced any wrong or grievance at the hands of those in authority that could justify a resort to armed resistance to our established Government; and whereas it is the duty of those who rule in the Church to guide the flock in the way of truth and righteousness and warn them against error and sin: therefore,

Resolved, That we, the Presbytery of St. Louis, acting upon a sense of duty to the churches over which we rule, do hereby earnestly entreat and warn all members of our churches to abstain from all participation in the present rebellion, or from giving countenance and encouragement thereto by word or deed, as such participation, countenance, or encouragement involves sin against God, and will expose those engaged therein to the penalties of ecclesiastical discipline.

PRESBYTERY OF RIPLEY, OHIO, APRIL, 1863.

Resolved, 1. That while the terrible judgments of God are inflicted upon the Government and people, there should be universal reformation. That all sinful practices should be abandoned, and that all systems of oppression and wrong should be abolished. Among these are intemperance, Sabbath-breaking, and slavery. These have been the most prominent sins of the nation.

2. That we recommend to the churches under our care to observe carefully the fast proclaimed by the President, to be kept on the 30th day of the present month.

3. That, as civil government is an ordinance of God, it is the duty of all persons to obey civil magistrates in all things that do not contravene the law of God.

4. That, upon full investigation, it is evident that the Government inflicted no wrong upon the slaveholding States, and that the rebellion of the slave power against the Government is the most enormous and criminal known to the world, and that the present calamitous war has been forced upon the Government, and, consequently, that it is the duty of all citizens to sustain the administration in suppressing the rebellion and the slaveholding combination by which it was instigated.

5. That disloyalty to the Government, as it tends to anarchy, robbery, and murder, is one of the highest crimes against God and man: consequently, that class of men in the free States who sympathize with the rebels of the South, oppose the administration, and aim to sustain the slave system, which has caused the murder of hundreds of thousands of the most brave and noble men of the nation, and has brought upon the whole country the most terrible calamities, are among the most depraved, dangerous, and abominably wicked men existing on the earth.

THE GENERAL CONVENTION OF CONGREGATIONAL
MINISTERS AND CHURCHES OF VERMONT, JUNE, 1863.
Whereas our beloved country continues to be the scene of
an unprincipled and wicked rebellion, the object of which, as
openly avowed by its leaders, is the overthrow of the Government established by the wisdom, the toils, and the sacrifices of
our fathers, the dismemberment of the Union, and the establishment within our limits of a Confederacy founded upon the
enormous wrong and outrage of human slavery: therefore,

Resolved, 1. That we reaffirm the principles and declarations relating to this subject, as set forth in the last meeting
of the Convention; solemnly renewing our pledge of fidelity
to the Government in the present fearful crisis, and of our
unwavering support by all lawful means at our command.

Resolved, 2. That as "the powers that be are ordained of
God," and submission to them is expressly required by the
Divine will, and as the existing administration of our Government, rightfully appointed, constitute for us "the powers that
be," for lawful government, we recognize the imperative duty
of all classes of citizens to render to the administration, striving in its appropriate sphere to put down the rebellion, their
hearty support and co-operation, such duty being involved in
their allegiance to God.

Resolved, 3. That we cordially approve of the proclamation
of emancipation, issued as a war measure by the President of
the United States, whereby millions of the enslaved are declared free, and promise is given that, as a nation, by the dreadful discipline of war, we are ere long to come to the realization
of the truth so prominently set forth in the Declaration of Independence, that all men are equally entitled to the privileges
of "life, liberty, and the pursuit of happiness." And we rejoice to
recognize the rapidly increasing favor with which the aforesaid
proclamation is regarded throughout the loyal States of the
Union, and by many who at first doubted its expediency.

Resolved, 4. That we highly commend the measures which
have been adopted for the comfort and instruction of the
slaves who, by means of the war and the President's procla-

mation, have availed themselves of the priceless boon of freedom; thus laying a foundation for their elevation to all that ennobles and blesses our common humanity.

Resolved, 5. That we tender the expression of our admiration and thanks to our soldiers who, at their country's call, with patriotic ardor, rushed to the field of danger to struggle for our national life. We assure them that whatever we can do for their comfort in camp and hospital shall be done; that when permitted to return to their loved homes, they will receive a hearty welcome; and those who shall have sacrificed life in our army and navy in the noble cause will long live in our grateful remembrance. And we tender our warmest sympathy to all the families who, by reason of this wicked rebellion, are mourning for fathers, husbands, brothers, and sons whose faces they see on earth no more.

Resolved, 6. That we commend the President of the United States, his Cabinet, and all to whom great public trusts are committed, to the special Divine guidance; that we acknowledge God's justice in our national calamities, and would humble ourselves under his mighty hand; and we earnestly beseech the God of our fathers that, instructed and purified by the things which we suffer, we may as a nation be established in truth and righteousness, and become indeed a light and blessing to the world.

The annual convention of the American Baptist Missionary Union held its forty-ninth anniversary, at Cleveland, Ohio, May, 1863, and passed the following paper. The President of the meeting was Hon. Ira Harris, Senator in Congress from New York.

The Committee appointed to prepare resolutions on the state of the country reported, through its chairman, Rev. Dr. Dowling, the following—

Whereas the officers and members of the American Baptist Missionary Union, at their last annual meeting in May, 1862, unanimously adopted a series of resolutions characterizing "the war now waged by the national Government to put down the unprovoked and wicked rebellion that has risen against it, and to establish anew the reign of order and of law, as a most righteous and holy one, sanctioned alike by God and all right-thinking men," and also expressive of their conviction that "the principal cause and origin of this attempt to destroy the Government has been the institution of slavery; and that a safe, solid, and lasting peace cannot be expected short of its complete overthrow:" therefore,

Resolved, That the developments of the year since elapsed, in connection with this attempt to destroy the best Government on earth, have tended only to deepen our conviction of the truth of the sentiments which we then expressed, and which we now and here solemnly reiterate and reaffirm.

Resolved, That the authors, aiders, and abettors of this slaveholders' rebellion, in their desperate efforts to nationalize the institution of slavery and to extend its despotic sway throughout the land, have themselves inflicted on that institution a series of most terrible and fatal and suicidal blows, from which, we believe, it can never recover, and they have themselves thus fixed its destiny and hastened its doom; and that, for thus overruling what appeared at first to be a terrible national calamity, to the production of results so unexpected and glorious, our gratitude and adoration are due to that wonder-working God who still "maketh the wrath of man to praise him, while the remainder of that wrath he restrains."—Psalm lxxvi. 10.

Resolved, That in the recent acts of Congress, abolishing slavery forever in the District of Columbia and the Territories, and in the noble proclamation of the President of the United States, declaring freedom to the slave in States in rebellion, we see cause for congratulation and joy, and we think we behold the dawn of that glorious day when, as in Israel's ancient jubilee, "liberty shall be proclaimed throughout all the land, unto all the inhabitants thereof."—Leviticus xxv. 10.

Resolved, That as American Christians we rejoice in the growing sympathy of the enlightened portion of our Christian brethren in Great Britain and other European nations with the Government and people of the United States in this righteous war; and that, while we cordially thank our friends across the water for all expressions of their confidence and approval, we embrace this opportunity of assuring them that, within our judgment, the United States possesses within herself the means, the men, and the courage necessary for the suppression of this rebellion, and that, while we ask no assistance from other nations, we will brook no intervention or interference with our national affairs while engaged in this arduous struggle, which we believe will soon be completely successful in utterly suppressing and subduing this rebellion.

Resolved, That we hereby pledge ourselves as ministers, and as Christians and patriots, to sustain the President of the United States and his associates in the administration by our prayers, our influence, and our personal sacrifices, till this rebellion shall be subdued, and peace, upon the basis of justice, freedom, and Union, shall be again restored.

MISSIONARIES ON THE REBELLION.

At the twenty-third annual meeting of the Mission to Western Turkey, the Rev. William Goodell, D.D., the Rev. William G. Schauffler, D.D., and the Rev. Cyrus Hamlin, D.D., were appointed a committee to draft resolutions on the state of our country. They reported the following, which were unanimously adopted by the mission—

CONSTANTINOPLE, May 30, 1863.

Resolved, 1. That, although we have been many years absent from our native land, yet we entertain the most loyal feelings towards our Government, and assure the President of our being in full sympathy with him, and with all loyal citizens in their efforts to suppress the great rebellion.

2. That, having given up to this cause some of our best and most promising sons, and one of our former missionary associates having fallen a sacrifice to it (Rev. Mr. Dunmore, near Helena, Arkansas), we are still ready for any further needed sacrifices for our country, and we earnestly pray that God may inspire all our fellow-citizens with true Christian patrio-

tism, to smite this rebellion with "the arrow of the Lord's deliverance," not, as Joash, thrice, but "five or six times," until it is utterly subdued.

3. That we recognize the righteous judgment of God in calling our beloved country to this reckoning of blood for the national sins of slavery, oppression, greed, and political corruption in high places, and that we regard national repentance, and the abandonment of these and other sins characterizing us as a people, as the only way to recover national safety and prosperity.

4. That whereas God has vindicated in so remarkable a manner, and before an attentive world, his glorious justice and mercy in pleading the cause of four millions of downtrodden, degraded, and despised slaves;

And whereas the Government has abolished slavery in the District of Columbia, and prohibited the same in all the Territories, and the President, as commander-in-chief, has issued his proclamation of freedom to the slaves of rebels; and whereas the prejudices so long cherished in our country by the white population against the colored race are evidently yielding to the imperious pressure of providential circumstances under the Divine discipline administered to our nation;

Therefore it is the clearest duty of all loyal citizens to fall in with this wonderful march of freedom and providence, and to count no sacrifices too dear in order to attain a solid peace upon the basis of *universal freedom and equal rights.*

5. That the courage, fidelity, sagacity, patient endurance, and absence of cruelty and vindictiveness, exhibited so generally by the colored race, under exasperating wrongs hardly paralleled in history, entitle it to the respect and sympathy of the civilized world.

6. That the distinct recognition which the President, Senate, and many officers of the army and navy have made of God and his law, of the Sabbath, and the necessity of prayer, is to us a matter of devout gratitude.

7. That it is our Christian duty to pray daily and earnestly for the President and his Cabinet, that they may have wis-

dom, energy, and firmness equal to this crisis; for the officers and Soldiers of the army and navy, that they may do valiantly for the Lord of hosts; for the millions of distracted Africans, that they may show themselves to be men fighting for freedom and a home, and in abstaining from bloody and lawless retaliation of wrong; for the deluded people of the South, that they may speedily renounce the tyranny of the slave-lords; and for the bereaved families of fallen patriots.

And may the God of peace shortly bruise Satan under our feet, and redeem our souls from deceit and violence.

J. F. Pettibone, *Chairman.*

Tillman C. Trowbridge, *Secretary.*

The following resolutions were passed at a State Sabbath-school Convention, Dayton, Ohio, May, 1863. They show the earnest Christian sympathy of Sabbath-schools throughout the nation with the country struggling with a gigantic rebellion, and were prepared and offered to the Convention by Rev. B. W. Chidlaw, a veteran in the cause of Sabbath-schools, and a faithful chaplain in the army.

Whereas our Sabbath-schools are so largely represented in the army and navy of our country, by our former associates in the Sabbath-school work, superintendents, teachers and scholars, now in the service, cheerfully and heroically bearing the burdens of duty and suffering, fighting for the flag, and living by the cross;

Resolved, 1. That the Ohio State Sabbath-School Convention, assembled in the city of Dayton, expresses its cordial greetings, and earnest sympathies with our brethren in arms.

2. That we urge upon every Sabbath-school at once to open and maintain a correspondence with its absent members, to cheer and encourage our loved ones in the camp, on the deck, or languishing in hospitals.

3. That we earnestly desire that all the children of our brave soldiers and noble sailors should be gathered into the Sabbath-school fold and taught the way of salvation.

4. That we would encourage all who at home have drilled in the Sabbath-school army and studied the heavenly tactics,

to fall into line, and establish a Sabbath-school in the camp, and keep its banners waving for the spiritual benefit of themselves and comrades.

THE REFORMED PRESBYTERIAN CHURCH, DECEMBER, 1862. The Rev. A. M. Milligan, of New Alexandria, Pennsylvania, and the Rev. J. R. W. Sloane, of New York, waited upon the President of the United States, and, on behalf of the Reformed Presbyterian (Old School Covenanter) Church in the United States, presented to him the following address—

TO HIS EXCELLENCY ABRAHAM LINCOLN, PRESIDENT OF
THE UNITED STATES.

We visit you, Mr. President, as the representatives of the Reformed Presbyterian, or, as it is frequently termed, "Scotch Covenanter" Church—a church whose sacrifices and sufferings in the cause of civil and religious liberty are a part of the world's history, and to which we are indebted, no less than to the Puritans, for those inestimable privileges so largely enjoyed in the free States of this Union, and which, true to its high lineage and ancient spirit, does not hold within its pale a single secessionist or sympathizer with rebellion in these United States.

Our Church has unanimously declared, by the voice of her highest court, that the world has never seen a conflict in which right was more clearly wholly upon the one side, and wrong upon the other, than in the present struggle of this Government with the slaveholders' rebellion. She has also unanimously declared her determination to assist the Government, by all lawful means in her power, in its conflict with this atrocious conspiracy, until it be utterly overthrown and annihilated.

Profoundly impressed with the immense importance of the issues involved in this contest, and with the solemn responsibilities which rest upon the Chief Magistrate in this time of the nation's peril, our brethren have commissioned us to come and address you words of sympathy and encouragement; also, to express to you views which, in their judgment, have an important bearing upon the present condition of affairs in our beloved country, to congratulate you on what has already been accomplished in crushing rebellion, and to exhort you to persevere an the work until it has been finally completed.

Entertaining no shadow of doubt as to the entire justice of the cause in which the nation is embarked, we nevertheless consider the war a just judgment of Almighty God for the sin of rejecting his authority and enslaving our fellow-men, and are firmly persuaded that his wrath will not be appeased, and that no permanent pence will be attained, until his authority be recognized and the abomination that maketh desolate utterly extirpated.

As an anti-slavery Church of the most radical school, believing slavery to be a heinous and aggravated sin both against God and man, and to be placed in the same category with piracy, murder, adultery, and theft, it is our solemn conviction that God, by his word and providence, is calling the nation to immediate unconditional, and universal emancipation. We hear his voice in these thunders of war, saying to us, "Let my people go." Nevertheless, we have hailed with delighted satisfaction the several steps which you have taken in the direction of emancipation; especially do we rejoice in your late proclamation declaring your intention to free the slaves in the rebel States on the 1st day of January, 1863—an act which, when carried out, will give the death-blow to rebellion, strike the fetters from millions of bondmen, and secure for its author a place among the wisest of rulers and noblest benefactors of the race. Permit us, then, Mr. President, most respectfully, yet most earnestly, to urge upon you the importance of enforcing that proclamation to the utmost extent of that power with which you are vested. Let it be placed on the highest grounds of Christian justice and philanthropy; let it be declared to be an act of national repentance for long complicity with the guilt of slavery; permit nothing to tarnish the glory of the act or rob it of its sublime moral significance and grandeur, and it cannot fail to meet a hearty response in the conscience of the nation, and to secure infinite blessings to our distracted country. Let not the declaration of the immortal Burke be verified in this instance—"Good works are commonly left in a rude and imperfect state, through the lame circumspection with which a timid prudence so frequently enervates beneficence. In doing good we are cold, languid, and sluggish, and of all things afraid of being too much in the right." We urge you, by every consideration drawn from the word of God and the present condition of our bleeding country, not to be moved from the path of duty on which you have so auspiciously entered, either by the threats or blandishments of the enemies of human progress, nor to permit this great act to lose its power through the fears of timid friends.

There is another point which we esteem of paramount importance, and to which we wish briefly to call your attention. The Constitution of the United States contains no acknowledgment of the authority of God, of his Christ, or of his law, as contained in the Holy Scriptures. This we deeply deplore as wholly inconsistent with all claims to be considered a Christian nation or to enjoy the protection and favor of God. The Lord Jesus Christ is above all earthly rulers, He is King of kings and Lord of lords. He is the one mediator between God and man, through whom alone either nations or individuals can secure the favor of the Most High. God is saying to us in these judgments, "Be wise now, therefore, O ye kings; be instructed, ye judges of the earth. Serve the Lord with fear. Kiss the Son, lest he be angry, and ye perish from the way when his wrath is kindled but a little. Blessed are all they that trust in him. For the nation and kingdom that will not serve thee shall perish; yea, those nations shall be utterly wasted."

This time appears to us most opportune for calling the nation to a recognition of the name and authority of God, to the claims of Him who will overturn, overturn, and overturn, until the kingdoms of this world become the kingdoms of our Lord and of his Christ. We indulge the hope, Mr. President, that you have been called, with your ardent love of liberty, your profound moral convictions manifested in your Sabbath proclamation and in your frequent declarations of dependence upon Divine Providence, to your present position of honor and influence, to free our beloved country from the curse of slavery and secure for it the favor of the great Ruler of the Universe. Shall we not now set the world an example of a Christian state, governed, not by the principles of mere political expediency, but acting under a sense of accountability to God and obedience to those laws of immutable morality which are binding alike upon nations and individuals?

Praying that you may be directed in your responsible position by Divine wisdom, that God may throw over you the shield of his protection, that we may soon see rebellion crushed, its cause removed, and our land become Immanuel's land, we subscribe ourselves, in behalf of the Reformed Presbyterian Church.

Yours, respectfully,

J. R. W. Sloane,
A. M. Milligan.

Messrs. Milligan and Sloane were introduced to the President by the Hon. John A. Bingham, M.C., of Ohio. They were very cordially received.

General Synod of the Reformed Presbyterian Church, May, 1863.

Whereas there is a God revealed to man in Holy Scripture as the Creator, Preserver, Redeemer, and Moral Governor of the world; and

Whereas nations, as well as individuals, are the creatures of his power, the dependants of his providence, and the subjects of his authority; and

Whereas civil government is an ordinance of God, deriving its ultimate sanctions from his appointment and permission; and

Whereas it is the duty of all men to acknowledge the true God in all the relations they sustain; and

Whereas there is no specific mention of the authority of God in the Federal Constitution of the United States of America, the fundamental law of their existence as a nation; and

Whereas that Constitution and the Government which it organizes and defines are now undergoing the trial of a defensive civil war against a rebellion of a large portion of its own citizens and for its own national existence; and

Whereas the exigencies of the war have brought the authorities of the nation, civil and military, subordinate and supreme, to formal recognitions of the being, providence, and grace of God and of Jesus Christ his Son, to an extent and with a distinctness such as the country has never witnessed before: therefore,

Resolved, 1. That in the judgment of this Synod the time is come for the proposal of such amendments to the Federal Constitution, in the way provided by itself, as will supply the omissions above referred to and secure a distinct recognition of the being and supremacy of the God of Divine revelation.

Resolved, 2. That in the judgment of Synod the amendments or additions to be made to the national Constitution should provide not only for a recognition of the existence and authority of God, but also of the mediatorial supremacy of Jesus Christ his Son, "the Prince of the kings of the earth and the Governor among the nations."

Resolved, 3. That, as several articles of the Federal Constitution have been and are construed in defence of slavery, Synod do earnestly ask the appropriate authorities to effect such change in them as will remove all ambiguity of phraseology on this subject, and make the Constitution, as its framers designed it to be, and as it really is in spirit, a document on the side of justice and liberty.

Resolved, 4. That Synod will petition the Congress of the United States, at its next meeting, to take measures for proposing and securing the amendments referred to, according to the due order.

Resolved, 5. That Synod will transmit a copy of such action as they may themselves adopt to the several religious bodies of the country, with the respectful request that they will take order on the subject.

Resolved, 6. That a committee be appointed, composed of a member from each of the Presbyteries in Synod, to whom this matter shall be referred, and whose duty it shall be to correspond with such Christian statesmen and other individuals of influence as they may find disposed to further this dutiful and momentous object.

THE GENERAL ASSEMBLY OF THE CUMBERLAND PRESBYTERIAN CHURCH, MAY, 1863.

Whereas this General Assembly of the Cumberland Presbyterian Church in the United States of America cannot conceal from itself the lamentable truth that the very existence of our Church and nation is endangered by a gigantic rebellion against the rightful authority of the General Government of the United States, which rebellion has plunged the nation into the most dreadful civil war; and

Whereas the Church is the light of the world, and cannot withhold her testimony upon great moral and religious questions, and upon measures so deeply affecting the great interests of Christian civilization, without becoming justly chargeable with the sin of hiding her light under a bushel: therefore,

Resolved, That loyalty and obedience to the General Government, in the exercise of its legitimate authority, are the imperative Christian duties of every citizen, and that treason and rebellion are not mere political offences of one section against another, but heinous sins against God and his authority.

Resolved, That the interest of our common Christianity, and the cause of Christian civilization and national freedom throughout the world, impels us to hope and pray God (in whom is all our trust) that this unnatural rebellion may be put down, and the rightful authority of the General Government re-established and maintained.

Resolved, That we deeply sympathize with our fellow-countrymen and brethren who, in the midst of great temptation and sufferings, have stood firm in their devotion to God and their country, and also with those who have been driven, contrary to their judgment and wishes, into the ranks of the rebellion.

Resolved, That in this time of trial and darkness we re-endorse the preamble and resolution adopted by the General Assembly of the Presbyterian Church at Clarksville, Tennessee, on the 24th day of May, 1850, which are as follows—

Whereas in the opinion of this General Assembly the preservation of the Union of these States is essential to the civil and religious liberty of the people, and it is regarded as proper and commendable in the Church, and more particularly in the branch which we represent (it having had its origin within the limits of the United States of America, and *that* soon after the blood of our Revolutionary fathers had ceased to flow, in that unequal contest through which they were successfully conducted by the strong arm of Jehovah), to express its devotion, on all suitable occasions, to the Government of their choice: therefore,

Resolved, That this General Assembly look with censure and disapprobation upon attempts, from any quarter, to dissolve this Union, and would regard the success of any such movement as exceedingly hazardous to the cause of religion as well as civil liberty. And this General Assembly would strongly recommend to all Christians to make it a subject of prayer to Almighty God to avert from our beloved country a catastrophe so direful and disastrous.

On the subject of American slavery, your committee submit that we should not view it as if it were about to be introduced, but as already in existence. We do not hesitate to declare that the introduction of slavery was an enormous crime, surpassed by few crimes that have disgraced the history of the world, and that there are at present great evils connected with it, and that we believe will more or less be connected with it while it exists. As to the remedy for these, the greatest and best minds of our country and the world have greatly differed and been much perplexed: therefore we would recommend to those who in the providence of God have been placed in connection with this institution, to continue prayerfully to study the word of God, to determine their duty in regard to their slaves and slavery; and to those who are not thus situated, that they exercise forbearance towards their brethren who are connected with slavery—as the agitation of this subject at the present time in that part of the Church where slavery does not exist cannot result in any good, either to the master or slave. Touching the subject of American slavery as set forth in the memorial before us, your committee are not prepared to make the simple holding of slaves a test of church-membership, as they understand the memorial before them to propose.

Resolved, That we disavow any connection with, or sympathy for, the extreme measures of ultra-abolitionists, whose efforts, as we believe, have been, and are now, aimed at the destruction of our civil Government in order to abolish slavery. The committee would say, in conclusion, that the report herein submitted is agreed upon as a compromise measure, to unite the whole energies of our beloved Church and harmonize all our interests in the future, and to bind the entire membership of our Church, if possible, in close bonds of Christianity and fellowship.

THE PRESBYTERIAN GENERAL ASSEMBLY (OLD SCHOOL), MAY, 1863.

Your committee believe that the design of the mover of the original resolution and of the large majority who apparently are ready to vote for its adoption, is simply to call forth from the Assembly a significant token of our sympathy with this Government in its earnest efforts to suppress a rebellion that now for over two years has wickedly stood in armed resistance to lawful and beneficent authority, But as there are many among us who are undoubtedly patriotic, who are willing to express any righteous principle to which this Assembly should give utterance touching the subjection and attachment of an American citizen to the Union and its institutions, who love the flag of our country and rejoice at its successes by sea and by land, and who yet do not esteem this particular act a testimonial of loyalty entirely becoming to a church court, and as many of these brethren by the pressing of this vote would be placed in a false position, as if they did not love the Union, of which that flag is the beloved symbol, your committee deem themselves authorized by the subsequent direction of the Assembly to propose a different action to be adopted by this venerable court.

It is well known, on the one hand, that the General Assembly has ever been reluctant to repeat its testimonies upon important matters of public interest, but, having given utterance to carefully considered words, is content to abide calmly by its recorded deliverances. Nothing that this Assembly can say can more fully express the wickedness of the rebellion that has cost so much blood and treasure, can declare in plainer terms the guilt, before God and man, of those who have inaugurated, or maintained or countenanced, for so little cause, the fratricidal strife, or can more impressively urge the solemn duty of Government to the lawful exercise of its authority, and of the people, each in his several place, to uphold the civil authorities, to the end that law and order may again reign throughout the entire nation, than these things have already been done by previous Assemblies. Nor need this body declare its solemn rebukes towards those ministers and members of the Church of Christ who have aided in bringing on and sustaining these immense calamities, or tender our kind sympathies to those who are overtaken by troubles they could not avoid, and who mourn and weep in secret places, not unseen by the Father's eye, or reprove all wilful disturbers of the public peace, or exhort those who are subject to our care to the careful discharge of every duty tending to uphold the free and beneficent Government under which we are, and this specially for conscience' sake and as in the sight of God, more than in regard to all these things the General Assembly has made its solemn deliverances since these troubles began.

But, on the other hand, it may be well for this General Assembly to reaffirm, as it now solemnly does, the great principles to which utterance has already been given. We do this the more readily because our beloved Church may thus be understood to take her deliberate and well-chosen stand, free from all imputations of haste or excitement; because we recognize an entire harmony between the duties of the citizen (especially in a land where the people frame their own laws and choose their own rulers) and the duties of the Christian to the Great Head of the Church; because, indeed, least of all persons should Christian citizens even seem to stand back from their duty when bad men press forward for mischief; and because a true love for our country in her times of peril should forbid us to withhold an expression of our attachment for the insufficient reason that we are not accustomed to repeat our utterances.

And because there are those among us who have scruples touching the propriety of any deliverance of a church court respecting civil matters, this Assembly would add that all strifes of party politics should indeed be banished from our ecclesiastical assemblies and from our pulpits, that Christian people should earnestly guard against promoting partisan divisions, and that the difficulty of accurately deciding, in some cases, what are general and what party principles, should make us careful in our judgments, but that our duty is none the less imperative to uphold the constituted authorities because minor delicate questions may possibly be involved. Rather, the sphere of the Church is wider and more searching, touching matters of great public interest, than the sphere of the civil magistrate, in this important respect, that the civil authorities can take cognizance only of overt acts, while the law of which the Church of God is the interpreter searches the heart makes every man subject to the civil authority for conscience' sake, and declares that man truly guilty who allows himself to be alienated in sympathy and feeling from any lawful duty, or who does not conscientiously prefer the welfare and especially the preservation of the Government to any party or partisan ends. Officers may not always command a citizen's confidence; measures may by him be deemed unwise; earnest, lawful efforts may be made for changes he may think desirable; but no causes now exist to vindicate the disloyalty of American citizens towards the United States Government.

This General Assembly would not withhold from the Government of the United States that expression of cordial sympathy which a loyal people should offer. We believe that God has afforded us ample resources to suppress this rebellion, and that, with his blessing, it will ere long be accomplished;

we would animate those who are discouraged by the continuance and fluctuations of these costly strifes to remember and rejoice in the supreme government of our God, who often leads through perplexity and darkness; we would exhort to penitence for all our national sins, to sobriety and humbleness of mind before the Great Ruler of all, and to constant prayerfulness for the Divine blessing; and we would entreat our people to beware of all schemes implying resistance to the lawfully constituted authorities, by any other means than are recognized as lawful to be openly prosecuted. And as this Assembly is ready to declare our unalterable attachment and adherence to the Union established by our fathers, and our unqualified condemnation of the rebellion, to proclaim to the world the United States, one and undivided, as our country the lawfully-chosen rulers of the land our rulers, the Government of the United States our civil Government and its honored flag our flag, and to affirm that we are bound in the truest and strictest fidelity to the duties of Christian citizens under a Government that has strewn its blessings with a profuse hand, your committee recommend that the particular act contemplated in the original resolution be no further urged upon the attention of this body.

The General Assembly of the Presbyterian Church, New School, May, 1863, passed the following paper, prepared by Rev. Albert Barnes—

Whereas a rebellion, most unjust and causeless in its origin and unholy in its objects, now exists in this country, against the Government established by the wisdom and sacrifice of our fathers, rendering necessary the employment of the armed forces of the nation to suppress it, and involving the land in the horrors of civil war; and

Whereas the distinctly avowed purpose of the leaders of this rebellion is the dissolution of our national Union, the dismemberment of the country, and the establishment of a new Confederacy within the present territorial limits of the United States, based on the system of human slavery as its chief corner-stone; and

Whereas from the relation of the General Assembly to the churches which they represent, and as citizens of the republic, and in accordance with the uniform action of our Church in times of great national peril, it is eminently proper that this General Assembly should give expression to its views in a matter so vitally affecting the interests of good government, liberty, and religion; and

Whereas on two previous occasions since the war commenced the General Assembly has declared its sentiments in regard to this rebellion, and its determination to sustain the Government in this crisis of our national existence; and

Whereas, unequivocal and decided as has been our testimony on all previous occasions, and true and devoted as has been the loyalty of our ministers, elders, and people, this General Assembly deem it a duty to the Church and the country to utter its deliberate judgment on the same general subject: therefore,

Resolved, That this General Assembly solemnly reaffirms the principles and repeats the declarations of previous General Assemblies of our Church, so far as applicable to this subject and to the present aspect of public affairs.

Resolved, That in explanation of our views, and as a further and solemn expression of the sentiments of the General Assembly of the Presbyterian Church in the United States of America, in regard to the duties of those whom we represent, and of all the American people at tho present time, we now declare—

First. That civil government is ordained of God, and that submission to a lawful Government and to its acts in its proper sphere is a duty binding on the conscience, and required by all the principles of our religion as a part of our allegiance to God.

Second. That while there is in certain respects a ground of distinction between a *Government* considered as referring to the Constitution of a country, and an *administration* considered as referring to the existing agencies through which the principles and provisions of the Constitution are administered, yet the Government of a country to which direct allegiance and loyalty are due at any time is the administration duly placed in power. Such an administration is the Government of a nation, having a right to execute the laws and demand the entire, unqualified, and prompt obedience of all who are under its authority; and resistance to such a Government is rebellion and treason.

Third. That the present Administration of the United States, duly elected under the Constitution is the Government in the land to which alone, under God, all the citizens of this nation owe allegiance; who, as such, are to be honored and obeyed; whose efforts to defend the Government against rebellion are to be sustained; and that all attempts to resist or set aside the action of the lawfully constituted authorities of the Government in any way, by speech or action to oppose or embarrass the measures which it may adopt to assert its lawful authority, except in accordance with the forms prescribed by the Constitution, are to be regarded as treason against the nation, as giving aid and comfort to its enemies, and as rebellion against God.

Fourth. That in the execution of the laws it is the religious duty of all good citizens promptly and cheerfully to sustain the Government by every means in their power; to stand by it in its peril, and to afford all needful aid in suppressing insurrection and rebellion and restoring obedience to lawful authority in every part of the land.

Resolved, That much as we lament the evils, the sorrows, the sufferings, the desolations, the sad moral influences of war, and its effect on the religion and character of the land, much as we have suffered in our most tender relations, yet the war, in our view, is to be prosecuted with all the vigor and power of the nation, until peace shall be the result of victory, till rebellion is completely subdued, till the legitimate power and authority of the Government be fully re-established over every part of our temporal domain, and till the flag of the nation shall wave as the emblem of its undisputed sovereignty, and that to the prosecution and attainment of this object all the resources of the nation, in men and wealth, should be solemnly pledged.

Resolved, That the Government of these United States, as provided for by the Constitution, is not only founded upon the great doctrine of human rights as vested by God in the individual man, but is also expressly declared to be the supreme civil authority in the land, forever excluding the modern doctrine of secession as a civil or political right. That since the existing rebellion finds no justification in the facts of the case, in the Constitution of the United States, in any law, human or divine, the Assembly can regard it only as treason against the nation, and a most offensive sin in the sight of God, justly exposing its authors to the retributive vengeance of earth and heaven; that this rebellion, in its origin, history, and measures, has been distinguished by those qualities which most sadly evince the depravity of our nature, especially in seeking to establish a new nationality on this continent, based on the perpetual enslavement and oppression of a weak and long-injured race; that the national forces are, in the view of this Assembly, called out not to wage war against another Government, but to suppress insurrection, preserve the supremacy of law and order, and save the country from anarchy and ruin.

Resolved, In such a contest, with such principles and interests at stake, affecting not only the peace, prosperity, and happiness of our beloved country for all future time, but involving the cause of human liberty throughout the world, loyalty, unreserved and unconditional, to the constitutionally elected Government of the United States, not as the transient passion of the hour, but as the intelligent and permanent state of the public conscience, rising above all questions of party politics, rebating and opposing the foul spirit of treason, whenever and in whatever form exhibited, speaking earnest words of truth and soberness, alike through the pulpit, the press, and in all the walks of domestic and social life, making devout supplications to God, and giving the most cordial support to those who are providentially intrusted with the enactment and execution of the laws, is not only a sacred obligation, but indispensable if we would save the nation and perpetuate the glorious inheritance we possess to future generations.

Resolved, That the system of human bondage, as existing in the slaveholding States, so palpably the root and cause of the whole insurrectionary movement, is not only a violation of the domestic rights of human nature, but essentially hostile to the letter and spirit of the Christian religion; that the evil character and demoralizing tendency of this system, so properly described, so justly condemned, by the General Assembly of our Church, especially, from 1818 to the present time, have been placed in the broad light of day by the history of the existing rebellion. That in the sacrifices and desolations, the cost of treasure and blood, ordained thereby, the Assembly recognize the chastening hand of God applied to the punishment of national sins, especially the sin of slavery; that in the proclamation of emancipation issued by the President as a war-measure, and submitted by him to the considerate judgment of mankind, the Assembly recognize with devout gratitude that wonder-working providence of God by which military necessities become the instruments of justice in breaking the yoke of oppression and causing the oppressed to go free; and, further, that the Assembly beseech Almighty God, in his own time, to remove the last vestige of slavery from the country, and give to the nation, preserved, disciplined, and purified, a peace that shall be based on the principles of eternal righteousness.

Resolved, That this General Assembly commends the President of the United States, and the members of his Cabinet, to the care and guidance of the Great Ruler of nations, praying that they may have that wisdom which is profitable to direct, and also that the patriotism and moral sense of the people may give to them all that support and co-operation which the emergencies of their position and the perils of the nation so urgently demand.

Resolved, That, in the ardor with which so many members of our churches and of the churches of all the religious denominations of our land have gone forth to the defence of our country, placing themselves upon her altar in the struggle for national life, we see an illustration, not only of the principles of our holy religion, but in the readiness with which such vast numbers have, at the call of the country, devoted themselves to its service, we see a demonstration which promises security to our institutions in all times of future danger. That we tender the expression of admiration and hearty thanks to all the officers of our army and navy, that those who have nobly fallen and those who survive have secured an imperishable monument in the hearts of their countrymen, and that this Assembly regard all efforts for the physical comfort or spiritual good of our heroic defenders as among the sweetest charities which gratitude can impose or grateful hands can minister.

Resolved, That this General Assembly expects all the churches and ministers connected with this branch of the Presbyterian Church, and all our countrymen, to stand by their country, to pray for it, to discountenance all forms of complicity with treason, to sustain those who are placed in civil or military authority over them, and to adopt every means, and at any cost, which an enlightened, self-sacrificing patriotism may suggest as appropriate to the wants of its honor, having on this subject one heart and one mind, waiting hopefully on Providence, patient amid delays, and animated by reverses, persistent and untiring in effort, till, by the blessing of God, the glorious motto, "One Country, one Constitution, and one Destiny," shall be enthroned in the sublime fact of the present and more sublime harbinger of the future.

Resolved, That this General Assembly tenders its affectionate condolence and heartfelt sympathy to the bereaved families of all the heroic men who have fallen in this contest for national life, and especially the families and officers of our churches who have poured out their lives on the altar of their country, with the assurance that they will not be forgotten in their bereavement by a grateful people.

Resolved, That a copy of this action, duly authenticated, be transmitted to the President of the United States, and that these resolutions be read in all our pulpits.

This patriotic Christian paper was republished in England, and noticed with distinguished favor by some of the leading journals of that country.

After the adjournment of the Assembly, some sixty-five members, as a committee, proceeded to Washington City and presented the resolutions to the President. They were introduced by Rev. Dr. John C. Smith, the oldest pastor in Washington, in appropriate remarks; and the Chairman, John A. Foote, of Cleveland, Ohio, read the resolutions. The President replied as follows—

> It has been my happiness to receive testimonies of a similar nature from, I believe, all denominations of Christians. They are all loyal, but perhaps not in the same degree, or in the same numbers; but I think they all claim to be loyal. This to me is most gratifying, because from the beginning I saw that the issues of our great struggle depended on the Divine interposition and favor. If we had that, all would be well. The proportions of this rebellion were not for a long time understood. I saw that it involved the greatest difficulties, and would call forth all the powers of the whole country. The end is not yet.
>
> The point made in your paper is well taken as to "the Government" and "the administration," in whose hands are these interests. I fully appreciate its correctness and justice. In my administration I may have committed some errors. It would be, indeed, remarkable if I had not. I have acted according to my best judgment in every case. The views expressed by the Committee accord with my own; and on this principle "the Government" is to be supported though the administration may not in every case wisely act. As a pilot, I have used my best exertions to keep afloat our ship of state, and shall be glad to resign my trust at the appointed time to another pilot more skillful and successful than I may prove. In every case, and at all hazards, the Government must be perpetuated. Relying, as I do, upon the Almighty Power, and encouraged as I am by these resolutions which you have just read, with the support which I receive from Christian men, I shall not hesitate to use all the means at my control to secure the termination of this rebellion, and will hope for success.
>
> I sincerely thank you for this interview, this pleasant mode of presentation, and the General Assembly for their patriotic support in these resolutions.

THE GENERAL SYNOD AND CONVENTION OF THE REFORMED
PROTESTANT DUTCH CHURCH, JUNE, 1863.

Whereas it is the duty of the Church of Christ, and of all those who minister at her altars, agreeably to the teachings of the Scriptures, and the injunctions of our standards and formularies of doctrine and worship, to yield at all times a cordial support, both by precept and example, to the legitimate Government of the land; and

Whereas this duty is especially incumbent at a period when the Government is assailed by armed violence and insubordination, and its very existence and integrity are sought to be subverted by a powerful and persevering rebellion: therefore,

Resolved, 1. That we tender to the Government of the United States, and those who represent it, the renewed expression of our warmest and deepest sympathy in its present protracted struggle to maintain its lawful authority and to preserve unbroken the integrity and union of these States.

2. That we hold it to be our imperative duty as ministers of the gospel and members of the Synod, while abstaining from all unseemly mixing up of ourselves with mere party politics, in our own appropriate sphere and by every possible means to strengthen the hands of the Government at the present imminent crisis, wherein are put at stake the national life and the noblest example and experiment of constitutional government the world has ever seen; and that we will yield a cordial support to all such measures, not incompatible with the great law of righteousness, as may be necessary to suppress the existing rebellion and to assert the complete authority of the Union over all proper territory and domain.

3. That we will hail with satisfaction the earliest practicable period for the introduction and establishment of a salutary peace—a peace founded on the full ascendency of law and rightful authority, and guaranteed in its permanency by the removal or the sufficient coercion and restraint of whatever causes tend necessarily to imperil the existence of the nation and to endanger the preservation of the Union; and until such a peace can be obtained, we hold it to be a sacred duty to

ourselves, our children, our country, the Church of God, and also to humanity at large, to prosecute to the last a war forced upon us by an imperative necessity, and waged on our part not in hatred or revenge, but in the great cause of constitutional liberty and rational self-government.

4. That we recognize devoutly our dependence upon God for a happy issue and termination to our present troubles; that we accept with profound humility and abasement the chastisements of his hand; that we make mention of our deep unworthiness and sin; and that we endeavor, by continual searching, repentance, and careful walking before God, to conciliate the Divine favor, so that ere long his heavy judgments in our national calamities may be removed, and a restoration may be accorded to us of the blessings of peace, fraternal harmony, fraternal union, and established government.

The Episcopal Convention of Pennsylvania, May, 1863.

Resolved, That, in the present crisis of our national existence, we feel called upon, as a Convention of the Church, not only to give to our beloved and bleeding country our earnest prayers, but to sustain the hands of the Government by a distinct expression of our loyal sentiments.

Resolved, therefore, That we pledge to the constituted authorities of the land our cordial sympathy and support in their efforts to suppress the existing rebellion and re-establish our national Union; and that we will continue to offer our constant prayers to Almighty God that he will be pleased to unite "the hearts of his people as the heart of one man in upholding the supremacy of law and the cause of justice and peace."

Resolved, That we do solemnly recognize and reaffirm, as pertaining to the character and requirements of our holy religion, the duty of hearty loyalty to the Constitution and Government under which God, in his good providence, has placed us, the duty of religiously abstaining from and boldly rebuking all sympathy or complicity with the privy conspiracy and rebellion from which we pray to be delivered, and the duty of humbly acknowledging the hand of Almighty God in the chastisements he inflicts, and of imploring his forbearance and forgiveness, and his gracious interposition in speedily restoring to us the blessings of union and peace, through Jesus Christ, our only Mediator and Redeemer.

Memorial of the Quakers to Congress

The following extract, taken from a memorial to Congress, presented in February, 1863, by "the representatives of the religious Society of Friends, commonly called Quakers, in Pennsylvania, New Jersey, Delaware, &c.," expresses the views of this body of American Christians on the rebellion. The memorial, after stating "that the Friends as a body have ever felt it a religious duty to live a quiet and peaceable life, to obey all laws which do not violate the precepts of our holy Redeemer," and that "we love our country, and thankfully appreciate the many privileges and benefits which, through the blessings of the Most High, have been vouchsafed to us under its mild and liberal government, and desire to do all we conscientiously can to maintain its integrity," and "that Friends have ever felt themselves religiously restrained from any participation in war," and that they cannot conscientiously pay penalties imposed as military fines, &c., concludes as follows—

> We deplore and utterly condemn the wicked rebellion, fomented by misguided and infatuated men, which has involved the nation in strife and bloodshed; and earnestly desire that, while the Lord's judgments are so awfully manifest, the inhabitants of the earth may learn righteousness, and through obedience to the requisitions of the only religion which we all profess we may happily secure the favor of Him who has all power in heaven and on earth, and by whose blessing only the nation can be preserved and prosper, so that peace may once more be restored throughout our whole land, and Christian liberty, harmony, and love universally prevail among the people.
>
> Signed on behalf and by direction of a meeting of the representatives aforesaid, held in Philadelphia, the 24th of the 2d month, 1863.
>
> Joseph Snowdon, *Clerk.*

A Convention of Methodist laymen met in the city of New York, in May, 1863, on ecclesiastical matters, and closed their deliberations by the passage of the following resolutions—

> *Resolved*, 1. That we deem the present a fitting occasion, on the assembling together of laymen of the Methodist Episcopal Church from different States of the Union, to give expression to our sentiments as Christian men, pledging our unqualified devotion and adherence to the Union and the enforcement of the laws; and that no effort of ours, becoming those who are devoted to the furtherance of the interests of humanity and religion, shall be spared to sustain the Government in this crisis of its history.
>
> *Resolved*, 2. We also recognize with great satisfaction the course of our papers, the patriotic services of many of our ministers in the army and navy at home and abroad in the national cause; and we indulge the hope that the day is not far distant when these noble men shall have the proud satisfaction of having contributed in no small degree in bringing about a restoration of our beloved country to the blessings of a glorious and permanent peace.
>
> *Resolved*, 3. That we extend to our brave brethren on the field and in the army, now exposing their lives in defence of our common interests, our cordial sympathy and support, and we pledge them an interest in our prayers for themselves and our concern for their families at home.

Numerous delegates, many of whom occupied high civil and military positions, were present from Ohio, Maryland, New Jersey, Connecticut, New York, Pennsylvania, Rhode Island, Massachusetts, Delaware, Indiana, Illinois, Michigan, Maine, the District of Columbia, and the cities of New York and Brooklyn. The Convention was presided over by Joseph A. Wright, of Indiana, who had been Governor of the State, a representative in Congress, Minister at the Court of Berlin, in Prussia, and during the first two years of the rebellion a Senator in Congress. He was distinguished for his efforts to extend Christian institutions and influences through the land, and for his devotion to the country in its imperilled condition. His views on the relation of Christianity to civil society are expressed in the following words—

> Too long has the sentiment of Lord Brougham been heralded forth, "The schoolmaster is abroad." The proper sentiment is, The BIBLE is abroad. Out of the word of God spring the hope, the life, the vitality of the nations of the earth; without note or comment, freely circulated among the people. Its principles underlie all civil institutions and social structure.
>
> Nations and men must fully recognize God's truth and providence in all their doings and actions. Our fathers fully realized it; and therein alone consisted their power and strength.

Governor Wright was connected with a beautiful, patriotic, and Christian incident in Berlin, the metropolis of Prussia. During his residence as minister to that court, he labored in a missionary German Sabbath-school; and, returning to that city in June, 1863, he bore from the capital of the American republic, where he had been a member of the Senate of the United States, a very beautiful Bible, which was sent as a present by the Sabbath-school connected with Wesley Chapel in Washington City. Governor Wright made a thrilling speech. The effect of the presentation and of the speech on the children and teachers was very marked, as was abundantly evidenced by smiling faces and falling tears. The Governor referred to the past history of the school, and his connection with it, and also to his intense anxiety for its future success. He spoke also of our present national troubles, and requested the whole school to kneel down and ask the God of our fathers to deliver us from this horrible rebellion. "It was cheering," says the writer, "to hear two or three hundred children and teachers, led by their pastor, offering up their earnest prayers that God would bless America, the home of Washington, the land that these children have learned to prize."

The National Convention of the Young Men's Christian Association of the United States and the British Provinces met in May, 1863, at Chicago, Illinois. Delegates were present from most of the Northern States, the District of Columbia, Canada, and England. The Association was presided over by George H. Stuart, of Philadelphia, and passed the following resolutions—

Resolved, That we hereby reaffirm our unconditional loyalty to the Government of the United States, and our determination to afford every required and Christian aid for the suppression of the infamous rebellion.

Resolved, That we are gratified at the steps already taken by the administration for the removal of the great sin of slavery—" the sum of all villainies,"—and must express our candid conviction that the war will last so long as its cause morally exists, and that when we as a nation do *fully* right, God will not delay to give success to our arms.

Resolved, That it is no time to confound liberty with lawlessness. We cherish the dearest boon of freedom with jealous vigilance, but remember that true freedom can only continue under restraints, and exist at all as guarded by law.

Resolved, That neither is this a time for doubtful, timid measures. The counsels of time-serving, self-seeking, inconsistent politicians are not to be heeded; but the loud voice of the loyal people, the heroic demands of our teeming volunteers, and the vigorous measures of unselfish and uncompromising generals are to be respected by those who rule over us.

Resolved, That we remember with honest gratitude the noble and immense work accomplished by the Young Men's Christian Association of our land, and the sanitary and spiritual fields opened up by the providence of God for our willing hearts and hands, and pledge that we will continue to pray for our army and navy, and to meet their wants in the future with greater fidelity, if possible.

Resolved, That we recommend to daily prayer-meetings connected with the Associations here represented to observe the usual hour of Monday following July 4, 1863, as a season of special prayer for the outpouring of the Holy Spirit on all brave defenders of our country.

Religion the Stay of the Government

Other ecclesiastical bodies and Christian associations, during the rebellion, passed resolutions similar in tone and sentiment to those recorded in this volume; and all show in a most eminent degree the harmonious action and sentiment of all denominations of Christians in sustaining the Government of the United States and preserving the integrity and nationality of the republic. As a historic fact, unfolding the free genius of the Christian religion and the loyalty of its ministers, members, and Churches to liberty and free government, it is full of instruction, and reflects the highest honor on American Christianity as developed in the Northern States.

As an important fact in the Christian history of the nation, the resolutions of American Churches during the rebellion on the subject of slavery correspond with the sentiments and action of the Churches previous to and during the Revolution. The Congregational Churches, Presbyterian Synods and Assemblies, Baptist Associations, and the Quakers, all passed resolutions against slavery and labored for its abolition. The facts demonstrating this historic harmony are too numerous to be given in this volume.

The action of Christian denominations, as expressed in their resolutions and sentiments, justifies the following statement, made by Rev. Mr. Duryea before the American Tract Society, May, 1863—

> You may talk of patriotism, but the Christian needs no other motive than Christianity. If he is a Christian, he will have patriotism. When patriotism has died out from all other hearts, you will find it warm and true in the hearts of the Christian Church.
>
> During the darkest hour of our trial, some of the Christian gentlemen of this land determined to go to the administration. I was made, unworthily, with Dr. Taylor, and Mr. Stuart, of Philadelphia, the spokesman. I told the President that the foundation of his strength had been in party constancy; when that should be gone, he might come down upon the people; but when the people should be divided, and he should find himself sinking, he need not despair, for in the lower depth he would find a new resting-place: he would strike *the Christian Church*, and then he would strike a rock. In high places in Washington, the secret tears rolled down the cheeks of our rulers when I told them that *Christian men and women, and even little children, with clasped hands, were praying for the*

President of the United States, his advisers and co-laborers; and the President said that that testimonial from the Christian Church had comforted and strengthened him, and he thanked us and God for it.

Proclamation of Emancipation

The Christian action of most of the Churches during the second and third years of the rebellion, as well as the civil and military policy of the Government, had reference to the following important state paper—

A PROCLAMATION

Whereas, on the twenty-second day of September, in the year of our Lord one thousand eight hundred and sixty-two, a proclamation was issued by the President of the United States, containing, among other things, the following, to wit:

"That on the first day of January, in the year of our Lord one thousand eight hundred and sixty-three, all persons held as slaves within any State, or designated part of a State, the people whereof shall then be in rebellion against the United States, shall be thenceforward and FOREVER FREE, and the Executive Government of the United States, including the military and naval authority thereof, will recognize and maintain the freedom of such persons, and will do no act or acts to repress such persons, or any of them, in any efforts they may make for their actual freedom.

"That the Executive will, on the first day of January aforesaid, by proclamation, designate the States and parts of States, if any, in which the people thereof respectively shall then be in rebellion against the United States; and the fact that any State, or the people thereof, shall on that day be in good faith represented in the Congress of the United States, by members chosen thereto at elections wherein a majority of the qualified voters of such State shall have participated, shall, in the absence of strong countervailing testimony, be deemed conclusive evidence that such State and the people thereof are not then in rebellion against the United States."

Now, therefore, I, Abraham Lincoln, President of the United States, by virtue of the power in me vested as Commander-in-Chief of the Army and Navy of the United States in time of actual armed rebellion against the authority and Government of the United States, and as a fit and necessary war-measure for suppressing said rebellion, do, on this first day of January, in the year of our Lord one thousand eight hundred and sixty-three, and in accordance with my purpose so to do, publicly proclaimed for the full period of one hundred days from the day first above mentioned, order and designate as the States and parts of States wherein the people thereof, respectively, are this day in rebellion against the United States, the following, to wit—

Arkansas, Texas, Louisiana (except parishes of St. Bernard, Plaquemines, Jefferson, St. John, St. Charles, St. James, Ascension, Assumption, Terre Bonne, Lafourche, St. Marie, St. Martin, and Orleans, including the city of New Orleans), Mississippi, Alabama, Florida, Georgia, South Carolina, North Carolina, and Virginia (except the forty-eight counties designated as West Virginia, and also the counties of Berkeley, Accomac, Northampton, Elizabeth City, York, Princess Anne, and Norfolk, including the cities of Norfolk and Portsmouth, and which excepted parts are, for the present, left precisely as if this proclamation were not issued).

And, by virtue of the power and for the purpose aforesaid, I do order and declare that ALL PERSONS HELD AS SLAVES within said designated States and parts of States ARE, AND HENCEFORWARD SHALL BE, FREE; and that the Executive Government of the United States, including the military and naval authorities thereof, will recognize and maintain the freedom of said persons.

And I hereby enjoin upon the people so declared to be free to abstain from all violence, unless in necessary self-defence; and I recommend to them that in all cases, when allowed, they labor faithfully for reasonable wages.

And I further declare and make known that such persons, of suitable condition, will be received into the armed service of the United States, to garrison forts, positions, stations, and other places, and to man vessels of all sorts in said service.

And upon this act, sincerely believed to be an act of justice, warranted by the Constitution, upon military necessity, I invoke the considerate judgment of mankind and the gracious favor of Almighty God.

In testimony whereof, I have hereunto set my hand and caused the seal of the United States to be affixed.

Done at the City of Washington, this first day of January, in the year of our Lord one thousand eight hundred and sixty-three, and of the independence of the United States of America the eighty-seventh.

Abraham Lincoln.

By the President:

William H. Seward, *Secretary of State.*

Christian Organizations

Made special efforts to cultivate and strengthen the religious element of the nation during the conflict. The American Bible Society distributed to the men in the army and navy more than a million of Bibles and Testaments. The American Tract Society of Boston had its head-quarters at Washington, and through its agent, Mr. Alvord, accomplished a great work. He says, "General Scott and his staff received the books with remarkable favor, and the old general himself bid him God-speed in the work of distribution. Government allowed the packages to go in the mails, and furnished every facility for distribution, by which the entire Army of the Potomac was reached once a week. The books and tracts were eagerly received."

The American Tract Society of New York made systematic and successful efforts to reach the army and navy with its Christian literature, and received every encouragement from the Government. Their work received from the President the following approval—

EXECUTIVE MANSION, WASHINGTON, D.C., SEPT. 6, 1881.

REV. O. EASTMAN, *Secretary American Tract Society, New York.*

DEAR SIR—I take pleasure in acknowledging for the President your kind and patriotic note of the 3d instant. Allow me to express for the President his warm approbation of the work in which your Society is engaged. *Religion and good government are sworn allies.*

Respectfully,

Jno. G. Nicolay, *Private Secretary.*

The President said to a member of the Society, "You may have every thing—transportation, free passes, can go where you please, and command the administration to the whole extent of its ability and means, to help you take care of the religious interests of the army.

The American Temperance Union was an efficient co-laborer in the moral and Christian work done for the army. Samuel F. Carey, of Ohio, distinguished for his devotion to the cause of temperance, and for his eloquence in defending the country against the rebellion, said "that during the present civil war volumes of facts can be adduced demonstrating that many of our most serious disasters are directly attributable to intemperance, and that intoxicating liquors do more than all other things to deteriorate the character of the soldier and to unfit him for the defence of his country. In efforts made to promote the temperance reformation, General Scott, the veteran soldier and world-renowned officer, early in the war gave a written order to admit a temperance-lecturer within the lines, and directed that every possible facility be afforded him to exert an influence among the soldiers. President Lincoln, the commander-in-chief of the army, warmly endorsed the movement; and when the advocate was denied an opportunity of performing his mission by liquor-loving officers, the President gave a written and imperative command to receive him and facilitate his object. Backed by this credential, he went from regiment to regiment in the Potomac army; and his influence for good was felt and acknowledged. Commodores Foote and Porter, of the navy, have in the most unqualified manner testified to the necessity of total abstinence for the efficient conduct of the navy.

"In view of the peculiar temptations in the army, and the dangers of our soldiers contracting intemperate habits, tracts have been prepared by Marsh, Delavan, Carey, and others, and millions of pages distributed gratuitously by philanthropic individuals and societies."

THE CHRISTIAN COMMISSION was an extensive and an efficient organization for the diffusion of religious influences during the war. It was organized on a national basis, with a large committee of the most distinguished ministers and laymen in the various Northern States, and had its unpaid agents everywhere in the army and navy, who were received with the most cordial welcome. The following is the official statement of its object—

> Their object is to promote the spiritual and temporal welfare of the brave men who are now in arms to put down a wicked rebellion. They propose to do this by aiding the chaplains and others in their work.
>
> 1. By furnishing to them religious tracts, periodicals, and books.
>
> 2. By aiding in the formation of religious associations in the several regiments.
>
> 3. By putting such associations in correspondence with the Christian public.
>
> 4. By cultivating, as far as possible, the religious sympathies and prayers of Christians in their behalf.
>
> 5. By obtaining and directing such gratuitous personal labor among the soldiers and sailors as may be practicable.
>
> 6. By improving such other opportunities and means as may, in the providence of God, be presented.
>
> 7. By furnishing, as far as possible, profitable reading other than religious, and, wherever there is a permanent military post, by establishing a general library of such works.
>
> 8. By establishing a medium of speedy and safe intercommunication between the men in the army and navy and their friends and families, by which small packages of clothing, books, and medicines, and mementoes of social affection, can be interchanged.
>
> We propose to encourage in them whatever is good and keep fresh in their remembrance the instructions of earlier years, and to develop, organize, and make effective the religious element in the army and navy. The field is open to us. We can have free access to their immortal souls; the chap-

lains desire and call for our aid; the Government wish it; and the men ask for and receive religious reading and teaching with an eagerness most touching. Thousands who at home never entered the house of God, and had none to care for their souls, now, in imminent peril, desire to know of Him who can give them the victory over death through our Lord Jesus Christ.

The following testimonials addressed to George H. Stuart, of Philadelphia, Chairman of the Christian Commission, show the value of this benevolent organization—

EXECUTIVE MANSION, WASHINGTON, DECEMBER 12, 1861.
MY DEAR SIR—Your Christian and benevolent undertaking for the benefit of the soldiers is too obviously proper and praiseworthy to admit any difference of opinion. I sincerely hope your plan may be as successful in execution as it is just and generous in conception.

A. Lincoln.

WAR DEPARTMENT, DECEMBER 13, 1861.
This Department is deeply interested in the "spiritual good of the soldiers in our army," as well as in their "intellectual improvement and social and physical comfort," and will cheerfully give its aid to the benevolent and patriotic of the land who desire to improve the condition of our troops. It confidently looks for beneficial results from so noble an enterprise, and begs you to express to the Commission its sincere wish for the success of this great work in behalf of the soldier.

Simon Cameron, *Secretary of War.*

NAVY DEPARTMENT, DECEMBER 10, 1861.
This Department will be gratified with any legitimate means to promote the welfare (present and future) of all who are in the service.

Gideon Welles, *Secretary of the Navy.*

WASHINGTON, JANUARY 5, 1863.
The Christian Commission have in hand a noble work, and are performing it, I am well assured, as only a labor of love can be performed.

M. Blair, *Postmaster-General.*

HEAD-QUARTERS, ARMY OF THE POTOMAC, WASHINGTON,
JUNE 5, 1862.
The objects of the Commission are such as meet my cordial approval, and will, if carried out in the proper spirit, prove of great value.

George B. McClellan.

WAR DEPARTMENT, WASHINGTON, JANUARY 24, 1863.
Bishop Janes is authorized to state that he has received assurance from the Secretary of War, E. M. Stanton, that every facility consistent with the exigencies of the service will be afforded to the Christian Commission, for the performance of their religious and benevolent purposes in the armies of the United States, and in the forts, garrisons and camps, and military posts.

BUREAU OF EQUIPMENT AND RECRUITING,
WASHINGTON, D.C., JANUARY 28, 1863.
The object and importance of your Commission cannot be overestimated. It will supply a *hiatus* long wanting in the army and navy, and must enlist the sympathies and prayers of all true Christian patriots. To supply the spiritual wants of the public service on the battle-field and upon the ocean, and to lead our warriors to go forward valiantly to the fight, acknowledlging God as our Ruler and looking to him for success, will, I have no doubt, soon cause this wicked rebellion to culminate in the restoration of our Union.

A. H. Foote, *Admiral in the Navy.*

Lieutenant-General Winfield Scott, at a public meeting of the Christian Commission held in New York, December, 1861, presided, and made the following address—

FELLOW-CITIZENS—The honor done me on this occasion, in calling me to occupy this chair upon an occasion of so much importance and worth, gladdens the heart of an old soldier and fills him with gratitude and love. New York has sent out her thousands upon thousands of brave sons to fight the battles of our Constitution and Union, and has not forgotten them in the field or upon their return home. Her care has been incessant. She has given them every aid, has cared for their families, and watched over the wounded, sick, lame, and halt upon their return. The objects of this Association will be explained to you by my colleague in the duties of the chair, more fully than I shall attempt upon this occasion. With such a cause, that God will prosper our efforts and give us triumph no Christian man can doubt.

General Scott, as chief of the army of the United States, and for a half-century distinguished in the military service of his country, and exerting a large influence on society and the Government, in public and in private, bore his testimony to the divinity of the Christian religion, and its vital necessity to the welfare and stability of human society and governments. In 1844, in a public letter, referring to the settlement of international difficulties, he said, "We should especially remember, *all things whatsoever ye would that men should do to you, do ye even so to them.* This Divine principle is of universal obligation: it is as applicable to rulers in their transactions with other nations as to private individuals in their daily intercourse with each other. Power is intrusted by the Author of peace and lover of concord 'to do good, and avoid evil.' Such is clearly the revealed will of God."

He inculcated the highest moral virtues with the character and conduct of an American officer and soldier, and enjoined, in a general order, in 1842, that "every officer shall give himself up entirely to the cultivation and practice of all the virtues and accomplishments which can elevate an honorable profession. ... The officers should unite a high degree of moral vigor with the courtesy that springs from the heart."

"To this distinguished man," said Dr. Channing, of Boston, "belongs the rare honor of uniting with military energy and daring the spirit of a philanthropist.... It would not be easy to find among us a man who has won a purer fame."

On Sabbath evening, February 22, 1863, the Christian Commission held a meeting in the hall of the House of Representatives, Washington City, which was one of the most remarkable meetings ever held in the Capitol of the nation.

Those who took part in the proceedings represented the widest range of the most important interests. Secretary Chase, who presided, represented the Government, the approval of which was given most cordially not only by him, but also by the letter received from the President, to the United States Christian Commission, and its great national work for the army and navy—

> EXECUTIVE MANSION, WASHINGTON, FEBRUARY 22, 1863.
> Whatever shall be sincerely and in God's name devised for the good of the soldiers and seamen in their hard spheres of duty can scarcely fail to be blessed. And whatever shall tend to turn our thoughts from the unreasoning and uncharitable passions, prejudices, and jealousies incident to a great national trouble such as ours, and to fix them upon the vast and long-enduring consequences for weal or for woe which are to result from this struggle, and especially to strengthen our reliance on the Supreme Being for the final triumph of the right, cannot but be well for us all.
>
> The birthday of Washington and the Christian Sabbath coinciding this year, and suggesting together the highest interests of this life and of that to come, is most propitious for the meeting proposed.
>
> A. Lincoln.

The Sabbath

In its proper observance and influence in the army and navy, enlisted the earnest efforts of the Christian public, The following petition was extensively circulated, and sent to the President—

> TO HIS EXCELLENCY THE PRESIDENT, COMMANDER-IN-CHIEF OF THE ARMY AND NAVY OF THE UNITED STATES.
> The petition of the subscribers, loyal citizens of the United States, and heartily pledging all righteous support to the national

Government, particularly in the present unhappy struggle with a rebellion most criminal and fearful, very respectfully showeth—

That we are, in fact, a Christian people, believing obedience to God's will, revealed in the Holy Scriptures, to be our sole security for his blessings; that our soldiers and sailors go forth usually from Christian communities and homes, with at least strong religious convictions; that many of them are communicants in Christian Churches; that our army and navy, therefore, are distinctly a Christian army and navy, and entitled, in war as well as in peace, to Christian care and privileges; that experience has conclusively proved that moral and religious improvement, and a reasonable respect paid to conscientious convictions, always promote the loyalty and efficiency of men engaged in warfare, while nothing can well demoralize and discourage them so thoroughly as an apprehension that God's favor has been forfeited by either themselves or their commanders; that men returning home debauched in a service characterized by vice and irreligion ever prove a bane to society; and that the Christian people of this land, in sending forth from their dwellings and churches those who are to fight the battles of the country, do therefore reasonably expect, as your petitioners do most earnestly pray, that your Excellency will give careful attention to the moral and religious interests of the whole army and navy under your command; and particularly—

1. That you will adopt the most stringent measures to banish, as far as possible, from our forces all temptation to intemperance or any other vice.

2. That you will employ your whole authority to secure the general appointment of chaplains, regularly ordained, and of good standing in their respective denominations, with a faithful discharge of duty on their part, and all proper encouragement and independence in the same, and to insure to both officers and privates entire religious liberty and the right of attending upon a ministry of their own choice.

3. That you will issue such orders respecting parades, reviews, receptions, the admission of visitors, military services,

and the giving of battle, as will, excepting in cases of absolute necessity, secure uninterrupted the rest and worship of the Sabbath, to none more important, for both body and soul, than to the soldier or sailor, and to him never more important than upon the eve of battle.

And your petitioners will ever pray, &c.

The ministers of Cincinnati, Ohio, addressed the President the following paper—

Cincinnati, Ohio, June 29, 1861.

To the President of the United States:

Sir—The undersigned, members of the "Union of Protestant Ministers of Cincinnati," desire to address you, briefly, on a subject which lies very near to our hearts. It respects the moral and religious welfare of the troops called forth to suppress the present causeless and wicked rebellion. Our Churches, as you are aware, have fully and without reserve entered into the purpose of the Government to defend and maintain the national life. They have freely given of the choicest of their members, and sent them to the camp and the fields of conflict, with their benedictions and their prayers.

At the same time, we cannot be indifferent to the moral dangers to which they are exposed. They are mostly young men; and, in their name and in the name of those with whom they are associated, we therefore ask the Government to do all that it consistently can to guard their morals and provide for their religious welfare. We would especially mention the steady encouragement of the observance of the Sabbath in the camp, and the furnishing of all reasonable facilities for religious instruction and edification. War, we know, has its own exigencies; and we would ask for nothing impracticable, or that would in the least impair the efficiency of the military arm. It is with great satisfaction, also, that we have learned the determination of the Government to provide for the maintenance of a chaplain in each regiment, while the army regulations in respect to religious matters must recommend themselves to every mind.

At the same time, we feel assured that the expression of the interest of the Government in the carrying out of these regulations, its expressly discouraging all unnecessary drilling and other work in the camp, and the making suitable provision for the erection of sheds or other temporary accommodations for religious worship in stationary camps, would have an exceedingly beneficial influence, and do much to strengthen the religious element, which, we are happy to know, prevails so largely among our troops, and which in all wars of principle has been found to contribute so essentially to the final result.

Invoking upon you, sir, and your Cabinet the blessings of Heaven, and assuring you of our fervent intercession, and those of our congregations, in public and in private, at the throne of grace, in your behalf,

We are, respectfully.

The President made the following reply—

EXECUTIVE MANSION, JULY 21, 1861.
REVEREND AND DEAR SIR—I am directed by the President to acknowledge the receipt of a communication signed by yourself and many others of the "Union of Protestant Ministers of Cincinnati."

The President desires me to express his deep appreciation of the motives which prompted your address, and his entire sympathy with the views you hold, and to assure you that, as far as practicable, the principles to which you give utterance shall guide the conduct of the Government in the troubled scenes upon which we are entering.

I have the honor to be your most obedient servant,

John Hay, *Assistant Secretary.*

ADDRESS OF THE NEW YORK SABBATH DEPUTATION TO THE PRESIDENT.

To the President:

We wait on you, Mr. President, as a Deputation from the New York Sabbath Committee, in conformity with the request of a meeting of influential citizens from all parts of the country, held last August at Saratoga Springs, to promote the better observance of Sunday in the army and navy of which you are the honored commander-in-chief. To this end we respectfully solicit your sanction of an appropriate General Order protecting the rights of our brave soldiers and sailors to their weekly season of rest and worship—the emergencies of the service excepted—and recommending such use of sacred time as will best secure its sanitary, moral, and religious benefits.

We deem it superfluous in this presence to discuss the civil or sacred relations of an institution as old as time and as prevalent as freedom and Christianity. We address the civil and military ruler of a republic whose busy population weekly pause in their industrial pursuits and throng the temples of Christian worship, attesting their reverence for the Lord's day and its Author, and whose laws and customs reflect, as they have ever done, the popular appreciation of the national rest-day. It is no unintelligent, superstitious principle that has moulded the legislation of more than thirty States of the Union and stamped its impress on the character of the nation. The law of periodical rest is written on the human constitution and on the framework of free, self-governing institutions, as indelibly as it is on the pages of revelation. A government of law must have its foundations in morality: its liberties inhere, under God, in its virtues. But it is the recorded axiom of the late Justice McLean, "Where there is no Christian Sabbath there is no Christian morality; and without this free institutions cannot long be sustained,"—a sentiment impressively illustrated by the fact that the only free nations in existence are those in which the civil Sabbath is incorporated in their laws, as is the sacred Sabbath in their cherished convictions and habits.

The respected Attorney-General of the United States has well defined the fundamental connection of the Sabbath with public morals, and so with regulated liberty. "The religious character," says Mr. Bates, "of an institution so ancient, so sacred, so lawful, and so necessary to the peace, the comfort, and the respectability of society, ought alone to be sufficient for its protection; but, that failing, surely the laws of the land made for its account ought to be as strictly enforced as the laws for the protection of person and property. Vice and crime are always progressive and cumulative. If the Sunday laws be neglected or despised, the laws of person and property will soon share their fate and be equally disregarded." The Deputation may be pardoned for alluding to the recent records of crime in New York City as a striking confirmation of the Attorney-General's views. They show that the partial suppression of Sunday abuses and temptations resulted in a relative change of sixty-five per cent, in the arrests for violating "the laws of person and property," as compared with the period when "the Sunday laws were neglected or despised." The Deputation appeal to the results of our national system of moral discipline in the general supremacy of law and liberty throughout the Northern States, even in a time of civil war, as revealing at once the root and the fruits of the tree under whose shadow the republic has sought its weekly repose and rendered its weekly homage.

Assuming, then, as we surely may, the President's patriotic and Christian respect for the Lord's day, we pass to the specific object of the Deputation.

In response to the call of the Government, nearly a million of citizens have become soldiers. They have been transferred from home, Church, and neighborhood influences, so fruitful in incitements to virtue and restraints from vice, and are exposed to the temptations of the camp and forecastle, The laws and habits of civil and domestic life are superseded by the military code and customs. It may be hoped that individuals or entire commands have borne the transition without injury to principle or character; but the tendency of the novel influences must be towards demoralization, and every available counteracting agency is demanded by the highest considerations of philanthropy, patriotism, and religion.

It is due to the army and navy. The common right of soldiers and sailors to their weekly rest, unless abridged by military necessity, will not be questioned; nor the correlative duty to observe the day according to its design. But tens of thousands of men have enlisted into one or other branch of the national service from Christian Churches. Bible classes, Sunday-schools, and religious homes—twenty-seven from a single Bible-class within our knowledge. We would vindicate the rights of these Christian men, and of all others who have moral sense enough to make good soldiers, to immunity from outrage of feeling or oppression of conscience in matters as sacred as life. They cherish, for example, a profound reverence for the name of God, and regard "profane cursing and swearing," as Washington did, as "a foolish and wicked practice," "a vice so mean and low that every man of sense and character detests and despises it." They esteem the Sabbath as sacred to rest and devotion, and have been taught from infancy "that the observance of the holy day of the God of mercy and of battles is our sacred duty." They have been trained to devout reliance on the Divine arm in their exposure of life itself in defence of a just cause, and they recoil from the violation of Divine statutes and from the wanton disregard of them by their companions in arms. They may justly claim such leadership and discipline as shall respect their most sacred convictions, when those convictions contain the elements of principled courage, unswerving obedience, and undying patriotism. If any of their officers lack the tact, self-respect, or principle to recognize these claims, superior authorities should exact the recognition, as the simplest justice to the men and the most obvious requisite of military discipline. Immorality and irreligion will sufficiently abound in spite of law and example: when these are lacking, the drift is fearful towards moral degeneracy and consequent military inefficiency.

The official intervention we seek is due to the country. The camp cannot become a school of vice without entailing irreparable injury on the numberless homes and hamlets represented in a vast volunteer army, nor without lasting damage to the morals and so to the liberties of the republic. Nor can the fact be overlooked that the cause itself for which the country and the army are contending is imperilled just in the measure in which impiety and immorality characterize its defenders and provoke the displeasure of Heaven.

It is conceded that the limit of official interposition in this matter is quite restricted. The rights of conscience are sacred. The exigencies of military service, too, must frequently overrule the choice of commanders and the natural rights of the soldier. But is there not a sphere within which the legitimate exercise of authority and moral influence may restrain the tendencies to evil that awaken alarm and grief among right-minded citizens?

The action we solicit might be mandatory so far as relates to needful weekly rest, the wanton invasion of Christian rights, and the choice of Sunday for aggressive warfare, due discretion being accorded to generals commanding, under their responsibility to God and the Government. Beyond this, paternal counsels only might suffice to encourage the virtuous and self-respecting, and to bring into disrepute the lawless trifling of officers or men with sacred interests.

The records of our Revolutionary period furnish memorable precedents for the action we venture to suggest. Repeatedly did the Father of his Country address orders to the army rebuking immorality, and encouraging purity of conduct as only befitting the holy cause for which they contended, and reminding officers and men, as we need to be reminded, that "we can have little hope of the blessing of Heaven on our arms if we insult it by our impiety and folly."

The President issued the following order—

EXECUTIVE MANSION, WASHINGTON, D.C., NOV. 18, 1862. The President, commander-in-chief of the army and navy, desires and enjoins the orderly observance of the Sabbath by the officers and men in the military and naval service. The importance for man and beast of the prescribed weekly rest, the sacred rights of Christian soldiers and sailors, a becoming deference to the best sentiment of a Christian people, and a due regard for the Divine will, demand that Sunday labor in the army and navy be reduced to the measure of strict necessity. The discipline and character of the national forces should not suffer, nor the cause they defend be imperilled, by the profanation of the day or the name of the Most High. At this time of public distress, adopting the words of Washington in 1776, "men may find enough to do in the service of God and their country, without abandoning themselves to vice and immorality." The first general order issued by the Father of his Country, after the Declaration of Independence, indicates the spirit in which our institutions were founded and should ever be defended—"The general hopes and trusts that every officer and man will endeavor to live and act as becomes a Christian soldier defending the dearest rights and privileges of his country."

Abraham Lincoln.

Views of Officers in the Army and Navy on the Sabbath

General McClellan, who for more than a year was commander of the Army of the Potomac, issued the following order—

GENERAL ORDERS NO. 7.

HEAD-QUARTERS ARMY OF THE POTOMAC, WASHINGTON,

SEPT. 7.

The Major-General commanding desires and requests that in future there may be a more perfect respect for the Sabbath on the part of his command. We are fighting in a holy cause, and should endeavor to deserve the benign favor of the Creator. Unless in case of an attack by the enemy, or some other extreme military necessity, it is commended to commanding officers that all work shall be suspended on the Sabbath; that no unnecessary movements shall be made on that day; that the men, as far as possible, shall be permitted to rest from their labors; that they shall attend Divine service after the customary morning inspection, and that officers and men alike use their influence to insure the utmost decorum and quiet on that day. The general commanding regards this as no idle form. One day's rest is necessary for man and animals. More than this, the observance of the holy day of the God of mercy and battles is our sacred duty.

Signed　　　　　　　　　　　　Geo. B. McClellan.
Major-General Commanding.

General Casey, a veteran officer of the United States army, at a public meeting in Washington in January, 1863, held to promote the observance of the Sabbath in the army, made the following statement—

> I have been thirty-six years in the military service, and I know that the army need a Sabbath. I was five years in the Florida War. In long marches better time will be made, and the men will go through in better condition, by resting on the Sabbath than by continuous marching. No prudent general will plan for a Sunday battle. I would appeal to the American people to save our American Sabbath. If our wealth is lost in this terrible war, it may be recovered; if our young men are killed off, others will grow up; *but if our Sabbath is lost, it can never be restored, and all is lost.*

Commodore Foote, who as a commander in the navy was distinguished for his eminent and practical piety, as well as for his patriotism and earnest efforts to serve his country and put down the rebellion, issued the following order in respect to the Sabbath and profanity—

> ### General Order No. 6.
>
> *A strict observance of the Sabbath,* so far as abstaining from all unnecessary work, and giving officers and men the opportunity of attending public worship on board, will be observed by all persons connected with the flotilla.
>
> It is the wish of the commander-in-chief that on the Sabbath the public worship of Almighty God may be observed on board of all the vessels composing the flotilla, and that the respective commanders will, either themselves, or cause other

persons, to pronounce prayers publicly on Sabbath, when as many of the officers and men as can be spared from duty may attend the public worship of Almighty God.

Profane swearing being forbidden by the laws for the better government of the navy, all officers and men will strictly observe this law; and every officer who uses profane language towards the men in carrying on duty will be held amenable for such gross violation of law and order.

Discipline, to be permanent, must be based on moral grounds, and officers must in themselves show a good example in morals, order, and patriotism, to secure those qualities in the men.

Andrew H. Foote,
Flag-Officer commanding U.S. Naval Forces on the Western Waters.

The Chaplains of the Army

Were from all denominations of Christians; and the following testimony to their fidelity and usefulness is from sources entitled to the highest credit. Rev. Granville Moody, who relinquished one of the largest and wealthiest pastorates of the Methodist Church in Cincinnati in order to accept the position of colonel in the army, and who was earnest and eloquent in infusing a spirit of patriotism into the people from the pulpit, bears the following testimony—

> As I have had the amplest opportunities for noticing the operations of chaplains in the army, allow me to pay a passing tribute to their worth and work.
>
> With very few exceptions, they have been men of one work, "watching for souls as they who must give account of the souls committed to their care" in the wise, Christian, patriotic, and humane provision for their office and work by our glorious Government.
>
> It is, indeed, refreshing to meet these men of God in all the departments of military operations. In camp, on the toilsome march, on the battle-fields, or in the hospitals with their crowded wards, we meet these humble ministers of peace,

vindicating their claims as successors to the apostles, evangelists, pastors, teachers, and helps, who have received their commissions from Him "who went about doing good" to the bodies and souls of men.

Pray for the chaplains in the army, in disseminating gospel truths, in advertising and applying God's remedy for man's misery, in the timely utterances of the precepts and promises of God, in restraining vice and encouraging virtue, in consoling the afflicted, comforting the comfortless, pointing sinners to the Lamb of God, sanctifying patriotism, sustaining Government, and serving their generation in their day. They are doing a great and glorious work, which will redound to the glory of God and the good of men.

As they appear before listening thousands in these sun-hot Southern groves, leading the solemn, simple, and sublime devotions of the Sabbath in camp, we are compelled to say, with Cowper—

> "There stands the solemn legate of the skies,
> His theme divine and his credentials clear.
> By him the violated law speaks out its thunders,
> And by him, in strains as sweet as angels use,
> The gospel whispers peace."

Long may the bright succession run, represented by those "who shall turn many to righteousness, and shine as the stars forever."
Granville Moody,
Colonel commanding 74th *Reg't O.V.I.*

Rev. Mr. Alvord, Secretary and Superintendent of the operations of the American Tract Society of Boston in its work among the soldiers, and who was with the Army of the Potomac in active Christian service for two years, and in frequent conferences with chaplains, testifies as follows to their power and influence—

> Give the chaplains *opportunity, facility, material*; they are the organic, established ministration to the army, "God's ordinance,"

therefore, to advance Christianity, They are to be strengthened, not *thrust aside*. Link them all back to the people at home for sympathies and supplies, and in every way rally the Christians of the army around them; then let all the volunteer agency be as "Aarons and Hurs," and, what-ever the Government or mere military men may do, religion will, under this Divine agency, magnify her supremacy and show her power to save. This is the way God is evidently now working. Christian appliances, *especially through the chaplains*, are rapidly gaining in effect.

Rev. Dr. Marks, as a chaplain in the Army of the Potomac, who by his fidelity and fitness for the work won a high distinction among the officers and soldiers, and who wrote a popular book on the military and Christian scenes of the Peninsular campaign, gives the following testimony—

During more than two years of my connection with the Potomac army I was most intimately acquainted with a large number of the chaplains in that service, and, with few exceptions, they were very excellent men, and, in spite of the difficulties of their position, accomplished an amount of good that never can be told. When sickness came, they were the most patient and sympathizing of nurses and friends. Their words of faith and loyalty cheered the soldiers in their long marches and on entering into battle. As a general thing, their office and character brought them into more intimate communion with the troops than any other officers, and the men felt that the chaplain was the link that bound them still to their homes, their churches, and their father's house.

And to the wounded and dying on the battlefield they were like angels sent of God. Many a dying soldier have I seen, with his hand grasping that of the chaplain as the friend to whom he clung in his last moments with the greatest confidence; and the presence and words of the good man encouraged and blessed the departing hero.

His work, from the nature of the case, could not find place in bulletins and despatches from the field, but was no less valuable because thus unheralded.

The various Christian agencies produced the most happy and beneficent results.

> The Christian sentiment of the loyal States was elicited to sustain the Government and to relieve and benefit our brave men of the army and navy. The Government was called on to confess and express its dependence upon God for support, and to manifest deep interest for the moral and religious welfare of our gallant defenders. *The Home and the Church* have been brought to the men in the field, and cheering, consoling intelligence from the men in the field to the Home and the Church. Thousands of lives have been saved to the country and to loving home-circles. Thousands have been led to the Saviour, and hundreds of thousands comforted, instructed, and cheered in the hour of agony, despondency, or death.

The army felt it was engaged in a most holy cause, and the inspirations of religion and righteousness imparted faith, courage, and resolution, in the protracted and terrible struggle for the life of the republic and its free institutions against the rebellion.

> No army was ever set on foot so thoroughly imbued with enlightened religious sentiment as ours. The Crimean army, with its Hedley Vickars, and the large class of devout soldiers of whom he was a type, the Indian army, with its Havelock, the Puritan hosts of Cromwell, are no exceptions. The respect of our soldiers for the Sabbath, their family altars in messes, their prayer-meetings, their devout observance of religious ordinances, and the numerous instances which have occurred even of conversions in the camp, are circumstances which fill the Christian heart with delight. Whole companies have been devoted, with prayer and self-consecration, to God's peculiar service.

The nation owe the heroic and patriotic men of the army and navy a boundless debt of gratitude, and theirs is the honor and imperishable glory of saving, under God, the republic, and handing it down to future ages. Let the meed of praise be given to the living, and a nation's tears and gratitude to the memories of the hundred thousand fallen in battle.

Patriotic and Christian Work and Influence of the Women

Of the Northern States, during the great conflict, in their unselfish and ceaseless works of patriotism and piety, received the following tribute from a leading religious journal—

> It is inspiring to see the abounding and ever-increasing enthusiasm of the intelligent Christian women of the North for the triumph of liberty, righteousness, and truth, in that momentous national controversy now coming at last to a conclusion and settlement through the dread and final arbitrament of battle. What multitudes of women have met during the last two years, in private houses, vestries, churches, with spontaneous alacrity hastening together to prepare beforehand for the wants of the wounded, or for the comfort and relief of the sick, in the campaign that is imminent! How many, with far more signal exhibition of their love for the right, have sent their own husbands, brothers, sons, into the field, or have bidden their betrothed go forth undaunted in the cause of God and their native land! How many pastors, preaching on the great and urgent theme and pouring their full souls into their message, have been encouraged, reinforced, lifted to higher levels of feeling, penetrated with more fervent and powerful conviction, by the responses they have met from the voices or the faces of those whose delicacy has been heretofore more conspicuous than their daring, and into whose dwelling no sound of strife was ever admitted! It is one of the most remarkable phenomena in that whole series of astonishing wonders which we have of late been permitted to see.
>
> Yet there is reason for this; and the fact has a vast and deep significance. Women have reason to love the land which is their ample, bounteous home. They have reason to value the social system which cherishes and guards them with its

chiefest care. They have reason to prize the great institutions of civil and religious freedom, which furnish them with the richest means of culture and advancement, which open to them the most varied paths to happiness and usefulness. No civilization that has ever existed on the face of the earth has had a larger, so large a claim on the love and loyalty of virtuous women as that which we have here enjoyed—that which now is threatened and assailed by the headstrong violence and the vindictive passion of the Southern slave-masters. It is well, therefore, that women should rally to contribute their part to maintain it—well and fit that they should give all that God enables them to give in defence of a past so glorious as ours, in defence of a present so sheltering and benign. They would be unmindful of the sources of their own highest prosperity, or ungrateful for the blessings that hitherto have distilled each day and hour upon them and their children, except they did this!

But there is yet another relation of this wide-sweeping, spontaneous enthusiasm, inspiring to contemplate. It indicates and vindicates the holiness of the cause in which our whole vast Northern force is now engaged. The moral instincts of such a multitude of Christian women could not possibly have been enlisted or conciliated by any enterprise of ambition or aggression, by any expedition prompted by desire of territorial expansion or of martial renown. Rather from such a scheme or purpose, however plausibly advanced and advocated, such is the Christian culture of the sex in our land and in our time, they would have been instantaneously repelled. As one immense, unconquerable host they would have set themselves in the way of its progress, and with infallible certainty have arrested it. It is because they, whose moral instincts are finer and more sensitive than man's, whose moral judgments are more immediate and more authoritative, whose souls stand nearer to God and to his Son, nearer the cross, nearer the crown—it is because they know and feel that this now coming and imminent war, however protracted, fierce, and terrific it may be, is still to be a war for freedom,

for truth, for the gospel, for the coming Christian civilization of the land, for the coming hope and glory of mankind,
therefore it is that they rise to the height of the sacrifice it
demands; that they give to it the verdict of enthusiastic acceptance; that they dedicate themselves already not only to
the mitigating of the sufferings it must cause, but to the furnishing of the ranks with their recruits, of the soldiers with
their equipments, of the whole army with their own temper
of intrepid, self-denying, and heroic faith.

God bless forever the worthy daughters of the glorious
and ever-honored Revolutionary mothers!

Two thousand women of St. Louis, Missouri, entered into the following—

PLEDGE

We, the undersigned women of St. Louis, believing that in
this hour of national peril to our country every influence,
moral as well as military, should be brought to bear in the
great struggle for national existence against a rebellion as
crafty as it is wicked, and that while our fathers, husbands,
sons, and brothers are giving their treasure and blood, it is
our duty to contribute the influence God has given us in our
social sphere to the same holy cause, and that in this solemn
crisis loyalty is bound to be outspoken, even in the case of
women, as truly as loyalty to our God:

We, therefore, do constitute ourselves as an association, to
be known as the Ladies' National League of St. Louis, and do
pledge our unconditional adherence to our national Government in its struggle against the present rebellion, engaging
to assist it by whatever means may be in our power, in the
maintenance of our national Union and the integrity of our
national domain.

To this end, we do further resolve and pledge ourselves to encourage and sustain our brave soldiers by acts of kindness and
patriotic cheer; to use every fitting opportunity of expressing
our unflinching determination to stand by our dear old flag and

to honor those who fight in its defence until the day of sure and permanent triumph; and to prove, in whatever way we can, that *loyalty to our country forms a part of our allegiance to God*.

The loyal women of New York formed an association and passed the following resolutions—

We, the undersigned, women of the United States, agree to become members of the "Women's Loyal National League," hereby pledging our most earnest influence in support of the Government in its prosecution of the war for freedom and for the restoration of the national unity.

Resolved, That for the present this League will concentrate all its efforts upon the single object of procuring to be signed by one million women and upward, and of preparing for presentation to Congress within the first week of its next session, a petition in the following words, to wit—

TO THE SENATE AND HOUSE OF REPRESENTATIVES OF THE UNITED STATES.

The undersigned, women of the United States, above the age of eighteen years, earnestly pray that your honorable body will pass, at the earliest practicable day, an act emancipating all persons of African descent held to involuntary service or labor in the United States.

Resolved, That, in furtherance of the above object, the Executive Committee of this League be instructed to cause to be prepared and stereotyped a pamphlet, not exceeding four printed octavo pages, briefly and plainly setting forth the importance of such a movement at the present juncture, a copy of the said pamphlet to be placed in the hands of each person who may undertake to procure signatures to the above petition, and for such further distribution as may be ordered by the said Executive Committee.

A "Loyal Women's League" was formed in Hartford, Connecticut, the members pledging themselves to "encourage and sustain our brave soldiers by constant tokens of love, but still more by the expression of a cheerful and unflinching determination to stand by the dear old flag till the day of its triumph, be it near or remote," and so to instruct their children, and all who may be dependent upon them, that "they may grow into such filial reverence for this best of all governments as shall make them always patriots, never mere partisans." These true-hearted women also declare that they will "in all ways endeavor to create such a sentiment of devoted loyalty in the circles in which they move, *that no traitor* to *liberty, or cowardly recreant, shall utter his sentiments in their presence unrebuked."* In token of their loyalty, they have determined to wear publicly a Union badge "until the day of our national triumph."

The loyal women of Philadelphia received the following tribute, for their devotion to the soldiers and the country, from the General Assembly of the Presbyterian Church, New School, which met in that city, May, 1863—

> *Resolved*, That the Assembly hereby express their high admiration of the manner in which the ladies of Philadelphia have contributed, and are contributing, to the comfort of the soldiers who pass through this city, and of those who return as sick and suffering to its hospitals, and that as citizens of the country, and in behalf of those whom we specially represent, we present to these ladies our hearty thanks.

"The politicians are not the great workers in a war of ideas and principles like ours. Noble women, now, as ever, are the great workers, the great feelers, the great hopers, the great lovers, who keep up the *morale* of men and create the atmosphere which their spirits breathe. Leaving the actual army-work out of the account, they do actually more than the men."

The leading journals of the Northern States, both political and religious, during the great conflict, and especially on the observance of the days of fasting and prayer and of thanksgiving designated by the Government, exerted a wide-spread and beneficent influence in diffusing and strengthening the Christian element, and in pervading the rulers and people of the republic with a just sense of their responsibilities to God. They discussed the religious aspects of the war, reviewed and rebuked the sins of the nation which they stated were the causes of the just judgments of God, exhorted the people to humiliation and repentance, advocated the fundamental principles of the Bible and an obedience to the laws of God as the only true basis of national existence and prosperity, and proclaimed the great truth that God must be honored and recognized in all governmental and political transactions as well as in the social and private walks of life, if the nation would be saved and preserved in its institutions and integrity. Extracts from the elaborate editorials of leading journals, on those great Christian principles which underlie all civil institutions, had been prepared for this volume; but the limits of the work forbid their record. It is, however, an important historic fact that the loyal political papers and all the Christian journals of the country exerted a powerful and a healthful influence in developing and diffusing the religious element.

The Ministers

Of religion, of all denominations, throughout the loyal States, in the great crisis of the nation, were, with but few exceptions, true to freedom and the country. Their pulpits were pillars of moral support and strength to the Government, and their influence aided effectively and powerfully in the suppression of the rebellion. Loyalty to the Government was a religious duty, which they in their sermons and examples inculcated upon their congregations and diffused through the nation. Many of them went into the army; and no class of men made greater sacrifices to save the republic and to purify and preserve the Government in its integrity and unity. The fundamental principles of Christianity, as related to civil government and political policies, and to the causes that brought on and sustained the rebellion, were by them thoroughly unfolded and applied, and thus pure and wide currents of Christian influences flowed over all the interests and through every department of the nation. A few illustrations of their earnest patriotism and piety can only be given in this volume.

An association of evangelical ministers of Cincinnati, in the summer of 1861, discussed the question, "How can ministers best serve the interests of our country at the present crisis?" and presented their views in the following paper—

> Deeply grateful to Almighty God, our heavenly Father, for his past mercies to this nation, and particularly noting at this time his gracious goodness in leading our fathers to establish and preserve for us a constitutional government unequalled among the governments of the earth in guarding the rights and promoting the entire welfare of a great people, we, the evangelical ministry of Cincinnati, have been led by a constraining sense of accountability to him, the Author of all our good, and by unfeigned love for our country, to adopt the following statement and resolutions—
>
> We are compelled to regard the rebellion which now afflicts our land and jeopardizes some of the most precious hopes of mankind as the result of a long-contemplated and wide-spread conspiracy against the principles of liberty, justice, mercy, and righteousness proclaimed in the word of God, sustained by our constitutional Government, and lying at the foundation of all public and private welfare. In the present conflict, therefore, our Government stands before us as representing the cause of God and man, against a rebellion threatening the nation with ruin in order to perpetuate and spread a system of unrighteous oppression. In this emergency, as ministers of God, we cannot hesitate to support, by every legitimate method, the Government in maintaining its authority unimpaired throughout the whole country and over this whole people: therefore,
>
> *Resolved*, 1. That all Christian ministers and people should be exhorted to unite their fervent supplications to the God of our fathers for his protection of the Government formed under his approving providence, without which neither an empire rises nor a sparrow falls.
>
> 2. That the interests of our country demand of all good citizens a firm, united, and loyal support of the Government in destroying the armed rebellion which has risen against it.
>
> 3. That, as ministers of the gospel, we will co-operate with the chaplains of the army, so far as we may, in securing reg-

ular services of divine worship in camps and hospitals, the freest circulation of a healthful religious literature, especially of the word of God and the happy influence of the Sabbath among the soldiers.

4. That we should be admonished by the present judgment of Almighty God to call upon our nation to repent of the sin of oppression, with all those other vices for which he has thus entered into controversy with us, so that iniquity may not be our ruin.

5. That we will remember, and seek also to impress upon the public mind, that those with whom the Government is thus brought into conflict are our brethren—misguided and criminal, but still our brethren, towards whom we should maintain the spirit of compassion and kindness even while waging war against them.

6. That, with humble faith, we fearlessly commit the issue of this conflict to the just and gracious God who presides over the destinies of nations, assured that in the answer to the prayers of his people he will cause the wrath of man to praise him and restrain the remainder thereof, until he sends forth judgment unto victory, and the work of righteousness be peace, and the effect of righteousness, quietness, and assurance forever.

The following address "On the Christian's Duty in the Present Crisis," is by Bishop McIlvaine, of the Episcopal Church, who is distinguished for his catholic Christian spirit towards all denominations, and for his influence in this country and in England. He visited England during the great conflict, and exerted a wide-spread influence in favor of the cause of the Government and of the loyal States in suppressing the rebellion. The address was published in 1861—

War is upon us—the worst, the most horrid, the most calamitous and sorrowful of all wars—not only *civil* war, but civil war in circumstances beyond precedent painful and productive of all the bitterest passions of man's evil nature. The cloud is exceedingly dark, But it reaches not to heaven. God's light is behind it, however hid. His ways, however unsearchable, and "a great deep" to our eye, are in wisdom and goodness; and still "God is our refuge, and a very present help in trouble." But what is *our* duty? I mean the duty of disciples of Christ—ours *as members of Christ's Church*, having brethren in Christ everywhere—in the States now in array against us, and even in the army now perhaps on the march against us?

First. Our duty is clearly, solemnly, steadily, patiently, bravely, earnestly, to sustain our Government, There is no room for hesitation here. Whatever may be said of persons or localities, or sections of people, our Government has not provoked this war, the *country* has not. We are *pro patria*, for our beloved country—not Ohio, not this State or that, not north, or east, or west, but our country, and our Government as the only representative of our country. All duty says so. And what we are and do in the discharge of this duty should be zealous, devoted, self-sacrificing, undaunted.

But, secondly, in what spirit as Christians? There is no necessity of coming down in the least from all that pertains to Christian spirit in the discharge of such duty, wherever it may carry us. Good soldiers, especially soldiers standing for their homes and institutions, repelling invasion, encircling around their Government, contending for the Union, have no need to borrow a spirit not their own. There need be no unhallowed passions, no spirit of bitter revenge, no cultivation of hate, no ceasing to pray for enemies, no passing away of actual kindness and readiness to do good to those arrayed against us, whenever *duty, loyalty* to our own cause, does not prevent. Especially with those who stay at home and do not plunge into the actual conflict—the great mass of praying, loving, Christian people—the highest measure of loyalty and of stern determination to sustain the Government is perfectly consistent with the cherishing in their hearts of all the tempers and spirit, the charities, the kindness, the doing good to them that may hate us, the praying for those who would "despitefully use us," which our blessed gospel requires.

Under these general views, what is duty?

1. Let us keep our hearts with all diligence, with special effort to prevent the encroachment of a war feeling and ex-

citement upon the proper domain of the Spirit of God within you. The danger is great. These strong excitements carry away the mind as with a flood. They overwhelm us, unless our dikes be well kept. Duty to God, the duty of a devotional mind, the duty of prayer, secret and daily and regular and spiritual, remains. Eternity is only the nearer. God's blessing and favor are only, if possible, the more needful. The more exciting the crisis, the more the need of God. If we want an army in the field with carnal weapons, we want also, and for the same cause, an army at the throne of grace, taking hold, by constant prayer, on the arm of the only real strength. In *that* army, while the other is composed only of those between certain ages, and it must exclude the aged, the feeble—in *that* army all can be marshalled; the praying child, the praying woman, the heart on a sick-bed, tottering age—all can contend in that, and make a great and mighty host before God, holding up the hands of those who go to the battle, praying for the blessings of peace, union, stability, and brotherly love. Let us keep our hearts with all diligence, that we may thus keep ourselves at the throne of grace. Never were praying people more needed in our country than now.

2. Let us watch against the growth in our hearts of all bitterness of spirit against those whom we must now call (most painful as it is) our enemies. Many there are whom we must thus place under that name who are enemies to us only because their cause is against ours, while the bonds of Christian charity and real brotherly love of Christian brethren towards us are not broken. I believe that most truly. So it is, and must be, among us towards them. It is awful to be thus arrayed, brother against brother. No greater affliction could come. It must not be made more awful, so far as religious people can help it, by the kindling of fires of evil passion, which the cause on neither side demands, and by which any cause must be disgraced. Let us stand by the right, but *righteously*, in the right mind, in the spirit of those whose rule of mind is the word of God, and who desire to "approve themselves unto God" and to have his blessing.

3. Let us still seek peace, and the measures that make for peace. The President seeks peace, and has done nothing inconsistent with his profession of a pacific spirit and aim. Let *us* seek it also, and, while preparing for war, still cherish the hope and the spirit of peace. We may not see the way by which, consistently with what we ought to maintain, peace can *now* be restored. But let us remember that *we see* but little of the ways and power of God. Our hope of peace is not destroyed because our eyes cannot detect its path or our Chief Magistrate and his counsellors cannot devise the means of obtaining it. The Lord reigneth, God is our refuge. "He hath his way in the sea, and his path in the mighty waters." When the disciples of Christ were on the billows, tempest-tossed, they knew not any path on those waves by which their Master could reach them, It was *"the fourth watch of the night."* But he had a path in the sea, and they saw him walking therein, and he came to them and the waves were still. If there be no way of peace, God can make one by dividing the sea. We are not hopeless of peace because we cannot tell how it could be brought about. Let us still hope, and still pray. With arms in hand let us do so. God be with us! God preserve and guide our counsellors, our Governors, our President. May they all learn humbly to feel and acknowledge their dependence on him for wisdom and strength. May the godlessness which has too long disgraced our public councils and affairs be cast away. May our President seek his help in God, and his Cabinet ask wisdom where only it is to be found, and our legislators know that God's blessing is worth their Seeking.

Bishop McIlvaine, in a second address, in 1863, to the clergy and laity of the diocese of Ohio, uttered similar sentiments. "We long," says he, "for such peace as the permanent interests of law and order, of justice and right, will permit our Government to seek and accept."

An important part of the bishop's address of 1863 is taken up with the statements of the Right Rev. James Henry Otey, D.D., LL.D., late Bishop of the Episcopal Church in Tennessee. Bishop Otey said, in 1861, "I am well satisfied that the majority of the people in the seceding States, if their voice could be fairly heard, would speak loudly in favor of Union."

> That which I fear most of all is, that God is about to visit us, and deservedly, for our national sins and ingratitude. The only foundation of my hope is that *"the Lord reigneth."* Oh, there is comfort in that declaration, precious, full, and abiding! Let what changes in government and overthrow of institutions come that may, we shall be safe under the shadow of His wings who "ruleth in the armies of heaven, and doeth all his pleasure among the inhabitants of the earth."

Dr. Stephen H. Tyng, pastor of one of the largest and most influential churches in the city of New York, in a sermon preached on fast-day, April 30, 1863, reflected the loyalty and sentiments of the American ministers on the great issues of the conflict. It was entitled "Christian Loyalty," and was founded on a passage expressive of the loyalty and love of the Hebrew people for their institutions and nationality. Brief extracts only can be given.

> "By the rivers of Babylon, there we sat down. Yea, we wept when we remembered Zion. We hanged our harps upon the willows in the midst thereof. If I forget thee, O Jerusalem, let my right hand forget her cunning. If I do not remember thee, let my tongue cleave to the roof of my mouth; if I prefer not Jerusalem above my chief joy."— Psalm cxxxvii. 1, 2, 5, 6.
>
> This (said Dr. Tyng) is the patriot's devotion to his country. It is a living spirit in his heart. It clings to his own land and people in their lowest depression as truly as in their highest prosperity. It is living and active within him, to whatever contumely and reproach it may expose him.
>
> 1. My loyalty to Jerusalem is my love of her people. I am loyal to my nation. I will never give my consent to its dismemberment or its separation. I cling to the one Federal American people—not to a confederacy of States, but to a consolidated nation. I desire not to live to see a disunion of them for any reasons or upon any terms. ... My loyalty is to the United

States of America, that great federal nation, which, wherever scattered or however collected, have dwelt together under one glorious government, as one perpetual, indivisible people.... Be one people; be one nation, ... Let Jerusalem be still a city at unity in itself, encircled with the walls of a common defence from foes abroad and bound together for a united subjugation of traitors at home.

2. My loyalty to Jerusalem is my love for her territory. I love my country; I love it with an intense affection. Every part of it is equally mine, and equally dear to me. I am a citizen of the United States. I will acknowledge no Northern rights nor Southern rights. I have a fee simple, indisputable right in every portion of this soil, from sea to sea, as a citizen of this nation. I will never consent to give it up. I am a citizen of the whole, I have a right to a domicile, a protected home, throughout the whole, which I will never yield. To separate this glorious hard-earned land, to divide it, to disintegrate it, cut it up, parcel it out to a set of wild conflicting provinces, farm it out to the ambition of petty contending satraps, gaining in blood a short-lived triumph, is a degradation and a social atrocity to which I will never consent, ...

Let the land of your fathers, the sacred revered abode of a nation of freemen, be transmitted, unbroken, solid, entire, untarnished, to the children who succeed you. Die, if it must be so, for it, but never give it up.

3. My loyalty to Jerusalem is my love for the freedom which she has established. Men may call the testimonies of her Declaration of Independence a tissue of "glittering generalities," when they have no affinity with the liberty which it proclaims and no sympathy with the grandly humanizing influence which it is designed and destined to exercise. To my mind, it stands on the highest platform of uninspired testimonies. In it the noblest emotions, aspirations, sentiments, and principles of the heart of man speak out in golden, crystal sounds. "We hold these truths to be self-evident, that all men are created equal; that they are endowed by their Creator with certain inalienable rights; that among these are life,

liberty, and the pursuit of happiness; that to secure these rights, governments are instituted among men, deriving their just powers from the consent of the governed." What nobler testimony for human freedom or human exaltation was ever given? When did the representative mind of progressive, rising humanity ever announce its convictions and its purposes in a loftier strain or in a grander formula? ... Never yield this priceless inheritance of human liberty; never sacrifice by any compromise the unrestricted, universal freedom of your nation; never consent to any arrangement in which you may not look back upon your fathers' line and home, and still triumphant say, "Jerusalem, the mother of us all, is free."

4. My loyalty to Jerusalem is my love for her *Constitution*. Jerusalem had her glorious constitution from the Divine gift—a book in the hands of every one, to be read at home, to be studied by children, to be talked of by the way. America has received her Constitution from the gracious providence of God—the grand result of ages of human experience and observation—the admired shape and cast of man's wisdom among the nations of the earth.

Never was there a more majestic exhibition of sovereign power; never was there a more honorable display of mutual concession and self-restraint.

Such is the American Constitution—a beautiful machinery of intellectual conception and of moral influence, working with its powers and restraints, its checks and balances, its provisions and prohibitions, in a thoroughly adjusted harmony, and in remarkable order and grandeur of operation. ... Never give up this contest for the Constitution. Compel this rebellion to submit to its authority. And, if you must perish, perish nobly maintaining the peerless cause of liberty, government, and order.

5. My loyalty to Jerusalem is my love for her government. Her Constitution is the charter of her government, the fixed and final scheme arranged for its construction and its perpetual control....

I love this Government. I love it in its origin. I love it in its simplicity. I love it in its supremacy. I love it in its individuality. I love it in its constitutional strength. I love it in its personal power, determination, and will. It combines for me all the possible freedom of liberty for the many consistent with order and tranquillity for the whole, and the vast security of absolute authority in an ultimate ruler from whom there is no appeal. It seems to me to have gathered the gems from all regions to make this new, last crown of a monarchical people—a ruling nation.

To my nation, to my country, to the principle of freedom, to the Constitution, to the Government, while I live, will I be faithful; and, however depressed or downcast or desponding may be the incidents and elements of the day, even though in captivity I sit by the river's of Babylon, I will never forget, dishonor, or deny the Jerusalem I have loved, beneath whose shade I have grown and been refreshed, and with whose sons and daughters I have gone to the house of God and taken sweet delight. Still in prayer for my beloved country will I look up to the King of kings and Lord of lords.

Dr. Byron Sunderland, pastor of the First Presbyterian Church in Washington City, and chaplain of the Senate of the United States, preached a sermon on the national fast-day, April 30, 1863, entitled "The Crisis of the Times," which was heard by an immense audience, and published by an "Association of patriotic citizens" and widely circulated through the country. The following is an extract—

When the ship of state, freighted as it is with all our memories and all our hopes, lies tossing in the tempest—when it is no longer a question of policy or preference as between rival parties and candidates in time of peace, but a deeper, broader, more vital question of the triumph of the Government and the *conscience* of the American people over a system of usurpation and despotism sustained by an organized and armed rebellion against them—now, when a fierce and bloody attempt is made to undermine the very foundations of social order and to pull down tho noblest structure of empire the sun has ever shone upon, and to sunder a land that was once most happy in all the arts and industries of advancing civilization, and to blot out from the face of the globe the unity of a mighty nation, and to impair forever the greatness and the usefulness of a people among whom the Divine principles and precepts of Christianity itself have had their freest and their noblest scope—would it not be thought a thing incredible that the Christian people and the Christian ministry of this land should stand aloof, should manifest a deep and profound indifference, should undertake to live and act and preach and speak and think and feel as though there were no war and no judgment of God among us whatever? And all this, too, while the whole history of the nation hitherto has been marked by one continued succession of providential interpositions for deliverance, one constant series of examples of the presence and influence of the Christian element in working out our national destiny! Without Christianity, the story of America could never have been told—these manifold and mighty monuments which cover the land could never have been reared. None but God can tell the effect of Christian prayer and fidelity in the testimony of Christian truth upon the fortunes of this nation. And now, in such a land, with such a record and such a prospect, and in such a condition, when we feel and know that blows are being struck which, if not repelled, must not only destroy our civil heritage, but also roll back the chariot of human salvation for a thousand years, can the disciples and ministers of this religion, which has more than all other things made the land a blessing, be excused from the duties and trials which now rest upon the nation? Nay, do you not look to the Christian sentiment and opinion of this country for countenance and support? Do you not rely on the loyalty and the prayers of the Christian people of this country as constituting, under God, the firmest and most unwavering prop and pillar of the nation's strength? If this be so, then I am here to declare, in the name of the Christian Church, and of all that follow the great Head of the Church in this land, that as they have never, heretofore, been found wanting in the hour of the country's need, so they will now not be found wanting. For, when it comes to this, the old religion which has for eighteen hundred years produced the heroes and martyrs of the world, will rise again and lead her mighty processions into the thickest of the contest. And not until the Church of Christ has been utterly overthrown, and not until her last prayer goes out and her last soul is offered up on the altar of expiring liberty, will it be time for men to say, "there is no longer any hope." And not until then can the cause of America, which we believe to be the cause of human nature everywhere, be ruined. And for this reason it is that in the name of the Church we lift up our voice, cry aloud and spare not, showing the people their sins and transgressions. The Christian mind of this nation beholds the spectacle we now present with a feeling of the deepest solemnity and the most painful suspense. The Christian mind of this nation interprets the afflictions we are suffering now, as the judgments of God for our moral obliquity. It holds that there is a righteousness which exalteth a nation, while sin is a reproach to any people. It holds that in a crisis like this there is but one inspiration that can carry us through in triumph, and that is the inspiration of the Almighty. It holds that among the first signs of the presence of such an inspiration is the general return of the people to sobriety and virtue; and therefore it views with pain and grief, with apprehension and alarm, the almost universal reign of vice, vulgarity, and impurity. And because the nation has been so long blind and indifferent to the principles of truth, and so long disobedient to the authority of God, he has not only kindled the fire of this furnace, but he is adding fuel to the flames, and holding us in them, that we may be either purified or consumed. That is the issue now before us—purification or destruction. It is comparatively of little account what may be the tidings from the great sieges or the battle-fields of our military or naval operations, what may be the condition of the currency or the result of local elections, or, indeed, what may be the daily contingencies or details that fall out to us in the history of this great time; but the true question is, whether amid all these millions of human beings a sufficient number may be found upon whom the inspiration of the Almighty has descended, to render it consistent with his most gracious purpose and with the character of his supreme government over men, to interpose and give us the victory. If this point in the moral and religious condition of the American people can be attained, then we have no fear for the remainder. The same power that delivered the Hebrew nation with a high hand and a stretched-out arm, the same power that shielded the people of the Netherlands against the combined attack of the greatest potentates of the time in Europe, the same power that brought our fathers through the bloody baptism of the Revolution, and gave to them, to bequeath to us, their children, this glorious inheritance, will thunder for us along all our lines of battle, and put our enemies to rout and confusion forever.

The Day of Fasting and Prayer

Appointed by the President, on Thursday, April 30, 1863, the proclamation for which is on the 558th page of this volume, was memorable in its Christian influence through the loyal States. Stirring and timely truths were preached in the pulpits, which tended greatly to impress the public mind and conscience with religious sentiments and responsibility to God, and to urge the people and all in civil and military authority to repentance and reformation. "We believe," says Bishop McIlvaine, in an address to the clergy and laity of the Diocese of Ohio, "the day was warmly welcomed by all the religious and patriotic people of the loyal States, and was observed with solemnity and prayerfulness in devout assemblies throughout those portions of our country." The resolution of the Senate requesting the President to appoint a day of fasting and prayer was gratifying to the Christian public especially, because it distinctly recognized Christ as mediator, and the New School Indianapolis Presbytery, in view of it, passed the following—

> *Resolved*, That this Presbytery, as an ecclesiastical court, called to witness for Christ before the world, cannot refrain

from a public expression of its gratification that the resolutions of the Senate of the United States, asking the appointment by the President of a national fast, make such distinct mention of our Lord Jesus Christ as the Heaven-appointed way of access to God the Father. This recognition of our Divine Mediator by our national authorities is as gratifying and appropriate as it is rare.

The Governors of several States, and the mayors of some of the larger cities and towns, responded to the proclamation of the President by issuing their own.

Washington City

PROCLAMATION BY THE MAYOR.

MAYOR'S OFFICE, APRIL 28, 1863.

The President, in compliance with a resolution of the Senate of the United States, having set apart a day for national prayer and humiliation, renders needless any thing of a like character from me. As requested in the following joint resolution, my fellow-citizens will doubtless manifest their appreciation of the occasion, as well as their respect for the high authority from whence it emanates, by abstaining from secular employment, and an observance of the day as enjoined on us, in common with the whole country, by the proclamation of the President.

RICHARD WALLACH, *MAYOR.*

—

Joint Resolution relative to the observance of Thursday, 80th April, as a day of fasting, humiliation, and prayer.

Whereas the President of the United States has, by public proclamation, recommended the observance of the 30th instant as a day of fasting, humiliation, and prayer throughout these United States, and whereas it is meet and proper that we should acknowledge our sins before Almighty God, and pray that the evils of civil war be removed from us: therefore

Be it Resolved, That the Mayor be, and is hereby, requested to issue his proclamation inviting and enjoining upon the citizens of Washington the observance of this day as a day of fasting, humiliation, and prayer, and requesting the suspension of all secular business on that day.

Alex. R. Shepherd,
President of the Board of Common Council.
Joseph F. Brown,
President of the Board of Aldermen.

Approved, April 28, 1863.

Richard Wallach, *Mayor.*

ORDER BY THE MILITARY GOVERNOR OF
THE DISTRICT OF COLUMBIA

GENERAL ORDERS, NO. 15.

HEAD-QUARTERS MILITARY DISTRICT OF WASHINGTON,
WASHINGTON, D.C., APRIL 29, 1863.

In compliance with the proclamation of the President of the United States, Thursday, the 30th of April instant, will be observed by officers and men in this command as a day of fasting and humiliation.

Within the limits of the city of Washington and the District of Columbia, the orders regulating the transaction of business and closing of shops, stores, and bars on Sunday will be applicable to Thursday, the 30th instant, and will be observed accordingly and enforced.

The President's proclamation devoutly recognizes the existence and presence of Almighty God. It is impossible that such a Being should not be interested in the affairs of men. No further appeal ought to be necessary to those who publicly profess a Christian faith.

But to others, who are inclined to ask, "What good can be gained by fasting?" the commanding general, while desiring their respectful co-operation in the observance of the day, suggests to them the following answer—

1. They will thereby manifest a *soldierly respect* to a recommendation which comes to them from the Commander-in-Chief of the Army and Navy of the United States; and the company or

regiment most imbued with that quality of respect affords signal evidence that it possesses the highest fighting quality.

2. A soldier who is moved to the performance of his duty in battle or elsewhere by the inspiration of God's presence in the mind and purposes will be incited by an influence of immense power.

Not the miraculous interposition of Divine agency, but the infusion of new determination and earnestness into our own hearts, will be the consequence, in the rudest minds, of our honest and manly observance of the fast recommended by the President.

A whole nation stimulated and exalted by such influences would be irresistible.

By command of Brigadier-General Martindale.

John P. Sherbourne, *A.A.G.*

GOVERNOR OF NEW YORK

The President of the United States having set apart the last Thursday of April as a day of national prayer, fasting, and humiliation, I, HORATIO SEYMOUR, Governor of the State of New York, do recommend that the day be observed throughout the State with suitable religious solemnities.

Humbly acknowledging the manifold offences of our rulers and people, let us humiliate ourselves before Almighty God, and fervently pray that our sins may be forgiven. Acknowledging our dependence upon his powers and mercy, let us put away pride and ingratitude, malice and uncharitableness, and implore him to deliver our land from seditious fury, conspiracy, and rebellion, and to restore the blessings of peace, concord, and union to the several States of our distracted and afflicted country.

In witness whereof, I have hereunto affixed the privy seal of the State, at the city of Albany, the 27th day of April, in the year of our Lord one thousand eight hundred and sixty-three.

Horatio Seymour.

By the Governor:

R. B. Miller, Jr., *Private Secretary.*

MAYOR OF NEW YORK

Whereas the President of the United States, in compliance with a resolution of the Senate, has issued his proclamation, setting apart Thursday, the 30th day of April, 1863, as a day of national humiliation, fasting, and prayer; and

Whereas the scourge of civil war which is now desolating our country and changing many of its happy homes into abodes of sorrow renders such solemn service peculiarly appropriate at the present time:

Now, therefore, in official recognition of said proclamation and its just and timely admonitions to the nation, I do hereby request that all the public offices in this city be closed on that day, and that the people, refraining from all secular pursuits, devote themselves with humble and contrite spirits to the religious duties suitable to the occasion.

Given under my hand and the seal of the Mayoralty, at the City Hall, in the city of New York, this twenty-seventh day of April, in the year of our Lord one thousand eight hundred and sixty-three.

George Opdyke, *Mayor.*

MAYOR OF BROOKLYN

MAYOR'S OFFICE, Tuesday, April 28, 1863.

Thursday, the 30th day of April, 1863, having been set apart by the president of the United States, in compliance with a resolution of the Senate, as a day of national humiliation, fasting, and prayer, in accordance therewith I do hereby direct that the various public offices of the city be closed on that day; and I respectfully recommend, also, that our citizens on that day refrain, as far as may be, from the pursuit of their ordinary business avocations. The suffering and misery and humiliation which during the past two years have fallen upon us as a nation would seem to render an earnest and universal appeal to the Divine mercy from us, as a people, especially a duty at this time; and I doubt not that the recommendation of the President will be appropriately responded to by our citizens.

Martin Kalbfleisch, *Mayor.*

MAYOR OF CINCINNATI

Now, therefore, in pursuance thereof, believing that our cause is just and righteous, feeling that in these times of trial to our beloved country we should humble ourselves before the Almighty in fasting and in prayer, ask his forgiveness for our sinfulness in the past and implore His blessings and favor upon the future, I earnestly desire all citizens to observe the day thus appointed by our Chief Magistrate in a becoming and reverent manner, and that all places of business and amusement shall then be closed.

Len. A. Harris, *Mayor of Cincinnati.*
CINCINNATI, April 28, 1863.

MAYOR OF PHILADELPHIA

Whereas the President of the United States, being moved thereto by the Federal Senate, has set apart Thursday next, the 30th day of April, as a day of national humiliation, fasting, and prayer; and whereas we have cause, as a people, to take shame to ourselves before all nations and before Almighty God that we have misused the civil blessings wherewith we have been signally favored, by setting at naught the wisdom of our fathers, betraying the trust of self-government, winking at unfaithfulness and corruption in high places, and giving ourselves to selfishness and disregard of ourselves as citizens:

Therefore it becomes us earnestly to beseech him that he will enlighten us to the honest discharge of our duties as freemen; that he will keep steadfast within us a true devotion to our country, to the confusion of all traitors and workers of sedition; that he will endow our rulers with wisdom and firmness, and that he will lead our hosts and give them strength in the conflict, that they may prevail over all rebellion, And I do hereby call upon the people of this city to keep such appointed day by foregoing the usual pursuits, closing their places of employment, and presenting themselves, after their respective manner of worship, before the Most High God; that, acknowledging his supreme power, and the righteousness of the judgments that he has visited upon our land, we may implore him mercifully to withhold his corrections from us, and give us welfare and peace through the speedy overthrow of all who resist the lawful authority of our national Government.

In testimony whereof, I have hereunto set my hand and caused the seal of the city of Philadelphia to be affixed, this twenty-seventh day of April, in the year of our Lord one thousand eight hundred and sixty-three.

Alexander Henry, Mayor of Philadelphia.

Thanksgiving-days for Victories

As a Christian nation, it has been the uniform practice of the civil authorities, when signal blessings were received or important victories obtained, to issue proclamations of thanksgiving and praise to Almighty God. During the winter and spring of 1862 important victories were won by the armies of the United States, at Mill Spring, Kentucky, at Fort Donelson and Pittsburg Landing, Tennessee, and at Pea Ridge, Missouri. In view of these victories, Congress passed the following resolution—

> *A Resolution giving the Thanks of Congress to the Officers, Soldiers, and Seamen of the Army and Navy, for their gallantry in the recent brilliant victories over the enemies of the Union and the Constitution.*
>
> *Resolved, by the Senate and House of Representatives of the United States of America, in Congress assembled,* That the thanks of Congress are due, and are hereby tendered, to the officers, soldiers, and seamen of the Army and Navy of the United States, for the heroic gallantry that, under the providence of Almighty God, has won the recent series of brilliant victories over the enemies of the Union and Constitution. Approved, February 22, 1862.

The President and Secretary of War issued the following papers—

A PROCLAMATION

Washington, April 10, 1862.

It has pleased Almighty God to vouchsafe signal victories to the land and naval forces engaged in suppressing an internal rebellion, and at the same time to avert from our country the dangers of foreign intervention and invasion. It is, therefore, recommended to the people of the United States that at their next weekly assemblages in their accustomed places of worship which shall occur after the notice of this proclamation shall have been received, that they especially acknowledge and render thanks to our heavenly Father for these inestimable blessings; that they then and there implore spiritual consolation in behalf of all those who have been brought into affliction by the casualties and calamities of sedition and civil war; and that they reverently invoke the Divine guidance for our national councils, to the end that they may speedily result in the restoring of peace and harmony and unity through-out our borders, and hasten the establishment of fraternal relations among all the countries of the earth.

In witness whereof, I have hereunto set my hand, and caused the seal of the United States to be affixed.

Done at the city of Washington, this 10th day of April, in the year of our Lord one thousand eight hundred and sixty-two.

(Signed)   Abraham Lincoln.

WAR DEPARTMENT, WASHINGTON, APRIL 9, 1862.
Order 1. That at meridian of the Sunday next after the reception of this order, at the head-quarters of every regiment in the armies of the United States, there shall be offered by its chaplain a prayer, giving thanks to the Lord of Hosts for the recent manifestations of his power in the overthrow of the rebels and traitors, and invoking the continuance of his aid in

delivering this nation, by the arms of patriotic soldiers, from the horrors of treason, rebellion, and civil war.

E. M. Stanton, Secretary of War.

The Secretary of War expressed the following sentiments—

> The glory of our recent victories belongs to the gallant officers and soldiers that fought the battles. No share of it belongs to me.
>
> Much has recently been said of military combinations and organizing victories. I hear such phrases with apprehension. They commenced in infidel France with the Italian campaign, and resulted in Waterloo. Who can organize victory? Who can combine the elements of success on the battle-field? We owe our recent victories to the Spirit of the Lord, that moved our soldiers to rush into battle and filled the hearts of our enemies with terror and dismay. The inspiration that conquered in battle was in the hearts of the soldiers and from on high; and wherever there is the same inspiration there will be the same results. Patriotic spirit, with resolute courage, in officers and men, is a military combination that never failed.
>
> We may well rejoice at the recent victories, for they teach us that battles are to be won now and by us in the same and only manner that they were ever won by any people or in any age since the days of Joshua—by boldly pursuing and striking the foe. What, under the blessing of Providence, I conceive to be the true organization of victory and military combination to end this war, was declared in a few words by General Grant's message to General Buckner—*"I propose to move immediately upon your works!"*

The thanksgiving appointed by the President was generally observed by the Churches in the loyal States. The following was a form used by the Episcopal churches in Ohio—

*To the clergy of the Protestant Episcopal Church
in the Diocese of Ohio.*

In obedience to the proclamation of the President of the United States, and responding cordially to his acknowledgment of the good hand of our God upon us in giving victory to our national forces, I hereby appoint and set forth the following collect of thanksgiving, and prayers for the wounded, sick, and dying, and for the bereaved, to be read during divine service in every church within this diocese, on the Sunday after the receipt of this notice, and at other times at the discretion of the minister. Affectionately,

G. T. Bedell, *Assistant Bishop in charge.*

—

COLLECT OF THANKSGIVING AFTER VICTORY.
To be used before the General Thanksgiving.
(ADAPTED.)

O Almighty God, the Sovereign Commander of all the world, in whose hand is power and might which none is able to withstand, we bless and magnify thy great and glorious name for these late happy victories. The whole glory thereof we do ascribe to thee, who art the only giver of victory. And, we beseech thee, give us grace to improve this great mercy to thy glory, the advancement of thy gospel, the honor of our country, and the speedy re-establishment of such peace as will maintain the supremacy of law, the securities of righteous liberty, and the welfare of the Union. And, we beseech thee, give us such a sense of this great mercy as may engage us to a true thankfulness, such as may appear in our lives by an humble, holy, and obedient walking before thee all our days, through Jesus Christ our Lord; to whom, with thee and the Holy Spirit, as for all thy mercies, so in particular for this victory and deliverance, be all glory and honor, world without end. Amen.

The following is the prayer of thanksgiving for our victories which Bishop Whittingham directed the Episcopal clergy of the Diocese of

Maryland to use on all occasions of public worship during the next eight days—

> O Almighty God, the Sovereign Commander of all the world, in whose hand is power and might, which none is able to withstand, we bless and magnify thy great and glorious name for the happy successes which thou hast of late vouchsafed in so many instances to the arms of this nation, and more especially for the deliverance of this city and district from the terrors of blockade and siege. And, we beseech thee, give to us and to all this people grace to use this great mercy shown towards us to thy glory, the advancement of thy gospel, the honor of our country, and, as much as in us lieth, the good of all mankind. Stir up our hearts, O Lord, to a true thankfulness, such as may appear in our lives by an humble, holy, and obedient walking before thee all our days, through Jesus Christ our Lord; to whom, with thee, O Father, and thee, O Holy Ghost, as for all thy mercies, so in particular for these victories and this deliverance, be all glory and honor, world without end. Amen.

Victory at Gettysburg

On the first three days of July, 1863, a great victory was won by the army of the United States, under General Meade, over the rebel army under General Lee. Pennsylvania and Maryland were invaded by the army of the rebels, which threatened to capture Harrisburg, Philadelphia, Baltimore, and Washington, the capital of the nation. The two armies, each numbering about a hundred thousand men, met on the field of battle at Gettysburg, Pennsylvania, and a victory, great and important in its immediate and future results, was won by the national army. On the 4th of July, memorable in its historic associations, the news of the defeat of the invading army spread through the nation, and the President of the United States issued the following brief; comprehensive, and Christian address of congratulation to the country—

Christian Address of the President to the Country

WASHINGTON, JULY 4, 10 A.M., 1863.
The President announces to the country that news from the Army of the Potomac up to ten P.M. of the 3d is such as to

cover that army with the highest honor, to promise a great success to the cause of the Union, and to claim the condolence of all for the many gallant fallen, and that for this he especially desires that on this day He whose will, not ours, should ever be done, be everywhere remembered and reverenced with profoundest gratitude.   ABRAHAM LINCOLN.

General Meade assumed the command of the Potomac army, by the appointment of the President, on the Sunday previous to this important and decisive battle. In his address to the army on Sabbath, June 28, 1863, he said—

> By direction of the President of the United States, I hereby assume command of the Army of the Potomac. The country looks to this army to release it from the devastation and disgrace of a hostile invasion. Whatever fatigues and sacrifices we may be called upon to undergo, let us have in view constantly the magnitude of the interest involved, and *let each man determine to do his duty, leaving to an all-controlling Providence the decision of the contest.*

General Meade's Thanksgiving Order to the Army

In General Meade these traits crown his conduct, that "no one looks with more favor upon the true Christian who ministers to the spiritual wants of the wounded," and "an humble recognition that victory is of the Lord, and that to him belongs its glory." This is seen in the following order—

> HEAD-QUARTERS ARMY OF THE POTOMAC, JULY 4, 1863. *General Order No. 68.*—The commanding general, in behalf of the country, thanks the Army of the Potomac for the glorious result of the recent operations.
>
> Our enemy, superior in numbers and flushed with the pride of a successful invasion, attempted to overcome or destroy this army. Utterly baffled and defeated, he has now

withdrawn from the contest. The privations and fatigues the army has endured, and the heroic courage and gallantry it has displayed, will be matters of history to be ever remembered.

Our task is not yet accomplished; and the commanding general looks to the army for greater efforts to drive from our soil every vestige of the presence of the invader.

It is right and proper that we should, on suitable occasions, return our grateful thanks to the Almighty Disposer of events, that, in the goodness of his providence, he has thought fit to give victory to the cause of the just.

By command of Major-General Meade.

S. Williams, *A.A.G.*

Victory at Vicksburg

On the 4th of July, 1863, Vicksburg, a strongly garrisoned town on the Mississippi River, and the key to the commerce of the Western States, surrendered to the national forces under Major-General U. S. Grant. This important event, occurring the same day with the news of the defeat of the invading army at Gettysburg, thrilled the national heart with gratitude and general joy. Thanksgivings to Almighty God ascended from the loyal people in all parts of the Northern States. The following scene at Philadelphia on the reception of the news on the 7th of July is one of great solemnity and sublimity, heightened by the associations and remembrances of the day on which these great victories were achieved, and the historic inspirations of Independence Hall. The ministers of religion who officiated in this scene of patriotism and piety stood exactly in the same spot where the Declaration of Independence was read eighty-seven years before. The editor of the "North American and United States Gazette," of Philadelphia, Morton McMichael, described the scene as follows—

We have read of the first prayer offered in the Continental Congress, and of the sublimity and impressiveness of the scene as the assembled body knelt while Jehovah was praised for the workings of his providence in ordaining freedom to America.

Independence Square yesterday saw a sight emulating it in solemn grandeur, and presenting a spectacle Philadelphia never before witnessed, never may again. The tidings of the progress of the Union arms brought it about. When first promulgated, a large number of the members of the Union League met coincidently at the League rooms. The throng increased until the place was nearly filled. Everybody had left their places of business, and the members instinctively sought the League House for mutual congratulation.

It was proposed that something more than an informal recognition of so bountiful a blessing of victory should be made, and the gentlemen present took steps to make it. Birgfeld's Band of forty-six instruments was secured, and, with this at its head, the Union League, headed by the Rev. Kingston Goddard and Rev. Dr. Brainerd, moved down Chestnut street to Independence Square, keeping step to the glad strains of national airs that have been familiar since the dear days of youth's earliest dreams.

As the end of the line reached the square, all were uncovered. The line filed to right and left, when Hon. Charles Gibbons ascended the steps of Independence Hall. The concourse of people that now poured into the square were thousands in number. They spread over a surface beyond earshot of the loudest enunciation.

Mr. Gibbons made a brief address. He said that this day the beginning of the end is in view. The rebels are losing their strongholds, the cause of the Union is approaching its final triumph. He drew a picture of what we were as a nation, what we are, and what, in God's providence, we shall be. He spoke briefly and to the point, but was so overwhelmed with cheers that we failed to catch his speech as he uttered it.

Rev. Dr. Brainerd now bared his head; and instinctively—we believe reverently, as by an intuitive impulse—every man present was uncovered. A hush fell upon the densely-crowded assemblage as the hand of the reverend doctor was raised and an invitation given to the multitude to follow him in rendering thanks to Heaven for its many mercies and for crowning the arms of the country with victory.

Amid more profound silence, we verily believe, than an equal number of people ever kept before, Dr. Brainerd gave praise. He thanked the Almighty for the victories that were now crowning our arms. He had chastened us in his displeasure, and alike in that chastening as now in the blessing upon our work he recognized the hand of the Omnipotent. He implored the Divine blessing upon the country and its people—that religion and truth and justice might take the place of pride and arrogance and vain-glory, and that this people might recognize in every event of life the ruling of Divine power. He prayed for the President and Cabinet, for the continued success of our arms and for the restoration of our national unity, for liberty to the oppressed, for freedom to worship God everywhere, and for the coming of that day when his kingdom shall extend over the whole earth.

When at the close of his prayer the Christian minister pronounced the word "Amen!" the whole multitude took up the Greek dissyllable, and as with one mighty voice re-echoed it, reverently and solemnly, "Amen!"

While this prayer was being offered, the band silently disappeared. As the final word of the supplication was pronounced, a strain of sacred music burst from overhead. The band had ascended to the State-House steeple, and there played, with effect that no tongue can adequately describe, the air of Old Hundred, written by Martin Luther more than three centuries ago.

Spontaneously a gentleman mounted a post, and started the melody to the words,

"Praise God, from whom all blessings flow."

The whole multitude caught it up, and a doxology was sung with a majesty that Philadelphia never before heard. Every voice united. The monster oratories that we have heard, with a vocal chorus of three hundred singers, dwindled into insignificance in comparison to it. Rev. Dr. Goddard then pronounced the benediction, and the vast audience again covered themselves and slowly dispersed. The whole scene was remarkable. It was a touching illustration of the fact that down deep in every man's heart, no matter what may be the utterance of his lips, or his daily walk and conversation, there is a recognition of the fact that the Lord reigneth.

PROCLAMATION BY THE GOVERNOR OF MARYLAND.
To the People of Maryland.
STATE OF MARYLAND, EXECUTIVE DEPARTMENT.
The recent occurrences within or near our borders are well calculated to profoundly excite the devotional feelings of our people, and incline their hearts to offer to Almighty God their earnest thanks for his agency in delivering the State from the dangers which recently threatened it, in driving the invaders from our soil, and in crowning with victory the efforts of those to whom, under his providence, we are indebted for that deliverance.

Humbly, therefore, acknowledging our dependence on his favor, so often before and now again so conspicuously extended to us, let us embrace the earliest opportunity of publicly confessing it.

I, therefore, earnestly recommend to the people of the State to unite, on Sunday next, the 19th instant, in their usual places of public worship, in humbling themselves before God in acknowledgment of his recent mercies; and, while we offer up our thanks for the deliverance he has sent and the victory he has vouchsafed to us, let us humbly entreat that his wisdom may so direct the councils of our rulers that the result of these achievements may be the speedy restoration of our beloved country to its former condition of a united, peaceful, and prosperous people.

Given under my hand and the great seal of the State, this fifteenth day of July, in the year eighteen hundred and sixty-three.

A. W. Bradford.

By the Governor:

Wm. B. Hill, *Secretary of State.*

The loyal ministers and Churches of Maryland responded to the appointment of the Governor, and the Bishop of the Episcopal Diocese issued the following circular letter—

> *To the Clergy and Laity of the Diocese of Maryland.*
> DEAR BRETHREN—The Governor of the State having recommended to the people to unite on Sunday next, the 19th instant, in their usual places of worship, in humiliating themselves before Almighty God in devout thanksgiving for his recent mercies, in delivering this State from invasion and crowning with victory the arms of its lawful Government, you are earnestly requested and recommended to give due and religious heed to this laudable recommendation of the civil authority; and, in order thereto, I hereby set forth for use at the Morning Prayer, instead of the *Venite*, the last "Psalm or Hymn of Praise" in the office of "Forms of Prayer to be used at Sea;" and in both Morning and Evening Prayers, after the *general thanksgiving*, the *collect* in the same office which follows the aforesaid Hymn of Praise.
>
> Your loving friend and brother,
> William Rollinson Whittingham,
Bishop of Maryland.
> Baltimore, July 16, 1863.

National Thanksgiving.

The President of the United States, in view of the important victories of the national armies, and in obedience to the wishes of the Christian public and his own feelings, issued the following—

> PROCLAMATION
> It has pleased Almighty God to hearken to the supplications and prayers of an afflicted people, and to vouchsafe to the army and the navy of the United States victories on the land and on the sea so signal and so effective as to furnish reasonable grounds for augmented confidence that the Union

of these States will be maintained, their Constitution preserved, and their peace and prosperity permanently restored. But these victories have been accorded not without sacrifices of life, limb, health, and liberty, incurred by brave, loyal, and patriotic citizens. Domestic affliction in every part of the country follows in the train of these fearful bereavements. It is meet and right to recognize and confess the presence of the Almighty Father and the power of his hand equally in these triumphs and in these sorrows.

Now, therefore, be it known that I do set apart Thursday, the sixth day of August next, to be observed as a day for national thanksgiving, praise, and prayer; and I invite the people of the United States to assemble on that occasion in their customary places of worship, and, in the forms approved by their own consciences, render the homage duo to the Divine Majesty for the wonderful things he has done in the nation's behalf, and invoke the influence of his Holy Spirit to subdue the anger which has produced and so long sustained a needless and cruel rebellion, to change the hearts of the insurgents, to guide the counsels of the Government with wisdom adequate to so great a national emergency, and to visit with tender care and consolation throughout the length and breath of our land all those who, through the vicissitudes of marches, voyages, battles, and sieges, have been brought to suffer in mind, body, or estate; and finally to lead the whole nation, through the paths of repentance and submission to the Divine will, back to the perfect enjoyment of union and fraternal peace.

In witness whereof, I have hereunto set my hand, and caused the seal of the United States to be affixed.

Done at the city of Washington, the fifteenth day of July, in the year of our Lord one thousand eight hundred and sixty-three, and of the Independence of the United States of America the eighty-eighth.

Abraham Lincoln.

By the President:

William H. Seward, *Secretary of State.*

Bishop Potter's Form of Thanksgiving

In obedience to the proclamation of the President, Bishop Alonzo Potter, of the Diocese of Pennsylvania, prepared and sent to the congregations under his pastoral care the following form of thanksgiving. It expressed the Christian feeling of the nation—

> Almighty and everlasting God, who art the author and giver of all good things, who visitest the earth and blessest it, crowning the year with thy goodness, and giving to all their meat in due season, we praise and bless thee for thy unbounded kindness to the people of this land. Our fathers hoped in thee, they trusted in thee, and thou didst deliver them. We thank thee, O Lord our God, for the goodly heritage which we enjoy, and for blessings unbounded, both temporal and spiritual, which through thy patience and long-suffering are still continued to us. We bless thee for civil and religious liberty, for the administration of justice, and for all the privileges which pertain to us as individuals and families, as Christians and as citizens. Grant that a sense of this thy great goodness may engage our hearts and lives in thy service. Give wisdom and strength and union to our public councils. Bless the Governor and magistrates of this Commonwealth, and all who exercise civil or military authority among us. Bless our Churches and all our religious institutions. Bring back once more peace and concord to our borders. Increase and multiply upon us thy mercy, that, thou being our ruler and guide, we may so pass through things temporal that we finally lose not the things eternal. All which we ask through Jesus Christ our Lord and Saviour. Amen.
>
> O Almighty God, the sovereign commander of all the world, in whose hand is power and might which none is able to withstand, we bless and magnify thy great and glorious name for these happy victories, the whole glory whereof we would ascribe to thee, who art the only giver of victory. And, we beseech thee, give us grace to improve this great mercy to thy glory, the advancement of thy gospel, the honor of our

country, and, as much as in us lieth, to the good of all mankind. Imprint deeply on our hearts such a lively and lasting sense of these great deliverances as may incite us to a true thankfulness, such as may appear in our lives by an humble, holy, and obedient walking before thee all our days; through Jesus Christ our Lord, to whom, with thee and the Holy Spirit, as for all thy mercies, so in particular for these victories, be all glory and honor, world without end. Amen.

O Eternal God, the shield of our help, beneath whose sovereign defence thy people dwell in safety, we bless and praise, we laud and magnify thy glorious name for all thy goodness to the people of this land, and especially for the success with which of late thou hast crowned our efforts to maintain the authority of law and to restore once more the blessings of union and peace. Inspire our souls with grateful love; lift up our voices in songs of thankfulness; make us humble and watchful in our prosperity, and prepare us for whatever reverses thou shalt see that we need. Give wisdom and grace to our rulers. Pour constancy and courage and charity towards all men into the hearts of our people. Draw towards us those who are now alienated from us in appearance or in heart, and hasten, O Lord of hosts, the blessed day when as one people we may once more give thanks unto thee in thy holy Church, and by our daily lives show forth thy praise, through Jesus Christ our most blessed Lord and Saviour. Amen.

National Influence of the Day of Thanksgiving

The Governors of several States, and the mayors of some of the larger cities and towns, issued proclamations in harmony with that of the President, in which there were official recognitions of God as the author of these national victories, and of the responsibility of the nation to the Divine government. Christian denominations gratefully and joyfully responded to these invitations, and the people went up to the temples of God and entered into his gates with thanksgiving and into his courts with praise. The day was memorable in the civil and Christian annals of the republic, and presented the sublime spectacle of a whole nation offering praise and prayer unto the Lord of hosts, who had ever been its shield and guide and who again had wrought this signal deliverance. It had the happy effect of diffusing and deepening the religious element of the nation, and giving to the public mind and conscience a more practical sense of dependence on God, and a higher appreciation of the value and vital necessity of the Christian religion to the perpetuity and permanent prosperity of the nation.

This volume, which traces to the Christian religion the life, character, genius, fruits, and fame of the civil institutions of the United States, closes while these songs of thanksgiving and praise are echoing through the land. The historic and Christian facts of the volume are full of sublime significance and instruction to all classes of American citizens, and reaffirm, in prophetic voice, the declaration of one of the purest patriots and most accomplished statesmen of the republic, "THAT THE BIBLE IS THE ONLY GENUINE MORAL CONSTITUTION OF SOCIETY, AND ITS PRINCIPLES THE ONLY SAFE FOUNDATION OF ALL CIVIL AND POLITICAL ESTABLISHMENTS."